POWER

BOATWORKS YACHT SALES

SAIL

DEALERS FOR: GRAND BANKS • EAST BAY • SABRELINE • SABRE • CALIBER • BLUE STAR

PLEASE CALL ONE OF OUR OFFICES:

Rowayton, CT – *203·866·0882*

Essex, CT – *860·767·3013*

Newport, RI – *401·846·8484*

Grand Banks 46 Europa • Fast 18 kt Cruiser tops at 22 kts w/435 HP cats, 2 Staterooms, 2 Heads, Palatial Aft Deck.

Saberline 42 • 2 Cabin galley down or up • 30 knot speed • Blue hull • Brand new design for 2001

East Bay 43 • Ray Hunt design • Very sea kindly 24 kt Cruise • 2 Staterooms built by American Marine to Grand Banks Standards.

Sabreline 36 • Twin 300 cats • 23 kt Cruise Sabre Quality • Island Queen Forward.

Blue Star 29.9 • 30 knot speed • Dinnette below • Full galley • Standing head w/shower • V-berth • L-settee • THE POCKET YACHT

Looking
for a
marina?

Robert Daly / Stone

Make your reservation
at **Marinalife.com**

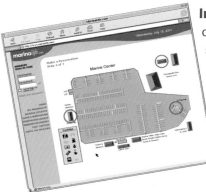

Introducing Marinalife.com. The online boat slip reservation system dedicated to helping you find and make reservations at a marina. With a few simple clicks, you can **view detailed maps of marinas at your destination,** e-mail your travel itinerary to friends and family, access your Marinalife reservations, and lots more. Or, you can call us at 1-800-RENT-A-SLIP and we will reserve a boat slip for you quickly...anywhere...anytime.

Marinalife.com. Making a slip reservation has never been this easy.

Long Island Sound

EIGHTH EDITION

MAPTECH®

Embassy®
Guides

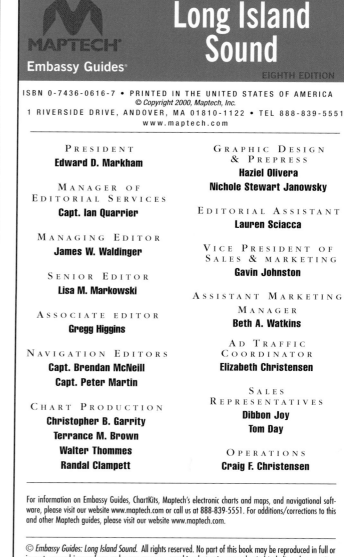

Long Island Sound

MAPTECH®

Embassy Guides®

EIGHTH EDITION

ISBN 0-7436-0616-7 • PRINTED IN THE UNITED STATES OF AMERICA
© Copyright 2000, Maptech, Inc.
1 RIVERSIDE DRIVE, ANDOVER, MA 01810-1122 • TEL 888-839-5551
www.maptech.com

PRESIDENT
Edward D. Markham

MANAGER OF
EDITORIAL SERVICES
Capt. Ian Quarrier

MANAGING EDITOR
James W. Waldinger

SENIOR EDITOR
Lisa M. Markowski

ASSOCIATE EDITOR
Gregg Higgins

NAVIGATION EDITORS
Capt. Brendan McNeill
Capt. Peter Martin

CHART PRODUCTION
Christopher B. Garrity
Terrance M. Brown
Walter Thommes
Randal Clampett

GRAPHIC DESIGN
& PREPRESS
Haziel Olivera
Nichole Stewart Janowsky

EDITORIAL ASSISTANT
Lauren Sciacca

VICE PRESIDENT OF
SALES & MARKETING
Gavin Johnston

ASSISTANT MARKETING
MANAGER
Beth A. Watkins

AD TRAFFIC
COORDINATOR
Elizabeth Christensen

SALES
REPRESENTATIVES
Dibbon Joy
Tom Day

OPERATIONS
Craig F. Christensen

For information on Embassy Guides, ChartKits, Maptech's electronic charts and maps, and navigational software, please visit our website www.maptech.com or call us at 888-839-5551. For additions/corrections to this and other Maptech guides, please visit our website www.maptech.com.

Show Your BoatU.S. Card And Discover a New World of Savings!

WANT THE DISCOUNTS? IT'S EASY!

Discounts on fuel, overnight slips, repairs and more, are available at over 575 BoatU.S. Cooperating Marinas from coast-to-coast. But to get the discounts you've got to be a BoatU.S. Member! Call 800-395-2628 to join for SPECIAL annual dues of only $14.00 for more than 26 Benefits & Services! Or visit us at www.BoatUS.com. Mention Code: TMMSM79T

Up to 15% OFF Repairs
25% OFF Transient Slip Rentals
10¢ OFF Per Gallon Fuel

Not all discounts are available from every marina. You must show BoatU.S. Membership card to obtain discounts. For more information about Credit Rebates, call 800-395-2628.

SHOW THE CARD. GET THE DISCOUNTS.

BoatU.S.
JAMES TAYLOR
#219320
MEMBER SINCE 1966
EXPIRES DEC 2000
On-the-Water Towing $50

BoatU.S. Cooperating Marinas - New York & Long Island Sound

VERMONT

Champlain Marina
Colchester, VT
802-658-4034

Champlain Bridge Marina, Inc.
Addison, VT
800-729-2469

CONNECTICUT

Mystic Shipyard, LLC
West Mystic, CT
860-536-6588

Haring's Marine
Noank, CT
860-536-2842

Spicer's
Noank, CT
860-536-4978

Pine Island Marina
Groton, CT
860-445-9729

Thamesport Marina
New London, CT
860-442-1151

Between the Bridges Marina and
Resort North & South
Old Saybrook, CT
860-388-1431

UK Sailmakers
Essex Connecticut Office
Essex, CT
860-767-9893

Quantum Eastern Long Island Sound
Quantum Sail Design Group
Westbrook, CT
860-399-0077

Pier 76 Marina
Westbrook, CT
860-399-7122

Yankee Boat Yard
Portland, CT
860-342-4735

Oyster Point Marina
New Haven, CT
203-624-5895

UK Sailmakers
Western Connecticut
Norwalk, CT
203-853-0676

Stamford Landing Marina
Stamford, CT
203-965-0065

Beacon Point Marine
Cos Cob, CT
203-661-4033

Palmer Point Marina
Cos Cob, CT
203-661-1243

NEW YORK / LONG ISLAND

South Minneford Yacht Club
City Island, NY
718-885-3113

UK Sailmakers New York
City Island, NY
718-885-1700

Manhasset Bay Marina
Port Washington, NY
516-883-8411

Quantum Western Long Island Sound
Quantum Sail Design Group
Port Washington, NY
516-944-5660

Toms Point Marina
Port Washington, NY
516-883-6630

The Jude Thaddeus Glen Cove Marina
Glen Cove, NY
516-759-3129

RV Bridge Marina Inc.
Bayville, NY
516-628-8688

Seymour's Boat Yard
Northport, NY
631-261-6574

Matt-A-Mar Marina
Mattituck, NY
631-298-4739

Cutchogue Harbor Marina
Cutchogue, NY
631-734-6993

Hampton Watercraft & Marine
Hampton Bays, NY
631-728-0922

Hampton Boat Service
Hampton Bays, NY
631-728-1114

Windswept Marina
East Moriches, NY
631-878-2100

Moriches Boat & Motor
East Moriches, NY
631-878-0023

Southwest Marina
Mastic Beach, NY
631-281-8244

Beaver Dam Boat Basin
Brookhaven, NY
631-286-7816

Morgan's Swan River Marina
Patchogue, NY
631-758-3524

West Sayville Boat Basin
West Sayville, NY
631-589-4141

Burnett Marine Service, Inc.
Bay Shore, NY
631-968-5213

Seaborn Marina, Inc.
Bay Shore, NY
631-665-0034

Theodore DeGarmo
Babylon, NY
631-669-0789

RPM-Marine
Lindenhurst, NY
631-957-1901

Bay Village Marina
Amityville, NY
631-691-4631

Pearl Grey Marine Service
Amityville, NY
631-598-3938

King's Plaza Marina
Brooklyn, NY
718-253-5434

Port Sheepshead Marina
Brooklyn, NY
718-332-4030

Marine Basin Marina
Brooklyn, NY
718-372-5700

NEW YORK / HUDSON RIVER

T & R Marina, Inc.
Piermont, NY
845-359-6308

Tarrytown Marina
Tarrytown, NY
914-631-1300

Minisceongo Yacht Club
Stonypoint, NY
914-786-8767

Hyde Park Marina
Poughkeepsie, NY
845-473-8283

Ulster Marine Center
Kingston, NY
800-640-3943

Castleton Boat Club
Castleton on the Hudson, NY
518-732-7077

Albany Yacht Club
Rensselaer, NY
518-445-9587

Troy Town Dock & Marina, Inc.
Troy, NY
518-272-5341

NEW YORK / UPSTATE

Harris Bay Yacht Club, Inc.
Cleverdale, NY
518-656-9028

Castaway Marina
Lake George, NY
518-656-3636

Lock 12 Marina, Inc.
Whitehall, NY
518-499-2049

Westport Marina
Westport, NY
518-962-4356

Essex Shipyard
Essex, NY
518-963-7700

Schenectady Yacht Club
Rexford, NY
518-384-9971

Oswego Marina
Oswego, NY
315-343-0436

Buoys Dockside Restaurant &
Anchorage
Brewerton, NY
315-676-3625

Winter Harbor, L.L.C.
Brewerton, NY
315-676-9276

Fisher Bay Marina
Bridgeport, NY
315-633-9657

Oneida Lake Marina
Canastota, NY
315-762-4865

Johnnie's Pier 31
Canastota, NY
315-697-7007

Lighthouse Marina
Pulaski, NY
315-298-6688

Lake Ontario Mariner's Marina
Henderson Harbor, NY
315-938-5222

Bill & Jack's Marina
Fishers Landing, NY
315-686-3592

Hutchinson's Boat Works
Alexandria Bay, NY 13607
315-482-9931

Shon's Boat Basin
Fair Haven, NY
315-947-6635

Pier Pointe East Marina
Sodus Point, NY
315-483-6947

Pier Pointe West Marina
Sodus Point, NY
315-483-6947

Shumway Marine
Rochester, NY
716-342-3030

Oak Orchard Riverside Marina
Kent, NY
716-682-4309

Eagle Bay Marina
Port Byron, NY
315-776-8468

Complete Boat Works
Auburn, NY
315-252-2833

Table of Contents

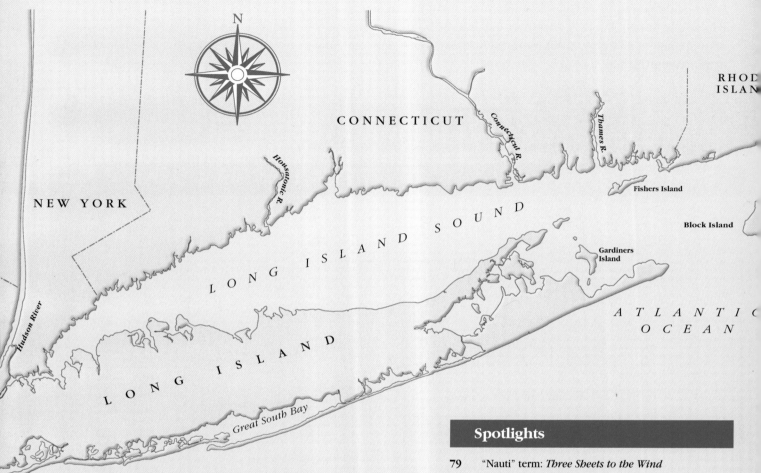

Reference 10

Index 410

Spotlights

(continued on page 8)

SWITLIK

Quality, Value and A Name You Trust

RESCUE POD-4

The RESCUE POD-4 is a very high quality inflatable flotation platform with canopy that supports four people and offers basic protection from the elements. The compact sizes of its fiberglass container or soft valise allow it to be carried aboard the smallest open sport fishing boat, day cruiser or sail boat. Although small in packed size, the RESCUE POD-4 is extremely tough and durable.

- Capacity: 4 persons
- Buoyancy: 205 lbs./person
- Floor Area: 3.0 sq. ft./person
- Container Size: 24" x 13" x 12.5"
- Soft Valise Size: 24" x 12" diam.
- Wt.: 44 lbs.
- Wt.: 33 lbs.

RESCUE POD-8

The RESCUE POD-8 is similar to our 4 person capacity RESCUE POD-4 and supports eight people. The double layer inflatable canopy design provides better hypothermia protection than the single layer canopy used on most standard Life Rafts. Upon inflation of the RESCUE POD-8, the canopy remains furled around the top of the buoyancy tube until needed. This allows for easier boarding from either the water or your vessel. Once in the POD, the occupants can immediately inflate the canopy using the CO_2 inflators.

- Capacity: 8 persons
- Buoyancy: 211 lbs./person
- Floor Area: 3.0 sq. ft./person
- Container Size: 31" x 21" x 14"
- Soft Valise Size: 32" x 19" x 14"
- Wt.: 98 lbs.
- Wt.: 79 lbs.

MD-2 6 PERSON LIFE RAFT

Designed for offshore use, the MD-2 Life Raft includes extended survival equipment and a twin tube configuration, allowing this raft to meet the requirements of the Offshore Racing Council (ORC). Two large canopy entrances and its unique single arch tube geometry provide more ventilation, lookout capability, and occupant headroom than any other raft in this class.

- Capacity: 6 persons
- Buoyancy: 217 lbs./person
- Floor Area: 4.0 sq. ft./person
- Container Size: 31" x 21" x 14"
- Soft Valise Size: 34" x 18" x 16"
- Wt.: 94 lbs.
- Wt.: 75 lbs.

SEARCH AND RESCUE MK-II 6 PERSON LIFE RAFT

Our Search & Rescue MK-II Life Raft is based on the original Military Specification configuration with an updated canopy design, which allows easier boarding from higher freeboard vessels. The Toroidal Stability Device (TSD), rigid boarding step, and Standard Range survival kit are included.

- Capacity: 6 persons
- Buoyancy: 257 lbs./person
- Floor Area: 4.0 sq. ft./person
- Container Size: 37" x 24" x 14" Wt.: 121 lbs. } Standard
- Soft Valise Size: 36" x 24" x 15" Wt.: 102 lbs. } Kit
- Container Size: 37" x 24" x 17" Wt.: 135 lbs. } Extended
- Soft Valise Size: 36" x 24" x 17" Wt.: 116 lbs. } Kit

USCG APPROVED/CLR-6 MK-II 6 PERSON LIFE RAFT

Approved by the USCG and the same basic configuration as our 6 person capacity SOLAS Life Raft, the CLR Life Raft's unique design is substantially better than many non-approved twin tube "Offshore" life rafts. With its buoyancy chamber inner-sleeves, it is the only single tube life raft that meets the Offshore Racing Council's (ORC) requirements. It features a self-erecting canopy with two canopy support arch tubes, two large canopy entrances, and the largest occupant space of any raft in this class.

- Capacity: 6 persons
- Buoyancy: 225 lbs./person
- Floor Area: 4.0 sq. ft./person
- Container Size: 31" x 21" x 14"
- Soft Valise Size: 30" x 20" x 16"
- Wt.: 115 lbs.
- Wt.: 93 lbs.

USCG APPROVED/CLR-10 MK-II 10 PERSON LIFE RAFT

The CLR-10 MK-II Life Raft is identical to our 10 Person Capacity U.S.C.G. Approved/ SOLAS MK-II Life Raft except the SOLAS equipment is replaced with a U.S.C.G. Approved Coastal Service equipment pack. This allows the CLR-10 to be packed into a smaller, lower profile, flat fiberglass container. Additional survival equipment appropriate to your vessel, crew, and area of operation should be packed in a separate Abandon Ship Bag. Twin "Gull-Wing" doors facilitate boarding from higher freeboard vessels and two counter-opposed canopy support arch tubes provide generous head and shoulder room for all occupants.

- Capacity: 10 persons
- Buoyancy: 218 lbs./person
- Floor Area: 4.0 sq. ft./person
- Container Size: 37" x 24" x 17"
- Wt.: 145 lbs.

USCG APPROVED/SOLAS MK-II 6 PERSON LIFE RAFT

Based on our USCG Approved CLR life raft design (described above), this configuration also includes a rigid boarding step, two double storm doors, double canopy and SOLAS "A" or "B" equipment. Inflatable floor, deck mounting cradle and USCG approved hydrostatic release are included as standard equipment.

- Capacity: 6 persons
- Buoyancy: 225 lbs./person
- Floor Area: 4.0 sq. ft./person
- Flat Container Size: 37" x 24" x 17"
- Round Container Size: 44" x 21"
- Refer to Brochure for Weights

USCG APPROVED/SOLAS MK-II 8,10,15,20,& 25 PERSON LIFE RAFTS

There is no better life raft available for offshore use than one approved by the United States Coast Guard and meeting international *SOLAS* standards. The configuration shown to the right is available in 8, 10, 15, 20, and 25 person capacities.

- Capacity: 8, 10, 15, 20, & 25 persons
- Buoyancy: 217 lbs./person
- Floor Area: 4.0 sq. ft./person
- Container Sizes: 54" x 24" diam. (8, 10, & 15 person)
  56" x 26" diam. (20 & 25 person)
- Refer to Brochure for Weights

Please Ask Your Dealer for Additional Information
Specifications Subject to Change Without Notice

SWITLIK   Established 1920

SWITLIK PARACHUTE COMPANY, INC.
1325 East State Street, Trenton, N.J. 08609, Phone: (609) 587-3300, Fax: (609) 586-6647 www.switlik.com

(continued from page 6)

Table of Contents

Embassy Guides

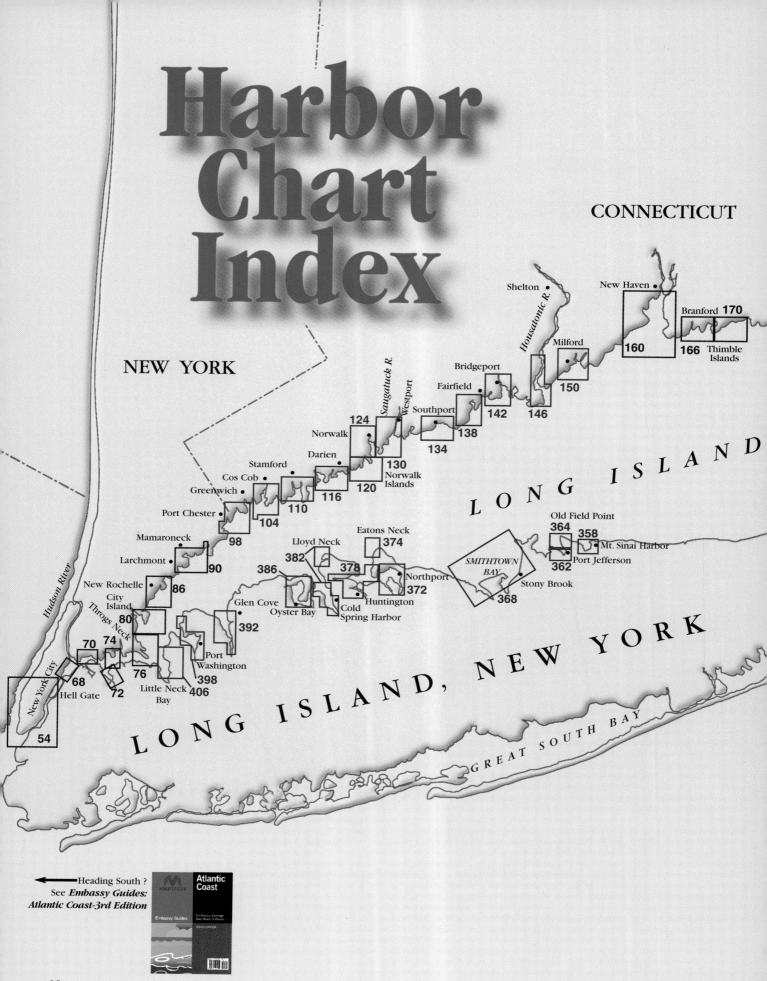

Harbor Chart Index

CONNECTICUT

NEW YORK

Shelton •

New Haven •

Branford **170**

160

166

Thimble Islands

Housatonic R.

Milford •

150

Bridgeport •

Fairfield •

142

146

Saugatuck R.

Westport

Southport •

138

124

134

Norwalk •

Darien •

130

Stamford •

Norwalk Islands

Cos Cob •

120

116

Greenwich •

110

Port Chester •

104

Mamaroneck •

98

LONG ISLAND

Larchmont •

90

Old Field Point

Eatons Neck

364

358

New Rochelle

Lloyd Neck

374

City Island

86

382

378

SMITHTOWN BAY

Mt. Sinai Harbor

362

Port Jefferson

Glen Cove •

386

372

Northport •

368

Stony Brook

Hudson River

80

Oyster Bay

Cold Spring Harbor

Huntington

Throgs Neck

70

74

392

76

Port Washington

398

New York City

68

72

Little Neck Bay

406

Hell Gate

54

LONG ISLAND, NEW YORK

GREAT SOUTH BAY

LONG ISLAND, NEW YORK

← Heading South ?
See *Embassy Guides:*
Atlantic Coast-3rd Edition

MAPTECH
Atlantic Coast
Continuous Coverage from Maine to Florida
Embassy Guides
THIRD EDITION

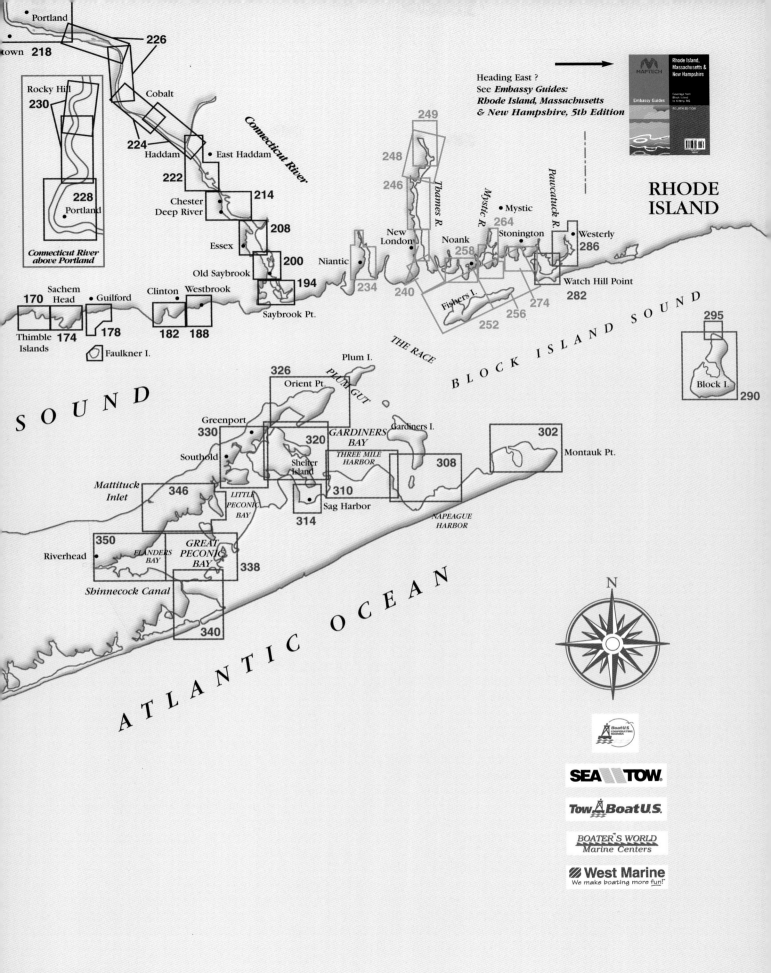

Portland

218 · town

226

Rocky Hill
230

Cobalt

224
Haddam · East Haddam

Connecticut River

222

Chester
Deep River
214

Essex
208

228
Portland ·

Connecticut River above Portland

Old Saybrook
200

Westbrook
194

Saybrook Pt.

Sachem Head
170
· Guilford

Clinton
182

Westbrook
188

Thimble Islands
174

178

· Faulkner I.

Niantic

234

Heading East ?
See *Embassy Guides:*
Rhode Island, Massachusetts
& New Hampshire, 5th Edition

MAPTECH
Rhode Island, Massachusetts & New Hampshire
Embassy Guides

249

248

246

Thames R.

New London

240

Mystic R.

· Mystic

Noank
258

264

Stonington

282

274

256

252

Fishers I.

Pawcatuck R.

Westerly
286

Watch Hill Point

RHODE ISLAND

295

Block I.
290

302

S O U N D

THE RACE

B L O C K   I S L A N D   S O U N D

Plum I.

326

Orient Pt.

PLUM GUT

Greenport
330

320

GARDINERS BAY

Gardiners I.

Southold

Shelter Island

THREE MILE HARBOR

308

Montauk Pt.

Mattituck Inlet
346

LITTLE PECONIC BAY

310

Sag Harbor

314

NAPEAGUE HARBOR

350

FLANDERS BAY

GREAT PECONIC BAY

338

Riverhead ·

Shinnecock Canal

340

A T L A N T I C   O C E A N

N

BoatUS
COOPERATING MARINA

SEA TOW.

Tow BoatU.S.

BOATER'S WORLD
Marine Centers

West Marine
We make boating more *fun!*

How To Use

Maptech's Embassy Guides

Dear Reader,

For nearly 15 years, we at Maptech's Embassy Guides have worked to bring boaters the most useful and useable cruising information available. Much has changed since we first embarked on our journey to create the "perfect" cruising guide. On the other hand, some things never change: our attention to detail, our firsthand research on the waters we cover, and the bottom line, our quality.

Maptech's Embassy Guides continues to create the most comprehensive, accurate, and attractive cruising guide available. You'll love to read our books not just when you're on the water, but when you're curled up at home. This book will be a valued crew member as well as a helpful planning tool.

Embassy Guides is proud to be part of the Maptech family, which offers boaters a suite of navigational information solutions including Maptech Navigational Software, ChartKit paper chartbooks, and Maptech Waterproof Charts.

To help keep you updated, we have added Additions/Corrections pages for each of our guides to our website (www.maptech.com). Click on Cruising Guides and then the appropriate addenda link. We'd love to hear your comments. Thank you, and have fun on the water!

~The Embassy Staff

REFERENCE

Table of Contents & Harbor Chart Index: Embassy Guides' Table of Contents and Introductory Harbor Chart provide a view of the big picture, pinpointing exactly where you can find the information you are looking for.

Features: Boating is more than just traveling from marina to marina—it is learning about and having fun in the areas you are visiting. To help you appreciate and understand what you see, we have asked the experts to give you a perspective on the worlds of history, geology, fishing, birding, and scuba diving. It's good reading and a great reference.

Boater's Reference: Embassy Guides' new Boater's Reference sections will appear at the beginning of every one of our cruising guides. This section includes important information for the mariner, like details on using GPS and radionavigation systems, as well as common weather patterns along the coast and where to pick up NOAA weather broadcasts.

CRUISING REGIONS

A. Regional Chapters: Each Embassy Guide is organized into Cruising Regions, which are signified by a color bar at the top of the page for easy reference. And every Cruising Region begins with a Regional Chapter, which provides an overview of the cruising region as well as navigation advice on moving from destination to destination.

B. Regional Map: Each Regional Chapter leads off with a Regional Map that identifies where you can find the destination harbors. It gives you a better sense of where destinations are located in relation to each other, aiding your trip-planning.

DESTINATIONS

C. Harbor Chapters: Within each region, Embassy Guides introduces you to all cruising destinations, from hot ports to quiet harbors. Each Harbor Chapter includes a Harbor Chart, Marine Facilities Table, color photographs, and text

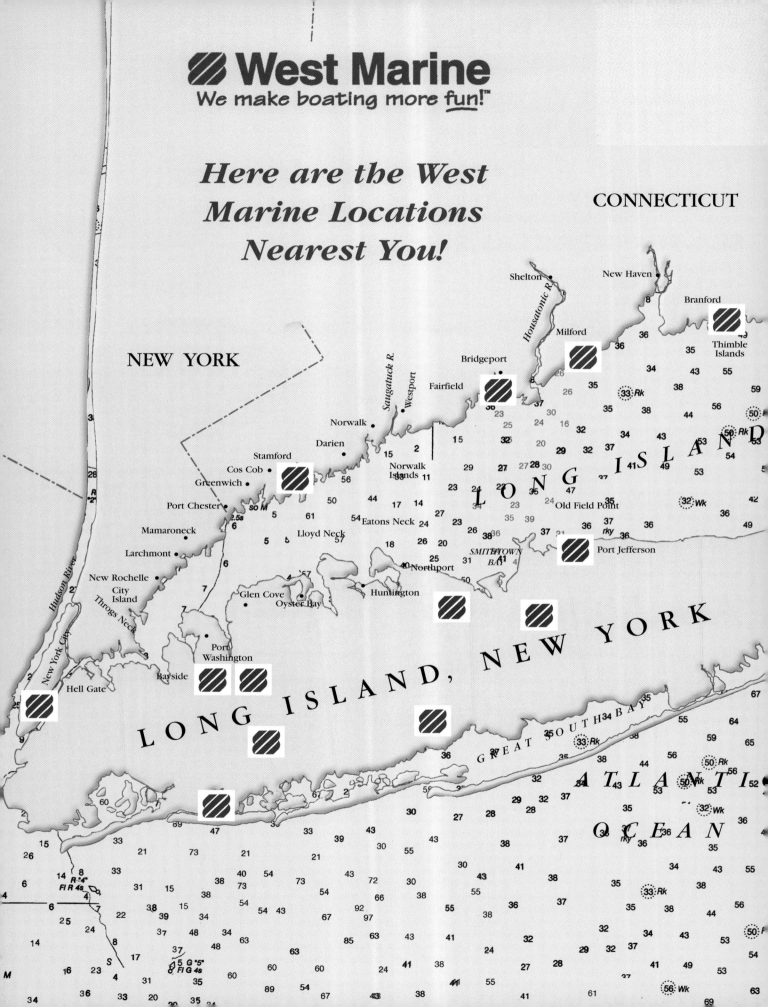

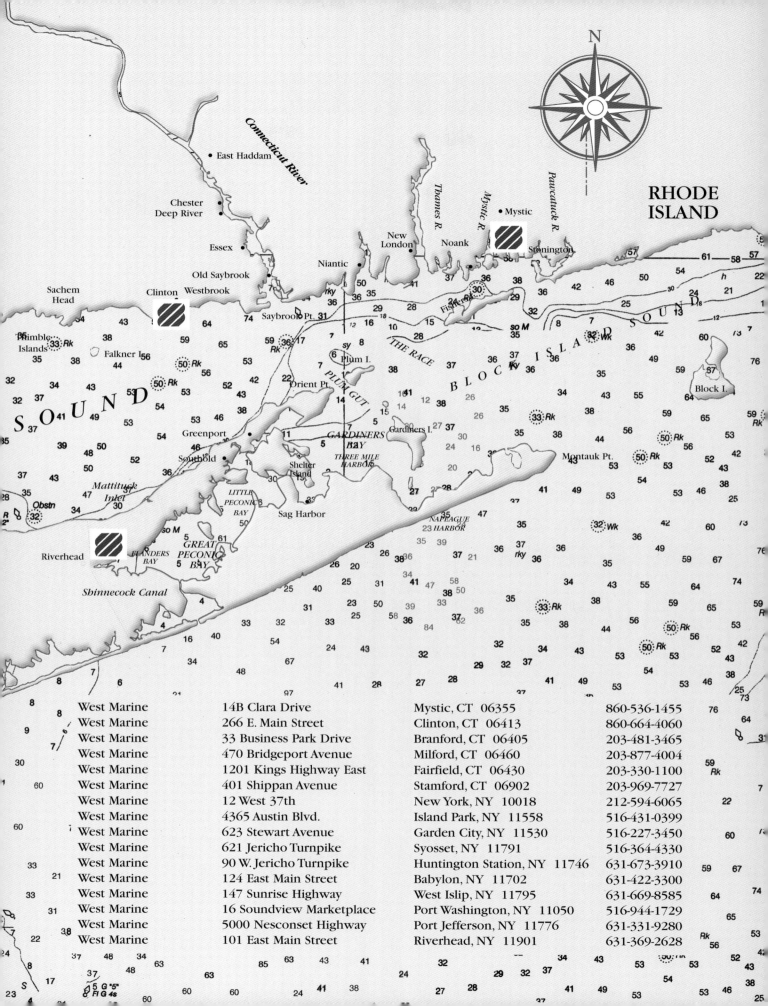

RHODE ISLAND

West Marine	14B Clara Drive	Mystic, CT 06355	860-536-1455
West Marine	266 E. Main Street	Clinton, CT 06413	860-664-4060
West Marine	33 Business Park Drive	Branford, CT 06405	203-481-3465
West Marine	470 Bridgeport Avenue	Milford, CT 06460	203-877-4004
West Marine	1201 Kings Highway East	Fairfield, CT 06430	203-330-1100
West Marine	401 Shippan Avenue	Stamford, CT 06902	203-969-7727
West Marine	12 West 37th	New York, NY 10018	212-594-6065
West Marine	4365 Austin Blvd.	Island Park, NY 11558	516-431-0399
West Marine	623 Stewart Avenue	Garden City, NY 11530	516-227-3450
West Marine	621 Jericho Turnpike	Syosset, NY 11791	516-364-4330
West Marine	90 W. Jericho Turnpike	Huntington Station, NY 11746	631-673-3910
West Marine	124 East Main Street	Babylon, NY 11702	631-422-3300
West Marine	147 Sunrise Highway	West Islip, NY 11795	631-669-8585
West Marine	16 Soundview Marketplace	Port Washington, NY 11050	516-944-1729
West Marine	5000 Nesconset Highway	Port Jefferson, NY 11776	631-331-9280
West Marine	101 East Main Street	Riverhead, NY 11901	631-369-2628

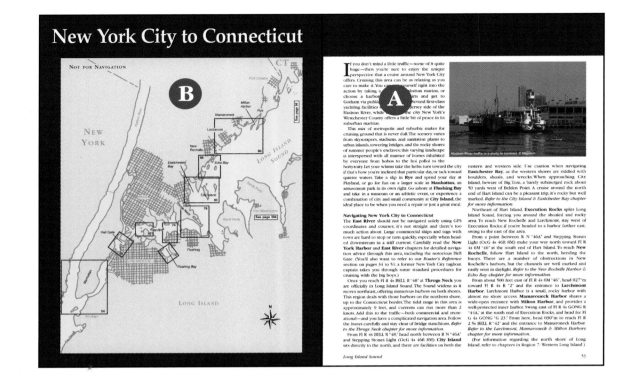

New York City to Connecticut

covering local history and activities, restaurants and provisions, and detailed navigation advice on local approaches and anchorages.

D. Harbor Charts: Every Harbor Chapter begins with a full-color section of the appropriate National Oceanic and Atmospheric Administration (NOAA) chart for the area. Information that we add to the chart is always over-printed in the appropriate regional color. These charts should be used to give you an idea of where marinas and anchorages are located. Refer to Maptech's Waterproof Charts and ChartKit, or NOAA charts for more extensive coverage. (Embassy Guides' Harbor Charts are marked "Not for Navigation," as required by NOAA of all private publishers. NOAA requires that this admonition be included on all charts that they themselves do not publish because they cannot control the reproductions and, hence, cannot guarantee their accuracy.)

E. Latitude and Longitude Border: Many Harbor Charts are surrounded by a latitude and longitude border, marked in degrees and minutes for easy locating of landmarks and navigational markers.

F. Waypoints: We have collected thousands of waypoints and located them on the Harbor Charts. The waypoints are listed in the Light List & Waypoints indexes in the front of the books, which you should read before using the waypoints.

G. Chart Information: On every Harbor Chart you will find all of the important chart information, like NOAA chart # and edition, plus the scale that the chart is printed at in the book.

H. Compass Rose: Every Harbor Chart contains a full or segmented compass rose showing the directions of true and magnetic north, the magnetic variation, and annual increase.

I. Marine Facility Locators: These show the location of virtually every marina, yacht club, boat yard, and dockside restaurant on the coast. The locators are cross-referenced to the chapter's Marine Facilities Table. A (R) symbol on the chart indicates a launching ramp. A ⚓ on the chart indicates an anchorage area—read the navigation text for more information about the spot.

J. Distance Scale: All of our Harbor Charts are reproduced at or near the same scale as the original NOAA charts.

K. Anchorages: For your convenience, popular anchorages are plotted right on the charts.

L. Chapter Text: There are four main components that you'll find in every chapter of Embassy Guides: the Introduction, Activities, Restaurants & Provisions, and Navigation & Anchorages.

    Introduction: This section gives you some interesting historical and cultural background on the harbor and the town, and a feel for what contributed to its development and character.

    Activities: This section describes the most popular attractions and events in the area. Telephone numbers are always given so that you can get up-to-the-minute information about schedules, admission rates, and the

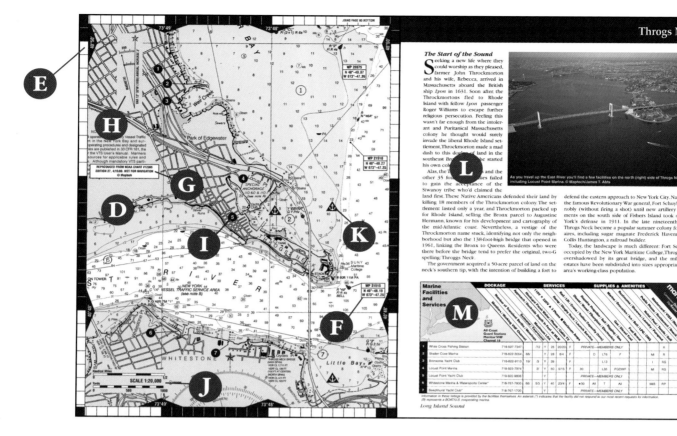

L. Chapter Text: continued

like. We also alert you to some of the free attractions of the area such as public beaches, wildlife preserves, walking trails, parks, and good fishing holes.

Restaurants & Provisions: Culinary tastes vary, so we try to present to you lots of choices in each harbor. We will mention most restaurants immediately accessible to the waterfront and get progressively more selective as you go farther afield. We will also tell you where to find groceries, marine supplies, laundromats, banks, pharmacies, and other useful establishments.

Navigation & Anchorages: Read this section before you head to a new harbor. Here you will find lots of local knowledge about the tricks to dealing with the tides, currents, or traffic; where the hidden rocks are and how to avoid them; and how to find the choice anchorages. The heart of the text is a detailed description of all the approaches and anchorages. All major landmarks and destinations are bold-faced for easy scanning.

ChartKit Reference Pages: For full chart coverage of a harbor and its approaches, we provide page references to specific ChartKits that cover the corresponding area.

Cautions & Notes: For those areas that are navigationally difficult, you'll find important information set apart as a caution or a note.

Shoreside & Emergency Services: Here are all the telephone numbers and VHF channels for important services ashore and afloat.

M. Marine Facilities Tables: Here you will find virtually every marina, yacht club, boat yard, and waterfront restaurant in the area, and the services, facilities, and amenities they offer. Most of the categories are self-evident. However, it should be noted that facility operators sometimes report their approach and dockside depths optimistically.

N. Color Photographs and Aerials: "A picture is worth a thousand words," so we usually give you at least one color photograph of each harbor to show you what to expect and to point out local landmarks. We include aerial photos of almost every harbor entrance to give you a "live" look at your approach, and a few around-town shots provide a feel for the destination.

Spotlights: We guarantee you will have fun reading these short feature articles. Read your way up the coast for a truly eclectic view of the people, ideas, and events that have shaped the cruising area. We also feature Nauti Words, which explain the origins of various nautical terms and idioms.

A Boater's Guide to
Marine Sewage Pumpouts
Located on Long Island Sound

A List of Pumpout Facilities Appears on the Next Two Pages

Boaters, perhaps more than any others, are aware of and concerned about pollution threats facing our coastal waters. While not a major source of pollution, boat sewage contributes to poor water quality in areas where boats congregate, such as sheltered harbors, rivers and embayments. Boat sewage is of particular concern as this waste may contain disease-causing bacteria and viruses that can contaminate shellfish beds and swimming areas. As a boater, you can do your part to help keep our waters clean by using and maintaining the appropriate type of marine sanitation device on your boat.

The Federal Clean Water Act requires all boats with an installed head to have one of three types of Coast Guard-approved Marine Sanitation Devices (MSDs) attached to the toilet.

✓ **A TYPE I MSD** treats sewage so that discharged effluent meets specified standards for bacteria content and contains no visible floating solids.

NOTE: A macerator is not considered to be an approved Type I or Type II treatment system. A macerator only grinds sewage—it does not treat it. Any system that allows for the direct overboard discharge of raw (untreated) sewage is illegal.

FOR MORE INFORMATION, check out these web sites:
Connecticut – *http://dep.state.ct.us/olisp/cva/cva.htm*
New York – *www.nysefc.org*

✓ **A TYPE II MSD** is similar to a Type I but must meet a higher standard of sewage treatment and is usually found on boats 50 ft. and larger.

✓ **A TYPE III MSD** is a holding tank that retains untreated sewage for shore based disposal or discharge beyond the U.S. Territorial Seas Demarcation Line. A Type III does not treat waste. Portable toilets, like holding tanks, also retain untreated waste and should be emptied at a dump station or pumpout station facility.

NOTE: It is not legal to discharge untreated sewage anywhere in Long island Sound or within 3 miles of the south shore of Long Island.

Many states are implementing "No Discharge Areas" with the approval of the Environmental Protection Agency (EPA). Within these areas, the discharge of sewage, treated or untreated, is prohibited.

Currently, the following "No Discharge Areas" in Long Island Sound and vicinity have been established by the EPA.

Connecticut:	None
New York:	Huntington Harbor, Lloyd Harbor, Mamaroneck Harbor and the eastern end of Long Island Sound
Rhode Island:	All waters

NOTE: Many local authorities have established no discharge areas. Boaters should heed posted signs.

Principal funding for the publication of the "Marine Sewage Pumpouts" pages provided under the Sports Fish Restoration Account, as established by the federal Clean Vessel Act. Additional funding provided by the Connecticut Department of Environmental Protection Boating Division, the New York State Department of Environmental Conservation, Division of Fish and Wildlife and the New York State Environmental Facilities Corporation.

MARINE SEWAGE PUMPOUTS
FACILITIES DIRECTORY

WESTERLY, RHODE ISLAND
1. Town of Westerly Pumpout Boat, VHF CH: 9
2. Westerly Yacht Club, CH: 10
3. Avondale Boat Yard Inc., CH: 9, 16
4. Norwest Marine •, CH: 68

STONINGTON, CONNECTICUT
5. Dodson Boatyard, CH: 78
6. Mystic Marine Basin, CH: 68
7. Mystic Pumpout Boat •, CH: 68
8. Mystic River Marina •, CH: 9
9. Brower's Cove Marina, CH: none
10. Mystic Cove Marina, CH: none
11. Brewer Yacht Yard at Mystic, CH: 9, 11

GROTON
12. Noank Village Boatyard, CH: 68
13. Noank Shipyard •, CH: 9
14. Atlantic Navigation Pumpout Boat, CH: 72
15. Mystic Pumpout Boat •, CH: 68
16. Spicer's Noank Marina, CH: 68
17. Pine Island Marina, CH: 68
18. Shennecossett Yacht Club, CH: 68
19. City of Groton, Wastewater Treatment Facility •, CH: 72

NORWICH
20. The Marina at American Wharf •, CH: 68

NEW LONDON
21. Crocker's Boatyard, Inc. •, CH: 9, 10
22. Ferry Slip Dockominium, CH: none
23. Burr's Yacht Haven •, CH: 9, 78
24. Thamesport Marina •, CH: 9, 68

EAST LYME
25. Bayreuther Boat Yard Inc., CH: 8, 9
26. Port Niantic Marina, CH: 9

OLD LYME
27. CT DEP Marine Headquarters •, CH: 9
28. CT DEP Pumpout Boat •, CH: 68

GLASTONBURY
29. Seaboard Marina, CH: 68

PORTLAND
30. Yankee Boat Yard & Marina •, CH: 68

HADDAM
31. Andrews Marina •, CH: none

CHESTER
32. Chrisholm Marina, CH: 9
33. Hays Haven Marina, CH: 9

DEEP RIVER
34. Brewer Deep River Marina •, CH: 9

ESSEX
35. Brewer Dauntless Shipyard, CH: 9
36. The Chandlery at Essex, CH: 68

OLD SAYBROOK
37. Between the Bridges Marina, CH: 9, 7
38. Saybrook Point Marina •, CH: 9

WESTBROOK
39. Harry's Marine Repair, CH: none
40. Brewer Pilot's Point Marina •, CH: 9

CLINTON
41. Cedar Island Marina Inc. •, CH: 9, 68
42. Riverside Basin Marina •, CH: 9

GUILFORD
43. Guilford Yacht Club •, CH: 71

BRANFORD
44. Brewer Bruce & Johnson's, CH: 9
45. Goodsell Point Marina, CH: none
46. Town of Branford Pumpout Boat •, CH: 9
47. Pier 66, CH: 9

WEST HAVEN
48. West Cove Marina •, CH: none

MILFORD
49. Milford Landing •, CH: 9
50. Milford Harbor Marina, CH: 68

STRATFORD
51. Marina at the Dock, CH: 9
52. Brewer Stratford Marina, CH: 9, 10

BRIDGEPORT
53. Cedar Marina •, CH: 9
54. City of Bridgeport Pumpout Boat •, CH: 6, 9, 13, 16
55. Captain's Cove Seaport, CH: 18

NEW YORK

FAIRFIELD
56. South Benson Marina •, CH: 9, 16
57. Pequot Yacht Club, CH: 69

WESTPORT
58. Compo Yacht Basin, CH: 11, 16

NORWALK
59. Soundkeeper Pumpout Boat •, CH: 77
60. Norwalk Cove Marina, CH: 9, 72
61. Norwalk Visitors' Dock •, CH: 9
62. Rex Marine Center •, CH: 9

63. The Boatworks Inc., Rowayton •, CH: 68

STAMFORD
64. Cove Mills Marina, CH: none
65. Cummings Park Marina, CH: none
66. Harbour Square Marina, CH: 9
67. Czescik Municipal Marina •, CH: none
68. Soundkeeper Pumpout Boat •, CH: 77
69. Stamford Landing Marina, CH: 9

GREENWICH
70. Mianus River Boat/Yacht, CH: none
71. Soundkeeper Pumpout Boat •, CH: 77
72. Greenwich Fuel Dock, CH: none

RYE, NEW YORK
73. Port Chester Municipal Marina •, CH: 79
74. Long Island Soundkeeper Boat •, CH: 77
75. Rye Municipal Boat Basin

MAMARONECK
76. Nichols Yacht Yard •, CH: none
77. Mamaroneck - Harbor Island •, CH: 16
78. Post Road Boat Yard

NEW ROCHELLE
79. New Rochelle Municipal Marina •, CH: 16

LONG ISLAND, NEW YORK

NORTH HEMPSTEAD
80. Manhasset Bay Marina •, CH: 9
81. North Hempstead Town Dock •, CH: 9
82. N. Hempstead Manhasset Bay Boat •, CH: 9
83. Haven Marina •
84. Inspiration Wharf •, CH: 9
85. N. Hempstead Manorhaven Beach Park •, CH: 9
86. Capri Marine & Yachting Ctr. •, CH: 9, 71
87. N. Hempstead Bar Beach Park •, CH: 9

GLEN COVE CITY
88. Brewer Marina •, CH: 9
89. City of Glen Cove Yacht Club •
90. Glen Cove Yacht Service & Repair •

OYSTER BAY
91. Sea Cliff Yacht Club •, CH: 9
92. Oyster Bay Tappen Beach & Boat Basin •, CH: 9
93. Oyster Bay Mobile Pumpout Boats West •, CH: 9
94. Oyster Bay Mobile Pumpout Boats East •, CH: 9
95. Oyster Bay Theodore Roosevelt Beach •, CH: 9
67. Tobay Beach & Boat Basin •, CH: 9
68. John Burns Park •, CH: 9

CONNECTICUT

HUNTINGTON
96. Huntington Boat Pumpout •, CH: 10
97. Huntington Yacht Club •, CH: 68
98. Huntington Halesite Marina Floating
    Pumpout •, CH: 10
99. Huntington Mill Dam Marina Floating
    Pumpout •, CH: 10
100. West Shore Marina
101. Village of Northport Pumpout Boat •, CH: 9
102. Huntington Woodbine Marina •, CH: 10
103. Britannia Marina & Yacht Club

SMITHTOWN
104. Smithtown Old Dock Road Boat Ramp •, CH: 16
105. Smithtown Long Beach Marina •, CH: 16
106. Smithtown Long Beach
     Mooring Area •, CH: 16

151. Windswept Marina •, CH: none
152. Morgan's Swan River Marina •, CH: none

SOUTHOLD
113. Claudio's Marina •, CH: 9
114. Port of Egypt Marine •
115. Albertson Marina •, CH: 9, 16
116. New Suffolk Shipyard •
117. Cutchogue Harbor Marina •
118. Strong's Marina •, CH: 68

RIVERHEAD
119. East Creek Marina/Boat Ramp •, CH: none
120. Great Peconic Bay Marina •, CH: none

121. Larry's Lighthouse Marina •, CH: none
122. Downtown Pumpout Station •, CH: none

SOUTHAMPTON
123. Dreamer's Cove Motel
124. Gateway Marina
125. Treasure Cove Marina
126. Southampton Peconic Bays Boat •, CH: 73
127. Southampton Sag Harbor Boat •, CH: 73
132. Shagwong Marina •, CH: none
133. Harbor Marina - Seacoast Enterprises

134. Three Mile Harbor Boat Yard
143. Southampton Shinnecock Bay Boat •, CH: 73
144. Mariner's Cove Marine
145. Sherry & Joe Carr's Boat Works
146. Southampton Tiana Bay Boat •, CH: 73
147. Remsenburg Marina •, CH: 16
148. Seatuck Cove Marina
149. Cerullo Brothers Marina
150. Southampton Moriches Bay Boat •, CH: 73

EAST HAMPTON
128. Sag Harbor Marine Park Docks •, CH: 9, 73
129. E. Hampton Trustees Pumpout Boat •
130. E. Hampton Point Marina •, CH: 9
131. E. Hampton Gann Road •, CH: 73
135. Montauk Sportsman's Dock •, CH: none
136. E. Hampton Star Island #2 Pumpout •, CH: 73
137. E. Hampton Star Island Pumpout Fac. •, CH: 73
138. Gone Fishing Marina •, CH: 19
139. Star Island Yacht Club

SHELTER ISLAND
140. Piccozzi's Dering Harbor Marina •, CH: 9
141. Coecles Harbor Marina & Boatyard •, CH: 9
142. The Island Boatyard •

ISLIP
153. Patchogue Marine
154. Dutchmen Cove Marina •, CH: none
155. West Sayville Basin Boat •, CH: 68
156. Timber Point County Marina •, CH: 16
157. Heckscher State Park •, CH: none

RHODE ISLAND

No Discharge Areas

158. Atlantique Beach Marina •, CH: 16
160. East Islip Marina •, CH: 16
161. Islip Dept. of Parks Bay Shore Marina •, CH: 16
162. Bay Shore Marina

BABYLON
159. Captree State Park •, CH: none
163. Bablyon Marina (aka, Argyle) •, CH: none
164. Surfside 3 Marina
165. Anchorage Marine
166. Delmarine

HEMPSTEAD
169. Precision Marine •, CH: none
170. Treasure Island Marine •
171. Blue Water Yacht Club •, CH: none
172. Al Grover's High & Dry Marina •, CH: none
173. Freeport Bay Marina •
174. Guy Lombardo Marina •, CH: 16
175. Mako Marine
176. Morgan's Marine Service
177. Empire Point Marina •, CH: 9
178. Jones Beach State Park •, CH: none
179. Crow's Nest Marina •, CH: 68, 72
180. East Marina •, CH: 16

NEW YORK CITY
181. Coney Island Marine Pumpout •, CH: none

KEY
• Funded by Clean Vessel Act
○ Federal "No Discharge Area"
–·–· U.S. Territorial Seas Demarcation
     Line (3-mile limit)
◯ Pumpout boat

Geology

It took a few hundred million years, but it turns out Mother Nature knew what she was doing when she created Long Island Sound. Its formation began well before North America started to take shape.

The land masses that would ultimately become Africa and North America were on a collision course. The ocean that separated them was slowly growing smaller, by a mere several inches per year. This ocean pre-dated the Atlantic (named for Atlas, the mythological Titan) and was therefore called the Iapetos Ocean, since Iapetos was the father of Atlas. The closing of the Iapetos Ocean and the movements of the ancestral African and North American continents were part of a larger process that brought all of the major early land masses of the earth together to form the supercontinent Pangaea (meaning "all-lands").

As the African and North American land masses came together their colliding edges crumpled, thrusting up the Appalachian Mountains. Pangaea survived as a supercontinent for roughly 50 million years, and about 200 million years ago, a different set of forces started moving the land masses apart again. These movements initiated the development of Africa, North America, and the Atlantic Ocean. At this same time, the geologic foundation of Long Island Sound began to take shape.

The crashing of continents and scraping of glaciers laid the foundation for Long Island Sound, but the glacial retreat that began 20,000 years ago is what fleshed out the Sound's present configuration. At this time sea level was about 300 feet lower than it is today because ocean water was trapped in the ice sheet advancing to the middle of Long Island. The glaciers deposited a pile of debris called a terminal moraine. The continental shelf was almost entirely above sea level, and the equivalent of an Atlantic coast beach like Fire Island was about 100 miles farther south.

By 19,000 years ago, the ice could no longer maintain itself at its terminal position because it was melting faster than new ice was being pushed south. The ice front slowly receded to the north. As the ice front retreated, it stuttered and paused a few times. At each of these pauses (recessional positions) it left a pile of glacial debris known as a recessional moraine. The bulk of the above-water portions of Fishers Island, Plum Island, and northernmost Long Island are composed of this recessional moraine debris. From Plum Island westward, this glacial debris sits atop the glacially-scoured erosional remnant of the coastal plain wedge and forms the high, sandy bluffs of the North Shore of Long Island.

Because the glacier paused on the high portion of the coastal-plain remnant, it left a long, thin, high line of deposits (the recessional moraine), which made an ideal dam. When the glacier resumed its northward recession, it began to back into the Long Island Sound basin that it had helped to create. This formed a low area between the ice front and the recessional moraine. The low area filled with melt water and a glacial lake formed.

The ice also stuttered as it retreated across the basin. It deposited a few small recessional moraines at Mystic, Old Saybrook, Hammonasset, and Madison near the Connecticut shore. These moraines have offshore extensions in Long Island Sound: Kimberly Reef, Branford Reef, and Crooked Shoal. The Captain and Norwalk islands are also moraine segments that were deposited about 17,000 years ago. The familiar sandy bluffs of Faulkner Island have a glacial origin, although they may be older than the most recent ice advance that left the other moraines.

By about 17,000 years ago the ice front had retreated out of southeastern Connecticut. The expanding

Continued on page 24...

NE 400 SERIES NORTHEAST

The Northeast 400 (above) a fast, stable, comfortable sailboat that is fun to sail. She features inside and outside steering stations, cruises at 8-9 knots, has a 100 hp engine that provokes reverse power for adverse conditons.

The Northwest 480 (right) is a bluewater 10-12 knot sailboat, with private staterooms, a library-computer den and gourmet galley. Push button sailing and dual steering stations.NW480

NONSUCH

For 150 years the simple catboat was a day sailor, a workboat and weekend racer. Then the idea of sticking a big windsurfer rig on a stable modern catboat was a "right on" solution.

1100 were built. One person, one sail, one sheet. Simple, stable and safe. We specialize in the wonderful boats called Nonsuch.

Hallberg-Rassy yachts are designed by German Frers and they are built in Sweden. Every boat is delivered with 100A55 certificate (unlimited ocean voyages). The finest interiors, the best systems and all the top hardware are found here.

A close look at Hallberg-Rassy will indicate a relationship between the highest of yacht quality and one of todays extraordinary buying opportunities. An investment today will be well appreciated tomorrow.

Hallberg-Rassy

HR 31   HR 34   HR 36   HR 39   HR 42   HR 46   HR 53   HR 62

EASTLAND
YACHTS INC.

33 Pratt Street • Essex, Connecticut 06426 • 860-767-8224 • Fax 860-767-9094 • www.eastlandyachts.com

glacial lake (Lake Connecticut) eventually filled the Long Island Sound basin, grew to about the same size as the present-day Sound, and began to fill in with clay sediments. At one time, this fresh water lake may have been connected with similar lakes in Block Island Sound and Buzzards Bay.

The history of the glacial lake in Long Island Sound is not completely understood. Up to 300 feet of glacial-lake clay deposits now partially fill the Long Island Sound basin, and it probably took about 3,500 years for this sediment to accumulate. If the clay deposit had not partially filled the basin, Long Island Sound would be much deeper than its 64-foot average depth. Rather than the few localized 300-foot water depths, 400- to 500-foot water depths would be more common.

The glacial lake is thought to have drained before sea level had risen sufficiently to allow marine waters to flood the Sound. For a relatively short time, the lake clays were exposed to the air, forming a broad plain which was cut by streams. Ocean waters probably began to enter the Long Island Sound basin about 15,000 years ago. We don't yet understand all the details of sea-level rise over the last 15,000 years, but present evidence indicates that the fertile tidal marshes were well developed at least 4,000 years ago.

In many areas of the world, we would have seen the shoreline change significantly over the last 4,000 years as the sea slowly rose. But Long Island Sound was in a fairly "low-energy nearshore environment." This means that geologic agents such as wave action and nearshore currents had a hard time dominating the shoreline. It takes time and energy to build wide, extensive beaches, or large bars and spits. Because it is sheltered by Long Island, the Sound environment provides for neither. As a result, previous upland features such as glacially-modified stream valleys and hills were not extensively changed as they were gradually submerged. Valleys became coves, harbors, and bays. Hills became headlands, promontories, or islands. Some beaches and spits did form but they did not really disrupt the overall shape of the submerged upland features that form the Sound shore of today.

If you sailed the Sound 4,000 years ago, only the major landmarks such as the Connecticut, Housatonic, and Thames Rivers or the high, sandy bluffs of the North Shore of Long Island would be recognizable. The water level would be 30 feet lower than it is presently so that hills and coves along the shore would look very different. The Thimble Islands would be a series of little hills with only their feet wet. Long Sand Shoal between Westbrook and the Connecticut River might be known as "Long Sand Dune." Of course, there would be no manmade structures except Indian settlements along the shore—smoke rising from the lodges, piles of oyster shells glistening on the beach, men working the stone fishing weirs extending out into the water. Those fishing weirs are still there today—30 feet under the surface of the Sound.

How much more will the sea encroach? In the natural scheme of things, beaches, tidal marshes, river mouths, and human settlements retreat before the rising sea. Modern man, with his sea-walls, jetties, and "permanent" structures has yet to learn the wisdom of such a strategic retreat. ♦

The Thimble Islands got dropped off during the glacial retreat. © Maptech/James T. Abts

Fishing Long Island Sound

© Maptech

Nurtured by rivers and streams, dotted with islands and reefs, sparkling with currents and eddies, Long Island Sound's sheltered estuaries provide exciting fishing for food and game. Marine fishing does not require a license in Connecticut or New York, but fishing inland waters does; check with your local tackle shop if you're planning on gunkholing very far upriver (for example, north of the Interstate 95 bridge in Old Saybrook on the Connecticut, or the Merritt Parkway on the Housatonic).

Equipment

The Long Island Sound has got the fish; all you need is the tackle to haul them in. Remember that you don't have to tap into Junior's college fund to buy good equipment. Nevertheless, the old adage holds true: you get what you pay for.

A quality reel prevents a tangled mess. The reel should have at least a 4-to-1 retrieval ratio and hold 150 to 200 yards of quality monofilament line. (Cheap bulk spools are more expensive in the long run.) Many anglers prefer conventional tackle to spinning gear: bait-fishing wears line harder, and rocks, barnacles, and other hazards require a stronger rig. Whether you're trolling, jigging, or bait-fishing, the conventional star drag reel has the advantage over spinning equipment.

© Maptech

Your rod should be strong and light, yet stiff enough to handle jigs, plugs, baits, and lead weights up to 12 ounces. Some fishermen carry a dozen different rods on board, but that's not always feasible. A 6.5- to 7-foot graphite rod with a reel filled with strong, supple line of 15- to 25-pound test should be adequate. Two spools—one with 15-pound line and one with 20- or 25-pound line—will give you greater flexibility.

How To Fish

There are five basic methods for landing the Big One: live bait, trolling, jigging, casting (plugging), and fly-fishing.

Live-lining (using live bait) catches the Sound's monster blues and trophy stripers on live bunker (menhaden) and eels. Sand worms are popular for striped bass, winter flounder, scup, and early blackfish. Summer blackfish favor green crabs and fiddler crabs, while fluke prefer live minnows. Pieces of clam and mussels make excellent baits for bottom-fishing. The odor and flavor of "chunk baits" entice fish to feed on these larger pieces.

Trolling allows you to cover a lot of Sound water effectively. Charter boat captains troll daily for striped bass and bluefish from hot spots like The Race, Plum Gut, and Montauk. You can troll with standard gear, but when the fish are down deep, you need special wire-line trolling outfits or down-riggers to get the bait down there.

Jigging is surefire for catching fish in schools. In Long Island Sound, spring mackerel and summertime blues are the prime targets. Jigging is the simple act of lowering a metal or lead jig into a school of fish, and then moving or jigging the rod in an up-and-down motion to make the lure dance. Eatons Neck and Middle Ground (Stratford Shoals) are favorite jigging spots where party fishing boats jig thousands of fish every season.

Surface casting with poppers and plugs is the favorite among thrill-seekers fishing stripers or blues. Once you've had a few surface slashing encounters, you'll be hooked.

Years ago, fly-rodders were a novelty in saltwater. Today, it's hard to miss the graceful curves of the long rods on the waters of the Sound. Saltwater fly-fishing is the fastest growing phenomenon in sportfishing, breaking records every season. This popularity is driving big improvements in fly-fishing technology. The saltwater outfits of today are more efficient, easier to use, and less expensive than those of a decade ago. The Sound has dozens of fly-fishing specialty shops, and many shops, fishing clubs, and equipment manufacturers offer seminars on what's best in today's tackle for your chosen destination.

Catch and release is an important topic for today's pressured fisheries. By following several simple steps you can return a healthy fish to the water. Terminal tackle and improper handling do the most damage to fish, but terminal tackle doesn't need to be deadly. Crimp or file down hook barbs first; on plugs or lures with two sets of treble hooks, remove the top set. For fastest return to the water, replace the bottom set with a single hook. A good pair of needlenose pliers removes hooks quickly and

effectively—and speed is good with your fingers in a mouth full of snapper teeth. Minimize air time and wet your hands when handling the fish, and take care not to damage its gills. If you're having trouble, cut the leader as close to the hook as possible and release the fish—its digestive juices will eventually dissolve the hook. Finally, a returning fish may need a little resuscitation. Move it slowly backward and forward, gently pushing water through its gills. A little care will go a long way toward ensuring a Sound fishery for the future.

What's Out There?
The kings of the circuit on Long Island Sound are striped bass and bluefish. After a long brush with extinction,

Striped Bass

stripers have recovered in great numbers. These nighttime feeders will take natural baits from sand- and bloodworms to squid, sand eels, menhaden (bunker), and mackerel. Try fishing the bottom with worms or chunk baits, trolling lure

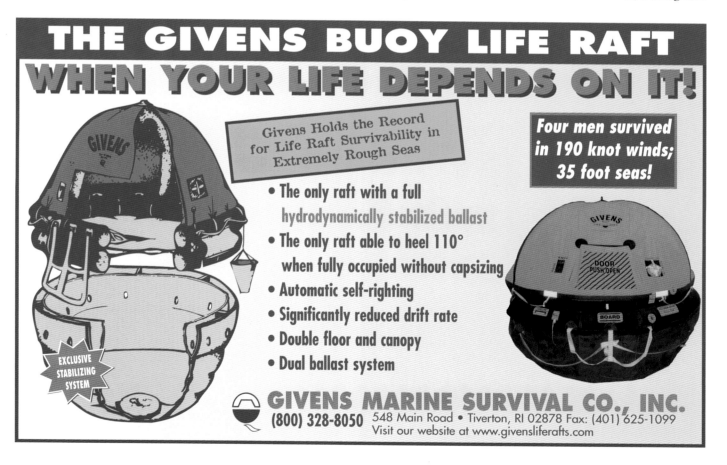

Quiet, Yes. Humble, No Way.

*The quiet strength
of Honda.*

You're out there on the open waters. You need dependable power to push through the pitching and rolling sea. But you don't need a noisy, vibrating, smoky two-stroke. Honda's legendary four-stroke technology provides clean, quiet power that is virtually free of noise, vibration, and smoke. Nobody else has Honda's 35 years of four-stroke outboard experience or offers you a selection so complete. Choose from more than 50 models, from two-horsepower to the BF130, the most powerful four-stroke outboard in the world. Honda pioneered the modern four-stroke outboard to give you what you really want – the power to cut through the waves, and the peace and quiet to enjoy it. For more information and the Honda Marine dealer nearest you, call 1-800-426-7701 or visit our Web site.

2006 EPA STANDARD

Power In Tune With Nature

www.honda-marine.com

Power In Tune With Nature

HONDA MARINE

*Whether at the dock, at sea, or at home,
you have a Honda Marine Dealer nearby...*

and worm baits, and drifting and live-lining mackerel, bunker, eels, or sea worms.

Anadromous bass thrive in both fresh and saltwater. Bass in western Long Island Sound come mainly from Hudson River stocks, while eastern Sound waters draw populations from the Chesapeake Bay and Atlantic seaboard. Bass travel in dense schools, and trophies have weighed in at more than 70 pounds; one lucky angler reeled in a 75.5-pound striper off New Haven, Connecticut, in 1992, just a half-pound shy of the Sound's 1981 record of 76 pounds in East Setauket, New York.

Bluefish

Mighty armies of **bluefish** invade Long Island Sound in May. Settling in for the summer, they haunt the trenches of the Sound by day and raid the beaches and estuaries at dawn and dusk, providing tremendous excitement for fishermen. Bluefish get bigger every season, with choppers of 20 pounds and more being recorded every year—the 1979 record of 24-plus pounds still stands, so go for it. Bluefish nicknames, graded by size, paint a warlike picture. This army has slammers, choppers, alligators and gorillas, tailors, harbor blues, and snappers too.

The Sound's most popular sport fish has an ominous future. Since 1990, biologists have recorded an 80-percent decline in bluefish stocks. Catches here in the Sound have dropped noticeably in recent years. A 10 fish per angler per day limit was imposed in 1994. Despite the decline, you can still snag blues most days in summer, and they normally linger through October and even past Thanksgiving.

Bait supply determines your method for blues. Abundant bunker (menhaden) ensures steady bottom-fishing action. Smaller baitfish like sand eels bring the blues up to surface plugs, where their savage attacks make excellent top-water sport. Wire-line trolling is also very productive. In western Long Island Sound, 100 yards of 40-pound test stainless-steel wire gets your lure down to the 30-foot mark. At the eastern end of the Sound, in stronger currents and deeper holes, heavier wire and chunk baits will land you a trophy blue.

Weakfish look like saltwater rainbow trout, as delicious as they are attractive. It can be a long time between successful weakfish seasons; they'll practically disappear for a few years, then show up in good numbers and bigger than ever. Their soft jaw requires a gentle touch, making them a favorite for fly rods and light tackle. They'll feed on the same baits as striped bass and bluefish, and their season runs year-round.

Mackerel used to show up in mid-April, sometimes staying only a week or two before advancing hordes of hungry bluefish chased them off. In recent years, they've favored outer waters, passing Long Island Sound in the spring and fall. When they do come back, backyard smokers are waiting for these big Boston mackerel that run from 2 to 3 pounds.

Frostbite fishermen favor flounder. The **winter flounder** season runs from April 1 to December 1 in the bays and rivers, and from April to late May you can stir them up in every harbor and sandy cove on Long Island Sound. Winter flounder are "right-eyed," as opposed to summer flounder or fluke whose eye migrates to the left side. Unfortunately, flounder numbers have dwindled dramatically. While you can still catch enough for a delicious dinner, the freezer full of flatfish has passed into legend. Connecticut has an 8-fish limit, and size limits change from year to year, so be sure to check the DEP angler's guide before heading out.

Fluke (summer flounder) also run in cycles, and the past couple of seasons have shown tremendous increases. Catch "left-eyes" with live killies (baitfish) on a spinner fluke rig, or rig a metal jig or bucktail with a belly strip from a sand eel or a strip of squid. They're summertime fish, usually arriving in the Sound in June and staying into October. Keeper fluke must be 15 inches; 2 to 4-pounders are common and the big "doormat" flatties can top 10 pounds.

T a u t o g (blackfish or tog) are tops in bottom-fishing. Famous for their spunky battles, the flavorful togs went long undiscovered. Blackfish season begins in May, when they feed on worms; into June, they'll prefer crab. Most tackle shops stock green crabs and fiddlers, but true blackfish buffs treasure hermit crabs as the very best bait for big tautog (limit 14 inches).

Tackle some tuna! **Little tunny** and **Atlantic bonito** are growing popular for fly rods and light tackle. These speedsters set drags screaming across the Sound in midsummer

© Maptech

Virtual Voyages

Welcome Aboard!

An Educational Voyage, on the Web and on the Water, is Coming to Your port city!

Beginning in 1999, Virtual Voyages, Inc., has run annual voyages out of Boston stopping at major ports in the Northeast. Students sail the boat and keep the log of the voyage that can be found at our web site. Schools along our route host our visit to their port and exhibit student work that relates school subjects to the sea. The ultimate goal of Virtual Voyages is to engage students from schools across the country in an ongoing learning experience.

Voyage 2001 will circumnavigate New England and Atlantic Canada stopping at the following ports: Boston, Plymouth, Martha's Vineyard, New Bedford,Newport, Fall River, New London, Greenport, New Haven, Port Jefferson, Stamford, City Island, Manhattan, Haverstraw, Kingston, Catskill, Albany, Troy, Burlington, Plattsburg, Montreal, Sorel, Trois Rivieres, Quebec, Tadusac, Rimouski, Matane, Fox River, Pictou, Summerside, Port Hawkesbury, Halifax, Lunenburg Shelburne, Bar Harbor, Brooklin, Rockland, Monhegan Island, Portland, York, Portsmouth, Gloucester, Lynn and Boston.

Virtual Voyages is always looking toward the next horizon seeking sponsors, consorts, host schools and other organizations to add to its list of ports and voyagers. If you, your school or organization would like to participate in the Virtual Voyages program, you can contact us via our website or call (617) 536-1343 in Boston or (860) 442-2704 in New London.

Join us aboard EASY WIND as we circumnavigate New England!

The website consists of:
- An interactive daily log
- "Discussion zone" on maritime issues
- Student projects and sailing skills
- Links to sponsors and other marine organizations

www.virtualvoyages.net

through early fall. More common around Watch Hill and The Race, they'll venture as far west as the Norwalk Islands and Great Captain islands. Fly fishermen most often catch (and release) them on baby anchovy and sand lance imitations.

Porgies (scup) are a scrappy little summertime species that run from half a pound to 2 pounds. From mid-July to mid-October, the day's catch is measured by the bucketful, not by the fish (keepers are 8 inches). They're very simple to catch with worms or clam pieces fished right on the bottom. Black sea bass are often a bonus catch when you're porgy fishing. Less delicious by-catches, like sea robins and sharks, are considered "trash fish."

Fall runs of **hickory shad** and **blueback herring** are gaining fans. Bluebacks often linger well into winter, congregating in boat basins all along the Sound. **Smelt** returned in numbers in the mid-1990's, and **white perch** are plentiful in the Connecticut and Housatonic rivers. The Connecticut River's spring shad run sets anglers salivating from Old Saybrook to Enfield for summer bakes and shad festivals. The Atlantic salmon restoration effort is making significant progress, but has not yet reopened for taking. It may be another decade before anglers can cast again for the "king of the game fish."

© Maptech

Where To Go

Every Sound community boasts good fishing sometime during the season, but several are consistently tops. Your boat will give you the angler's advantage, especially in western Long Island Sound where public access can be a problem.

Huntington and **Northport** harbors offer excellent bottom fishing for flounder in spring and fall. Cast or troll **Eatons Neck** for blues during the summer, and pick up porgies around Sand City and the LILCO plant.

Farther east, fishermen are always talking about **Crane's Neck**, whether it's trolling for blues, casting the rocks for big stripers, or bouncing the bottom for blackfish. You can fill your scuppers with scup here too. Busy **Port Jefferson** boasts excellent fishing inside the harbor, but G C "11" northeast of the entrance is the spot for bluefish, fluke, and weakfish. A quick drop-off makes for some fine trolling and often surface action too. To the east, the area G C "9" is a recognized early-

morning hot spot, famous for top-water bluefish action.

Mattituck has a great reputation for sea bass. The blue fishing is excellent year-round, with plenty of porgies and blackfish in season. **Orient Point** earns its regard as one of the finest spots for black fishing in Long Island Sound. Fierce currents and ocean chop on a calm day make **Plum Gut** the place to pull up bass and bluefish with heavy jigs and buck tails.

Peconic Bay boasts strong spring weakfish runs and summer and fall fishing for scup, as well as its share of bass, blues, and blackfish. The May run of weakfish here makes an excellent barometer for the entire Sound fishing season.

Montauk Point is a sport fishing mecca of the Northeast. It's the jumping-off point for offshore tuna, marlin, and big sharks. Closer to the point itself there are daily sorties with big bluefish, some fine fluke in the north rips, and some of the biggest porgies found anywhere. On crisp autumn nights, monster striped bass prowl the tidal rips, taking clam baits off the bottom. You may want to try your luck at surfcasting here also.

Waters off **Mamaroneck** and **Rye** offer fine flounder in spring and fall, but the big excitement for several summers now has been a barrage of bluefish invading harbors and coves to corner schools of bunker. **Greenwich** hot spots include Great Captain's Island, Todd's Point, and Greenwich Point; blackfish feed heavily here and around Cormorant Reef and Hens & Chickens.

The **Norwalk Islands** provide fantastic fishing from April to November. Top bass spots include Cockenoe Island, Sheffield Island, and Brown's Point. Flounder fishing is better off Norwalk than most areas; Sprite Island, Calf Pasture Beach and waters outside Goose and Copps islands near Fl R 4s BELL R "26" are good during the summer months. Blackfish are very strong here as well—try Greens Ledge, Smiths Reef, Copps Island rocks, and Fl R 2.5s BELL R "24" off Cockenoe Island.

One of Fairfield's prime spots is **Penfield Reef**. This mile-long bar to the lighthouse is hot for bass and blues and weakfish. Fluke fishermen sing its praises, and in the spring, it's one of the first to produce big flounder. The outer reaches near the light are studded with big boulders, so beware; but monster blackfish and stripers nestle in there, and there's even better blackfish action outside the lighthouse.

The **Housatonic River** is consistently hot for bass, bluefish, and fluke fishing, and it's notable for winter flounder and white perch too. When the exotics show up, you can bet it will be here on the Housy.

At Charles Island off **Milford**, scup and blackfish share top honors. Then of course there's **Middle Ground** (Stratford Shoal), where blackfish and blues run big, and big humpback porgies replace the little sand porgies closer to shore. The lighthouse marks this area's strong tides and rough waters.

New Haven blackfish cooperate well at Townshend's Ledge, and snapper blues invade the Quinnipiac and West rivers and New Haven Harbor in early fall. Keep an eye out for stripers too—this is where the 75-pounder tied the record in 1992.

The **Connecticut River** is probably the Sound's best all-around fishing spot. More bass are caught and released in this river every year. Finding bluefish is a different story: where they once cavorted almost daily along the river, they're more elusive now. Spring shad runs may not rival those of olden days, but Enfield Dam still sees lots of action in April and May.

The **Thames River** near New London boasts a terrific winter fishery for striped bass. Eastern Connecticut fishermen run offshore from Niantic, Noank, or New London after tuna, marlin, and shark, or jump out to **Race Rock** for consistent blackfish and fabulous blue fishing. A friend who's a charter boat skipper put it best: "If there's a best spot for bluefish along the eastern seaboard, The Race has to be it."

Niantic Bay's excellent state ramp matches its fishing. The Millstone Power Plant offers some very early bluefish, as well as good bottom fishing for flounder, porgies, and fluke. However, Niantic Bay's strongest point is its scalloping season; permits are available in tackle stores.

Farther east, **Mystic** and **Stonington** are known for fluke, flounder, and porgy, while **Watch Hill** and **Napatree** points are renowned for bountiful blues and stripers. This has also become a favorite late-summer hunting ground for little tunny and Atlantic bonito.

The Sound's many boat ramps, boat rental facilities, and public access areas make opportunities for great fishing ashore and afloat. First-timers can wet their reels aboard party boats sailing from Groton, New London, or Niantic/Waterford.

For even more fun and expert advice, charter a boat at almost any harbor along the Sound. Be sure not to overlook your local tackle shop: the people at those business are well-versed on the wheres, whens, and hows of fishing in their particular area, and they'd be crazy not to share a bit of advice to ensure your success.

Embassy Guides' Boater's Reference

Long Island Sound is alive with boating opportunities. Whether you're headed out for a day sail or making your way from harbor to harbor along the shores, Long Island Sound cruising presents enough challenges, opportunities, and rewards to satisfy even the most seasoned cruising veteran. Even experienced skippers should take the time to become fully acquainted with every form of boating communication before casting off. To be safe, a boater needs to know everything about how to gain and maintain contact with ships and shore in the event of an emergency. In addition, boaters need to know all they can to make cruising safer and easier, whether it concerns charting, weather, or boating among large tugs and barges.

Here, Embassy Guides condenses some basic boating knowledge into a few simple articles, providing you with resources to obtain the proper information. In our Boater's Reference, we separate the information into these topics: VHF Marine Radio, Shoreside Communications, Radio-navigation Systems, Electronic Charting Systems, Cruising Alongside Commercial Vessels, Atlantic Coast Weather, Long Island Sound Currents, and Embassy's Light List and Waypoints.

Good luck and safe boating!

VHF Marine Radio

A VHF marine radio is the single most important radio system you can buy. It provides a link between you and other vessels or the shore in the event of an emergency. But your radio is more than just a safety device—it can keep you connected in today's electronic world. You can use it to call ahead to a marina to reserve a slip, obtain a pilot for tricky passage, or ask around the harbor to see who is selling fresh lobster for dinner. Knowing and practicing proper communications procedures is the mark of a seasoned yachter.

VHF marine radio is used for short-range communications, generally 5 to 10 miles, and most often for ship-to-ship contact when not in port. Recreational vessels less than 66 feet (20 meters) in length are not required to carry a marine radio, but if they do so voluntarily they must maintain a watch on VHF channel 16 (156.800 MHz) whenever the radio is operating and not being used to communicate. Such vessels may alternatively maintain a watch on VHF channel 09 (156.450 MHz), the boaters' calling channel.

VHF Channel 16
The primary purpose of electronic communication devices is for boaters to contact others when they run into trouble—a distress call. VHF channel 16 (VHF 16) has been designated as a distress, safety, and calling frequency. This channel is monitored by the U.S. Coast Guard.

When to make a distress call
A distress call (MAYDAY) is a very serious matter and should be made only when your vessel is in dire need of assistance. Situations that warrant a MAYDAY call include a burning or foundering boat. Urgency calls (PAN-PAN), on the other hand, can be used when the threat to your vessel is less immediate.

How to make a distress call
The U.S. Coast Guard recommends the following procedure when making a distress call:

If you have a MF/HF marine radio and know you are outside VHF range of shore and ships, tune your MF/HF radiotelephone to 2182 kHz and send the radiotelephone alarm signal if one is available *(see Shoreside Communications)*. Otherwise, tune to VHF 16.

1) Repeat "MAYDAY" three times.
2) Say "This is (your name)."
3) State the name of the vessel in distress (spoken three times) and call sign or boat registration number (spoken once).
4) Repeat "MAYDAY" and the name of your vessel (spoken once).
5) Provide the position of your vessel by latitude or longitude, or by bearing (true or magnetic, state which) and distance to a well-known landmark such as a navigational aid or an island. Include any information on vessel movement such as course, speed, and destination.
6) State the nature of distress (sinking, fire, etc.).
7) State the kind of assistance needed.
8) State the number of persons on board.
9) Supply any other information that might facilitate rescue, such as length or tonnage of vessel, number of persons needing medical attention, color of hull, cabin, masks, etc.
10) When finished, say "OVER."
11) Stay close to the radio if possible. Even after the message has been received, the Coast Guard can find you more quickly if you can transmit a signal on which a rescue boat or aircraft can home.
12) Repeat at intervals until an answer is received.

What do you do if you hear a distress call?

If you hear a distress message from a vessel and it is not answered by anyone else, then *you must answer*. If you are reasonably sure that the distressed vessel is not in your vicinity, you should wait a short time for others to acknowledge. Do not use VHF 16 if a vessel in distress is being assisted on that frequency.

MAYDAY Radio Checks and other Hoaxes

A growing number of boaters unsuccessful in getting a radio check on VHF 16 are calling MAYDAY to get a response. Every hoax, including MAYDAY radio checks, is subject to prosecution as a Class D felony under Title 14, Section 85, of the U.S. Code, and the perpetrator is liable for a $5,000 fine plus all costs the Coast Guard incurs as a result of his or her action.

The Coast Guard First District (New England, south to northern New Jersey) is now answering radio checks on VHF 16, operations permitting. Radio checks will not be answered when Coast Guard radio operators are handling distress communications. The purpose of this policy change is to help reduce hoax MAYDAY calls. Radio checks with the Coast Guard are not permitted in any other location. Radio checks with the Coast Guard Communications Stations on DSC and HF radiotelephone are allowed.

VHF Channel 09

The Federal Communications Commission has established VHF 09 as a supplementary calling channel for recreational boaters. A ship or shore unit wishing to call a boater should do so on VHF 09. The purpose of the FCC regulation is to relieve congestion on VHF 16, the distress, safety, and calling frequency. FCC regulations require boaters having VHF radios to maintain a watch on either VHF 09 or 16 whenever the radio is turned on and not communicating with another station.

NOTE: The First Coast Guard District (waters off the coast of northern New Jersey, New York, and New England) ceased announcing weather warnings on VHF 09 at the start of the 2000 boating season. Boaters in that area should revert back to VHF 16.

Procedure for Calling a Ship by Radio

VHF 16 is primarily an emergency channel, but it may be used to hail a ship. When using VHF 16, *you must be brief*. The procedure below applies to VHF 09 as well as VHF 16.

Sonrisas: "*Paradise Island*, this is *Sonrisas*" (the name of the vessel being called may be said more than once if necessary)

Paradise Island: "*Sonrisas*, this is *Paradise Island*. Reply 68" (or some other proper working channel)

Sonrisas: "68" or "Roger"

U.S. VHF Marine Radio Channels and Frequencies

Ch. #	Ship Transmit/ Receive MHz	Use
01A	156.05/156.05	Available only in New Orleans/Lower Mississippi area
05A	156.25/156.25	Available in the Houston, New Orleans and Seattle areas
06	156.3/156.3	Intership Safety
07A	156.35/156.35	Commercial
08	156.4/156.4	Commercial (Intership only)
09	156.45/156.45	Boater Calling. Commercial and Non-Comm.
10	156.5/156.5	Commercial
11	156.55/156.55	Commercial. VTS in selected areas.
12	156.6/156.6	Port Operations. VTS in selected areas.
13	156.65/156.65	Intership Navigation Safety (Bridge-to-bridge). Ships 20m length maintain a listening watch on this channel in U.S. waters.
14	156.7/156.7	Port Operations. VTS in selected areas.
15	—/156.75	Environmental (Receive only). Used by Class C EPIRBs.
16	156.8/156.8	International Distress, Safety and Calling. All ships and U.S. Coast Guard Stations.
17	156.85/156.85	State Control
18A	156.9/156.9	Commercial
19A	156.95/156.95	Commercial
20	157/161.6	Port Operations (duplex)
20A	157/157	Port Operations
21A	157.05/157.05	U.S. Coast Guard only
22A	157.1/157.1	Coast Guard Liaison and Maritime Safety Information Broadcasts. Broadcasts announced on channel 16.
23A	157.15/157.15	U.S. Coast Guard only
24	157.2/161.8	Public Correspondence (Marine Operator)
25	157.25/161.85	Public Correspondence (Marine Operator)
26	157.3/161.9	Public Correspondence (Marine Operator)
27	157.35/161.95	Public Correspondence (Marine Operator)
28	157.4/162	Public Correspondence (Marine Operator)
63A	156.175/156.175	Port Operations, available only in Lower Mississippi area.
65A	156.275/156.275	Port Operations
66A	156.325/156.325	Port Operations
67	156.375/156.375	Commercial. Bridge-to-bridge communications
68	156.425/156.425	Non-Commercial
69	156.475/156.475	Non-Commercial
70	156.525/156.525	Digital Selective Calling
71	156.575/156.575	Non-Commercial
72	156.625/156.625	Non-Commercial (Intership only)
73	156.675/156.675	Port Operations
74	156.725/156.725	Port Operations
77	156.875/156.875	Port Operations (Intership only)
78A	156.925/156.925	Non-Commercial
79A	156.975/156.975	Commercial. Non-Commercial in Great Lakes only
80A	157.025/157.025	Commercial. Non-Commercial in Great Lakes only
81A	157.075/157.075	U.S. Government only - Environ. protection operations
82A	157.125/157.125	U.S. Government only
83A	157.175/157.175	U.S. Coast Guard only
84	157.225/161.825	Public Correspondence (Marine Operator)
85	157.275/161.875	Public Correspondence (Marine Operator)
86	157.325/161.925	Public Correspondence (Marine Operator)
87	157.375/161.975	Public Correspondence (Marine Operator)
88	157.425/162.025	Public Correspondence only near Canadian border.
88A	157.425/157.425	Commercial, Intership only.

121.5 MHz EPIRBs Phased Out

Maptech's navigation editor Capt. Brendan McNeill, a former navigating officer in the British Merchant Navy, knows the value of emergency position-indicating radio beacons, or EPIRBs. He also knows how temperamental they can be.

"About ten years ago, one of my colleagues was a mate on a survey boat out of Morgan City, Louisiana," Brendan said. "One August afternoon Coast Guardsmen were walking the docks, searching for a 121.5 MHz EPIRB that had been activated up in bayou country. The 'distress' signal was reported to the Coast Guard by the Soviet Consulate. It seems that a Russian satellite picked up the signal. The EPIRB, which ended up being located on a mud boat, had been inadvertently activated when someone removed it from its cradle to paint the vessel's handrail."

This is not an isolated incident. In fact, false alarms have become such a nuisance that the COSPAS-SARSAT Program will soon eliminate the problem. (COSPAS is from the Russian words *cosmicheskaya sistyema poiska avariynich sudov,* meaning "space system for the search of vessels in distress;" SARSAT stands for "search and rescue satellite-aided tracking.") The Coast Guard is deactivating 121.5 MHz emergency beacons, switching to the more reliable and accurate 406 MHz beacons. The main reason for the switch stems from the false alerts that 121.5 MHz beacons give authorities. The switch is part of the International COSPAS-SARSAT Program, which operates the satellites that relay distress signals to search and rescue authorities worldwide.

Despite their increased accuracy, the $1,000 price of the 406 MHz beacons— versus $250 for the 121.5 MHz ones— discourages many boaters. However, the BoatU.S. Foundation and Coast Guard have launched an EPIRB rental project that has proved very popular. Any recreational boater can rent a 406 MHz EPIRB for $45 per week. Call the BoatU.S. Foundation at 888-663-7472

Shoreside Communications

With single sideband (SSB) equipment you can make ship-to-shore calls from long distances offshore via high seas radiotelephone. SSB transmits over longer distances than either VHF or cellular, and is more reliable while cruising. If you have a SSB contact on the mainland to relay messages, it's a reliable way to stay in touch with family and friends. VHF is primarily used for ship-to-ship communications. Satellite telephone is a much more costly option, but one that is increasingly available to boaters through Atlantic Radiotelephone (ART) and other providers.

For high seas shore-to-ship calls to the Atlantic Ocean, the on-shore party should call 800-SEA-CALL. Be sure to monitor your radio if you expect a call. For more information on VHF or SSB, please consult the Maritime Radio Users Handbook, available from the Radio Technical Commission for Maritime Services (RTCM), Box 19087, Washington, D.C. 20036. Or write to the FCC, 201 Varick Street, New York, New York 10014.

MARITEL

MariTEL (888-MARINE2) is the main radiotelephone operator along the coast, with a range of 50 miles offshore from Maine to Florida. When making a high seas call using MariTEL, follow this procedure: 1) Tune to the nearest MariTEL channel on your VHF or SSB radio; 2) Depress and hold your microphone button for six seconds. You will automatically be connected with the tower and hear a recording asking you to hold your button for another six seconds; 3) A MariTEL operator will answer and ask for your subscriber number and the phone number you wish to call.

AT&T

AT&T High Seas service is expensive but excellent as a ship-to-shore communications backup. They offer two daily traffic lists you can monitor. Call AT&T High Seas Operator (800-392-2067 or www.attmobsat.com) for signup and pre-billing information.

ART

Atlantic Radiotelephone (ART) offers radiotelephone service to support the Global Marine Distress and Safety System (GMDSS). The International Maritime Organization (IMO) developed the GMDSS to guarantee that complying vessels will be able to communicate with a shore station or ship at any time. GMDSS was implemented in 1992 and became mandatory for all ships (almost all commercial vessels) in 1999. Call ART (800-940-9636) for service information

Radiotelephone Alarm Signal

The radiotelephone alarm signal is used only in distress, including when a person has been lost overboard and the assistance of other vessels is required. This signal consists of two audio tones transmitted alternatively on the distress frequency 2182 kHz. It is not used over VHF marine radio in the United States, although it may be used on VHF in Canada. This signal is similar in sound to a two-tone siren used by some ambulances. When generated by automated means, it shall be sent continuously over a period of not less than 30 seconds nor more than 1 minute. The purpose of the signal is to attract attention or to activate automatic devices receiving the alarm. The radiotelephone navigation warning signal, a single 2200 Hz tone transmitted twice per second, is used to announce a storm or similar warning.

Radionavigation Systems

This introduction to electronic navigation is not intended to serve as a treatise on GPS or any other electronic system. There are several excellent sources available, like the U.S. Coast Guard Navigation Center (www.uscg.navcen.mil) and the industry standard *Chapman's Piloting*, that go into detail about the theory and operation of each system. You should also consult the owner's manual supplied with your unit for its particular specifications and operation procedures. Here, Embassy Guides will provide you with a basic overview of the uses of each radionavigation system.

Global Positioning System (GPS)

The Global Positioning System (GPS) has become such a staple on today's boat, some consider it a necessity. GPS is a satellite-based radionavigation system developed and operated by the U.S. Department of Defense (DOD). It permits land, sea, and airborne users to determine their three-dimensional position, velocity, and time 24 hours a day, in all weather conditions, anywhere in the world, with a precision and accuracy within 10 meters, or 36 feet (see below). Twenty-four satellites (with more scheduled to be launched) orbit the earth in six circular orbits. The satellites are spaced so that at any time a minimum of six satellites will be available to a given user anywhere in the world.

GPS receivers collect signals from available satellites, and display the user's position, velocity, and time as needed for their marine, terrestrial, or aeronautical applications. Some display additional data, such as distance and bearing to selected waypoints or digital charts.

GPS More Accurate Than Ever

Your GPS readings are now 10 times more accurate than they were before May 2000. This means that GPS signals will be as accurate as what the military receives, placing you within 10 meters (36 feet) of your unit's latitude and longitude.

Before May 2000, civilian signals were degraded using selective availability (SA), which diminishes accuracy. But with the U.S. government's setting of the intentional SA to zero, the inaccuracies are effectively wiped away.

The caveat to this move is that the government's National Command Authority (NCA) can still degrade the signal in the event of war or threat to national security. Technological advances have enabled the NCA to increase the SA setting in one corner of the world without affecting the boater on this side of the globe.

In 1999, the U.S. government announced plans to modernize GPS by adding two new civilian signals in order to enhance public and commercial service. There are up to 18 additional satellites that are awaiting launch or are in production.

DGPS

The decisions to set SA to zero would appear to have effectively eliminated the benefits of Differential GPS (or DGPS). This is not the case. Government testing has found that DGPS can yield positions accurate to 3 meters (10 feet), in some instances. Continued improvements in the DGPS system may reap improved accuracy for navigation in the future.

LORAN-C

Loran-C was specifically designed as a radionavigation tool for United States coastal cruising. Using a host of radio beacons along the coastline, the system geometrically determines a unit's location. A boater with a Loran-C unit on board can return to previously recorded position with an accuracy of 50 meters (165 feet) or better. Twenty-four U.S. Loran-C stations provide better than 0.25-nautical mile accuracy all along the U.S. coastline, and in parts of Alaska. The system works along with Canadian and Russian stations to provide coverage into Canadian waters, as well as the Bering Sea.

The age of the Loran-C unit and especially weather conditions can severely hamper the accuracy of the system. Beginning in the 1980s and continuing today, Loran-C's popularity has waned with the explosion of the much more accurate and lighter GPS units.

The 1996 Federal Radionavigation Plan all but did away with Loran-C operations, essentially terminating the system in the United States by December 31, 2000. With pleas from aeronautical pilots and those who do not feel comfortable relying on just one source of radionavigation, the U.S. government reconsidered the system's termination.

Nondirectional Radiobeacons

Unlike Loran-C, which can triangulate your position using several signals, nondirectional radiobeacons only provide a bearing from a specific tower. Due to their limited utility, these radio beacons, and the "old-fashioned" Radio Direction Finders (RDF) used to find them, are currently being phased out if they are not carrying a DGPS signal.

NAVCEN

When you're in need of radionavigation system user information, who are you going to call? The Coast Guard's Navigation Information Service (NIS), of course. Operated by NAVCEN (Coast Guard Navigation Center), the NIS provides information in many media 24 hours a day, seven days a week. This information includes status, policy, and general information for GPS, DGPS, and Loran-C. The NIS also disseminates Maritime Safety Broadcasts and Local Notices to Mariners. You can contact NIS via the internet (ftp://ftp.navcen.uscg.mil) for information on status and outages, or telephone (703-313-5900) for user inquiries. The NIS also provides a taped recording of GPS status forecasts (703-313-5907).

Cruising with the Tugs

What to do when in the vicinity of a tug and tow By Capt. Peter Martin

There's no way to get around it—if you cruise Long Island Sound, you are going to encounter tugs and barges. Long Island Sound coastal towns receive much of their gasoline, home heating oil, diesel, kerosene, and even coal via tugs and barges. Frequently, the commercial terminals are located within the vicinity of recreational marinas, yacht clubs, and popular anchorages. The more you know, the better equipped you'll be to handle these encounters.

During my time captaining tugs in New York City, I had my fair share of encounters with recreational boaters. In a nutshell, there are three main things that recreational boaters can do to make a meeting safe and anxiety-free. First, communicate with the tug and tow. Second, know the Rules of the Road. Finally, be responsible out on the water.

Communication

A tug and tow captain doesn't know what you're thinking, and you don't know what he's thinking. So, you have a couple of choices: you can guess and take the risk that something bad happens, or you can communicate with the tug and tow captain. Naturally, communication between vessels is the best way to avoid a dangerous situation.

The single most effective tool you have on board is your VHF marine radio. Most recent VHFs are equipped with a scan memory, which enables you to monitor more than one channel at a time. Tugs monitor VHF 13. Monitoring it will provide you with valuable information that is passed along through what are termed "security calls." Basically, you'll find out vessel positions, routes, and type of tow. If you have any doubt about a tug and tow's intentions, hail the vessel's captain using VHF 13—discretion is the better part of valor.

Know the Rules of the Road

They are called the 72 ColRegs, but you probably know them as the Rules of the Road. While the law requires vessels more than 65 feet (20 meters) to carry a copy on board, it would behoove any seaman to read them and know them. One of the most important rules when dealing with a tug and tow is Rule 9(b): "A vessel of less than 20 meters or a sailing vessel shall not impede the passage of a vessel that can safely navigate only within a narrow channel or fairway." Basically, keep an eye out for large vessels and get out of their path.

Responsible Cruising

A wise captain once told me "speed kills." After working as a tug captain for eight years, I can't stress this enough: operate your vessel in a prudent manner and at a safe speed.

I remember one time I was on my way to New Haven, Connecticut, with a barge filled with 1.6 million gallons of gasoline when a 40-foot sportfishing boat attempted to overtake me. He decided he was fast enough to pass across my bow. As he began to cross my path he lost an engine and slowed dramatically—his prop must have caught a lobster pot. I placed my engines full astern, but even though I was traveling only 8 knots it still would have taken me a mile to fully stop. This was the sportfisher's lucky day—he had just enough left in his engines to skim within 15 feet of my tug. He nearly lost his vessel, and possibly his life.

* * *

There are numerous courses, seminars, books, and professional mariners available to help answer questions and teach you all aspects of boating safety. Some of these resources are as close as your local library, yacht club, power squadron, or Coast Guard station.

Captain Peter Martin is a fourth-generation mariner who served on tugboats in New York City from 1992 to 2000. He is a graduate of the Massachusetts Maritime Academy and is now one of Maptech's Navigation Editors.

Electronic Charting Systems

As electronic systems have become accepted aids to navigation, the electronic chart industry has flourished. The National Oceanic and Atmospheric Administration (NOAA), the publisher of U.S. marine paper charts, has a partnership with Maptech to produce and distribute electronic versions of official government data. These digital charts are created using a method called "raster scanning." This type of scanning effectively photocopies the original charts in full color. They are then geo-referenced to latitude and longitude, extra data is embedded, and the information is packaged onto CDs by region for use on most major navigational software. The CDs contain faithful digital renditions of the paper charts, along with chart indexes, help files, and a chart viewer.

Naturally, we believe that Maptech's navigation programs are the best in the industry, but there are other companies that produce navigation software, each with their own strengths and weaknesses. You can connect your global positioning satellite base unit (GPS) to one of these electronic navigation programs with electronic charts and watch real-time vessel position on-screen mimic your on-the-water course and speed. You can plan future routes and monitor a current route, or use overlays to position alarm areas, routes, waypoints, marks, and range and bearings lines. Maptech's software programs also allow you to create your own default or personalized chart directories as well as view tide and current tables, coast pilots, and the light list. If you're having trouble finding a place on a chart, use the sophisticated Geographic Names Information System (GNIS) or Marine Facilities search functions. The software can even print lists of all overlays, route plans, and charts.

Additional Content

International charts are added daily to the digital library, and topographic maps can now be used with marine programs, too. Other formats have been introduced as well, such as overhead, geo-referenced photographs—both aerial and satellite images—that can assist in real-time navigation. Augment the overhead views with line-of-sight pictures for harbor entrances and channels, making it much easier for boat operators to safely navigate unfamiliar waters.

The most recent additions to the Maptech line are contour charts that display multi-colored, three-dimensional renditions of the ocean floor and interface with Maptech software, GPS input, and vessel positioning. It is now possible to track your vessel on a geo-referenced photograph tiled with a NOAA chart that is in turn tiled to a contour chart. All of this can run simultaneously while still monitoring vessel progress via data windows and performing future or current route-planning functions.

Maptech's Notice to Mariners

Updating your charts is no longer tedious in the digital world. Maptech's Professional series chart CDs enable boaters to access a weekly Notice to Mariners (NTM) service—no more pencils and tape, just download an update from the web. A simple mouse click replaces hours of painstaking corrections.

CAUTION: Prudent mariners use every source of information at their disposal while navigating. Charts need constant updating and revision, and are only a reference. There is no substitute for experience and keen observation.

Personal computers are opening an ocean of opportunity. Boaters can add marine software for celestial navigation, sail or powerboat simulations, watch logging, and vessel and event management. Wireless web links allow cyberspace connections for destination research, reservations, or even dinner orders. Electronic charting and marine computer software make boating easier, safer, and more fun.

Weather in Long Island Sound

© Maptech

"One of the brightest gems in the New England weather," Mark Twain once said, "is the dazzling uncertainty of it. There is only one thing certain about it: you are certain there is going to be plenty of weather."

Twain was not far off the mark, as you can expect a little bit of everything when cruising Long Island Sound. But over the years we have learned a thing or two about the more common weather conditions that circulate through the Sound. Let's take a look at the types of weather conditions that boaters should know about.

Cold Fronts

These sharp boundaries between relatively warm and cold air usually approach the Atlantic Coast from the west and head north. Ahead of the front, winds often blow out of the south through southwest. Atmospheric pressure falls moderately and seas become choppy; showers, and sometimes thunderstorms, appear.

In spring and summer, a line of thunderstorms known as a squall line may develop. These instability lines can form 50 to 300 miles ahead of a fast-moving front. Once the front passes, winds shift rapidly to the west and northwest. Strong gusts and squalls continue. Clearing usually occurs a short distance behind the front as the cold air moves in.

Cold fronts can move through quite rapidly. Their frequency decreases with latitude.

Thunderstorms

Thunderstorms form when a cold front moves through an area with dropping temperatures, gusting winds, and heavy rain from towering clouds, called thunderheads. Two severe hazards of thunderstorms are lightning, which can strike masts and any vessel alone on the water, and the lesser-known downbursts. These localized strong winds can exceed 130 mph and can capsize either sail or power vessels with the heavy seas they raise. Downbursts usually last less than 10 minutes, but a squall line of thunderstorms can produce downbursts all along its length. If you see a squall line approaching, or feel a gusting, cold breeze with a thunderhead behind it, reef your sails and run for shelter. It'll be over quickly, and you can bask in the clear, dry weather that follows a thunderstorm.

Nor'easters

The most frequent powerful storms in the Northeast, especially in winter, are the extratropical cyclones called Nor'easters. These intense storms are named not for the

Northeast region they hit hardest, or for the direction they usually move, but for the gale force winds that blow ashore from the northeast as the storm develops. These storms are most common from October to April, but can develop any time of year. Nor'easters have an irregular core of cold air and can blow up to 50 knots or more across more than 1,000 miles. These fickle but usually well-forecasted storms hit hard, battering the coast with rough seas, surging tides, driving rain, and wintry blizzards. Nor'easters can generate 30-foot seas, and can whip up in less than 24 hours from a weak frontal disturbance to a full-blown storm system that can rage for a full week.

Tropical Cyclones: Depressions, Storms, and Hurricanes

Tropical cyclones include tropical depressions, tropical storms, and hurricanes, which are the most disastrous storms of the North Atlantic.

In small hurricanes, the diameter of the area of destructive winds may not exceed 25 miles. In some of the greatest storms, the diameter may be as large as 500 miles. At the center is a comparative calm known as the "eye of the storm," which may be as little as 7 miles in diameter but is rarely more than 30 miles.

An average of nine tropical cyclones form yearly, reaching at least tropical storm density. About five of these reach hurricane strength, and about two reach the United States. The Caribbean area, the Bahamas, the Gulf of Mexico, and the Atlantic Coast are subject to these storms during the hurricane season, from June through October (peaking in September). Infrequently, hurricanes have developed in May and November, and even in other months. New England occasionally gets hit hard, though it usually receives the remnants of the hurricane, which come in the form of rains.

Fortunately, the National Hurricane Center (www.nhc.noaa.gov) tracks and reports all tropical depressions, storms, and hurricanes. Learn and listen for these storm definitions:

Storm Terms

Tropical Depression: sustained surface winds of 33 knots or less.
Tropical Storm Watch: tropical storm conditions are possible in your area within the next 36 hours.
Tropical Storm Warning: expect tropical storm conditions in your area within the next 24 hours.
Tropical Storm: sustained winds between 34 knots and 63 knots.
Hurricane Watch: hurricane conditions are possible in your area within 36 hours.
Hurricane Warning: expect hurricane conditions in a specified area within 24 hours.
Hurricane: sustained surface wind of 64 knots or more.
Your best prediction of an approaching storm is a falling barometer. If the pressure drops more than 2 Mb in 3 hours, a strong storm is heading your way. For more information

Heed the two red flags—gale force winds are near. © Maptech

on nor'easters and hurricanes, check out The Weather Channel (www.weather.com).

Storm Safety

The best way to deal with hurricanes and nor'easters is to avoid them. Stay tuned to regional forecasts, especially from June to November during hurricane season. If a major storm is forecast, run for the nearest hurricane hole and get your vessel out of the water if possible. Most importantly, get off the boat! Don't ride out a hurricane on board—the risks are not worth the adventure. As you disembark, here are some safety precautions.

- Remove all valuables from the boat for safekeeping.
- Secure some personal identification on deck in a waterproof container, like a soda bottle. If your vessel is carried away, this will let its rescuers reach you.
- If your boat is docked to a fixed structure, double up your lines and put out extra fenders.
- If anchoring, set two bow anchors at 60-degree angles with plenty of scope. This will let your vessel ride out the storm as smoothly as possible. If you have more anchors, set another off your stern. Choose the best anchors for local bottom conditions, secure the bitter ends extra carefully, and stay as clear of other vessels as possible.
- Reduce your topside load as much as possible. Stow

Beaufort Wind Scale

Back in 1805, Sir Francis Beaufort of England developed a scale for determining the effects of wind speeds on water conditions. The Beaufort Scale of force has been only slightly modified in almost two centuries.

Force	ForceWind (Knots)	Common Reference	Appearance on water
0	Less than 1	Calm	Sea surface smooth and mirror-like
1	1-3	Light Air	Scaly ripples, no foam crests
2	4-6	Light Breeze	Small wavelets, crests glassy, no breaking
3	7-10	Gentle Breeze	Large wavelets, crests begin to break, scattered whitecaps
4	11-16	Moderate Breeze	Small waves 1-4 feet becoming longer, numerous whitecaps
5	17-21	Fresh Breeze	Moderate waves 4-8 feet taking longer form, many whitecaps, some spray
6	22-27	Strong Breeze	Larger waves 8-13 feet, whitecaps common, more spray
7	28-33	Near Gale Sea	Sea heaps up, waves 13-20 feet, white foam streaks off breakers
8	34-40	Gale	Moderately high (13-20 feet), waves of greater length, edges of crests begin to break into spindrift, foam blown in streaks
9	41-47	Strong Gale	High waves (20 feet) sea begins to roll, dense streaks of foam, spray may reduce visibility
10	48-55	Storm	Very high waves (20-30 feet) with overhanging crests, sea white with densely blown foam, heavy rolling, lowered visibility
11	56-63	Violent Storm	Exceptionally high (30-45 feet) waves, foam patches cover sea, visibility more reduced
12	64+	Hurricane	Air filled with foam, waves over 45 feet, sea completely white with driving spray, visibility greatly reduced

sails, electronics, and anything else that might come loose and flail around.

• Belowdecks, secure any loose gears in cabins and lockers. Close all hatch covers securely.

• Check all your valves and lines and make sure your pump is working properly.

With your boat secured, find yourself a comfortable spot to ride out the storm. In all likelihood, you'll be back on the water soon.

Fog

Meteorologically speaking, fog is simply water suspended in air. Fog forms when the air cools to its dew point, so that water vapor condenses into minute droplets just big enough to be visible—and to reduce your visibility to zero. Warming air means the air can hold more water; cooling air means fog will form. There are all types of fog: radiation fog forms over land on clear, cold nights in low-lying valleys; upslope fog forms when air flows up a mountain, cooling and expanding as it rises; precipitation fog forms when rain or snow passes through a cooler layer of air on its way

down to earth; advection fog forms when warm, moist air moves over a colder surface, so its water vapor condenses.

One New England fisherman gave us the best advice we've heard yet for navigating in fog. "Know the Rules of the Road, plain and simple." We couldn't have said it better. In 1972, the International Convention for the Prevention of Collisions at Sea developed the 72 ColRegs, as they're known to professional navigators. You probably know them as the Rules of the Road. If you don't already own a copy of this U.S. Coast Guard publication, it's available at any marine store. Here's the most important Rule of the Road in fog: if you hear a vessel forward of your beam, reduce speed to the minimum needed to hold your course. If necessary, stop until all danger of collision is past.

The easiest way to navigate fog is to avoid it. If you don't see it coming or can't steer clear of it, slow down and proceed with caution. Set a bow watch, and use your radar and GPS, if available, as you navigate with care. Use every navigation aid available; many buoys are placed precisely to provide the best route in fog. Your ears augment your eyes in the fog. Turn off the music—switch to weather radio, and turn it low. Ease up on the throttle, and listen. Check your chart for bell, whistle, and gong buoys and lights with foghorns; use their characteristics to note your position. Listen for other boats' engines, and especially for breakers on a ledge or surf on a looming shore. Use your horn and bell, as well as your VHF, to communicate with other vessels in your area, and listen for the signals below to determine what other vessels near you are doing. Sound the signal appropriate for your vessel.

Fog Signals

Vessel Power	State in water	Signal
Using Power	Underway and making way	1 prolonged blast (4-6 seconds; intervals less than 2 minutes)
Using Power	Not anchored, but not making way	2 prolonged blasts (intervals less than 2 minutes)
Using Sail*	Underway	1 prolonged blast and 2 short (1 second) blasts
Power or Sail	At anchor	Ring bell for 5 seconds (intervals less than 1 minutes)

* If your sailboat is using its engine for propulsion, regardless of whether or not the sails are up, it is considered a power-driven vessel.

NOAA Weather Broadcasts

With more than 400 FM transmitters on seven frequencies in the VHF band, NOAA Weather Radio (www.aoml.noaa. gov/general/lib/radio.html) is an important tool for coastal mariners. NOAA provides continuous broadcasts of weather information from local National Weather Service offices. The messages are repeated every five minutes, and updated every three hours— more often during heavy atmospheric activity.

Each station reports on its broadcast area. NOAA Weather Radio coverage is limited to within 40 miles of the transmitter, so listen to the nearest station (see table) for local conditions.

Tune in to local VHF channels and listen for the fishermen's broadcasts for some of the best local knowledge available on approaching weather conditions. If there's heavy weather coming, fishing boats will know. They can also usually advise you of the closest port in a storm.

On the following page, Embassy Guides has listed each NOAA Weather Broadcast channel along the Atlantic Coast. The list is separated into states for easy use.

NWR Transmitter	Call	Freq MHz	Watts	Programming Office
NEW HAMPSHIRE				
CONCORD	WXJ40	162.400	330	PORTLAND, ME
MASSACHUSETTS				
BOSTON	KHB35	162.475	500	BOSTON, MA
HYANNIS (Camp Edwards)	KEC73	162.550	1000	BOSTON, MA
WORCESTER	WXL93	162.550	500	BOSTON, MA
RHODE ISLAND				
PROVIDENCE	WXJ39	162.400	500	BOSTON, MA
CONNECTICUT				
HARTFORD	WXJ41	162.475	300	BOSTON, MA
MERIDEN	WXJ42	162.400	500	NEW YORK CITY, NY
NEW LONDON	KHB47	162.550	500	NEW YORK CITY, NY
NEW YORK				
ALBANY	WXL34	162.550	1000	ALBANY, NY
BINGHAMTON	WXL38	162.475	1000	BINGHAMTON, NY
KINGSTON	WXL37	162.475	1000	ALBANY, NY
NEW YORK CITY	KWO35	162.550	500	NEW YORK, NY
RIVERHEAD	WXM80	162.475	1000	NEW YORK, NY

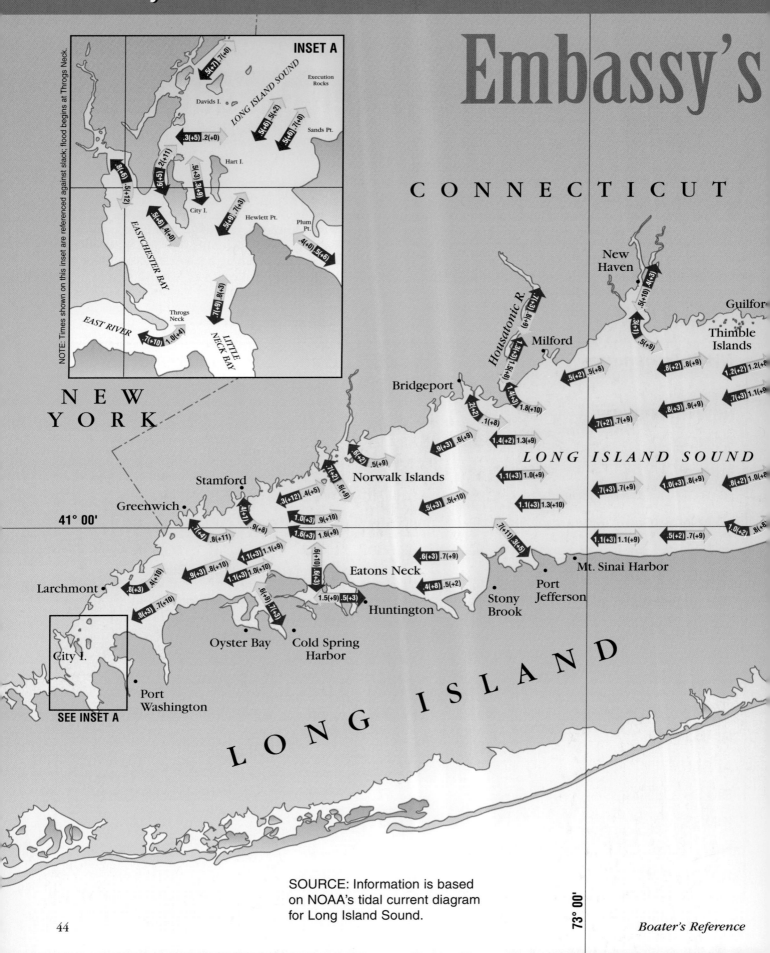

Embassy's

INSET A

LONG ISLAND SOUND

Execution Rocks

Davids I.

Sands Pt.

.5(+7) .7(+0)

.5(+6) .5(+2)

.3(+5) .2(+0)

.5(+6) .7(+0)

Hart I.

.2(+11)

.8(+6)

.6(+5)

.5(+12)

.5(+3) .3(+9)

City I.

.5(+6) .4(+0)

.5(+9) .7(+3)

Hewlett Pt.

Plum Pt.

.4(+0) .5(+6)

EASTCHESTER BAY

Throgs Neck

.7(+4) .8(+3)

EAST RIVER

.7(+10) 1.0(+4)

LITTLE NECK BAY

NOTE: Times shown on this inset are referenced against slack; flood begins at Throgs Neck.

C O N N E C T I C U T

New Haven

.5(+10) .4(+3)

Guilfor

.3(+1)

.5(+9)

Thimble Islands

Housatonic R.

.7(+6) .8(+9)

.4(+3) .5(+8)

.8(+2) .8(+9)

1.2(+2) 1.2(+9

Milford

.5(+2) .5(+8)

.8(+3) .9(+9)

.7(+3) 1.1(+9

Bridgeport

.4(+3)

1.8(+10)

.7(+2) .7(+9)

.2(+2)

.1(+8)

.9(+3) .6(+9)

1.4(+2) 1.3(+9)

L O N G   I S L A N D   S O U N D

.6(+2)

.5(+9)

1.1(+3) 1.0(+9)

Norwalk Islands

.1(+2) .6(+9)

.7(+3) .7(+9)

1.0(+3) .8(+9)

.8(+2) 1.0(+8

Stamford

.3(+12) .4(+5)

.5(+3) .5(+9)

Greenwich

.4(+1)

1.0(+3) .9(+10)

1.1(+3) 1.3(+10)

41° 00'

.7(+7)

.8(+11)

.9(+8)

1.6(+3) 1.6(+9)

.7(+11) .3(+5)

1.1(+3) 1.1(+9)

.5(+2) .7(+9)

1.0(+2) .8(+8

Larchmont

.8(+3)

.4(+10)

1.1(+3) 1.1(+9)

.6(+10)

.6(+3)

.6(+3) .7(+9)

Mt. Sinai Harbor

.9(+3) .8(+10)

1.1(+3) 1.0(+10)

Eatons Neck

.8(+3) .7(+10)

.6(+9) .7(+3)

1.5(+9) .5(+3)

.4(+8) .5(+2)

Huntington

Stony Brook

Port Jefferson

**N E W
Y O R K**

City I.

SEE INSET A

Port Washington

Oyster Bay

Cold Spring Harbor

L O N G   I S L A N D

SOURCE: Information is based on NOAA's tidal current diagram for Long Island Sound.

73° 00'

Current Chart®

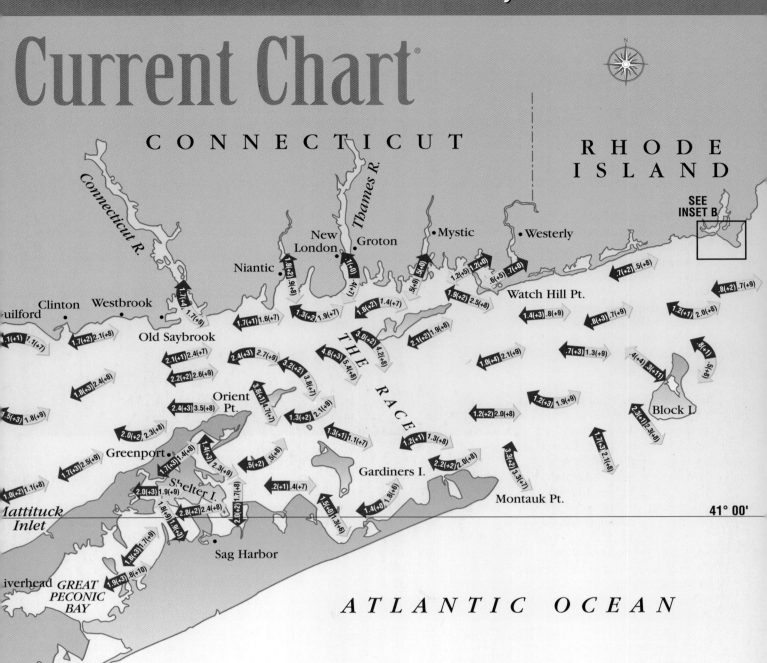

CONNECTICUT

RHODE ISLAND

Connecticut R.

Thames R.

SEE INSET B

New London • • Groton • Mystic • Westerly

Niantic

Watch Hill Pt.

Clinton Westbrook

Guilford

Old Saybrook

Orient Pt.

THE RACE

Block I.

Greenport

Shelter I.

Gardiners I.

Mattituck Inlet

Montauk Pt.

41° 00'

Sag Harbor

Riverhead GREAT PECONIC BAY

ATLANTIC OCEAN

Embassy's Current Chart © shows the approximate speed, direction, and times at which spring tidal currents are at maximum flow. The **PURPLE** heads of the arrows are **FLOOD** tides. The Gold heads are ebb tides. All times are referenced against *"SLACK; FLOOD BEGINS AT THE RACE."* For example: The **FLOOD** tide at Niantic reaches a maximum speed of 1.8 knots, running in a northerly direction two (+2) hours after *"SLACK; FLOOD BEGINS AT THE RACE."* The ebb tide reaches a maximum speed of .9 knots eight (+8) hours after *"SLACK, FLOOD BEGINS AT THE RACE."*

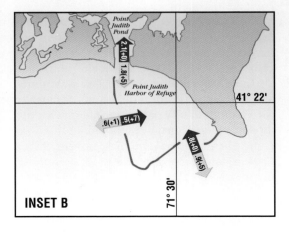

Point Judith Pond

2.1(+0) 1.8(+5)

Point Judith Harbor of Refuge

.6(+1) .5(+7)

.8(+0) .9(+5)

41° 22'

71° 30'

INSET B

Embassy's Light List & Waypoints

The GPS (Global Positioning System) has become the preferred method of electronic navigation and has greatly expanded the cruising range of many boaters. When used with soundings, lights, buoys, radar, up-to-date charts, and proper plotting techniques, a GPS will enhance your abilities as a navigator. It should never be used as a primary navigation system.

This introduction is not intended to serve as a treatise on GPS or its use. There are several excellent books available, from the U.S. Coast Guard as well as from private publishers, that go into detail about the theory and operation of the system.

© Maptech

You should also consult the owner's manual supplied with your GPS receiver for its particular specifications and operating procedures. The Internet is an excellent resource for navigation information.

Under presidential directive, the Department of Defense set Selective Availability (SA) to zero on May 1, 2000. Zero SA will yield positions accurate to within 30 feet. Selective availability is the "dumbing down" of the GPS signal; an intentional error. Be warned that for reasons of national security the government reserves the right and the ability to increase selective availability settings as necessary. Errors of up to 100 meters are not beyond the realm of possibility. Again, GPS should never be used as a primary navigation system.

The latitude and longitude coordinates you'll find on *Maptech's Embassy Guides: Long Island Sound* harbor charts were derived from official NOAA electronic charts developed by Maptech, Inc., using Maptech's Offshore Navigator software. The waypoints were plotted at the charted position of the aid or close to the mark on the channel or safe side as prudent, with the approximate directions and distances noted in the Waypoint Index. Light List numbers and names correspond to the U.S. Coast Guard Light List, Volume 1, Atlantic Coast. The page number(s) of the waypoint, shown immediately to the right of the Light List number, indicate where to turn in this book for a harbor chart with plotted waypoints. The indicated latitude and longitude reflect the plotted position relative to the mark. In addition to coordinates provided for daybeacons, buoys, and lights on the harbor charts, we include data for additional aids to navigation, some inshore and others along the Sound, indicated by "LIS" in the page number column.

CAUTION: This data should be used for reference only; mariners should collect their own readings on-site as they become familiar with an area. Additionally, cruising guides should be used in conjunction with the most current nautical charts for your cruising area, corrected with Notices to Mariners.

The latitude and longitude positions shown are for reference and planning purposes only. Under no circumstances are they to be used for navigation. When plotting your own courses, be sure to correct for deviation, set, drift, and leeway. As noted in the U.S. Coast Guard Light List, "Buoys' positions represented on nautical charts are approximate positions only due to the practical limitations of positioning and maintaining buoys and their sinkers in precise geographical locations."

For these reasons, Maptech cannot guarantee the accuracy of the information contained herein, and will in no way be responsible for any loss or damage caused by the use or misuse of this information.

No.	WP	Name	Characteristic	Position	Latitude	Longitude
650	LIS	Southwest Ledge Lighted BELL Buoy	Fl R 2.5s BELL R "2" Racon B (-...)	On mark	N 41°-06.72	W 071°-40.27
19460	LIS	Point Judith Lighted WHISTLE Buoy	Fl R 4s WHISTLE R "2"	On mark	N 41°-18.46	W 071°-28.35
19465	LIS	Point Judith BELL Buoy	BELL R "4"	On mark	N 41°-20.93	W 071°-30.42
19470	LIS	Nebraska Shoal Buoy	R N "2NS"	S 0.1nm	N 41°-20.87	W 071°-34.50
19475	LIS	Block Island North Reef Lighted BELL Buoy	Fl G 4s BELL G "1BI"	On mark	N 41°-15.49	W 071°-34.55
19490	LIS	Point Judith East Entrance Light	Fl G 4s 39ft 5M "3"	E 450ft	N 41°-21.59	W 07°-29.78
19500	LIS	Point Judith West Entrance Light	Fl R 4s 35ft 5M R "2"	NW 0.1nm	N 41°-21.78	W 071°-30.87
19510	LIS	South Lump Buoy	RG N	On mark	N 41°-21.81	W 071°-30.46
19685	288	Block Island Northeast WHISTLE Buoy	WHISTLE G "5"	On mark	N 41°-12.61	W 071°-32.02
19690	288	Block Island Old Harbor Channel BELL Buoy	BELL G "1"	On mark	N 41°-11.17	W 071°-33.23
19715	288	Block Island Southeast Point Buoy	G C "1"	SE 0.1nm	N 41°-08.85	W 071°-32.67
19720	288	Block Island Breakwater Light	F G 27ft 11M HORN "3"	NW 400ft	N 41°-10.69	W 071°-33.28
19730	288	Block Island Black Rock Point Buoy	R N "2"	S 550ft	N 41°-08.32	W 071°-35.74
19735	288	Block Island Southwest Point Lighted WHISTLE Buoy	Fl R 6s WHISTLE R "4"	On mark	N 41°-08.70	W 071°-37.36
19740	288	Dickens Point Shoal BELL Buoy	BELL R "6"	W 975ft	N 41°-09.56	W 071°-37.36
19745	288	Great Salt Pond Entrance BELL Buoy	BELL R "2"	On mark	N 41°-12.09	W 071°-35.66
19780	288	Great Salt Pond Buoy	R N "12" & G C "11"	Between	N 41°-11.62	W 071°-35.18
19805	LIS	Watch Hill Lighted WHISTLE Buoy	Mo (A) WHISTLE RW "WH"	On mark	N 41°-15.83	W 071°-50.92
19810	LIS	Cerberus Shoal Lighted GONG Buoy	Fl G 4s GONG G "9"	On mark	N 41°-10.44	W 071°-57.12
19815	250	Race Rock Light	Fl R 10s 67 ft 16M HORN	SW 0.3nm	N 41°-14.38	W 072°-03.08
19825	LIS	Valiant Rock Lighted BELL Buoy	Q G BELL G "11" Racon B (-...)	NE 0.4nm	N 41°-14.09	W 072°-03.72
19840	LIS	Little Gull Island Reef Buoy	G C "1"	NE 0.2nm	N 41°-12.65	W 072°-05.93
19850	LIS	Endeavor Shoals Lighted GONG Buoy	Fl G 4s GONG G "1"	On mark	N 41°-06.06	W 071°-46.24
19865	LIS	Shagwong Reef Lighted BELL Buoy	Fl G 2.5s BELL G "7SR"	NE 0.1nm	N 41°-07.14	W 071°-54.75
19870	300	Montauk Entrance Lighted BELL Buoy	Mo (A) BELL RW "M"	On mark	N 41°-05.11	W 071°-56.38
20005	254	Lords Passage Lighted WHISTLE Buoy	Mo(A) WHISTLE RW "L"	On mark	N 41°-17.38	W 071°-54.32
20015	254	Wicopesset Passage BELL Buoy	BELL RW "W"	On mark	N 41°-17.47	W 071°-54.96
20025	280	Gangway Rock Lighted BELL Buoy	Fl R 6s BELL "R 2" & G C "3"	Between	N 41°-17.94	W 071°-51.59
20045	254, 280	Napatree Point Ledge Lighted BELL Buoy	Fl R 4s BELL R "6"	S 900ft	N 41°-17.86	W 071°-53.32
20085	254	Latimer Reef Light	Fl W 6s 55ft 9M BELL	S 0.2nm	N 41°-18.07	W 071°-56.00
20095	262, 272	Eel Grass Ground Southeast Buoy	R N "16"	On mark	N 41°-18.51	W 071°-56.70
20110	250, 254, 256	Ram Island Reef Lighted BELL Buoy	Fl R 4s BELL R "20"	SSW 0.2nm	N 41°-18.00	W 071°-58.38
20145	250	North Dumpling Light	F W (Red Sector) 94 ft 7M HORN	NW 0.2nm	N 41°-17.41	W 072°-01.34
20155	238, 256	Seaflower Reef Light	Fl W 4s 28ft 7M	S 0.2nm	N 41°-17.54	W 072°-02.00
20160	272	Stonington Harbor Approach Buoy	R N "2"	W 400ft	N 41°-18.57	W 071°-54.67
20175	272	Stonington Breakwater Light	Fl G 4s 31ft 5M G "5"	E 575ft	N 41°-19.52	W 071°-54.66
20180	272	Stonington Point Junction Buoy	RG N "SP"	On mark	N 41°-19.49	W 071°-54.37
20185	272	Stonington Inner Breakwater Light	Fl R 4s 5M R "8"	WSW 275ft	N 41°-19.82	W 071°-54.62
20490	250, 256	Mystic Harbor West Approach Buoy	G C "1"	On mark	N 41°-18.40	W 071°-59.42
20500	256	Mystic Harbor West Approach Buoy	G C "3" & R N "2"	Between	N 41°-18.60	W 071°-59.46
20975	250, 254	East Harbor Buoy	R N "2E" & G C "1E"	Between	N 41°-17.23	W 071°-56.96
20985	LIS	West Harbor East Channel Buoy	R N "2W" & C G "1W"	Between	N 41°-17.25	W 071°-58.18
20990	LIS	West Harbor East Channel Buoy	R N "4" & G C "5"	Between	N 41°-17.01	W 071°-59.51
21020	250	Flat Hammock Buoy	R N "2" & G C "1"	Between	N 41°-17.22	W 072°-00.09
21025	250	West Harbor Entrance Lighted BELL Buoy	Fl R 2.5s BELL R "2" & G C "3"	Between	N 41°-16.82	W 072°-01.22
21040	250	West Harbor Channel Lighted Buoy	Fl R 4s R "6"	N 400ft	N 41°-16.36	W 072°-00.32
21055	250	Silver Eel Pond Entrance Lighted BELL Buoy	Fl R 4s BELL R "2"	On mark	N 41°-15.54	W 072°-02.22
21065	LIS	Bartlett Reef Lighted BELL Buoy	Fl R 4s BELL R "4"	On mark	N 41°-15.57	W 072°-08.35
21070	LIS	Bartlett Reef Light	Fl W 5s 35ft 12M HORN	S 0.2nm	N 41°-16.27	W 072°-08.20

*The Waypoint number listed is the same as the U.S. Coast Guard Light List number.

WYPT #	PAGE	NAME & LOCATION	CHARACTERISTIC	LOCATION	LATITUDE	LONGITUDE	NOTES
21080	LIS	Plum Island Lighted WHISTLE Buoy	Mo (A) WHISTLE RW "PI"	On mark	N 41°-13.28	W 072°-10.79	
21090	324	Plum Gut Light	Fl W 2.5s 50ft 5M	SW 0.4nm	N 41°-10.06	W 072°-12.85	
21100	LIS	Hatchett Reef Buoy	R N "6"	S 475ft	N 41°-15.83	W 072°-16.00	
21105	LIS	Saybrook Bar Lighted BELL Buoy	Fl R 4s BELL R "8"	WSW 0.2nm	N 41°-14.77	W 072°-19.07	
21135	LIS	Long Sand Shoal Lighted BELL Buoy	QR BELL R "8A"	On mark	N 41°-13.50	W 072°-23.14	
21145	LIS	Long Sand Shoal West End Lighted Buoy	Fl (2+1) R 6s HORN RG "W"	On mark	N 41°-13.59	W 072°-27.27	
21155	LIS	Sixmile Reef Lighted BELL Buoy	Fl R 4s BELL R "8C"	On mark	N 41°-10.79	W 072°-29.43	
21160	LIS	Twenty-Eight Foot Shoal Lighted Buoy	Fl (2+1) R 6s RG "TE" Racon T (-)	On mark	N 41°-09.28	W 072°-30.40	
21165	LIS	Kimberly Reef Lighted HORN Buoy	Fl (2+1) R 6s HORN RG "KR"	On mark	N 41°-12.84	W 072°-37.42	
21175	178	Goose Island Lighted BELL Buoy	Fl R 4s BELL R "10GI"	On mark	N 41°-12.10	W 072°-40.50	
21185	LIS	Branford Reef Light	Fl W 6s 30ft 7M	S 0.2nm	N 41°-13.07	W 072°-48.26	
21190	LIS	Townsend Ledge Lighted BELL Buoy	Fl R 4s BELL R "10A"	On mark	N 41°-12.52	W 072°-51.77	
21205	LIS	New Haven Harbor Lighted WHISTLE Buoy	Mo(A) WHISTLE RW "NH"	On mark	N 41°-12.13	W 072°-53.79	
21220	LIS	Pond Point Shoal Buoy	R N "12"	S 400ft	N 41°-11.88	W 073°-01.05	
21225	150	Charles Island Lighted BELL Buoy	Fl R 4s BELL R "16"	On mark	N 41°-11.02	W 073°-03.09	
21245	LIS	Stratford Point Lighted BELL Buoy	Fl R 6s BELL R "18"	On mark	N 41°-06.81	W 073°-08.16	
21255	LIS	Stratford Shoal Buoy	G C "3"	On mark	N 41°-04.60	W 073°-06.26	
21265	LIS	Middle Ground Lighted BELL Buoy	Fl R 4s BELL R "2"	On mark	N 41°-03.06	W 073°-06.21	
21270	LIS	Mt. Misery Shoal Buoy	G C "11"	NE 400ft	N 40°-59.26	W 073°-04.72	
21285	LIS	Old Field Point GONG Buoy	GONG G "11A"	On mark	N 40°-59.22	W 073°-07.29	
21290	138	Penfield Reef Light	Fl R 6s 51ft 18M HORN	S 0.3nm	N 41°-06.76	W 073°-13.34	
21295	134	Pine Creek Point Lighted BELL Buoy	Fl R 4s BELL R "22"	S 475ft	N 41°-06.42	W 073°-15.78	
21300	LIS	Cockenoe Shoal Island Lighted BELL Buoy	Fl R 2.5s BELL R "24"	SE 0.1nm	N 41°-04.45	W 073°-19.67	
21305	LIS	Norwalk Islands Lighted BELL Buoy	Fl R 4s BELL R "26"	SE 0.1nm	N 41°-03.61	W 073°-21.88	
21310	LIS	Eatons Neck Point Lighted GONG Buoy	Fl G 4s BELL G "11B"	On mark	N 41°-00.02	W 073°-23.70	
21320	374	Eatons Neck Point Shoal Buoy	G C "13"	On mark	N 40°-58.20	W 073°-23.64	
21330	LIS	Cable & Anchor Reef Lighted BELL Buoy	Fl R 4s BELL R "28C"	On mark	N 41°-00.56	W 073°-25.14	
21335	LIS	Great Reef Buoy	R N "28"	S 0.1nm	N 41°-02.42	W 073°-25.51	
21340	LIS	Greens Ledge Light	Al WR 24s 62ft 15M HORN	W 0.3nm	N 41°-02.50	W 073°-26.98	
21355	LIS	Smith Reef Lighted Buoy	Fl R 4s R "30"	S 0.1nm	N 41°-01.40	W 073°-29.49	
21360	LIS	Lloyd Point Shoal Lighted GONG Buoy	Fl G 4s GONG G "15"	On mark	N 40°-57.68	W 073°-29.26	
21365	LIS	The Cows Lighted Buoy	Fl R 6s R "32"	S 400ft	N 41°-00.15	W 073°-31.42	
21380	LIS	Twenty-six Foot Spot Lighted BELL Buoy	Fl R 2.5s BELL R "32A"	On mark	N 40°-58.12	W 073°-32.81	
21385	LIS	Centre Island Reef BELL Buoy	BELL G "17"	NW 0.2nm	N 40°-56.12	W 073°-31.83	
21390	LIS	Oak Neck Point Buoy	G C "19"	On mark	N 40°-55.45	W 073°-34.19	
21395	104	Woolsey Reef Buoy	R N "34"	SW 875ft	N 40°-59.82	W 073°-34.00	
21405	LIS	Bluefish Shoal BELL Buoy	BELL R "36"	SE 0.1nm	N 40°-58.06	W 073°-38.69	
21410	LIS	Rye Beach Lighted BELL Buoy	Fl R 4s BELL R "38"	SE 500ft	N 40°-57.46	W 073°-39.53	
21415	LIS	Parsonage Point Lighted Buoy	Fl R 6s R "40"	SE 500ft	N 40°-56.78	W 073°-40.42	
21420	LIS	Matinecock Point Shoal Lighted GONG Buoy	Fl G 4s GONG G "21"	N 450ft	N 40°-54.60	W 073°-38.19	
21425	90	Milton Point Buoy	R N "40A"	On mark	N 40°-56.13	W 073°-41.29	
21430	90	Scotch Caps Lighted BELL Buoy	Fl R 2.5s BELL R "42"	On mark	N 40°-55.48	W 073°-42.16	
21435	LIS	Prospect Point Lighted GONG Buoy	Fl G 4s GONG G "23"	WNW 0.1nm	N 40°-52.76	W 073°-43.34	
21450	LIS	Execution Rocks Shoal North End Buoy	G C "1"	N 0.1nm	N 40°-53.58	W 073°-44.14	
21475	LIS	Sands Point Reef Lighted Buoy	Fl G 2.5s G "25"	N 0.1nm	N 40°-52.23	W 073°-44.27	
21485	398	Gangway Rock GONG Buoy	GONG G "27"	NW 400ft	N 40°-51.54	W 073°-44.86	
21495	LIS	Hewlett Point Lighted Buoy	Fl G 4s G "29"	NW 0.1nm	N 40°-50.55	W 073°-45.45	
21500	LIS	Hart Island Light	Fl R 5s 23ft 10M "46"	SE 0.2nm	N 40°-50.60	W 073°-45.76	
21505	406	Stepping Stones Light	Oc G 4s 46ft 8M	WNW 0.2nm	N 40°-49.52	W 073°-46.75	
21510	76	Locust Point Buoy	R N "46A"	SSW 0.2nm	N 40°-49.27	W 073°-47.25	

Waypoint	Light List	Name	Characteristic	Position	Latitude	Longitude
21515	76	Throgs Neck Lighted BELL Buoy	Fl R 4s BELL R "48"	On mark	N 40°-48.19	W 073°-47.25
21530	LIS	Cornfield Point Shoal Lighted BELL Buoy	Fl R 4s BELL R "2"	On mark	N 41°-15.03	W 072°-23.05
21565	LIS	Crane Reef Buoy	R N "4"	On mark	N 41°-14.89	W 072°-25.37
21570	188	Duck Island Reef Buoy	R N "6"	S 0.1nm	N 41°-14.74	W 072°-28.47
21580	182	Hammonasset Point Reef Buoy	R N "10"	S 0.1nm	N 41°-14.65	W 072°-33.22
21585	LIS	Charles Reef Buoy	R N "14"	S 400ft	N 41°-14.78	W 072°-37.42
21590	178	Faulkner Island Reef Lighted GONG Buoy	Fl G 4s GONG G "15"	On mark	N 41°-13.38	W 072°-39.26
21610	174	Goose Rocks Shoal Lighted BELL Buoy	Fl R 4s BELL R "22"	SE 400ft	N 41°-14.33	W 072°-43.41
21615	LIS	Browns Reef Lighted BELL Buoy	Fl R 4s BELL R "26"	S 425ft	N 41°-13.74	W 072°-46.23
21625	166	Five Foot Rock Buoy	R N "32"	SW 450ft	N 41°-14.38	W 072°-50.00
21630	LIS	Cow and Calf Lighted BELL Buoy	Fl R 2.5s R "34"	S 325ft	N 41°-14.24	W 072°-50.54
21645	LIS	Mattituck Inlet GONG Buoy	GONG G "3A"	On mark	N 41°-01.85	W 072°-33.96
21650	344	Mattituck Inlet Breakwater Light	Fl W 4s 25ft 6M "MI"	N 0.2nm	N 41°-01.12	W 072°-33.73
21770	238	Rapid Rock Buoy	G R C "R"	S 0.1nm	N 41°-17.16	W 072°-06.09
21790	238	New London Harbor Channel Lighted Buoy	Fl 2.5s R "2" & Fl 2.5s G "1"	Between	N 41°-17.60	W 072°-04.72
21850	238	New London Harbor Channel Lighted Buoy	Fl 2.5s G "5" & Fl 2.5s R "6"	Between	N 41°-19.30	W 072°-04.92
22275	232	White Rock Lighted BELL Buoy	Fl R 4s BELL R "6"	On mark	N 41°-18.00	W 072°-10.49
22285	232	Black Rock Buoy	R N "8"	W 0.1nm	N 41°-18.58	W 072°-10.85
22305	232	Niantic River Channel Day Beacon	G "1"	SW 325ft	N 41°-19.11	W 072°-10.91
22495	194	Saybrook Breakwater Light	Fl G 6s 58ft 11M HORN	SE 375ft	N 41°-15.74	W 072°-20.51
22525	194	Connecticut River Lighted Buoy	Fl G 4s G "5"	E 175ft	N 41°-16.31	W 072°-20.46
22540	194	Connecticut River Lighted Buoy	Fl R 4s R "8"	S 400ft	N 41°-16.64	W 072°-20.62
22550	194	Connecticut River Lighted Buoy	Fl R 4s R "14"	W 325ft	N 41°-17.34	W 072°-21.02
22580	200	Connecticut River Lighted Buoy	Fl G 4s G "19"	NNE 0.6nm	N 41°-18.45	W 072°-20.95
23410	188	Patchogue River Channel Lighted Buoy	Fl R 4s R "2"	SW 275ft	N 41°-15.94	W 072°-28.38
23455	182	Kelsey Point Breakwater Light	Fl W 2.5s 33ft 7M	SW 350ft	N 41°-14.57	W 072°-30.52
23465	182	Clinton Harbor Lighted Buoy	Fl G 4s G "3"	On mark	N 41°-15.39	W 072°-31.66
23715	178	Guilford Harbor Lighted BELL Buoy	Fl R 4s BELL R "4"	WSW 525ft	N 41°-15.00	W 072°-39.33
23735	178	Guilford Harbor Channel Lighted Buoy	Fl 4sG "7"	SE 0.1nm	N 41°-15.67	W 072°-39.76
23820	170	Thimble Shoals Buoy	R N "4"	SW 275ft	N 41°-14.96	W 072°-44.56
23910	170	Pine Orchard Approach Lighted Buoy	Fl R 4s R "4A" & G C "3"	Between	N 41°-14.59	W 072°-46.81
23925	170	Pine Orchard Approach Lighted Buoy	Fl R 4s R "8"	W 475ft	N 41°-15.31	W 072°-46.32
23950	166	Blyn Rock Lighted Buoy	Fl R 4s R "2"	WNW 575ft	N 41°-14.84	W 072°-50.00
23975	166	Farm River Approach Buoy	G C "1"	NE 450ft	N 41°-14.49	W 072°-51.41
24055	160	New Haven Harbor Entrance Channel Buoy	Fl G 2.5s G "7"	E 275ft	N 41°-14.06	W 072°-55.03
24075	160	New Haven West Breakwater Light	Fl W 4s 35ft 7M & Fl R 4s 38ft 4M	Between	N 41°-13.36	W 072°-56.34
24080	160	New Haven West Breakwater West End Light	Fl R 6s 29ft 4M "2"	W 0.1nm	N 41°-13.54	W 072°-57.52
24140	160	New Haven Harbor Channel Lighted Buoy	Fl G 2.5s G "15"	E 200ft	N 41°-16.31	W 072°-54.70
24295	LIS	Welches Point Buoy	R N "2"	S 400ft	N 41°-11.86	W 073°-02.17
24300	150	Charles Island Buoy	G C "1"	E 150ft	N 41°-11.61	W 073°-03.02
24305	150	Milford Harbor Channel Lighted Buoy	Fl R 4s R "4"	W 100ft	N 41°-12.27	W 073°-02.96
24355	146	Housatonic River Entrance Channel Lighted BELL Buoy	Fl G 2.5s BELL G "1"	On Mark	N 41°-09.40	W 073°-05.44
24545	LIS	Bridgeport Harbor Channel Approach Lighted WHISTLE Buoy	Mo(A) WHISTLE RW "BH"	On mark	N 41°-06.24	W 073°-11.73
24590	142	Bridgeport Harbor Entrance Channel Lighted BELL Buoy	Fl R 2.5s R "10" & G C "11"	Between	N 41°-08.92	W 073°-10.87
24630	142	Bridgeport Inner Harbor Buoy	Fl R 2.5s R "16" & G C "15"	Between	N 41°-09.66	W 073°-10.64
24675	138	Black Rock Harbor Entrance Light	Fl R 4s 43ft 4M "2A"	SW 0.1nm	N 41°-08.16	W 073°-13.16
24735	138	Ash Creek Buoy	G C "1" & R N "2"	Between	N 41°-08.42	W 073°-13.79
24765	134	Southport Harbor Entrance Buoy	R N "2"	W 125ft	N 41°-07.18	W 073°-17.16
24815	LIS	Georges Rock Lighted Buoy	Fl G 2.5 s G "1"	E 0.1nm	N 41°-05.21	W 073°-19.33
24820	LIS	Saugatuck River Entrance Lighted Buoy	Fl G 4s G "3"	NE 250ft	N 41°-05.91	W 073°-21.18

*The Waypoint number listed is the same as the U.S. Coast Guard Light List number.

WYPT #	PAGE	NAME & LOCATION	CHARACTERISTIC	LOCATION	LATITUDE	LONGITUDE	NOTES
24825	130	Saugatuck River Buoy	R N "6" & G C "5"	Between	N 41°-05.99	W 073°-21.50	
24915	LIS	Norwalk East Approach Buoy	R N "2"	S 400ft	N 41°-04.35	W 073°-21.72	
24920	130	Norwalk East Approach Buoy	R N "4" & G C "5"	Between	N 41°-04.59	W 073°-21.91	
24930	130	Peck Ledge Light	Fl W 4s 61ft 7M	NE 525ft	N 41°-04.72	W 073°-22.14	
24935	120, 130	Grassy Hammock Light	Fl R 4s 26ft 5M "8"	S 425ft	N 41°-04.54	W 073°-23.02	
24945	120	Norwalk East Approach Buoy	G C "1"	On mark	N 41°-04.40	W 073°-23.83	
24960	120	Norwalk Channel Lighted Buoy	Fl R 2.5s R "2" & G C "3"	Between	N 41°-03.52	W 073°-25.10	
25030	LIS	Norwalk Channel Light	Q R 26ft 4M "14"	SW 250 ft	N 41°-04.69	W 073°-24.03	
25085	116	Five Mile River Entrance Channel Buoy	Fl G 4s G "3" & R N "4"	Between	N 41°-03.37	W 073°-26.79	
25100	116	Goodwives River Entrance Lighted Buoy	Fl G 4s G "1"	NE 250ft	N 41°-02.28	W 073°-28.98	
25135	110	Westcott Cove East Entrance Buoy	Fl G 4s G "1" & R N "2"	Between	N 41°-01.72	W 073°-30.48	
25205	110	Stamford Harbor Entrance Buoy	R N "2"	W 475ft	N 41°-00.75	W 073°-32.19	
25530	LIS	Little Captain Island East Reef Lighted GONG Buoy	Fl G 2.5s GONG G "1"	SE 0.1nm	N 40°-59.54	W 073°-35.75	
25340	104	Newfoundland Reef Lighted Buoy	Fl R 4s R "4"	SSW 0.2nm	N 41°-00.27	W 073°-36.29	
25365	98	Jones Rocks Light	Fl G 4s 25ft 5M "3"	SE 525ft	N 40°-59.25	W 073°-38.00	
25370	98	Cormorant Reef Buoy	R N "4"	W 175ft	N 40°-59.47	W 073°-37.91	
25490	98	Greenwich Harbor Channel Buoy	R N "4" & G C "3"	Between	N 41°-00.19	W 073°-37.33	
25535	98	Great Captain Rocks Lighted Buoy	Fl R 4s R "2" & G C "3"	Between	N 40°-58.94	W 073°-39.19	
25585	90	Mamaroneck Harbor Entrance Buoy	G C "3"	E 425ft	N 40°-55.57	W 073°-43.04	
25605	90	Outer Steamboat Rock Buoy	Fl G 4s G "5"	E 175ft	N 40°-56.24	W 073°-42.99	
25720	90	Larchmont Harbor East Entrance Light	Fl R 4s 26ft 5M "2"	S 0.1nm	N 40°-54.98	W 073°-43.84	
25730	LIS	Hens and Chickens South Lighted Buoy	Fl R 4s R "2"	SE 0.1nm	N 40°-54.11	W 073°-44.22	
25735	86	Hicks Ledge Junction Buoy	G R C "HL"	S 375ft	N 40°-54.12	W 073°-45.14	
25780	86	Bailey Rock Lighted Buoy	Fl G 4s G "3BR" & R N "4"	Between	N 40°-54.29	W 073°-45.71	
25810	86	Emerald Rock Buoy	G R C	WSW 475ft	N 40°-53.70	W 073°-45.93	
25815	86	Huckleberry Island Lighted Buoy	Fl R 4s R "2"	SE 275 ft	N 40°-53.42	W 073°-45.35	
25820	86	Old Tom Head Rocks Buoy	R N "4" & Fl G 4s G "5"	Between	N 40°-53.48	W 073°-46.11	
25850	LIS	Hart Island East Side GONG Buoy	GONG G "1"	E 400ft	N 40°-51.43	W 073°-45.67	
25860	80	South Nonations Reef Lighted BELL Buoy	Fl R 4s BELL R "4"	S 375ft	N 40°-51.82	W 073°-46.28	
25870	80	Chimney Sweeps Lighted Buoy	Fl G 4s G "1"	ENE 300ft	N 40°-51.77	W 073°-46.73	
25890	86	Machaux Rock Lighted BELL Buoy	Fl R 4s BELL R "6" & G C "7"	Between	N 40°-52.42	W 073°-46.72	
25975	76	City Island Lighted Buoy	Fl R 4s R "2"	On Mark	N 40°-49.97	W 073°-47.36	
26010	80	Cuban Ledge Lighted Buoy	Fl R 4s R "2"	W 0.1nm	N 40°-50.44	W 073°-48.37	
26065	LIS	Mt. Sinai Harbor Approach Buoy	RW "M"	On Mark	N 40°-58.20	W 073°-02.63	
26125	LIS	Port Jefferson Approach Lighted WHISTLE Buoy	Mo(A) WHISTLE RW "PJ"	On Mark	N 40°-59.28	W 073°-06.45	
26130	360	Port Jefferson Harbor Entrance Lighted Buoy	Fl 2.5s BELL R "2" & Fl G 2.5s G "1"	Between	N 40°-58.39	W 073°-05.66	
26205	368	Stony Brook Harbor Entrance Lighted Buoy	Fl G 4s G "1"	On mark	N 40°-56.26	W 073°-09.78	
26315	368	Nissequogue River Entrance Lighted Buoy	Mo(A) RW "NR"	On mark	N 40°-55.39	W 073°-13.73	
26365	LIS	Northport Platform West Light	Q W 26ft HORN Private	N 0.3nm	N 40°-57.56	W 073°-20.58	
26420	374	Eatons Neck Lighted Buoy	Fl G 2.5s G "1"	WSW 0.1nm	N 40°-56.83	W 073°-24.38	
26465	LIS	Huntington Bay Approach Buoy	R N "2"	NE 0.1nm	N 40°-57.36	W 073°-28.59	
26475	LIS	Huntington Bay Approach Buoy	R N "4"	NE 0.1nm	N 40°-56.82	W 073°-27.49	
26480	LIS	Huntington Bay Approach Buoy	R N "6"	NE 0.1nm	N 40°-56.62	W 073°-26.24	
26485	LIS	Huntington Bay Lighted BELL Buoy	Fl R 4s BELL R "8"	NE 0.1nm	N 40°-55.92	W 073°-25.29	
26530	LIS	Huntington Harbor Light	Iso W 6s 42ft 6M HORN	NE 0.1nm	N 40°-54.70	W 073°-25.75	
26680	LIS	Northport Bay Entrance Lighted Buoy	Fl G 4s G "1"	S 300ft	N 40°-54.83	W 073°-24.35	
26690	372	Northport Bay Buoy	G C "3"	SE 250ft	N 40°-54.83	W 073°-24.00	
26705	378	Northport Bay Lighted Buoy	Fl R 4s R "8"	N 500ft	N 40°-55.09	W 073°-22.54	
26865	LIS	Oyster Bay GONG Buoy	GONG G "4"	SW 0.1nm	N 40°-55.48	W 073°-30.34	
26870	382	Cold Spring Harbor Light	F W (Red Sector) 37ft 7M	E 575ft	N 40°-54.87	W 073°-29.46	

WYPT #	PAGE	NAME & LOCATION	CHARACTERISTIC	LOCATION	LATITUDE	LONGITUDE	NOTES
26880	382, 386	Oyster Bay Buoy	R N "4"	S 0.1nm	N 40°-54.00	W 073°-30.39	
26885	382, 386	Oyster Bay Lighted Buoy	Fl G 4s G "5"	NW 0.1nm	N 40°-53.92	W 073°-30.67	
26890	386	Oyster Bay Buoy	R N "6"	SE 425ft	N 40°-53.10	W 073°-31.00	
27050	LIS	Hempstead Harbor Buoy	R N "2"	NE 0.1nm	N 40°-52.55	W 073°-42.61	
27055	LIS	Prospect Point Buoy	R N "4"	NE 0.1nm	N 40°-52.28	W 073°-41.92	
27060	392	Mott Point BELL Buoy	BELL R "6"	E 0.3nm	N 40°-51.66	W 073°-40.00	
27065	392	Glen Cove Breakwater Light	Fl G 4s 24ft 4M "5"	W 0.3nm	N 40°-51.72	W 073°-39.93	
27070	392	Hempstead Harbor Buoy	R N "8"	E 0.2nm	N 40°-51.33	W 073°-39.54	
27075	392	Hempstead Harbor Anchorage Buoy	Y C "A" & Y N "B"	Between	N 40°-51.11	W 073°-39.54	
27115	398	Plum Point Lighted Buoy	Fl G 4s G "1"	S 400ft	N 40°-49.86	W 073°-43.72	
27160	406	Elm Point Buoy	R N "4"	On mark	N 40°-49.02	W 073°-46.05	
27175	406	Little Neck Bay Approach Channel Buoy	RW C "LN"	On mark	N 40°-47.26	W 073°-45.77	
27660	LIS	Constellation Rock Buoy	R N "2"	S 0.1nm	N 41°-10.37	W 072°-06.57	
27665	LIS	Gardiners Island Lighted GONG Buoy	Fl G 4s GONG G "1Gl"	On mark	N 41°-08.99	W 072°-08.94	
27730	306	Gardiners Bay South Entrance BELL Buoy	Mo(A) BELL "RW "S"	On mark	N 41°-02.20	W 072°-03.09	
27735	LIS	Gardiners Bay South Entrance Buoy	R N "2"	WSW 225ft	N 41°-01.49	W 072°-03.76	
27745	LIS	Gardiners Bay South Entrance Buoy	R N "4"	WSW 450ft	N 41°-00.90	W 072°-04.74	
27750	LIS	Gardiners Bay South Entrance Buoy	R N "6"	On mark	N 41°-00.89	W 072°-06.69	
27755	LIS	Gardiners Bay South Entrance Buoy	R N "8"	SW 450ft	N 41°-01.28	W 072°-07.26	
27760	LIS	Gardiners Bay South Entrance Buoy	G C "11"	E 0.3nm	N 41°-02.74	W 072°-07.56	
27770	LIS	Crow Shoal Buoy	R N "14"	S 0.3nm	N 41°-04.29	W 072°-10.55	
27775	308	Three Mile Entrance Lighted BELL Buoy	Mo(A) BELL RW "TM"	On mark	N 41°-02.66	W 072°-11.31	
27960	318	Shelter Island Sound No. Channel Lighted Buoy	Mo (A) RW "N"	On mark	N 41°-05.99	W 072°-15.68	
27965	318	Shelter Island Sound No. Channel Lighted Buoy	Fl R 4s BELL "R "2" & G C "3"	Between	N 41°-06.14	W 072°-18.21	
28045	318	Shelter Island Sound No. Channel Buoy	R N "8"	E 400ft	N 41°-06.89	W 072°-19.88	
28050	318, 328	Greenport Harbor Light	Fl R 4s 19ft 4M "8A"	SE 0.1nm	N 41°-06.15	W 072°-20.75	
28070	328	Stirling Basin Buoy	R N "10"	SE 500ft	N 41°-05.40	W 072°-21.60	
28135	328	Shelter Island Sound No. Channel Lighted Buoy	Fl G 4s G "11"	NE 0.1nm	N 41°-04.44	W 072°-23.10	
28145	328	Town Creek Lighted Buoy	G C "1" Private & R "2" Fl R 4s R "2" Private	Between	N 41°-03.52	W 072°-24.76	
28180	328	Shelter Island Sound No. Channel Lighted Buoy	Fl R 4s R "12"	E 0.1nm	N 41°-03.00	W 072°-22.56	
28200	318	Coecles Harbor Lighted Buoy	Fl G 4s G "1"	On mark	N 41°-04.02	W 072°-16.19	
28235	308	Shelter Island South Channel Buoy	R N "2" & G C "1"	Between	N 41°-03.25	W 072°-14.02	
28245	308	Cedar Island Light	Fl G 4s 57ft 5M "3Cl" & R N "6"	Between	N 41°-02.37	W 072°-15.95	
28255	308	Barcelona Point Light	Fl G 4s 10ft 4M "7" & R N "8"	Between	N 41°-01.05	W 072°-16.16	
28310	312	Sand Spit Light	Fl R 4s 10ft 4M "10A"	S 0.1nm	N 41°-00.86	W 072°-16.95	
28325	312	Sag Harbor Breakwater Light	Fl G 2.5s 12ft 4M "1SH"	NW 425ft	N 41°-00.59	W 072°-17.74	
28405	312, 318	Shelter Island Sound So. Channel Lighted Buoy	Fl G 4s G "15"	NE 0.1nm	N 41°-02.73	W 072°-18.61	
28415	312, 318	West Neck Harbor Lighted Buoy	Fl R 4s R "2" Private	On mark	N 41°-02.83	W 072°-20.30	
28450	312, 318, 328	Shelter Island Sound So. Channel Lighted Buoy	Fl R 4s R "16"	S 0.1nm	N 41°-01.62	W 072°-21.24	
28505	312, 328	Little Peconic Bay Lighted Buoy	Fl G 4s G "17"	NW 500ft	N 41°-01.57	W 072°-22.98	
28510	LIS	Little Peconic Bay Buoy	R N "18"	E 0.2nm	N 41°-00.69	W 072°-23.62	
28570	LIS	Little Peconic Bay Lighted Buoy	Fl R 4s R "22"	SE 0.2nm	N 40°-58.40	W 072°-25.62	
28685	344	North Race Buoy	G C "1"	NE 575ft	N 40°-59.28	W 072°-26.83	
28690	344	North Race Lighted Buoy	Fl G 4s G "3"	N 400ft	N 40°-59.21	W 072°-28.30	
28750	336	Great Peconic Bay Lighted Buoy	Fl R 2.5s R "26"	SE 500ft	N 40°-57.07	W 072°-27.00	
28820	336	Sebonac Creek Lighted Buoy	Fl W 5s R "2" Private	NW 525ft	N 40°-55.20	W 072°-27.57	
28850	336	Cold Spring Pond Approach Light	Fl G 5s G "1" & R N "2"	Between	N 40°-54.15	W 072°-28.81	
28860	336	Shinnecock Canal Entrance Lighted Buoy	Fl G 4s G "1"	N 0.2nm	N 40°-54.16	W 072°-30.26	
28910	348	Flanders Bay Lighted Buoy	Fl R 4s R "4"	On mark	N 40°-55.62	W 072°-34.36	
28975	348	Peconic River Lighted Buoy	Fl R 2s R "2"	SSW 0.1nm	N 40°-55.68	W 072°-32.72	

*The Waypoint number listed is the same as the U.S. Coast Guard Light List number.

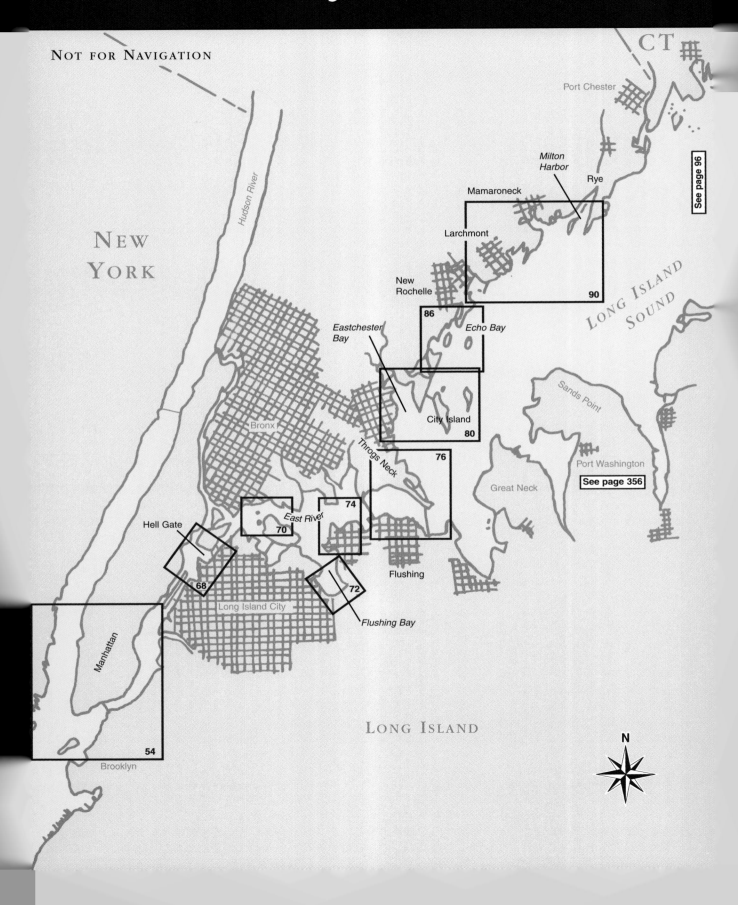

NOT FOR NAVIGATION

CT

Port Chester

Milton Harbor

Rye

Mamaroneck

Larchmont

See page 96

New
Rochelle

86

Eastchester Bay

Echo Bay

90

LONG ISLAND SOUND

NEW

YORK

Hudson River

Sands Point

Bronx

City Island

80

Throgs Neck

76

Port Washington

Great Neck

See page 356

Hell Gate

East River

74

70

68

72

Flushing

Long Island City

Flushing Bay

Manhattan

54

Brooklyn

LONG ISLAND

N

If you don't mind a little traffic—some of it quite huge—then you're sure to enjoy the unique perspective that a cruise around New York City offers. Cruising this area can be as relaxing as you care to make it. You can put yourself right into the action by taking a slip at a Manhattan marina, or choose a harbor on the outskirts and get to Gotham via public transportation. Several first-class yachting facilities serve the New Jersey side of the Hudson River, while north of the city New York's Westchester County offers a little bit of peace in its suburban marinas.

This mix of metropolis and suburbia makes for cruising ground that is never dull. The scenery varies from skyscrapers, stadiums, and sanitation plants to urban islands, towering bridges, and the rocky shores of summer people's enclaves; this varying landscape is interspersed with all manner of homes inhabited by everyone from hobos to the hoi polloi to the hoity-toity. Let your whims take the helm: turn toward the city if that's how you're inclined that particular day, or tack toward quieter waters. Take a slip in **Rye** and spend your day at Playland, or go for fun on a larger scale in **Manhattan**, an amusement park in its own right. Go ashore at **Flushing Bay** and take in a museum or an athletic event, or experience a combination of city and small community at **City Island**, the ideal place to be when you need a repair or just a great meal.

Hudson River traffic is a study in contrasts. © Maptech

Navigating New York City to Connecticut

The **East River** should not be navigated solely using GPS coordinates and courses; it's not straight and there's too much action about. Large commercial ships and tugs with tows are hard to stop or turn quickly, especially when headed downstream in a stiff current. Carefully read the **New York Harbor** and **East River** chapters for detailed navigation advice through this area, including the notorious Hell Gate. (You'll also want to refer to our *Boater's Reference* section on pages 34 to 51; a former New York City tugboat captain takes you through some standard procedures for cruising with the big boys.)

Once you reach Fl R 4s BELL R "48" at **Throgs Neck** you are officially in Long Island Sound. The Sound widens as it moves northeast, offering numerous harbors on both shores. This region deals with those harbors on the northern shore, up to the Connecticut border. The tidal range in this area is approximately 9 feet, and currents can run more than 2 knots. Add this to the traffic—both commercial and recreational—and you have a complicated navigation area. Follow the buoys carefully and stay clear of bridge stanchions. *Refer to the Throgs Neck chapter for more information.*

From Fl R 4s BELL R "48," head north between R N "46A" and Stepping Stones Light (OcG 4s 46ft 8M). **City Island** sits directly to the north, and there are facilities on both the eastern and western side. Use caution when navigating **Eastchester Bay**, as the western shores are riddled with boulders, shoals, and wrecks. When approaching City Island, beware of Big Tom, a barely submerged rock about 50 yards west of Belden Point. A cruise around the north end of Hart Island can be a pleasant trip; it's rocky but well marked. *Refer to the City Island & Eastchester Bay chapter for more information.*

Northeast of Hart Island, **Execution Rocks** splits Long Island Sound, forcing you around the shoaled and rocky area. To reach New Rochelle and Larchmont, stay west of Execution Rocks; if you're headed to a harbor farther east, swing to the east of the area.

From a point between R N "46A" and Stepping Stones Light (OcG 4s 46ft 8M) make your way north toward Fl R 4s 6M "46" at the south end of Hart Island. To reach **New Rochelle**, follow Hart Island to the north, heeding the buoys. There are a number of obstructions in New Rochelle's harbors, but the channels are well marked and easily seen in daylight. *Refer to the New Rochelle Harbor & Echo Bay chapter for more information.*

From about 500 feet east of Fl R 4s 6M "46", head 027°m toward Fl R 4s R "2" and the entrance to **Larchmont Harbor**. Larchmont Harbor is a small, rocky harbor with almost no shore access. **Mamaroneck Harbor** shares a wide-open entrance with **Milton Harbor**, and provides a well-protected inner harbor. Swing east of Fl R 4s GONG R "44A," at the south end of Execution Rocks, and head for Fl G 4s GONG "G 23." From here, head 030°m to reach Fl R 2.5s BELL R "42" and the entrance to Mamaroneck Harbor. *Refer to the Larchmont, Mamaroneck & Milton Harbors chapter for more information.*

(For information regarding the north shore of Long Island, refer to chapters in Region 7: Western Long Island.)

Dutch Treat

In a letter home to his mother, 17-year-old Samuel Langhorne Clemens, in New York City for the first time, wrote, "I have taken a liking to the abominable place, and every time I get ready to leave I put it off a day or so."

True, New York City wasn't quite the banks of the mighty Mississippi, but the aspiring writer and publisher had had enough of those muddy waters for the time being. While he was grateful to Hannibal, Missouri, for providing novel inspiration as well as his Mark Twain pen name, he knew that success would come only from the glittering streets of Gotham.

After a number of years away in which he kept busy with short-lived careers as a Confederate soldier, gold and silver miner, and steamboat pilot, Clemens returned to New York to carve his sure path to success. Known by this time by his nautical nomenclature, Mark Twain, he jumped headlong into social opportunity—he frequented the library, visited the World's Fair, met his future bride, and attended Broadway shows—and career opportunity, progressing from reporting and writing humorous essays to lecturing and publishing.

At roughly the same time that Twain was making his mark, financier Jay Gould was tackling Wall Street. Gould, a savvy and astute (if not always scrupulous) businessman, built an amazing fortune by purchasing small railroad holdings and watching them skyrocket seemingly in an instant under his golden touch. Thanks to the contributions of these two 19th-century men, New York remains tops in the world in the publishing and finance industries.

Since the time of Twain and Gould, many generations have headed to Manhattan in search of fame, fortune, or just a little fun. Credit the intrepid Adriaen Block for discovering this island, as he did so many others, and claiming

A sail provides momentary peace from the hub-bub ashore. © Maptech

Marine Facilities and Services

All Coast Guard Stations Monitor VHF Channel 16

marinalife.com — Convenient Online Boat Slip Reservations

#	Marine Facilities and Services	Phone	Monitors / Working VHF Channel	Number of Transient Berths / Moorings	Seasonal / Year-round	Maximum LOA	Approach / Dockside Depth in Feet at MLW	Hookups: Fresh Water / Phone / Cable TV	110V* 220V▲ 3 Phase■ Maximum Amps	Ramp / Dinghy Dock / Launch Service	Rail / Lift / Crane / Trailer: Capacity (tons)	Repairs: Propellor / Sail / Rigging / Electronics	Marine / Groceries / Ice / Bait / LPG / CNG	Gas / Diesel Fuel	Fuel Brand	Restrooms / Showers / Laundry / Pumpout	Public Phone / Restaurant / Snack Bar	Hotel / Pool / Tennis / Golf	Mastercard / VISA / Discover / AmEx
1	Marine Basin Marina	718-372-5700	16/68	10/	Y	100	8/8	FP	★▲50		C55	All	IB	GD		RS		P	MVA
2	New York Skyports Marina Inc.	212-686-4548	16/	5/	S	100	9/8	F	★50								R		MVA
3	South Street Seaport Museum*	212-748-8600	MUSEUM—NO DOCKAGE AVAILABLE																
4	North Cove Yacht Harbor	212-938-9000	69/	26/	Y	180		All	★▲■										MVA
5	SURFSIDE 3 (p. 57)	212-336-7873	68/	15/	S	200	8/8	All	★▲50				MB			RS	G	PR	MVA
6	West 79th St. Boat Basin (p. 63)	212-496-2105	9/16	9/10	Y	35	/1	FP	★50	D							P		P

Continued on next page…

The *Adirondack's* bowsprit gets some attention at Chelsea Piers. © Maptech

it for the Dutch, who purchased it in 1626 from the Native Americans for $24 worth of rum and trinkets. But Nieuw Amsterdam, as they called it, remained under Dutch possession only until 1664, when it was ceded to England and renamed New York.

New York City prospered as a shipping center, because of its well-protected, accommodating harbor. The first port stood three blocks inland of today's South Street Seaport, but as the debris of civilization accumulated, the island expanded. Pearl Street, along the original waterfront, was replaced by Water Street, which was replaced by Front Street and finally, South Street. Where it could be said that Wall Street and Park and Fifth avenues were

paved in gold, South Street was paved in the scales of fish. Scores of fishing boats tied up daily at the Fulton Fish Market, still among the world's largest—although all seafood now arrives on refrigerated trucks.

ACTIVITIES: If ever there was a place to be seen and done, The City that Never Sleeps is it. Access to Manhattan from the New Jersey side of the Hudson is quick and easy: NY Waterway (800-53-FERRY) has ferries running from Weehawken, Hoboken, and Jersey City to West 38th Street and the World Financial Center, with free connecting buses to Chelsea Piers. The PATH train (800-234-PATH) makes a stop at the Newport Marina and runs to a terminus in Greenwich Village.

If you're not sure where to begin, head over to the New York Convention & Visitors Bureau (212-484-1222) at 59th Street and Columbus Circle. They'll give you a handle on how to spend your visit.

Ellis Island (212-363-3200), just southeast of the Battery, is where more than 16 million immigrants made landfall between 1892 and 1932. The restored, main building now houses a Wall of Honor, an Oral History Studio, and a computerized database containing records on many of the immigrants who came ashore here. A ferry (212-269-5755) to the island departs from Castle Clinton in Battery Park. Don't try landing on Ellis Island in your own boat—you'll be evicted by the Park Police.

Marine Facilities and Services		Number of Transient Berths / Monitors / Working VHF Channel	Approach / Dockside Depth in Feet at MLW	Seasonal / Year-round / Moorings	Maximum LOA	Hookups: Fresh Water / Phone / Cable TV	110V ★ 220V ▲ 3 Phase ■ Maximum Amps	Ramp / Dinghy Dock / Launch Service	Rail / Lift / Crane / Trailer: Capacity (tons)	Diesel / Wood / Fiberglass / Electronics	Repairs: Propeller / Sail / Rigging / Gas	Marine / Groceries / Ice / Bait / LPG / CNG	Restrooms / Showers / Laundry / Pumpout	Gas / Diesel Fuel / Fuel Brand	Public Phone / Restaurant / Snack Bar	Hotel / Pool / Tennis / Golf	Mastercard / VISA / Discover / AmEx
7 PORT IMPERIAL MARINA (B) p. 61	201-902-8787	88/	100/	S	100	27/8	FP	★▲■100	L	L35		PGFE	GD	MI	All	PS	MVA
8 LINCOLN HARBOR YACHT CLUB p. 59	800-205-6987	74/	250/	Y	200	45/8	All	100					All	D		All	P	All
9 NEWPORT MARINA p. 67	201-626-5550	16/72	30/	Y	180	12/10	FC	★▲■100	D						MGI	All	P	MVA
10 Liberty Harbor Marina & R.V. Park	201-451-1000	68/68	12/	Y	100	18/12	F	▲50		L60		PGDWFE	GD	IB	All	All	All
11 LIBERTY LANDING MARINA p. 65	201-985-8000	72/72		Y	250	18/18	All	★▲50	All	L60		All	GD	I	All	PR	All

Information in these listings is provided by the facilities themselves. An asterisk (*) indicates that the facility did not respond to our most recent requests for information. (B) represents a BOAT/U.S. cooperating marina.

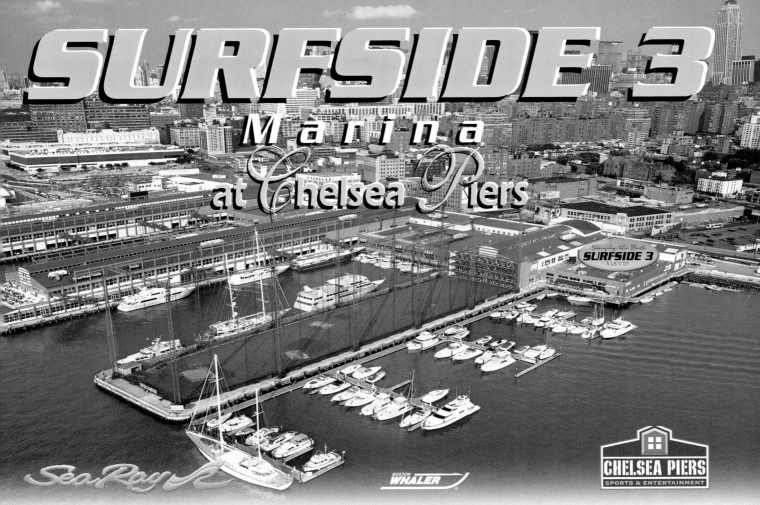

SURFSIDE 3
Marina
at Chelsea Piers

Manhattan's Most Exciting Marina & Entertainment Complex

Cruise in to Surfside 3 Marina, Chelsea Piers in Manhattan. All-new Chelsea Piers is New York's most exciting marina, recreation and entertainment complex. From fine dining to active sports, it's all here for you to enjoy.

As for Surfside 3, we're a full-service marina, offering the niceties that make owning a boat an equally pleasurable experience on land and at sea.

Whether you're just visiting or looking to be a part of the action, check out Surfside 3 and all it has to offer. We're located on the West Side right where 23rd Street meets the Hudson River, Pier 59. At our state-of-the-art complex you will meet our professional, experienced staff ready to accommodate your every need.

Surfside 3 at Chelsea Piers

- Concierge Service
- New Boat Sales
- Dock and Dining
- Seasonal Dockage
- Transient Dockage
- In-Water Displays
- Yacht Brokerage
- Ship's Store

Simply the Best
SURFSIDE 3
Marina

23rd St. & The Hudson River, New York City
1-800-650-SURF ▪ 212-336-SURF
www.surfside3.com

The World's Largest Retail *SeaRay* Dealer!

LINDENHURST	COPIAGUE	HUNTINGTON	NORWALK, CT
631-957-5900	631-842-5900	631-424-2710	203-831-6311

Frederic Bartholdi originally intended to place his Lady Liberty sculpture at the entrance to the Suez Canal. When the Sultan of Egypt turned down the plan, Bartholdi looked to the New World for a suitable site and found a taker in 1886. The Statue of Liberty's (212-363-3200; call for tour information) current location atop old Fort Wood on Liberty Island is certainly spectacular—so thank the persnickety sultan as you drift past.

For the cheapest ride in the city, try a round-trip on the Staten Island Ferry (718-390-5253), departing from a terminal at South and State Streets. For just 50 cents, the trip offers some of the best—and least expensive—views of the harbor and New York's skyline.

A more expensive and inclusive tour is offered by Circle Line (212-563-3200). Departing from Pier 83 at the end of West 42nd Street, the line's 12 daily cruises circumnavigate Manhattan—past the Statue of Liberty, up the East and Harlem rivers and back down the Hudson. There's also a shorter option, which will take you down to the Statue and back up again.

Whether you're an athlete or a shopoholic, you'll be glad you found the Chelsea Piers complex. Choose from ice and roller rinks, basketball courts, batting cages, and an indoor field house for soccer, lacrosse, and field hockey. The Golf Club at Chelsea Piers (212-336-6400) boasts a multi-tiered, all-weather driving range, open year-round. Those interested in another kind of action can rock the boat on a Spirit Cruise vessel, offering dining, dancing, and live shows. There's even a moonlight cruise departing at 1:30 a.m. The City never sleeps, so why should you?

On Labor Day Weekend, the Annual Intrepid Tugboat Challenge (212-957-7049) is held in the area of the 79th Street Boat Basin and the Intrepid Museum. Tugs compete in various races and other competitions, including Nose-to-Nose Pushing contests, and awards are given for the Best Crew Tattoo and Best Tug Mascot. In honor of Popeye, there's a spinach-eating contest, as well as a temporary tattoo booth.

Every boater should visit the South Street Seaport (212-732-7678), a shopping area and historic site loaded with pubs and restaurants. Check out the Museum Book & Chart Store (212-748-8600), with a full stock of nautical prints and maritime literature. Tour the four-masted bark *Peking* and the lightship *Ambrose*, or join the crew on the schooner *Pioneer* for a hands-on sail. Visiting training ships and ships of state often stop here as well. Stop by the Visitors Center at Fulton and Water streets for tickets or more information.

If you're staying in New Jersey, don't miss a visit to the Liberty Science Center (201-200-1000), offering IMAX films, plus exhibits and displays on inventions, health, and the environment, including tanks of live fish and insects. The Meadowlands Sports Complex (201-935-3900), the home of the New York Giants, New York Jets, New Jersey

Look Before You Launch!

Before you commit to a berth for the season check out Lincoln Harbor Yacht Club.

Positioned on the Hudson directly across from Midtown Manhattan, we provide a Country Club setting and an excellent location for boats cruising the Tri-State area. Right outside our gate you'll find four restaurants, a 165 room all suite hotel, mini-mall and ferry service to New York City.

Our 250 floating docks with full fingered slips and our wide, deep water fairways allows ease of maneuvering for any type of vessel. 170 of our slips can accommodate vessels from 40' to 120' and our face dock can handle mega yachts up to 200'

If that's not enough, our on-site amenities include: • A professional staff ready to assist you with docking 24 hours a day • Excellent security with electronic gates, closed circuit TV monitoring and 24 hour roving patrol • Cable Television • Private phone connection • Conference Room and Business Services • Mini work-out center • Yacht detailing and Mechanic on-site • Yacht Brokerage • Diesel Fuel.

For a copy of our brochure and dockage rates please call 201-319-5100. Ask about our unique Float Plan which allows you to take advantage of our in season monthly rate without committing to a 30-day consecutive stay.

LINCOLN HARBOR YACHT CLUB

1-800-205-6987 • 201-319-5100
Latitude 40° 45' 35"...Longitude 74° 01' 12"
•1500 Harbor Blvd., Weehawken, NJ 07087
Fax: 201-319-5111 • VHF 74
http://www.lincolnharbor.com

The little red lighthouse is overwhelmed underneath the mighty George Washington Bridge. © Maptech

Devils, and New Jersey Nets, is just a short trip away by cab or bus.

RESTAURANTS & PROVISIONS: Since you won't be doing much sleeping here, you'll really need sustenance. And if you've made it here, you can make it anywhere—Italy, Greece, Jamaica, Mexico, China—without even raising the main. New York is a melting pot, all right, and when it comes to restaurants it's a pot of gold. Of course, for the finest places, you'll need to bring the gold...your gold card, that is.

Around South Street Seaport, you need only turn your head to find whatever you're craving, be it a menus-and-cloth-napkin place or a pay-first kind of place. For *deliciozo* Italian dishes just like Mama's, try Gianni's (212-608-7300). Got your Sunday best aboard? Make reservations for a steak at Delmonico's (212-422-4747), one of the oldest restaurants in the city.

When those growling stomachs get to be unbearable, you've got your choice at Surfside 3 Marina at Chelsea Piers. Take the family to Crab House (212-366-4111) for seafood in a fun atmosphere, or sit by the glass wall at Chelsea Brewing Company (212-336-6440) and watch the brew crew churn out barrels of suds while you put away traditional pub fare.

If you stay in New Jersey, your dining options are almost as unlimited. Near Lincoln Harbor in Weehawken, Ruth's Chris (201-863-5100) is sure to satisfy the steak and potato crowd. Houlihan's (201-863-4000) is the place for burgers and salads, and the new Chart House (201-348-6628) offers steak, seafood, and a great view of the Manhattan skyline. There's also an on-site food court with a deli, pizzeria, and Chinese restaurant.

Arthur's Landing (201-867-0777) at Port Imperial Marina, specializes in seafood, duck, and steak. In the vicinity of Newport Marina, the Café Newport (201-626-7200) serves a mix of popular Italian and American dishes. Hoboken and Jersey City are home to many more fine restaurants, just a cab ride away. Ruth's Chris and Arthur's Landing offer the pre-theater crowd a prix-fixe dinner deal including tickets for the Port Imperial Ferry and shuttle service to the theater district.

No need to worry if you find yourself low on supplies in Manhattan. Almost everything you need can be found within walking distance, even an all-night grocery.

NAVIGATION & ANCHORAGES: Use ChartKit Region 3, page 51; Maptech™ Waterproof Chart 8; and Maptech™ electronic and NOAA paper charts 12339 (1:10,000), 12335 (1:10,000), 12334 (1:10,000), 12402 (1:15,000), 12401 (1:15,000), and 12327 (1:40,000). Use tide tables for New York. High tide at Hell Gate, Hallets Point, is 2 hours, 4 minutes later; low tide is 2 hours, 7 minutes later. Multiply height of tide at New York by 1.1 for height of tide at Hallets Point. Mean tidal range is 5.1 feet. At Fort Wadsworth, the Narrows, use tide tables for Sandy Hook.

Embassy Guides

Boats moored along the Hudson. © Maptech

Coming from Hell Gate down the East River to the Battery, there is only one marina—the New York Skyports Marina at the end of East 23rd Street. Heavy currents, commercial traffic, and partially submerged debris mean that you can't lollygag through this stretch of the river. For information on navigating Hell Gate, see the next chapter.

South of Mill Rock, the East River's channel splits at Roosevelt Island, formerly called Welfare Island because of the prisoners and mentally ill who were once kept there. The west channel is preferred by most traffic because it's the deeper of the two, and the east channel is spanned by a lift bridge with only 40 feet of vertical clearance when closed (mhw). Six-hour notice is needed to raise the bridge. Currents in both channels can run as high as 5.2 knots, which can significantly alter your course and that of other vessels; be especially careful in this area.

High and low tides at the Narrows are 6 minutes later. Use height of tide at Sandy Hook for height of tide at the Narrows. Mean tidal range is 4.8 feet.

Few places in the world, if any, are as awe-inspiring as the Big Apple. Though the navigable waters are wide and deep, commercial traffic can be thick—know your navigational rules, and keep your eyes open.

CAUTION: Tugs, barges, and large ships have less maneuverability (especially in the East River), and therefore, the right of way. As this harbor is very busy, it is highly recommended that you maintain a listening watch on VHF 13. All commercial traffic monitors and converses (bridge to bridge) on this channel. Important information, such as position and route of commercial traffic, can be heard over VHF 13. By using this valuable resource, you may be able to avoid potentially dangerous situations.

CAUTION: Sailboats should stay west of Roosevelt Island. The Lift Bridge on the east side of the island has only 40 feet of vertical clearance when closed (mhw); a 4-5 knot current here can make it very difficult for some sailboats to turn around.

You'll find Fl G 4s 6M "17" on Belmont Island, at the southern tip of Roosevelt Island. Do not pass between Roosevelt and Belmont Islands—a pretty nasty shoal awaits you. Just north of the Williamsburg Bridge, you will come upon Fl R 2.5s R "18," which appears to be in the middle of the river. The preferred passage is to the east; however, most deep-draft and commercial traffic use this eastern passage in conjunction with the "Poorhouse Flats Range."

If you see a parade of traffic to and from Hell Gate, take the western side of the buoy, as the depths are similar. When navigating around Corlears Hook, just after the Williamsburg Bridge, stick to the Manhattan side, as it will keep you clear of traffic proceeding eastbound.

The next stretch of bridges is easily navigable, and it's an inviting setting to snap some photos. One mile southwest of the Williamsburg Bridge is the Manhattan Bridge, followed by the spectacular Brooklyn Bridge, after which you'll see some tall ships to the northwest. This is the South Street Seaport, well worth a visit for its nautical history, though it no longer offers transient dockage. At the Battery, the southern tip of Manhattan, the view is awesome, but don't get caught up in the scenery as ferries and other commercial traffic make for busy waters.

City of New York
Parks & Recreation
Rudolph W. Giuliani, Mayor
Henry J. Stern, Commissioner

West 79th St. Boat Basin

West 79th Street and the Hudson River
New York, NY 10024
(212) 496-2105 • (212) 496-2157 (Fax)

⚓ Located at river mile 1.9, just North of the USS Intrepid Air and Space Museum

⚓ Close to the Subway

⚓ Restaurants

⚓ Transients boaters welcome

⚓ Within walking distance of many Museums, Riverside and Central Park

⚓ Conveniently located on the Upper West Side of Manhattan

⚓ MSD Pump Out Station

⚓ Fresh Water and Phone Hook ups

⚓ Loading dock for guests and provisions

⚓ 24 hour security

THE RECREATIONAL BOATING GATEWAY TO NEW YORK CITY

Sister Marina *World's Fair Marina* located in Flushing Bay, contact information (718) 478-0480

⚓ Contact information at Dockmaster's office 212-496-2105 or 212-496-2157 (fax)

⚓ Monitiors Channel 9, 13 and 16

⚓ Self service Mooring fields and secure Dinghy Dock.

Governors Island is where the Dutch settlers established a toehold before taking Manhattan. The "Lady of the Harbor" awaits as you pass north of Governors Island and into the Upper Bay. Landing on either Liberty Island or Ellis Island to the north is strictly prohibited. You may get caught up in the moment with the view of the Statue of Liberty, but be cautious as it gets a bit rocky around Liberty Island. The holding ground south of Liberty is soft and muddy—ideal for anchoring. The west side of the island, parts of which are reduced to mud at low water, is designated for recreational boats, with the more open water reserved for commercial traffic.

The Hudson River is home to a number of marinas that cater to transients, including the West 79th Street Boat Basin, a year-round facility for smaller boats. The Chelsea Piers Sports and Entertainment Complex/Surfside 3 Marina stands out with its pier-side golfing range, and red, white, and blue buildings. Lincoln Harbor Yacht Club, opposite the Empire State Building, is a full-service marina with fuel (available by appointment on summer weekends), concierge, and 24-hour security. Similar amenities are available at Liberty Landing Marina, which is in a protected basin at the river's mouth.

Port Imperial Marina, north of Lincoln Harbor, is a 300-slip, full-service facility, with a fully-stocked ship's store and a restaurant. Farther south is Newport Marina, another facility that seems to have it all.

The Hudson River is wide and deep, and it can take you on a majestically landscaped journey upstate. Maptech Waterproof Chart #4: Hudson River, can assist you on your way with information on marina facilities, services, and sightseeing activities.

Though there are few, if any, natural obstructions in the river, commercial traffic is heavy near the Upper Bay. With all of the huge ships and debris (everything from timber to tires) floating in the water, you need to be alert. The center of the river is generally free of man-made obstructions. When navigating close to shore, be aware of old pilings.

CAUTION: For night-time navigation, be familiar with the navigation lights of powerboats, sailboats, and commercial vessels. There are so many lighted buoys, vessels, and buildings in the area that it begins to look like a planetarium show.

If you're headed for the Lower Bay, to Marine Basin Marina, a full-service marina, or points beyond, you can duck east of Governor's Island via the sheltered Buttermilk Channel and set a course for the Narrows, making sure to stay west of Bay Ridge Flats (marked by Fl

Lady Liberty looks over New York Harbor. © Maptech/James T. Abts

LIBERTY LANDING MARINA

A Full Service Marina
with a Spectacular View of Manhattan!

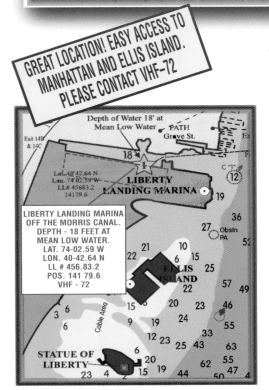
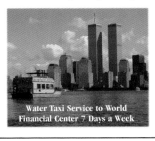

Looking north over Governors Island, with Manhattan in the background. © Maptech/James T. Abts

Y 4s Y "A" and Fl Y 4s Y "C"). Except for the Jersey side, there's plenty of water in the Upper Bay.

In a strong easterly or southeasterly wind, take advantage of the Red Hook and Bay Ridge channels, as you will be sheltered by the Brooklyn shore. In these winds, the Upper Bay can become very choppy, especially on the ebb side. Stay in the channel, passing east of Bay Ridge Flats, and set your course for the Narrows. Once past Fl G 2.5s "5" you can navigate freely to the bridge, keeping in mind to stay well off the Brooklyn shore from Owls Head sanitation dock southward to the Verrazano Narrows Bridge.

When heading to sea from the Narrows, you'll have plenty of water unless you stray into Romer Shoal, at the intersection of the Ambrose, Swash, and Chapel Hill North channels, or parts of Eastbank, a shallow area between Coney Island and Ambrose Channel. The channels here are wide and clearly marked.

Departing the Lower Bay, you'll have two options. One is to take the Ambrose Channel, starting between Fl G 4s GONG G "19" and Fl R 4s BELL R "20." The second is a combination of the Chapel Hill North Channel, from about where the Ambrose starts, to the Swash Channel at R G N "CH," to the east section of the Sandy Hook Channel at Fl R 4s BELL R "8." When using the Ambrose Channel,

keep in mind that outbound traffic will stay to the green side and inbound traffic will stay to the red side. If you stay in the channels you shouldn't have much of a problem. Expect to find a lot of commercial traffic in this area, including small fishing boats in the early hours.

Shoreside & Emergency Services
Airport:
—Port Authority of NY/NJ (800-AIR-RIDE)
Bus:
—NYC Travel Authority (718-330-1234)
Coast Guard: Sandy Hook (732-872-3428)
—Fort Totten (718-352-4422)
Ferry:
—NY Waterway (800-53-FERRY)
Police, Fire, Ambulance: 911
Subway: (718-330-1234)
Tow Service:
SEA TOW. —24-Hour Dispatch (800-4SEATOW)
— Western Long Island Sound (914-698-6523)
Tow BoatU.S. —24-Hour Dispatch (800-391-4869)
— Upper New York (718-885-3420)
Train: PATH (800-234-PATH)
—Amtrak (800-USA-RAIL)
—Metro-North (800-638-7646)

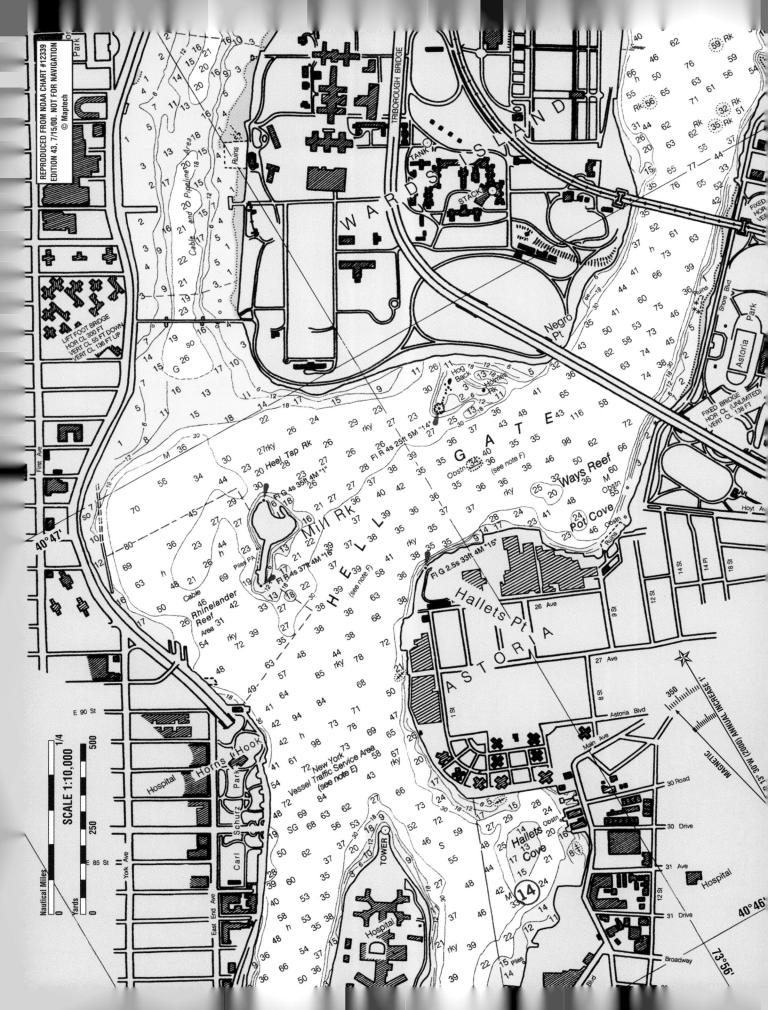

Location, Location, Location

From 1913 to 1957, the Brooklyn Dodgers played in Flatbush's Ebbets Field, to the delight of those no-nonsense New Yorkers who swore they bled "Dodger blue." But when owner Walter O'Malley's request for a plot of land on which to build a new stadium was denied, he announced that he was packing up his team for the dream-filled west coast. And so, after the 1957 season, those young men went west, saying hello to Hollywood. The New York Giants went too, to escape dwindling attendance at the aging Polo Grounds in a promising new San Francisco home. When Ebbets Field was demolished in 1960, its light towers were among the salvaged parts; you can see them today in use at Downing Stadium on Randalls Island.

The Unisphere and U.S. Tennis Center, as seen from Shea Stadium. All are part of Flushing Meadows Corona Park. © Maptech

Betrayed National League fans in the boroughs were left with only the American League's Yankees to root for. But it was too easy for these nitty-gritty folks to be Yankees fans; the team from the Bronx won too much and too easily for it to be satisfying. The void was filled in 1962 with the birth of the New York Metropolitans, who took as their colors the Dodger's blue and the Giants' orange. After playing in Manhattan's Polo Grounds in '62 (when they lost 120 games) and '63, the Mets moved into Shea Stadium, their new home in Queens, in time for the 1964 season. Designed by Robert Moses as a multi-purpose venue (football's Jets played there, as did the Beatles), Shea was built in time for the 1964 World's Fair along with the Unisphere sculpture and the aptly-named World's Fair Marina, but it is now used solely for baseball. In 1969 the Amazin' Mets took it all, winning the World Series despite having been in last place as late as August.

They've since made three World Series appearances, winning the championship in 1986.

The East River's reputation as a tricky passage is well deserved. It's not—and probably will never be—a popular spot for casual boating. New York was built around the East River, and though its role is diminished, the river still offers a unique view of the city's inner workings: the massive piers, power plants, and waste treatment plants that serve the population's most fundamental needs. If you're not too busy fighting a foul tide (remember your timing!), you're sure to come away from the passage awed by the vast scale of New York City.

Successfully running Hell Gate is primarily a matter of good timing. The Dutch explorer Adriaen Block, the first European to navigate the East River, gave the Gate its name. The Dutch word "hellegat" means "beautiful pass," leading us to believe Block must have caught the tide right (and with-

	Marine Facilities and Services	DOCKAGE							SERVICES				SUPPLIES & AMENITIES					
1	Point Yacht Club	718-378-8932			Y					*PRIVATE—MEMBERS ONLY*									
2	College Point Yacht Club	718-463-9841			Y					*PRIVATE—MEMBERS ONLY*									
3	Frank Tiborsky Marine Ltd.	718-353-2653			Y	25	20/8				C								DA
4	The Boat Yard*	718-886-5113			Y														
5	Arrow Yacht Club	718-359-9229			Y					*PRIVATE—MEMBERS ONLY*									
6	Williamsburg Yacht Club	718-359-9147			Y					*PRIVATE—MEMBERS ONLY*									
7	WORLD'S FAIR MARINA	718-478-0480 p. 75	71/	20/	Y	120	15/11	F	★50		L50	All	GD	Tex	MIB	RSP		PR	

Information in these listings is provided by the facilities themselves. An asterisk (*) indicates that the facility did not respond to our most recent requests for information. (B) represents a BOAT/U.S. cooperating marina.

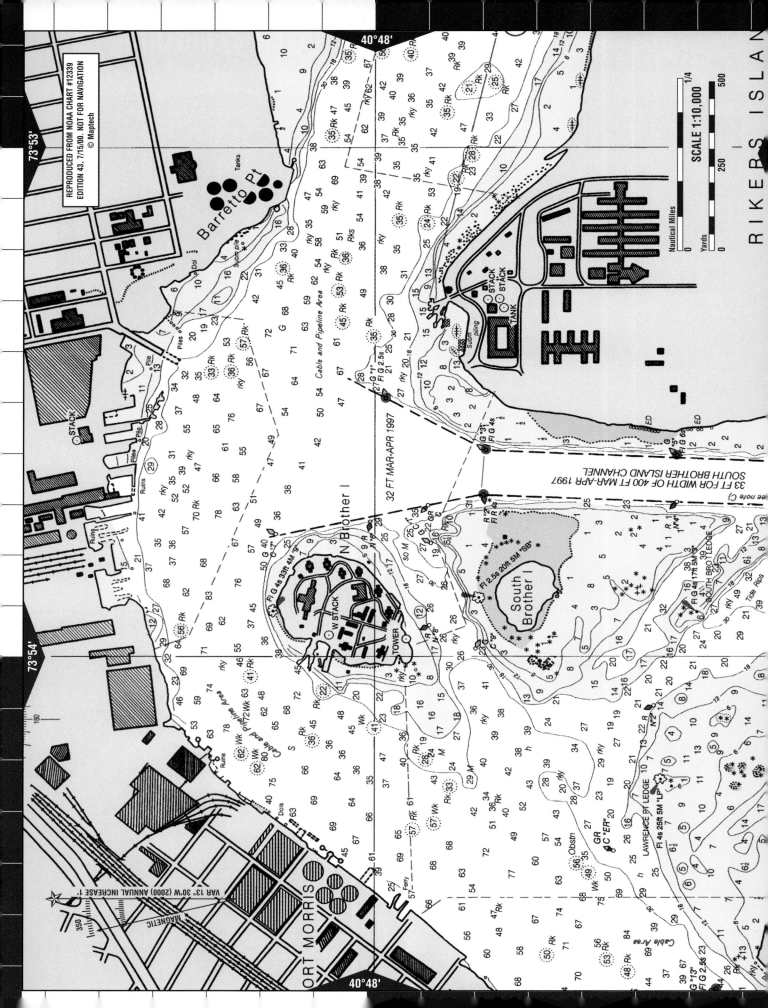

out the benefit of the Staten Island Ferry Terminal's huge clock). Less fortunate English-speaking sailors may have seized upon the Dutch word's infernal-sounding connotations and rewrote it on their charts.

ACTIVITIES: Flushing Bay has many old factories and sanitation plants, and the jets constantly flying overhead to and from LaGuardia Airport can make it too loud for you to think (although the Mets seem to have gotten used to it). It may not be the most picturesque place, but its sheltered bay offers great access to professional tennis and baseball.

From World's Fair Marina, it's an easy walk to Flushing Meadows Corona Park and everything it offers, including playgrounds, ball fields, basketball and tennis courts, a mini-golf course, and a model airplane field. Flushing Meadows is also home to the New York Mets (718-507-TIXX); big, blue Shea Stadium dominates the landscape, along with the Unisphere sculpture from the 1964 World's Fair and the Tennis Center. If you're visiting in September, check out the U.S. Open action.

On the grounds of the World's Fair in Flushing, the Hall of Science (718-669-0005), built as the Science Pavilion for the fair of 1964-65, is the city's only hands-on museum of science and technology. Also in the shadow of the Unisphere is the Queens Art Museum (718-592-9700), an engaging place without a trace of stuffiness. If you're around on the first Thursday evening of any month, check out their First Thursday program—it's a fun open house featuring music & dancing, films, refreshments, games and activities.

Horseracing is big in these parts. The Aqueduct Race Track (718-641-4700) and Belmont Park Race Track (718-641-4700) hold top-notch racing events, including the Belmont Stakes, one of the Triple Crown events. You'll need a taxi to reach these venues. A cab can also take you to Randalls Island, where concerts and other events are sometimes held in Downing Stadium (212-860-1828). If there's no musical event to attend, you can still take the crew to Family Golf Center (212-427-5689).

Few, if any, places in the world have a livelier arts scene than New York. You can really get a feel for the city through its fairs, festivals, exhibits, and concerts. The Queens Council on the Arts (718-647-3377), a borough-wide, cultural event information organization, can update you on everything that's happening when you pull into port.

Not far from Flushing Bay, you'll see vestiges of the city's early years. The Bowne House (718-359-0528), built in 1661, and the Kingsland Homestead (718-939-0647), a colonial farmhouse circa 1785, are each a short ride from the bay. If the concrete, asphalt, and roaring jets have made you a little daffy, the 38-acre Queens Botanical Gardens (718-886-3800) on Main Street will quell your yearning for something natural. Or visit the Queens Wildlife Center (718-271-1500), with 11 acres of North American fauna.

RESTAURANTS & PROVISIONS: In the 16th century William Shakespeare wrote that "people are the city." How right

Buzzing past the Pepsi plant on the East River. © Maptech

he was, and what better place to experience that than in New York City? The area's cultural variations make it what it is, and the diversity in Queens gives you wide-ranging, delectable dining.

A stop in Flushing Bay leads you to Queens, home to more Greeks than any other city but Athens. A four-mile cab ride to Astoria will bring you to Elias Corner (718-932-1510), Telly's Taverna (718-728-9056), and Taverna Vraka (718-721-3007) for a taste of highly authentic Hellenic cuisine. Other recommended spots include Jai Ya Thai (212-889-1330), serving spicy, inexpensive Thai dishes on Broadway at 81st Street, and London Lennie's (718-894-8084), a popular fish house on Woodhaven Boulevard at 63rd Drive.

You need not go any farther than the water if you stay at World's Fair Marina, where the Grand Bay Restaurant (718-898-3663) can set you up with a nice steak dinner.

A stay at one of the boat basins on College Point gives you access to a few restaurants and pizzeria-type pubs. College Point Boulevard, the area's main strip, is big on choices, including McDonald's, and with a sizable Asian community, there are a number of Chinese and Thai restaurants to choose from.

Though Queens is the largest of New York's five boroughs, the College Point area is not really a transient-friendly place when it comes to food and provisions. This is not to say that the people aren't friendly, just that there aren't a lot of places that cater to boaters.

NAVIGATION & ANCHORAGES: Use ChartKit Region 3, page 51, 52, and 52A; Maptech™ Waterproof Charts 1, 8, and 16; and Maptech™ electronic and NOAA paper charts 12339 (1:10,000), 12342 (1:10,000), 12335 (1:10,000), and 12364 (1:40,000). On the East River, use tide tables for New York. High tide at Hell Gate, Hallets Point, is 2 hours, 4 minutes later. Multiply height of tide at New York by 1.1 for height of tide at Hallets Point. Mean tidal range is 5.1 feet.

CAUTION: Large commercial ships are hard to stop or turn quickly, especially when headed downstream in a stiff

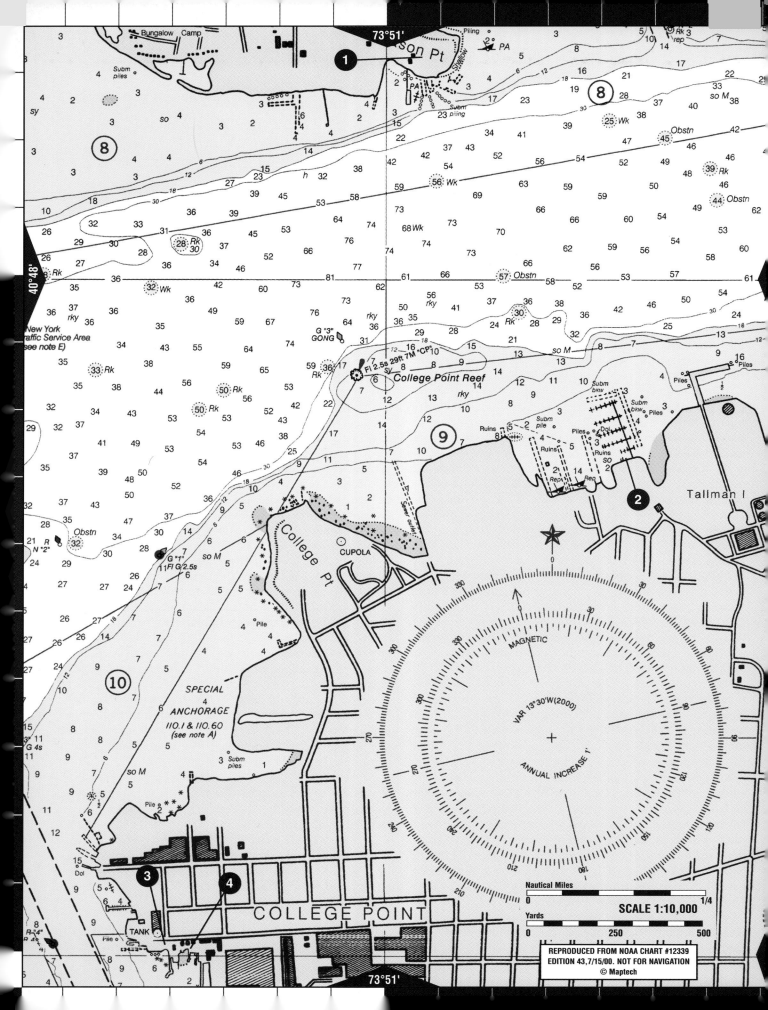

current. If evasive actions are required, you'll be the one who has to make them.

The deep channel leading west from Throgs Neck is about 0.4nm wide all the way to Rikers Island, where it narrows. Once past the Whitestone Bridge, you'll pass north of College Point Reef Fl 2.5s 29ft 7M "CP" on a riprap island, and you'll see and hear jets at La Guardia Airport to the southwest.

Flushing Bay is a shallow, well-protected harbor bordered by College Point to the east and La Guardia to the west. A well-marked, 15-foot channel runs southeast about 1.5nm to the bay's head. To enter Flushing Bay from the east, proceed southwest from GONG G "3" (just north of College Point Reef), and pass between Fl G 2.5s G "1" and R N "2." Aim for Fl G 4s G "3" at the start of the dredged channel. From the west, pass north of Fl G 2.5s G "5" before turning southeast between R N "2" and Fl G 2.5s G "1." This course avoids the long, lighted pier extending northeast from one of La Guardia's runways.

Looking north over Roosevelt Island and the East River. At the top you'll see the oft-mentioned Hell Gate. © Maptech/James T. Abts

Stay within the well-marked channel as far as the turning basin. Also, keep an eye out for garbage barges heading to and from the sanitation pier just south of Cape Ruth, and note the submerged dike running along the west edge of the channel.

Though it's not exactly quaint, Flushing Bay is a fine place to pull in for the night. Several of the marinas offer transient spaces. The bay provides good protection in all but northeasterly winds and even then the southern reaches of the harbor, protected by a long bar, remain calm. World's Fair Marina, at the head of the bay, is a secure, deep-water marina with a large restaurant.

Northwest of Fl G 2.5s G "5" is the Hunts Point Sanitation Pier. At press time this facility was idle, due in large part to the continuing effort of the New York Sanitation Department to reduce the amount of garbage transported to Staten Island's Fresh Kills landfill. To the southwest is Rikers Island, where you can get long-term accommodations if you run afoul of the law. Farther west you'll see North and South Brother islands, with a shallow channel between them that can be very turbulent. Under-powered boats should avoid this route. The preferred channel runs to the north of North Brother Island, where "Typhoid Mary" was incarcerated for a time. There is a long bar stretching southwest from North Brother Island, where the currents can be turbulent.

If you're heading east from Hell Gate, toward Long Island Sound, it's easy to get confused when traveling between the islands. There are a good number of lights and buoys in the area, which can be disorienting. We're told it's not uncommon for boaters unfamiliar with the area to head south of South Brother Island by mistake. This will not only add time to your journey, but a lot of headache.

The infamous Hell Gate, about 1.5nm southwest of North Brother Island, is where the strong currents of the East River combine with the waters of the Harlem River around Mill Rock. The area has a reputation for strong, reversing currents

and large standing waves, and there are (unfounded) rumors of eddies ready to swallow the unprepared. The river's reputation as a place to practice prudent navigation and piloting techniques is, however, justified. You'll make a blind "S" turn through Hell Gate, so be on your toes in case a 1,500-plus ton tanker or large tug/barge unit "suddenly" appears in front of you when rounding the corner.

A local mariner suggests staying as far away from the center as possible while transiting the river, especially if you have a small or under-powered boat, because the stiffest current runs in the deeper water. Traveling close to shore isn't a problem in the East River, because it's pretty deep, but keep an eye out for old pilings.

The tides and currents in the East River vary with location. Generally, flood currents run northeast into Long Island Sound and ebb currents run southwest into New York Harbor, the opposite of Long Island Sound currents. At either end of East River, currents are fairly weak, but at Hell Gate, 4- to 5-knot currents combine with strong winds, heavy traffic, and fluctuating depths to make navigation difficult if you go through at the wrong time. Consult your current tables for daily predictions for Hell Gate, and follow a few rules of thumb:

1. Plan ahead! Go with the current and avoid maximum flood or ebb currents in Hell Gate, especially in small or under-powered boats. When planning your passage through the Gate, remember that slack water only lasts about 4 minutes. If you're running late, don't push it; plan on dropping anchor or overnighting at a marina.

2. Use proper charts and keep track of your position. (The bridges make great landmarks.)

3. Monitor VHF 13; commercial vessels will be making their passing agreements and position announcements as required by law.

4. Wear lifejackets while on the river. Getting a person back aboard will take longer than in open water due to the traffic and currents.

FLUSHING BAY

COLLEG

SCALE 1:10,000

15 FT FOR MID-WIDTH OF 150 FT JAN 1995

SPECIAL ANCHORAGE
110.1 & 110.60 (see note A)

SPECIAL
ANCHORAGE
110.1 & 110.60
(see note A)

RESTRICTED AREA
162.20 (see note B)

SPECIAL ANCHORAGE
110.1 & 110.60 (see note A)

6 FEET JAN 1995

15 FEET JAN 1995

14 FT FOR WIDTH OF 200 FT JAN 1995

SPECIAL ANCHORAGE
110.1 & 110.60 (see note A)

Cape Ruth

Breakwater

Pipeline and Cable Area

FIXED BRIDGES
HOR CL 140 FT
VERT CL 34 FT

MAGNETIC

350

VAR 13° 30'W (2000) ANNUAL INCREASE 1'

5. In general, navigate to the right of center of the channels, and always be on the lookout for large vessels that can't change course quickly. It's your responsibility to move in this narrow channel.

When meeting head on, vessels navigating Hell Gate on a rising tide sometimes pass starboard-to-starboard because of the strong currents between Hallets Point and Negro Point. Outside this area the normal convention of port-to-port passing is observed.

Clearance is not a problem at any of the eight bridges crossing the river, with the possible exception of the vertical lift bridge at 36th Street on the east side of Roosevelt Island, with a clearance of 40 feet in the closed position. You need six-hour notice to raise that bridge.

CAUTION: Sailboats should stay west of Roosevelt Island. The Lift Bridge on the east side of the island has only a 40-foot vertical clearance when closed; a 4-5 knot current here can make it difficult for some sailboats to get turned around.

Although the waterways in and around New York City are much cleaner than ever before, there can still be a lot of debris floating at or just below the surface. Keep a sharp lookout and travel at a safe speed, especially after an abnormally high tide. Rafts of debris tend to bunch together along the edges of the channels or where there's swirling action.

Just north of Hell Gate, in the middle of the Harlem River entrance, is Mill Rock, marked with lights on both ends. The tiny island is actually a city park, and though we don't encourage it, you're welcome to go ashore if you don't mind bucking the 5-knot current. This island was where the Army Corps of Engineers manufactured the explosives used to blast Flood Rock out of Hell Gate—the largest manmade explosion before the atomic bomb. South of Mill Rock, the channel splits at Roosevelt Island.

For more information on traveling through the lower East River and New York Harbor, see the previous chapter.

Shoreside & Emergency Services
Airport: Port Authority of NY/NJ (800-AIR-RIDE)
Bus: NYC Travel Authority (718-330-1234)
Coast Guard: Fort Totten (718-352-4422) or VHF 16
Police, Fire, Ambulance: 911
Taxi: Caprice (718-460-3434)
Tow Service:
SEA TOW —24-Hour Dispatch (800-4SEATOW)
—Western L.I. Sound (914-698-6523)
Tow BoatU.S.—24-Hour Dispatch (800-391-4869)
—Upper New York (718-885-3420)
Train: Amtrak (800-US-RAIL)
—Metro-North (800-638-7646)

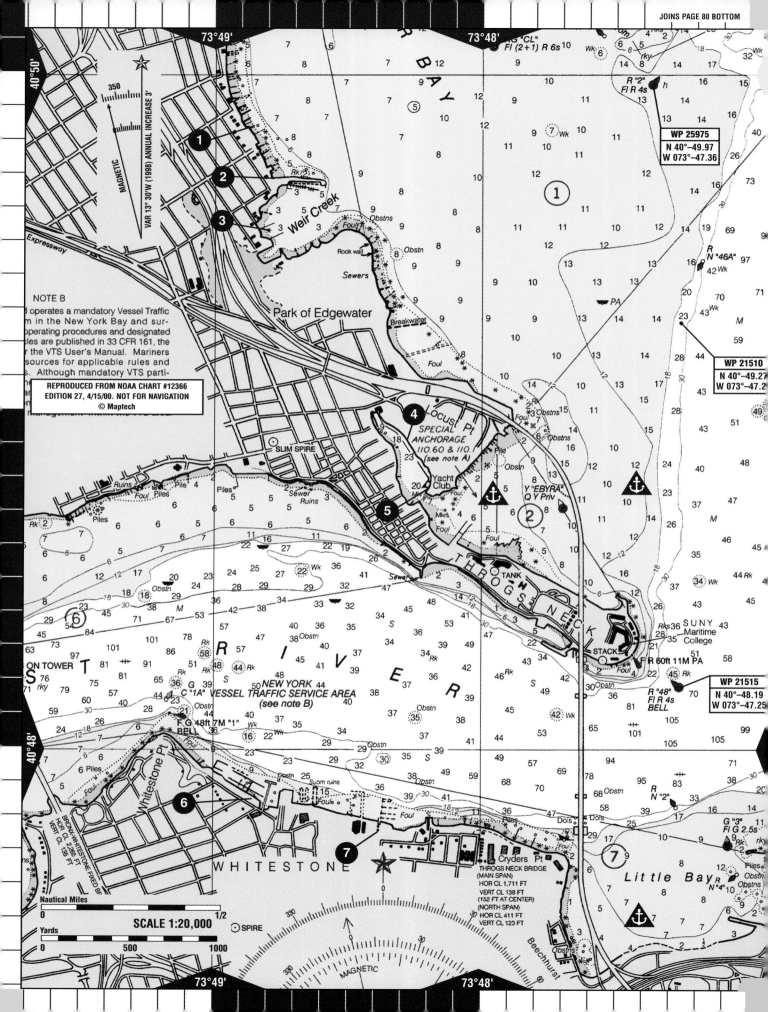

73°49' 73°48'

40°50'

NOTE B

...perates a mandatory Vessel Traffic
...m in the New York Bay and sur-
...perating procedures and designated
...les are published in 33 CFR 161, the
...r the VTS User's Manual. Mariners
...sources for applicable rules and
... Although mandatory VTS parti-

REPRODUCED FROM NOAA CHART #12366
EDITION 27, 4/15/00. NOT FOR NAVIGATION
© Maptech

VAR 13° 30'W (1998) ANNUAL INCREASE 3'

MAGNETIC

350

Weir Creek

Park of Edgewater

Sewers

Breakwater

Foul

SLIM SPIRE

Locust Pt
SPECIAL
ANCHORAGE
110.60 & 110.1
(see note A)

Yacht
Club

Ruins

Sewer
Ruins

Piles

Mkrs

Foul

THROGS NECK

TANK

Y "EBYRA"
Q Y Priv

WP 25975
N 40°–49.97
W 073°–47.36

①

R "2"
Fl R 4s

N "46A"
Wk

PA

WP 21510
N 40°–49.27
W 073°–47.2

②

N E W Y O R K   R I V E R

C "1A" VESSEL TRAFFIC SERVICE AREA
(see note B)

ON TOWER

F G 48ft 7M "1"
BELL

Whitestone Pt

⑥

W H I T E S T O N E

Subm ruins

Foul

Cryders Pt

THROGS NECK BRIDGE
(MAIN SPAN)
HOR CL 1,711 FT
VERT CL 138 FT
(152 FT AT CENTER)
(NORTH SPAN)
HOR CL 411 FT
VERT CL 123 FT

BRONX-WHITESTONE
HOR CL 2,205 FT
VERT CL 135 FT

FIXED BR

⑦

SUNY
Maritime
College

STACK

F R 60ft 11M PA

WP 21515
N 40°–48.19
W 073°–47.25

R "48"
Fl R 4s
BELL

R
N "2"

G "3"
Fl G 2.5s

Little Bay

R
N "4"

Obstn

⑦

40°48'

Nautical Miles
0   1/2

SCALE 1:20,000

Yards
0   500   1000

SPIRE

MAGNETIC

Beechhurst

73°49' 73°48'

The Start of the Sound

Seeking a new life where they could worship as they pleased, farmer John Throckmorton and his wife, Rebecca, arrived in Massachusetts aboard the British ship *Lyon* in 1631. Soon after, the Throckmortons fled to Rhode Island with fellow *Lyon* passenger Roger Williams to escape further religious persecution. Feeling this wasn't far enough from the intolerant and Puritanical Massachusetts colony he thought would surely invade the liberal Rhode Island settlement, Throckmorton made a mad dash to this dogleg of land in the southeast Bronx, where he started his own colony in 1643.

Alas, the Throckmortons and the other 35 founding families failed to gain the acceptance of the Siwanoy tribe who'd claimed the land first. These Native Americans defended their land by killing 18 members of the Throckmorton colony. The settlement lasted only a year, and Throckmorton packed up for Rhode Island, selling the Bronx parcel to Augustine Hermann, known for his development and cartography of the mid-Atlantic coast. Nevertheless, a vestige of the Throckmorton name stuck, identifying not only the neighborhood but also the 138-foot-high bridge that opened in 1961, linking the Bronx to Queens. Residents who were there before the bridge tend to prefer the original, two-G spelling: Throggs Neck.

The government acquired a 50-acre parcel of land on the neck's southern tip, with the intention of building a fort to defend the eastern approach to New York City. Named after the famous Revolutionary War general, Fort Schuyler served nobly (without firing a shot) until new artillery emplacements on the south side of Fishers Island took over New York's defense in 1911. In the late nineteenth century Throgs Neck became a popular summer colony for millionaires, including sugar magnate Frederick Havemeyer, and Collis Huntington, a railroad builder.

Today, the landscape is much different: Fort Schuyler is occupied by the New York Maritime College, Throgs Neck is overshadowed by its great bridge, and the millionaires' estates have been subdivided into sizes appropriate for the area's working-class population.

As you travel up the East River you'll find a few facilities on the north (right) side of Throgs Neck, including Locust Point Marina. © Maptech/James T. Abts

Marine Facilities and Services

	Facility	Phone	Monitors/Working VHF Channel	Transient Berths	Seasonal/Year-round Moorings	Hookups (110V ★ 220V ▲ 3 Phase ■; Water/Phone/Cable TV; Max Amps)	Max LOA	Approach/Dockside Depth (ft at MLW)	Ramp/Dinghy Dock/Launch Service	Rail/Lift/Crane/Trailer: Capacity (tons)	Repairs: Prop/Sail/Rigging; Diesel/Wood/Fiberglass/Electronics	Marine/Groceries/Ice/Bait/LPG/CNG	Gas/Diesel Fuel	Fuel Brand	Restrooms/Showers/Laundry/Pumpout	Public Phone/Restaurant/Snack Bar	Hotel/Pool/Tennis/Golf	Mastercard/VISA/Discover/AmEx
1	White Cross Fishing Station	718-597-7347			/12	Y	25	20/20	F	*PRIVATE—MEMBERS ONLY*					R			
2	Shelter Cove Marina	718-822-3054	68/			Y	28	8/4	F	LT6	D	MI	F		R	P		MVA
3	Bronxonia Yacht Club	718-822-9113	18/		/3	Y	38		F	L13		I			RS			
4	Locust Point Marina	718-822-7974			2/	Y	50	5/15	F	30 / L35	PGDWF	MI			RS	P		
5	Locust Point Yacht Club	718-822-9806				Y				*PRIVATE—MEMBERS ONLY*								
6	Whitestone Marina & Watersports Center*	718-767-7800	68/		5/5	Y	40	23/4	F	★30 / T	All	MIB	All		RP	S		MVA
7	Beechhurst Yacht Club*	718-767-1700				Y				*PRIVATE—MEMBERS ONLY*								

Information in these listings is provided by the facilities themselves. An asterisk (*) indicates that the facility did not respond to our most recent requests for information.
(B) represents a BOAT/U.S. cooperating marina.

All Coast Guard Stations Monitor VHF Channel 16

marinalife.com — Convenient Online Boat Slip Reservations

ACTIVITIES: In 1938, Fort Schuyler became the State of New York Maritime College (718-409-7200). You'll easily spot the yellow smokestacks and white hull of the college's large training ship, *The Empire State VI*. Tours of the college are available from September to April, but you must call ahead to schedule one.

The Throgs Neck area really isn't an anchorage, so there aren't too many attractions accessible by boat. The most interesting sight is the sweeping panorama of the Throgs Neck and Whitestone bridges, with the Manhattan skyline beyond.

If you're staying at Locust Point Marina when the Mets are in town, take a cab ride to Shea Stadium (718-699-4220), get some peanuts and CrackerJack, and enjoy the game.

RESTAURANTS & PROVISIONS: The marine facilities at Throgs Neck and to the north are surrounded by dense residential areas. From any of the Throgs Neck marinas, it's a short cab ride or a long walk to East Tremont Avenue, where you'll find small pizzerias, markets, drugstores, and eateries. If you want more variety, take a cab to Manhattan or City Island. There are small grocery stores in the Weir Creek area. Around Whitestone you'll find larger shopping centers, but you'll need a taxi to reach them.

NAVIGATION & ANCHORAGES: Use ChartKit Region 3, page 20; Maptech™ Waterproof Charts 1, 4, 8, and 16; and Maptech™

electronic and NOAA paper charts 12363 (1:80,000), 12366 (1:20,000), 12364 (1:40,000), and 12339 (1:10,000). Around Throgs Neck, use tide tables for Willets Point. High tide at Throgs Neck is 8 minutes later; low tide is 12 minutes later. Use the height of tide at Willets Point for the height of tide at Throgs Neck. Mean tidal range is 7 feet.

The Throgs Neck Bridge is the generally accepted demarcation between the Sound and the East River. The tip of Throgs Neck, a narrow peninsula jutting southeast from the Bronx, is 2nm from Belden Point, City Island, and 1.7nm from the Whitestone Bridge. Opposite Throgs Neck, 0.7nm away, is the granite-walled Fort Totten Coast Guard Station on Willets Point.

Willets Point forms the eastern boundary of Little Bay, the first anchorage in Long Island Sound. Little Bay (not to be confused with Little Neck Bay) holds an average depth of 6 to 10 feet, with more anchoring room on the western side. Stay out from under the approach ramp for the bridge, which crosses the eastern part of the bay and marks the beginning of shallow water. Also, stay clear of the Coast Guard docks on the east side of the bay, and note the obstruction just southeast of R N "4" off the Coast Guard docks.

From the Throgs Neck Light (F R 60ft 11M PA), it's about 1.4nm north-northeast to the first major navigational aid in the Sound, the Stepping Stones Lighthouse (Oc G 4s 46ft 8M). When rounding Throgs Neck, stay south and east of Fl R 4s BELL R "48" marking shoal ground off Throgs Neck.

Between the north side of Throgs Neck and Locust Point is a popular anchorage enclosed by the north span of the bridge. Part of the bay is wide open to the east, but is well protected by Throgs Neck from the prevailing southwesterly winds. The northern section, inside the Locust Point Yacht Club, is called Hammond Cove by residents, though it's unnamed on the chart. Hammond Cove is completely protected and has plenty of water, so it's likely to be crowded. In the cove, you'll find the Locust Point Marina, which keeps a few transient berths available.

When passing under the north span of the Throgs Neck Bridge into this anchorage, you'll have many channels to choose from between the bridge supports, but don't pass through the first five sections on either end—they are shoaled up. In the middle of this section of the bridge, the vertical clearance is as much as 60 feet (mhw).

Once past the bridge, getting into Hammond Cove can be tricky. Although the cove itself has plenty of water, the entrance channel is shallow and narrow (no more than 15 feet wide). The Locust Point Yacht Club maintains the channel markers: a tall pair of pilings painted red and green. Past these markers is another red piling, with deep water beyond. If you have a sailboat or other deep-draft boat, wait until high tide to attempt this passage.

To the north, between Weir Creek and Locust Point, watch out for stake buoys where tugs and barges often tie up. These 6-foot, steel balls will win any battle with your boat. Also, R N "46A," northeast of Locust Point, is unlit and difficult to see at night against the city lights.

Looking northeast over the Throgs Neck Bridge and into Eastchester Bay. City Island sits off in the distance. © Maptech/James T. Abts

CAUTION: If you're motoring through Hell Gate, fuel up before heading into New York Harbor. Use your tide tables, current tables, and current charts to figure out the best time to run the Gate. See the previous chapter on Hell Gate and East River for more information.

The Throgs Neck area can be mean and tricky. The tidal range is up to 9 feet, and the current can run 2 knots or more, with tide rips that mean business. Big commercial ships tend to hog the middle of the channel and swing wide when rounding Throgs Neck. Other commercial and recreational traffic runs in all directions, kicking up a confused sea. The traffic under the bridge can be particularly heavy, with crosscurrents and eddies reminiscent of Hell Gate developing around the bridge fenders, making steering difficult. To complicate matters further, the lighted aids to navigation in this area may be hard to pick out at night, obscured by the lights of the city in the background.

Follow the buoys carefully, stay clear of the bridge stanchions, and keep well to starboard. Once past the bridge, heading west, keep an eye out for the barges moored well off the north shore of the river, about a mile west-northwest of Fort Schuyler.

CAUTION: Large commercial ships are hard to stop or turn quickly, especially when headed downstream in a stiff current. If evasive maneuvers are required, you'll be the one who has to make them.

Shoreside & Emergency Services
Airport: Port Authority of NY/NJ (800-AIR-RIDE)
Bus: NYC Transit Authority (718-330-1234)
Coast Guard:
—Fort Totten, NY (718-352-4422) or VHF 16
Police, Fire, Ambulance: 911
Taxi: Zero's (718-822-2222)
Tow Service:
SEA TOW —24-Hour Dispatch (800-4SEATOW)
—City Island (718-885-0101)
TowBoatU.S.—24-Hour Dispatch (800-391-4869)
—Sound Tow (718-885-3420)
Train: Amtrak (800-US-RAIL)
—Metro-North (800-638-7646)

"Nauti" term

Three Sheets to the Wind: *a sheet is a line that controls the tension on the downwind side of a sail. If, on a fully-rigged, three-masted ship, the sheets of the three lower sails are loose they will flutter in the wind. In his condition, the ship will stagger aimlessly downwind.*

So when you see a mate stumble from a tavern door, be sure to tighten those sheets, and point him in the right direction.

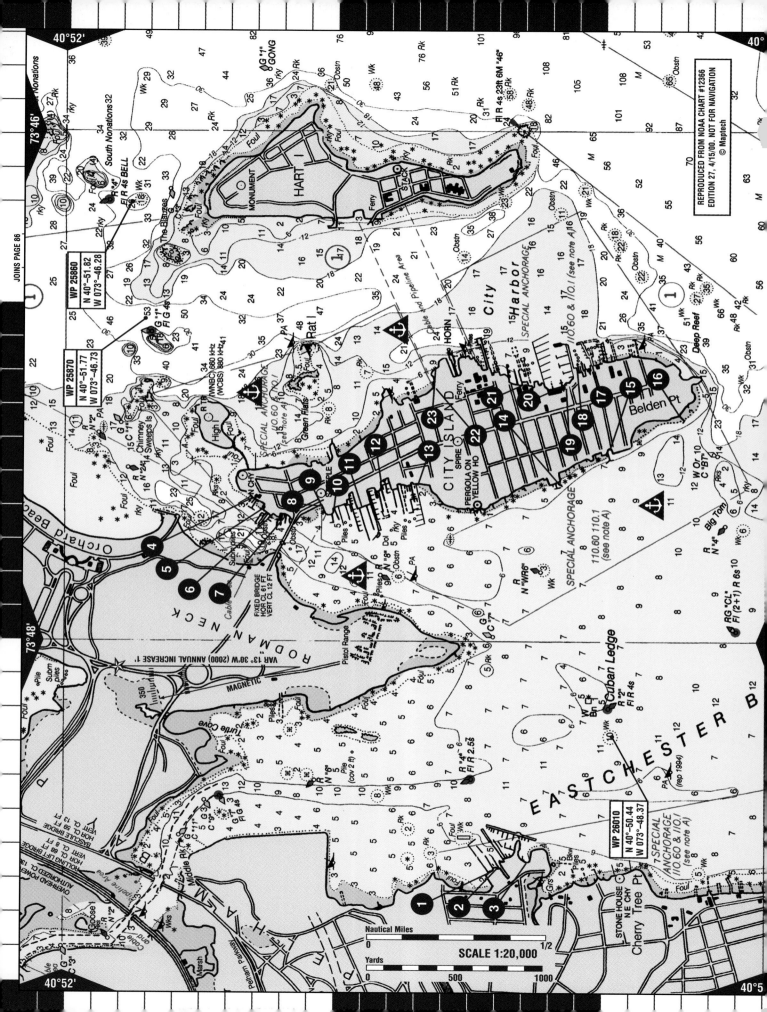

The Mariner's Mile

Although City Island will never be mistaken for a Cape Cod village, you still may have to remind yourself that it's part of the Bronx. Only from the perspective of the cityscape to its south does the maritime enclave seem unusual. After all, at the island's north end only a small bridge separates City Island from Rodman Neck, site of Orchard Beach and the sylvan beauty of Pelham Bay Park (New York City's largest park). After traveling through that almost country-like parcel, those arriving by land probably aren't expecting to see skyscrapers on the island, anyway.

City Island was settled by the Dutch, who called it Minnewits Island. Under American rule, the island developed into a major fishing and shipbuilding center. Some of the finest racing and cruising yachts in the world were built on this 230-acre dot of land. Yachts designed by Sparkman & Stephens were once built here, and Ratsey Lapthorn Sailmakers also plied their trade on the island. Minneford's Shipyard, builders of many America's Cup boats—most recently, *Freedom* in 1980—was known

The sun sets over Rodman Neck. © Maptech

worldwide for its craftsmanship. Although foreign shipbuilding competition has taken the wind out of City Island's sails in recent years, this maritime neighborhood still offers a wealth of facilities for the yachtsman.

Despite the island's metropolitan location, the pace of life here is far from hectic (actually, you may hear some gunfire as you're pulling into harbor—don't worry; it's just the

	Marine Facilities and Services		Monitors / Working VHF Channel	Number of Transient Berths / Seasonal / Yearround	Approach / Dockside Depth in Feet at MLW	Maximum LOA	110V • 220V ▲ 3 Phase ■ Maximum Amps	Ramp / Dinghy Dock / Launch Service	Rail / Lift / Crane / Trailer Capacity (tons)	Repairs: Propellor / Sail / Rigging / Wood / Fiberglass / Electronics	Diesel / Gas / Diesel Fuel	Marine / Groceries / Ice / Bait / LPG / CNG	Restrooms / Showers / Laundry / Pumpout	Public Phone / Pool / Tennis / Golf	Hotel / Restaurant / Snack Bar	Mastercard / VISA / Discover / AmEx
1	Sunrise Marina*	718-823-3847		5/	Y	55	7/7	F	★▲	D	LT10			M		
2	Pelambar Corporation	718-824-7171		2/	S	40	7/7	F	★30		RC20	PSRDWF		I	RS	P
3	Evers Marina	718-863-9111	16/74		S	100	8/8	F	★30	RL	L30	PGDWFE			R	PS
4	Portside Marina Inc.*	718-885-2211		40/	S	25	5/5	F		D	CT25	GDWE		M	R	P
5	Lobster House	718-885-1459		10/	Y	25									R	All
6	City Island Yacht Sales	718-885-2300	9/	10/	S	55	8/6	F	★50		L30	PGWFE	G	Tex	MI		P	All
7	Rosenberger's Boat Livery*	718-885-1843	16/9		S		10/3	F		R				GIB	R	P	MVD
8	Sea Shore Restaurant & Marina	718-885-0300	68/	15/	Y	30	8/8	F							R	PR	All
9	The Harbor Restaurant	718-885-1373	24/		Y	70	12/8								R	PR	All
10	Jack's Bait & Tackle*	718-885-2042			Y								MB			All
11	Royal Marina	718-885-1800	72/	7/	Y	85	5.5/5.5	FP	★30		L25	PGDF		M	RS	P
12	STELTER MARINE SALES, INC. p. 85	718-885-1300			Y	28	4/4	F	★30		L10	PGDF		M		P
13	Harlem Yacht Club	718-885-1225	72/		S		8/	F		DL	R18				RS	All	All

All Coast Guard Stations Monitor VHF Channel 16

Facilities continued on next page...

police firing range on Rodman Neck). Initially, residents may display a hard-boiled exterior to visitors. But once they begin to talk about their town, you'll realize just how unique—and beloved—a place this is.

ACTIVITIES: The east, or "commercial," side of City Islalnd is jammed with marinas, boatyards, and outfitters. Here, you'll find the South Minneford Yacht Club, catering to transient boaters. The northwest coast of the island is also packed with yards and retail operations like Royal Marine and Stelter Marine Sales. The southwest side, with its views of the Manhattan skyline, is often called the "social side." Here, you'll find the Harlem, Stuyvesant, City Island, and Morris yacht clubs, as well as most of the island's residential areas.

The North Wind Nautical Museum (718-885-0701), housed in an ornate, red-roofed, Victorian-style captain's home on City Island Avenue, is certain to catch your eye. With the intention of increasing children's awareness of environmental issues, founders Michael Sandlofer and musician Richie Havens started the museum in 1976. The disappointing news as of this writing is that the museum is temporarily closed. If it hasn't yet reopened by the time you visit, you can still check out the front yard: a museum in itself. Otherwise, go inside to see the fine whale exhibits, the collection of nautical art, and the "rescuarium" housing injured animals.

The tiny City Island Public Library (718-885-1703), at 320 City Island Avenue, has the largest collection of maritime literature in New York City: over 2,000 volumes covering the past, present, and future of sailing and the sea. The library's hours vary.

If you visit City Island on the first Sunday in June, you can take part in the Blessing of the Fleet. Early in the afternoon, boaters sail by the docks at Fordham Street and have their boats blessed by a local priest, rabbi, or minister. For more information, write the Power Squadron at P.O. Box 154, City Island, NY 10464.

If you cross the bridge connecting City Island to the mainland (the bridge was built in 1897 using recycled steel from the battleship *North Carolina*), you'll be in Pelham Bay Park, New York City's largest. There, you'll find a driving range (718-885-2646) and golf course (718-885-1258), as well as the Pelham Bit Stables (718-885-0551) for those who might enjoy some horseback riding. Orchard Beach, open to the public, is nearby—about a 20-minute walk.

The New York Botanical Gardens (718-817-8705) and the Bronx Zoo (718-367-1010) are relatively close—just hop onto a bus or hail a cab.

RESTAURANTS & PROVISIONS: Everyone loves a meal on City Island. The restaurants get busy early on weekend evenings and Sunday afternoons, as hand-holding couples and families in station wagons head down the avenue to compete with city-escapers and the boating crowd for the good tables.

If you're undecided on where to dine, walk the length of the island and check out all of the offerings. It'll only take you about 30 minutes to walk the full length of the island, which is crowded with more than 20 restaurants among the marinas, chandleries, and yacht clubs. Most of the bigger eateries cater to tourists and aren't hard to

	Marine Facilities and Services		Monitors / Working VHF Channel	Number of Transient Berths	Seasonal / Year-round Moorings	Approach / Dockside Depth in Feet at MLW	Maximum LOA	110V • 220V ▲ 3 Phase ■ Maximum Amps	Hookups: Fresh Water / Phone / Cable TV	Rail / Lift / Crane / Trailer / Launch Service	Ramp / Dinghy Dock / Launch Service	Repairs: Propellor / Sail / Rigging / Electronics	Diesel / Wood / Fiberglass	Marine / Groceries / Ice / Bait / LPG / CNG	Gas / Diesel Fuel	Fuel Brand	Restrooms / Showers / Laundry / Pumpout	Public Phone / Pool / Tennis / Golf	Hotel / Restaurant / Snack Bar	Mastercard / VISA / Discover / AmEx
14	Stuyvesant Yacht Club	718-885-9840	72/	5/	S	45	5.8/	F	★30	L	L15				B	RS		All	
15	City Island Yacht Club	718-885-2487	72/	/6	S	45	7/6	F	▲■100	L					I	RS		PR	MVA
16	Morris Yacht & Beach Club*	718-885-0574	68/	/10	Y	45	12/6	F	★15	DL	T					RS		PS	MV
17	Consolidated Yachts Inc.	718-885-1900	69/	5/	Y	65	12/6	F	★50	D	LT60	All			B	RS		P	MVD
18	SOUTH MINNEFORD YACHT CLUB (B) p. 85	718-885-3113	69/69		Y	110	14/10	FP	★▲■50	D	T				MGB	RS			MV
19	Boathaven Marineland*	718-885-2000		50/	Y								S		I	RSP		P	MVA
20	North Minneford Yacht Club*	718-885-2000	77/	5/5	S	60	12/12	FP	★▲■		LC45	All				RS		P	
21	Sailmaker Marina at City Island	718-885-2700		4/	S	45	12/3	F	★▲50							RSP		P	
22	Fenton Marine*	718-885-0844			Y	50	12/5	F		L									
23	Barron Boat Yard	718-885-9802	16/9		Y	52	12/10	F	★30	DL	LC30	All				RS		P	MV

All Coast Guard Stations Monitor VHF Channel 16

Information in these listings is provided by the facilities themselves. An asterisk (*) indicates that the facility did not respond to our most recent requests for information. (B) represents a BOAT/U.S. cooperating marina.

spot—look for bright lights and big signs.

Several restaurants offer dockage for patrons. Harbor Restaurant (718-885-1373) serves seafood, steaks, chops, pastas, and salads, with indoor or outdoor dining. The Sea Shore Restaurant & Marina (718-885-0300) offers fine dining on seafood and Italian with a grand sunset view. At the north end of the island is The City Island Lobster House (718-885-1459).

If you're not dockage-dependent, there are plenty of other choices along City Island Avenue, from seafood to Continental to Italian. Ask a marina operator or a friendly-looking islander for a recommendation; everyone has an opinion, especially in New York. Indulge yourself with a meal at Le Refuge Inn (718-885-2478), or if you're on a tight budget, try the small and unpretentious City Island Diner (718-885-9867) at Fordham and City Island avenues. Lobster Box (718-885-1952) is more upscale, offering fine Italian dishes and seafood, punctuated by desserts fit for the gods. Or you can shell out a few bucks at the Crab Shanty (718-885-1810) for a delightful lunch or dinner.

At the end of City Island Avenue, you'll find a good, family restaurant on either side of the street: Johnny's Reef Restaurant (718-885-2086) and Tony's Pier Restaurant (718-885-1424). Both serve seafood in a casual outdoor setting.

City Island Avenue is supply central. Both New Way Supermarket and City Island Supermarket/IGA (718-885-0881) have all you'll need for the galley. Buddy's Hardware & Yacht (718-885-1447) sells all types of marine goods, and on wash day, you've got your choice of two laundromats.

NAVIGATION & ANCHORAGES: Use ChartKit Region 3, page 20; Maptech™ Waterproof Charts 1, 4, 8, and 16; and Maptech™ electronic and NOAA paper charts 12366

Hungry and tired after a long day at work, this man contemplates some City Island seafood. © Maptech

(1:20,000), 12364 (1:40,000), and 12363 (1:80,000). Use tide tables for Willets Point. High tide at City Island is 3 minutes later; low tide is 5 minutes earlier. Use height of tide at Willets Point for height of tide at City Island. Mean tidal range is 7.2 feet.

City Island lies 2nm from Throgs Neck and 2.1nm from Davenport Neck. Between Throgs Neck and City Island lies Eastchester Bay, with depths of 6 to 12 feet in its southern part.

Use caution when navigating Eastchester Bay: the shores to the west are fringed with boulders, shoals, and wrecks. A dredged channel leads from Eastchester Bay north to the Hutchinson River, which has a controlling depth of less than 6 feet. This river has little to offer the recreational boater, unless you like dodging barges and gazing at oil and cement plants. The channel is narrow and has many obstructions.

From the south or west, approaching City Island, beware of Big Tom, a barely submerged rock about 500 yards west of Belden Point, and Cuban Ledge, in the center of Eastchester

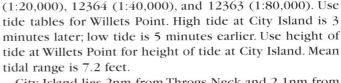

Bay. Big Tom is well marked by a triangle of buoys: Fl R 4s R "2" on the south, R N "4" on the west, and W Or C "BT" on the east. The problem is that on a busy summer weekend the buoys may be "buried" by boats moored or anchored outside the special anchorage area, and thus difficult or impossible to spot. The same problem can occur with R N "WR6," which marks a 3-foot spot 0.5nm north-northwest of Big Tom.

CAUTION: Beware of Cuban Ledge, almost in the center of Eastchester Bay. Do not pass between Fl R 4s R "2" on the west side of the ledge and Fl (2+1) R 6s R G "CL" about 400 yards to the southeast. Also, be careful of the 5-foot spot about 0.3nm northeast of Weir Creek. You'll pass right over it if you leave Weir Creek and head directly toward the spire on City Island.

Around Cuban Ledge, keep a sharp eye out for the tug and barge traffic heading north into the Hutchinson River and the infrequent (but startling) air taxis that fly in and out of Evers Seaplane Base & Marina. Both the South Minneford Yacht Club and Sailmaker Marina at City Island are located on this eastern side of City Island and are great places to stop and explore the island.

From the north or east, there are two approaches to City Island: around the southern end of Hart Island, or through the rocky but navigable waters to the north. As a part of the New York City Prison System, the island is off limits to everyone and you'll be promptly arrested if you try to go ashore.

A cruise around the north end of Hart Island can be a pleasant trip. Some boaters are intimidated by the many rocks here, but the area is well marked; go slowly and follow the aids. As you pass to the north of Hart Island, stay between Fl R 4s BELL R "4" at the South Nonations and G C "3," swinging north and wide around The Blauzes.

CAUTION: Never pass between the South and East Nonations, or between The Blauzes and Hart Island, where you can run hard aground. Be careful when heading down the channel 500 yards south of Twin Island and 200 yards northwest of Chimney Sweeps Island. Follow those buoys!

If you're heading for one of the marinas north of the bridge connecting City Island to the mainland, proceed carefully. There's plenty of water but the channel is unmarked. From R N "2A" off Orchard Beach, aim for the middle of the bridge to stay mid-channel. The longest of the piers to port comes all the way out into the channel.

The channel northeast of Hart Island leads to the south entrance of New Rochelle Harbor and some very nice anchorages between Davids, Hunter, and Glen islands.

Looking west over City Island. © Maptech/James T. Abts

Embassy Guides

If you want to anchor off City Island instead of staying at one of the marinas or yacht clubs, you can do so in Eastchester Bay, west of the island, although the anchorage is filled with yacht club and commercial moorings and is often packed with boats. Every year it seems that more moorings appear, spilling farther west into the channel.

The most popular anchorage is south of the fixed bridge that connects City Island to Rodman Neck, in an area dominated by powerboats. If you're in a deep-draft boat, be aware of the 3- to 4-foot areas just off the shores on either side. Since the bridge has a vertical clearance of only 12 feet (mhw), circumnavigating the island is possible only for small powerboats. Currents can run 1 to 2 knots in the area around the bridge. You may find more room to anchor in City Island Harbor, also known as Hart Island Roads, to the east of City Island. City Island Harbor is somewhat better protected but offers only fair holding ground.

The best bet for anchoring is south of Green Flats and Rat Island. Keep in mind that in a northeast or east wind, the area north of Rat Island is very exposed, and there are at least 50 miles of fetch behind those waves. Residents tell us that boats anchored north of Rat Island rock hard on the high swells, while at the same time those anchored south of the island, protected by Hart Island, roll gently. Wherever you choose to drop anchor, you'll have plenty of company.

Give Green Flats, just west of Rat Island, plenty of room; it's exposed at low water and always dangerous. The fixed bridge connecting High Island and the WNBC and WCBS radio towers with City Island has no water under it at low tide.

If your boat is in need of repair, head to Royal Marina, a full-service marina with slips for transients. Nearby is Stelter Marine Sales for sales and service, including repairs on propellers, gas and diesel engines, and fiberglass hulls.

Stay within the 5-mph speed limit around the island, or pay the price—the NYPD Harbor Unit patrols these waters diligently. They're especially on the lookout for drunken skippers.

Shoreside & Emergency Services
Airport:
—Port Authority of NY/NJ (800-AIR-RIDE)
Bus:
—MTA NYC Transit Authority (718-330-1234)
Coast Guard:
—Fort Totten, NY (718-352-4422) or VHF 16
Police, Fire, Ambulance: 911
Taxi:
—Zero's (718-822-2222)
Tow Service:
SEA TOW —24-Hour Dispatch (800-4SEATOW)
—City Island (718-885-0101)
Tow BoatU.S.—24-Hour Dispatch (800-391-4869)
—City Island (718-885-3420)
Train: Amtrak (800-US-RAIL)
—Metro-North (800-638-7646)

73°46'

Premium
Mill Pond

NEW ROCHELLE

ECHO BAY HARBOR
The controlling depth at M.L.L.W. was 8½ feet
for a mid-width of 50 feet to Turning Basin at
Beaufort Pt., and 7 feet in Turning Basin.

Oct. 1985

CAUTION
This chart has been corrected from the Notice to Mariners published weekly
by the National Imagery and Mapping Agency and the Local Notice to Mariners
issued periodically by each U.S. Coast Guard district to the date shown in the
lower left hand corner.

Premium Pt
MIDDLE OF ARCADE

GENERAL ANCH
110.155
(see note A)

Hicks Ledge

SPECIAL ANCH
110.60 & 110.1
(see note A)

WP 25780
N 40°-54.29
W 073°-45.71

WP 25735
N 40°-54.12
W 073°-45.14

GENERAL ANCH
110.155
(see note A)

DAVENPORT
NECK

WP 25820
N 40°-53.48
W 073°-46.11

WP 25810
N 40°-53.70
W 073°-45.93

Middle Ground

WP 25815
N 40°-53.4
W 073°-45.3

Huckleberry I

TANK
Cable and
Pipeline Areas

BASCULE BRIDGE
HOR CL 59 FT
VERT CL 13 FT

SPECIAL ANCH
110.60 & 110.1
(see note A)

SQUARE CHY

Stevens Rock

Columbia I

Pea I

Pipeline Area

WP 25890
N 40°-52.42
W 073°-46.72

TWIN I

Machaux Rock

Middle Reef

73°47'   73°46'

The Swing Palace of Westchester

Glen Island used to be one swingin' place. For two decades, the once-famous Glen Island Casino, built in 1930, shook to its rafters with happy people dancing into the night to the sounds of big band swing music. The Glenn Miller Orchestra broke through with a 1938 performance at the Casino, when they debuted their song "In the Mood" and watched the mood on the dance floor rise to one of gleeful appreciation.

Casino crowds also raved over the Dorsey Brothers, a staple act there in the mid-30s. Tommy and Jimmy Dorsey made great music together until some brotherly bickering led to their breakup. Each brother then started his own band, with Tommy getting the edge in popularity after hiring a young and virtually unknown singer, Frank Sinatra....ah, but that's another story entirely.

Even before the swing bands swung in, Glen Island had always been a good-time place. Lewis August DePau bought the parcel in 1847 and had a mansion built on it so that he could entertain his highbrow friends. Then, in 1881, developer John Starin opened Glen Island Park, a family-oriented amusement park, which was hugely popular until the steamer *General Slocum* burned with 1,000 passengers aboard. Starin took the disaster so hard that he closed Glen Island Park.

In 1924 under parks commissioner William Ward, Westchester County acquired Glen Island and some smaller islands on its fringes for the recreational benefit of citizens.

Looking northwest over New Rochelle Harbor and its many facilities. © Maptech

Later, they joined the islets to Glen Island to create one large land mass. These days, Glen Island is open for recreation to residents of Westchester County. Glen Island Casino remains open as an upscale restaurant and banquet hall.

ACTIVITIES: Of New Rochelle's two harbor areas, the larger and more popular is around Glen Island, a park and beach for Westchester County residents only. Five Islands Park lies on the north side of Echo Bay. There's a clubhouse and picnic area on Clifford Island, connected by footbridges to the two Harrison Islands where there are footpaths, picnic sites, and a small beach for sunbathing only.

Marine Facilities and Services

All Coast Guard Stations Monitor VHF Channel 16

marinalife.com — Convenient Online Boat Slip Reservations

#	Facility	Phone	Monitors/Working VHF Channel	Number of Transient Berths/Moorings	Seasonal/Year-round	Maximum LOA	Approach/Dockside Depth in Feet at MLW	Hookups: Fresh Water/Phone/Cable TV	110V∗ 220V▲ 3Phase■ Max Amps	Ramp/Dinghy Dock/Launch Service	Rail/Lift/Crane/Trailer: Capacity (tons)	Repairs: Propellor/Sail/Rigging/Electronics; Diesel/Wood/Fiberglass/Electronics	Gas/Diesel Fuel	Fuel Brand	Marine/Groceries/Ice/Bait/LPG/CNG	Restrooms/Showers/Laundry/Pumpout	Public Phone/Restaurant/Snack Bar	Hotel/Pool/Tennis/Golf	Mastercard/VISA/Discover/AmEx
1	New Rochelle Municipal Marina	914-235-6930	16/	10/	S	45	7/4	F	★30		L20	All	GD		MGIBC	All	PR		MV
2	Polychron Marina Company	914-632-4088			S	30	4/4	F	★30		C30		G		IB	R	R		
3	Echo Bay Yacht Club*	Unlisted			Y					*PRIVATE—MEMBERS ONLY*									
4	New York Athletic Club Yacht Club	914-738-0065			Y					*PRIVATE—MEMBERS ONLY*									
5	West Harbor Yacht Service	914-636-1524		2/	Y	60	8/8	F	★30	D	LC25	PSRGDWF				RSL		P	
6	Huguenot Yacht Club	914-636-6300			Y					*PRIVATE—MEMBERS ONLY*									
7	Wright Island Marina (p. 89)	914-235-8013		10/	Y	65	11/11	All	★▲50	D	L50	All	GD	BP	I	All	P	All	MV
8	Hayes Harbor Club*	914-235-5979			Y					*PRIVATE—MEMBERS ONLY*									
9	Mill Pond Cove Marina*	914-762-7580			S	26	6/5	F	■30	D	T								
10	Imperial Yacht Club	914-636-1122	9/	10/	Y	65	14/10	All	★▲■50	R	L70	All	GD	Mob	I	RSL	PT	All	MV
11	Neptune Boat Club	914-636-9764			S	40	8/7		50		C45	All				RS		P	
12	Castaways Yacht Club (p. 89)	914-636-8444		2/	Y	65	14/7	All	★▲■50		L35	All	GD		MGI	RSL	PT	All	MVA

Information in these listings is provided by the facilities themselves. An asterisk (*) indicates that the facility did not respond to our most recent requests for information. (B) represents a BOAT/U.S. cooperating marina.

Thomas Paine, the Revolutionary War-era author of *The Rights of Man*, *The Age of Reason*, and the famous *Common Sense*, once lived in a New Rochelle cottage. Since he'd received honorary French citizenship during their Revolution, New Rochelle's officials considered him a citizen of France and would not allow him to vote. Nor was his body allowed to permanently rest in peace after his 1809 death. After a Quaker cemetery refused to accept his remains, he was buried on the grounds of his estate. Ten years later, an admirer disinterred Paine's remains in 1819 and moved them to England. For more on Thomas Paine in New Rochelle, visit the Paine Monument, Paine Cottage, or the Paine Memorial House, open Fridays, Saturdays, and Sundays, and maintained by the Huguenot/Thomas Paine Historical Association (914-632-5376).

RESTAURANTS & PROVISIONS: You'll find few eateries around the residential waterfront. Dudley's Parkview Restaurant, (914-636-9491) at the Polychron Marina, is an unpretentious spot serving pub fare. At the Municipal Marina, don't pass on the sports bar/restaurant On The Waterfront (914-632-9625).

To the south, between Echo Bay and New Rochelle Harbor on Pelham Road, Frank & John's Ristorante (914-636-6611) features steaks, seafood, and Italian meals. Farther south on Pelham Road, you'll find a large A&P supermarket, with Hacker's Bakery in the plaza next door.

Get some eats with a bit of scenery on Marina Restaurant's (914-235-5252) second-floor deck, on the grounds of Wright Island Marina. If you need supplies of any kind, you're in business—just around the corner is a shopping center with eateries, a market, a hardware store, and a laundromat.

On Davenport Neck, you'll find the Yacht Café (914-636-9449) at the Imperial Yacht Club, serving steaks and seafood. Downtown New Rochelle, with a variety of shops and restaurants, is on Main Street (Route 1), only a half-mile up from the Echo Bay waterfront. You'll also find groceries and a laundromat on Main Street.

NAVIGATION & ANCHORAGES: Use ChartKit Region 3, pages 20 and 21; Maptech™ Waterproof Charts 1 and 16; and Maptech™ electronic and NOAA paper charts 12366 (1:20,000), 12367 (1:20,000), 12364 (1:40,000), and 12363 (1:80,000). Use tide tables for Willets Point. High tide at New Rochelle is 18 minutes earlier; low tide is 21 minutes earlier. Use the height of tide at Willets Point for the height of tide at New Rochelle. Mean tidal range is 7.3 feet.

New Rochelle

New Rochelle has two harbor areas, New Rochelle Harbor and Echo Bay. Both are strewn with rocks and small islands. Davids Island, southeast of the entrance to New Rochelle Harbor, is 2nm from City Island Harbor, 2nm from Sands Point on Long Island, and 4nm from Mamaroneck Harbor. Echo Bay sits between Premium Point and the northeastern end of Davenport Neck.

CAUTION: There are some obstructions in New Rochelle's harbors, but the channels are well marked. Use your searchlight when navigating after dark.

From the east, the main approach to the area around Glen Island is between Middle Ground and Huckleberry Island. Pass south of Fl R 4s R "2." It is also possible to approach from Echo Bay, passing between Middle Ground and Davenport Neck. Head for GR C Emerald Rock marking the middle of the channel, and keep east of the rocks found up to 300 yards northeast of R N "4." There are fair anchorages northeast of Davids Island, northwest of Huckleberry Island, and just off the Glen Island Casino. Be warned, however: a reader tells us that the bird rookery on Huckleberry Island is the source of an incredible din during the nesting season.

Follow the chart closely. Once you're past Middle Ground on either approach, pass between R N "4" and Fl G 4s G "5" north of Davids Island. From the east, it's a straight shot from Fl R 4s R "2" north of Huckleberry Island. From R N "4," follow the buoyed channel. Stay clear of Spindle Rock, marked by G C "9."

At Q R R "14" between Davenport Neck and Glen Island, turn northwest. Pass east of Fl G 4s 20ft 5M "15." You have the choice of turning north to go into upper New Rochelle Harbor or south to go behind Glen Island in the lower harbor. If you require more than 13 feet of vertical clearance, one long and one short blast of your horn will alert the Glen Island Bascule Bridge tender to open the draw.

From the south, there are two approaches to Glen Island and New Rochelle Harbor. Your best bet is to follow the dredged channel from Fl R 4s BELL R "6," found between Middle Reef and Twin Island. The channel runs north-northeast to Davids Island and Goose Island. The area on the west side of the channel is an anchorage—very peaceful and fairly well-protected.

Head toward Fl R 4s 24ft 6M "10" at Aunt Phebe Rock, turn northwest between it and G C "9," and steer into the harbor. Be aware that there are some charted but unbuoyed rocks in this area. You'll spot a few of them at low tide. Inside New Rochelle Harbor you'll find Wright Island Marina and Castaways Yacht Club. Both are full-service facilities catering to transients.

The second and more difficult approach also starts at Fl R 4s BELL R "6," but it runs south of Glen Island and into the lower harbor. The controlling depth is only 6 or 7 feet, so approaching at high tide will help if you are unfamiliar with the area. The channel is very narrow, but big sailboats pass through it regularly. Keep it slow and watch the chart. The Bronx-New Rochelle border, incidentally, runs nearly straight up the middle of the channel. There's a well-protected anchorage on the south side of Travers Island. One of our readers who anchors here tells us that the spot is so peaceful that it's hard to believe it's only 10 miles from Manhattan. The anchorage is not free from personal watercraft and their ilk, so serenity is not guaranteed.

The channel on the west side of Glen Island is crowded with assigned moorings and floats. It's also the home of the very exclusive New York Athletic Club Yacht Club (look for the huge white clubhouse with a red roof), the Huguenot Yacht Club, and West Harbor Yacht Service, which handles all types of repairs and may have an available slip for transients (sailboats only). A big sewer pipe crosses the bottom of this channel; it's not a hazard for most of us, but big sailboats with drafts of 7 feet or more have been known to bump into it on occasion at low tide.

CAUTION: Don't try to round the eastern side of Davids Island—foul ground surrounds it. Also, keep clear of Pea Island. Landing on either island is prohibited.

Echo Bay

Echo Bay Harbor is easier to enter but offers fewer places to stay. The harbor is generally shallow, except in the dredged approach channel, and usually is packed. Be especially alert for small sailboats. Approaching Echo Bay is much simpler than the approach to New Rochelle Harbor.

From the south, you can go to the west of Middle Ground, marked by RG C at Emerald Rock. Once past tiny Pine Island, off Davenport Neck, it's a clear shot north-northeast to Fl G 4s G "3BR," then northwest to the channel entrance.

From the east, approaching Echo Bay is even easier. The best landmarks are the gold-domed clock tower of the New Rochelle Rowing Club on Beaufort Point, and the long, red clubhouse of the Echo Bay Yacht Club on Echo Island. Start at Fl R 4s R "2" about 1nm east-northeast of Middle Ground, and head west for GR C "HL" at Hicks Ledge. Pass south of Hicks Ledge to avoid the 6-foot spot north of the can, and continue west for Fl G 4s G "3BR."

There is a 4-mph speed limit in the harbor. For a little more room to swing (or less commotion), try one of the general anchorages either northwest of Middle Ground or between Hicks Ledge and Premium Point, just outside the bay.

Shoreside & Emergency Services
Airport: Westchester County (914-285-4860)
—Port Authority of NY/NJ (800-AIR-RIDE)
Bus: Westchester County Bee Line (914-682-2020)
Coast Guard: Fort Totten (718-352-4422) or VHF 16
Police, Fire, Ambulance: 911
Taxi: Blue Bird Taxi (914-632-0909)
—Deluxe Taxi (914-632-8000)
Tow Service:
SEA TOW—24-Hour Dispatch (800-4SEATOW)
—Southern Connecticut (203-331-0410)
Tow BoatU.S.—24-Hour Dispatch (800-391-4869)
—Norwalk (516-624-3483)
Train: Amtrak (800-USA-RAIL)
—Metro-North (800-638-7646)

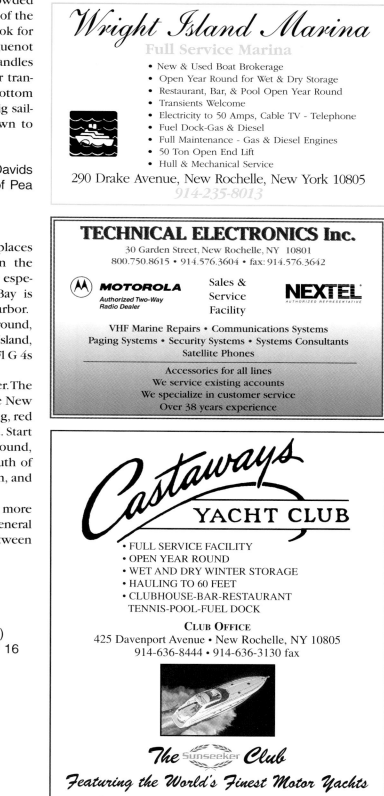

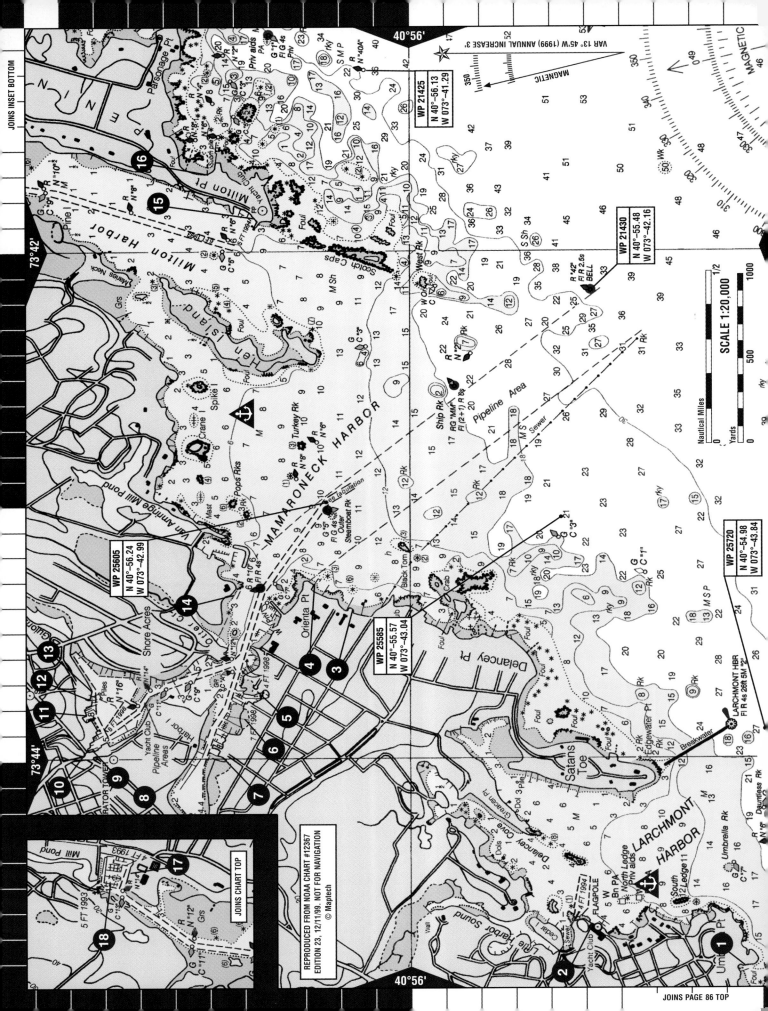

JOINS INSET BOTTOM

JOINS CHART TOP

JOINS PAGE 86 TOP

SCALE 1:20,000

Nautical Miles

Yards

WP 21425
N 40°-56.13
W 073°-41.29

WP 21430
N 40°-55.48
W 073°-42.16

WP 25720
N 40°-54.98
W 073°-43.84

WP 25585
N 40°-55.57
W 073°-43.04

WP 25605
N 40°-56.24
W 073°-42.99

VAR 13°45'W ANNUAL INCREASE 3'

MAGNETIC

MAMARONECK HARBOR

Milton Harbor

Milton Pt

Hen Island

Van Amringe Mill Pond

Shore Acres

Orienta Pt

Delancey Pt

Satans Toe

LARCHMONT HARBOR

Little Harbor Sound

Mill Pond

Puffs of Pureness

Clean air is important to residents of Larchmont. They need it for breathing, of course, but they also need it to fill out the canvas: Larchmont is a sailing mecca, boasting one of the oldest yacht clubs in the country. So strong is the racing fever in the area that even in the dead of winter, you'll find hardy "frostbiters" racing tiny Interclub sailboats in Larchmont Harbor.

Peter Jay Munro, John Jay's nephew, built the Manor House at Elm and Prospect streets in Larchmont Manor in 1797. Looking for a tall, quick-growing tree to protect his property from the dust and noise of the Boston Post Road, Munro obtained some larch seeds from Scotland. The delicate conifers grew quickly and did the trick—at least in spring and summer. Munro may or may not have known that the larch is a deciduous species, dropping its needles in autumn.

Nevertheless, clean air being his goal, Munro made a better choice than a scientist of the time could have known. Recent studies show that the larch is a powerhouse when it comes to processing and retaining carbon dioxide, meaning the "greenhouse effect" is lessened. Larchmont officials are doing what they can to uphold the clean air around the provincial streets; for instance, an ordinance prevents the use of gas-powered leaf blowers between June 1st and September 30th.

If you're looking for marine facilities, head next door to Mamaroneck Harbor, which is almost entirely man-made. Harbor Island, the site of the municipal marina, was once called Quahog Island—at only 4.5 acres, it wasn't much bigger than a clam. The East Basin was navigable only at high water and the West Basin was marsh. In 1912 the village dredged the East Basin and partially filled in the marsh between the island (by then known as "Hog Island") and the mainland. Finally, during the 1930s the West Basin was dredged and the island was expanded to its present 44 acres to become Harbor Island. Today, in addition to the municipal marina, the island is home to what must be the Sound's most architecturally inspiring sewage treatment plant.

Derecktor Shipyard (it's the large building at the head of the East Basin with the rooftop parking lot) built Dennis Connor's 12-meter *Stars & Stripes*, an America's

#	Marine Facilities and Services	Monitors / Working VHF Channel	Number of Transient Berths	Seasonal / Year-round Moorings	Approach / Dockside Depth in Feet at MLW	Maximum LOA	110V ★ 220V ▲ 3 Phase ■ Maximum Amps	Hookups: Fresh Water / Phone / Cable TV	Ramp / Dinghy Dock / Launch Service	Rail / Lift / Crane / Trailer Capacity (tons)	Repairs Propellor / Sail / Rigging / Gas	Diesel / Wood / Fiberglass / Electronics	Marine / Groceries / Ice / Bait / LPG / CNG	Gas / Diesel Fuel Fuel Brand	Restrooms / Showers / Laundry / Pumpout	Public Phone / Restaurant / Snack Bar	Hotel / Pool / Tennis / Golf	Mastercard / VISA / Discover / AmEx
1	Horseshoe Harbor Yacht Club	914-834-9418		Y						PRIVATE—MEMBERS ONLY							
2	Larchmont Yacht Club	914-834-2440	72/	/20	Y	85	9/5			DL		GD		I	RSP	PT	All	All
3	Orienta Beach Club	914-698-1900		Y						PRIVATE—MEMBERS ONLY							
4	Beach Point Club	914-698-1600		Y						PRIVATE—MEMBERS ONLY							
5	McMichael Rushmore Yard	914-381-2100	16/	2/	Y	30	8/5				PDWFE						MVD
6	Total Marine Ltd.	914-698-2700		Y	40	8/8	F	★30		L30		G		I	RS		P	MV
7	Nichols Yacht Yard	914-698-6065		2/	Y	70	10/10	F	★30		LC35	All		M	RSP		P	All
8	Harbor Island Municipal Marina	914-777-7744	16/	2/	S	50	9/9	F		RD					RP		P	
9	R.G. Brewer	914-698-3232		Y					MARINE HARDWARE & SUPPLIES		M			
10	**BREWER POST ROAD Boat Yard** (Inside Back Cover)	914-698-0295	9/	2/1	Y	65	10/9	FP	★▲■50		LC50	All	GD	ML	RS		P	All
11	Derecktor Shipyard	800-691-2100	9/72		S	180	12/20	FP	★▲■100	D	CT110	All	G	LC		P	All
12	Orienta Yacht Club*	914-698-9858	68/	/1	S	42	8/8			PRIVATE—MEMBERS ONLY				RS		P	
13	McMichael Yacht Yard	914-698-4957	72/		Y	50	6/10		★30		C20	All		R			MVD
14	Mamaroneck Yacht Club	914-698-1130		Y						PRIVATE—MEMBERS ONLY							
15	American Yacht Club	914-967-4800		Y						PRIVATE—MEMBERS ONLY							
16	Shenorock Shore Club	914-967-3700		Y						PRIVATE—MEMBERS ONLY							
17	Rye Municipal Boat Basin*	914-967-2011	16/	3/5	S	37	6/6	F		RD	T			RP		PR	
18	The Shongut Marine	914-967-3842		S	35	6/12	F	★		C6	PRGWF		MI	R		All

All Coast Guard Stations Monitor VHF Channel 16

marinalife.com — Convenient Online Boat Slip Reservations

Information in these listings is provided by the facilities themselves. An asterisk (*) indicates that the facility did not respond to our most recent requests for information. (B) represents a BOAT/U.S. cooperating marina.

A ruby-red sailboat moored in Mamaroneck reflects its simple beauty.
© Maptech

Cup winner. There's always an impressive collection of racing and cruising yachts in the yard's service slips.

ACTIVITIES: The biggest draw around here is Rye Playland (914-925-2701), which was used as a location for the film *Big*, starring Tom Hanks. You can't miss this Art Deco wonder from the water, as its trademark white tower and roller coaster make unmistakable landmarks; just to the west you'll see the enormous, white stucco pavilion at Rye Beach. Playland puts on a fireworks display every Wednesday and Friday night at 9:30. Besides rides, it features a beach, pool, and a 19-hole miniature golf course. You might even be able to catch a glimpse of the New York Rangers hockey team, which holds practice sessions (sometimes open to spectators) at Playland's Ice Casino.

One of the oldest yacht clubs in the country, Larchmont has held its annual Race Week every July since 1895. During the event (typically the second week of July), as many as 500 boats of every class blanket the harbor. Some call it exciting, while others describe it as mayhem. Either way, be prepared for lots of company if you plan to cruise here during Race Week.

In Mamaroneck, antiquers shouldn't miss Chatsworth Auction Rooms (914-698-1001) on Mamaroneck Avenue. Opened in 1924 by Irish immigrant Sam Lightbody, the huge shop is bursting at the doors with a large selection of estate furniture, silver, china, and even a piano or two. For more shopping and dining, Larchmont, New Rochelle, and even White Plains are just a quick cab ride away.

If you're interested in fishing near Execution Rocks Lighthouse, remember that it's surrounded by heavy commercial traffic, and occasionally, by currents strong enough to set you onto the rocks if you're not careful. The only safe place to come in close and anchor is on the south side. The rocks on the west side are particularly dangerous.

RESTAURANTS & PROVISIONS: Everything you need onshore is easily accessible from Mamaroneck Harbor. There's a bait, tackle, and boat rental shop next to the public launch ramp on Harbor Island. From there, it's an easy walk to Mamaroneck Avenue and Boston Post Road, each loaded with shops and restaurants of all kinds. On the Post Road just north of Harbor Island, Charlie Brown's Steakhouse (914-698-6610) specializes in beef, chicken, and seafood. Just a little bit farther down the Post Road you'll find the new Mamaroneck Diner (914-698-3564), a casual spot for a BLT, turkey club, or other standard diner fare.

A short walk up Mamaroneck Avenue, Satsuma-ya (914-381-0200) serves sushi, sashimi, and other Japanese food, with a French accent. You'll also find diners, delis, and pizzerias on the avenue. Sal's Pizzeria (914-381-2022) comes highly recommended from one of our readers. Do-it-yourselfers will find a couple of small markets on the avenue, as well as a pharmacy and hardware store.

At the head of Milton Harbor, your choices are more limited. Across the street from Shongut Marina and the Rye Municipal Marina there's a small deli. La Panatière Restaurant (914-967-8140) is a short walk from the marina, and Milton Plaza, a block north, offers Bobby D's Deli (914-921-4010) and Piazza Pizzeria (914-921-4444), which is a big hit in this area. A stop at Brewer Post Road Boat Yard offers access to R.G. Brewer and its selection of marine supplies and hardware.

In Larchmont, unless you stay at the yacht club, there is no easy way to go ashore. So, if you're in need of supplies or a meal ashore, you would do better to head for New Rochelle or Mamaroneck. If you'd like to do some "real estating," however, stroll around the neighborhood of palatial homes and tree-lined streets near Larchmont Yacht Club.

NAVIGATION & ANCHORAGES: Use ChartKit Region 3, pages 20 and 21; Maptech™ Waterproof Charts 1 and 16; and Maptech™ electronic and NOAA paper charts 12367 (1:20,000), 12364 (1:40,000), and 12363 (1:80:000). Use tide tables for Willets Point. High tide at Mamaroneck is 2 minutes earlier; low tide is 13 minutes earlier. Use height of tide at Willets Point for height of tide at Mamaroneck. Mean tidal range is 7.3 feet.

Larchmont Harbor, a small, rocky harbor with almost no shore access, is 2.6nm from the entrance to New Rochelle Harbor, 7.2nm from Byram Harbor, and 3nm from Sands

Looking northwest over Satans Toe (right) and Larchmont Harbor. © Maptech/James T. Abts

Point on Long Island. Mamaroneck Harbor has a wide-open entrance which it shares with Milton Harbor, and a well-protected, divided inner harbor. The entrance to Mamaroneck Harbor is 1.5nm from Larchmont Harbor.

Larchmont Harbor

Larchmont Harbor can be approached from either side of Hen and Chickens, about 0.4nm south-southeast of Umbrella Point. However, if you are a newcomer to the area, you would be much safer taking the main entrance between the Hen and Chickens, marked by Fl G 4s BELL G "1," and the breakwater, marked by Fl R 4s 26 ft 5M "2." Keep G C "3" marking Dauntless Rock well to the west.

CAUTION: Opposite the inner end of the breakwater is a pile known as Umbrella Rocks, the remains of an abandoned breakwater project. The pile is completely submerged at high tide, so keep an eye out for G C "7," just southeast of the hazard.

Do not try to pass between the north end of the breakwater and Satans Toe. The mean tidal range is 7.3 feet, and sometimes over 9 feet, so what looks like good water now may leave you high and dry 6 hours later. Stick to the main entrance.

Inside Larchmont Harbor, the depth is pretty good (5 to 13 feet) anywhere you see moored yachts. Spot the various rock spindles and avoid them. Going between the two spindles of North Ledge (directly off the yacht club) is a no-no; the rocks are exposed at low tide. You can't go very far into Delancey Cove except at high water. The cove between Greacen Point and Satans Toe is not worth trying because there is no room to anchor. Do your exploring in the dinghy, not with your keel.

There is good water for anchoring near the first moorings you come to, a few of which are guest moorings for the Larchmont Yacht Club. Moorings are available to members, members of reciprocating clubs, and transients. Reservations are requested. The club's main dock is off-limits, even to members. Guests may tie up briefly at the work dock to the right of the club. At low tide you'll find about 4 feet of water there, as there's a small shoal before you get to the dock. Call the launch operator for instructions on VHF 72.

Mamaroneck Harbor

Mamaroneck Harbor, approximately 1.5nm northeast of Larchmont Harbor, encompasses everything from Delancey Point to Scotch Caps. The outer harbor is open to everything out of the south, but it's good in northerly weather, and the area north of Turkey Rocks gives the best overall protection in the outer harbor. The town recently upgraded its sewage treatment plant and extended the outfall pipe farther into the sound, so swimming in the harbor is again a recreational option. The tricky part about entering Mamaroneck Harbor is that the outer buoys also serve Rye and Milton harbors.

From the east, the simplest and safest way to enter Mamaroneck Harbor is to observe Fl R 2.5s BELL R "42," which local boaters call the "42nd Street Buoy" because of all the traffic. Then turn northwest and follow the main channel into Mamaroneck Harbor, passing well west of R N "2" and Fl (2+1) R 6s R G "MM" Ship Rock.

Heading into Mamaroneck, a good landmark from Fl R 2.5s BELL R "42" is the pair of gray, cone-shaped towers of the Mamaroneck Yacht Club at the inner harbor entrance. Observe Fl G 4s G "5" at Outer Steamboat Rock, 400 yards east-southeast of Orienta Point. Even though you may see big boats moored to the west of it, it marks one bad rock. The harbormaster can show you a sonar image of it—tall and narrow like a chimney, and jagged! Pass south of R N "6" and R N "8," marking rocks that show at low water. Continuing into Mamaroneck Harbor, the first two facilities are private clubs. Farther in, GR C "A" marks the junction of the East and West basins. The channel to the West Basin is narrow and unmarked, but straight. There is about 5 feet of water at low tide.

The Municipal Marina keeps a guest float on a first-come, first-served basis. The harbormaster can be reached on VHF 16, as can the Coast Guard Auxiliary (914-698-0323), and the Harbor Patrol (914-777-1122). Both maintain bases at the Municipal Marina. The Auxiliary also offers free safety examinations for your boat during the summer; call for more details.

The channel into the East Basin is deeper (about 9.5 feet) and buoyed. Make your turn into the channel at R N "12" (opposite GR C "A"), as this marks the eastern boundary of the channel. Do not cut the last nun—between R N "14" and R N "16" is a nasty shoal very near the channel. All the water

behind it is also shallow, as evidenced by the absence of moored boats in the area. You can come closer to the beach on the port side than you think, but your best bet is to stay in the middle of the channel.

Farther in, each "aisle" between the moored boats has deep water. There is obviously no room for anchoring, but you might have occasion to enter for supplies or repairs at one of the facilities here. Brewer Post Road Boat Yard is a full-service yard with a few transient slips and a well-stocked retail store; they also sell gas and diesel. Remember, there's a 5-mph speed limit in the harbor.

CAUTION: There is a rock right off the end of the fuel dock at the Brewer Post Road Boat Yard that has been hit by deep-draft boats.

When leaving Mamaroneck Harbor to head east, many local skippers cut to the north of Fl R 2.5s BELL R "42," but as we said earlier, it's not something you want to try if you're unfamiliar with the area. Stay at least 0.5nm to the west and south of W Or C when rounding West Rock.

Milton Harbor
From Fl R 2.5s BELL R "42," you will head northwest and then pass between Fl (2+1) R 6s RG "MM" at Ship Rock and R N "2," and then leave G C "3" to port.

Milton Harbor is full of moored sailboats. (If you can find a powerboat in there, let us know.) Up to Milton Point there is about 7 feet of water, and from there about 6 feet in the

Looking northwest over Mamaroneck Harbor. Hen Island sits in the center. Your entrance into Milton Harbor is nicely outlined by the moored boats, heading off to the right. © Mantech/James T. Ahts

Looking north into Milton Harbor. The American Yacht Club is in the foreground. © Maptech

narrow, dredged channel. Be careful of the rock north of G C "5," and don't ignore the 5-mph speed limit sign.

In addition to the two clubs on the east side of Milton Harbor, you'll see the large, brick clubhouse of the Durland Boy Scout Nautical Training Facility. It's one of the country's largest Sea Scout centers, where teenagers can learn day sailing, scuba diving, and snorkeling.

The trip up the harbor will be peaceful. Shongut Marina, the Rye Municipal Boat Basin, and the harbormaster are located at the head of the harbor. You may go aground off the main dock, but it's soft mud.

Shoreside & Emergency Services
Airport: Westchester, White Plains, NY (914-285-4860)
Bus: Westchester County Bee Line (914-682-2020)
Coast Guard: Fort Totten (718-352-4422) or VHF 16
—Eatons Neck (631-261-6868) or VHF 16
Police, Fire, Ambulance: 911
Taxi: Leon's Taxi (Larchmont) (914-834-4000)
—Mamaroneck Taxi (914-698-2000)
—Rye Cab Co. (914-967-0500)
Tow Service:
SEA TOW —24-Hour Dispatch (800-4SEATOW)
—Southern Connecticut (203-331-0410)
Tow BoatU.S.—24-Hour Dispatch (800-391-4869)
—City Island (718-885-3420)

Western Connecticut Coast

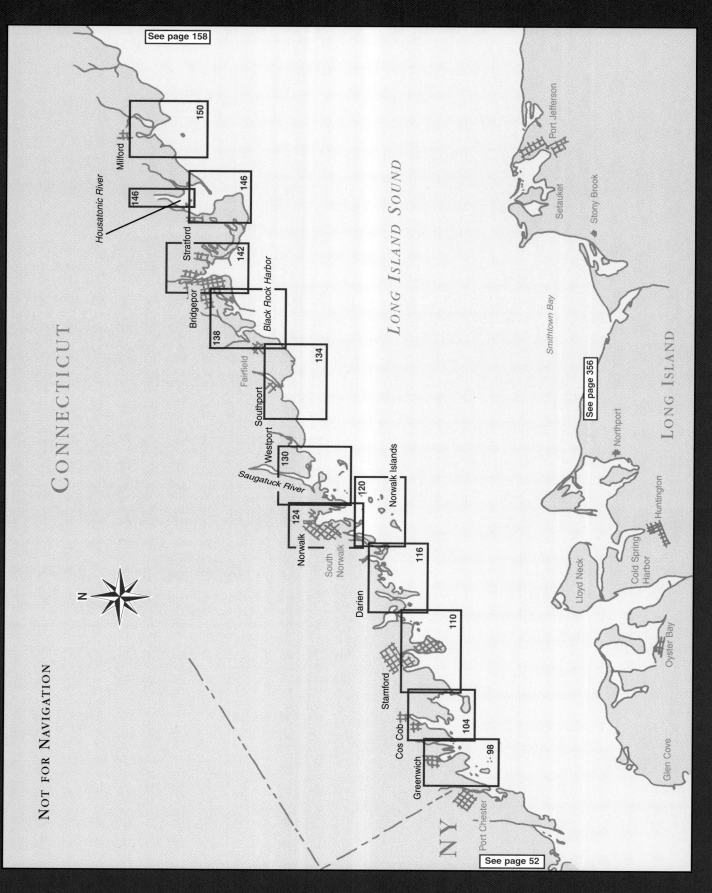

See page 158

150

Milford

Housatonic River

146

146

Stratford

142

Bridgepor

Black Rock Harbor

138

Fairfield

134

Southport

130

Westport

Saugatuck River

120

Norwalk Islands

124

Norwalk

South Norwalk

116

Darien

110

Stamford

104

Cos Cob

98

Greenwich

NY

Port Chester

CONNECTICUT

LONG ISLAND SOUND

Smithtown Bay

See page 356

Port Jefferson

Setauket

Stony Brook

Northport

LONG ISLAND

Huntington

Cold Spring Harbor

Lloyd Neck

Oyster Bay

Glen Cove

N

NOT FOR NAVIGATION

See page 52

From **Greenwich** to **Milford** the Connecticut shoreline ebbs and flows, sometimes rushing far inland along one of the area's many rivers, and sometimes staying fast to form a more finite harbor. Cruisers of this region will find that the atmosphere ashore varies from town to town as much as the water's edge varies from harbor to harbor.

In **Greenwich**, your landing party will experience New York's lushest suburb. This is less of a cruising destination than it is a wealthy suburb that makes small allowances for visitors. As you travel east along the coastline, with stops in **Cos Cob** and **Stamford**, you'll witness the transformation from suburbia to city. Stamford is the first real city this side of New York. It's not a stunning or architecturally beautiful city, but it's likeable, has a busy atmosphere with plenty to do, and it has lots of places to dock, to buy provisions, and to enjoy a late meal or drink.

Just to the east, the quiet of suburbia prevails through **Darien** and up the **Fivemile River** before again succumbing to a city atmosphere, this time in **Norwalk**. A lot of Norwalk's waterfront is crowded with marine industry. For marine repairs of any sort, this is the place to be. Past Norwalk, in **Westport** and **Southport**, you will have come full circle on your journey through this region. Both towns are smallish, have money, and enjoy a quiet, homey atmosphere. On the plus side for cruisers, the marine facilities, restaurants, and provisions make themselves accesible to visitors.

Navigating the Western Connecticut Coast

If you're coming from the Big Apple, begin your approach to this region from Fl G GONG G "23," located between Execution Rocks and Prospect Point. From here, head 053°m for 8.9nm toward Fl G 2.5s GONG G "1" and the entrance to Captain Harbor, which gives you access to Greenwich Harbor, Cos Cob Harbor and Greenwich Cove. Keep Fl G 2.5s GONG G "1" to your west before swinging northwest into the harbor. You can enter **Captain Harbor** from its western side, but it's a bit trickier. *Refer to the Greenwich Harbor & the Captain Islands chapter, and the Cos Cob Harbor and Greenwich Cove chapter for more information.*

Simply continue east and round Greenwich Point, keeping R N "34" to the north, and **Stamford Harbor** awaits. Head for the channel that runs between the two breakwaters. If you're traveling east to west, be sure to round Fl R 6s BELL R "32" before heading toward the breakwaters—The Cows are dangerous. *Refer to the Stamford Harbor & Westcott Cove chapter for more information.*

From Fl R 6s BELL R "32" a course of 077°m will take you to Fl R 2.5s BELL R "24," southeast of Cockenoe Island, and will keep you in safe water past the **Norwalk Islands**. Heed the buoys, especially R N "28" off Greens Ledge, along the way. To approach **Norwalk Harbor** from this route, swing to the north and pass west of Al W R 24s 62ft 15M HORN at the

An ideal way to spend the day in Fairfield, Connecticut. © Maptech

eastern end of Greens Ledge. A series of buoys and a dredged channel lead you to Norwalk Harbor. You can also approach Norwalk Harbor from the Norwalk Islands' eastern end. Head north at Fl R 4s BELL R "26" and pick up Fl 4s 61ft 7M. Follow the series of buoys. *Refer to the Norwalk Harbor chapter and the Norwalk Islands chapter for more information.*

To head into the **Saugatuck River**, turn to the northeast at Fl R 2.5s BELL R "24," keeping it and Fl G 2.5s G "1" to your west before heading toward Fl G 4s G "3." From the east, the water is deep and clear to Fl G 4s G "3." *Refer to the Westport & the Saugatuck River chapter for more information.*

Steer northeast from Fl R 2.5s BELL R "24" to reach G C "3" and R N "2" at the entrance channel to **Southport Harbor**. *Refer to the Southport Harbor chapter for more information.*

From Fl R 2.5s BELL R "24" you can head 089°m toward Fl R 6s BELL R "18" in order to continue eastward. This will take you past the **Bridgeport Harbor** channel approach buoy. Before reaching Fl R 2.5s GONG R "2" and G C "3," about 1.1nm north of Mo(A) WHIS RW "BH," swing wide around Black Rock and the Little Cows, marked with only W Bn, in order to reach **Black Rock Harbor**. Head for Fl R 4s 43ft 4M "2A." *Refer to the Black Rock Harbor chapter and the Bridgeport Harbor chapter for more information.*

Continuing east, you'll round Stratford Point, with its Fl (2) 20s 52ft 16M Light. Keep offshore about 0.3nm to escape the shallows, avoiding R N "20," which marks an 11-foot spot and a wreck. Head for Fl G 2.5s BELL G "1," about 0.7nm northeast of Fl (2) 20s 52ft 16M, to enter the channel leading to the **Housatonic River**. *Refer to the Housatonic River chapter for more information.*

Northeast of the Housatonic River's entrance, Fl R 4s BELL R "16" marks the way to **Milford Harbor**. Keep this mark to the north and head into The Gulf. *Refer to the Milford Harbor chapter for more information.*

To bypass these harbors, steer for Mo(A) WHIS RW "NH," the approach buoy to **New Haven Harbor**.

73°40'
73°38'
73°37'

Puddys Grove

PORT CHESTER HARBOR

FIXED BR
HOR CL
VERT CL

STACK

Fox I
Marine
Yacht
Railway
Club

for a
trance
width
a mid-

1993

Kirby Pond

JOINS CHART LEFT

Grs

Belle Haven

Marine
Railway

GREENWICH HARBOR

Round I

Grass

Smith Cove

Indian Harbor

Tweed I

Wk

BYRAM HARBOR

Field Pt

Fence

WP 25490
N 41°—00.19
W 073°—37.33

Grs

n Park

Rich I

Farwells I

Game Cock I

Wilson Head

Shore

Otter Rks

R
N "4"

G
C "3"

R "2"
Fl R 4s

G
C "1"

TOWER

Foul

Bowers I

JOINS PAGE 104 LEFT

Calf Islands

Foul

WP 25365
N 40°—59.25
W 073°—38.00

Grassy Rk

Jones Rks

Fl G 4s
25ft 5M "3"

WP 25370
N 40°—59.47
W 073°—37.91

R
N "4"

Rk

Cormorant Reef

Foul
Incinerator

PAVILION

Byram R

Wk

Channel Rk

Fl R 2.5s 28ft 5M "4"

rky

G
C "1"

Rk Great
Captain I

G
C "1"

Foul

Great Captain Rks

G
C "3"

Fl R 4s

Wk
rky

R "2"

Manursing I Reef

Cable Area

Rocky

GREAT CAPTAIN ISLAND
Al WR 12s 62ft 12M
HORN

WP 25535
N 40°—58.94
W 073°—39.19

Fourfoot Rks

GR
C "F"

R
N "2"

Payeaa Reach

Nautical Miles
0   1/2

SCALE 1:20,000

Yards
0   500   1000

VAR 13° 45'W (1999) ANNUAL INCREASE 3'

MAGNETIC

① ② ③ ④ ⑤ ⑥ ⑦ ⑧ ⑨ ⑩ ⑪ ⑫ ⑬ ⑭ ⑮ ⑯

Suburb Central

Named for Greenwich, England, this Connecticut Gold Coast town was known for many years as "Horseneck" because of its fine grazing land. Legend has it that the land was bought from the Indians for 25 coats, making it one of history's greatest real-estate deals, since Greenwich today is one of the nation's wealthiest communities.

Since its inception Greenwich meant little to workers in New York City. But in 1848 the railroad came to town, and ever since, Greenwich has been the quintessential commuter's suburb of The Big Apple.

In addition to wealth, Greenwich has had its share of historic figures, starting with Captain David Patrick. Great Captain Island was named in honor of the brave (but not so likeable) Capt. Patrick, one of the original settlers of Greenwich. In 1656 he was appointed the military commander in charge of protecting Greenwich and the islands from the Petuquapaen Indians. He had great success, or so the story goes, and as a tribute to himself he named one island "Great Captain" Island. Modest guy, eh?

Another notorious Greenwich figure was Tammany Hall kingpin William "Boss" Tweed, who had Tweed Island named after him. This small grass island was once the home of the Americus Club, a yacht club where Tweed and his cronies could gather and plot ways to swindle New York City out of

Repeat visitors will recognize this Greenwich Harbor regular. © Maptech

	Marine Facilities and Services		Monitors / Working VHF Channel	Number of Transient Berths / Moorings	Approach / Dockside Depth in Feet at MLW	Seasonal / Year-round	Hookups: Fresh Water / Phone / Cable TV	110v • 220v ▲ 3 Phase ■ Maximum Amps	Rail / Lift / Crane / Launch Service	Ramp / Dinghy Dock	Repairs: Propellor / Sail / Rigging / Electronics	Diesel / Wood / Fiberglass / Electronics	Marine / Groceries / Ice / Bait / LPG / CNG	Gas / Diesel Fuel	Fuel Brand	Restrooms / Showers / Laundry / Pumpout	Public Phone / Restaurant / Snack Bar	Hotel / Pool / Tennis / Golf	Mastercard / VISA / Discover / AmEx
1	Tide Mill Yacht Basin	914-967-2995	68/	2/	S	70	7/7	F	★▲50		L35	DWFE		GD	Citgo	M	RS		P	MVA
2	Port Chester Yacht Club*	914-939-9687			S	21		F	★	R	R						R		P	
3	Cahill's Marina	914-939-8286			Y															
4	Pearl of the Atlantic Boatyard*	914-939-4227			Y	75	21/16		★						Tex					
5	Rudy's Tackle Barn	203-531-5928		1/	Y	25	12/12	F	★30	RD	CT5						MGIB			MVD
6	J. Catalano & Sons Inc.	203-531-9207			Y		6/6				C15	PDEF		G	Tex		R			MV
7	Port Chester Municipal Marina*	914-939-5226		25/25	S	23						All		GD		GIB		All	
8	Byram Shore Boat Club*	203-531-9858			Y			*PRIVATE—MEMBERS ONLY*												
9	Greenwich Bay Marina	203-531-9255		10/	S	25	16/4	F	★30			All		G	Citgo	GIB	R		P	MVA
10	West Chester Marina Services	914-937-1352	16/11	5/	S	39	12/8	F	★▲	D	CT40	All		G		MIB	RSL		P	All
11	Byram Park Greenwich Municipal Boat Basin*	203-531-9879			Y			*RESIDENTS ONLY*												
12	Belle Haven Yacht Club*	203-861-5353			Y			*PRIVATE—MEMBERS ONLY*												
13	Greenwich Boat & Yacht Club*	203-622-9558		/2	Y	42	4/7										I	RS		
14	Grass Island Marina	203-869-9689	9/	2/	S	44	7/7		★▲50	R	L10			GD	Tex	I	RP		PS	All
15	Greenwich Harbor Inn	203-661-9800			Y			*UNDERGOING RENOVATIONS—CLOSED UNTIL 2001*												
16	Indian Harbor Yacht Club	203-869-2484	68/		Y												RSL		PR	MV

All Coast Guard Stations Monitor VHF Channel 16

Information in these listings is provided by the facilities themselves. An asterisk (*) indicates that the facility did not respond to our most recent requests for information. (B) represents a BOAT/U.S. cooperating marina.

its money. In 1871, the gang managed to rig the election for state senator, bringing to office J.H. Woodward, an Americus Club member. Tweed's deeds were eventually unearthed, sending him to the big house, and leaving the name of the island the only reminder of his legacy in Greenwich.

Not all Greenwich names are founded in hard facts, like the Byram River. Separating Port Chester from Greenwich and, in turn, New York from Connecticut, the origin of the name of the Byram River is not concrete. Folklore has it that there used to be an Indian trading post on the river where natives would "buy rum."

Call it what you will, the town of Greenwich is very proud of its history and intent on preserving its uniqueness. If you're fortunate enough to land a slip, you'll be able to explore the interesting nooks and crannies of Greenwich yourself.

ACTIVITIES: Greenwich is the great escape, especially for those fleeing the Big Apple. It's only 29 miles from Times Square, yet you're a world away.

Across the street from the Greenwich Harbor Inn are the exhibits of art and natural history at the Bruce Museum (203-869-0376). Here, the sights and sounds of New England woodlands come to life, and you'll find some interesting exhibits on wildlife and marine life. Next door is the beautiful Bruce Park. If you've been out at sea too long, the Greenwich Arts Center Gallery (203-622-3998), in the center of town, is a fine place to catch up on the culture scene.

The beaches around Greenwich are beautiful, but you'll see signs everywhere that read "Residents Only." This gorgeously landscaped coastline is quite a sight from sea, and unfortunately, that's how you'll have to view much of it.

There are no restrictions on shopping, however, and Greenwich has plenty of that. Get your credit card ready—or hide it—as Greenwich Avenue is a shopaholic's paradise. Blocks of boutiques and shops, most of which are very posh (i.e. not too cheap), are mixed with some of the better known retail stores.

Take a cab up to the Audubon Center (203-869-5272) and its 485-acre bird sanctuary with 15 miles of nature trails. It's about a 20-minute ride from the water and includes a section of the Byram River that's only a babbling brook.

Remember, no matter where you are in Greenwich, New York City is never far. Hop on the Metro-North Railroad (800-638-7646) from a station in Greenwich, Cos Cob, Riverside, or Old Greenwich, and you'll be in the Big Apple in less than an hour.

The true salts can forget land altogether and drop anchor off the protected Captain Islands. Legend says Capt. Kidd buried treasure on Great Captain Island, though nearly every rock that sticks above the water in these parts makes such claims. In any case, enjoy the peacefulness, and keep an eye out for any of them thar' gold trinkets.

These waters are littered with rocks and wrecks, so drop a line and try to hook a porgy or tautog, if you're just sitting around.

RESTAURANTS & PROVISIONS: Whether it's a day at sea, or one exploring the shops, Greenwich can really stir up a hunger. Greenwich Avenue has more than enough options, from simple delis to expensive eateries you'd expect from the "Gold Coast."

For a taste of the Orient, try the sushi bar at Kagetsu Restaurant (203-622-9264). For the seafood and burger crowd, try Benny's Italian Seafood (203-661-6108), or the Thataway Café (203-622-0947).

If you end up staying on the Byram River, Port Chester has a few selections itself. Steaks and chops are cooked to a tee at the fancy Willet House (914-939-7500), next to

Oh, rats!

You'd probably prefer that your vessel be free of any pesky stowaways, but maybe this little bit of lore will make you think again. Sailors often welcomed common rats onto their ships, regarding them as pets and valuing them as good luck charms and predictors of unsafe voyages. Before a ship left port, sailors would watch to see if the rats stayed aboard or not, believing that rats knew whether or not a ship was doomed and would abandon it if they sensed a sinking. (Ostensibly, these wise critters who deserted went on to new careers as wharf rats, while the foolish ones who stayed aboard met a watery death, going down like rats from a sinking ship.)

On the other hand, if a sailor "smelled a rat," he wasn't likely to be upset—it probably just meant that it was dinnertime. When food supplies were low the men often betrayed their beady-eyed bunkmates and made the vermin into vittles (which was only right, considering that the rodents had probably eaten half the food in the hold, anyway).

Sailors' views on rats changed when the stowaways began spreading maladies such as the bubonic plague: a condition that would make any person turn his back on the pet who gave it to him, if he lived to do so. Thus, the preferred maritime companion animal became *Felis domestica*, the rat-killing cat.

the Port Chester Municipal Marina. Mark Anthony's (914-937-3357) serves international cuisine, and you can get a good Italian dinner at Per Voi Ristorante (914-937-3200).

Port Chester has a good number of small grocery stores, like Stop One Food. ATMs can be found near several of the restaurants as well.

NAVIGATION & ANCHORAGES: Use ChartKit Region 3, page 22; Maptech™ Waterproof Charts 1 and 16, and Maptech™ electronic and NOAA paper charts 12367 (1:20,000), 12364 (1:40,000), and 12363 (1:80,000). Use tide tables for Bridgeport. High tide at Greenwich is 1 minute later; low tide is 1 minute later. Multiply height of tide at Bridgeport by 1.1 for height of tide at Greenwich. Mean tidal range is 7.4 feet.

Whether you're on your way to the Big Apple or beginning your journey along the coast, Greenwich is a pleasant stop. The entrance to the Byram River is 4.4nm from Fl R 2.5s BELL R "42" at the Mamaroneck Harbor entrance and 1.7nm from Greenwich Harbor. Matinecock Point is 4.8nm away. From Fl R 2.5s BELL R "32A" halfway between Captain Harbor and Oyster Bay, a course of about 320°m will take you to the eastern entrance of Captain Harbor.

Port Chester

From the south or west, it's safest to pass between BELL R "36" at Bluefish Shoal and G R C "F" marking Fourfoot Rocks. Pass to the east of BELL R "36" at Bluefish Shoal, as hazards such as Glover Reef, to the west, are not buoyed. Keep an eye out for the large, unlighted, steel mooring buoys used by the commercial gravel barges. Pass west of G R C "F," and leave Fl R 4s R "2" at Great Captain Rocks at least 200 yards to the east, as it shoals north and east of the buoy. Once past Great Captain Rocks, swing northwest around G C "3," passing Fl R 2.5s 28ft 5M "4" on the breakwater off Byram Point.

From the north and east, pass south of Fl R 4s R "2" and stay at least 200 yards west of the buoy when rounding. Do not attempt to pass between Great Captain Rocks and Channel Rocks off Byram Point. Leave this passage to those with local knowledge. If you're new to this area, come in on a rising tide, as the tidal range is about 7.4 feet. Once in the main channel, there's a good, though small, anchorage south of Fl G 4s 25ft 5M "5" in the middle of the harbor. There are mudflats north of the flasher.

The channel down to the Tide Mill Yacht Basin is dredged to 7 feet, and privately marked. The dredged channel up the river is about a mile long and has an approximate depth of 10 feet up to the Interstate 95 bridge (vertical clearance: 60 feet mhw), and beyond that, approximately 7.5 feet to the turning basin. You'll be able to see plenty of boats, but it may be difficult to distinguish between marinas. One boater tells us he even has trouble finding his marina sometimes because signs are few. The channel shallows to 5 feet or less at the turning basin in Port Chester.

CAUTION: For such a narrow river, there's an amazing amount of commercial traffic (including tugs with barges

Looking north over Greenwich Harbor. © Maptech/James T. Abts

Looking northwest over Byram Harbor. © Maptech/James T. Abts

base of Jones Rocks is easily spotted and makes a good landmark. Stay northwest of the shoal extending southeast from R N "4."

CAUTION: We concur with local wisdom and recommend against entering the harbor between Great Captain and Little Captain islands. Many of the rocks you see exposed at low tide are deceptively covered much of the time. If you happen to witness a boat doing so successfully, chalk it up to a lot of experience.

Once in Captain Harbor, you have easy access to Byram Harbor and Greenwich Harbor. Captain Harbor affords fair shelter and some good anchorages. Two secluded anchorages can be found in the 7- to 8-foot area northeast of Calf Islands, and in the 7- to 9-foot area west of the islands. This is also a nice place to drop a baited hook and try your chances on landing a winter flounder or blackfish. Both of these anchorages are visible to each other, but don't try to pass between them directly, unless in your dinghy. Reefs extend from the mainland past the islands and out to Jones Rocks, so you'll have to transit all the way around.

A good daytime anchorage is northwest of Great Captain Island, although it's exposed to the prevailing southwesterly winds. One of our readers tells us it's a nice swim to the beach from there.

and oil tankers). A few enormous barges may be tied up at the cement plants, further reducing the width of the channel.

Captain Harbor

If you're sailing along the Sound, Captain Harbor is a good spot to tack into to get away from an unfavorable current, or for protection in a blow. Great Captain Island is to the west of Little Captain Island, and is easily distinguishable by its 62-foot skeleton tower (Al W R 12s 62ft 12M HORN) at the end of the island. Even easier to see is the island's old stone lighthouse tower.

The two main approaches to Captain Harbor—and hence Byram Harbor, Greenwich Harbor, Indian Harbor, Cos Cob Harbor, and Greenwich Cove—are from the east and west.

From the east is the safest course. Use the passage between Fl G 2.5s GONG G "1" and R N "2" off Flat Neck Point. Leave G C "1A" to the west to avoid Hen and Chickens. Once past "1A" you'll be in Captain Harbor with Greenwich Harbor directly ahead to the northwest. Cos Cob Harbor will be to the north.

CAUTION: Don't cut between Wee Captain Island and G C "1A." It may look possible on the chart, but the Hen and Chickens claim a good number of boats every summer and keep the marine division quite busy.

From the south or west, pass between R "36" BELL and R N "2" off the southwest tip of Great Captain Island. Leave G R C "F," marking Fourfoot Rocks, to the west and pass south of G C "1" before heading north between Fl G 4s 25ft 5M "3" at Jones Rocks, and R N "4" northwest of Cormorant Reef. The 25-foot skeleton tower and concrete

Byram Harbor

Byram Harbor, suitable only for shallow-draft boats in good weather, is about 2nm northeast of the Byram River. The entrance to the inner harbor is between Rich Island and Farwells Island, and you may not want to enter at dead low tide. Another 1nm to the northeast lies Greenwich Harbor. Both Byram and Greenwich harbors are accessible only from Captain Harbor, which is bordered on the west by Calf Islands and on the south by Little Captain and Great Captain Islands.

The approach to Byram Harbor is north of Bowers Island, between G C "1" and Fl R 4s R "2." The moorings you pass to starboard belong to the Belle Haven Yacht Club, which doesn't cater to transients. It does, however, offer reciprocal privileges to members of other clubs.

Don't try squeezing between tiny Bowers Island and Calf Islands to get into this area or you'll be in trouble. The town marina and the club in Byram Harbor are open to members and residents only, but if you do enter the little basin at Byram Park, hug the Rich Island (north) side of the entrance to avoid shoaling on the south side.

Smith Cove and Greenwich Harbor from the southwest. Tweed Island is in the foreground. © Maptech/James T. Abts

Greenwich Harbor

Greenwich Harbor's entrance is marked by R N "2," 0.3nm southeast of Field Point, well out in Captain Harbor. The mile-long channel takes you past the famous green-tile-roofed Indian Harbor Yacht Club, founded in 1889, which has guest moorings for members of other clubs. Advance reservations are usually necessary. As we went to press, it was closed for renovations and scheduled to re-open in 2001. On the west side is the fancy residential neighborhood of Belle Haven. Passing R N "4" you'll see a scale model of the Brooklyn Bridge ashore. This fine replica was built by John Augustus Roebling before he undertook the real thing.

Farther into the harbor you'll find the Greenwich Harbor Inn. This inn/marina has been one of Connecticut's premier stops for cruising boaters. As we went to press, it was closed for renovations and scheduled to re-open in 2001. On the west side of the harbor is Grass Island, a town marina with transient docking from April 15th through November 15th. For booking call 203-618-7651 or on weekends 203-618-9695. There's a 5-mph speed limit in the harbor. At the head of the harbor on the west side are the docks for the Greenwich Marine Police boat, and the Captain Islands and Calf Islands ferries.

Keep an eye out for Red Rock southeast of Tweed Island (R G N "R"), which is a frequent cause of trouble for visitors. Tweed Island also marks the entrance to the very pretty Indian Harbor, which is too grassy and shallow to accommodate most cruising boats.

Shoreside & Emergency Services

Airport: Westchester, White Plains, NY (914-285-4860)
Coast Guard: Eatons Neck (631-261-6868) or VHF 16
Police, Fire, Ambulance: 911
Taxi: Greenwich Taxi (203-869-6000)
Tow Service:
SEA TOW —24-Hour Dispatch (800-4SEATOW)
—Southern Connecticut (800-331-0410)
Tow BoatU.S.—24-Hour Dispatch (800-391-4869)
—Norwalk (203-855-7918)
Train: Amtrak (800-USA-TRAIN)
—Metro-North (800-638-7646)

From Artists to Boaters

Greenwich's five harbors make it a busy and popular stop for boaters. Cos Cob, part of Greenwich, is one of those stops. It was a popular haven for artists in the late 19th and early 20th centuries, when painters and writers from New York City summered in Connecticut to get away from the heat and stress of the city and to get their creative juices flowing again. The Bush-Holley House found itself at the center of this artistic wave.

Built in the late 1600s when Greenwich was still under the jurisdiction of New Amsterdam as New York City was then called, the Bush-Holley House was later used by the famous Revolutionary War General Israel Putnam, who, it's said, lived in it so that he could keep an eye on the strategic saltworks. The British, under General Tryon, still managed to plunder the saltworks and the surrounding area before being chased away by American troops.

This has always been a popular place. Adriaen Block brought the first settlement here in 1614, the same year the Dutch captain also discovered the Connecticut River. The strategic location of Greenwich made it an important stronghold from the time of the French and Indian War to the War of 1812. Today, Cos Cob is a small but upscale bedroom community preferred by Manhattan executives. New York City boaters like to escape to here, too, so finding a slip on a weekend may not be easy.

Fjord Fisheries can fulfill your craving for fresh fish. © Maptech

	Marine Facilities and Services		Monitors / Working VHF Channel	Number of Transient Berths	Approach / Dockside Depth in Feet at MLW	Seasonal / Yearround Moorings	Hookups: Fresh Water / Phone / Cable TV	110v + 220v ▲ 3 Phase ■ Maximum Amps	Maximum LOA	Rail / Lift / Crane / Trailer: Capacity (tons)	Ramp / Dinghy Dock / Launch Service	Diesel / Wood / Fiberglass / Electronics	Repairs: Propellor / Sail / Rigging / Gas	Marine / Groceries / Ice / Bait / LPG / CNG	Gas / Diesel Fuel	Fuel Brand	Restrooms / Showers / Laundry / Pumpout	Public Phone / Pool / Tennis / Golf	Hotel / Restaurant / Snack Bar	Mastercard / VISA / Discover / AmEx
1	Mianus River Boat & Yacht Club	203-869-4689		Y					*PRIVATE—MEMBERS ONLY*											
2	**PALMER POINT MARINA & SHIPS STORE** p. 109	203-661-1243	/1	Y	55	6/6	All	★▲50		L35	All		GD	Tex	MI	RS		All	All	
3	Riverscape Marina	203-661-0471		1/	Y	60	6/6	All	★▲50		L25	PWFE			IB	RS				
4	**Beacon Point Marine** (B) p. 107	203-661-4033	9/	10/	Y	70	6/6	All	★▲		LCT35	PRGDWFE			MI	All		P	MVA	
5	Mianus Marine, Inc.	203-869-2253		2/	S	50	6/6	F	★30		C50	All				R		P		
6	Albin Marine	203-661-4341	/68	Y	45	5.5/5.5	F	★30		C50	All						P			
7	**OMA** Full Service Marine Facility p. 106	203-661-4283		2/	Y	35	5/5	F	★30		C30	All			I	RS				
8	Drenckhahn Boat Basin	203-869-1892	9/	3/	Y	40	7/7	F	★30		C35	All			I	R				
8	Mianus Marine Engine Corp.*	203-661-7678		Y						L25	PGD							D		
9	Riverside Yacht Club	203-637-1706	74/	Y					*RECIPROCAL PRIVILEGES*											
10	Longmeadow Creek Marine*	203-637-0115		Y							L2	PGWF							MV	
11	Old Greenwich Yacht Club*	203-637-1961		Y					*PRIVATE—MEMBERS ONLY*											

Information in these listings is provided by the facilities themselves. An asterisk (*) indicates that the facility did not respond to our most recent requests for information.
(B) represents a BOAT/U.S. cooperating marina.

All Coast Guard Stations Monitor VHF Channel 16

marinalife.com Convenient Online Boat Slip Reservations

Looking northwest into Cos Cob Harbor, with the entrance to Greenwich Cove to the right. © Maptech/James T. Abts

ACTIVITIES: Pleasant marinas with pleasant folks and easy access to amenities and fine restaurants are reason enough to plot a course for Cos Cob Harbor. Greenwich Cove is one of the most attractive and best protected anchorages in Long Island Sound, unspoiled by commercial wharves or buildings or, for that matter, amenities. If you're going for quiet beauty, Greenwich Cove is the place to be, especially on weekdays when there are few, if any, of the rafting-boat parties you'll see on weekends.

Pelican Island and Greenwich Island are fair picnic grounds, but watch out for poison ivy and water rats on Greenwich Island. Alas, that tempting stretch of sand on the northwest shore of the cove is private property.

Walk off those sea legs and head ashore to the Bush-Holley House, just a stone's throw from the marinas along the Mianus River. This 1732 saltbox was once a gathering spot for the American Impressionist colony, and it now houses the Historical Society of the Town of Greenwich (203-869-6899). You'll find a fine collection of antique furniture and art, particularly works of the American impressionists who summered here. The house has secret passageways and trap doors that lead to a dark and eerie cellar—great romance novel material.

Done enough relaxing on the water? Head for New York. Find a slip in Cos Cob, and Metro-North Railroad (800-638-7646) will take you to the core of the Big Apple in about an hour.

RESTAURANTS & PROVISIONS: Whether your palate yearns for fast food or expensive cuisine, Cos Cob delivers (in some cases literally).

Enjoy a great selection of salads, pastas, and interesting entrées at Sevilla Restuarant (203-629-9029) in the Mill Pond Shopping Center. Three blocks west is Bella Nonna's (203-869-4445). If you're not in the mood to make decisions, Domino's Pizza (203-661-2202) can provide a familiar flavor. At River Road and Route 1 is Fonda La Paloma (203-661-9395), serving reasonably priced Mexican cuisine.

Take care of your provisioning and basic cleaning needs on Route 1, where you'll find Food Mart (203-629-2100), a post office (203-869-1470), and Center Hardware and

Embassy Guides

Housewares (203-869-9254). Just north of River Road, Hay Day Country Market (203-637-7600) has baked goods, a deli, gourmet foods and whole meals. If you're looking to spend a night ashore, check in at the elegant Cos Cob Inn, directly across the street from Beacon Point Marine.

NAVIGATION & ANCHORAGES: Use ChartKit Region 3, page 26; Maptech™ Waterproof Charts 1 and 16; and Maptech™ electronic and NOAA paper charts 12367 (1:20,000), 12364 (1:40,000), and 12363 (1:80,000). Use tide tables for Bridgeport. High tide at Cos Cob Harbor is 5 minutes later; low tide is 11 minutes later. Multiply height of tide at Bridgeport by 1.1 for height of tide at Cos Cob Harbor. Mean tidal range is 7.2 feet.

Cos Cob Harbor, where the Mianus River meets Captain Harbor, is the most popular destination for transient boaters among Greenwich's harbors, offering the most marine facilities and the best shore access. Hitchcock Rock, marking the outer entrance to Cos Cob Harbor, is 3.8nm from the Stamford Harbor breakwaters, 1nm from R N "2" at the entrance to Greenwich Harbor, and 2.7nm from Port Chester Harbor. From Fl R 2.5s BELL "32A," halfway between Captain Harbor and Oyster Bay, a course of about 320°m will take you to the eastern entrance to Captain Harbor, 2.8nm away.

From any direction, you'll first have to get into Captain Harbor. Your best, and safest, bet is to enter from the east, between Fl G 2.5s GONG G "1," east of Hen and Chickens, and R N "2" off Flat Neck Point. Leave G C "1A" to the west to avoid Hen and Chickens.

CAUTION: Do not attempt to cut short of G C "1A." The Hen and Chickens will surely "peck" a hole in your itinerary, if not your hull.

Once you're in Captain Harbor you have easy access to Cos Cob Harbor and Greenwich Cove. If you enter Captain Harbor from the west, do so between Jones Rocks, signified by Fl G 4s 25ft 5M "3," and Great Captain Island. (See the preceding chapter for navigational information on Captain Harbor, Byram Harbor, and Greenwich Harbor.)

Cos Cob Harbor

Cos Cob Harbor appears tricky, but is perfectly safe if you follow the markers. Look for Fl R 4s R "4" marking Newfoundland Reef as you enter Captain Harbor. Leave Newfoundland Reef to the east and head for Fl R 4s R "2" at Hitchcock Rock. Pass west and north of Hitchcock Rock and follow G C "1," G C "3," and G C "5," to the well-marked inner channel.

You may notice boats cutting straight into Cos Cob Harbor, east of Bluff and Diving islands. Rest assured, these are local mariners, and even they need to use caution. Play it safe and follow the markers.

If you want to enter the Special Anchorage south of the Riverside Yacht Club, be careful of the rock east of R N

"8." The channel leads you past Riverside Yacht Club on the east bank.

There's a mooring area and an anchorage opposite the club on the west side of the channel. If you drop anchor here, stay close to the channel or well south of the shoal in the middle of the Special Anchorage area. The deepest water is just northwest of G C "7." The chart doesn't accurately portray the heavy shoaling that has diminished the anchorage area. Also, with a strong west wind the channel becomes much narrower as moored boats at the yacht club swing outward. If you want to drop anchor, local mariners recommend simply heading over to Greenwich Cove, or better yet, Captain Harbor.

Powerboats with a vertical clearance of less than 20 feet and drafts of no more than 5 feet can proceed up the Mianus River to the many marinas above the bascule railroad bridge. Sailboats will have to wait for the bridge to open. Sound a long and a short blast of your horn to get the bridgetender's attention, or hail him on VHF 13 between 5 a.m. and 9 p.m. Overnight, the bridge is usually not manned and will be opened only at the Metro-North Railroad's discretion. Unless it's an emergency, you'll have to stay put until morning.

There's not much room to maneuver in the channel since the area near the bridge has silted up. Just upstream of the railroad bridge is the infamous I-95 bridge, part of which fell into the river in 1983, killing several motorists. Note that the

The Ways of the Wind

Every boater knows to watch the wind to plan a day on the water. But what exactly is this invisible force that dictates your cruising plans? Here's a very quick earth science lesson in the ways of the wind.

Air is a gas, made up primarily of oxygen molecules. These molecules have weight—in fact, when you're at sea level, there's about 14 pounds of air above you. This weight is called air pressure. Air is very predictable; it likes to move from areas of high pressure to areas of low pressure. When two air masses of different pressures meet, air molecules rush from the high-pressure mass to the low-pressure mass.

Easy enough, but when and where are high and low pressure areas? They form in response to both global and local forces. Global wind currents move huge air masses around the world much like ocean currents, creating fronts where warm and cold air masses meet. Warm air is "lighter" than cooler air, which is much denser because the molecules are not moving around. Warm air rises and cold air sinks, so a cold front will "push" a rounded air mass below warmer air, while a warm front forms a V-shaped wedge above the cooler air beneath it. You can usually smell a cold front coming, heralded by brisk winds and often a swift shower and followed by crisp blue skies. Warm fronts sneak in more gradually, and their slow, small rains can last for several days along the coast—long after a cold front has blown through. Water vapor is one of the components of air. Warm air can hold more gaseous water than cool air, so as air cools, the water precipitates as dew, rain, or fog (see Maine Weather page 35).

Coastal cruisers pay close attention to local winds. Land warms and cools faster than water, so on sunny days, heat rises and warms the air above the land in the morning. The land air then cools and sinks toward evening. Water, by contrast, absorbs much of the sun's energy and remains at a fairly constant temperature day and night. In the morning, cooler, denser air over water rushes toward the lower pressure over land, producing sea breezes blowing onshore from the water. Toward evening, land air cools and sinks, creating a land breeze blowing offshore from land. Daytime heating is generally stronger than nighttime cooling, so sea breezes are much more intense than land breezes—they're not simply opposites. Any sailor knows that early morning is the best time to catch the breeze, and now you know why.

channel is not a straight one; it bends slightly. Around Riverscape Marina the channel is filling, so stay in the center of the channel.

As you move upriver there are several marinas, including Palmer Point Marina, Beacon Point Marine, and OMA. Each provides transients with slips and great access to the main strip in town.

Greenwich Cove

Entering Greenwich Cove, give R N "2" marking Cove Rock a wide berth (its mooring sometimes drags), and pass north of Pelican Island to starboard. Don't try passing between Pelican Island and Flat Neck Point.

Near the tall tower on the northwestern tip of Flat Neck Point is the Old Greenwich Yacht Club. It's located on Greenwich Point, a town park that requires resident beach cards (of course). The park closes at sunset so it is no good as a landing for reaching town. However, if you just want to row your dink ashore to explore the point, no one will bother you.

In the cove, there's a no-wake speed limit, strictly enforced. You can anchor anywhere among the moored boats of your size, but stay out of the midcove channel. The holding ground in the cove is so good that if you feel you need a mooring, you really need a bigger anchor. Don't go too far north unless you like heeling over on the mud at low tide.

Resist the temptation to go east of Greenwich Island. Numerous grass islands (only a few are indicated on the chart) are barely submerged at high tide until late spring when the grass gets tall enough to show their locations.

Don't be fooled by the natives who take their cruising boats inside of Greenwich Island at high tide. They know where the grass islands are; they've probably studied some of them at really close range—for four or five hours.

Shoreside & Emergency Services
Airport: Westchester, White Plains, NY(914-285-4860)
Coast Guard: Eatons Neck (631-261-6868), or VHF 16
Police, Fire, Ambulance: 911
Taxi: Greenwich Taxi (203-869-6000)
Tow Service:
SEA TOW. —24-Hour Dispatch (800-4SEATOW)
—Southern Connecticut (203-331-0410)
Tow BoatU.S.—24-Hour Dispatch (800-391-4869)
—City Island (718-885-3420)
Train: Amtrak (800-USA-RAIL)
—Metro-North (800-638-7646)

You'd be hard pressed to find a nicer anchorage than Greenwich Cove. Greenwich Island is the small island with trees in the left center of the photo. © Maptech

From Farmers to Financiers

Although Stamford never engaged in battle, it played a vital role in the American Revolution. The city, which was settled in 1641, served as a focal point for the supply, training, and encampment of American soldiers. Also, local men patrolled Long Island Sound in a fleet of whaleboats, harassing the British soldiers. After the war, Stamford's attention shifted first to farming and later to manufacturing.

Beginning with Linus Yale's invention of the cylinder block in 1848, Stamford became a major manufacturing center. Although companies profited, Stamford was never really a place visitors yearned to get to. In the past several decades, though, things have changed: Stamford has become the state's financial capital. Two dozen Fortune 500 companies thrive within city limits, the third-highest concentration in the United States. In fact, Swiss Bank has located its North American headquarters in Stamford, the first major investment bank to leave the confines of Manhattan. These financial developments have changed the face of the city; a diverse cultural scene, vibrant nightlife, and an active waterfront can now be found here.

The Stamford skyline, as seen from Southfield Park along Stamford Harbor's West Branch. © Maptech

Stamford's resurgence has affected the boating scene, too. Just take a look at Stamford's waters on a typical day: sailboats circle the horizon like a school of white-finned sharks as runabouts skim across the water like skipping stones. That doesn't even include all the PWCs and sailboards.

Marine Facilities and Services

All Coast Guard Stations Monitor VHF Channel 16

marinalife.com — Convenient Online Boat Slip Reservations

#	Facility	Phone	Monitors/Working VHF Channel	No. of Transient Berths	Seasonal (S) / Year-round (Y)	Maximum LOA	Approach/Dockside Depth (ft at MLW)	Ramp/Dinghy Dock/Launch Service	110V★ 220V▲ 3 Phase■ Max Amps	Repairs: Propellor/Sail/Rigging	Rail/Lift/Crane/Trailer Capacity (tons)	Diesel/Wood/Fiberglass/Electronics	Gas/Diesel Fuel	Fuel Brand	Marine/Groceries/Ice/Bait	Restrooms/Showers/Laundry/Pumpout	Public Phone/Restaurant/Snack Bar/Hotel/Pool/Tennis/Golf	Mastercard/VISA/Discover/AmEx
1	Stamford Landing Marina (B)	203-965-0065	9/	2/	Y	50	15/9	All	★▲50						I	All	PR	MVA
2	Hathaway, Reiser & Raymond — p. 114	203-324-9581			Y	SAILMAKING & RIGGING								M	R		All
3	Ponus Yacht Club	203-323-7157		3/	Y	33	/4	F		R						R	PR	
4	MacDonald Yacht Rigging	203-323-5431			Y					SRE								MV
5	Brewer Yacht Haven — Inside Back Cover	203-359-4500	9/5	100/	Y	125	11/8.5	FP	★▲		L60	All	GD	Tex	ILC	RSL	P	MVA
6	Harbour Square Marina	203-324-3331	9/	15/	Y	200	15/8	F	★▲100		L	All	GD	Tex	I	All	PR	All
7	Czescik Municipal Marina*	203-977-4645			S	28	5/5									R		
8	Schooner Cove*	203-357-8563			Y	PRIVATE—MEMBERS ONLY												
9	Stamford Yacht Club	203-323-3161			Y													
10	Seaview House Marina — p. 113	203-602-9900	9/71	5/	S	45	8/8	All	★▲50	D	T		GD	Tex	I	RS	PS	All
11	Halloween Yacht Club	203-348-5510	63/	1/	S	36	6/6	FP	★60	D					I	RS	P	
12	Cummings Park Marina*	203-977-4645			S	22	2/2									R		
13	Cove Marina*	203-327-8992			S	22	4/3									R		

Information in these listings is provided by the facilities themselves. An asterisk (*) indicates that the facility did not respond to our most recent requests for information. (B) represents a BOAT/U.S. cooperating marina.

Looking west, with Westcott Cove in the foreground and Stamford Harbor in the background. In Westcott Cove you can see Seaview House Marina, the Halloween Yacht Club, and Cummings Park Marina. © Maptech/James T. Abts

It's hard to imagine Stamford as it once was: a soft-spoken little farm town, with its inhabitants rowing around in whaleboats. From the mini- and mega-yachts floating in the harbor, to the factories, office buildings, condos, and all-around activity ashore, the Stamford of today will make you feel busy, even if you're not.

ACTIVITIES: If you're looking for something to do, you've come to the right place. Stamford moves and shakes from dawn to dusk, and then some. You can get a good feel for the city and its people during its cultural festivals, fairs, and exhibitions. Call the Greater Stamford Chamber of Commerce (203-359-4761) for details on what's going on during your stay. Don't miss the annual Fourth of July seaside celebration, complete with orchestral music and fireworks.

Both the Stamford Center for the Arts (203-358-2305) and the Palace Theatre (203-325-4466) host plays and concerts throughout the year, and are located just five minutes from the water. You can't get any more cultured than a trip to the Stamford Symphony (203-325-1407), or a play at the Stamford Theater Works (203-359-4414). The Whitney Museum of American Art (203-358-7630) hosts exhibits throughout the year.

Stamford is known for its nightlife. Somebody's always having a ball at Bobby Valentine's Sports Gallery (203-348-0010). Named for its owner, who is the New York Mets' manager as well as a Stamford native, the restaurant features a sports-themed menu of pub appetizers, salads, sandwiches, burgers, and pasta. Puff on a cigar at Violet's Dinner Club (203-316-0278) next door, as you listen to live music. Across the street is the Art Bar (203-973-0300), a New York-style bar. It's hip, man, it's happenin', it's... well, you might think it's just plain weird, but it's worth a visit. Head over to the Terrace Restaurant (203-359-1300) to dance the night away.

If you're into ultramodern architecture, take a cab to downtown Stamford and check out some of the shapes, sizes, and colors you'll find there. You'll think a few square blocks of Manhattan were transported 35 miles east.

Stamford doesn't restrict itself to a concrete-laden downtown. The Stamford Museum and Nature Center (203-322-1646) has acres of woodlands, a working farm, and exhibits on the history of the area. For more information on the historical sights around the city, call the Stamford Historical Society (203-329-1183).

Catch a cab to the Mianus River Park to take in the great outdoors. From mountain biking, to walking to fishing, there are miles of wooded trails with streams and hills for you to take advantage of. It's a dog's paradise if Spot is getting a little bored on board. Sterling Farms Public Golf Course (203-461-9090) is also within cab distance.

Racing is in the blood of the yachtsmen here. The Stamford Yacht Club sponsors two races: the Stamford-Denmark Friendship Race, a buoy race in the middle of Long Island Sound, and the Vineyard Race from Stamford to Martha's Vineyard and back each Memorial Day weekend. The Halloween Yacht Club sponsors the Mayor's Cup Race every June.

Though you're in a fine city, remember that The City—New York—is but 40 miles away. Metro-North Railroad (800-638-7646) can get you there in a jiffy.

RESTAURANTS & PROVISIONS: No matter what your stomach growls for, Stamford can supply the goods. The city has a few spots on the water, and though you'll have to take a cab, there are a good number of restaurants inland. Pull your boat up to the Crab Shell (203-967-7229), where you can view the water from the patio and enjoy one of the best seafood restaurants in Connecticut.

You need not travel far if a stop in Stamford lands you at Harbour Square Marina. The Dock House Deli (203-324-3331) offers a selection of hot and cold sandwiches. Next door is the Eclisse Restaurant of Stamford (203-325-3773), for an elegant meal. At Stamford Landing Marina, the Paradise Bar & Grill (203-323-1116) offers good food and a water view.

A Celtic feel may run through you when you step inside Kennedy's (203-325-1131), or the Playwright (203-353-1120); don't be alarmed, you didn't miscalculate your course. The Irish music sets a truly Gaelic atmosphere in downtown Stamford. Oh yes, they'll pull you a pint if you'd like.

Also on Summer Street is a fine Mexican eatery, Hacienda Don Emilio (203-324-0577). Locals rave about the authentic Mexican menu, and accolades pour in from such places as the New York Post and the Stamford Advocate. Amadeus (203-348-7775) is also recommended, serving a cosmopolitan menu with a Viennese flair.

As for provisions, you'll find everything you need within walking distance. Grade A (203-964-9500) can stock the galley with ease.

NAVIGATION & ANCHORAGES: Use ChartKit Region 3, page 26; Maptech™ Waterproof Charts 1 and 16; and Maptech™ electronic and NOAA paper charts 12368 (1:20,000), 12364 (1:40,000), and 12363 (1:80,000). Use tide tables for Bridgeport. High tide at Stamford is 3 minutes later; low tide is 8 minutes later. Multiply height of tide at Brideport by 1.1 for height of tide at Stamford. Mean tidal range is 7.2 feet.

Stamford Harbor is Y-shaped, including a large, relatively exposed outer harbor and two, inner-harbor channels, the East and West branches. The Stamford Harbor breakwaters are about 3.5nm from Greenwich Cove, and 2.7nm from Westcott Cove.

A view of Stamford Harbor's East Branch. © Maptech

Amid all the Fortune 500 talk, recreational boating has its place in Stamford at Seaview House Marina. © Maptech

Seaview House Marina calls Westcott Cove home. © Maptech

From the west, you have a clear shot from Greenwich Point R N "34" to GONG G "1," marking rocks and a wreck. Pass south of GONG G "1" and then into the harbor.

CAUTION: From the east, don't be tempted to cut north of Fl R 6s BELL R "32" at The Cows, 0.8nm south-southeast of Shippan Point. As little as 2 feet of water covers the treacherous rocks that reach for 800 yards north of the bell. Likewise, rocks extend 800 yards south and east of Shippan Point, leaving little room between the two shoals, with no buoys to guide you.

While these rocks are troublesome for yachters, they are a favorite hangout for blackfish, winter flounder, and striped bass—hence, fishermen.

From the entrance between the breakwaters the channel leads about 1nm north through the outer harbor and then divides into the East Branch and the West Branch. The range is the Q 27ft light at the junction of the two branches, below the Iso R 6s 38ft light on Cemetary Point. You should have no trouble shooting straight up to the divide. There is a 6-mph speed limit throughout the harbor. Even with the breakwaters, the outer harbor is exposed to the south and can get uncomfortable during the summer since the prevailing winds are from the southwest.

There are a number of rocks in the outer harbor you'll want to keep an eye on, but there is also room between them to swing at anchor. The average tidal range is 7.2 feet, so if you don't see the rocks now, just wait six hours.

One popular anchorage is just west of Highwater Rock, where the west breakwater offers protection from the southwest. You might also find anchoring room southwest of the Stamford Yacht Club, on the east side of the harbor, south of Rhode Island Rocks. The area is not as well protected as the Highwater Rock area, and is often full of the yacht club's moorings. There is a channel marked with privately maintained red and green buoys from R N "10" east into the club's docks. The club offers launch service until late in the evening, free with a mooring rental.

Stay away from the commercial barge mooring area adjacent to the channel and south of G C "7." A tug headed in there will need to maneuver and may not be able to make way for you.

The West Branch of the harbor is more commercial but has several marinas, one of which—Brewer Yacht Haven—has a fuel dock. The first facility you see to the west is the Southfield Park Marina, which is operated by the city and is used mostly by commercial fishermen. Brewer Yacht Haven West, however, is a complete repair facility that caters to transients. You'll notice condominiums (and dockominiums) to the west as you approach the head of the West Branch. There's also a breakwater protecting the docks at Brewer Yacht Haven West. For all of your sail and rigging needs, head to Hathaway, Reiser & Raymond.

Brewer Yacht Haven East, just inside the East Branch, has all the amenities one could ask for. Farther up the East Branch is the hurricane barrier that is designed to protect Stamford from unusually high storm tides such as those that flooded the town in the hurricane of September 1938. To the chagrin of the facility operators, the hurricane barrier also intimidates some visiting boaters. Fear not; the channel is easy to navigate (90 feet wide at the barrier, carrying 15 feet of water), and it offers the easiest access to downtown Stamford.

The town marina at Czesik Park is for residents only, but transients may tie up for 15 minutes for loading and unloading. At Harbour Square Marina, transient slips, fuel, supplies, and a pump-out station are available.

Westcott Cove

Westcott Cove is a snug, little harbor about 2.7nm from the Stamford breakwaters and 2nm from Long Neck Point. It is the home of the Halloween Yacht Club, Cummings Park Marina, and Seaview House Marina, which has transient slips available.

Looking north over Shippan Point and into Stamford. © Maptech/James T. Abts

From the west, keep south of Fl R 6s R "32" at The Cows, then head north-northeast toward Fl G 4s G "1," southeast of Westcott Cove. Pass east of Fl G 4s G "1" before turning northwest to the channel entrance.

From the east, keep south of the Fl R 4s R "30" at Smith Reef and then shoot between R N "2" at Cove Rocks and Fl G 4s G "1."

Once past Cove Rocks, pick up Fl R 4s R "4" at the entrance to the outer harbor and follow the channel into the marina at Cummings Park. There's been some shoaling in the channel, especially between GC "7" and RN "8," and at low tide, a sandbar nearly blocks the channel 100 feet north of GC "9" and RN "10," opposite the fishing pier. If you draw more than 4 feet, you won't make it past the bar at low tide.

Cummings Park Marina is for residents only. The ramp on the west side of Westcott Cove may be used by anyone, but there's a fee. The float at the end of the ramp is also one of the two emergency medical pick-up points in Stamford (the other is at the Texaco fuel dock at Brewer Yacht Haven West). Boats may use this float for loading or unloading from trailers only. Anyone tying up here is subject to a summons. The same restrictions apply to the

Cove Island Park Marina, about 0.7nm northeast of Westcott Cove in Cove Harbor. Full of small to medium powerboats, Cove Harbor has some 4-foot spots at the entrance but carries 7 feet or more inside. If you draw more than 4 feet, don't try to get in there at low water. The inner harbor is a narrow channel neatly bordered by stone walls.

Shoreside & Emergency Services
Airport:
—Westchester County, White Plains, NY (914-285-4860)
Coast Guard: Eatons Neck (516-261-6868) or VHF 16
Police, Fire, Ambulance: 911
Taxi: Yellow Cab (203-967-3633)
—Stamford Taxi (203-325-2611)
Tow Service:
SEA TOW —24-Hour Dispatch (800-4SEATOW)
—Southern Connecticut (203-331-0410)
Tow BoatU.S. —24-Hour Dispatch (800-391-4869)
—Norwalk (516-624-3483)
Train: Metro-North (800-638-7646)
—Amtrak (800-USA-RAIL)

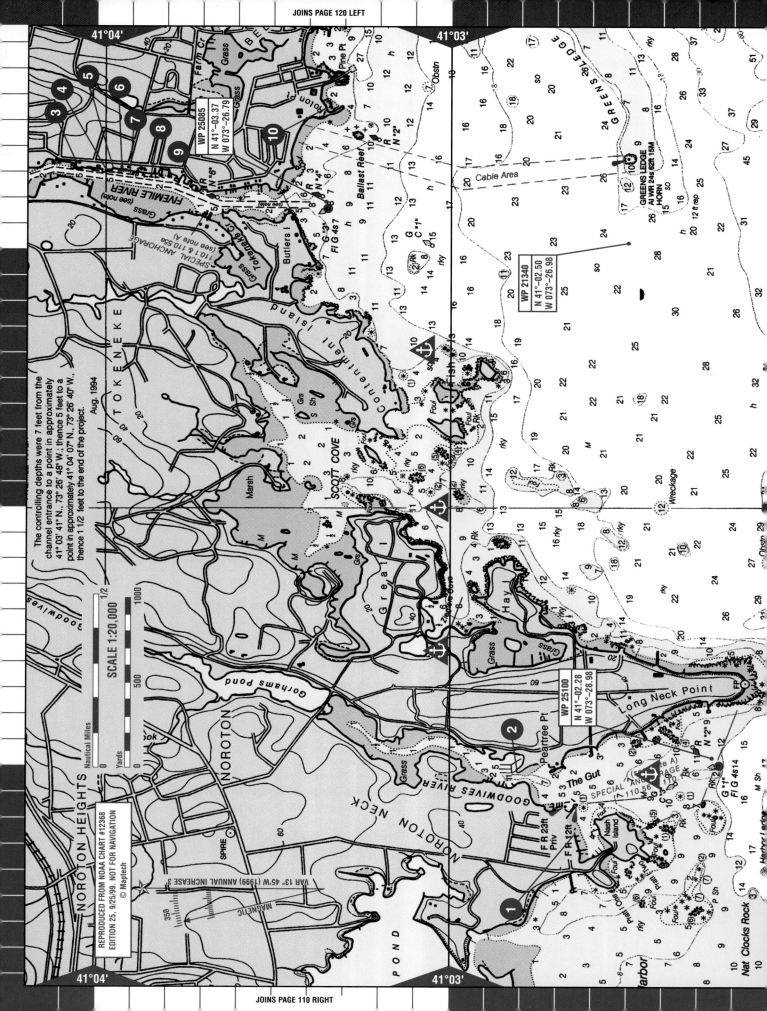

A Big City Neighbor

Darien is a quiet oasis bordered by Stamford and Norwalk, a place of solitude amid all the big-city distractions and chaos. It's a shame not many boaters visit this part of Connecticut's coast. Yes, the harbors are relatively small, and rocks and reefs are more abundant than whitecaps during a nor'easter, but you'll be rewarded with some quiet, pleasant gunkholes and friendly marinas.

The water supplies all the excitement in this area. Like their neighbors in Stamford, the Noroton Yacht Club's members are no strangers to yacht racing. The club is known nationally for its junior and adult sailors, and every Sunday during the summer months the club runs races for its one-design classes. The competition is fierce and the action can get very exciting, setting even the hearts of spectators... well, racing.

Greens Ledge Light, a prominent landmark you'll see when approaching Darien from the east, was built in 1902 as a replacement for the Sheffield Island Lighthouse (built in 1868). Apparently, few boats landed on the island, but many discovered the reef that extends about a mile out from Sheffield Island—something you'll want to keep in mind when cruising this area.

ACTIVITIES: As with any good gunkholing spot, the best things to see and do in Darien involve more seeing than doing. North of Fish Island, east of Zieglers Cove, is a

Masts line the Five Mile River's channel. © Maptech

favorite swimming spot. Plan your activities for high tide unless you're up for pushing your boat through the mud. It's shallow, but the holding ground is sandy. Zieglers Cove is a fine anchorage as well, but enter either cautiously—the area's pretty rocky.

With a little effort you can find interesting spots to visit on land. Go ashore at one of the marinas on the east bank of the Five Mile River and you'll be on Rowayton Avenue (Route 136), which is lined with shops, restaurants, and delis. This is a quiet, low-key place, good for a relaxing walk or bike ride.

Marine Facilities and Services		Number of Transient Berths / Moorings	Seasonal / Yearround	Approach / Dockside Depth in Feet at MLW	Maximum LOA	Hookups: Fresh Water / Phone / Cable TV	110V ★ 220V ▲ 3 Phase ■ Maximum Amps	Rail / Lift / Crane / Trailer: Capacity (tons)	Diesel Wood / Fiberglass / Electronics	Repairs Propellor / Sail / Rigging / Gas	Marine / Groceries / Ice / Bait / LPG / CNG	Gas / Diesel Fuel	Fuel Brand	Public Phone / Restaurant / Snack Bar	Hotel / Pool / Tennis / Golf	Restrooms / Showers / Laundry / Pumpout	Mastercard / VISA / Discover / AmEx
1	Noroton Yacht Club* 203-655-7686	72/	/10	S	60	6/8	F	★20	All	LT2				I		RS	T PS
2	Darien Boat Club 203-655-1927			S													
3	Conel Inc. 203-853-6602			S	60	6/6	F	▲50	R		WE						MV
4	**Five Mile Riverworks** 203-866-4226 p. 119		1/1	Y	40	7/7	F	★▲■50	D	CT35	PGDWE				R		
5	B & G Marine 203-853-9599	16/	/5	Y	40	8/8	F	★30			All						
6	Village Marine 203-866-1739			Y	40	/8	F	★			All			M			MV
7	The Bait Shop, Inc. 203-853-3811 p. 119			Y	30	12/10	F	★	L	C17	PD			MB	R	P	MV
8	The Boatworks Inc. 203-866-9295	68/	5/3	Y	50	6/6	F	★30	D	C45	All	D		M	RP		MV
9	Rowayton Commission Beach Dock 203-852-8095		/1	S	22	7/		D									
10	Roton Point Club 203-838-1606			Y					*PRIVATE—MEMBERS ONLY*								

Information in these listings is provided by the facilities themselves. An asterisk (*) indicates that the facility did not respond to our most recent requests for information. (B) represents a BOAT/U.S. cooperating marina.

For an explanation of all the historic houses and sites you encounter on your journey, head to the Darien Historical Society (203-655-9233) at the Bates-Scofield Homestead. Built in 1737, this authentically furnished colonial homestead has a reference library and gallery.

If Mother Nature doesn't want to cooperate, there's always the big screen. Call the United Artists Darien Playhouse (203-655-7655) for a list of what's showing.

RESTAURANTS & PROVISIONS: You don't have to lose sight of Five Mile River to find a few places to eat. Simply tie up to Rowayton Seafood's (203-838-7473) dock and take your pick of the day's fresh catch. Next door is The Restaurant (203-866-4488), which serves seafood and more seafood. Call ahead and they'll try to make room for your boat on their dock. Rowayton Pizza (203-853-7555), and across the street, Wendall's Deli (203-853-1050), are within walking distance. On Rowayton Avenue, check out River Cat Grille (203-854-0860). For do-it-yourselfers, there's White Bridge Deli (203-655-9533) down the street, after the White Bridge Marina.

Take care of your provisioning needs at Rowayton Market (203-852-0011) or head to The Bait Shop (203-853-3811) for any marine hardware and accessory needs. They also have a good selection of fishing equipment in case that big one snapped your line and took your best lure. A great spot for marine supplies and nautical gifts is Boatworks Boatique & Marine Supplies (203-866-9295). For more eating options, take a cab to Boston Post Road, the main strip in Darien.

Fleet Bank and First Union have ATMs eager to spit out money so you can go to Palmer's (203-655-2077), a grocery store. If you're sick of picking out the day's wardrobe from a pile, go to Darien Tailors & Cleaners (203-655-9086) to tidy up your fashion options.

NAVIGATION & ANCHORAGES: Use ChartKit Region 3, page 26; Maptech™ Waterproof Charts 1 and 16; and Maptech™ electronic and NOAA paper charts 12368 (1:20,000), 12364 (1:40,000), and 12363 (1:80,000). Use tide tables for Bridgeport. High tide at Greens Ledge is 2 minutes earlier; low tide is 1 minute earlier. Multiply height of tide at Bridgeport by 1.1 for the height of tide at Greens Ledge. Mean tidal range is 7.2 feet.

The tip of Long Neck Point, marking the outer approach to the Goodwives River, is 3.7nm from the entrance to Stamford Harbor. The Greens Ledge Light off Sheffield Island is 1.6nm from Long Neck Point. From Fl R 4s BELL R "28C" at Cable and Anchor Reef, a course of 340°m for 2.2nm will take you to the Greens Ledge Light (Al W R 24s 62ft 15M HORN) and the approach to the Five Mile River.

Noroton Harbor, labeled "The Gut" or Goodwives River on your chart, has a crowded anchorage between Noroton Neck and Long Neck Point, marked by a prominent house and a flagpole.

From the west, keep well south of Fl R 4s R "30" marking Smith Reef. Don't cut inside the Smith Reef buoy; every year several boats get hung up there. Once well east of the reef, head for the east side of Fl G 4s G "1" off Long Neck Point.

CAUTION: Favor R N "2" to avoid the 6-foot spot to the west, especially if you're in a deep-draft boat.

Looking north into the Five Mile River. To the right you'll find the northern end of Sheffield Harbor and Wilson Cove. © Maptech/James T. Abts

From the south, you have a clear shot up to Fl G 4s G "1" so long as you stay a minimum of 400 yards off Long Neck Point. Between Nash Island and the yacht club is a small and crowded but well-protected mooring area.

From the east, you'll have to contend with Greens Ledge, extending about 1nm west-southwest from Sheffield Island. Don't think of cutting between the light (Al W R 24s 62ft 15M HORN) and Sheffield Island without local knowledge. The closer to Sheffield Island, the more hazardous it becomes with rocks, including Old Baldy— he claims his share of boats annually.

NOTE: Fl R 4s R "2A" has been added to the northern side of Greens Ledge, east of the lighthouse.

Keep in mind, the entire area west of Long Neck Point to Nash Island and up to the Darien Boat Club is a special anchorage, so moored or anchored boats will not be lighted. There is seldom space to anchor except near the tip of Long Neck Point.

Around the eastern side of Long Neck Point is the popular Zieglers Cove, named for the owners of an enormous estate that surrounds it. North of Hay Island, it's a gem of a gunkhole except in a strong easterly. To get to Zieglers Cove from Long Neck Point, go 0.8nm north-northeast and look for the exposed rock off the east side of Hay Island. Head due north for 200 yards past the exposed rock before turning west into the cove, where there's about 6 to 9 feet (mlw) waiting for you. The south side of Great Island is lined with a sheer rock cliff; boaters traditionally enter Zieglers Cove along this stretch, where there's good water.

The marshes and wooded shores of Scotts Cove make it a beautiful gunkhole if you draw less than 3 feet. The chart shows as much as 9 feet of water due east of Great Island, but be sure to stay well off Great Island because of the nasty rocks on its east side. Scott Cove is a nice spot to explore in your dinghy, and we're told you can go all the way up to the north end of Contentment Island.

Both Ziegler and Scotts Cove are beautiful places to dinghy around, but local knowledge is recommended to enter either.

The approaches to the Five Mile River from the east and west are pretty straightforward. Buoy G C "1," about 0.3nm south of Butlers Island, marks a nasty rock 2 feet under the surface—stay east of this buoy. The narrow, but well marked, channel up the river shoals the farther you go up, but carries 5 feet mlw except in the extreme northern end. The channel begins at Fl G 4s G "3," paired with R N "4."

On the east bank of the river in Rowayton, the protection is excellent. Although the river itself is well marked, the channel does get a bit thin. A nice anchorage spot is behind Fish Island, at the tip of Contentment Island. The Five Mile River Commission (203-852-8095), offers three transient moorings (fore and aft) near R N "6." They're available on a first-come, first-served basis. Across from the moorings is a community dock where you can access Rowayton.

There are several full-service facilities in the river for small and medium-sized craft. Five Mile Riverworks (203-866-4266) and The Bait Shop (203-853-3811) do repairs and refit work. Both have transient slips and moorings available, but you may want to check ahead of time as space can be scarce. The lines of moored boats on the west side of the channel make turning a medium-sized boat difficult. It goes without saying there's no room to anchor.

Shoreside & Emergency Services
Airport: Bridgeport Sikorsky Memorial (203-576-7498)
Bus: Greyhound Bus Lines, Stamford (203-348-6200)
Coast Guard: Eatons Neck (631-261-6868) or VHF 16 —New Haven (203-468-4450) or VHF 16
Police, Fire, Ambulance: 911
Radio Telephone: MARITEL VHF 27
Taxi: Darien Yellow Cab (203-655-8779)
Tow Service:
SEA TOW. —24-Hour Dispatch (800-4SEATOW)
—Southern Connecticut (203-331-0410)
Tow BoatU.S. —24-Hour Dispatch (800-391-4869)
—Norwalk (516-624-3483)

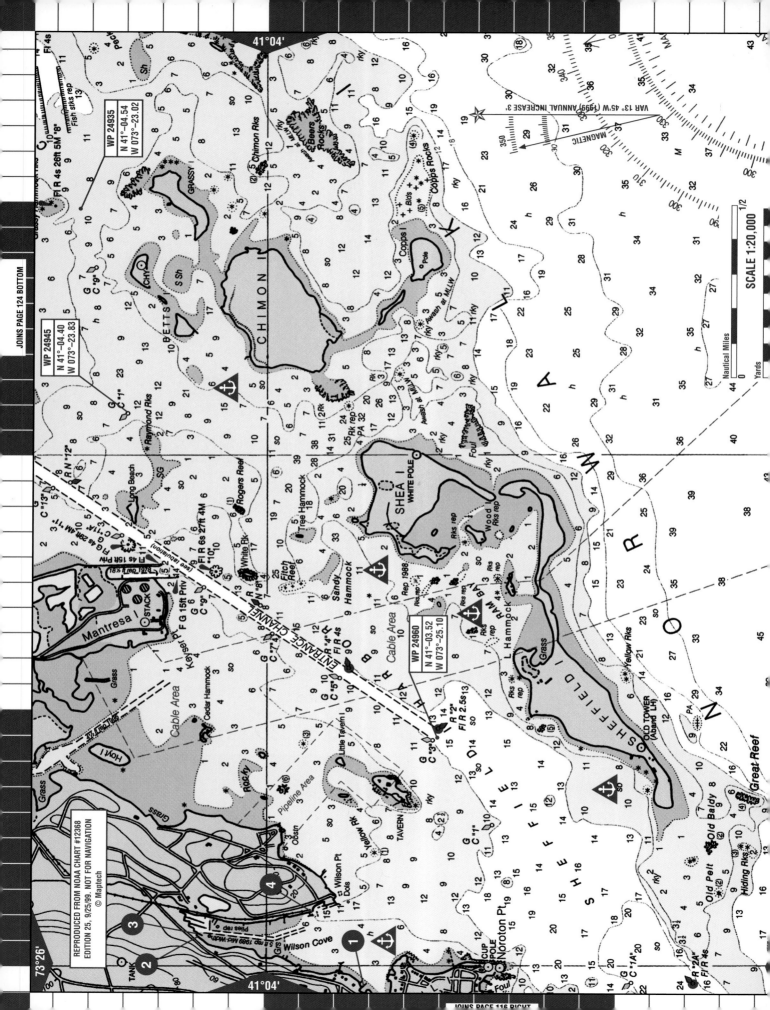

Birding Paradise

Move over boaters, these Norwalk Islands are for the birds. Since 1984, Sheffield Island and Chimon Island have been the center of the Stewart B. McKinney National Wildlife Refuge. Consisting of 145 acres of islands and coastlands in Connecticut, the refuge also includes Milford Point and Faulkner Island, off Guilford. Chimon's 70 acres support the most important heron rookery in the state and one of the three largest colonies of wading birds in the northeast.

Developers have always salivated over the islands' resort potential. A few lavish clubhouses were attempted, but they were doomed by storms, logistical problems, and a lack of fresh water. Chimon Island is the only one with a freshwater supply, but the creation of the McKinney Refuge put an end to any thought of building a resort. Tavern Island, once called Pilot Island, got its name during Prohibition, when it was reputedly a speakeasy. Now, along with Sheffield Island, it's a favorite watering hole for herds of seahorses. Of the island's many owners, none was more famous than Billy Rose, a champion shorthander and typist who wrote and produced Broadway musicals. Rose went to the altar many times; local savants say that there is a statue on Tavern Island for each of Billy Rose's five wives, one of whom was comedienne-singer-actress Fanny Brice. He later made a fortune as a Wall Street stockbroker, owning more AT&T stock than any other person.

Legend says Goose Island is bare because it was stripped of vegetation by treasure hunters madly searching for Captain Kidd's buried booty. Of course, there's not an island in Long Island Sound without a Captain Kidd legend attached to it. Truth is he wasn't a very good pirate, nor did he spend much time in the Sound. The moral: if someone wants to sell you a tiny island with some of Captain Kidd's treasure buried on it, offer to swap it for the Brooklyn Bridge.

Just north of Goose Island you'll spot the solar-powered Pecks Ledge Lighthouse, built in 1906 and said to be haunted by the ghost of one of the keepers. During World War II both the Pecks Ledge and Greens Ledge lighthouses were

These boats call Wilson Cove home. © Maptech

manned by Coast Guard personnel on the lookout for German submarines.

ACTIVITIES: Most of the 16 islands are privately owned, but several of the larger ones are open to public exploration. Nestle into one of the fine anchorages found among the islands, bars, coves, and bays, and enjoy.

Sheffield Island, about 1nm east of Greens Ledge Light, is the westernmost of the Norwalk Islands. Most of the island

	Marine Facilities and Services		Number of Transient Berths / Moorings	Monitors / Working VHF Channel	Approach / Dockside Depth in Feet at MLW	Hookups: Fresh Water / Phone / Cable TV	110V ★ 220V ▲ 3 Phase ■ Maximum Amps	Seasonal / Year-round	Maximum LOA	Ramp / Dinghy Dock / Launch Service	Rail / Lift / Crane / Trailer Capacity (tons)	Repairs: Propellor / Sail / Rigging / Electronics	Diesel / Wood / Fiberglass	Marine / Groceries / Ice / Bait / LPG / CNG	Gas / Diesel Fuel	Fuel Brand	Restrooms / Showers / Laundry / Pumpout	Public Phone / Pool / Tennis / Golf	Hotel / Restaurant / Snack Bar	Mastercard / VISA / Discover / AmEx
1	Rowayton Yacht Club	203-854-0807	68/	/10	S				F			L					RS		P	MV
2	Wilson Cove Yacht Club	203-853-8463			Y				PRIVATE—MEMBERS ONLY											
3	Wilson Cove Marina	203-866-7020			Y	55	6/6	F	★50		D	LC25	All				RS		P	
4	Norwalk Yacht Club	203-866-6624			Y				PRIVATE—MEMBERS ONLY											

All Coast Guard Stations Monitor VHF Channel 16

Information in these listings is provided by the facilities themselves. An asterisk (*) indicates that the facility did not respond to our most recent requests for information. (B) represents a BOAT/U.S. cooperating marina.

is part of the McKinney Refuge, but the Norwalk Seaport Association (203-838-9444) owns the old lighthouse—which is now a museum listed in the National Register of Historic Places—on the western end. Tour the lighthouse and view some of the workings and nautical artifacts collected by the group. Picnic tables, an old (but still functioning) hand-pump well, and other facilities are on the grounds. Pull up to the docks on the north side of the island for mooring instructions.

The city of Norwalk owns Grassy Island, Shea Island, and the beach on the west side of Chimon Island. Each is open to the public for boating, swimming, and picnicking from dawn to dusk. You'll find a popular beach and camping area along the eastern shore of Shea. Call the department of Parks and Recreation (203-854-7806) for permit information. The area is marked by a tall white flagpole, which appears on the chart. On Sheffield and Chimon (part of the Stuart B. McKinney National Wildlife Refuge), hiking is prohibited during the nesting season (April 15 to August 15).

Putting in a long day at Calf Pasture Beach. © Maptech

RESTAURANTS & PROVISIONS: You stocked your galley before you left, didn't you? If not, you're out of luck in the islands. For restaurant and provisioning suggestions in Norwalk Harbor, see the Norwalk Harbor chapter.

NAVIGATION & ANCHORAGES: Use ChartKit Region 3, pages 26 and 27; Maptech™ Waterproof Charts 1 and 16; and Maptech™ electronic and NOAA paper charts 12368 (1:20,000), 12364 (1:40,000), and 12363 (1:80,000). Use tide tables for Bridgeport. High tide at Greens Ledge is 2 minutes earlier; low tide is 1 minute earlier. Multiply height of tide at Bridgeport by 1.1 for height of tide at Greens Ledge. Mean tidal range is 7.2 feet.

Greens Ledge Light (Al W R 24s 62ft 15M HORN) marks the western end of the Norwalk Islands. The light is 5.2nm from the entrance to Stamford Harbor and 8nm from the entrance to the Saugatuck River. Eatons Neck Point is 5.6nm away.

From Fl R 4s BELL R "28C" at Cable and Anchor Reef, a course of about 340°m for 2.2nm will take you to Greens Ledge Light and the approach to Sheffield and Norwalk Harbors.

The eastern approach to Cockenoe Harbor—and hence Norwalk Harbor—goes past Peck Ledge Light (Fl 4s 61ft 7M) just north of Goose Island. Even if you're coming from Westport or Southport, the only safe approach to Cockenoe Harbor from the east is to go east of Georges Rock Fl G 2.5s G "1" and Fl R 2.5s BELL R "24," then south of R N "2" off Cockenoe Shoal. Between any of these buoys and Cockenoe Island there are dangerous rocks and shoals. Once past R N "2," head northwest for Peck Ledge Light, staying north of the light and GONG G "5" and south of R N "4."

After passing Peck Ledge Light, turn hard west-southwest and head for Fl R 4s 26ft 5M "8" at Grassy Hammock Rocks. Keep a keen lookout for the many oyster stakes and lobster pots. Leave G C "9" and Betts Island to the south, and make sure you continue toward G C "11" marking Raymond Rocks. Then make a dogleg turn to the northwest toward the Q R 26ft 4M "14" light off Round Beach. Pass south of the light and then turn north up the main channel. Watch out for the shallows southeast of the light and northwest of G C "11."

CAUTION: Avoid using the east approach in reduced visibility. Even when it's clear, assign a lookout. The aids to navigation can be hard to spot, and shallow spots are abundant.

Although there is no speed limit around the islands, be on constant lookout for swimmers, windsurfers, and daysailers. For information on Cockenoe Island, the easternmost of the Norwalk Islands, see the chapter on Westport and the Saugatuck River.

To the west, Wilson Cove is the first shoreside anchorage east of Greens Ledge Light (Al W R 24s 62ft 15M HORN). The cove is lined with beautiful homes, two yacht clubs, and a marina, but it doesn't take much wind to make it uncomfortable there.

The area just to the north and west of Sheffield and Shea islands makes a convenient stopover anchorage for those traveling along the Sound, since it's easily reached and not far off the main channel. It's exposed to the southwest, but the holding ground is good. For best results, drop a Danforth anchor.

Don't cut between Sheffield Island and the Greens Ledge Light at low tide. The ledge (rock, not sand) goes all the way from the island out to the light, but many boats pass over the ledge close to the east side of the light. Fl R 4s R "2A" marks this ledge. If you pass to the west of it, you should have at least 7 feet at mlw.

Looking southwest over the Norwalk Islands. Chimon Island is in the center. © Maptech/James T. Abts

There are no marinas on the islands, so if you're looking for a slip, head to Norwalk Harbor. The entrance channel for Norwalk Harbor begins 400 yards southeast of Tavern Island at G C "3" and Fl R 2.5s R "2." The channel is also used by oyster boats, coastal oil tankers, tugs, and barges, along with all the pleasure boats. Give a wide berth to Fl G 4s 29ft 4M "11" east of Manresa Island, because of a shoal reaching out from its base. Don't stray too far over to the right side of the channel as the shoal area off Long Beach (opposite G C "11A") extends out to the limit of the dredged channel. The red lights on top of the tall stacks of the United Illuminating Company power plant on Manresa Island are excellent landmarks and can be seen for many miles. Keep a lookout for the tugs and barges maneuvering in and out of the power plant, as it is operational year-round. Note that the 6-mph speed limit for Norwalk Harbor begins at Fl R 6s 27ft 4M "10," just south of the power plant.

About 0.4nm northeast of Fl G 4s 29ft 4M "11," the channel turns to the north and then to the northwest before dividing into two channels at Fitch Point. For more information on Norwalk Harbor and the entrance channel north of Manresa Island, see the following chapter.

To visit Shea Island, formerly Ram Island, anchor offshore and take your dinghy in. The easiest dinghy approach is from the north, followed by northeast, southeast, and finally south, by way of Wood Island.

The area between Shea Island and Chimon Island is known as the "Middle Passage." Like the Middle Ages, this is not something that you would want to go through. It is narrow, unbuoyed, and filled with rocks. Many of the local boaters zip between the two islands in their runabouts, but they already know where the rocks are and use them to scrape the barnacles off their hulls. If you want to try it in your dink, head north for the sand bar on the west side of Copps Island and turn to the northwest, clearing the reefs off the southwest side of Chimon. Go on a rising tide and go slow.

If you've brought rod and reel, there's good fishing all over the Norwalk Islands' coves, reefs, and tidal rips. Blackfish and flounder flourish on the south side of Copps Island. Copps Island itself is privately owned and is none too inviting because of water rats. For bass, try Brown's Point and Cockenoe and Sheffield islands.

CAUTION: If you're cruising outside the Norwalk Islands, be sure to keep well away from Copps Island. Copps Rocks extend almost 0.5nm to the southeast.

When approaching Chimon Island from the north, stay at least 350 yards west of Betts Island and the same distance west of Chimon. Put G C "11" at Raymond Rocks dead astern and aim for the flagpole on Shea Island until you're due west of the beach. Then make for land. This way you shouldn't go aground on the shoals that surround most of the island. The area northwest of Chimon is also a nice anchorage, well protected from easterlies.

Shoreside & Emergency Services
Coast Guard:
—Eatons Neck (631-261-6868) or VHF 16
Police, Fire, Ambulance: 911
Tow Service:
SEA TOW —24-Hour Dispatch (800-4SEATOW)
—Southern Connecticut (203-331-0410)
Tow BoatU.S.—24-Hour Dispatch (800-391-4869)
—Norwalk (203-855-7918)

Bountiful Bivalves

Connecticut, Norwalk especially, has always been on the vanguard of the oyster industry. Legends exist about foot-long oysters with five-pound meats, growing in beds sizeable enough to restrict navigation. For the last half of the 19th century and for two decades into the 20th, the oyster was the most popular shellfish in the United States. Connecticut was blessed with natural oyster beds spanning many square miles, and it held the crown as the bivalve's major producer. Those of you who thought that these tasty mollusks were under-appreciated, will be happy to know that Connecticut adopted the oyster as its state shellfish in 1898.

ACTIVITIES: From festivals to art galleries, there's a whole lot to see and do in Norwalk. The Seaport Association sponsors Norwalk's biggest event of the year: the Norwalk Oyster Festival, held the first weekend after Labor Day. The festival features tall ships, continuous entertainment, arts & crafts shows, international food, boat-building competitions, and oysters. Norwalk constantly competes with the town of Milford as the unofficial "Oyster Capital of Fairfield County." While you're traveling along the coast, you might want to stop in on both and be the judge yourself.

There are many other events going on during the summer in South Norwalk, including the SoNo Arts Celebration, featuring sculpture, painting, storytelling,

This light leads the way to Sono Seaport Seafood. © Maptech

	Marine Facilities and Services	DOCKAGE							SERVICES				SUPPLIES & AMENITIES							
1	South Norwalk Boat Club	203-866-6624			Y						*PRIVATE—MEMBERS ONLY*										
2	Total Marine	203-838-3210			Y	60	8/8		F	★30		LC35	All			I	RSL		P	MV
3	≋REX Marine Center — Since 1936 — p. 127	203-866-5555	9/72	2/	Y	45	10/6		F	★30		L35	PGDWFE			MI	RSP		P	All
4	INFLATABLE BOATS p. 129	203-838-6990			Y						*INFLATABLE BOAT SALES & SERVICE*										
5	New England Fiberglass Repair p. 128	203-866-1690			Y			All	★▲■		RLC	All		GD	MGIBL	All		All		
										FIBERGLASS STRUCTURAL REPAIRS—POWER & SAIL											
6	Ischoda Yacht Club	203-853-8886			Y						*PRIVATE—MEMBERS ONLY*										
7	NORWEST MARINE p. 129	203-853-2822	68/		Y	40	/4		F	★30		LC40	PGDFE		GD	MI			P	All
8	Maurice Marine	203-866-5169	9/68	2/	Y	30	3/3		F	★30	D	C5	PG			I				
9	Sono Seaport Seafood	203-854-9483		6/	Y	40	20/6													MVA
10	Maritime Aquarium at Norwalk*	203-852-0700			Y											R			PS	MV
11	United Marine Inc.	203-853-1174	69/		Y	50	10/8		F	★30		C50	All			M	R			MVA

Facilities continued on next page...

Looking west over Norwalk Harbor's entrance. Norwalk Cove Marina is in the foreground.
© Maptech/James T. Abts

Sound side of the Point you can fish away the day on the pier. For those seeking something more physical, the water off Calf Pasture Point is ideal sailboarding territory.

Farther up Norwalk Harbor, the Maritime Aquarium at Norwalk (203-852-0700) is a place you won't mind spending the entire day. You'll find exhibits on boatbuilding and Connecticut history, lots of hands-on demonstrations, aquaria showing the ecosystems of Long Island Sound and the Atlantic, and tanks filled with seals, sharks, otters, and fish from the Sound. Don't miss the twice-daily feedings at the shark tank and seal colony; the center also runs short documentary films on its IMAX screen.

Hop aboard the Aquarium's *R/V Oceanic* for a hands-on, three-hour cruise. You'll learn all about the Sound and get to meet its residents up close—starfish, flounder, crabs, or whatever the net drag brings up. Inquire about other educational offerings for children and adults at the Aquarium.

The restored SoNo shopping district features everything from art galleries, fashion clothing stores, antique shops, bookstores, and boutiques to a wide variety of restaurants and delicatessens. The restoration of the area

dance, all types of music and fine food, and even a block party. There's also the Norwalk Boat Show held mid-September at Norwalk Cove Marina. Call Coastal Fairfield County Convention & Visitors Bureau (800-866-7925) for a complete summer schedule.

While down by Norwalk Cove Marina and Calf Pasture Point, take advantage of the outdoors. Near the marina, putt your way over to the miniature golf course, and on the

	Marine Facilities and Services		Number of Transient Berths / Monitors / Working VHF Channel	Approach / Dockside Depth in Feet at MLW	Seasonal / Year-round Moorings	Maximum LOA	Hookups: Fresh Water / Phone / Cable TV	110V ★ 220V ▲ 3 Phase ■ Maximum Amps	Ramp / Dinghy Dock / Launch Service	Rail / Lift / Crane / Trailer: Capacity (tons)	Repairs: Propellor / Sail / Rigging / Electronics	Diesel / Wood / Fiberglass	Marine / Groceries / Ice / Bait / LPG / CNG	Restrooms / Showers / Laundry / Pumpout	Gas / Diesel Fuel	Fuel Brand	Public Phone / Restaurant / Snack Bar	Hotel / Pool / Tennis / Golf	Mastercard / VISA / Discover / AmEx
12	Norwalk Boat Club*	203-853-8801			Y				PRIVATE—MEMBERS ONLY										
13	St. Ann Club Marina	203-853-8777			Y				PRIVATE—MEMBERS ONLY										
14	Oyster Bend Marina*	203-854-6666	13/	12/	Y	100	8/8	All	▲50	R					GI	RSL		P	
15	SoNo Wharf*	203-855-9270			Y														
16	Conn. Fireboat Corp.*				Y				DESIGNERS & BUILDERS OF COMMERCIAL VESSELS										
17	Norwalk Visitors Dock	203-849-8823	9/	20/2	S	60	10/6	F			All						RP	P	
18	Pastime Boat Club	203-853-8613			Y				PRIVATE—MEMBERS ONLY										
19	East Norwalk Boating & Yacht Club	203-853-8696			Y				PRIVATE—MEMBERS ONLY										
20	Bloom Bros. Marine	203-838-9273			S	30	6/6				C5		G		G		I	R	
21	Shore and Country Club	203-838-7507			Y				PRIVATE—MEMBERS ONLY										
22	**NORWALK COVE MARINA** INC. p. 127	203-838-5899	9/72	10/	Y	170	12/10	F	★▲■100	D	LC160	PRGDWFE	GD	Gulf	MI	All		PR	All

Information in these listings is provided by the facilities themselves. An asterisk (*) indicates that the facility did not respond to our most recent requests for information. (B) represents a BOAT/U.S. cooperating marina.

has left intact the brick façades and gas lamps of the old district, which add to the atmosphere. At Shenanigan's Nite Club (203-853-0142) on Washington Street you'll find live entertainment every night, including well-known national performers.

One of the most intriguing sights in Norwalk is the enormous Lockwood-Mathews Mansion (203-838-1434). The 50-room mansion is the ultimate in Victorian architecture. To some it's beautiful; others would call it extravagant or gaudy, but everyone agrees it's unique. Back in 1868 it cost $2 million to build. Saving it from the wrecking ball, the city acquired the abode in 1938 and reopened it as a museum. Though the mansion is within

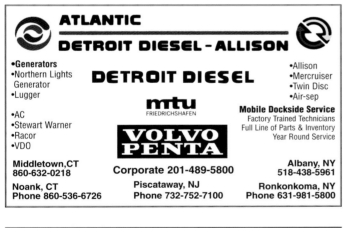

walking distance of the marinas in South Norwalk, you might be better off calling a cab to get there—Route 1 is pretty busy.

RESTAURANTS & PROVISIONS: When your stomach's rumbling tells you it's time to refuel, there's no need to go farther than SoNo's Washington Street. This veritable Restaurant Row includes the aforementioned Shenanigan's and El Acapulco (203-853-6217), where you'll find a Mexican dish or two. Amberjacks Coastal Grill (203-853-4332) serves avant-garde seafood, but if you're looking for Italian, Pasta Nostra (203-854-9700) will be more to your liking. And then there's Rattlesnake Southwestern Grill (203-852-1716). Just take a walk down the street and let your stomach lead the way.

Nearby, just before the bascule bridge you'll spot an ornamental lighthouse to the west, luring you to SoNo Seaport Seafood (203-854-9483) where you can purchase fresh seafood or enjoy dockside dining. SoNo Seaport has a few slips for diners, but you can expect a wait. Just to the south, the Ischoda Yacht Club (203-853-8886) serves American fare in a casual atmosphere.

If you're tied up at the Visitors Dock or have come by launch, there are lots of other choices from fancy to humble in the seaport and Maritime Center area. Across the street from Veterans Park is Papa's Pizza Café (203-831-9921), for California-style, designer pizza. In the same block are the basics—Italian at Abruzzi Kitchen (203-838-6776), and American at the Oceanview Café (203-854-0770), serving breakfast and lunch only.

While at Norwalk Cove Marina, dine on dishes of chicken and seafood at the Sunset Grille (203-866-4177).

NAVIGATION & ANCHORAGES: Use ChartKit Region 3, pages 26 and 83; Maptech™ Waterproof Charts 1 and 16; and Maptech™ electronic and NOAA paper charts 12368 (1:20,000), 12364 (1:40,000), and 12363 (1:80,000). Use tide tables for Bridgeport. High tide at South Norwalk is 9 minutes later; low tide is 15 minutes later. Use height of tide at Bridgeport for height of tide at South Norwalk. Mean tidal range is 7.1 feet.

The main approach channel to Norwalk Harbor begins at Fl R 2.5s R "2" between Sheffield and Tavern islands, about 1.7nm southwest of Norwalk Harbor itself and 6.8nm northeast of the Stamford breakwaters. Huntington Bay on Long Island is 8.3nm to the south.

There are two approaches to Norwalk Harbor: from the west via Greens Ledge Light and from the east via Peck Ledge Light. The commercial channel from Greens Ledge Light is much easier and is the only approach you should use if you're unfamiliar with the area, when visibility is restricted, or if you're coming in at night.

NOTE: Both approaches go through the Norwalk Islands. See the previous chapter for a complete description of the passages through the islands.

From Q R 26ft 4M "14," west of Round Beach, the dredged channel is well marked and easy to follow. Be careful not to cut the corner passing G C "13," G C "15," and G C "17," as there is little water outside the channel. Charles Creek has undergone extensive dredging (to at least 8 feet) to accommodate hundreds of boats. Norwalk Cove Marina, a large, full-service yard with transient slips available, is the only commercial facility in Charles Creek. The docks farther up the creek belong to condo developments.

To get into Charles Creek, turn northeast just before G C "17" and follow the channel, staying in the middle between the bulkheads and docks to the east and the breakwaters to the west. Although the harbor is wide, it is shallow except at the main dock and in the channel.

Half a mile north of the entrance to Charles Creek is the East Norwalk Channel (unnamed on the chart), with its entrance marked by Fl G 2.5s 29ft 4M "1" and R N "2" in about 6 feet of water. There are several small-boat facilities up the channel. At Bloom Brothers Marine or Overton's you can rent small skiffs for fishing.

Continuing up the main channel you'll find a number of marinas and yacht clubs. Rex Marine Center, to the west, is one of the area's largest marine stores as well as a full-service marina. Also here are Inflatable Boats and New England Fiberglass Repair. Just to the north, Norwest Marine has plenty of transient berths, and can fill you up with gas or diesel. Call on American Yacht Services (203-838-7797) on Water Street for any repair needs you have or performance upgrades you want. Just before the Washington Street Bridge, on the east side, is the Norwalk Visitors Dock, offering 350 feet of floating concrete docks for transient boats only.

Once you've passed the Maritime Aquarium and the Metro-North railroad bridge, there are more choices for the transient in search of a slip. You'll find at least 7.5 feet of water in the channel nearly all the way up the harbor. Keep an eye out for the occasional tug or barge heading for the warehouses, stone docks, and oil depot at the head of the harbor. (The tugs and barges maintain the channel by churning up the bottom and keeping it from silting up).

Shoreside & Emergency Services
Airport: Sikorsky Memorial (203-576-7498)
Bus: Wheels Bus (203-852-0000)
Coast Guard: Eatons Neck (631-261-6868)
Harbormaster: (203-849-8823)
Police, Fire, Ambulance: 911
—Marine Police (203-838-0111)
Taxi: Yellow Cab (203-853-1267)
Tow Service:
SEA TOW —24-Hour Dispatch (800-4SEATOW)
—Southern Connecticut (203-331-0410)
Tow BoatU.S.—24-Hour Dispatch (800-391-4869)
—Norwalk (203-855-7918)
Train: Amtrak (800-USA-RAIL)
—Metro-North (800-638-7646)

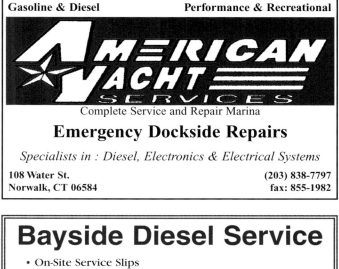

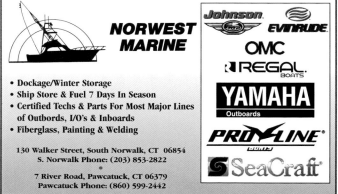

A Celebrated Retreat

Westport is the getaway of getaways, so to speak. Consider that celebrities such as Paul Newman, Ron Howard, Martha Stewart, and Kathie Lee Gifford live in Westport, trying to escape the non-stop buzz of the Big Apple. It's a celebrity outpost, of sorts.

In the fervent days of the Revolution, Westport was an outpost of a different kind. Approximately two thousand British Redcoats disembarked from warships at the mouth of the Saugatuck River, then landed at Compo Beach and marched inland to raid the supply depot at Danbury. Saugatuck later became a favorite launching place for retaliatory raids by the Colonists.

Such a hostile demeanor didn't last, and early in the 20th century Westport was little more than a few shops and homes along Boston Post Road. The town's artists and writers congregated at the Manor House, a local hotel. Over the years, Westport has managed to retain its charm despite the urban sprawl nearby. Note the very striking, palatial homes that you'll get a look at as you cruise up the lower Saugatuck River.

Another aspect that sets this "Gold Coast" town apart is its population of wacky watercraft. Witness the Great Race Festival, held each July on the Saugatuck River. Recent years' entries have included a huge, bubbly bar of Ivory Soap, a raft of balloons, and a "houseboat" (a shed atop a catamaran). The vivid vessels are judged on creativity, originality in overall design, appearance, and propulsion technique, with prizes ranging up to $1000 cash.

If you have the time, try to make par at Longshore Club Park's 18-hole golf course. © Maptech

ACTIVITIES: There's a reason why many of America's rich and famous call Westport at least a part-time home: relaxation comes easily here. Parks and beaches line the coast and are easily accessible, depending on where you decide to come ashore.

Sherwood Island State Park (203-226-6983) is located east of Compo Beach. With 218 acres of sandy beach, marshes, linden and maple trees, and a large pavilion with an observation deck, the park will entertain your entire crew. Established in 1914, Sherwood Island was the first state park in Connecticut and one of the first in the nation. Landing at the beach is not permitted.

	Marine Facilities and Services		Number of Transient Berths / Monitors / Working VHF Channel	Seasonal / Yearround Moorings	Approach / Dockside Depth in Feet at MLW	Maximum LOA	110V ★ 220V ▲ 3 Phase ■ Maximum Amps Hookups: Fresh Water / Phone / Cable TV	Ramp / Dinghy Dock / Launch Service Rail / Lift / Crane / Trailer Capacity (tons)	Repairs: Propellor / Sail / Rigging / Gas Diesel / Wood / Fiberglass / Electronics	Gas / Diesel Fuel	Fuel Brand	Marine / Groceries / Ice / Bait / LPG / CNG Restrooms / Showers / Laundry / Pumpout	Public Phone / Restaurant / Snack Bar Hotel / Pool / Tennis / Golf	Mastercard / VISA / Discover / AmEx
1	Sprite Island Yacht Club	203-866-7879	9/	S					*PRIVATE—MEMBERS ONLY*			I	S	
2	Cedar Point Yacht Club*	203-266-7411	78/	5/	Y	50	11/6	F ★▲30	RD	T			I	RS	T	PS
3	Saugatuck Harbor Yacht Club	203-227-3607	71/	5/	S	60		F ★▲50	*PRIVATE*		GD		I	All	P	P
4	Coastwise Marina	203-226-0735			Y	30	8/10	F	D	WF			MI	R		All
5	Bridgebrook Marina	203-454-8900			Y											
5	Northrop's Landing	203-226-1915	8/	4/4	S	40	6/6	F ★30	All	T	All			R		P
6	E.R. Strait Marina	203-226-3688			S	35	6/6	F ★30			G	Tex		R		P	All
7	Compo Yacht Basin	203-227-9136	16/11	6/	Y	47	9/9	F ★30	RD	T	G	Tex	I	RP		PS	All

Information in these listings is provided by the facilities themselves. An asterisk (*) indicates that the facility did not respond to our most recent requests for information. (B) represents a BOAT/U.S. cooperating marina.

Looking north over Saugatuck Shores and the Cedar Point Yacht Club.
© Maptech/James T. Abts

The E.R. Strait Marina, located at Longshore Club Park, is owned and operated by the town of Westport. The marina gives you access to the park and all of its amenities, including tennis courts and an 18-hole golf course. But first you'll have to visit the town's recreation department (203-341-5090) for a pass.

The Westport Country Playhouse (203-227-4177), one of New England's best-known summer theaters, has provided stellar entertainment for more than 60 seasons. The Nature Center for Environmental Activities (203-227-7253) is only a few miles from the river with 53 wooded acres of trails and streams, a science museum, a hands-on aquarium, and more—a great visit for the kids.

RESTAURANTS & PROVISIONS: If you find the Saugatuck River appealing enough to stay for more than a few days, there's one thing you won't have to worry about: variety in your diet. Surrounding Coastwise Marina and the railroad bridge, eight delectable restaurants await, so take your time and check out all of them.

The Black Duck (203-227-7978) just north of the railroad bridge is a Westport landmark of sorts. It's an old riverboat-turned-restaurant that's been left in otherwise original condition. Food and drinks are inexpensive. Farther north on Riverside Avenue, on the other side of the I-95 overpass, you'll find DeRosa's (203-227-7596), widely considered one of the best Italian restaurants in Fairfield County. You'll pay for the quality, but you have to expect that along Connecticut's Gold Coast.

Across the street from DeRosa's, John Harvard's Brew House (203-454-2337) offers pub fare and then some, and 187th Arthur Avenue (203-221-1551) mirrors the 187th Avenue in the Bronx. If you've never been to that part of New York City, it's the Bronx's Little Italy. You can expect various Italian specialties, pizza, fresh pasta, and cappuccino.

For seafood, continue up Riverside to the Mansion Clam House (203-454-7979). If your tastes run spicy, wild, and free, check out the Mexican food and fun atmosphere at Viva Zapata (203-227-8226), across the street.

Down near the railroad station, Mario's (203-226-0308) serves a good meal and enough local gossip to fill you up. Next door, try Tarantino's (203-454-3188), yet another eatery with a flair for Italian.

Give your galley a lift with provisions from Peter's Bridge Market (203-227-0602) or Elvira's Deli and Market (203-341-8582), where you can scare up some sandwiches.

NAVIGATION & ANCHORAGES: Use ChartKit Region 3, page 27; Maptech™ Waterproof Charts 1 and 16; and Maptech™ electronic and NOAA paper charts 12368 (1:20,000), 12364 (1:40,000), and 12363 (1:80,000). Use tide tables for Bridgeport. Height of tide at Bridgeport is the same as the Saugatuck River entrance. High tide at the Saugatuck River entrance is 2 minutes earlier; low tide is 1 minute later. Mean tidal range is 7 feet.

The mouth of the Saugatuck River, marked by Fl G 4s G "3," is 3.2nm west of the entrance to Southport Harbor. Peck Ledge Light, marking the eastern approach to Norwalk Harbor, is 4.2nm to the southwest.

From Mo(A) WHIS R W "BH" southeast of Penfield Light, a course of approximately 280°m should bring Fl G 4s G "3" within sight; be sure to stay clear of Hanford Rock, north of Cockenoe Island.

If you're running down the center of the Sound, your marker should be Fl R 4s BELL R "2" at the southern tip of Middle Ground; steering a course of about 297°m should also lead you to Fl G 4s G "3" outside the entrance to the Saugatuck River.

North of Cockenoe Island, between Bluff and Cedar points, the shallow Saugatuck River leads to Westport. You can't reach the river from the west inside the Norwalk Islands because at mlw you can walk between Cockenoe and the mainland and barely get your shoes wet. If you're just harbor-hopping between Westport and Norwalk, it can be frustrating to take the long, but necessary, trip around Cockenoe Island. Avoid the Saugatuck at night. The channel is well marked but extremely narrow and snakelike, slithering through the mud flats on either side. Generally, the channel follows the western shore.

From the west, stay outside Cockenoe Shoal and Reef, turn north at Fl R 2.5s BELL R "24" and keep east of Fl G 2.5s G "1" off Georges Rock. Head for Fl G 4s G "3," which will be in line with the first pair of river buoys, G C "5" and R N "6."

From Cedar Point on there is a 5-mph speed limit that the active marine patrols enforce. Because of the speed limit, narrow channel, and tremendous number of small, one-design sailboats and windsurfers crowding the harbor, it can be a 20- or 30-minute trip up to the railroad bridge. Most of the marinas have floating finger piers because of the 7-foot variation in the tides.

Just inside Cedar Point is the Compo Yacht Basin, which you may enter by rounding R N "8." The basin can be congested, and anchoring is impossible. Just 800 yards to the west is the E.R. Strait Marina, also town-operated. Guest berths aren't usually available at either facility, so call ahead.

North of Bluff Point the channel twists in horseshoe fashion toward the west, then south, then west again, and finally north. Bluff Point is home to the Cedar Point Yacht Club. The entrance is better protected than Compo or Saugatuck Harbor, but the basin is usually filled.

Upriver to the west you'll see the Saugatuck Harbor Yacht Club at the head of Duck Creek, a nice little shelter. The Saugatuck can be so filled that it may discourage you from staying overnight. The river carries a charted depth of at least 5 feet at mlw up to the railroad and highway bridges. However, we once headed up the river at spring tide (when the moon is new or full, resulting in a greater than average tidal range) and found 4 feet or less in the channel at low water.

If you have a shallow-draft boat, pass through the bascule railroad bridge and go upstream by signaling the bridge tender with the usual long and short blasts of your horn. Just past the railroad bridge, Coastwise Marina services outboards and I/Os, and has high-octane gas, marine supplies, and a well-stocked parts department. North of the railroad bridge is the I-95 bridge, but beyond that most of the depth disappears. Another 200 yards north is a small swing bridge that no longer opens, with a vertical clearance of 7 feet at high tide. If this is enough overhead room for you, and you have a shallow-draft boat, you can proceed safely up the river into downtown Westport at Post Road. The depths in this part of the river are only 1 to 5 feet at mlw.

Back outside the Saugatuck River is the easternmost of the Norwalk Islands, Cockenoe Island. Owned by the town of Westport, Cockenoe is one of Long Island Sound's best picnic sites. You can reach the island only by dinghy, and the best approach is from the northwest side. It's shallow in the bay, but the bottom is hard sand and mud. If you have a very shallow draft, you can spend the night in the bay: anchor at the mouth, toward the northeast fork. Deeper-draft boats will want to anchor out in Cockenoe Harbor. Don't approach the island from the east—there are too many unmarked rocks and reefs.

Northwest of Cockenoe Island is Bermuda Lagoon, a privately dredged basin (entered through Cockenoe Harbor) surrounded by private homes and docks. The lagoon itself is quite deep, but the entrance channel has

Looking north over Compo Basin and Cedar Point. © Maptech/James T. Abts

been dredged only partway out into the shallow northern section of the harbor, so many boats can enter only at half-tide or better.

Cockenoe Harbor, via Peck Ledge Light, is also the eastern approach to Norwalk Harbor. Like the Saugatuck River, this is not a passage to try for the first time at night. Round north of Fl 4s 61ft 7M at Peck Ledge, then turn west and head south to Fl R 4s 26ft 5M "8" at Grassy Hammock Rocks.

CAUTION: Don't be tempted to run for the next red flasher you see off Round Beach: you will end up stuck in the mud. A better course is to head for G C "11" off Raymond Rocks, then turn northwest toward Q R 26ft 4M "14." Watch out for the shallows southeast of this light and northwest of G C "11."

From here, the channel is fairly well marked but can be tricky. See the previous two chapters for descriptions of the channel up to the city of Norwalk and for more information on the Norwalk Islands.

Shoreside & Emergency Services
Airport: Bridgeport Sikorsky Memorial (203-576-7498)
Bus: Westport Transit District Minibus (203-226-7171)
Coast Guard: Eatons Neck (631-261-6868) or VHF 16
Police, Fire, Ambulance: 911
Taxi: Westport Star Taxi (203-227-5157)
Tow Service:
SEA TOW —24-Hour Dispatch (800-4SEATOW)
—Southern Connecticut (203-331-0410)
TowBoatU.S.—24-Hour Dispatch (800-391-4869)
—Norwalk (516-624-3483)

The Cream of the Crop

The town of Southport is a cameo of the "good life" in Fairfield County. In fact, if all the harbors in Connecticut were milk, Southport would be the cream—it's very rich, but there's not much of it. The harbor is quiet and beautiful, and you might feel as though you're in the middle of a picture postcard. Houses nestle in the woods to the west, while the hills and fairways of Fairfield Country Club roll a wide, green carpet to the east.

This ground of gracious living was also the site of the Great Swamp Battle of 1637. Here, the last of the Pequot Indians, having escaped the massacre at Mystic, were run down and killed in a Southport swamp by the English settlers of eastern Connecticut.

In the Revolutionary days of 1779, General Tryon was the nominal

Southport Harbor on a beautiful, early fall day. © Maptech

British Military Governor of New York. He and his Hessian troops burned 85 public buildings and private homes in the town of Fairfield. The rebuilt town now enjoys several beautiful historic districts, including the west side of Southport Harbor. It is ironic that a town that suffered so heavily during the Revolution sits close to Black Rock Harbor, the home port of a full-scale working replica of the British warship H.M.S. *Rose*.

The subsequent history of the town is far from bloody. The settlers were farmers, and Southport was mostly onion fields. The federal government began improving to the harbor in 1831 so that more boats could reach Southport (and more people could enjoy Southport's onions). Teams of oxen pulled crude scoop buckets to dredge the Mill River, and schlepped heavy, wooden sleds loaded with granite boulders across the mud flats to build the breakwater at the entrance of Southport Harbor.

All of that hard, manual labor has been much appreciated by the many recreational boaters, who have since taken advantage of the small but snug harbor of Southport and turned it into a charming port, smooth and rich like cream.

ACTIVITIES: Southport Harbor is small, and so is the list of activities. Keep in mind, however, that Southport Harbor is just a cab ride away from the posh shopping districts in downtown Westport and Fairfield.

In summer there is often entertainment at the gazebo on the Sherman green, in Fairfield, which is about three miles from the water. Off the green is the Community Theater (203-255-6555). Their terrific neon marquee is pure art deco.

Fairfield is headquarters of the Audubon Society of Connecticut (203-259-6305). Locally, Audubon runs the Birdcraft Sanctuary Museum (203-259-0416) and the Larson Sanctuary, a nature preserve with 6 miles of year-round nature trails.

The Fairfield Historical Society (203-259-1598) features art of the American Revolution, especially images of sea captains and ships, and antique navigational aids. The

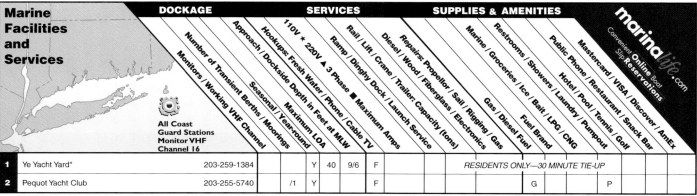

Marine Facilities and Services		Number of Transient Berths / Moorings	Monitors / Working VHF Channel	Approach / Dockside Depth in Feet at MLW	Hookups: Fresh Water / Phone / Cable TV	Seasonal / Yearround	Maximum LOA	110V * 220V ▲ 3 Phase ■ Maximum Amps	Ramp / Dinghy Dock / Launch Service	Rail / Lift / Crane / Trailer: Capacity (tons)	Diesel / Wood / Fiberglass / Electronics	Repairs: Propellor / Sail / Rigging / Gas	Marine / Groceries / Ice / Bait / LPG / CNG	Gas / Diesel Fuel	Restrooms / Showers / Laundry / Pumpout	Fuel Brand	Public Phone / Restaurant / Snack Bar	Hotel / Pool / Tennis / Golf	Mastercard / VISA / Discover / AmEx
1	Ye Yacht Yard*	203-259-1384		Y	40	9/6		F									RESIDENTS ONLY—30 MINUTE TIE-UP		
2	Pequot Yacht Club	203-255-5740	/1	Y				F					G				P		

Information in these listings is provided by the facilities themselves. An asterisk (*) indicates that the facility did not respond to our most recent requests for information. (B) represents a BOAT/U.S. cooperating marina.

Some of ye Southport residents dock their boats at Ye Yacht Yard. © Maptech

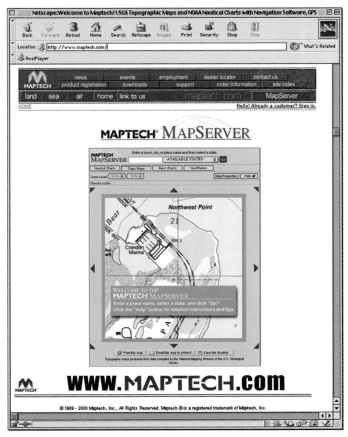

Society also sponsors summer walking tours of historic Fairfield, including their 18th-century Ogden House.

RESTAURANTS & PROVISIONS: Southport's village center is about a mile from the town dock, but at least one restaurant makes the walk worthwhile. Paci (203-259-9600), at the town railroad depot, has won awards for its outstanding restaurant design and impressive wine selection, and we're sure it will win over your appetite as well. If you're in port for more than a day, make a repeat visit here, as the menu changes daily.

Nearby, you'll also find the Driftwood Sandwich Shop (203-255-1975), known for its fantastic sandwiches, and the Horseshoe Café (203-255-8624). Just outside of town, the Southport Brewing Company (203-256-2337), can quench your thirst and quell your hunger.

To stock up on provisions, visit the Spic & Span Market (203-259-1688) or Zamary's Southport Market (203-259-8377), which has a good selection of produce and meat. If you need non-food supplies, Switzer's Pharmacy (203-259-7891) and Village Hardware (203-259-0425) will be at your service.

For more substantial dinnertime fare you'll need a cab to get to downtown Fairfield. Here, across from Sherman Green, Tommy's (203-254-1478) specializes in Northern Italian cuisine (reservations are recommended). By the railroad tracks you'll find Archie Moore's (203-256-9295), and Avellino's (203-254-2339).

NAVIGATION & ANCHORAGES: Use ChartKit Region 3, page 27; Maptech™ Waterproof Charts 1 and 16; and Maptech™ electronic and NOAA paper charts 12369 (1:20,000), 12364 (1:40,000), and 12363 (1:80,000). Use tide tables for Bridgeport. High tide at the Black Rock Harbor entrance is 4 minutes earlier; low tide is 3 minutes earlier. Use height of tide at Bridgeport for height of tide at Black Rock Harbor entrance. Mean tidal range is 6.9 feet.

The entrance to the Southport Harbor channel is 3.4nm to the northeast of the outer approach to the Saugatuck River, and 4.7nm to the west of the outer entrance to Bridgeport Harbor.

From Mo(A) WHIS R W "BH" southeast of Penfield Light (Fl R 6s 51ft 15M HORN), a course of approximately 288°m should bring you to Fl R 4s BELL R "22." You should see the entrance markers to Southport Harbor from here.

CAUTION: Don't cut inside Fl R 4s BELL "22" off Pine Creek Point, or you may run into Sasco Reef, which lies just below the surface.

The approach to Southport Harbor is unobstructed except for the rocks off Frost Creek Point and Pine Creek Point and a few oyster stakes in the shallows of the bay. Stay south of Fl R 4s BELL R "22" off Pine Creek Point.

You have clear sailing up to the first buoys, G C "3" and R N "2." Keep at least 0.5nm offshore on your approach.

Looking north over Southport Harbor. © Maptech/James T. Abts

The first light is Fl G 4s 32ft 4M "7." Farther up, Fl R 4s 28ft 4M "12" marks the end of the breakwater.

The channel is very narrow—never more than 50 to 75 feet wide—until you reach the Pequot Yacht Club basin. The good folks at the club tell us that the main channel has been shoaling, so after passing R N "10," favor the western side of the center of the channel for the deepest water. There you'll have at least 6 feet of water at mlw.

Unfortunately for transients, there's not much here in the way of marinas. The yacht club sells fuel and has pump-out service and transient moorings available. You'll need to head for Black Rock Harbor or Westport for repair service or dockage. If you're looking for a slip or mooring, call ahead.

The harbor is less than a mile long and is usually full of moored boats. On the west side is the town dock (known locally, and somewhat whimsically, as "Ye Yacht Yard") which has about 6 feet of water beside it at mlw. You can tie up there for a maximum of 30 minutes to load or unload, but no overnight docking is allowed. Contact the harbormaster for information about town facilities. There is a no-wake speed limit within the harbor.

Shoreside & Emergency Services
Airport:
—Bridgeport Sikorsky Memorial (203-576-7498)
Bus:
—Greater Bridgeport Transit District (203-333-3031)
Coast Guard:
—Eatons Neck (631-261-6868) or VHF 16
Harbormaster: (203-259-5571)
Police, Fire, Ambulance: 911
Taxi:
—Fairfield Cab Co. (203-255-5797)
Tow Service:
SEA TOW —24-Hour Dispatch (800-4SEATOW)
—Southern Connecticut (203-331-0410)
Tow BoatU.S.—24-Hour Dispatch (800-391-4869)
—Norwalk (203-855-7918)

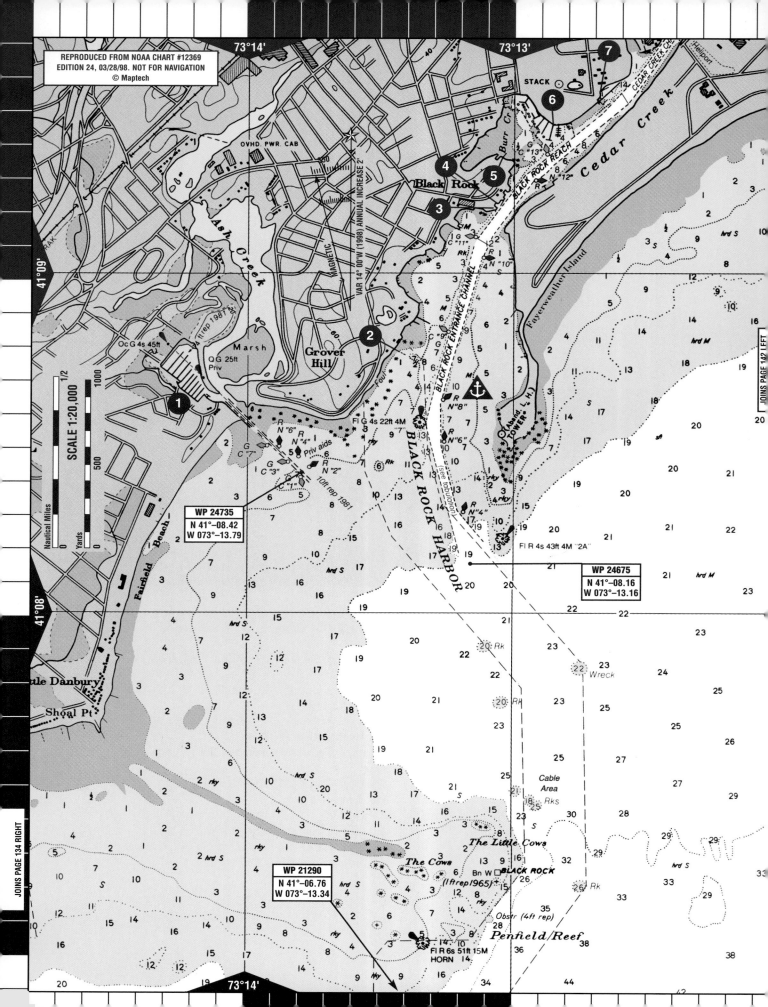

Keep the Lights Burning

Two lighthouses mark the approach to Black Rock Harbor. From the west, Penfield Light warns of a reef extending a mile offshore from Fairfield. And at the eastern edge of the harbor entrance, Fayerweather Light sits on an island of the same name. While it has been abandoned and is no longer used as a navigational aid, Fayerweather Light has not been forgotten. To residents it's both a welcoming landmark and a symbol that Black Rock is a survivor.

In 1808, a light station was established at Fayerweather Island and the present tower was built there in 1823. At that time, critics feared that the small stones and timbers used to build the 47-foot tower would not hold.

Fayerweather Island Light was decommissioned in 1932, given to the city of Bridgeport, and became part of Seaside Park. Vandals gradually gutted Fayerweather Light's interior, and then burned the 1879 keeper's house in 1977. The exterior of the lighthouse was never seriously damaged. In 1983, Fayerweather Island and its lighthouse got a good scrubbing; alas, they would again succumb to vandals and neglect.

In 1993, two local people, a caterer and an artist, started a fund to preserve the lighthouse. Shortly afterward, lighthouse activists danced the night away at the first annual Preservation Ball, an event that is still held today. Restoration began in 1998 and was completed a year later. Mortar matching the original lighthouse was used. The lantern room was reglazed, all the rust was removed, and a protective stone seawall was reconstructed to save the foundation. Expensive, graffiti-resistant paint and steel-paned "windows" deter vandals. Solar panels and equipment

Fayerweather Light welcomes visitors to Black Rock. © Maptech

for lighting, not to be used for navigation but to show off the structure at night, were donated by local power companies. Workers and volunteers came from all over, but most were based at the Black Rock marinas and yacht clubs. After all, it is their lighthouse, an icon that has survived for nearly 180 years and continues to greet sailors.

ACTIVITIES: Most of the action in Black Rock Harbor takes place at Captain's Cove Seaport (203-335-1433). Years ago, the harbor was grimy and rundown, but the tremendous improvements made at Captain's Cove have livened up the area. For a day of fishing or diving, you will find charter boats at the docks. The boardwalk features gift shops with a nautical flavor and on weekends, the place is hopping with entertainment. Along with dockside tours and sea chantey

Marine Facilities and Services		Monitors / Working VHF Channel	Number of Transient Berths / Moorings	Approach / Dockside Depth in Feet at MLW	Hookups: Seasonal / Year-round	Maximum LOA	110V • 220V ▲ 3 Phase ■ Maximum Amps	Fresh Water / Phone / Cable TV	Ramp / Dinghy Dock / Launch Service	Rail / Lift / Crane / Trailer: Capacity (tons)	Repairs: Propellor / Sail / Rigging / Electronics	Diesel / Wood / Fiberglass	Gas / Diesel Fuel	Marine / Groceries / Ice / Bait / LPG / CNG	Restrooms / Showers / Laundry / Pumpout	Fuel Brand	Public Phone / Restaurant / Snack Bar	Hotel / Pool / Tennis / Golf	Mastercard / VISA / Discover / AmEx
1	South Benson Marina 203-256-3010	16/9	2/	S	36	6/6	F		PRIVATE—RECIPROCAL PRIVILEGES ONLY						IB		RP		PS	M
2	Black Rock Yacht Club 203-335-0587	14/	/5	Y	45	25/5			NO OVERNIGHT DOCKAGE						I		RS		All	M
3	Port 5 Naval Veterans Assn. 203-576-9366			Y													R		R	
4	Fayerweather Yacht Club 203-576-6796	14/		Y		8/4	F	★		L	C3			G			R		All	MV
5	Fayerweather Boatyard 203-334-4403	9/		Y	40						L25	All				M				
6	Captain's • Cove • Seaport 203-335-1433 p. 141	18/	40/	Y	150	25/15	F	★▲■50		L85	PSRDWFE	GD		MGI	All		All		All	MV
7	Cedar Marina Inc. 203-335-6262	9/72	6/	Y	65	18/8	All	★30		LC15	PRGDWFE			M	All		S			MVD

All Coast Guard Stations Monitor VHF Channel 16

Information in these listings is provided by the facilities themselves. An asterisk (*) indicates that the facility did not respond to our most recent requests for information. (B) represents a BOAT/U.S. cooperating marina.

Looking west over the entrances to Black Rock Harbor (foreground) and Ash Creek (background).
© Maptech/James T. Abts

cab ride to downtown Bridgeport or Fairfield is necessary.

NAVIGATION & ANCHORAGES: Use ChartKit Region 3, page 28; Maptech™ Waterproof Charts 1 and 16; and Maptech™ electronic and NOAA paper charts 12369 (1:20,000), 12364 (1:40,000), and 12363 (1:80,000). Use tide tables for Bridgeport. High tide at the Black Rock Harbor entrance is 4 minutes earlier; low tide is 3 minutes earlier. Use height of tide at Bridgeport for height of tide at Black Rock Harbor entrance. Mean tidal range is 6.9 feet.

The Fl R 4s 43ft 4M "2A" light at the entrance to Black Rock Harbor is 1.6nm from Penfield Reef Light, and 1.8nm from Fl R 2.5s BELL R "10" outside Bridgeport Harbor. The breakwaters at Port Jefferson Harbor are 11.4nm away.

From Fl R 4s BELL R "2" at **Middle Ground** (Stratford Shoal), a course of about 330°m will take you across the main Bridgeport channel and into the approach to Black Rock Harbor.

CAUTION: When approaching Black Rock Harbor from the west or south, give Penfield Reef Light (Fl R 6s 51ft 15M HORN) plenty of room. It marks the southern tip of the reef, not the eastern tip. Little Cows just breaks the surface at low tide, and Black Rock is marked with W Bn, known locally as "the lollipop." Do not pass between the shore and Penfield Reef Light.

Stay well east of W Bn before turning north into Black Rock Harbor. Don't let the name fool you; the Little Cows are anything but little, claiming many boats every year. Occasionally, a newcomer traveling east after dark will somehow mistake the red Penfield Reef Light for the white flasher at Middle Ground, 6.5nm to the southeast, and end up on the rocks.

Another problem to contend with is the bar extending from Shoal Point out toward Penfield Reef. Every year, dozens of unwary boaters roar out of Black Rock Harbor toward the wide expanse of water west-northwest of Penfield Reef Light that beckons them out to the Sound, only to go aground on the bar. Lots of bets are made as to whether the fathometer or the captain will scream first. Pay attention to the charts: the rocks and the sandbar are real!

Fishermen with shallow-draft boats can anchor within 30 feet of the landing platform on the north side of the Penfield Reef Light (Fl R 6s 51ft 15M HORN). But be forewarned: the foghorn may drive you cuckoo.

Another cluster of rocks barely visible at low tide is off Saint Mary's, southwest of Fl G 4s 22ft 4M "7" at the head of the harbor. You can recognize Saint Mary's by the sea wall along the shore road, lined with street lights.

concerts for the public, nautical buffs will revel in the Nantucket Lightship that is docked here.

Captain's Cove is also the home port of the H.M.S. *Rose*, the world's largest active wooden sailing vessel. The *Rose* is a replica of a full-rigged, 24-gun, 18th century Royal Navy frigate that cruised the American coast during the Revolutionary War. Adventure and educational voyages are now held throughout the year. If you're lucky she'll be in port when you visit. At 179 feet long, with a beam of 32 feet, and a main mast at 130 feet, the *Rose* will be hard to miss.

The neighboring Seaside Park provides access to the Fayerweather Island Light via a stone breakwall. For more on information on Seaside Park and other attractions in Bridgeport, refer to that chapter. Remember, though it goes by the name Black Rock it's still part of Bridgeport. It's safer to call a cab or ask your marina for a ride, than to walk, even if you're going just a few blocks.

RESTAURANTS & PROVISIONS: If you want to stay in the harbor for a meal, the Black Rock Yacht Club (203-335-0587) and Captain's Cove Seaport (203-335-7104) both feature good restaurants (take-out is available at Captain's Cove). Your other option is the Fayerweather Yacht Club (203-576-6796), which offers a good lunch menu at reasonable prices.

The restaurant at Captain's Cove has a 40-foot model of the *Titanic* hanging from the ceiling above the bar, which is built around the pilothouse of a steam tugboat, circa 1900. It's a hot spot for the singles crowd on weekends. The Seaport also boasts 20 specialty shops, including a small grocery and fish market. If you're looking for boat hardware, you'll find limited supplies at Captain's Cove and Cedar Marina. Apart from the waterfront eateries, the harbor is surrounded by factories and warehouses, so a

The channel into Black Rock Harbor is dredged to a minimum depth of 14 feet (shallowing to 9 feet at the sides), but there's considerably less water outside the channel. Honor the nuns and cans and stay in the channel. The average tidal range here is 6.9 feet, so all the marinas have floating docks. Keep alert for the commercial vessels that transit through Black Rock Harbor enroute to the East and West branch of Cedar Creek.

At the entrance to Burr Creek, you'll find Captain's Cove Seaport, a full-service, transient facility that's also an amusement center. On the port side up by Captain's Cove, you'll find 4 to 5 feet of water. There are some muddy shoals in the creek, so enter with care. While the Seaport caters to transients, there are limited transient slips available on the Burr Creek side. If they are full, you'll be sent directly across the channel to another set of docks that do not have electrical hookups or water. Launch service is provided to the main Seaport facility.

Cedar Marina, north of the seaport, also caters to transients. Most of the nice parts of Bridgeport and Fairfield are not accessible by foot from Black Rock Harbor, so call a cab if you plan to go any farther afield than the seaport.

Just to the south of Burr Creek, Fayerweather Yacht Club members are generally the hospitable, do-it-yourself type. The large number of permanently moored boats leaves little room for anchoring in the inner harbor, but there is usually room in the excellent anchorage to the west of the old lighthouse on Fayerweather Island. Again, keep the anchor lights burning.

The area south of R N "10," off Fayerweather Island, is full of private moorings. If you grab one, expect to be kicked off.

Directly to the west of this anchorage is the Black Rock Yacht Club, which offers some guest moorings, a restaurant, a pool, and tennis courts. Dockside depths at the club can be skimpy at low tide. It's best to call ahead on VHF 9 for advice.

For launching trailered boats, there is a weathered town ramp with a parking lot at the end of the road on Fayerweather Island, north of R N "10." Also on Fayerweather Island, due east of G C "9," is a public fishing pier.

The harbor is open to the prevailing southwesterly winds, but otherwise offers good protection, thanks in part to the artificial windbreak of the old landfill. This has been completely covered with grass, so you don't notice it, but because of the sewage-treatment plant, Black Rock still isn't the place to be on hot, windless days.

Although there has been a great deal of progress made in the last few years, it will be several more years before the water in the harbor is clean enough for swimming. The warm water from the sewage-treatment plant may keep the wintertime ice at bay, but it also promotes the growth of barnacles and such on the bottom of your boat.

Another protected spot is Ash Creek. Ash Creek has an approach depth of about 10 feet, but inside at the South Benson Marina there's less than 4 feet at the docks. If you draw more than 3.5 feet, wait until at least half tide to approach the marina. When entering Ash Creek, especially at night, be sure to line up the two range markers: the Q G 25ft under the Oc G 4s 45ft. Note that several of the entrance buoys may be slightly different from their charted position; be sure to heed them.

The area to the west of GC "1," outside the entrance to Ash Creek, is reserved for small-boat sailing. Powerboats are prohibited from entering.

There's a no-wake speed limit in the dredged channel to the South Benson Boat Basin, which is owned and operated by the Town of Fairfield. The marina has a slip or two available for transients, and you can fuel up and grab some snacks at the gas dock. The area just inside the Ash Creek entrance offers great protection in a blow.

Shoreside & Emergency Services
Airport: Bridgeport Sikorsky (203-576-7498)
Bus: Greater Bridgeport Transit (203-333-3031)
Coast Guard: New Haven (203-468-4450)
—Eatons Neck (631-261-6868)
Police, Fire, Ambulance: 911
Taxi: Fairfield Cab Co. (203-255-5797)
Tow Service:
SEA TOW. —24-Hour Dispatch (800-4SEATOW)
—Southern Connecticut (203-331-0410)
Tow BoatU.S.—24-Hour Dispatch (800-391-4869)
—Norwalk (203-855-7918)

The Greatest Show on Earth

Bluefish that play baseball. Tigers that play ice hockey. It could only happen in Bridgeport, where "the greatest showman on Earth," P.T. Barnum, made his home for most of his life. Based on the history of Connecticut's largest city, the circus promoter picked a perfect place to establish himself.

When the area was first settled in 1639, it was called Pequonnock, after the river where the Indians of the same name lived. The town at the mouth of the Pequonnock sought an identity much like a Barnum act, undergoing numerous name changes. It was called Fairfield Village in 1694, then Stratfield Village in 1701, and Newfield Village in 1798. Two years later, when the first drawbridge was erected over the Pequonnock River, it was then changed again, for the final time, to Bridgeport. And, now you know why P.T. Barnum came here.

Born in Bethel, Connecticut in 1810, Barnum is well-known for his circus, which wintered in Bridgeport, but he made a good deal of his fortune through real estate in the city and investments in local banks, utilities, and the Bridgeport & Port Jefferson Steamboat Company. He also laid out parks and roads, built magnificent homes, and even designed Mountain Grove Cemetery where he is buried. Barnum, once a mayor of the city, is credited with bringing Elias Howe and his Singer sewing machines to Bridgeport in the early 19th century, changing this port city into a major manufacturing center.

Throughout most of its history, Bridgeport has been an industrial powerhouse, producing everything from brass products, machine tools, carriages, corsets, and sewing machines, to military equipment and supplies. The city's official motto in Latin is *Industria Crescimus*, or "by industry we thrive." Over the last 50 years, however, the city's fortunes and population have changed.

Monumental Seaside Park welcomes all to Bridgeport. © Maptech

Today's trades are more service-oriented. Many families of former factory workers moved into the suburbs with their cars, and a citizenry made up of new immigrants, mostly minorities, replaced them. The ethnic diversity brought educational and economic disparity in the region, and the polarization resulted in more crime and an unwanted reputation.

Marine Facilities and Services — DOCKAGE | SERVICES | SUPPLIES & AMENITIES — marina life.com Convenient Online Boat Slip Reservations

All Coast Guard Stations Monitor VHF Channel 16

#	Marine Facilities and Services	Phone	Monitors/Working VHF Channel	Number of Transient Berths/Moorings	Seasonal/Year-round	Maximum LOA	Approach/Dockside Depth in Feet at MLW	Hookups: Fresh Water/Phone/Cable TV	110V ★ 220V ▲ 3 Phase ■ / Max Amps	Ramp/Dinghy Dock/Launch Service	Rail/Lift/Crane/Trailer Capacity (tons)	Repairs: Propellor/Sail/Rigging/Electronics	Gas/Diesel Fuel	Fuel Brand	Marine/Groceries/Ice/Bait/LPG/CNG	Restrooms/Showers/Laundry/Pumpout	Public Phone/Restaurant/Snack Bar	Hotel/Pool/Tennis/Golf	Mastercard/VISA/Discover/AmEx
1	Pequonnock Yacht Club (SP)	203-334-5708	9/		Y							PRIVATE—MEMBERS ONLY				R			
2	M.O.V.E. Yacht Club (SP)	203-333-9987			Y							PRIVATE—RECIPROCAL PRIVILEGES							
3	Riverside Marine (SP)	203-335-7068	9/10		Y	35	15/15		★30		LC30	GD	GD	Tex	I	R			MV
4	Ryan's Marine Services (SP)	203-579-1319	10/5	/1	Y	50	22/10		★▲30	RD	LC30	All				RP			MV
5	Dolphin's Cove Marina & Restaurant	203-335-3301	6/10		Y	37	10/15	F	★▲■30							R	All		All
6	Lou's Boat Basin	203-336-9809	6/	1/	S	40	10/3	F	★				GD	Gulf	IB	P			
7	Miamogue Yacht Club*	203-344-9882	9/		Y	42	12/12	F	★			D	G	Citgo		R	All		MV
8	East End Yacht Club	203-366-3330			Y							PRIVATE—MEMBERS ONLY							

Information in these listings is provided by the facilities themselves. An asterisk (*) indicates that the facility did not respond to our most recent requests for information. (B) represents a BOAT/U.S. cooperating marina. (SP) represents facilities located on Steel Point—these facilities will relocate or close due to a municipal project. Please call the facility for up-to-date information.

The new millennium has brought revitalization to a city that needs it. The reconstruction of the highways intersecting the city and proposals for a new, multi-million-dollar Steel Point waterfront, complete with retail, hotel, and boardwalk space, are signs of change. Pleasure Beach, the island on the harbor's eastern entrance that was once an amusement center, is slated for more improvements as a public recreation area.

Bridgeport is a regional hub. The downtown area is a center of government, transportation, communications, and employment for the residents of Fairfield, Easton, Monroe, Trumbull, and Stratford. These towns also rely on the city's hospitals. The region is now looking to Bridgeport as a source of family entertainment, too. The presence of minor-league baseball and hockey teams with their multi-purpose arenas will bring other sporting events, concerts, and, yes, the circus. This resurgence would make P.T. Barnum proud.

ACTIVITIES: Popularly referred to as the "Park City," Bridgeport is home to more than 1,200 acres of parks, recreation areas, shoreline, and Connecticut's only zoo. Expansive Seaside Park, on the harbor's west shore, and Pleasure Beach, the island to the east, offer beautiful spots to picnic, fish, and get some sun just a short dinghy ride from the anchorage. Pleasure Beach also has hot showers.

You'll need to take a cab to the Beardsley Zoo (203-394-6565), located in a park of the same name in the city's North End, but don't expect to see the animals performing any circus acts. To get a better look at those types of activities, visit the Barnum Museum (203-331-1104) downtown. The museum's core exhibits center on Bridgeport and old P.T. himself, but you can also take the kids to the miniature three-ring circus or check out the exhibit wing.

If you're fortunate enough to be in Bridgeport in July, don't miss the Barnum Festival (203-367-8495). His circus and other entertaining acts in the 1800s spawned a craze for the bizarre that lasts today. The summer fete attempts to re-create P.T. Barnum's antics with a parade, fireworks, concerts, and other events such as the Tom Thumb and Lavinia Warren (Thumb's wife) look-alike contest.

Summer also means the Bluefish (203-345-4800) are biting…well, hitting and pitching. The Harbor Yard Ballpark is reminiscent of Baltimore's Camden Yards and other retro-stadiums, albeit on a smaller scale. Situated on an 18-acre site that industry once called home, the Ballpark cost $19 million to build and is a big part of the city's revitalization. The neighboring arena is home to the Sound Tigers, a new addition to the American Hockey League, and is slated for other activities, too.

Check with the chamber of commerce (203-335-3800) for a calendar of events during the boating season. You'll likely find an exhibition at the Housatonic Museum of Art (203-332-5052) or a visual performance at the Downtown Cabaret Theatre (203-576-1636), Polka Dot Playhouse (203-333-3666), or Klein Memorial Auditorium (203-576-8115).

The Discovery Museum (203-372-3521) definitely lives up to its name. You'll find art, hands-on science exhibits, and planetarium shows on its 11-acre site. The museum is especially popular with kids and offers special programs for disadvantaged and special-needs children.

RESTAURANTS & PROVISIONS: While you won't spot many eateries from the water, a venture into town reveals a few choices. We recommend you hop into a cab to get there. If you're banking on a great Italian dinner, Roberto's (203-368-6599), at the corner of Main and State streets, may be the place for you. After all, this beautifully decorated marble building was the birthplace of People's Bank. Roberto's décor is truly unique, replete with high ceilings, detailed marble etchings, and wait stations that resemble tellers' windows. In case the open lobby doesn't suit you, private dining vaults are also available.

And there's always Ralph & Richards (203-366-3597), located on Wall Street, for great Italian continental cuisine. This is a regional favorite for anyone coming into downtown. Locals say the name so fast that almost everyone knows it as "Ralphenriches." That's what you should ask for if you're lost. Your other Italian option is La Scogliera (203-333-0673) on Madison Avenue. For you vegetarians—and even for those of you who are not—Bloodroot (203-576-9168) offers a very nice menu, plus patio dining right on the Sound.

The only place to dock and dine is at Dolphin's Cove Marina & Restaurant (203-335-3301). Downtown Bridgeport has a few convenience stores, banks, pharmacies, and fast-food joints, but you won't find marine supplies.

NAVIGATION & ANCHORAGES: Use ChartKit Region 3, page 28; Maptech™ Waterproof Charts 1 and 16; and Maptech™ electronic and NOAA paper charts 12369 (1:20,000), 12364 (1:40,000), and 12363 (1:80,000). Use tide tables for Bridgeport. Mean tidal range is 6.8 feet.

The approach to Bridgeport Harbor, starting at Mo(A) WHIS RW "BH," is 4.7nm from the entrance to Southport Harbor and 5.8nm from the entrance to the Housatonic River. The entrance to Port Jefferson Harbor is 9.2nm away.

From Fl R 4s BELL R "2" at Middle Ground (Stratford Shoal), a course of about 330°m will put you between Mo(A) WHIS RW "BH" and the first set of entrance buoys to the main Bridgeport channel. Bridgeport is hard to miss. Even if you can't see its many large industrial and office buildings, you will see the red-and-white horizontally-striped smokestack of the United Illuminating Company (UI) power plant on Tongue Point.

Mo(A) WHIS RW "BH" has a ball topmark, which identifies it as a fairway marker. About 1nm north-northeast of Mo(A) WHIS RW "BH," channel buoys begin at Fl R 2.5s GONG R "2."

Small craft need not run the length of the entrance channel; if you're coming from the east or west, just make for Fl R 2.5s BELL R "10" and then keep to the channel into the harbor.

Tidal currents reach about 0.7 knots between the breakwaters at flood and ebb. To the west will be the 200-acre strip of Seaside Park and the campus of the University of Bridgeport just behind it. To the east, Pleasure and Long beaches stretch off toward Stratford.

The first possible anchorage, protected from the north and east, lies inside the eastern breakwater off Pleasure Beach. The old pier from the defunct amusement park has been rebuilt and is now a public fishing pier. The sandy soil offers good holding ground. Be careful where you drop the hook as there is a large steel mooring buoy for commercial vessels in this anchorage. If you arrive in darkness, seek it out with your

Looking northeast into Bridgeport Harbor. Seaside Park and the breakwater are in the foreground. © Maptech/James T. Abts

searchlight, so you don't wake up right next to an oil or gravel barge. The harbormaster's office runs a pump-out boat during season. Hail it on VHF 9, 13 or 16, should you need service.

Bridgeport Harbor has three channels, the first being Johnsons Creek, north and east of Pleasure Beach and home of the Miamogue and East End yacht clubs. When entering the creek, pass north of R N "2," which marks the channel, as it also marks a shoal that extends north off Pleasure Beach.

The wooden swing bridge across Johnsons Creek was the victim of a June 1996 fire that destroyed the approach span from the island. It should pose no problem to boaters.

The city boat ramp at Newfield Avenue is adjacent to Lou's Boat Basin. Docking for launching and retrieval of boats is limited to 20 minutes. Watch the traffic coming in and out of this area.

To the west of Johnsons Creek and Dolphin's Cove Marina is the banana boat dock, as locals call it. Look out for the 400-foot-long vessel that comes in every three weeks. It docks stern-to and sticks out into the channel. Opposite here, on the west side of the harbor, is Tongue Point's "Bug Light" (Fl G 4s 31ft 5M), which gets its name for being as dim as a lightning bug. Just to the west is an oil-barge terminal which you would do well to avoid.

Farther up the harbor is the Yellow Mill Channel, home of the Pequonnock Yacht Club, M.O.V.E. Yacht Club, Riverside Marine, and Ryan's. The Pequonnock and Ryan's both welcome transients.

NOTE: The Steel Point project south of I-95 proposes a multi-million-dollar retail and waterfront complex that will relocate, and possibly close, the four marinas and yacht clubs residing here. The battle for this area was ongoing as we went to press.

To avoid the infamous mud flats at the Pequonnock Yacht Club, pass south of GR C "YM." Then as you approach the club, you'll see a dock extending eastward from the charted docks. The people at the club tell us that to avoid getting stuck you should hug the docks on into the marina. For more advice, call the club on VHF 9.

Riverside Marine has a fuel dock but offers no slips. To get upstream to Ryan's, you'll have to pass through or under the Yellow Mill bascule bridge, vertical clearance 11 feet (mhw). You may have to give as much as 6 hours notice to have it opened.

Directly opposite Steel Point, just south of I-95, is the Water Street dock for the Bridgeport-Port Jefferson Ferry. It is possible to travel farther up the Pequonnock River, but it is not recommended as there is nothing of any visual value there. You will also have to pass a series of bridges—Stratford Avenue, MetroNorth Railroad, and Congress Street—with vertical clearances between 8 feet and 18 feet (mhw). Occassionally, you will see a tug or barge heading to or from the oil terminal just past the Congress Street Bridge.

Shoreside & Emergency Services

Airport: Bridgeport-Sikorsky Memorial (203-576-7498)
Bus: Greater Bridgeport Transit District (203-333-3031)
Coast Guard: New Haven (203-468-4450) or VHF 16
—Eatons Neck (631-261-6868) or VHF 16
Police, Fire, Ambulance: 911
Taxi: Fairfield Cab Co. (203-255-5797)
Tow Service:
SEA TOW —24-Hour Dispatch (800-4SEATOW)
—Southern Connecticut (203-331-0410)
Tow BoatU.S. —24-Hour Dispatch (800-391-4869)
—Norwalk (203-855-7918)

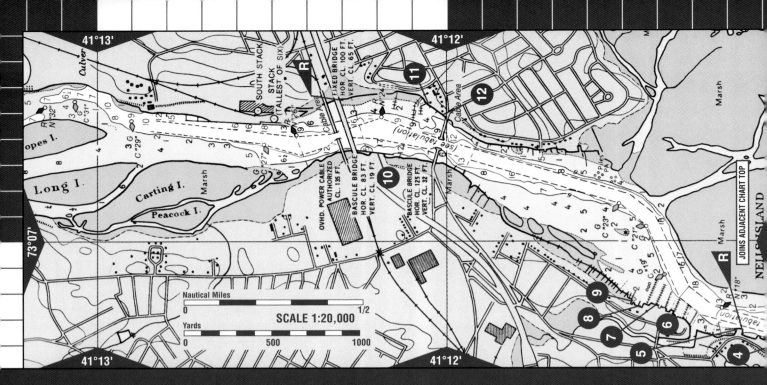

NELLS ISLAND

Nautical Miles
0   1/2
SCALE 1:20,000
Yards
0   500   1000

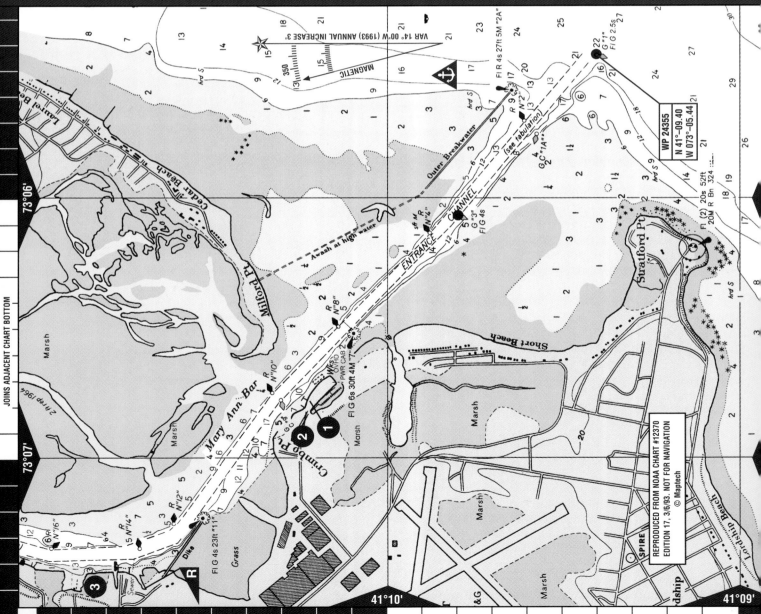

VAR 14°00'W (1993) ANNUAL INCREASE 3'
MAGNETIC

WP 24355
N 41°-09.40
W 073°-05.44

REPRODUCED FROM NOAA CHART #12370
EDITION 17, 3/6/93. NOT FOR NAVIGATION
© Maptech

Protecting the estuary

From its headwaters in the Berkshires of western Massachusetts, the Housatonic runs for nearly 150 miles and pours more fresh water into briny Long Island Sound than any river but the mighty Connecticut herself. Dutch explorer Adrian Block made the first recorded European visit to the Housatonic in 1614. In 1639, a group of English colonists from Wethersfield followed Indian trails to the shoreline, settling on the Housatonic's western shore in a protected area that the Paugussetts called Cupheag, or the harbor. Four years later, the colonists named the place Stratford, after William Shakespeare's birthplace, Stratford-upon-Avon, England.

Shakespeare could have easily written a tragedy about the Housatonic. As the colonists moved up the river valley, driving out most of the Indians, they harvested lumber, crops, livestock, and fish for trade with Boston, New York, England, and the Caribbean. Lumber and flour mills sprouted along the Housatonic's banks. Shipbuilding flourished from the mid-1600s to the late 19th century.

When the Housatonic Dam was built in Shelton and Derby in 1870, the river's flow changed, which caused silt to build up below the dam. No longer were ocean-going vessels able to make it up river. Industrial development during the turn of the 20th century lined the river valley, bringing pollution from factories and overpopulation. The legacy of those years of neglect by businesses and residents is still here today, even though the Federal Clean Water Act over the past few decades has brought incremental improvements to the river.

Tourism helps the Housatonic River by drawing attention to the fact that clean water is necessary for boating, fishing,

Looking northwest into the entrance to the Housatonic River. © Maptech/James T. Abts

Marine Facilities and Services

All Coast Guard Stations Monitor VHF Channel 16

#	Facility	Phone	Monitors/Working VHF	Transient Berths	Seasonal/Year-round/Moorings	Max LOA	Approach/Dockside Depth (MLW)	Hookups (Fresh Water/Phone/Cable)	110V/220V/3Ph Max Amps	Ramp/Dinghy Dock/Launch	Rail/Lift/Crane/Trailer (tons)	Repairs: Propellor/Sail/Rigging/Elec	Diesel/Wood/Fiberglass	Gas/Diesel Fuel	Fuel Brand	Marine/Groceries/Ice/Bait/LPG/CNG	Restrooms/Showers/Laundry/Pumpout	Public Phone/Restaurant/Snack Bar	Hotel/Pool/Tennis/Golf	Mastercard/VISA/Discover/AmEx
1	Breakwater Key	203-380-8475			Y							*PRIVATE*								
2	Knapp's Landing*	203-378-5999			S	40	12/12					R		GD			R	PR		MVA
3	Harbour Woods Yacht Club*	203-377-9766			Y							*PRIVATE*								
4	Housatonic Boat Club	203-377-9195			Y							*PRIVATE*								
5	Brown's Boat Works*	203-377-9303		7/	S	45	4.5/4.5	F	★	RL	C7		WF			IB	RS	R		All
6	Brewer Stratford Marina (Inside Back Cover)	203-377-4477	9/10	10/	Y	80	13/6	All	★▲50	R	L35		PGDWFE	GD	Tex	MGI	All	All		All
7	Paul's Diesel Service, Inc.	203-377-7741			Y									D						All
8	Housatonic Marina	203-375-1840			Y				*BOAT SALES*							All		M		All
9	Pootatauk Yacht Club	203-377-9068			Y							*PRIVATE*								
10	The Marina at The Dock (p. 149)	203-378-9300	9/	20/	Y	110	20/8	All	★▲50		L50		All			GI	All	All		MV
11	Flagship Marina Inc.	203-874-1783		3/	Y	35	8/6	F	★30	R						M	RS	P		MV
12	Valley Yacht Club*	203-874-9673			Y							*PRIVATE*								

marinalife.com — Convenient Online Boat Slip Reservations

Information in these listings is provided by the facilities themselves. An asterisk (*) indicates that the facility did not respond to our most recent requests for information. (B) represents a BOAT/U.S. cooperating marina.

hunting, bird watching, and other activities. As the open space along the resilient estuary is being preserved, and government, business, and citizens manage the protection and cleanup, the river is enjoying a renaissance. When conditions are right, as they are quickly becoming, the Housatonic River supports a great variety of plant and animal life. The tidal wetlands, mud flats, marshes, and sand spits here make fertile grounds for microscopic animals, shellfish, fish, and insects, which in turn attract predators such as larger fish, rodents, deer, hawks, bats, egrets, and osprey, to name a few. Hopefully, the years to come will show that the Housatonic has made a complete recovery.

ACTIVITIES: The Housatonic offers lots of beauty from its mouth all the way to the head of navigation at Derby. Get an up-close experience of an estuarine habitat in the salt marshes, mud flats, and sand bars around Milford Point, a protected area that is maintained by the Connecticut Department of Envirnomental Protection (860-485-0226). The Connecticut Audubon Coastal Center (203-878-7440) takes up an 8-acre site here that was once a hotel. Observation decks and a small tower provide excellent views of the river and of more than 50 species of shorebirds, wading birds, and waterfowl that migrate to this part of the Atlantic flyway. The Charles E. Wheeler Wildlife Area is made up of Nells Island and its 840 acres of salt marsh, which are primarily used for waterfowl hunting.

Milford Point and the Great Meadows refuge near the Sikorsky Airport are the only two units of the Stewart B. McKinney National Wildlife Refuge (860-399-2513) that are open to the public. The other protected areas require permits to use and are located in Westbrook, the Norwalk Islands, Falkner Island, and the Outer Islands off Branford.

Between the river's mouth and the bridges are some of the sate's richest oyster beds. This estuarine section of the river produces huge quantities of seed oysters each year, and you'll often see small outboards dredging for the baby oysters. The oysters are moved to cleaner areas of Long Island Sound before they are harvested. Efforts are ongoing to reduce the pollution and PCBs released by industrial sites upriver. The river is cleaner now, so take a dip if you want, but only fish for sport—toss your catch back (the carp and eels are especially contaminated).

When you're finished exploring the estuary, comb Short Beach, north of Stratford Point, for some relaxation. From the beach parking lot, walk southeast down Prospect Drive to Stratford Point Lighthouse, the Sound's second most powerful beacon. The current light was constructed in 1881 to replace the original built in 1821. Check in with the lightkeeper before going onto the grounds.

RESTAURANTS & PROVISIONS: Arrive at the mouth of the Housatonic River at lunch or dinner and your mouth will water at the sight of Knapps Landing Restaurant (203-378-5999), where there is dockage for diners. If you're staying at Brewer's Stratford Marina, you'll get caught up on the fish

specialties and the local gossip at Outriggers (203-377-8815). Your only other option for docking and dining is at The Dock, of course, where De Pizza Man (203-332-1594) is de place for de pie.

Selections for restaurants around the Housatonic River will depend on your appetite and how far you want to go. Near the bridges on the east side of the river, La Cucina (203-874-5300) sets the table with scrumptous Italian dishes at reasonable prices. About 2 miles west on Route 1, Salerno's Apizza (203-377-2436) is the place to be, but you'll need a taxi from the marinas. The bus makes a stop there, but it's not recommended—if you miss your stop you'll end up in the worst sections of Bridgeport. All along Route 1 you'll find family restaurants and fast-food joints, pharmacies and banks, and an array of shopping centers. Of course, if you're going shopping, go to the Dock, where Stop & Shop (203-375-8787) features a pharmacy, delicatessen, bake shop, beverages, and everything else you'll need.

You should know that the Milford side of the Housatonic River is called Devon, where Route 1 is known as Bridgeport Avenue. In Stratford, Route 1 is actually Barnum Avenue.

NAVIGATION & ANCHORAGES: Use ChartKit Region 3 page 29; Maptech™ Waterproof Charts 1 and 16; and Maptech™ electronic and NOAA paper charts 12370 (1:20,000), 12369 (1:20,000), 12364 (1:40,000), and 12354 (1:80,000). Use tide tables for Bridgeport. High tide at Stratford is 26 minutes later; low tide is 1 hour and 1 minute later. Multiply height of tide at Bridgeport by 0.8 for height of tide at Stratford. Mean tidal range is 5.5 feet.

The outer entrance to the Housatonic River, marked by Fl G 2.5s BELL G "1," is 5.8nm from Stratford Shoal Light (Fl 5s 60ft 13M HORN), 2.6nm from Charles Island at Milford, and 5.8nm from the entrance to Bridgeport Harbor.

From RN "20" south of Lordship Beach in Stratford, a course of about 60°m for 2.3nm will take you just south of Fl G 2.5s BELL G "1" at the entrance to the Housatonic River. From Fl R 4s BELL R "16" south of Charles Island in Milford, a course of about 240°m for 2.4nm will also get you to the mouth of the Housatonic.

Built in 1822, the Stratford Point Light (Fl (2) 20s 52ft 16M) is a white, conical tower with a brown band, making an excellent landmark for you to see when you're heading toward the entrance of the Housatonic.

From the south, there is more than enough water around Stratford Shoal, but because the shoal itself is so shallow relative to the surrounding waters, a nasty chop often arises when the wind and current oppose.

From the west, look for Fl R 6s BELL R "18," about 3.6nm southwest of Stratford Point. From there, head for the Fl G 2.5s BELL G "1" at the mouth of the Housatonic River. During the day, you'll see two, black stacks located 3.8nm upriver in the town of Devon that make excellent landmarks. However, entering the river at night for the first time can be tricky. Keep east of Fl G 2.5s BELL G "1" at the channel entrance; there are several 6-foot spots between this buoy and GC "1A" to the northwest.

The breakwater extending from Milford Point is marked at its far end by FL R 4s 27ft 5M "2A," and the channel leading upriver from this point is 200 feet wide with a depth of about 12 feet (mlw). Stay as close to the center of the channel as possible, because there are a few shoal spots along the edge leading to and southeast of RN "4." A steerage speed (no-wake) zone is located 500 feet downstream from Fl G 4s G "3" and 500 feet upstream from RN "4."

When current and wind are opposed, you'll run into little hillocks of sea near the breakwater. Whether thrilling, challenging, or scary, these crazy waters should always be approached with care.

You must be cautious of the many oyster stakes marking the underwater shellfish beds; they are nearly as plentiful as the oysters themselves.

CAUTION: Be aware of the current that can run 2 to 4 knots. It sets strong at the river's mouth and quickens considerably in the channel. When under sail, it's best to wait for an incoming or slack current with your engine running.

Also, be aware of small fishing boats anchored along the river, especially inside the channel entrance and near Knapp's Landing. East of the outer breakwater, you'll find a nice, daytime anchorage, and a great place to catch blackfish, blues, and spider crabs. The area is well protected against weather from the southwest, but to the east you'll find nothing but water as far as Portugal; we suggest you don't risk a wind shift by staying overnight.

Part of the inner breakwater, marked by Fl G 4s 23ft 4M "11," is underwater at high tide. East of here, you'll see the extensive marshes and protected wildlife areas that are mentioned in Activities.

North of RN "14," the channel depth drops to 9 feet MLW (centerline) and narrows to approximately 100 feet. Continuing past RN "16," you'll find the Housatonic Boat Club, offering guest moorings. Brewer Stratford Marina, located at G C "19," has more than 100 slips, and excellent facilities. From here, the dredged channel again drops slightly to 8 feet mlw (centerline).

The Route-1 Bridge is manned 24 hours and the bridgetender can be reached on VHF 13. Between the Route 1 bridge and the Interstate-95 Bridge on the west side is the Marina at the Dock, a full-service facility with accommodations for transients. Remember that there is an enforced steerage speed limit/no-wake zone near all marine facilities and between the Route-1 Bridge and railroad bridge.

If you need to have the bascule railroad bridge in Devon opened, you must give Metro-North (212-340-2050) 24 hours notice. The Interstate-95 Bridge marks the line between saltwater fishing areas, where a license is not required, and the freshwater areas, where a license is required. South of the bridge is the state launching ramp on the east shore in Milford. The Stratford fishing pier and town

ramp, called Bond's Dock (203-385-4085), is located on the river's west shore between Brown's Boatyard and the Housatonic Boat Club.

The Housatonic River can be explored as far north as Derby and Shelton, about 11.5nm upstream of Stratford Point; just be sure to keep your eye on the depth-sounder as you travel upriver.

High tide at Shelton is 1 hour 35 minutes later than Bridgeport; low tide is 2 hours 44 minutes later. Multiply height of tide at Bridgeport by 0.7 for height of tide at Shelton. Mean tidal range is 5.0 feet.

Above Devon, the river runs 3 feet deep, and the hydroelectric dam near Derby is the end of navigable water. At this point, the Naugatuck River runs into the Housatonic.

Shoreside & Emergency Services
Airport: Bridgeport Sikorsky (203-576-7498)
Bus: Greater Bridgeport Transit (203-333-3031)
Coast Guard: New Haven (203-468-4464) or VHF 16
Police, Fire, Ambulance: 911
Tow Service:
SEA TOW —24-Hour Dispatch (800-4SEATOW)
—Southern Connecticut (203-331-0410)
Tow BoatU.S.—24-Hour Dispatch (800-391-4869)
—Milford (203-874-6109)
Train: Amtrak (800-USA-RAIL)
—Metro-North (800-638-7646)

Oyster Country

The Paugussett Indians settled Milford because of its location beside Long Island Sound, the Oyster River and the Housatonic River, and among the Wepawaug and Indian Rivers. They knew that the rivers, tidal flats, and marshes would provide an abundant supply of fish, clams, and oysters. After years of successful harvesting, they sold the land in 1639 to English colonists from the nearby Quinnipiac colony, now New Haven.

The 15 Puritan families who settled here established a stern church society governed by members called "The Seven Pillars," in reference to the Biblical passage on which their strict lifestyle was based. Granting suffrage to six non-members of the church fellowship proved they weren't too rigid, although that act did keep the town from being admitted to the New Haven Colony until 1643. Both became part of the Connecticut Colony in 1664.

Much like those early settlers, today's visitors will find the water is very important to Milfordites. Oystering remains a big industry in this city of 50,000. In fact, Connecticut oysters are widely regarded as the best-tasting in the U.S. and they net the highest returns, thanks to cold, clean water and fine aquaculture techniques. Having the longest coastline in Connecticut, Milford is also proud of its beaches, six of which are open to the public.

With its waters such an economically important asset, Milford was one of the first coastal communities in the state to develop a Harbor Management Plan. Two old sewage treatment plants were shut down in favor of a new one, leading directly to significantly cleaner water in the harbor. Other towns have followed Milford's shining example—good news for the health and future of Long Island Sound.

The serene Milford Green is New England's second-longest town green. © Maptech

All Coast Guard Stations Monitor VHF Channel 16

marinalife — Convenient Online Boat Slip Reservations .com

Marine Facilities and Services	Phone	Monitors / Working VHF Channel	Number of Transient Berths / Moorings	Seasonal / Year-round	Maximum LOA	Approach / Dockside Depth in Feet at MLW	Hookups: Fresh Water / Phone / Cable TV	110V ★ 220V ▲ 3 Phase ■ / Maximum Amps	Ramp / Dinghy Dock / Launch Service	Rail / Lift / Crane / Trailer Capacity (tons)	Diesel / Wood / Fiberglass / Electronics	Repairs: Propellor / Sail / Rigging / Gas	Gas / Diesel Fuel	Fuel Brand	Marine / Groceries / Ice / Bait / LPG / CNG	Restrooms / Showers / Laundry / Pumpout	Public Phone / Restaurant / Snack Bar	Hotel / Pool / Tennis / Golf	Mastercard / VISA / Discover / AmEx
1 Milford Yacht Club	203-877-1261						Y				PRIVATE								
2 PORT MILFORD (p. 155)	203-877-7802		10/	Y	55	10/8	FP	★■50	DL	L35	All				MGIB	RS		All	MV
3 Milford Harbor Marina	203-878-2900	68/	20/	Y	50	8/8	F	★50	D				GD	Tex	MI	All	P		All
4 MILFORD BOAT WORKS (p. 157)	203-877-1475	68/	10/	Y	50	7/8	F	★50	D	LC35	All		GD		MI	All	P		All
5 Milford Landing (p. 153)	203-874-1610	9/	40/	S	65	10/9	F	★▲■50	RD						I	All	T	P	MV
6 Spencer's Marina	203-874-4173			S	45	10/6				L12		G	GD	Tex	MI	RS	P		All

Information in these listings is provided by the facilities themselves. An asterisk (*) indicates that the facility did not respond to our most recent requests for information. (B) represents a BOAT/U.S. cooperating marina.

Sitting pretty in Milford Harbor. © Maptech

best place to begin stretching your legs, window shopping, picking up provisions, and getting a bite to eat. That's how most visitors spend their time here, but there's more to do.

Milford and oysters go hand in hand. The Wepawaug River's tidal flats and the shallow waters of The Gulf provide the perfect breeding ground for these tasty bivalves, which need an influx of fresh water in order to produce. West of the bar leading to Charles Island are some of the state's only shellfishing beds that are entirely open to the public. You don't need a permit, and the restrictions are simple: use hand tools, respect private property, and restrict your take to a half-bushel per person each day. Shellfishing is prohibited at the following beaches: Silver, Gulf, Gulf Pond, Fort Trumbull, Cedar, and Calf Pen Creek. Call the Environmental Health Deptment (203-783-3287) for more information on where to take your rake.

Anglers are permitted to drop a line into Gulf Pond. The tidal surge under the bridge makes this a favorite spot for bunkers and blues. Gulf Pond is also an excellent spot for birding, as huge rafts of ducks collect on the safe waters of the preserve (avid birdwatchers should check out the viewing platforms).

ACTIVITIES: Just steps from the harbor, New England's second-longest green (Boston Common is No. 1) stretches the breadth of downtown, welcoming you to Milford like a giant red—well, green—carpet. This is where Milford's motto rings true, "a small city…with a big heart." The town center is the

Standing about a half-mile offshore, connected to the mainland by a sandbar, or tombolo, is Charles Island. This partially wooded island is rich in local lore. An Indian chief supposedly put a curse on it when his daughter was captured. Like every other bit of land in the Sound, Charles Island is said to have some of Captain Kidd's treasure buried on it. A religious retreat occupied the island until 1938, when the infamous hurricane swept it away. The island then changed hands during World War II and was closed to the public until the state bought it and made it accessible once again. You may explore the ruins while daydreaming of the pirates who spent time here. In recent years, the island has suffered at the hands of careless tourists, who have left behind their garbage, attracting a herd of large rats. So remember, if you carry it in, carry it out. Also be aware that several species of birds nest here and should not be disturbed. Finally, watch for the tide change, as the bar leading to the harbor is fully covered with a swift current when the water's up.

Aficionados of the arts will find a variety of presentations put on by the Milford Fine Arts Council (203-878-6647), which is located at the train station downtown. Their annual sandcastle competition, held in late July or early August when the tides are best for the event, is renowned throughout New England.

Milford was once a deep-water port, and the town still maintains some of its old seaport atmosphere. With 17 miles of coastline and the Wharf Lane Complex of historic homes maintained by the Milford Historical Society (203-874-2664), you'll have no trouble finding seaside enjoyment.

RESTAURANTS & PROVISIONS: In Milford, when you're in port, you're in town. Finding a restaurant, a bar, or just a snack near the water is easy, as all are just a few steps from the marinas. An added benefit is that the walk back to the docks is somewhat downhill, just in case you've indulged too much.

If you like fresh seafood, try the Stonebridge Restaurant (203-874-7947), next to its namesake bridge and a lovely waterfall on the Wepawaug River. The scene here is often who's being seen here, as the outdoor setting in summer makes it a favorite spot for socializing.

Seven Seas (203-877-SEAS) is a casual stop in downtown that's locally famous for its pub grub. Night owls flock to Archie Moore's (203-876-5088), where the kitchen's open every night 'til midnight. The popular hangout is known all over the world—or at least the state—for its Buffalo wings. Across the lot, you'll find a lot at Warner's Harborview (203-877-7237), where they dish up fish specialties nightly, along with the American standbys of steak, prime rib, and chicken.

If you're feeling adventurous like Columbus and are craving his homeland's delights, Armellino's (203-874-6509) is about 2 miles west of the green on Bridgeport Avenue. In the other direction, La Cantina (203-877-1170) is a mile away on New Haven Avenue. Both places treat

CLAM UP—THIS IS OYSTER COUNTRY!

There are more than 55,000 acres of public and private oyster beds in Connecticut waters today. *Crassostrea virginica*, the common eastern oyster, is the most valuable shellfish taken from the Sound, with major beds in the waters off Milford, New Haven, Bridgeport, and Norwalk. In the past few years the state has made major new commitments to further expand the seed-oyster beds. During the last half of the 19th century, and for two decades into the 20th, the oyster was the most widely eaten shellfish in the United States. Connecticut, blessed with natural oyster beds square miles in size, was the major producer in New England.

The enormous supply of the slimy (but delicous) bivalves did not escape the attention of the earliest Connecticut settlers. There were stories of foot-long oysters with five-pound meats, and oyster beds thick enough to block navigable waters. Unfortunately for fortune hunters, Long Island Sound oysters do not produce pearls as do their cousins in tropical waters.

By the early 1700s, many natural oyster beds were nearly gone. (The idea of cultivating the beds didn't occur to anyone for another century.) A law was passed prohibiting harvesting from May to August, allowing the oysters to spawn in peace.

Though New Englanders and New Yorkers could not compete with Chesapeake Bay oystermen for sheer production, the northern industry in the late 1800s had several advantages over the southern: the world's largest fleet of power oyster boats; more acres of private oyster grounds; and an oyster that kept longer in shipment. Connecticut's oysters also were more valuable, usually selling for about $10 more per bushel than did those from the Chesapeake Bay because of their superior taste and keeping capacity.

Oystering declined in the 1920s due to pollution, overharvesting, severe winter storms, and changing land use patterns. The low point came after the great hurricane of 1938, when thousands of oyster beds were buried under a layer of silt.

Today there are more than 40,000 acres of shellfish beds leased or franchised by the industry from the state. In addition, several Connecticut towns transplant oysters from polluted inshore waters to clean beds of their shores for later harvest. Private citizens wanting to harvest local oysters for personal use should contact their local municipality for more information and permits.

you like family. Scribner's (203-878-7019), farther east and out on Village Road, has a sparkling reputation throughout New England, owed to its serious shellfish menu. Reservations and a cab are recommended.

Beachgoers like to stop at Park Lane Deli (203-878-1498) or Harborwalk Deli & Caterers (203-783-1627) for sandwiches to scarf on the sand. Or put one footlong in front of the other and step into Subway (203-878-4059). No baloney, but Milford is this fast-growing franchise's world headquarters.

An affordable breakfast—or lunch—is the specialty at the Milford Diner (203-877-2093), a local landmark situated just a stone's throw from the Stonebridge. Another good spot for early-risers is The Corner (203-882-1150), offering the old standbys with a twist, as in stuffed French toast. Elfie's European Bakery (203-878-8393) can set you up with more calories than you can shake a cinnamon stick at. The Dunkin' Donuts on the green adds the modern American flair to the town's fare.

Where are you? Scoopy Doo's at Milford Landing satisfies those begging for a treat. Or head over to Rainbow Gardens (203-878-2500), where a homemade and hearty dessert— we bet you can't finish yours—is an additional pot of gold after their gourmet lunch or dinner.

Harrison Hardware (203-878-2491), within walking distance of the docks, sells much of what you will need to make repairs to your vessel. There's also a convenience store, pharmacy, camera shop, and bank around the green. For galley-provisioning on a larger scale, the Shop Rite (203-876-7868) supermarket is less than a mile away on Cherry Street.

NAVIGATION & ANCHORAGES: Use ChartKit Region 3, page 29; Maptech™ Waterproof Charts 1 and 16; and Maptech™ electronic and NOAA paper charts 12370 (1:20,000), 12364 (1:40,000), and 12354 (1:80,000). Use tide tables for Bridgeport. High tide at Milford Harbor is 8 minutes earlier; low tide is 10 minutes earlier. Use height of tide at Bridgeport for height of tide at Milford Harbor. Mean tidal range is 6.6 feet.

The Fl R 4s 27ft 5M "10" at the entrance to Milford Harbor is 4.6nm from Stratford Point and 7nm from the channel entrance between the New Haven Harbor breakwaters.

From the east, you'll see Pond Point and RN "12," and Welches Point and RN "2." They both have a number of rocks just off shore, so stay south of the nuns.

From the south and west, you'll want to be careful of the shoals to the east and south of Charles Island, between Fl R 4s BELL R "16" and GC "1."

CAUTION: At high tide, you may see local boaters cutting across the bar to Charles Island, but we suggest you go around, rather than going aground.

At 7 to 20 feet deep, the body of water between Charles Island and Welches Point, known as The Gulf, is a fine

Looking north over Burns Point and into Milford Harbor. © Maptech/James T. Abts

anchorage, except in a south or southeasterly blow. The water shallows gradually leading to the north shore, except where the dredged channel leads into Milford Harbor. You'll find the most desirable anchorage north of Charles Island; be sure to anchor far enough offshore so

that the mosquitoes don't arrive on the wings of a slight westerly breeze.

The farther from shore you drop your hook, the more likely you'll encounter some swells; these will rock you to sleep, although some boaters have met unexpected rotary currents in this anchorage. The bottom of The Gulf is hard sand, but it gets softer nearer shore. Be sure to watch for oyster stakes along both the east and west shores.

The channel leading into Milford Harbor is about 100 feet wide and well marked. The controlling depth of the channel is charted at 7 feet in the inner channel and 9 feet in the outer channel (see note below). Be aware that heavy silting has reduced depths outside the channel to only about 1 foot in many cases, and you may still see an occasional fisherman propped against a buoy, rod in hand.

NOTE: With the expansion of Milford Landing, the Milford channel has been dredged to 9 feet MLW past Wilcox Park (7 feet MLW at the very top).

The Milford Yacht Club sponsors small boat races, so on weekends expect the channel to be crowded with sailors on their way to the race course. Sailors entering the harbor against an ebb tide may have difficulty with the current. A strong southerly can cause waves to pile up in the channel, making it more difficult to enter.

"Nauti" words

Longshoreman: *a person employed on the wharves of a port, as in loading and unloading vessels* (circa 1805—1815).

But what is "long" doing in the word *longshoreman*? Because these men worked such *long* days? Because they were in this career for the *long* haul? Because the work was strenuous and boring, leaving them *long* in the face?

Some or all of the above conditions may have been accurate, but the etymological answer is that *longshore* originated as a variant of *alongshore*. When ships were unloaded, the sailors passed the goods from their ships to the men *'long* the shore.

And while his title sounds a bit fancier, a *stevedore* toils just the same as a longshoreman. This term derives from the Spanish *estibador*, meaning "one who packs or stows."

Gulf Pond empties into Milford Harbor just inside the eastern breakwater, which is marked by Fl R 4s 27ft 5M "10." When the current ebbs, the rush of water forced under the bridge at the mouth of Gulf Pond is tremendous; if you're not careful, you may be set onto Burns Point to the west.

There's a no-wake speed limit in Milford Harbor, while in the outer channel it's 5 mph. The bottom is a mixture of sand and mud, but there's no anchoring as space is limited, and there is no swing room. Several facilities, including Port Milford, Milford Boat Works, and Milford Landing, have transient slips available.

Shoreside & Emergency Services
Airport: Tweed New Haven (203-466-8833)
Bus: Connecticut Transit (203-624-0151)
Coast Guard: New Haven (203-468-4450) or VHF 16
Police, Fire, Ambulance: 911
Radio Telephone: MARITEL VHF 27
Taxi: Milford Taxi (203-877-1468)
Tow Service:
SEA TOW —24-Hour Dispatch (800-4SEATOW)
—Southern Connecticut (203-331-0410)
Tow BoatU.S.—24-Hour Dispatch (800-391-4869)
—Norwalk (203-855-7918)

© Maptech

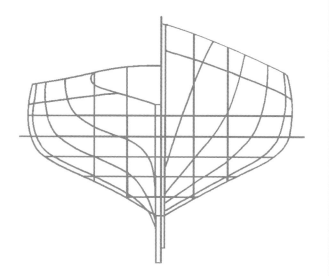

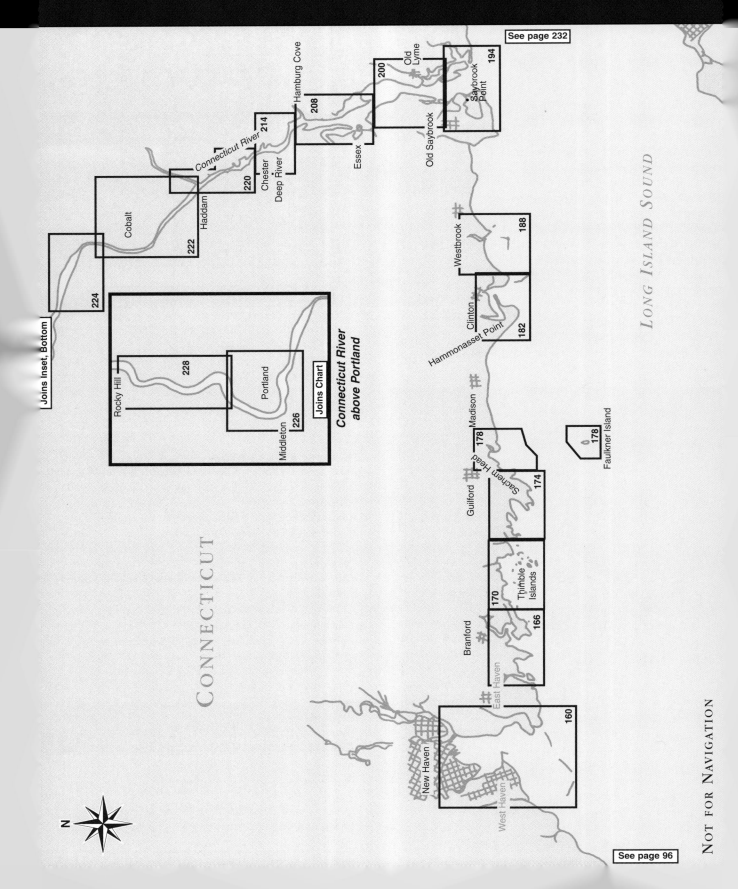

See page 232

194

Saybrook Point

200

Old Lyme

208

Hamburg Cove

214

Connecticut River

220

Chester

Deep River

Essex

Old Saybrook

222

Haddam

Cobalt

224

Joins Inset, Bottom

228

Rocky Hill

226

Portland

Middleton

Joins Chart

Connecticut River above Portland

188

Westbrook

182

Clinton

Hammonasset Point

178

Madison

178

Faulkner Island

178

Guilford

Sachem Head

174

170

Thimble Islands

166

Branford

East Haven

160

New Haven

West Haven

CONNECTICUT

LONG ISLAND SOUND

N

NOT FOR NAVIGATION

See page 96

New York City's grasp on Connecticut begins to wane as you enter the Central Connecticut Coast. Distinct New England-style towns and harbors emerge, welcoming you to the beginning of old-time New England.

New Haven, the intellectual epicenter of the state, begins your journey eastward. Home to Yale University, the Elm City is technically a commercial port, but transient-friendly marinas offer a key to this exciting city. Next comes **Branford** and the **Thimble Islands**. The latter offers top-notch facilities and the former a slice of Maine: granite islands scattered about an area perfect for anchoring. **Guilford** offers one of the nicest town greens around, surrounded by pleasant shops. **Clinton** serves as the mid-way point between New York City and Newport; as such, it's quite busy, and it certainly caters to transients. Westbrook is a boater's dream where you'll find restaurants, chandleries, bait shops, and grocery stores.

North Cove flowers, © Maptech

The Connecticut, the largest river in New England, twists and turns past **East Haddam** and **Glastonbury** for 43 miles up to the state capital—Hartford. Along the way, you'll see **Old Saybrook** and **Old Lyme**, just a few miles north of the mouth. Charming **Essex** lives up to its reputation of being one of the nicest small towns in America, and **Chester** and **Deep River** offer glimpses of suburban Connecticut life.

Navigating the Central Connecticut Coast

Approach **New Haven Harbor** from Mo(A) WHIS RW "NH," Approximately 2.5nm south of Morgan Point. New Haven Harbor is the second-largest commercial port in Connecticut. The channels are well marked, but be on the lookout for the many commercial vessels you'll encounter. If necessary, try hailing them on VHF 13 or 16. *Refer to the New Haven Harbor chapter for more information.*

From Mo(A) WHIS RW "NH," head 063°m to approach Cow & Calf, your welcome to **Branford Harbor**. Be certain to keep Fl R 2.5s BELL R "34" at Cow & Calf to your north before entering the harbor. Heed the markers as you approach. The Branford Channel carries about 8 feet of water but shallows to 6.5 feet in the river. You'll find plenty of hospitable facilities up here. *Refer to the Branford Harbor chapter for more information.*

Again, **from Mo(A) WHIS RW "NH,"** if you simply want to skip along the coast, steer a course of 097°m. On this route, once you pass Fl R 4s BELL R "10A" at Townshend Ledge, you can head 078°m to approach the **Thimble Islands**. Keep Branford Reef Light (Fl 6s 30ft 7M) to your south on that approach. Use caution when poking about in the Thimbles: all of the underwater obstructions are made of granite, not sand, so bumping bottom can do some damage.

Refer to the Thimble Islands chapter for more information.

Once abeam of Fl R 4s BELL R "26" at Browns Reef, turn to 067°m and head for Fl R 4s BELL R "22" to find a cozy anchorage near **Sachem's Head**. Once abeam of Fl R 4s BELL R "10GI," located at the western edge of Faulkners Island's shoals, you'll have a clear approach to **Guilford Harbor**. Steer toward G C "1." You'll find two facilities in the West River, and the town marina in the East River. Entrances to both rivers can be reached from Fl R 4s BELL R "4." *Refer to the Guilford, Madison & Faulker Island chapter for more information.*

The aforementioned course of 097°m from New Haven Harbor approach buoy Mo(A) WHIS RW "NH," will take you to Fl G 4s GONG G "15," located north of **Faulkners Island**. From this mark, continue along a course of 100°m for access the upcoming harbors. This course will lead you toward Fl R 4s BELL R "8," located south-southeast of the Connecticut River's mouth.

The approaches to the harbors along the way are quite simple. About 5nm on this route, once abeam of Hammonasset Point, you can turn into **Clinton Harbor**. Make way for Fl G 4s G "3." The entrance channel is straightforward as long as you follow the markers closely. *Refer to the Clinton Harbor chapter for more information.*

Heading into the Menunketesuck and Patchogue rivers—where all of the facilities are located—stick to the channel or you'll get stuck in the mud. Once you've entered the channel at Fl R 4s R "2," a no-wake speed limit is in effect. *Refer to the Clinton Harbor chapter for more information.*

While continuing east toward Duck Island Roads, the entrance to Westbrook sits to your port side, northeast of R N "8." Once abeam of Fl R 4s BELL R "2" at Cornfield Point Shoal, you can make way toward the lights on the Saybrook Breakwater. The well-marked river meanders north, passing Old Saybrook, Old Lyme, Essex, Chester, Deep River, and East Haddam along the way. *Refer to the Connecticut River chapters for more information on these destinations.*

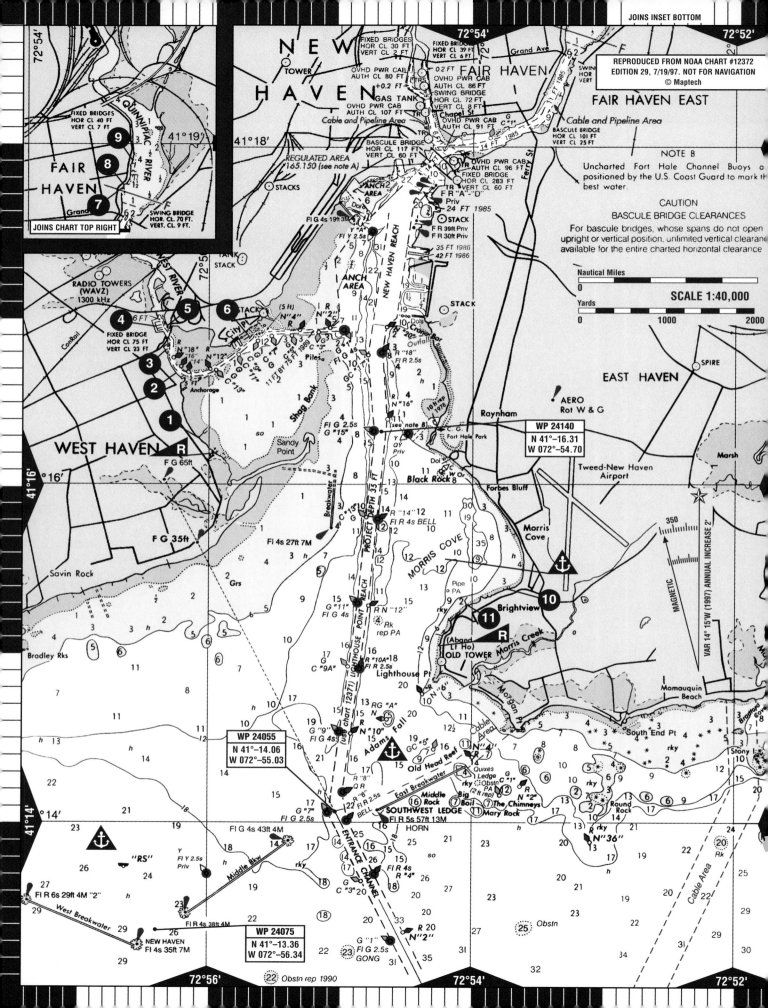

Culinary Creations & History

What do a meat cleaver, a tomato pie, and a pie plate have in common? They all helped change the course of American culture. At least that's New Haven's take on things, because it was right here in the Elm City where these three "items" whimsically played a role in American history.

It started in 1900 when Louis Lassen's meat cleaver took a few swift chops. Lassen cut up the raw trimmings from some steaks, placed it between two pieces of bread, and the All-American hamburger was born. It was that easy. His eatery, Louis' Lunch, has become a legendary New Haven landmark.

Not long after the hamburger became a household word, pizza (or more correctly, apizza) made its debut in New Haven. It's widely held that Italian immigrant Frank Pepe was the first in the world to go commercial with pizza when he opened his shop in the Wooster Square section of town in the 1930s. His 12-inch "tomato pies" were baked in brick ovens still used at Pepe's Pizzeria today. Salvatore (Sally) Consiglio opened shop eight years after Pepe and baked pizza in similar fashion a few doors down. Long lines—really long on weekends—are standard fare at both Sally's and Pepe's.

The freedom schooner *Amistad* sits at Long Wharf for all to visit. © Maptech

In a very different sense, another popular food made in New Haven is probably as important a contribution to American culture—the Frisbee. The Frisbee Pie Company, bakers of Mrs. Frisbee's Pies, was actually located in Bridgeport, Connecticut. In a nutshell, the story goes that in the 1920s Yale students took to flinging the empty pie tins—each one stamped with the Frisbee name—across the New Haven Green. The sport caught on amongst the

	Marine Facilities and Services		Number of Transient Berths	Monitors / Working VHF Channel	Approach / Dockside Depth in Feet at MLW	Seasonal / Year-round	Maximum LOA	110V ∗ 220V ▲ 3 Phase ■ Maximum Amps	Hookups: Fresh Water / Phone / Cable TV	Ramp / Dinghy Dock / Launch Service	Rail / Lift / Crane / Trailer Capacity (tons)	Diesel / Wood / Fiberglass / Electronics	Repairs: Propellor / Sail / Rigging / Gas	Marine / Groceries / Ice / Bait / LPG / CNG	Gas / Diesel Fuel	Fuel Brand	Restrooms / Showers / Laundry / Pumpout	Public Phone / Pool / Tennis / Golf	Mastercard / VISA / Discover / AmEx	Hotel / Restaurant / Snack Bar
1	Marine General	203-933-3208				Y					SHIP STORE—BOATING ACCESSORIES									
2	West Haven Yacht Club	203-933-9825				Y					PRIVATE—MEMBERS ONLY									
3	Shiner's Cove Marina	203-934-2182				Y	28	11/11	F			L500	PGWFE				MI	R	P	P	All
4	**WEST COVE MARINA** p. 165	203-933-3000		6/	S	45	10/8	F	★▲■50		T35			G	Tex	I	All	P	P	MVA
5	City Point Yacht Club	203-789-9301		2/	S	40	15/6		PRIVATE—RECIPROCAL PRIVILEGES							RS		P		
6	**OYSTER POINT MARINA** (B) p. 163	203-624-5895	9/	6/	Y	85	10/8	F	★30		L10			GD		MG	All		All	All
7	Waucoma Yacht Club	203-789-9530		6/	S	40	4/4	FP	★▲50	All	L30			G		I	RS		S	
8	Fair Haven Marina	203-777-0523	9/	6/	Y	40	4/4	F	★15	All	LT10	PGDE		G		MI	R			
9	Farren's Marina*	203-777-3844	9/	3/	S	55	5/5	F	★30							I			RS	
10	New Haven Yacht Club*	203-469-9608	68/		S	35	15/2			D	LT2						RS		P	
11	New Haven Marina*	203-469-8230			S	25	3/2	F			L5						R			

All Coast Guard Stations Monitor VHF Channel 16

marinalife.com — Convenient Online Boat Slip Reservations

Information in these listings is provided by the facilities themselves. An asterisk (*) indicates that the facility did not respond to our most recent request for information. (B) represents a BOAT/U.S. cooperating marina.

You'll pass lighthouse Point Park, Morris Creek, and Morgan Point to the east as you enter New Haven Harbor. © Maptech/James T. Abts

college set, where its popularity still resides. Mrs. Frisbee's pies are long gone, but their legacy remains. Today's "tins" are plastic, but in New Haven lies their endearing origin.

ACTIVITIES: From the marine facilities on the Quinnipiac River, you're going to need access to some wheels—be it a cab, a friend, or a loaner—in order to enjoy all New Haven has to offer. Once in the car, head for the Visitor Information Center (203-777-8550, 800-332-STAY, or www.newhavencvb.org) at Long Wharf, open Memorial Day to Labor Day from 10 a.m. to 7 p.m., to get the scoop on what's going on in port.

Cast against a background of industry, the schooner *Amistad* stands out among the industrial backdrop. Climb aboard for an educational journey into the past and learn about the well-known slave revolt that began off Cuba and ended in New Haven. The 1839 mutiny aboard the Spanish vessel, *La Amistad*, was chronicled by Steven Spielberg in the film *Amistad*. You can't miss the ship—it's within eyeshot of the Visitor's Information Center.

Yale University, the intellectual epicenter of Connecticut, has enough sights and activities to keep you busy for a few days. The history and architecture of the school are fascinating; an inspiring, free tour is offered by the Admissions Office (203-432-2300). Embrace the opportunity to go along, if you don't mind being watched by the many gargoyles peering from their cornice perches all over campus. Stop at the Whitney House Art Gallery (203-281-3562) to enjoy one of the best collections in the state. If you're interested in more dramatic renderings, spend an afternoon gawking at the huge dinosaur fossils at the Peabody Museum of Natural History (203-432-5050). The gigantic

Tyrannosaurus rex head and even larger fossil of a prehistoric sea turtle are magnificent.

Historic sights abound in the city of New Haven. Call the New Haven Colony Historical Society (203-562-4183) or the Eli Whitney Museum (203-777-1833), both on Whitney Avenue, to discover more about the heritage of the "Elm City."

New Haven is blessed with more theaters than any other city in the Nutmeg State, and you're bound to see some good acts. Numerous stars, including Dustin Hoffman and Meryl Streep, got their start at the Yale School of Drama. For prime viewing, try these theaters: the Shubert (203-624-1825), Long Wharf (203-787-4282), Yale Repertory (203-432-1234), and Palace (203-789-2120). The Arts Council of Greater New Haven (203-772-2788) can fill you in on all the current exhibitions during your stay.

Take your family out to a New Haven Ravens (203-782-1666) baseball game, take them out to the crowd. Buy them some peanuts and crackerjack, they won't care if they never get back... you get the picture. The Ravens are the Colorado Rockies' AA Eastern League affiliate, and at minor league prices, you won't find a better entertainment bargain.

Big-name musical acts find their way to New Haven at joints like Toad's Place (203-624-8623), but you sports-aholics will want to want to watch out for Sports Haven (203-821-3100). It's a nighttime hot spot where you can tune into nearly every game being played. If you're not in the mood for the tube, Sports Haven has a restaurant and nightclub as well.

RESTAURANTS & PROVISIONS: New Haven provides opportunities to satiate all different taste buds—American, French,

Italian, Jamaican, Indian, and more. Right at Oyster Point Marina, treat yourself to the popular Sage American Bar & Grill (203-787-3466). Also close by, Dockside Market & Deli (203-562-4947) can put together some tasty sandwiches, not to mention help stock the galley with the basics. The Rusty Scupper (203-777-5711), at the north end of Long Wharf, also serves good seafood. Or pull into Morris Cove, drop anchor, and dinghy up to Amarante's (203-467-2531). This seaside restaurant serves a continental menu, and if you're lucky, you might catch one of their clambakes.

A trip to New Haven is not complete without a slice of 'za. New Haven is famous for its pizza—after all, it was invented here. Modern Apizza (203-776-5306) on State Street serves some of the best and most interesting pizzas around. Service can be slow but you'll be rewarded for your patience with some great food.

On Wooster Street you'll find two pizza legends: Frank Pepe Pizzeria (203-865-5762) and Sally's Apizza (203-624-5271). You'll most likely be greeted by a line, but it's worth it. It's so good, many customers order extra pies to take home to the freezer. What is not very well known is that there's a little restaurant in the back of Pepe's called The Spot (203-865-7602). It's owned by Pepe's and serves the exact same tomato pies (as they're called at Pepe's), but The Spot rarely has a line. Shhhh—you didn't hear it from us.

Nestled among the houses on Willow Street you'll find a tiny restaurant and pub called Archie Moore's (203-773-9870).

Walk through the hallowed doors of Yale University and you enter the intellectual epicenter of Connecticut. © Maptech

Looking north over New Haven Harbor. © Maptech/James T. Abts

Take a seat in a very casual atmosphere and dig in to great food including fabulous chicken wings.

But the most famous of them all is—a drum roll please—Louis' Lunch (203-562-5507). The reputed home of the first hamburger is a local icon, especially with college students.

NAVIGATION & ANCHORAGES: Use ChartKit Region 3, page 20; Maptech™ Waterproof Chart 1, 16, and 17; and Maptech™ electronic and NOAA paper charts 12371 (1:20,000), 12372SC (1:40,000), and 12354 (1:80,000). Use tide tables for Bridgeport. High tide at New Haven City Dock is 1 minute later; low tide is 1 minute earlier. Multiply height of tide at Bridgeport by 0.9 for height of tide at New Haven City Dock. Mean tidal range is 6 feet.

The breakwaters marking the main entrance to New Haven Harbor are 4.7nm from Blyn Rock outside Branford Harbor, and 7.4nm from The Gulf at Milford Harbor. The Port Jefferson Harbor entrance is 17.5nm away.

New Haven Harbor is the second-largest commercial port in Connecticut, so you can expect the channels to be well marked and the water deep. From Long Island Sound on a clear day, you should be able to spot the Soldiers and Sailors Monument atop East Rock and the strobe marking the smoke stack of the United Illuminating power plant on the east shore. If you get close enough, the abandoned lighthouse in Lighthouse Point Park is visible as well.

Be cautious of the many commercial vessels you'll encounter in the area. They are less maneuverable, so give them the right of way. If you can't see the pilothouse, they probably can't see you; if necessary, try hailing them on VHF 13 or 16.

From the east or south, most boaters can approach the entrance between the east and middle breakwaters from any angle; just be sure to stay near to the center of the channel, so as not to be set onto the breakwaters by the current. To play it safe, pick up Mo(A) WHIS RW "NH," south of the New Haven Harbor entrance channel, and head about 348°m. This will take you to the channel between the middle and east outer breakwaters, marked on the east end of the middle breakwater by Fl G 4s 43ft 4M and Southwest Ledge Light (Fl R 5s 57ft 13M HORN), on the west end of the east breakwater. Line up the range lights in West Haven (F G 65ft over F G 35ft) and that will lead you up the channel between the breakwaters.

In good weather, cruising boats can avoid the traffic in the shipping lane by using the channel between the east breakwater and Morgan Point. Don't cut north of R N "36" south of Round Rock. Follow the buoys east of Quixes Ledge, pass between the breakwater and R N "4" (favor the R N "4" side as it shoals near the breakwater), and pass south of R N "6" off Lighthouse Point. This route takes you to the main channel north or R N "10."

Give Adams Fall, marked by R G N "A" a wide berth, as it's only about 5 feet deep, and keep clear of the 4-foot spot southeast of R N "12."

North of the east breakwater, you'll find a good anchorage. Also try Morris Cove, located north of the lighthouse, for good holding ground, but be aware that the ride will be rough in the prevailing southwest winds. The New Haven Yacht Club maintains moorings in the cove, and some should be available to members of other yacht clubs on a reciprocal basis. The yacht club also offers launch service during the summer daylight hours. Be aware that Black Rock, south of Fort Hale Park on the east shore and marked by a W Or C, often grabs unwary visitors and keeps them grounded for a while.

From the west, you'll have plenty of room to enter the harbor between the mainland and the west breakwater. The west end of the breakwater is marked by Fl R 6s 29ft 4M "2." New Haven Light (Fl 4s 35ft 7M) is on the east end of the breakwater. The middle breakwater is marked by Fl R 4s 38ft 4M on its west end and FL G 4s 43ft 4M on its east end.

Behind the breakwaters, you'll see a number of anglers fishing for blues. Except during bad weather, this is a decent spot to anchor for a while or slip out of an unfavorable current. You'll also find a few tugs and barges anchored here as they await an open berth in one of the inner harbors, or if they're waiting for more favorable weather before departing.

South of Sandy Point, New Haven looks like much of the rest of the Connecticut coast; north of the point, you'll surely notice the heavy industrialization. The inner harbor begins at Sandy Point and stretches from the west shore all the way to Fort Hale and the Coast Guard Station (203-773-2400) on the east shore. The waters outside the channel in the inner harbor are often very shallow.

CAUTION: Do not stray from the channel when approaching the inner harbor. The breakwater south of Sandy Point is submerged at high tide.

Choices for anchoring in the inner harbor are mostly limited to the western side due to the many commercial facilities along the eastern shore. If you'd like more comfortable accommodations, we suggest heading toward Oyster Point Marina at City Point or continuing up the West River to West Cove Marina. Both facilities have berths for transients, along with amenities.

The channel into the West River runs about 8.5 feet deep up to R N "18." City Point is perhaps the quietest place in the harbor and offers easy cab access to West Haven and downtown New Haven. You'll find a small deli and market at City Point, and there is courtesy dockage available through Oyster Point Marina. Because the tidal

range in the harbor is 6 feet, you may see small runabouts cutting across Shag Bank to City Point, but we suggest you stay to the channel.

You may also want to anchor up beyond the Tomlinson Bridge on the Quinnipiac River. The bridge has an 11-foot vertical clearance (mhw) when closed, but will open if you call the bridgetender on VHF 13. However, the bridge doesn't always work correctly, as it has been slammed frequently by commercial vessels. In the summer, the bridge often overheats and gets stuck until the fire department can arrive to cool it down. Immediately following the Tomlinson Bridge is the I-95 bridge, often referred to as the "Q Bridge," which has a vertical clearance of about 60 feet (mhw).

The two other bridges upstream, at Ferry Street and Grand Avenue, monitor VHF 13 and can be signaled with blasts of your horn. The channel markers disappear after Grand Avenue and so does the water; you should stay to the left side of the channel on your way to Fair Haven Marina or the Waucoma Yacht Club. Also be prepared to face currents of up to 6 knots.

Shoreside & Emergency Services
Airport:
—Tweed New Haven (203-466-8833)
Bus:
—Connecticut Transit (203-624-0151)
Coast Guard:
—New Haven (203-468-4464) or VHF 16
—203-468-4455) emergency
Police, Fire, Ambulance: 911
Taxi:
—Taxi Service (203-466-6666)
Tow Service:
SEA TOW —24-Hour Dispatch (800-4SEATOW)
—Central Conn. (860-395-0405)
Tow BoatU.S.—24-Hour Dispatch (800-391-4869)
—Clinton (860-388-4065)

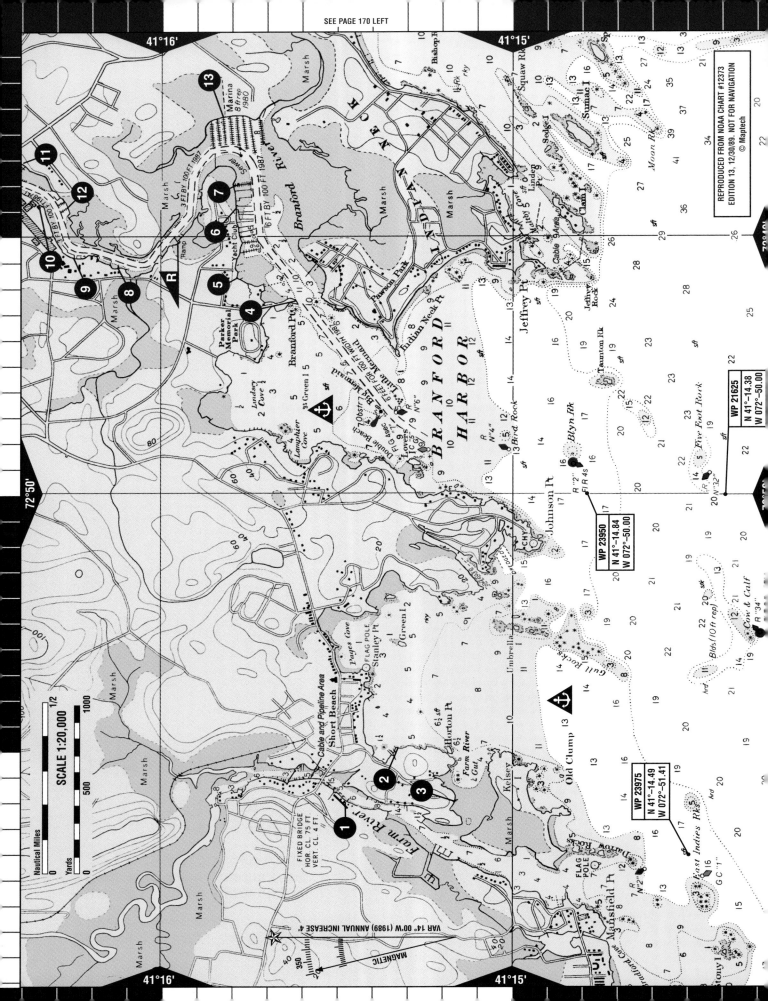

Streetcars and Granite

When the trolley came to the quiet coastal town of Branford in 1900, opportunity followed. There were opportunities for city folk to move outside of town and commute to work, and there were opportunities for citizens to move about conveniently and inexpensively. But by mid-century, urbanites began to spread out into the suburbs, making trolley lines less convenient. In August of 1941, the local newspaper, the *New Haven Register* summed up the fate of the trolley: "…Like the buffalo, lumbering yellow electric cars are fast becoming extinct, vanishing from city streets…"

The streetcars soon vanished from the streets, but Branford kept its grip on the trolley era by creating a museum, (now the oldest trolley museum in the country) the Shore Line Trolley Museum. The museum boasts nearly 100 vintage vehicles built between 1878 and 1962, from passenger streetcars to larger rapid transit

The Branford River plays home to a host of marine facilities, as well as some wildlife. © Maptech

cars to rubber-tired vehicles. A few cars are still in working order, and they can take you on a three-mile round-trip over original tracks.

	Marine Facilities and Services	Monitors / Working VHF Channel	Number of Transient Berths / Moorings	Approach / Dockside Depth in Feet at MLW	Seasonal / Year-round	110V + 220V ▲ 3 Phase ■ Maximum Amps	Hookups: Fresh Water / Phone / Cable TV	Maximum LOA	Ramp / Dinghy Dock / Launch Service	Rail / Lift / Crane / Trailer: Capacity (tons)	Diesel / Wood / Fiberglass / Electronics	Repairs: Propellor / Sail / Rigging / Gas	Gas / Diesel Fuel	Fuel Brand	Marine / Groceries / Ice / Bait / LPG / CNG	Restrooms / Showers / Laundry / Pumpout	Public Phone / Restaurant / Snack Bar	Hotel / Pool / Tennis / Golf	Mastercard / VISA / Discover / AmEx
1	C.T. Marina*		203-481-3067			Y	25			WINTER STORAGE									
2	Yale Corinthian Yacht Club		203-488-9330			Y				PRIVATE—MEMBERS ONLY									
3	Kelsey's Boat Yard	13/68	203-488-9567	/2		Y	40	2/2							W				
4	Branford Town Dock		203-488-8394			Y	80	7/6											
5	Branford Yacht Club*	9/	203-488-9798	1/1		Y	60	9/9	F	★50	D			GD	Tex	I	RS		P	MVD
6	**Pier 66** p. 169	9/	203-488-5613	6/2		S	50	10/10	All	★▲	D	CT40	PSRG	GD	Gulf	MGIB	RSP		P	All
7	Goodsell Point Marina*		203-488-5292	5/		S	45	8/7	F			LC50	RGDF				RP		P	
8	Branford River Marine	9/11	203-488-8921			S	40	10/8				C40							MV
9	Dutch Wharf Marina & Boatyard*		203-488-9000	1/		Y	65	10/10	F	★▲	D	LT35	All			M	RS		
10	Branford Landing		203-483-6544			Y	50	6/6	F	★30		L50	PGDWFE			MI	RS		R
11	Branford Marine Railway*		203-488-9224			Y	36	6/6	F	▲	L	L20	All			M	RP		P	All
12	Indian Neck Yacht Club*	9/	203-488-9276			S	40	7/	F	★	D						RS		PS
13	**Brewer Bruce & Johnson's Cove Marina** Inside Back Cover	9/	203-488-8329	10/		Y	50	8/8	FC	★50		L50	All			M	All	P	PR	All
13	**marinefabricators** p. 169		203-488-7093			Y				CUSTOM YACHT METAL WORK									

All Coast Guard Stations Monitor VHF Channel 16

Information in these listings is provided by the facilities themselves. An asterisk (*) indicates that the facility did not respond to our most recent requests for information. (B) represents a BOAT/U.S. cooperating marina.

Long Island Sound

Looking northwest over the Branford River. Brewer Bruce & Johnson's Marina is the large facility to the right of the channel; Marine Fabricators, Pier 66, and Goodsell Point Marina are to the left of center. © Maptech/James T. Abts

are not your usual 90s mini-mall. Here, wood carvers, leather workers, glass blowers, and potters ply their trades.

Built in 1720, the Harrison House is now the home of the Branford Historical Society (203-488-4828). It's worth a visit to view their furniture and authentic farm implements, as well as the only standing outhouse in Branford. We bring this up because this simple structure has apparently caused a small controversy among local historians who can't agree on its age. The oddest thing about this primitive commode is its door, which for some reason faces the house.

Fishing is always a viable option in this harbor. The rocky seabed shelters a number of bottom-dwelling species. On any given day, the Branford Point dock will be lined with fishing poles leaning up against pilings, their lines disappearing into the water. You might as well drop a line in yourself.

Branford's greatest natural resource—granite—is also its biggest cruising hazard. The coarse-grained rock looks fine on buildings and monuments, but will wreak havoc with the hull of your boat. This is why Branford never became a big port, settled instead by farmers and fishermen.

ACTIVITIES: Beautiful homes line the rocky coast of Branford. While it may be pleasing to the eye, this residential area can be inconvenient for boaters. Most shopping and eating will require a cab ride.

As we said before, the Shore Line Trolley Museum (203-467-6927), operated by the Branford Electric Railway Association, is possibly the area's biggest attraction. Antique trolley cars can take you on rides or a guided tour. The museum might surprise you—it's interesting even if you're not into trolleys.

Try the Branford Craft Village (203-488-4689) for a unique shopping experience. The nearly two dozen shops

RESTAURANTS & PROVISIONS: Although most everything in Branford is inland, Sam's Dockside Restaurant (203-488-3007) breaks the rule. Sam's serves seafood, sandwiches, and burgers at Brewer Bruce & Johnson's Cove Marina. If you want to head into town, try Lenny's Indian Head Inn (203-488-1500) near the Branford River. A few miles inland, on Route 1, try Su Casa (203-481-5001). It serves some of the best Mexican food around, and not surprisingly, is one of the more popular joints in town. For an Asian twist, try Kampai Japanese Restaurant (203-481-4536), or for Chinese, Fortune Village (203-481-3568).

While you're in town, take care of your laundry at Qwik Wash Laundromat (203-483-7873) on Main Street. There are about a dozen grocery stores, including Budd's Indian Neck Market, to help with your provisioning. You can take care of any repair needs at Marine Fabricators, located at Brewer Bruce & Johnson's Marina.

NAVIGATION & ANCHORAGES: Use ChartKit Region 3, pages 6, 30, and 31; Maptech™ Waterproof Charts 1 and 17; and Maptech™ electronic and NOAA charts 12373 (1:20,000), 12372 (1:40,000), and 12354 (1:80,000). Use tide tables for Bridgeport. High tide at Branford Harbor is 8 minutes earlier; low tide is 18 minutes earlier. Multiply height of tide at Bridgeport by 0.9 for height of tide at Branford. Mean tidal range is 5.9 feet.

The outer approach to Branford Harbor is marked by Fl R 4s R "2" at Blyn Rock, 4.1nm from the New Haven

Harbor breakwaters, and about 8.5nm from Fl G 4s GONG G "15" at Faulkner (spelled Falkner on the chart) Island. Outer Island, the southernmost of the Thimble Islands, is 3.5nm away.

From the west, approach from Mo(A) WHIS RW "NH." From here, travel 063°m for 3.3nm to Fl R 2.5s BELL R "34" at Cow and Calf. Stay well east of the mark, between it and R N "32" at Five Foot Rock. Proceed northeast to Fl R 4s R "2" at Blyn Rock. Give Stony Island and East Indies Rocks a wide berth but be mindful of the 5-foot spot 500 yards east of G C "1."

If gunkholing is on your itinerary, an approach from the west takes you past the Farm River, known locally as the East Haven River. It hasn't been dredged since the turn of the 20ᵗʰ century, but there was a time when coastal schooners could be pulled all the way up the river to the East Haven town green. Today the river is a pleasant gunk-hole accessible to shallow-draft boats. Wait for high tide before entering the river if you draw more than 3 feet. At any tide, rocks and a crooked channel make the river difficult to enter. Stay east of G C "1" at East Indies Rocks, then steer west before rounding R N "2," marking Darrow Rocks. From here on, the river is unmarked.

Short Beach Bay, locally known as Granite Bay (not a good sign) just east of Farm River, is wide open to the south, so it rarely attracts a large crowd. An unprotected anchorage lies at the southern end of the bay between Old Clump and Gull Rocks. Don't attempt to seek protection by going farther into the bay—it's hazardous. The harbormaster sent us a photo of the rocks that riddle the bay, and it's not a pretty picture. Avoid it if possible.

From the east, the coast is riddled with rocks, so heed the buoys. From Fl R 4s R "28," south of Negro Heads, you can head between the mainland and Taunton Rock, but it's unmarked and best left to those in the know. Play it safe and head about 291°m toward Fl R 2.5s BELL R "34" at Cow & Calf. Swing to the north once you round R N "2" toward Fl R 4s R "2" at Blyn Rock.

Keep Blyn Rock to the east and head north to R N "4," keeping that mark to the east as well. The dredged channel begins to the north-northeast between G C "5" and R N "6." Head for Fl G 4s 28ft 5M "7" to pick up the channel.

The outer harbor area between Johnson Point, Indian Neck Point, and Jeffrey Point has plenty of water and good holding ground. It offers good protection except from the south. The harbormaster says the area north of the Mermaids offers better protection.

Stay between Big Mermaid and Little Mermaid and you won't have any trouble going up the Branford River. Currents in the river reach 2 to 3 knots at full flow. The town dock on Branford Point marks the beginning of the inner harbor, which offers protection and has excellent facilities. You can tie up on this dock, but it leaves you somewhat abandoned—nothing is particularly close. There is a 12-inch wake limit from the Mermaids to the town dock, and from the town dock north is a no-wake

zone. There is a 6-mph speed limit within 100 yards of the Branford shoreline, including the Thimble Islands. Speed limits are enforced by the harbormaster.

The Branford Channel carries about 8 feet of water but shallows to 6.5 feet in the river. You'll find plenty of hospitable facilities up here. Pier 66 Marina is one of the first facilities you encounter on the north shore, and it offers a range of amenities, as well as fuel. At the first big bend, Brewer Bruce & Johnson's Cove Marina offers an opportunity to get some repairs done while enjoying its many amenities.

Shoreside & Emergency Services
Airport:
—Tweed-New Haven (203-466-8833)
Bus:
—Connecticut Transit (203-624-0151)
Coast Guard:
—New Haven (203-468-4464) or VHF 16
Harbormaster: (203-488-8394, ext 134)
Police, Fire, Ambulance: 911
Taxi: Metro Taxi (203-777-7777)
Tow Service:
SEA TOW —24-Hour Dispatch (800-4SEATOW)
—Central Conn. (860-395-0405)
Tow BoatU.S.—24-Hour Dispatch (800-391-4869)
—Clinton (860-388-4065)

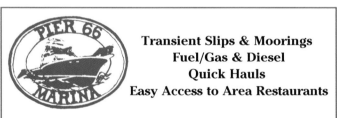

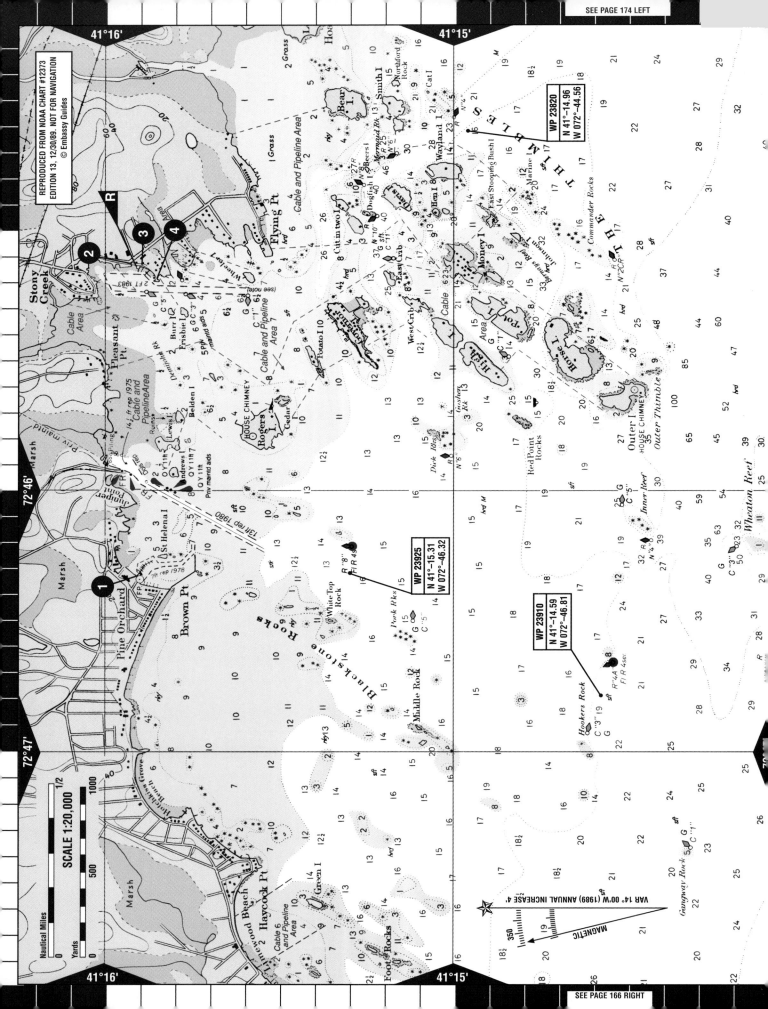

WP 23820
N 41°–14.96
W 072°–44.56

WP 23925
N 41°–15.31
W 072°–46.32

WP 23910
N 41°–14.59
W 072°–46.81

SCALE 1:20,000

Nautical Miles
1/2

Yards
0   500   1000

VAR 14° 00'W (1989) ANNUAL INCREASE 4'

MAGNETIC

A Search for Capt. Kidd's Treasure?

Whether you're looking at President Taft's summer cottage or hearing the legend of Captain Kidd's treasure (which has yet to be found), motoring around the pink granite of the Thimble Islands will stir your imagination.

In colonial times, the Thimble Islands (probably named because of the thimbleberry bushes once found on them) were considered too small and rocky to be of much use. A few settlers grazed sheep on the larger island while others quarried granite, but for the most part the Thimbles went unused.

Legend claims that Captain Kidd found the islands' seclusion ideal for hiding himself, and his fabled treasure. The area between the two sections of High Island is known locally as Kidd's Cove, and Money Island gets its name from the riches Kidd supposedly buried there. While the locals didn't mind pirates burying treasure, they were inspired by the British presence during the Revolutionary War to cut down the islands' trees so enemy masts could be readily spotted in the local channels.

Attracted by the beauty and mystique of being on an island, not to mention tales of Captain Kidd's treasure, the Thimbles became a popular summer resort in the beginning of the 20th century. Hotels and resorts popped up, the rich came to vacation, and this archipelago became known as "the Newport of Connecticut."

Today, the islands are all privately owned and the larger spits have at least one home on their shores. Islanders start arriving in late April and stay through October. A few hardy souls have even tried braving the winter, but the harbor's ice has always made the stay impossible.

A lone dinghy holds tight to the Stony Creek town dock. © Maptech

While Money Island is the most populated (they're still trying to find that treasure, no doubt), the largest island, Horse Island, is owned by Yale University and used for marine biological research. Currently, they're leaving the island be, trying to find what plant and animal species are indigenous to the area. Part of Outer Island has been donated to Southern Connecticut State University and is also used as a marine research station.

No public accommodations exist in the Thimbles today, and residents don't take kindly to visitors landing ashore. By carefully maneuvering through the minefield of rocks, you can find a quiet anchorage. So sit back and let the beauty and lore of the area whisk you away.

ACTIVITIES: A trip to the Thimble Islands is associated with relaxing. You come here for the view and the quiet serenity that pervades the area. It's the perfect place for a few leisurely hours of kayaking.

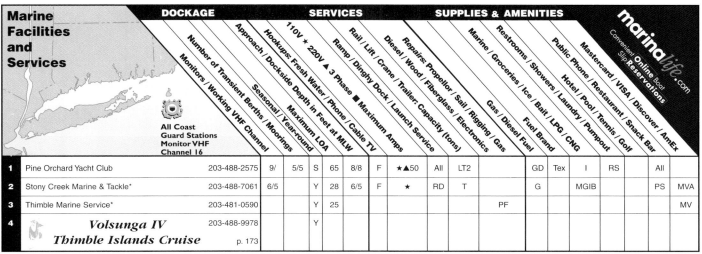

	Marine Facilities and Services		Number of Transient Berths / Moorings	Monitors / Working VHF Channel	Approach / Dockside Depth in Feet at MLW	Seasonal / Year-round	Maximum LOA	110V ★ 220V ▲ 3 Phase ■ Maximum Amps	Hookups: Fresh Water / Phone / Cable TV	Ramp / Dinghy Dock / Launch Service	Rail / Lift / Crane / Trailer Capacity (tons)	Repairs: Propellor / Sail / Rigging / Electronics	Diesel / Wood / Fiberglass / Electronics	Marine / Groceries / Ice / Bait / LPG / CNG	Gas / Diesel Fuel	Restrooms / Showers / Laundry / Pumpout	Fuel Brand	Public Phone / Pool / Tennis / Golf	Hotel / Restaurant / Snack Bar	Mastercard / VISA / Discover / AmEx
1	Pine Orchard Yacht Club	203-488-2575	9/	5/5	S	65	8/8	F	★▲50	All	LT2			GD	Tex		I	RS		All
2	Stony Creek Marine & Tackle*	203-488-7061	6/5		Y	28	6/5	F	★	RD	T			G		MGIB			PS	MVA
3	Thimble Marine Service*	203-481-0590			Y	25						PF								MV
4	*Volsunga IV* **Thimble Islands Cruise** p. 173	203-488-9978			Y															

Information in these listings is provided by the facilities themselves. An asterisk (*) indicates that the facility did not respond to our most recent requests for information. (B) represents a BOAT/U.S. cooperating marina.

Looking northeast over the Thimble Islands. In the foreground, right, is Outer Island with Horse Island, Potato Island, and High Island behind. Between Potato and High islands is a popular anchorage.
© Maptech/James T. Abts

The beautiful pink granite that composes the islands has its down side: the bottom of your boat won't like it much. So, sit back and let those who know the terrain show you around. The *Volsunga IV* (203-488-9978) makes hourly trips through the islands, all the while entertaining you with amusing stories of history and lore.

Performances of popular plays and musicals take place at the Puppet House Theater (203-488-5752), pretty close to the water. Birdwatching is popular in these parts. We suggest a dinghy to get close to the small islands. Binoculars and a field guide will come in handy, as 100 species of birds were recently tagged on Horse Island.

RESTAURANTS & PROVISIONS: Stony Creek doesn't offer a heck of a lot, but there's a small deli in Stony Creek Marine & Tackle (203-488-7061). You'll have to travel a few miles inland to enjoy seafood and chowder at the Chowder Pot (203-481-2356). They have a good brunch on Sunday and live bands for late-night dancing on weekends. Lenny's (203-488-1500) specializes in seafood and steak, but it is in Branford: a bit of a hike. For other area restaurants, see the Branford chapter.

Pick up any nautical provisions at Stony Creek Marine & Tackle and stock the galley down the street at Stony Creek Market (203-488-0145).

NAVIGATION & ANCHORAGES: Use ChartKit Region 3, pages 6, 30, and 31; Maptech™ Waterproof Charts 1 and 17; and Maptech™ electronic and NOAA paper charts 12373 (1:20,000), 12372 (1:40,000), and 12354 (1:80,000). Use tide tables for Bridgeport. High tide at Money Island is 12 minutes earlier; low tide is 23 minutes earlier. Multiply height of tide at Bridgeport by 0.8 for height of tide at

Money Island. Mean tidal range is 5.6 feet.

Before entering the Thimble Islands, please note that some buoy positions may have changed slightly from their charted position. As a group of islands, the Thimbles have no real port or harbor. The village of Stony Creek, about 0.5nm north of Governor Island, serves as the supply point and landing for the Thimbles. You can tie up your dinghy or other small boat for four-hour stays at the town dock (203-488-8394). At low tide, there's less than 4 feet of water off the dock, so don't arrive in anything other than a shallow-draft boat. Most provisions and supplies are available within a short walk of the town dock.

Outer Island, the southernmost of the Thimble Islands, is about 7nm from the New Haven Harbor breakwaters, and 2.4nm from Sachem's Head.

From Fl R 4s BELL R "10A" at Townshend Ledge, a course of about 080°m for 3.3nm will take you north of Branford Reef Light (Fl 6s 30ft 7M) to a spot just south of Fl R 4s R "28" at Negro Heads, west of the Thimble Islands. From the east, as from Fl R 4s BELL R "10GI" southeast of Faulkner Island, a course of about 305°m for 4.6nm will take you to a spot south of Fl R 4s BELL R "26" at Browns Reef, just south of the Thimble Islands.

The first thing to remember about cruising in the Thimbles is that they (and all their underwater obstructions) are made of granite, not sand. Because most cruising boats weigh several tons, it's possible to build up a lot of momentum when traveling at only a few knots. You get only one chance here—if you hit anything in the Thimbles, you're sure to hit hard.

From Sachem Head, pass south of Goose Rocks Shoals, which is marked at its southern end by Fl R 4s BELL R "22." Also beware of Leetes Rocks, about 0.5nm north of R "22." They are unmarked.

From the east, enter the channel west of R N "4" off Wayland Island, and pass west of R N "6" at Mermaid Rock. Then favor Davis Island toward R N "8." From there you have access to Stony Creek. Pass south of R N "10" and steer north of G C "11" before turning for Stony Creek. There is a 3-foot spot southwest of Cut-in-Two Island.

Local boaters recommend that you anchor between G C "11" off East Crib and G C "1" off High Island. Be warned that this area is located in the middle of a Cable Area. Anchor here at your own risk. In fact, there are underwater cables and pipelines everywhere among the islands.

The rocky bottom makes for lousy holding ground around much of the Thimbles. A strong northeast wind and an outgoing tide will give you problems, so after you've set anchor, observe your position periodically to make sure the boat isn't dragging.

CAUTION: From the west, the approaches are complicated by offshore reefs and the number of local buoys. In this area the buoys seem to function more as obstruction markers than channel markers, so study the chart carefully and keep a sharp lookout.

From the west, as from Branford Harbor, your best course is to stay south of Fl R 4s R "28" at Negro Heads and G C "1" at Gangway Rock. Be careful not to confuse the two channels ahead of you. To the northeast, both G C "3" at Hookers Rock and Fl R 4s R "4A" mark the approach to Pine Orchard and the Tilcon-Tomasso docks. The main approach to the Thimbles is farther east, south of Inner Reef.

Less than a mile west of Stony Creek is the tiny village and harbor of Pine Orchard. Heading for Pine Orchard, pass east of G C "1" at Gangway Rock before heading for Fl R 4s R "4A." From here, stay near to and west of Fl R 4s R "8," and look for local aids to navigation taking you along the channel and into the harbor. A breakwater extends 300 yards southwest from Brown Point to protect the Pine Orchard yacht basin. On the west shore of the harbor is the Pine Orchard Yacht Club.

Anchoring is not permitted in the yacht basin. Just east of Pine Orchard is the Tilcon-Tomasso wharf, where gravel from North Branford is loaded on barges and shipped around the northeast. The straight channel marked on the chart is for the barges, and you'll see three yellow flashing beacons to lead the tugs into the wharf.

CAUTION: When entering the Pine Orchard basin, avoid the chain of rocks south of Saint Helena Island. Stay close to the privately maintained marker at the end of the breakwater and give the tiny island a wide berth.

Those who pass Pine Orchard in favor of the Thimbles and Stony Creek will continue east between R N "4" at Inner Reef and G C "3" at Wheaton Reef. Don't cut between Northwest, Browns, East, and Wheaton reefs, as many boats get hung up there. After passing safely south and east of Inner Reef, turn northeast between Outer Island and G C "5," then head for G C "1" off High Island. Outer Island will be closest to you. Look for a cement sea wall on its west side. Scoot up the main channel between the two lines of islands, exiting around Davis Island or turning north-northeast at G C "11" to head into Stony Creek.

CAUTION: Be careful of the shoals south of East Crib, west of Davis Island, and north of Money Island.

The same course is also best for those under sail who want to take a tour through the islands. Coming from the southeast, pass east of East Reef and G C "1," and shoot between Inner Reef and Outer Island.

Because of the highly variable tide and wind conditions caused by the islands, we suggest that novices not try to sail through the Thimbles. The channel requires precise handling because of the number of fixed and floating obstructions.

There are many private moorings north of Cut-in-Two Island, but this area is unmarked and should be entered cautiously, with one eye on the depth sounder and the other on the moored boats. This is a good anchorage in early spring and late fall when fewer boats are moored.

If you are headed directly for Stony Creek and want to skip the islands, you should head northeast, being certain to pass west of Inner Reef and Dick Rocks before turning between Governor and Potato islands. Leave at least a 250-yard cushion to starboard when passing R N "6," and don't cut between Potato and Governor until you have left Dick Rocks well behind. There is a dangerous submerged rock centered between Governors Island and Dick Rocks, which claims about a dozen boats a year.

Don't try passing between Potato and Cedar or Rogers islands—there are too many rocks and shoals for safety. After passing between Potato and Governor islands, follow the marked and dredged channel up to the turning basin.

The town maintains a no-wake speed limit within 100 yards of shore. You'll see water skiers and PWCs around the Thimbles, even in the anchorage between High and Pot islands, so keep an eye out and mind your speed.

Shoreside & Emergency Services
Airport: Tweed/New Haven (203-466-8833)
Coast Guard:
—New Haven (203-468-4464) or VHF 16
Ferry: Volsunga IV (203-488-9978) or VHF 68
—Sea Mist II (203-488-8905)
—Connecticut Sea Ventures (203-397-3921)
Police, Fire, Ambulance: 911
Taxi: Yellow Cab (203-777-5555)
Tow Service:
SEA TOW —24-Hour Dispatch (800-4SEATOW)
—Central Connecticut (203-488-3442)
Tow BoatU.S. —24-Hour Dispatch (800-391-4869)
—Branford (203-874-6109)

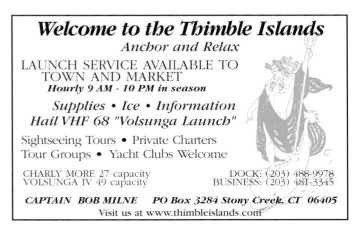

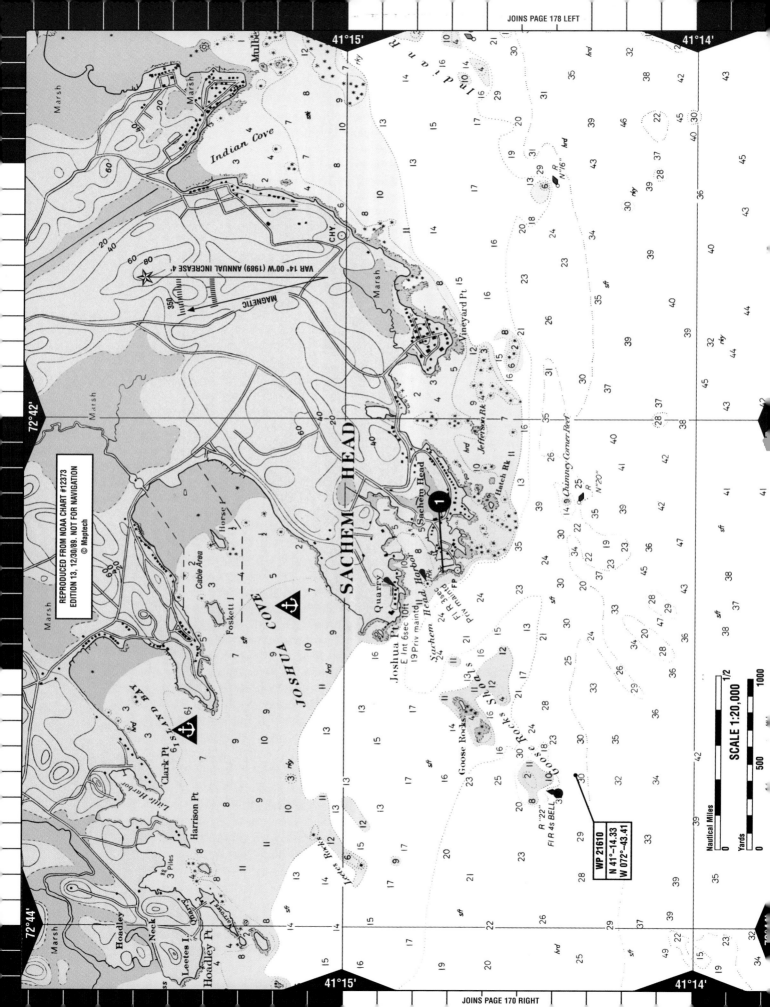

SACHEM HEAD

JOSHUA COVE

Indian Cove

Marsh

Marsh

Marsh

Marsh

Mulberry

VAR 14° 00'W. ANNUAL INCREASE 4'
MAGNETIC

REPRODUCED FROM NOAA CHART #12373
EDITION 13, 12/30/89. NOT FOR NAVIGATION
© Maptech

Cable Area

Foskett I

Horse Pt

Vineyard Pt

Jefferson Rk

Hatch Rk

Sachem Head

Joshua Pt
E Int 6sec 10ft
Priv maintd
Sachem Head Harbor
Fl R 3sec
Priv marina
Quarry

Goose Rocks Shoal

Leetes Rocks

Clark Pt

Harrison Pt

Little Harbor

Hoadley Neck

Leetes I

Hoadley Pt

ISLAND BAY

Chimney Corner Reef

R "16"

R N"20"

14 9 Chimney Corner Reef

R "22"
Fl R 4s BELL

WP 21610
N 41°–14.33
W 072°–43.41

CHY

SCALE 1:20,000

Nautical Miles
0   1/2

Yards
0   500   1000

Don't Take It Literally

If you're thinking that the name "Sachem's Head" must mean something other than its literal meaning, you're wrong. This peninsula is indeed named after the head of a Pequot sachem that was "displayed" many years ago. Long Island Sound is peppered with place names as thick in lore and legend as grandma's molasses cookies.

It started in the summer of 1637, during what was to be known as the Pequot War. The English settlers of Connecticut, with the help of the Mohegan Indians, intended to eliminate the aggressive and powerful Pequot tribe that controlled the eastern end of the state.

After a massacre of Pequot at Mystic, the remnants of Pequot Nation traveled west down the Connecticut coast toward Fairfield. The Pequot families moved slowly and were forced to break up into separate parties to forage for food.

A pursuing force of Mohegans, under the leadership of Uncas, was gaining rapidly on the straggling Pequot survivors; at the same time, an English force chased them by boat. Uncas and his warriors finally found a small party of Pequots camped at the head of what is now called "Bloody Cove" in Sachem Head. One of the two, lesser Pequot sachems, or chiefs, was killed and the other, with a few followers, escaped, with a few followers, onto the peninsula that forms the western shore of Sachem Head Harbor.

Pursued by the Mohegans, the remaining Pequots were forced to swim across the harbor from Prospect Point to Uncas Point, where Uncas and his men were waiting for them. The Pequot Sachem was executed and the others taken prisoner. Legend has it the sachem's head was placed in the fork of an oak tree overlooking the Sound, where it remained for years as a grisly reminder of Uncas' victory.

Looking northeast over Sachem Head. The private yacht club is to the right. © Maptech/James T. Abts

The end of the Pequot War came shortly after, in a swamp at Southport, where the remaining Pequots were killed by the English. As for the tree that held the sachem's skull on Uncas Point, it is long gone—as is the bluff on which it stood, destroyed by 19th-century quarriers. Today, the waters surrounding Sachem's Head bear no resemblance to the area's tumultuous past. Instead, you'll find quiet anchorages and beautiful scenery.

ACTIVITIES: Sachem Head is a little short when it comes to sightseeing and eating establishments. It's a part of Guilford, so check out the following chapter on Guilford and Madison, or the previous chapter on the Thimble Islands for activities in the area. Better yet, just throw down your anchor, sit back, and enjoy.

RESTAURANTS & PROVISIONS: Refer to the Guilford chapter if you want to head into town.

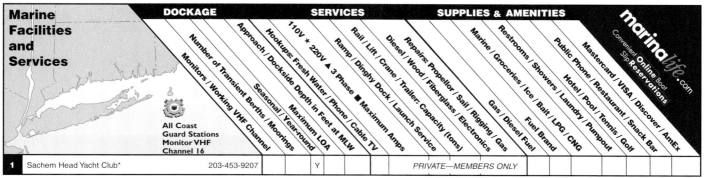

Marine Facilities and Services		DOCKAGE					SERVICES					SUPPLIES & AMENITIES							marinalife.com
	Monitors / Working VHF Channel	Number of Transient Berths	Seasonal / Year-round Moorings	Approach / Dockside Depth in Feet at MLW	Maximum LOA	Hookups: Fresh Water / Phone / Cable TV	110V + 220V ▲ 3 Phase ■ Maximum Amps	Ramp / Dinghy Dock / Launch Service	Rail / Lift / Crane / Trailer Capacity (tons)	Diesel / Wood / Fiberglass / Electronics	Repairs: Propellor / Sail / Rigging / Gas	Marine / Groceries / Ice / Bait / LPG / CNG	Gas / Diesel Fuel	Restrooms / Showers / Laundry / Pumpout	Fuel Brand	Public Phone / Restaurant / Snack Bar	Hotel / Pool / Tennis / Golf	Mastercard / VISA / Discover / AmEx	Convenient Online Boat Slip Reservations
1 Sachem Head Yacht Club*	203-453-9207			Y						*PRIVATE—MEMBERS ONLY*									

Information in these listings is provided by the facilities themselves. An asterisk (*) indicates that the facility did not respond to our most recent requests for information. (B) represents a BOAT/U.S. cooperating marina.

MODEL SHIPS

Models of ships have been around just about as long as people have been building real boats; the earliest known models, of Mesopotamian origin, date as far back as 5000 B.C.! From models of funeral boats found in Egyptian tombs to modern kits, ship models have served many purposes over the years, from the functional to the frivolous.

Alabaster models have been found in the tombs of Pharaohs and powerful Egyptians dating to 2600 B.C., and were thought to be "spirit ships" assisting the soul's passage over the Nile. In the lands of Greece and Cyprus, models used in burials served more practically as a representation of the deceased's status or profession. The practice of placing ship models in churches and holy places as "votive offerings" began around the same time, usually as a fulfillment of some vow. Such models were made by seamen and presented to a seafaring or personal deity for protection on an upcoming journey, thanks for a successful voyage, or as a "tithe" for a particularly profitable excursion. Votive models in the Renaissance were presented for the Church's blessing, and some were even used on altars to hold burning incense.

In the late Renaissance, when much was created that was ornamental, ship models were made purely for decorative purposes for the first time. Many models were made as children's toys, though their intricacy far surpassed what children play with today. Other models were made into clocks or other functional household items, often fashioned of gold and silver; you can be sure that in late 18th-century France, some aristocratic lady had one sailing the powdered hair of her wig.

The British Admiralty, among others, used extremely detailed models of warships as blueprints and research tools from the 17th century until the early days of iron ships. These "dockyard models" were also used for training naval seamen in the intricacies of a ship's sails and rigging.

The sailors themselves have produced some of the most interesting models in the history of the art. During the Napoleonic wars between France and England, hundreds of models were constructed by prisoners-of-war, who used any material they could get their idle hands on—bone from rations, scraps of wood, and even their own hair for rigging! And it was the common sailor who also began the tradition of building ships in bottles, a fascinating and delicate art in its own right.

Building ship models is still popular with "armchair sailors" and marine artists. For those devoted to the "pure" form of the art, models are scratch-built from extensive research and plans, just like the real thing. Wooden ships are framed and planked just as their full-sized ancestors were. For sailing ships, the thousands of feet of line in the rigging is reduced to a few yards of thread running through miniature blocks. More modern iron or steel ships are constructed just as carefully. The details that define them are different but executed with the same care and patience. Commercially produced kits of varying complexity allow those without the time, skill, or patience required of scratch-builders to construct their own models recreating their favorite ships. Technological advances have resulted in the current popularity of sailing yacht models via remote control by enthusiasts everywhere.

One unusual use of "model" ships is for training supertanker captains. They learn to pilot 100,000-ton tankers by driving 40-foot models powered by electric trolling motors. All is to scale, the handling characteristics are the same, but the cost of a mistake is mere pocket change compared to the billions of dollars and environmental devastation an oil spill would incur.

And let's not underestimate the appreciation of models as a fine art form. Throughout all these periods of history, ship models have graced the dwelling places of kings and queens, the nobility, great thinkers, and prominent citizens of cultures from Egypt to England. The collection of these works of art springs from a long-established tradition that continues to this day. In corporate offices, private homes, and aboard the modern yacht, fine ship models are proudly displayed by those who appreciate the union of artistic creativity, man's pioneering spirit, and the endless, boundless sea.

NAVIGATION & ANCHORAGES: Use ChartKit Region 3, pages 6 and 31; Maptech™ Waterproof Charts 1 and 17; and Maptech™ electronic and NOAA paper charts 12373 (1:20,000), 12372 (1:40,000), and 12354 (1:80,000). Use tide tables for Bridgeport. High tide at Sachem's Head is 11 minutes earlier; low tide is 15 minutes earlier. Multiply height of tide at Bridgeport by 0.8 for height of tide at Sachem Head. Mean tidal range is 5.4 feet.

Sachem Head Harbor is 2.5nm from Flying Point in Stony Creek, 3.5nm from Guilford Harbor, and 15.4nm from Mattituck Inlet, on Long Island.

From Fl R 4s BELL R "10GI" south of Goose Island, a course of about 340°m for 3.1nm will take you to a spot just in front of the entrance to Sachem Head Harbor. From Fl R 4s BELL R "26" south of Browns and East reefs, a course of about 90°m for 2.2nm will take you to Fl R 4s BELL R "22" marking Goose Rocks Shoals. From here, steer toward R N "20" for about 0.5nm, passing well east of Goose Rocks Shoals, before turning north to the entrance of Sachem Head Harbor. Stay clear of the rocks south and west of Sachem's Head.

From the south, you have a clear shot up to Fl R 3s PRIV light (maintained by the yacht club from June to September) on the south side of the harbor. From here, a turn to the east will place you smack-dab in the tiny, rock-ribbed harbor.

From the east, pass south of R N "20" at Chimney Corner Reef. Continue west for 600 yards before heading north to the harbor in order to clear the rocks to the south of the yacht club.

Coming from Stony Creek and the Thimble Islands requires some caution. Your main concern will be the unmarked Leetes Rocks, which are exposed at low water. There is also a 3-foot spot 300 yards northeast of the northernmost rock.

Sachem Head Harbor is about 0.3nm long, 300 yards wide, and has 5 to 10 feet of water at the floats and moorings. This snug size offers good protection except against southwesterly winds, which prevail during the summer. There is usually room in the harbor in the spring and fall, but during the summer, space is at a premium. There may be guest moorings available through the yacht club. Call ahead to avoid entering the harbor only to find no place to stay.

All is quiet and civilized in Sachem Head these days. With the old chief's skull long gone, Sachem Head Yacht Club presides over one of the quietest harbors you'll ever visit. The club is located on what is called Prospect Point, an island connected to the mainland by a footbridge just to the south of the harbor entrance. You'll find no place to land apart from the club, and if you head ashore, you'll find the surrounding area consists of nothing more than beautiful woods and private homes. As mentioned previously, if you're looking for dinner or supplies, Sachem Head is not the place to stop. Rather, you should head for Stony Creek to the west, or Guilford to the east.

Despite these debates, you may find fairly good protection in the area marked "Joshua Cove" on your chart, though

it will get bumpy in weather out of the south or southwest—prevalent during the summer. At low tide, you'll find about 5 to 10 feet of water up to Foskett Island, and then 2 to 3 feet at the head of the cove. The soft mud makes fair holding ground.

Island Bay can also be used as an anchorage, though not many people choose it as the waters get rough in a southwesterly breeze, as does the northern part of Joshua Cove. In the northernmost part of Island Bay is Shell Beach, which is run by the town.

Little Harbor is a snug, little gunkhole just west of Island Bay, with 2 to 3 feet of water at low tide. Jetties protect both sides of the entrance between Harrison and Clark points. Unfortunately, it also gets rough when the winds blow out of the south, especially due to its shallowness.

If your boat draws less than 3 feet, you may attempt the unnamed cove between Harrison Point and Narrows Island. Note that the rocks shown on the chart at the entrance to this cove are actually a bit farther to the northeast. This cove is best explored in a dinghy.

Shoreside & Emergency Services
Airport:
—Tweed/New Haven (203-466-8833)
Coast Guard:
—New Haven (203-468-4464) or VHF 16
—Eatons Neck (631-261-6868) or VHF 16
Police, Fire, Ambulance: 911
Tow Service:
SEA TOW. —24-Hour Dispatch (800-4SEATOW)
—Central Connecticut (203-488-3442)
Tow BoatU.S.—24-Hour Dispatch (800-391-4869)
—Clinton (860-388-4065)
Train:
—Amtrak (800-USA-RAIL)
—Metro-North (800-638-7646)

DID YOU KNOW...

Many moons ago, rudders were always mounted on a ship's right side. Because of this, the captain had to dock with the left side of the ship facing the port, hence the adoption of port, meaning "left." And what of starboard? Was it named thusly because this left-side docking exposed the right side to the stars? Nice guess, but not quite. The star in starboard is either a corruption of steer, going back to the positioning of the right-mounted rudder (the "steer board"), or the word steor, meaning "helm" or "rudder."

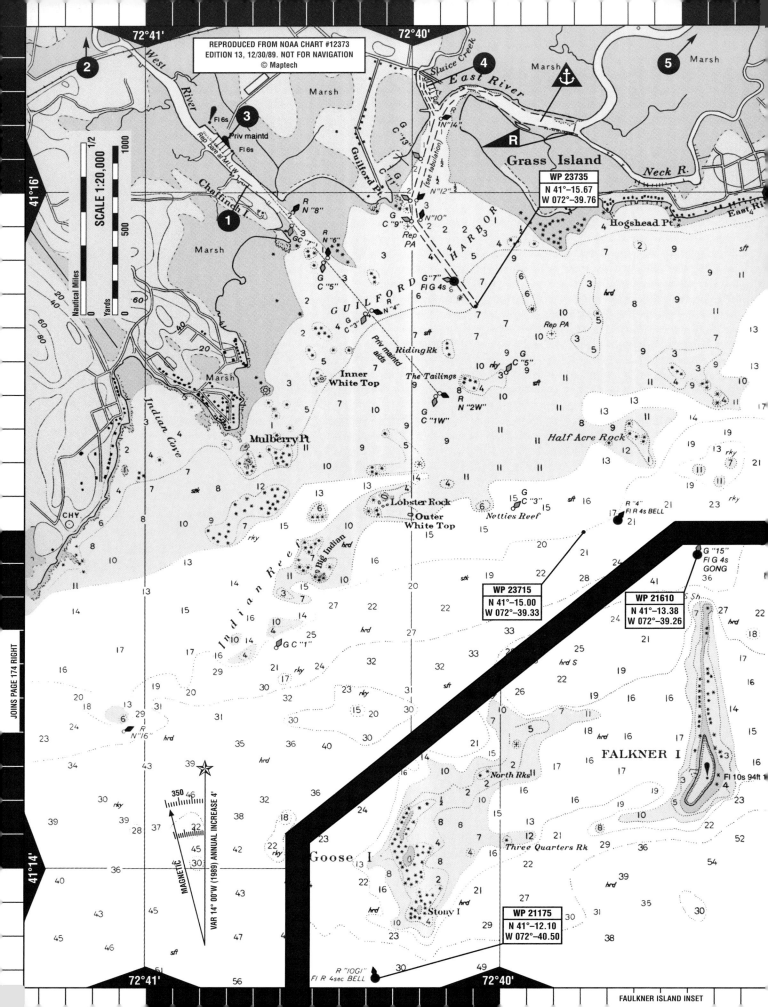

Safety on the Sea

America's founding fathers knew the importance of safe navigation, leading many to take an active role in choosing the locations of the country's first lighthouses. The early federal lighthouses were very well-built, many surviving even today. One such relic of the country's early years stands about three and a half miles off Guilford's coast, on Faulkner Island. Commissioned by none other than President Thomas Jefferson, the lighthouse was built in 1802 for $325. It's the second-oldest lighthouse in Connecticut.

The position of the light created quite a stir in the latter days of the 20th century. Years of wind erosion on the east side of the island have brought the lighthouse perilously close to falling off the edge. In 1991 the Faulkner Light Brigade set out to save this historic treasure and important navigational landmark. Through the Brigade's efforts, Congress has appropriated $4.5 million to the restoration and protection of the lighthouse and island.

Regardless, the light and the island let you know you're close to the pleasant towns of Guilford and Madison. The Reverend Henry Whitfield settled Guilford with a group of colonists by buying parcels of land a little at a time. In 1639, the pieces became the last independent colony in Connecticut, taking its place alongside Hartford, Saybrooke, and New Haven.

Much like other coastal Connecticut towns, Madison went through a period right after the American Revolution when fishing was crucial. Catches here were usually white-

Faulkner Island Light— the second-oldest lighthouse in Connecticut. © Maptech/James T. Abts

fish, which was used as fertilizer. A porpoise fishery also arose in Madison, providing lamp oil in the squalid tradition of whaling. Today, both towns are quiet and residential, known for their nice town greens and beaches.

ACTIVITIES: The towns of Guilford and Madison don't offer non-stop activities as much as provide you the solitude of a pleasant New England village. No doubt, there are tourist attractions, but it's the sights, sounds, and smells—a true New England ambience—that make a stay in these ports worthwhile.

The Guilford Yacht Club (203-458-3048) offers free use of their bikes for transients. About a mile from the water you'll find one of the nicest town greens around, Guilford Green. The lush, shaded lawn is bordered by shops and stores and

Marine Facilities and Services	All Coast Guard Stations Monitor VHF Channel 16	Monitors / Working VHF Channel	Number of Transient Berths	Approach / Dockside Depth in Feet at MLW	110V ★ 220V ▲ 3 Phase ■ Maximum Amps / Hookups: Fresh Water / Phone / Cable TV	Seasonal / Year-round / Maximum LOA	Rail / Lift / Crane / Ramp / Dinghy Dock / Launch Service	Repairs: Propellor / Sail / Rigging / Gas / Diesel / Wood / Fiberglass / Electronics	Marine / Groceries / Ice / Bait / LPG / CNG	Restrooms / Showers / Laundry / Pumpout	Gas / Diesel Fuel	Fuel Brand	Public Phone / Restaurant / Snack Bar	Hotel / Pool / Tennis / Golf	Mastercard / VISA / Discover / AmEx
1 **BROWN'S BOAT YARD** p. 181	203-453-6283	9/	1/	Y 35 5/5	F	★30		L25	PGDWF	GD		M		MVD
2 Guilford Boat Yards Inc.*	203-453-5031		2/	Y 32 1/6	F	★15		L15	All			M	R	MVD
3 **The Guilford Yacht Club** p. 181	203-458-3048	71/	5/	Y 45 8/8	F	★30	RD	T				I	RSP P P	MV
4 Guilford Town Marina	203-453-8092	9/11	2/1	S 36 4/4	F	★30	RD						R	All
5 Beebe Marine	203-245-8665		1/	Y 23 3/8	F	★30		C10	PG				R	

Information in these listings is provided by the facilities themselves. An asterisk (*) indicates that the facility did not respond to our most recent requests for information.
(B) represents a BOAT/U.S. cooperating marina.

Looking north up the West River in Guilford. Upriver you'll see Brown's Boat Yard (left) and the Guilford Yacht Club (right). © Maptech/James T. Abts

hosts a continuous lineup of events throughout the year. Norman Rockwell could not have pictured a better setting.

While rolling through the streets, stop in on some of the many historic sights, like the Hyland House (203-453-9477) and the Thomas Griswold House (203-453-3176). There's also Reverend Henry Whitfield's stone house (203-453-2457), supposedly the oldest stone house in New England (built in 1639), and the Allis-Bushnell House and Museum, home to the Madison Historical Society (203-245-4567).

There's plenty to do on the waterfront. The Guilford town beach, west of the town marina, is open to the public. You may explore the beaches of Grass Island, but the north beach just up the first turn of the East River has the best water.

For most of the year, Faulkner Island is off-limits because of its concentration of birds, including the endangered roseate tern. Around Labor Day, you can step upon the much-talked-about island. Call the Faulkner Island Lighthouse Brigade (203-453-8400/1111) for more information.

There is little doubt about what the biggest summer draw is around here: Hammonasset State Park (203-245-1817) in Madison. Connecticut isn't known for its abundance of public beaches, but Hammonasset is one of the finest in the state, and it's open year-round. Camping is also allowed in season. You can't dock at or anchor off the beaches, so you'll have to ride a bicycle from your marina to reach Hammonasset. Aside from the obvious attraction, miles of roadway within the park make for prime inline-skating territory as well.

RESTAURANTS & PROVISIONS: In Guilford Harbor, call the Guilford dockmaster (203-453-8092) to receive a berth across from the Stone House Restaurant (203-458-3700) or alongside the Guilford Mooring Restaurant (203-458-2921), where you can enjoy good seafood overlooking the water. Next door is the Guilford Lobster Pound (203-453-6122),

where you can get fresh lobster, of course. While you stock up on live or frozen bait and tackle, The Bait House (203-458-2554) offers up good portions of breakfast and lunch.

In downtown Guilford, be sure to try Esteva (203-458-1300) with a hip gourmet menu. East of downtown, on Boston Post Road, try Chips Pub II (203-453-0615) for great baby back ribs and a view of the game. For that rustic New England setting with an elegant atmosphere, stop in at the Guilford Tavern (203-453-2216).

Head to the Dolly Madison Inn & Restaurant (203-245-7377) in Madison for chicken, pasta, or seafood. Another good option is The Wharf (203-245-0005), for fine seafood and steaks on the beach.

On Guilford's green, Guilford Food Center (203-453-4849) can help with supplies; they deliver. There's a bank nearby as well. Call a cab and head to Boston Post Road for enough choices to stock your provisioning cabinet.

NAVIGATION & ANCHORAGES: Use ChartKit Region 3, pages 6 and 31; Maptech™ Waterproof Charts 1 and 17; and Maptech™ electronic and NOAA paper charts 12373 (1:20,000), 12372 (1:40,000), and 12354 (1:80,000). Use tide tables for Bridgeport. High tide at Faulkner Island is 14 minutes earlier; low tide is 25 minutes earlier. Multiply height of tide at Bridgeport by 0.8 for height of tide at Faulkner Island. Mean tidal range is 5.4 feet.

The approach to Guilford Harbor, beginning at Fl R 4s BELL R "4" S at Half Acre Rock, is 5.0nm from Outer Island in the Thimbles, and 5.9nm from Clinton Harbor. Mattituck Inlet, on Long Island, is 15nm away. From Fl G 4s GONG G "15," north of Faulkner Island, a course of 014°m for 1.6nm will take you to Fl R 4s BELL R "4." From here a course of 342°m for 0.8nm will take you east of G C "5" in route to Fl G 4s G "7" at the mouth of the Guilford Harbor entrance channel.

Embassy Guides

Entering Guilford Harbor presents no problems as long as you follow the buoys. There are some rocks and other foul ground outside the harbor entrance. Arriving from Sachem's Head Harbor, 3.5nm to the southwest, you'll want to keep R N "16" to port and stay well south of G C "1" at Indian Reef. From Indian Reef it is about 0.8nm northeast to G C "3" at Netties Reef and the approach to the harbor.

CAUTION: Do not let the strong wind and currents in this area set you outside the channel where there are numerous rocks and reefs.

From Clinton and other points east, your safest route follows a path south of Madison Reef and R N "14" at Charles Reef. Always pass on the south of Fl R 4s BELL R "4" marking Half Acre Rock, and don't round the buoy too sharply, because you want to stay west of the rock on your approach to the harbor.

Turning northwest toward the harbor, you'll pass east of The Tailings G C "5" before proceeding into the dredged channel. If you're boating really late in the season, you may not see Fl G 4s G "7" at the entrance, since it is removed by the Coast Guard in December. Be aware that many of the entrance buoys to Guilford have been moved slightly from their charted positions.

NOTE: there is a rock southeast of Fl G 4s G "7," just west of the channel.

The channel into the marina and the harbor of refuge in the East River carries about 5 feet of water at low tide. All slips and moorings at the town marina are reserved for residents, but call the dockmaster (203-453-8092 or VHF 9) for one of the moorings on the north side of Grass Island. If nothing is available, just drop your hook beyond the town moorings in the dredged basin up the East River—you'll have plenty of company on weekends. You can then take a dinghy into the town launching ramp and tie up behind its floating dock.

From the west, use the same approaches and cautions for the West River as for the East River, but head west of the Tailings from Netties Reef G C "3." Simply pick up the range lights and a dredged (8 feet), straight channel will lead you to two hospitable basins: Brown's Boat Yard and the Guilford Yacht Club. Brown's offers transient space and the only gas or diesel in Guilford. Plus, if you need any repairs, including carpentry work, Brown's is the place to go. Across the river, the yacht club offers a pool and clubhouse. Beyond the Guilford Yacht Club there's shallow water at low tide up to the railroad bridge and beyond to the Guilford Boat Yard. The current here runs about 1 knot.

Faulkner Island Light (Fl 10s 94ft 13M) lies about 3.5nm south-southeast of the Guilford Town Marina. The light is 3.1nm southeast of Sachems Head Harbor and 6.7nm southwest of Cedar Island in Clinton.

If you want to go between Faulkner and Goose islands, go slowly and favor the east side of this passage. Divers tell us that there are many uncharted rocks and plenty of wrecks. You also have to be careful of the tidal currents of 1 to 2 knots, which can set you well off course.

CAUTION: Don't attempt to pass between Faulkner Island and Fl G 4s GONG "15," because there is a bar extending this entire length.

The west side of Faulkner Island is a nice place for a swim on hot summer afternoons, but again be careful of the currents—the mainland is a long way off. On relatively calm nights you can settle into the lee of one of the islands for an anchorage, but the islands don't offer much protection.

Shoreside & Emergency Services
Airport: Tweed-New Haven (203-466-8833)
Coast Guard:
— New Haven (203-468-4464) or VHF 16
— Emergency (203-468-4455)
Police, Fire, Ambulance: 911
Tow Service:
SEA TOW —24-Hour Dispatch (800-4SEATOW)
— Central Conn. (860-395-0405)
Tow BoatU.S.—24-Hour Dispatch (800-391-4869)
— Clinton (860-388-4065)
Train:
— Amtrak (800-USA-RAIL)
— Metro-North (800-638-7646)

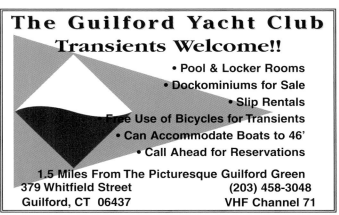

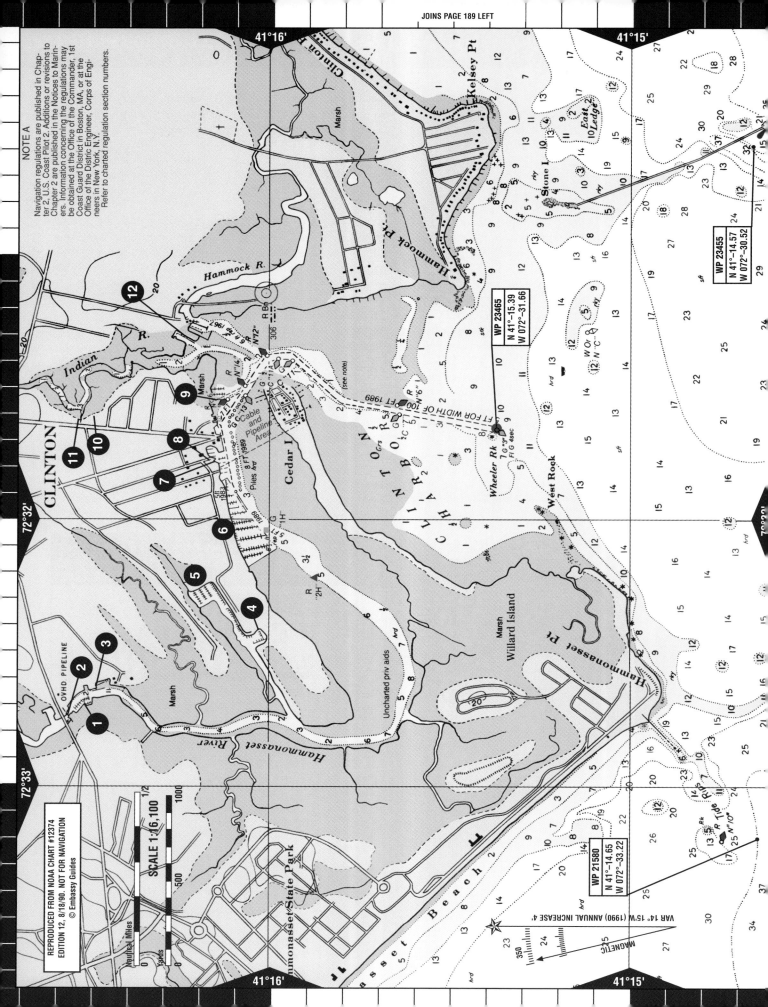

SCALE 1:16,100

Nautical Miles

NOTE A

Navigation regulations are published in Chapter 2, U.S. Coast Pilot 2. Additions or revisions to Chapter 2 are published in the Notices to Mariners. Information concerning the regulations may be obtained at the Office of the Commander, 1st Coast Guard District in Boston, MA, or at the Office of the District Engineer, Corps of Engineers in New York, N.Y.
  Refer to charted regulation section numbers.

CLINTON

Indian R.

Hammock R.

Hammock Pt

Kelsey Pt

Marsh

Stone I.

East
Ledge

WP 23465
N 41°-15.39
W 072°-31.66

WP 23455
N 41°-14.57
W 072°-30.52

Wheeler Rk

West Rock

Willard Island

Marsh

Hammonasset Pt

Cedar I.

Hammonasset River

Hammonasset State Park

Beach

WP 21580
N 41°-14.65
W 072°-33.22

VAR 14° 15'W (1990) ANNUAL INCREASE 4'

MAGNETIC

OVHD PIPELINE

Cable and Pipeline Area

Uncharted priv aids

72°33'

72°32'

41°16'

41°15'

Not That Clinton

Contrary to what supporters of our 42nd president would like to think, Clinton, Connecticut, was not named after him. The town was, however, named after a politician—Dewitt Clinton, mayor of New York City and later governor of New York state. Clinton was noted for his work on seeing the Erie Canal through fruition.

In its early days, Clinton—the town—was graced with the presence of two outstanding citizens; both were men of the cloth. The Reverend Abraham Pierson held classes in the local parsonage of the Collegiate School during 1701, classes that turned out to be the first in the long and distinguished history of Yale University.

Clinton's other outstanding man of the cloth was the Reverend Jared Eliot, a preacher said to have delivered more than 4,000 sermons, never missing a Sunday in nearly 40 years. Beyond his sermons, Eliot achieved fame as one of New England's leading physicians and as the discoverer of a way to convert black sand, found on many coastal beaches, into usable iron. This breakthrough earned Eliot membership in the Royal Society of London.

Like many coastal Connecticut towns during the 19th century, Clinton had a sizable shipbuilding industry. At one time there were three shipyards along the Indian River (which is now mostly marsh) in the center of town. One local resident even became famous as a captain; Charles W. Morgan led the ship that bears his name on many a voyage around the globe in search of the great leviathan. Today, his vessel, the *Charles W. Morgan*, is the last remaining wooden whaling ship in the world and is the centerpiece of the wooden boat collection at the Mystic Seaport museum.

Welcome to one of the most visted ports in all of Long Island Sound. © Maptech

Marine Facilities and Services

All Coast Guard Stations Monitor VHF Channel 16

marina*life*.com — Convenient Online Boat Slip Reservations

#	Facility (Phone)	Monitors / Working VHF	Transient Berths / Moorings	Seasonal(S) / Yearround(Y)	Max LOA	Approach / Dockside Depth (ft at MLW)	Ramp / Dinghy Dock / Launch Service	110V+220V ▲3Phase ■Max Amps	Rail/Lift/Crane/Trailer: Capacity (tons)	Repairs: Propeller/Sail/Rigging/Electronics, Diesel/Wood/Fiberglass	Gas / Diesel Fuel	Fuel Brand	Marine/Groceries/Ice/Bait/LPG/CNG	Restrooms/Showers/Laundry/Pumpout	Public Phone/Restaurant/Snack Bar	Hotel/Pool/Tennis/Golf	Mastercard/VISA/Discover/AmEx
1	BAYLINER BOAT CENTER — 800-840-9064 (p. 187)		15/	Y	44	3/3	F	★30	LC25	PDWFE			M	RS		P	All
2	Cerino's Marine — 860-669-5675			Y	50	4/9				PGDWFE			MI				MVD
3	Free Spirit Marine — 860-245-7242		15/	Y	44	4/9	F	★30	LC25	PGF			M	RS		P	All
4	Clinton Yacht Haven — 860-669-7716	9/72	10/	Y	50	4/9	All	★50	L30	PSGDWF			MI	All	P	P	MV
5	Riverside Basin Marina Inc. — 860-669-1503	9/	10/	Y	39	4/6	FC	★25	LC25	PGDWF			MI	RSP		P	MV
6	Cedar Island Marina Inc. — 860-669-8681 (p. 185)	9/68	70/	Y	120	8/8	All	★▲■100	LC30	PGDWF	GD	Gulf	MIB	All	P	All	All
7	Clinton Town Dock — 860-669-7475	16/	4/3	S	50	8/8	F	★30	RL					R		PS	
8	Clinton Harborside Marina — 860-669-1705	16/69		Y	45	6/4	FC	★30	L15	PSGDWF			M	RS			All
9	Port Clinton Marina — 860-669-4563	9/	10/	S	55	9/7	F	★▲50	L50	All				RS		P	MV
10	Indian River Marina* — 860-453-9343		1/	S	24	3/5	F		R					R			
11	Graves Marina* — 860-669-6809			S													
12	Old Harbor Marina — 860-669-8361	9/	10/	Y	40	5/5	F	★30	RD C35	PSWF			I	RS		PR	MV

Information in these listings is provided by the facilities themselves. An asterisk (*) indicates that the facility did not respond to our most recent requests for information. (B) represents a BOAT/U.S. cooperating marina.

Looking west over Clinton Harbor. You can't miss the many boats of Cedar Island Marina, located in the center of the photo. © Maptech/James T. Abts

Clinton is now a quiet New England town, although it has a curious distinction as headquarters of a major cosmetics firm. Chesebrough-Pond's operation began years ago when they started making Pond's Extract from witch hazel cut in the surrounding woods. More recently, Clinton's woods have become home to an upscale outlet mall called Clinton Crossing, featuring name-brand factory stores and off-5th-Avenue "outlets."

ACTIVITIES: Conveniently located between New York and Newport, Clinton remains one of the most visited ports in Long Island Sound. In summer, the waterway is often busy with sail and power boats stopping over for supplies or to visit one of the three state-owned, saltwater bathing beaches in the area.

Just west of Clinton Harbor you'll find Hammonasset State Park (203-245-1817). The beaches are open year-round, and camping is allowed in season, all for a small fee. From the Sound, the park can easily be recognized by the large pavilion and flagpole, as well as by the throngs of surf and sun worshipers. The straight coastline along the beach lets the current pick up speed, creating riptides off Hammonasset Point. When swimming or diving, be careful of the undertow. Underwater visibility is usually poor here, due to sediment brought down by the rivers emptying into Clinton Harbor and the Connecticut River to the east; if you snorkel on a good day, however, you may get to see a few squid and even some seahorses.

If you prefer swimming pools to beaches, Cedar Island Marina (860-669-8681), which bills itself as Connecticut's "family boating resort," has just what you are looking for. They also feature shuffleboard and basketball courts, lawn chairs, picnic tables, barbecues, and much more. If you're in harbor in mid-July, stay right where you are and get the first look-see at next year's boating trends at the Clinton Harbor Boat Show, held right at Cedar Island Marina. More than 50 dealers display more than 200 boats on land and in the water.

In mid-August, Clinton becomes the "Bluefish Capital," celebrating sportfishing for three days with parades, antique shows, concerts, and raft, inner tube and canoe races and, of course, fish bakes. If you're interested in either the fishing or the festival, call the Chamber of Commerce (860-669-3889).

Historic attractions in town include the Captain Elisha White House on East Main Street, built of red brick in the 18th century, or the Stanton House (860-669-2132), built in 1790. The historic room at the town hall, with its collection of china, dolls, glass, and silver, also attracts history buffs.

You and your crew have the rainy day blues? For those of you staying at Cedar Island Marina hop aboard the free shuttle and head over to Clinton Crossing (860-664-0700). From caramel-coated apples to camel-colored cashmere coats, these shops have it all.

RESTAURANTS & PROVISIONS: Right at Cedar Island Marina, Aqua (860-664-3788) serves up some everything from sandwiches to elegant dinners, not to mention a nice view

Embassy Guides

Looking northeast up the Hammonasset River. To the right is the extension that leads to Clinton Yacht Haven and Riverside Basin Marina. Follow the Hammonasset to the left and you're brought to Bayliner Boat Center and Free Spirit Marine, as well as Cerino's Marine. © Maptech/James T. Abts

of Clinton's inner harbor. Also at Cedar Island Marina, a pool-side snack bar serves up breakfast and sandwiches until 5:30 p.m. But that's as far as service on the water goes. For more selections, you'll have to head into town.

A 15- or 20-minute walk up Commerce Street and into town offers access to a variety of shops and restaurants, as well as a bank, pharmacy, and laundromat. If you need to restock the galley, Saldamarco's (860-669-3469) offers a variety of good quality meats and specialty provisions. Supermarket shopping will require a short ride, as shops are located about two miles east or west of town on Route 1. Cedar Island Marina customers can conveniently hop aboard a free shuttle bus into town.

In Clinton, you'll find 9 East Main (860-664-3828), which serves seafood, poultry, and Italian dishes. Also on East Main is Clinton Pizza (860-669-5577), which we hear is quite good. Farther up, on Boston Post Road in Westbrook, we suggest you try Lenny & Joe's Fish Tale Restaurant (860-669-0767), serving excellent local seafood. If you head west on Main Street, you'll find Chip's Pub III (860-669-3463) within a block or two. They have an American menu, entertainment, and a lively bar.

NAVIGATION & ANCHORAGES: Use ChartKit Region 3, pages 6 and 32; Maptech™ Waterproof Charts 1 and 17; and Maptech™ electronic and NOAA paper charts 12374 (1:20,000), 12372 (1:40,000), and 12354 (1:80,000). Use tide tables for Bridgeport. High tide at Duck Island (Westbrook) is 26 minutes earlier; low tide is 35 minutes

earlier. Multiply height of tide at Bridgeport by 0.7 for height of tide at Duck Island. Mean tidal range is 4.5 feet.

The entrance to Clinton Harbor at Wheeler Rock is 3.8nm from the entrance to Westbrook Harbor and 6.2nm from the approach to Guilford Harbor at Half Acre Rock. Mattituck Inlet on Long Island is 14.8nm away.

From Kelsey Point Breakwater Light (Fl 2.5s 33ft 7M), a course of about 325°m for 1.2nm will take you west of R N "2" marking a 5-foot spot to Fl G 4s G "3" at the entrance to the Clinton Harbor channel.

From the east, when approaching Clinton beware of lobster pots in the outer harbor area, particularly around Kelsey Point Breakwater. The current is strong enough to pull the markers under the surface, making them hard to spot, so stay at least 50 yards off the breakwater and keep your eyes peeled.

CAUTION: The entire area around Hammonasset Point develops a nasty chop from tidal rips.

The approach from the west is mostly open, and the problem areas are well marked. You can pass both Faulkner (spelled Falkner on the NOAA chart) Island and Kimberley Reef to either side.

When passing Faulkner Island to the north, stay north of Fl G 4s GONG G "15" or you'll go hard aground. Once at Hammonasset Point, remember to stay south of R N "10" and to give the point a wide berth in order to avoid the heavy tide rips.

NOTE: The Army Corps of Engineers dredged the Clinton Harbor channel in June 2000. The channel is now 100 feet wide and 8 feet deep at mlw.

Entering Clinton Harbor is straightforward as long as you follow the buoys closely. The outer harbor is shallow, but the channel leading in is well marked. When entering the channel, give Fl G 4s G "3" fair berth, as it marks Wheeler Rock, which is covered by only about one foot of water at low tide. Just ahead, the recently dredged channel begins to round Cedar Island. Watch for the bend marked by G C "9" and R N "8" (which are not charted, as they are frequently moved).

Once you're inside the harbor there are quite a few marinas with slips available, namely Cedar Island Marina. Here, you'll find a full range of boating services including fuel, and their 400 berths and top-notch amenities certainly appeal to the transient.

Also in harbor, you'll find Old Harbor Marina and Harborside Marina. When the tide and current are opposed, docking along the Hammonasset River can be difficult and requires care. There are also four slips available at the town dock; call the First Selectman's office to check on availability.

The river is a complex waterway that demands attention. First off, note that a 6-mph speed limit begins at Wheeler Rock, though you won't see anything posted until you reach G C "9." If you have a deep-draft boat, you should be aware of encroaching mud just inside the row of moorings on the south side of the channel. And keep an eye out for water-skiers near the "Cable and Pipeline Area" north of Cedar Island.

There are several facilities up the Hammonasset River, including Free Spirit Marine and Bayliner Boat Center, but you shouldn't try taking a cruising boat up the channel until high tide. This same precaution applies to the Indian River, which has two small-boat facilities and a lot of mud at low water.

Shoreside & Emergency Services
Airport:
—Action airlines (800-243-8623)
Coast Guard:
—New Haven (203-468-4464) or VHF 16
Police, Fire, Ambulance: 911
Tow Service:
SEA TOW. —24-Hour Dispatch (800-4SEATOW)
—Central Conn. (860-395-0405)
Tow BoatUS.—24-Hour Dispatch (800-391-4869)
—Clinton (860-388-4065)
Train:
—Amtrak (800-USA-RAIL)
—Metro-North (800-638-7646)

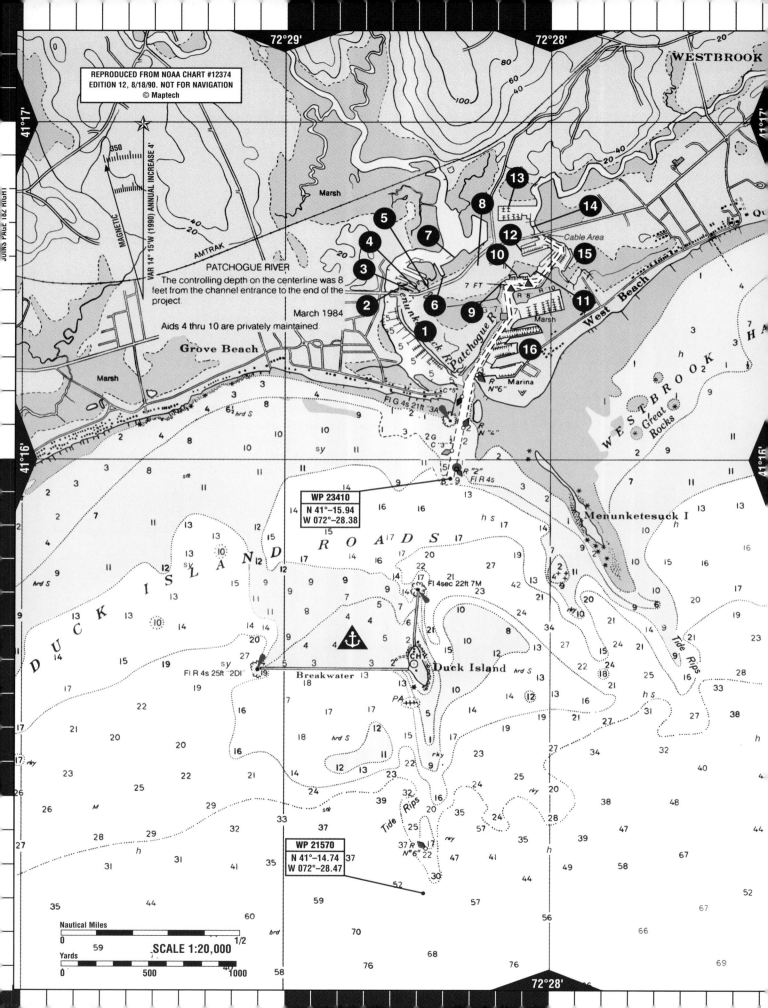

The Great American Turtle

As Westbrook town historian Michael Wells once wrote, the history of a town lays in the history of the great persons who shaped it. During the town's early years, those doing the shaping where in the shipbuilding business. Though not as well known as Essex, Westbrook's shipbuilding prowess is embodied in the town's greatest shipwright—David Bushnell. Bushnell's most famous accomplishment came in 1740 when he invented the first submarine, the *American Turtle*. Long unrecognized as one of the great mechanical minds in American history, Bushnell has only recently taken his place with Benjamin Franklin and Thomas Edison among the great creative minds of invention.

From subs to cruising sailboats—Westbrook takes advantage of its waters. © Maptech

Shipbuilding dominated the Westbrook shoreline for many years, as it did with many other coastal towns. Westbrook outfitted privateers during the Revolution and the War of 1812. But by mid-century, the industry went belly-up and the town lost a third of its population. That wouldn't last too long—the beginning of the 20th century brought a need to vacation and Westbrook was "discovered" again. Westbrook remains a summer beach-and-boating town. If you care to take a walk from any one of the marinas, you will find streets crammed with boating facilities. The coast itself is mostly marshland, home to waterfowl, crabs, and innumerable other marine creatures, though humans have clearly laid claim to the long sandy beaches.

ACTIVITIES: Westbrook is an ideal cruising destination; everything, including the nightlife; is right off your bow. The town comes equipped with numerous and sprawling marine facilities, a fine selection of restaurants, and plenty of outdoor activities.

First, the activities provided by nature. We suggest you spend some time exploring both the Patchogue and Menunketesuck rivers. You might find some osprey nesting in the extensive marshes just upstream of the Route 1

	Marine Facilities and Services		Number of Transient Berths / Moorings	Seasonal / Year-round	Hookups: Fresh Water / Phone / Cable TV	Maximum LOA	110V ★ 220V ▲ 3 Phase ■ Maximum Amps	Ramp / Dinghy Dock / Launch Service	Rail / Lift / Crane / Trailer Capacity (tons)	Repairs: Propellor / Sail / Rigging / Electronics	Diesel / Wood / Fiberglass	Marine / Groceries / Ice / Bait	Gas / Diesel Fuel	Fuel Brand	Restrooms / Showers / Laundry / Pumpout	Public Phone / Restaurant / Snack Bar	Hotel / Pool / Tennis / Golf	Mastercard / VISA / Discover / AmEx
1	Brewer Pilot's Point Marina North Yard Inside Back Cover	860-399-5128	9/		Y	130	8/8	FC	★▲50		LC30	All			MI	RSP	PT	All	All
2	Dick's Marina & Beach Nut Sports Center	860-399-6534	2/		Y	26	3/3	F	★20		*DIVE SHOP*				B	R			All
3	Paul's Custom Tackle	860-399-2271			Y					*BAIT & TACKLE SHOP*									
4	KAPPA SAILS p. 193	888-527-7265			Y							S							
5	Wetmore's Marina*	860-399-9728	5/	S	26	4/4	F	★	R							IB	RS		
6	Marshview Marina	860-399-4364	2/		Y	28	4/4	F		All	T						R		
7	Louis Marine Ltd.	860-399-5554	69/		Y	27	4/4	F	★30	RD	RT	GDWFE			M	R			MV
8	Atlantic Outboard*	800-399-6773			Y				*SALES & REPAIR*		PGDF				M				MVA

Facilities continued on next page…

There is no shortage of masts to be found in the Patchogue River. © Maptech

bridges. Swans, geese, terns, and heron can be seen swimming, wading, and swooping about these waters.

Duck Island may once have been used as a hospital for smallpox and tuberculosis, and there are stories that it was a drop-off for rumrunners during Prohibition, but now it's used as a boater's gathering place. Carefully make your way among the anchored vessels and drop a hook behind the protective jetties of Duck Island. Perfect for a picnic and a swim, you can also visit the island itself—row your dinghy in and explore the remains of an old building or walk the small beach; just be careful not to disturb the terns, and be aware that much of the island is covered with poison ivy.

If it's activity you're looking for, Pilot's Point Marina offers everything from tennis to volleyball to swimming pools spread over their three yards. Enhance your skills by enrolling in the Sailing School; inquire at your yard's dock office to find out what's available there. From the South and East yards, the Westbrook Public Beach is a short walk away. It's a great place to bask in the sun or cool off in the Sound.

Military buffs may want to visit the Company of Military Historians Museum (860-399-9460) and view the war memorabilia. Or perhaps you'd rather spend some time at the annual Westbrook muster and parade, held on the third Saturday in August. The event is usually attended by fife-and-drum corps from all over Connecticut and other parts of the United States, as well as from countries as far away as Switzerland. Even if you're not into this sort of thing, you'll surely enjoy the eating, drinking, and general merriment. For more information about the fife-and-drum muster and other events like the Potato Festival (a spud lover's dream), call the Town Hall (860-399-3044).

Marine Facilities and Services

All Coast Guard Stations Monitor VHF Channel 16

DOCKAGE | SERVICES | SUPPLIES & AMENITIES | marinalife.com Convenient Online Book / Slip Reservations

#	Facility	Contact	Monitors / Working VHF Channel	Number of Transient Berths / Moorings	Seasonal / Year-round	Maximum LOA	Approach / Dockside Depth in Feet at MLW	Hookups: Fresh Water / Phone / Cable TV	110V ★ 220V ▲ 3 Phase ■ Maximum Amps	Ramp / Dinghy Dock / Launch Service	Rail / Lift / Crane / Trailer: Capacity (tons)	Repairs: Propellor / Sail / Rigging / Electronics; Diesel / Wood / Fiberglass / Electronics	Gas / Diesel Fuel	Fuel Brand	Marine / Groceries / Ice / Bait / LPG / CNG	Restrooms / Showers / Laundry / Pumpout	Public Phone / Restaurant / Snack Bar	Hotel / Pool / Tennis / Golf	Mastercard / VISA / Discover / AmEx
9	Westbrook Town Dock	860-399-9406		/2	S	36	8/8												
10	Harry's Marine Repair	860-399-6165		3/	Y	52	7/7	FP	★▲		LC10	PGDWFE	G	Mobil	MI	RSP		P	MV
11	Duck Island Yacht Club*	860-399-4066		2/1	S	40	8/8	F	★30							RS		P	
12	RITTS MARINE CENTER (p. 193)	860-399-8467			Y	48	6/6	F	★30	L	L	PRGDF				RS	S		MV
13	Pier 76 (B)	860-399-7122		40/	Y	22	6/3	F		R		PDWE			MIB	R	PR		All
14	Bill's Seafood Restaurant	860-399-7224			Y	23	4/4			D						R	PR		
15	Brewer Pilot's Point Marina South Yard (Inside Back Cover)	860-399-7906	9/	50/	S	125	10/12	FC	★▲50	D	LCT80	All	GD	Tex	All	All	All	PTG	All
16	Brewer Pilot's Point Marina East Yard (Inside Back Cover)	860-399-6421			Y		7/7	All	★▲■30	D	L25	All				RSP		P	MVA

Information in these listings is provided by the facilities themselves. An asterisk (*) indicates that the facility did not respond to our most recent requests for information. (B) represents a BOAT/U.S. cooperating marina.

If stormy weather is delaying your trip, take the opportunity to visit the Westbrook Factory Outlet Stores (860-399-8656), where you'll find deals at Levi's, J. Crew, Nine West, and many others. It's a bit too far to walk, especially with all the bags.

RESTAURANTS & PROVISIONS: Dining options surround you in Westbrook. Let's start at the marinas: at Brewer Pilot's Point South, South East Galley (860-399-8161) offers up a menu featuring sandwiches, soups, and other light fare. On the other side of Route 1, next to the "singing bridge" is a Westbrook hangout—Bill's Seafood Restaurant (860-399-7224). Here you can dine on the patio and enjoy the music while watching striped bass battle for fries tossed from the deck. Bill's now has a creamery, so after a nice dinner you can top the night off with an ice cream. Nearby, Humphrey's Grill and Bar (860-399-5923) gives you that hometown feel.

Those looking for a meal can head to Frankie's (860-399-5524) for seafood and steak; those looking for a good time can head to Frankie's Upper Deck and partake in the summer evening tradition of beverages and conversation. You'll find many restaurants along Route 1, east of the marinas. The New Deal Steakplace (860-399-0015) serves—you guessed it—steak, as well as seafood, ribs, and chicken.

Farther from the water, Lenny & Joe's Fish Tale Restaurant (860-669-0767) is a summertime favorite. It's located in Clinton, about one mile from the Westbrook marinas, but the trek is worth it. Water's Edge Inn & Resort (860-399-5901) offers seafood and continental food in an elegant setting. For more spice, grab a cab and try the Mexican and Cajun food at the Cuckoo's Nest (860-399-9060) in Old Saybrook. The Cajun swordfish is excellent and the mango margaritas give new meaning to Jimmy Buffett's "(Wasting away again in) Margaritaville." These last two require access to some wheels.

Kenni General Stores, just east of Pilot's Point's south yard, along Route 1, provides some of the basics. But most provisioning in town requires a short ride. The Food Center (860-399-6915), across from the town green, is a mini-grocery store and deli with excellent quality meats. If you have heavy provisioning to do, head south on Route 1 toward Clinton, where you'll find supermarkets. There's no need to go far for nautical needs—Ritts Marine Center is right in the thick of things. So is Kappa Sails for any sail repairs.

NAVIGATION & ANCHORAGES: Use ChartKit Region 3, pages 6, 7, and 32; Maptech™ Waterproof Charts 6 and 17; and

On the blocks or in the water, Westbrook has a place for you. © Maptech

Maptech™ electronic and NOAA paper charts 12374 (1:20,000), 12372 (1:40,000), and 12354 (1:80,000). Use tide tables for Bridgeport. High tide at Duck Island Roads is 24 minutes earlier; low tide is 32 minutes earlier. Multiply height of tide at Bridgeport by 0.6 for height of tide at Duck Island Roads. Mean tidal range is 4.1 feet.

The Fl R 4s R "2" marking the entrance to the Westbrook channel is 6.6nm from the breakwaters at the entrance to the Connecticut River, and 3.4nm from Clinton Harbor. Plum Gut is 14.6nm away.

From Fl (2+1) R 6s HORN R G "W," west of Long Island Shoal, a course due north (000°m) for 2.4nm will get you to Fl R 4s R "2" marking the entrance to the channel leading into Westbrook. From Kelsey Point Breakwater Light (Fl 2.5s 33ft 7M), a course of about 065°m for 2.1nm will take you to Fl R 4s R "2" in Westbrook.

Most people think of the Patchogue and Menunketesuck rivers as Westbrook Harbor. Technically, however, Westbrook Harbor is the bight just east of Menunketesuck Island. This area is not used much as an anchorage because it is unprotected and scattered with many large boulders.

CAUTION: There are many lobster pots along the waterways of Westbrook, particularly near the breakwaters and Menunketesuck Island. Tidal currents often pull the pot markers below the surface. Navigate with caution. You do not want to foul your rudder and props a few yards off these rocks.

From the west, you will pass to the south of the Kelsey Point Breakwater, which protects Duck Island Roads from southwest winds. Normally you'll want to stay south of R N "8," 400 yards off the breakwater—there can be tide rips to the north.

When arriving at night, look for Kelsey Point Breakwater Light (Fl 2.5s 33ft 7M) as a landmark, but be sure to give it an even wider berth. Then swing northeast and run about 1.3nm passing north of Fl R 4s 25ft 5M "2DI" on the end of the Duck Island breakwater, giving it a wide berth. There are strong tidal currents around the Duck Island breakwaters, so keep a safe distance at all times.

From the south, pick up Fl (2+1) R 6s HORN R G "W" at the end of Long Sand Shoal and follow a course of due north magnetic to the buoys at the river's entrance. Don't cut between R N "6" and Duck Island. There is a shoal extending for more than half the distance out to this buoy, and there are strong tide rips, especially when wind and tide are opposed. If you have a shallow draft, this is a good place to find fish, like blackfish (or tautog), blues, and bass.

From the east, the major obstacle when approaching Westbrook is Long Sand Shoal. Generally speaking, the tides are slightly stronger south of the shoal, so when heading against the current, stay north; when you're going with the current, stay south. Depending on the draft of your boat, you may not want to cross the 6-mile-long shoal, which can be as shallow as 4 feet and has a hard, lumpy bottom. Assuming the tides are favorable, most mariners will opt to sail along the north side of Long Sand Shoal while keeping south of Fl R 4s BELL R "2" at Cornfield Point Shoal and R N "4" at Crane Reef.

There is a passage inside Cornfield Point Shoal that is close to shore and has a depth of about 15 feet. Passage here can be more interesting than a trip outside but requires careful navigation and a sharp lookout for Halftide Rock (W Or "A") and Hens and Chickens (W Or C). Cornfield Point in

Saybrook is a good landmark when approaching Westbrook from the east and is easily recognized by the huge stone walls and red tile roofs of Castle Inn.

Closer to Duck Island Roads, you will want to stay well south of Menunketesuck Island. This is often confused with Duck Island, but Menunketesuck can be recognized as the island without a tall chimney. Shallow ground extends about 500 yards south of the island, causing yet another set of nasty tide rips.

When heading for the rivers, keep well south and west of Menunketesuck Island to avoid a patch of rocks that lies southwest of the island. These rocks are now marked by two private buoys W Or C. One buoy is about 600 yards southwest of the southern tip of the island; the other marks the shoal 400 yards southeast of the island. Between these buoys there are many lobster pots—definitely stay clear.

Heading into the rivers, stay to the channel or you'll get stuck in the mud. Once you've entered the channel at Fl R 4s R "2," a no-wake speed limit is in effect.

The currents in the rivers are not usually swift, but you should be aware that when traveling up the channel at ebb tide, the currents will work to set your vessel onto the rocks to the east.

The Menunketesuck River tends to shoal on the west side and is less than 5 feet deep at mid-tide. However, if you stay close to the marina slips, you'll find deeper water. The Route 1 bridge cuts off the river prematurely for most cruising boats, but there are plenty of smaller boats berthed upstream. The chart doesn't show it, but the 5-foot-deep channel up the Menunketesuck is marked by privately maintained buoys. There are a number of marine facilities on or near the river, including Kappa Sails and Louis Marine Ltd.

Of the two rivers in Westbrook, the Patchogue is the more heavily developed. Its channel has been dredged to 8-plus feet to accommodate several marinas and boat yards, including Ritts Marine Center, a commercial fishing wharf, and a town dock. You may tie up at the town dock for as long as 2 hours, but you can't stay overnight. The town also supplies two free bow-and-stern moorings directly across the channel from the dock.

Westbrook is a boater's dream. You will find restaurants, chandleries, fishing stores, and grocery stores to fill your belly, tool box, tackle box, and ice chest—even a laundromat to empty your hamper. It's also hard to miss Brewer Pilot's Point Marina. With nearly 1,000 slips at three locations, this is one of the largest marinas on the Sound.

Traveling up the Patchogue, the "Singing Bridge" on the Boston Post Road cuts off river travel for large boats but doesn't stop the smaller ones. Listen when a car crosses the bridge at 40 mph, and you'll understand its name.

No anchoring is allowed on either of the rivers, but if you'd like to anchor outside the rivers, head for the triangle formed by the breakwaters at Duck Island. It's

---

"Nauti" words

Regatta: a boat race.

You'll surely encounter a local regatta or two as you cruise through the Sound. Almost every day, dinghies and yachts zip around courses to earn, well...bragging rights. It wasn't much different in the Middle Ages.

It was a Venetian custom to sail to a local beach to practice throwing slings, which was important for the region's defense. This leisurely sail to the beach eventually turned into a race. To make things fair, all the boats started from a line. The Italian word for line is *riga*, and that is where we get *regatta*.

Looking south over Westbrook and the Patchogue River. The Brewer Pilot's Point Yards are visible top center (South Yard), top right (North Yard), and bottom left (East Yard). Ritt's Marine Center is center foreground, with Kappa Sails is just right of center. © Maptech/James T. Abts

protected except in weather from the northwest, which may blow you onto the breakwaters or Duck Island if you're not careful.

Also be cautious of the 3-foot spot inside the "triangle;" it's just south of the midway point between the two flashers on the breakwaters. Long ago the area inside the Duck Island breakwaters was dredged to a depth of 15 feet, but now carries only 4 to 5 feet. The mud bottom does give a good hold for your anchor, but again, be careful of the hordes of lobster pots all around the area. If you're planning to anchor here, leave yourself plenty of room and scope, because you're sure to swing at least 180° when the tides change.

Shoreside & Emergency Services
Airport: Action Airlines (800-243-8623)
—Shoreline Aviation (203-468-8639)
Coast Guard: New Haven (203-468-4464) or VHF 16
Police, Fire, Ambulance: 911
Taxi: Essex Taxi (860-767-RIDE/7433)
Tow Service:
SEA TOW —24-Hour Dispatch (800-4SEATOW)
—Central Connecticut (203-488-3442)
Tow BoatU.S.—24-Hour Dispatch (800-391-4869)
—Clinton (860-388-4065)
Train: Amtrak (800-USA-RAIL)
—Metro-North (800-638-7646)

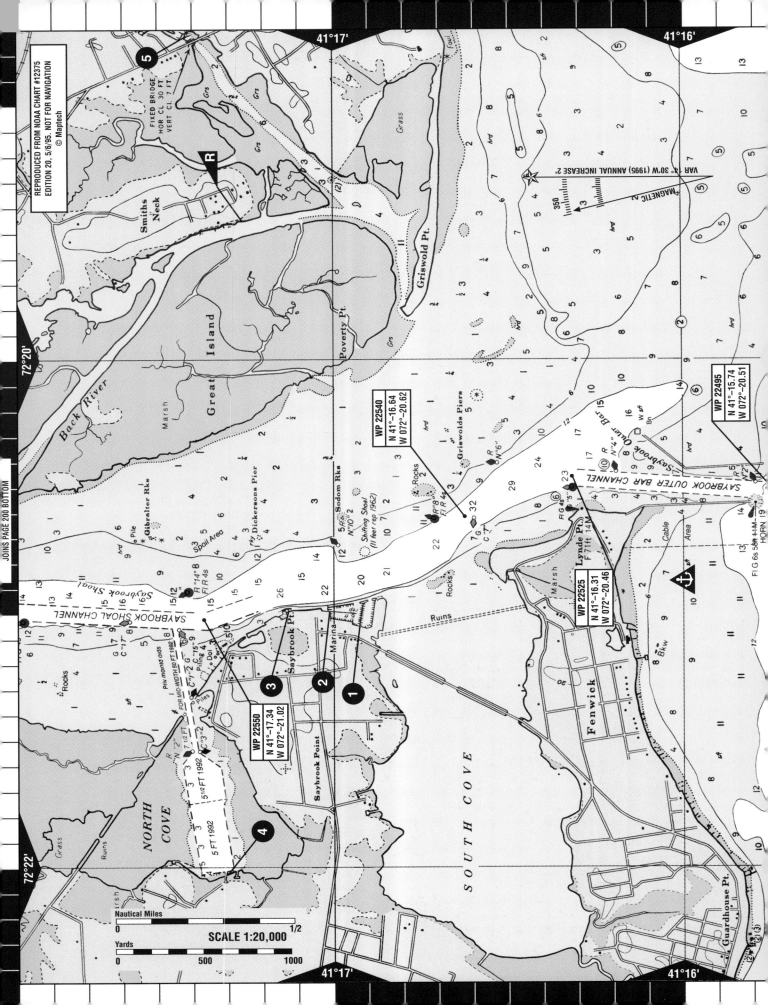

41°17'

41°16'

72°20'

72°22'

41°17'

41°16'

JOINS PAGE 200 BOTTOM

FIXED BRIDGE
HOR CL 30 FT
VERT CL 7 FT

R

Smiths Neck

Griswold Pt.

Poverty Pt.

Great Island

Back River

Marsh

Grass

Grass

Grass

Grass

VAR 14° 30'W (1995) ANNUAL INCREASE 2'

MAGNETIC 2'

350

WP 22495
N 41°–15.74
W 072°–20.51

WP 22540
N 41°–16.64
W 072°–20.62

Griswolds Piers

R "6"

R "8"
Fl R 4s

Sodom Rks
N "10" 2

Shifting Shoal
(11 feet rep 1962)

Rocks

7 G
C "7"

Dickersons Pier

Spoil Area

Gibralter Rks

Pile

Saybrook Shoal

R "14" 8
Fl R 4s

R "14"
12

SAYBROOK SHOAL CHANNEL

Priv maint'd aids
5 FT 1992

G 7
C "7"

G 5
C "5"

Dol 3

Piling

Piles

FOR MID-WIDTH 50 FT 1992

R "2"

5½ FT 1992

C "3"

5½ FT 1992

5 FT 1992

Ruins

NORTH COVE

WP 22550
N 41°–17.34
W 072°–21.02

Saybrook Point

Saybrook Pt.

Marina

Ruins

Rocks

SAYBROOK OUTER BAR CHANNEL

Saybrook Outer Bar

R "4"

R "2"

Fl G 4s

Lynde Pt.
F 71ft 14M

Marsh

WP 22525
N 41°–16.31
W 072°–20.46

Fenwick

Bkw

Guardhouse Pt.

HORN

FIG 6s 58ft 11M

Cable
Area

SOUTH COVE

1
2
3
4
5

R

Welcome to an American Heritage River

Adriaen Block first explored this "long tidal river" in 1614. Poking about in his 50-foot *Onrust*, with its shallow six-foot draft, Block had little trouble crossing the infamous Saybrook Bar. In fact, the stout boat of Manhattan oak carried Block 60 miles upriver, to Enfield Falls. Of course, he had much more experience than Einstein (read about the physicist's travails on page 196), and sailed freely, without performing for a curious public.

The Connecticut River is the longest and largest river in New England. From its source just south of the Canadian border, the river runs 410 miles, draining 11,000 square miles of land and pouring an average of 10 billion gallons of fresh water per day into Long Island Sound.

During the colonial period, the river provided New Englanders with both transportation and food. At one time, Middletown attracted more business than any other port between New York and Boston, and enough fish could be caught during the annual spring shad and salmon runs to supply settlers with food for months.

Over the years, however, the river's tributaries were dammed one by one, cutting off spawning grounds for most of the shad and all of the salmon. In addition, the increasingly concentrated population along the banks of the Connecticut led to a steadily worsening water quality, until the river became known as "the nation's most beautifully landscaped sewer."

Thanks to the efforts of the Connecticut River Watershed Council (860-528-3588), the Federal Clean Air and Water Acts, and many other groups and individuals, the Connecticut has undergone one of the most successful restoration efforts in the country. Twenty-five years ago, only 20 percent of the river was suitable for swimming

This black-hulled beauty rests along the scenic Connecticut River. © Maptech

and fishing; now at least 80 percent of the water is that clean or cleaner. The shad run has rebounded, and salmon have been reintroduced with some success. Between the Sound and East Haddam, 16 miles upriver, the Connecticut is protected by a unique regional agency called the Gateway Commission (860-388-3497). Established by local towns, this group works to limit development along the river in order to preserve its scenic beauty.

The Connecticut River's importance was affirmed in 1998 when it was the first river in the country to be named an American Heritage River (800-40-RIVER). President Clinton selected the Connecticut along with 13 other rivers

#	Marine Facilities and Services		DOCKAGE							SERVICES						SUPPLIES & AMENITIES							
			Monitors / Working VHF Channel	Number of Transient Berths / Moorings	Approach / Dockside Depth in Feet at MLW	Seasonal / Year-round	Maximum LOA	Hookups: Fresh Water / Phone / Cable TV	110V ★ 220V ▲ 3 Phase ■ Maximum Amps	Ramp / Dinghy Dock / Launch Service	Rail / Lift / Crane / Trailer Capacity (tons)	Diesel / Wood / Fiberglass / Electronics	Repairs: Propellor / Sail / Rigging / Gas	Gas / Diesel Fuel	Marine / Groceries / Ice / Bait / LPG / CNG	Fuel Brand	Restrooms / Showers / Laundry / Pumpout	Public Phone / Restaurant / Snack Bar	Hotel / Pool / Tennis / Golf	Mastercard / VISA / Discover / AmEx	marinalife.com Convenient Online Boat Slip Reservations
1	**Harbor One Marina** p. 199	860-388-9208	9/10	10/	S	150	20/8	All	★▲■200			PGDWFE		GD	Tex	MI	RSL	P	PS	All	
2	SAYBROOK POINT MARINA p. 197	860-395-3080	9/11	20/	Y	200	18/7	FC	★▲■200					GD	Tex	MI	All	HP	All	All	
3	Dock and Dine	860-388-4665		10/	Y	120		*DOCKING FOR RESTAURANT PATRONS ONLY*								R		All	All		
4	North Cove Yacht Club	860-388-9087	9/	/1	S	45	6/5	F		DL							RS	P			
5	Black Hall Marina	860-434-9680		50/	S	22		F	★30	R						MIB	R		MV		

Information in these listings is provided by the facilities themselves. An asterisk (*) indicates that the facility did not respond to our most recent requests for information.
(B) represents a BOAT/U.S. cooperating marina.

for this honorable status, which entitles the waterways to federal funding for various projects.

ACTIVITIES: Mother Nature provides most of the attractions at the entrance to the Connecticut River. Griswold Point and Great Island, on the eastern side of the river, harbor the largest nesting population of ospreys in Connecticut and are two of the best bird-watching sites in the state. Remember to keep your distance from the wildlife so as not to disturb them.

Although a breach in the beach at Griswold Point has cut off land access to the tip at all but low tide, this area is still a favorite swimming spot. Pets are not welcome at the preserve because of the trouble they can cause for the nesting birds. If you want to cross from one side of the spit to the other, you might want to use one of the designated trails in order not to trample the dune grass that helps stabilize the area. Actually, nothing really holds the spit in place, as the breach can attest.

Great Island and the Back and Black Hall rivers are fun to explore by dinghy, canoe, or small outboard; Between the Bridges South Yard (860-388-3614) has rentals. You'll see ospreys, egrets, sandpipers, and herons stalking the tidal flats at low tide and peering through the marshes at higher water. On sunny weekends from June through October there's usually someone on every bridge, angling for the blue crabs in the brackish water below. Some use special folding traps, but most use the traditional net and a chicken wing or some other leftovers tied to a string.

On the western side of the river is the borough of Fenwick, a beautiful and exclusive summer community. Fenwick has a public golf course (860-388-2516) that's open to non-residents on a limited/same day call-in basis, except on weekends during the high season.

Some people remember the old Terra Mar Marina and Hotel that once stood on Saybrook Point. In its heyday, it was the glitziest resort on the Sound, until it was closed and left to rot. In the late 1980s, a new group of investors bought the property, completely rebuilt the marina, and created a new complex that includes a luxury hotel, condominiums, and a conference center. Today, the site (renamed Saybrook Point Inn, Marina, & Spa) is once again making quite a name for itself.

If you're a Yale graduate or a lover of history, you'll want to stop off at Saybrook Point to see Fort Saybrook Monument Park, the statue of Lion Gardiner, the tomb of Lady Fenwick, and the boulder marking the site where Yale University stood from 1707 to 1716. Legend tells of a riot when the books were moved from the library here to Yale's present New Haven site.

To visit downtown Old Saybrook, you'll need to hop onto your bike or the local trolley, or call a cab—it's a pretty long walk. See the following chapter for more information on the downtown area.

RESTAURANTS & PROVISIONS: If you're staying at one of the Saybrook Point marinas, you have two very convenient dining choices. Terra Mar Grill (860-388-1111), the restaurant at Saybrook Point Inn, Marina, & Spa, offers fine waterfront dining either inside or outside on the terrace. Saybrook Point Dock & Dine (860-388-4665) serves a variety of seafood and other entrees, and dockage is available for patrons. If you're in the mood for a light bite or some fresh baked goods, stop in at the Bagel Bakery at Harbor One Marina.

Downtown Old Saybrook is about a mile away from the facilities at Saybrook Point, and half a mile or less from North Cove. We suggest Wine & Roses (860-388-9646) on Main Street, specializing in regional American cuisine. If

Einstein Miscalculated?

Although Albert Einstein was comfortable in a laboratory, he was a bit perplexed by sailing vessels. While visiting Old Lyme in the summer of 1935, the professor spent some time on the river in a small sailboat, and apparently had more than his share of troubles. One day, caught between the wind, the tide, and a shoal, he ran aground.

Our readers know that the mouth of the Connecticut River causes problems for even the most experienced navigators, so they will surely forgive the scientist his mistakes, but the *New London Day* was not so considerate. Wasting no time, the newspaper gleefully trumpeted Einstein's misadventures the next morning under the headline: "Einstein's Miscalculations Leave Him Stuck on Bar of Lower Connecticut River."

Einstein had simply rediscovered what residents of Old Saybrook knew many years ago: the sandbar at the river's mouth is a pain in the neck. Unlike most other major rivers of the world, because of its steep pitch and many rapids, the Connecticut has never been open to much heavy shipping. For this reason it has never developed a major metropolitan port along its banks. Instead, you'll find the estuary lined with small towns and wildlife preserves, and the waters dotted with peaceful anchorages.

you'd like to grab your food and go, try Orsini's Sausages, Inc. (860-388-5937) or Walt's Food Market (860-388-3308), both featuring hearty take-out sandwiches. For more information on Old Saybrook, see the following chapter.

NAVIGATION & ANCHORAGES: Use ChartKit Region 3, pages 7 and 33; Maptech™ Waterproof Charts 1, 2, and 17; and Maptech™ electronic and NOAA paper charts 12375 (1:20,000), 12372 (1:40,000), and 12354 (1:80,000). Use tide tables for New London. High tide at Saybrook Point is 1 hour 11 minutes later; low tide is 53 minutes later. Multiply height of tide at New London by 1.2 for height of tide at Saybrook Point. Mean tidal range is 3.2 feet.

Saybrook Breakwater Light (Fl G 6s 58ft 11M HORN) is 6.2nm from Duck Island in Westbrook, and 7.5nm from Black Point and the entrance to Niantic Bay. Plum Gut is 8.1nm away.

From the southeast at Fl R 4s BELL R "8," a course of 320°m for 1.5nm will take you to a spot between R N "2"

and Fl G 6s 58ft 11M HORN at the Saybrook outer bar channel. From here, follow the buoys upriver being sure (especially at night) to avoid floating debris.

From the west, look for Fl G 6s 58ft 11M HORN on the southern end of the breakwater. On a clear day, you can see the white tower for many miles. West of the breakwater is a nice anchorage for lunch and a swim. It is unprotected, however, so don't stay overnight.

When crossing the Sound from Plum Gut, or coming from the west and traveling south of Long Sand Shoal, pass on either side of the RG N "E" at the east end of the shoal. One of the first things you'll see is a large white house with two chimneys in Fenwick. Be sure not to confuse Lynde Point Light (Fl 71ft 14M) with the shorter outer light on the breakwater.

From the east, pass south of Hatchett Reef R N "6" off Old Lyme Shores. Then pass south and west of Fl R 4s BELL R "8" before swinging to the northwest and heading for the breakwaters.

CAUTION: Do not attempt to pass over the Saybrook Sand Bar. The ruins of the old shad-fishing piers on the east side of the river are real. You may see fishing boats heading through here—don't follow them.

As you head north through the breakwaters, keep R N "2" to the east, as it marks a shoal area on the eastern side of the channel. On weekends, the mouth of the river is heavily congested with all types of boats. And during an ebb tide, the current can run anywhere from 4 to 5 knots. You will also face some crosscurrent at the southern end of the breakwater, so take care not to get swept into the rocks. Be sure to give a wide berth to large commercial vessels, as

they aren't very maneuverable and can't alter course once within the restricted width of the dredged channel. The only other consideration is a set of earplugs. Once the "cigarette boats" are past the outer light—and sometimes before—they have the throttle wide open.

NOTE: A "steerage only" speed limit exists from the breakwater entrance to Fl G 4s G "5" and then again from just north of Fl R 4s R "8" to Fl R 4s R "14" opposite North Cove.

The 71-foot Lynde Point Inner Light was erected in 1803, making it the second-oldest lighthouse in Connecticut. After you pass both the light and G C "7," Old Saybrook's South Cove will be to the west. The remains of an old causeway at the mouth of this cove make it accessible only to very shallow-draft boats. At exceptionally low tides, you may be able to see the remains of the steamboat *Granite State*, which sank in 1883 near the mouth of the cove.

Saybrook Point is located between South Cove and North Cove. There are two excellent marinas here—Harbor One Marina and Saybrook Point Inn, Marina, & Spa. Because of their proximity to the open water of the Sound, they are favorite stopovers for large cruising boats on their way to Newport or New York.

North Cove in Old Saybrook has a dredged channel with a depth of 7.5 feet, making it accessible to most cruising boats. (The cove itself only carries a depth of 5.5 feet at

mlw.) North of G C "15" turn sharply to the west and stay between the local markers. There are some 150 permanent moorings here, so you'll find little space to drop anchor. The town of Old Saybrook welcomes transient boaters and maintains a few guest moorings available at no charge. All other vacant moorings are available on a temporary basis; however, you must remain aboard. If you have questions, North Cove Yacht Club (VHF 9) may be able to help. The club offers launch service, showers, restrooms, and other services for a modest fee.

Shoreside & Emergency Services
Airport:
—Tweed New Haven (203-466-8833)
Coast Guard:
—New London (860-442-4464) or VHF 16
Harbormaster: (860-399-6183)
Police, Fire, Ambulance: 911
Taxi:
—Essex Taxi (860-767-RIDE/7433)
Tow Service:
SEA TOW.—24-Hour Dispatch (800-4SEATOW)
—Central Conn. (860-395-0405)
Tow BoatU.S.—24-Hour Dispatch (800-391-4869)
— Old Saybrook (860-388-4065)
Train:
—Amtrak (800-USA-RAIL)
—Metro-North (800-638-7646)

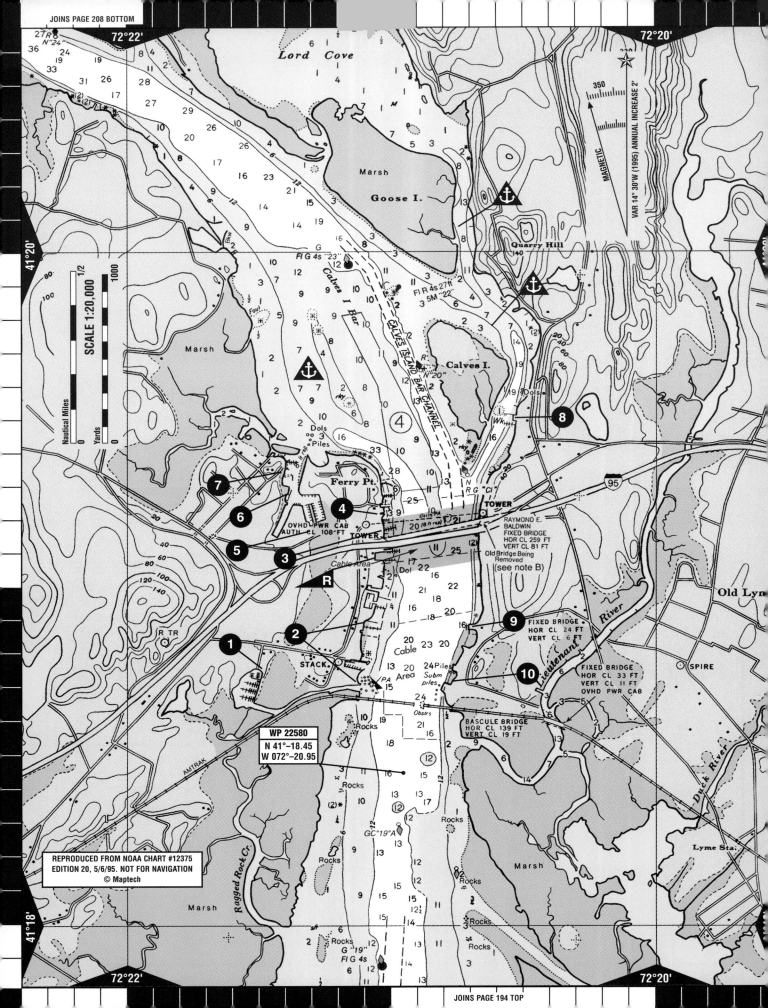

72°22'

72°20'

Lord Cove

Marsh

Goose I.

MAGNETIC

VAR 14° 30'W (1995) ANNUAL INCREASE 2'

350

Quarry Hill
140

41°20'

SCALE 1:20,000

Calves I Bar

Fl G 4s "23"

FL R 4s 27ft
3 5M "22"

Calves I.

Marsh

CALVES ISLAND BAR CHANNEL

Foul

④

Dols
Piles

N "20"

Wk

8

95

7

Ferry Pt.

N R G "C1"

TOWER

RAYMOND E.
BALDWIN
FIXED BRIDGE
HOR CL 259 FT
VERT CL 81 FT

6

4

TOWER

Old Bridge Being
Removed

(see note B)

5

3

OVHD PWR CAB
AUTH CL 108 FT

Cable Area

Dol

R

River

Old Lyn

9

FIXED BRIDGE
HOR CL 24 FT
VERT CL 6 FT

1

2

Cable

Lieutenant

FIXED BRIDGE
HOR CL 33 FT
VERT CL 11 FT
OVHD PWR CAB

R TR

STACK

Cable
Area

Piles
Subm
piles

10

SPIRE

WP 22580
N 41°–18.45
W 072°–20.95

Obstrs

BASCULE BRIDGE
HOR CL 139 FT
VERT CL 19 FT

Rocks

AMTRAK

⑫

Duck River

⑫

Rocks

GC "19"A

Lyme Sta.

Ragged Rock Cr.

Marsh

Rocks

Marsh

Rocks

Rocks

G "19"
Fl G 4s

41°18'

72°22'

72°20'

Puritans and Pugilists

In 1707 Saybrook Point became the new home of the Collegiate School, which had been established six years earlier at Branford. The institution served to educate young men who wished to become Congregationalist ministers. Treasurer Nathaniel Lynde donated the building and 10-acre campus on the condition that the school not be moved from that location.

Money talks. And while Nathaniel Lynde had some, Elihu Yale, a Massachusetts-born transplant to England, had more (or else his simply talked louder). Yale, an administrator with the East India Company, donated books to the school, which moved to New Haven in 1917. The following year, preacher and writer Cotton Mather penned a letter to Elihu Yale, hinting that if he were to make another ample donation the college would be named in his honor. The British benefactor obliged, and the prestigious Ivy League institution has held his name ever since.

If you spend any time on the opposite shore of the Connecticut River, you'll likely peg Old Lyme as a refined town preferred by artists, moneyed retirees, and weekend wedding parties. That's accurate but this polished façade belies less sophisticated beginnings. Officials in 1670 settled a boundary dispute with New London by way of a fistfight. Each community chose its champion brawler, agreeing that the man left standing would secure the land

You'll always find a spot to dock in this neck of the river. © Maptech

Marine Facilities and Services		DOCKAGE						SERVICES					SUPPLIES & AMENITIES								
		Monitors / Working VHF Channel	Number of Transient Berths / Moorings	Approach / Dockside Depth in Feet at MLW	Seasonal / Yearround	Hookups: Fresh Water / Phone / Cable TV	110V ★ 220V ▲ 3 Phase ■ Maximum Amps	Maximum LOA	Ramp / Dinghy Dock / Launch Service	Rail / Lift / Crane / Trailer: Capacity (tons)	Repairs: Propellor / Sail / Rigging / Gas	Diesel / Wood / Fiberglass / Electronics	Marine / Groceries / Ice / Bait / LPG / CNG	Gas / Diesel Fuel	Fuel Brand	Restrooms / Showers / Laundry / Pumpout	Public Phone / Restaurant / Snack Bar	Hotel / Pool / Tennis / Golf	Mastercard / VISA / Discover / AmEx		
1	**RAGGED ROCK MARINA** p. 206	860-388-1049	/68	3/	Y	55	5/10	All	★	RD	L20	All				MI	All		P	MV	
2	BETWEEN THE BRIDGES MARINA (B) p. 203	860-388-1431	9/7	50/	Y	120	14/14	All	★▲200		L65	PGDWFE	GD	Tex		MGI	All	P	All	All	
3	**OAK LEAF MARINA, INC.** p. 207	860-388-9817	9/11	10/	Y	110	30/20	F	★▲100		LCT25	PGDWF				MG	RSL		P	All	
4	Seth Persson Boat Builders	860-388-2343			Y	*CONSTRUCTION OF BOATS*					All					R		P			
5	Ferry Point Marina	860-388-3260		5/	S	45	6/6	All	★▲50		L25	All	GD	Tex		M	RS		P		
6	Offshore East Marina	860-388-4532		2/	S	40	8/8	F	★30	D	L20	PSRGDWF				MI	RS				
7	Island Cove Marina	860-388-1275	16/9	5/5	Y	45	12/7	FP	★35	All						I	RSL		P		
8	Old Lyme Marina	860-434-1272	9/68	5/5	Y	65	15/15	F	★▲50	D	LC25	All				MI	RS		P	All	
9	**Old Lyme Dock Co.** p. 205	860-434-2267	9/7	4/2	S	175	16/13	FP	★▲100	D			GD	Tex		MI	RSL			All	
10	State of CT DEP-Marine Division p. 19	860-434-8638			Y																

Information in these listings is provided by the facilities themselves. An asterisk (*) indicates that the facility did not respond to our most recent requests for information.
(B) represents a BOAT/U.S. cooperating marina.

Looking north over the marine facilities along Old Lyme's shore. © Maptech/James T. Abts

in question for his town. Several pints of blood later, Old Lyme's pugilist stood victorious.

The settlement of this Saybrooke Colony had been conceived by 15 English lords of Puritan descent (two of the 15 gentlemen, Lord Saye and Lord Brooke, lent their names to the colony). Given a large tract of land along the lower Connecticut River by the Earl of Warwick, these gentlemen were determined to create a colony of large estates for "men of distinction and qualitie." Namely, themselves.

In 1635, soldiers employed by the founders landed near the mouth of the river, and within a year, Lion Gardiner, future proprietor of Gardiner's Island, had built a fort on Saybrook Point. While Saybrooke never developed into the elite haven envisioned by its founders, the huge tract of land did become one of Connecticut's most beautiful areas. By 1663, Lyme had split from the rest of the colony, and over the next 300 years, the remaining land would be broken up into the five smaller towns of Chester, Deep River, Essex, Old Saybrook, and Westbrook.

Old Saybrook has managed to retain much of its charm despite its growth, especially along Main Street and the shore roads, but Old Lyme corners the market on peace and prettiness. Gracious captains' homes still sit back from tree-lined streets, and the town possesses a sense of lovely calm, never hurried or ruffled. Both towns provide a quiet and storm-safe spot for cruisers to recharge in the midst of natural beauty.

Looking northwest over Old Lyme Marina. Essex can be seen in the distance. © Maptech/James T. Abts

ACTIVITIES: In Old Saybrook, there's not an abundance of things to see and do, but you're sure to find any supplies or equipment you'll need for your boat (although you'll need to take a bike or taxi into town). You can also inquire at one of the marinas about the local trolley—if it's running, it makes for fairly convenient access to and around town. If you're into fishing, canoeing, and the outdoors, or are just looking for an interesting store to explore, be sure to stop in at North Cove Outfitters (860-388-6585) on Main Street. They have a wide selection of outdoor clothing and equipment that will interest everyone.

The opportunities for viewing art and nature are greater in Old Lyme than at any other point along the Connecticut River. Don't skip the Florence Griswold Museum of American Impressionist Paintings (860-434-5542), a National Historic Landmark within walking distance of Old Lyme Marina. This was an artists' colony, where talented Impressionists lived and painted—even directly on the walls and doors. The Lyme Art Association (860-434-7802) and the Lyme Academy of Fine Arts (860-434-5232) are also located in town; both have rotating exhibits of contemporary work.

Lord Cove's marshes offer fantastic birdwatching, and you're likely to see ospreys, herons, egrets, hawks, kestrels, and other shoreside birds here. If you happen to be in the area during the winter, keep your eyes peeled for bald eagles that visit when the river is frozen farther north. They ride the ice floes, hunting for big fish swimming just below the surface and for unwary ducks or gulls.

In June, the marshes fill with yellow and purple flags in bloom. By summer, the pink flowers of the swamp rose mallow burst into blossom. At dawn and dusk, muskrat, deer, and foxes come down to the water's edge, and recently there have been a few coyotes in town—back in 1962, there was even a moose.

Fishermen should be aware that the waters north of the Interstate-95 bridge are considered inland, so you'll need a fishing license to chase the blues, stripers, and so on in that area. North Cove Outfitters and River's End Bait & Tackle (860-388-2283) can help with the whens, wheres, and what baits to use, and they can provide the equipment to ensure

your success. Check with one of the tackle shops or town clerks for license information.

RESTAURANTS & PROVISIONS: Today, Old Saybrook remains the commercial hub of the region. This status may be partly due to the town's historic role as the center of the colony, but it's also because of the town's strategic location at the junction of I-95 and Route 9. Zoning laws have also allowed Old Saybrook more commercial development than other towns, with small shopping malls, auto dealerships, fast-food restaurants, and even some light industry.

For eating on the water, Between the Bridges Marina is the place, as it offers a restaurant and snack bar. Just down the road from the marinas at Ferry Point, the Saybrook Fish House (860-388-4836) offers healthy servings of some of the finest seafood in the state, as well as steak, chicken, and delicious salads. Toward town, Cloud Nine Cool Catering & Café (860-388-0800) has a creative selection of soups, sandwiches, salads, and baked goods. If you're in the mood for a real taste of summer (we mean deep-fried clams, onion rings, and chowder), go for Johnny Ad's (860-388-4032).

Downtown Old Saybrook is about a mile from the marinas and can be reached by bike, trolley, or cab. They also offer catering and delivery for those who'd rather stay aboard. If you have kids along, don't miss Pizzaworks (860-388-2218) at the Saybrook Junction. In addition to sumptuous pies and salads, you and your young'uns will be awed and entertained

Old Lyme Marina customers receive a launch to their mooring. © Maptech

Looking north over Between the Bridges Marina in Old Saybrook. © Maptech/James T. Abts

by the extensive model train sets. On the other side of the tracks, Pat's Kountry Kitchen (860-388-4784) offers home-style cooking including their famous clam hash.

Main Street features several good dining choices, including Wine & Roses (860-388-9646), as well as a hardware store, pharmacy, bank, and small grocery, Walt's (860-388-3308), which also sells wonderful deli sandwiches. You'll find more groceries than your boat can hold at the Stop & Shop on Elm Street. Remember, reaching this area will require some wheels.

In Old Lyme there are several fine restaurants not far from the marinas. Both the Old Lyme Inn (860-434-2600) and the Bee & Thistle Inn (860-434-1667) serve excellent food in elegant and comfortable settings. Reservations are suggested for both.

Old Lyme has a small plaza on either side of Halls Road, each with eateries. Try Anne's Bistro (860-434-9837) in the Old Lyme Market Place, or the Hideaway (860-434-3335) in the Old Lyme Shopping Center. If your galley is empty, the A & P Supermarket is the answer to your prayers. All of this is an easy walk from the marinas.

NAVIGATION & ANCHORAGES: Use ChartKit Region 3, page 33; Maptech™ Waterproof Charts 2 and 17; and Maptech™ electronic and NOAA paper charts 12375 (1:20,000), 12372 (1:40,000), and 12354 (1:80,000). Use tide tables for New London. High tide at the Lyme Highway Bridge is 1 hour 25 minutes later; low tide is 1 hour 10 minutes later. Multiply height of tide at New London by 1.2 for height of tide at the Lyme Highway Bridge. The mean tidal range is 3.1 feet.

The Interstate-95 bridge between Old Saybrook and Old Lyme is 2.9nm north of Lynde Point at the river's mouth; from the highway bridge, it is another 2.6nm north and west to the Connecticut River Museum docks at the foot of Main Street in Essex.

There are two separate waterfront areas in Old Saybrook. One, around Saybrook Point, is discussed in the previous chapter; the other, around Ferry Point, is often referred to as the place "up there by the bridges."

The Amtrak railroad crosses the Connecticut on the Old Lyme Drawbridge, about two miles from the river's mouth. The bridge has a vertical clearance of 19 feet (mhw); small powerboats can pass beneath it when it is closed. In the past, boaters with higher rigs circled endlessly, waiting for the bridge to open, but Amtrak has been working to speed things up. From May 15 to Oct. 15, the bridge will open immediately after a train passes and remain open until the next train approaches. When the bridge is closed a digital display shows the number of minutes until it will open again.

The bridgetender may be contacted on VHF 13, but will only answer if you ask for the Old Lyme drawbridge, not Old Saybrook. You may also contact the bridge with one long and one short blast of your horn; if you receive a similar horn signal, then the bridge will open shortly. If, however, you receive a single, 5-second blast, then the train is on its way, and you'll have to wait.

Just north of the railroad bridge are the I-95 bridges—vertical clearance on both spans is 81 feet (mhw). Just before passing under the bridges, you'll see the revamped, state-owned launching ramp and pier on the Saybrook shore.

Both shorelines around the bridges have several full-service marinas, all of which have transient slips and are equipped to handle any of your repair needs. North of the railroad bridge, on the west shore, are Ragged Rock Marina, Between the Bridges Marina, and Oak Leaf Marina, as well as the Connecticut DEP's docks.

On the east shore, the first set of docks belongs to the Marine Patrol Division and the Marine Fisheries Program of the Connecticut Department of Environmental Protection. About halfway between the railroad bridge and the I-95 bridges is the Old Lyme Dock Co., and just above the I-95 bridges is Old Lyme Marina.

North of the highway bridges, you'll find several nice, scenic anchorages. Those in medium-draft boats will want to check out the area east of Calves Island, a pleasant place to drop a hook away from the heavy wash that creeps up so steadily near the main channel. You may have a fair number of neighbors while visiting there, so get a good bite when setting anchor, as you may not be able to use a lot of scope.

For more privacy, head about 0.25nm into Lord Cove, just east of Goose Island. You'll have good water up to the

northeast corner of the island, but then the shallows take over, making further exploration difficult in anything but a dinghy. You may also want to anchor north of Ferry Point, across from Calves Island. You'll have more water here, but also more noise and more wakes from traffic in the channel.

CAUTION: The rocky shoals in the center of the river, north of Ferry Point, are unmarked and regularly snag unwary boaters.

Shoreside & Emergency Services
Coast Guard:
—New London (860-442-4471) or VHF 16
Harbormaster:
—Old Saybrook (860-399-6183)
Police, Fire, Ambulance: 911
Taxi:
—Essex Taxi (860-767-RIDE)
Tow Service:
SEA TOW —24-Hour Dispatch (800-4SEATOW)
—Central Connecticut (860-395-0405)
Tow BoatU.S.—24-Hour Dispatch (800-391-4869)
—Old Saybrook (860-388-4065)
Train:
—Amtrak (800-USA-RAIL)
—Metro-North (800-638-7646)

REPRODUCED FROM NOAA CHART #12375
EDITION 20, 5/6/95. NOT FOR NAVIGATION
© Maptech

From Sailing Ships to Steam Trains

Shipbuilding in Essex began in 1733. The 24-gun *Oliver Cromwell*, the first warship of the Revolutionary War, was built at Uriah Hayden's shipyard. Water in the coves ran deeper in the 19th century than today, and Essex boasted a number of other very busy shipyards that turned out schooners, packets, and other vessels for use mainly in foreign trade. The industry was so big in this town that a bell, suspended from a tree in the village, was rung each morning to awaken the laborers and tell them that it was time to head to work. Apparently the bell had been purposely cracked to give it a unique tone that would resonate farther to reach the ears of the dozing men.

The town's major role in shipbuilding was no secret: the British knew all about it. During the War of 1812 they launched a midnight raid against the town to destroy the local warships and hinder future production. While no one was hurt during the 12-hour raid, 23 vessels at anchor or under construction burned, and the British managed to commandeer a great many supplies from local chandleries, including all the town's rum.

Later on during the Age of Steam, Essex was busy with visits from the Connecticut Valley Railroad as well as the 243-foot

July is a festive time in downtown Essex. © Maptech

sister ships *Middletown* and *Hartford*. Although the steamships offered the most glamorous means of transportation in that time, they were also quite dangerous. Two ships suffered boiler explosions off the Essex shore: the *Ellsworth* in 1827, and the *New England* in 1833. Steamboat travel lived on for about 100 years after these tragedies, at which time the more convenient automobile stole the show.

Marine Facilities and Services — All Coast Guard Stations Monitor VHF Channel 16 — marinalife.com · Convenient Online Boat Slip Reservations

#	Facility	Phone	Monitors / Working VHF Channel	Number of Transient Berths	Seasonal / Year-round Moorings	Maximum LOA	Approach / Dockside Depth in Feet at MLW	Hookups: Fresh Water / Phone / Cable TV	110V★ 220V▲ 3 Phase■ Max Amps	Ramp / Dinghy Dock / Launch Service	Rail / Lift / Crane / Trailer Capacity (tons)	Repairs: Diesel/Wood/Fiberglass/Electronics · Propellor/Sail/Rigging/Gas	Gas / Diesel Fuel	Fuel Brand	Marine / Groceries / Ice / Bait / LPG / CNG	Restrooms / Showers / Laundry / Pumpout	Public Phone / Restaurant / Snack Bar	Hotel / Pool / Tennis / Golf	Mastercard / VISA / Discover / AmEx
1	Essex Yacht Club*	860-767-8121	68/	/10	S	50	13/8	F	★30	DL					I	RS	All		MV
2	THE CHANDLERY AT ESSEX (p. 211)	860-767-8267	68/68	1/55	Y	120	12/12	F	★▲■50	DL			GD	Mob	MIC	All		P	All
2	Essex Corinthian Yacht Club*	860-767-3239		/3	Y					RD						RS			All
3	Connecticut River Museum	860-767-8269		2/2	Y	120	5/5									R			MV
4	Middle Cove Marina	860-767-2641			Y	40	8/7	All	▲50							RS		P	
5	ESSEX BOAT WORKS, INC. (p. 212)	860-767-8276	16/9	6/6	Y	70	10/10	F	★▲50	D	LC50	All				R		P	All
6	Essex Island Marina (p. 211)	860-767-1267	9/68	75/	Y	200	7/6	FC	★▲■100		L30	PGDWF	GD	Tex	MGI	RSL	P	All	MVA
7	Essex Landing	860-767-3904	9/	4/	Y	55	12/8	F	★▲50			P			MI	RS			MV
8	Brewer Dauntless Shipyard (Inside Back Cover)	860-767-2483	9/	8/	Y	110	10/12	All	★▲50		LC35	All			MI	All	P	All	MVA
9	Pettipaug Yacht Club*	860-767-8893			Y	*PRIVATE—MEMBERS ONLY*													
10	Cove Landing Marina	860-434-5240		/15	S	80	6/9	F	★▲50	D	L35	All			MGI	RSP			
11	Reynolds' Garage & Marine	860-434-0028			S	50	5/5	F	★30	D	RT10					RS			All

Information in these listings is provided by the facilities themselves. An asterisk (*) indicates that the facility did not respond to our most recent requests for information. (B) represents a BOAT/U.S. cooperating marina.

Lucky for cruising boaters, yachting never left Essex. The town's location on a peninsula is one reason for this. Surrounded by water on three sides, the village offers cruising boaters all they need within a short walk of the water. Beautiful Federal and Colonial period homes and shops line the streets, attracting hordes of visitors during the summer (and mere crowds the rest of the year).

ACTIVITIES: A stroll around Essex Village could be ample entertainment for water-weary visitors. It's a treat you'll remember long after Old Man Winter makes his appearance.

The Connecticut River Museum (860-767-8269), right next to the town dock, is a highly-regarded showcase of regional history. Along with the best view of the harbor, the museum has outstanding exhibits on the animal life and geology of the Connecticut River Valley, native Americans, shipbuilding, brownstone quarries, and more. The pride of the museum is a working, full-size replica of the *American Turtle*—the first submarine, invented in 1776 by David Bushnell of Westbrook.

Train fanatics will be thrilled out of their shoes at the Valley Railroad Company (860-767-0103). On their yard you'll see a large collection of old steam and diesel locomotives as well as freight and passenger cars, and other pieces of machinery associated with a working railroad. Daily steam train rides take passengers upriver with the option of joining a sightseeing boat for a cruise along the river. The railroad also offers fall foliage rides, dinner excursions, and special Christmas trips.

Call Essex Taxi for a lift to the Ivoryton Playhouse (860-767-8348), where Katharine Hepburn got her start in 1931 (Eva Gabor, Marlon Brando, and Faye Dunaway have performed there as well). A little farther down the road in Ivoryton is the Company of Fifers and Drummers Museum (860-767-2237). This part of Connecticut is a hotbed of wailing fifes and pounding drums—they come out to strut their stuff and make "joyful noise" at every opportunity.

There isn't much going on in the town of Hamburg (of course, its serene beauty is its main appeal), save for the annual country fair (860-434-2494) held the third weekend of August.

RESTAURANTS & PROVISIONS: Essex Village may not be overflowing with eateries, but if you're like us, you value quality over quantity, anyway. Everyone ends up eventually at the Griswold Inn (860-767-1776), locally known as "The Gris," be it for lunch, dinner, or Sunday's Hunt Breakfast. A sign over the taproom door reads, "Because we cater to yachtsmen, a coat and tie are not required." The interior of the Gris, which has been in continuous operation since 1776, is filled with marine paintings and prints, as well as an excellent display of antique firearms. The restaurant is usually packed, so reservations are suggested.

A block up Main Street you'll find the Black Seal Seafood Grille (860-767-0233), with a pub and dining room. In keeping with the town's maritime ties, "The

Seal" is tastefully strewn with artifacts from the sea. The restaurant serves good grub at reasonable prices, and the bar is popular without being rowdy. If you decide to have a bite after some grog, check out the "daily specials" as they are, indeed, usually that.

If you're looking for a quicker bite, the Crow's Nest (860-767-3288) at the Dauntless Shipyard serves breakfast and lunch overlooking the marinas and the Connecticut River. Here you'll find everything from Belgian waffles to creative sandwiches, homestyle soup, salads, and fresh baked goods (we're wild about the scones). Dinners are served in season. Olive Oyl's Carry Out Cuisine (860-767-4909), just across the street from the Griswold, also serves sandwiches, quiche, salad, and soup. At Essex Coffee & Tea Co. (860-767-7804), you can enjoy a pastry and "the Captain's Cup" filled with a hot or cold beverage. While you're re-energizing, admire the model ships and nautical art, or just pore through a newspaper. Screaming for ice cream? Grab a cone at Sweet P's (860-767-7805), then go sit for a spell on the museum docks.

You'll have a moving experience dining aboard the Essex Clipper Dinner Train (860-767-0103), which runs Friday through Sunday from June to October and. The 2-hour excursion, which leaves from the Connecticut Valley Railroad depot in Essex, gives you ample time to savor both the meal and the scenery.

Before you can say, "homarus americanus," a cab can buzz you over to Oliver's Taverne (860-767-2633), where lobster dominates the menu. You won't have to shell out a lot for a great dinner, and afterwards you can retreat to the popular pub upstairs. In Centerbrook, Steve's Centerbrook Café (860-767-1277) offers very good, creative dishes.

Those who find price no object must try the Copper Beech Inn (860-767-0330). Located on Main Street in the village of Ivoryton, it's one of the finest restaurants in the state.

Back in downtown Essex, Village Provision Company (860-767-7376) is a small but complete convenience market, with deli meats, groceries, and even frozen birthday cakes, if someone in your crew is celebrating at sea. They also offer bicycle rentals and laundry service. A short cab ride will take you to Bennie's (860-767-8448), a small, upscale market, or to Bokum Plaza, where you'll find Colonial IGA (860-767-9029) as well as a pharmacy, ATM, and Chinese restaurant.

For marine supplies and accessories you'll find The Chandlery at Essex (860-767-8267). If you have the unfortunate experience of dropping your keys, jewelry, or some other valuable item over the side of your boat, give Divers' Cove (860-767-1960) a call. In addition to carrying a complete line of scuba equipment, they also rescue precious pieces that have inadvertently been tossed overboard.

In Hamburg, your choice for provisions is Jane's general store (860-434-2494). Whether you came for it or not, it's here: milk, bread, soda in a vintage Coca-Cola cooler, dollhouse furniture, old postcards, tag sale items, anti-Lyme Disease souvenirs—this is one-stop shopping at its

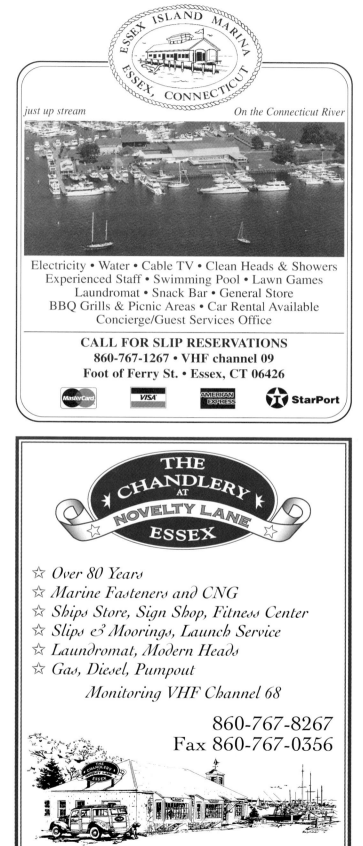

best. The store is open 'til 6:00 six days a week, but only 'til noon on Sunday.

NAVIGATION & ANCHORAGES: Use ChartKit Region 3, page 33; Maptech™ Waterproof Chart 2; and Maptech™ electronic and NOAA paper charts 12375 (1:20,000), 12372 (1:40,000), and 12354 (1:80,000). Use tide tables for New London. High tide at Essex is 1 hour 39 minutes later; low tide is 1 hour 38 minutes later. Multiply height of tide at New London by 1.2 for height of tide at Essex. Mean tidal range is 3.0 feet.

It's impossible to miss Essex—there are boats everywhere, most of them sporting masts. You'll see a large mooring area with two channels (marked by yellow cans) leading through the masses to the marinas and town. At night, the lights of town are alluring, and without the sound of speedboats on the river, this is a peaceful place.

The dock at the Connecticut River Museum, at the foot of Main Street, is 6nm upriver of the Saybrook Breakwater Light, and 2.6nm upriver of the Interstate-95 Baldwin Bridge.

From the south, follow the Coast Guard buoys up to Haydens Point, pass well east of Fl G 4s 27ft 5M "25." Be sure to pass south of R N "24" on the southwest side of Nott Island (several boats a year make a stand in the sand). Then follow the private buoys past the moored fleet into the marina or club of your choice.

South Cove's entrance is between Thatchbed Island and Haydens Point. Although it's too shallow for anchoring, it is home to a diversity of wildlife. Middle Cove, lined with beautiful homes, a marina, and the town green, is much more hospitable, and has a dredged channel about 6 feet deep. Some silting has occurred, so sailboats will want to enter on a rising tide.

Essex Island Marina, at the entrance to North Cove, and Brewer Dauntless Shipyard, just inside, are almost resorts. Essex Boat Works as well as the aforementioned yards can handle any type of repair or service your vessel requires. You'll find Clark Sailmakers in this area as well. Although there are many types of boats in Essex, it remains a very active sailor's port. Several of the yacht clubs have small boat racing groups—frostbiters—active through the late fall.

Due to the large number of moorings between the river channel and the marinas, there is no anchoring here. Check with The Chandlery at Essex or one of the other local facilities if you'd like to pick up a mooring or you need a launch ride. There is a 6-mph speed limit in effect between Fl G 4s 27ft 5M "25" at the South Cove entrance and R N "28" at the north end of the main mooring area.

If you want a quiet anchorage away from it all, try the far side of Nott Island, a.k.a. "Six Mile Island." Most boats will only be able to approach the anchorage from the south due to the shoals and marshes at the north end of the island, but there is 7 to 12 feet of water here, and usually lots of solitude. You'll also find a nice beach on the northwest side of the island. The water in this part of the Connecticut River is acceptable for both swimming and fishing.

Looking north over Essex. © Maptech/James T. Abts

From the north, keep an eye out for the rocks and sandbars that surround Brockway Island: insurance has paid for far too many boats beached and broken on this island. Take note of the sandbar and shallows extending north of the island.

Brockway Island is opposite the entrance to Hamburg Cove, 1.5nm north of Essex. The entrance to the cove is somewhat unimpressive, with a grass island right in the middle.

Once past the narrow, buoyed channel, the cove opens up to a deep hemlock-lined bowl. The channel inside the cove is marked by a series of green cans to port and red daymarkers to starboard. Heed the buoys, stay well inside the channel, and proceed cautiously. What's revealed inside is worth the trip.

Because of the many swimmers and moored boats, there is a 5-mph speed limit throughout Hamburg Cove. The tide range is under 3 feet, but the tidal and river currents can add up to 4 knots in the entrance channel. When under sail, plan your trip to take advantage of the tides.

Surrounded by hills and completely protected, Hamburg Cove is an excellent hurricane hole, but it often gets extremely crowded during the summer, with rafting parties or club rendezvous almost every weekend. Because of the poor holding and crowded conditions, the harbormaster recommends picking up a mooring (the size should be indicated on the float), but remain aboard in case the owner returns. Almost no wind gets in here, so it can get hot, and there's nothing to blow the mosquitoes away. One of our readers claims the cove is also her favorite spot to ride out a thunderstorm, because of the way the sound bounces off the hills.

Continuing south to Essex, you'll see the masts and waterfront of town once you leave the entrance to Hamburg Cove. Proceed until you see the no-wake markers and then begin to look for the private markers leading you through the mooring area to the marinas. Because of the town's popularity, it's best to call ahead to reserve a mooring or slip.

Shoreside & Emergency Services
Airport: Chester (860-526-4321)
Coast Guard: New London (860-442-4471) or VHF 16
—New Haven (203-468-4464) or VHF 16
Harbormaster: (860-767-0504)
Police, Fire, Ambulance: 911
Taxi: Essex Taxi (860-767-RIDE)
Tow Service:
SEA TOW —24-Hour Dispatch (800-4SEATOW)
—Central Connecticut (860-488-3442)
Tow BoatU.S.—24-Hour Dispatch (800-391-4869)
—Old Saybrook (860-388-4065)

More Power to 'em

In days long past, wherever you found industry you'd find its power source: flowing water. The force of a river running downhill toward the ocean generates more usable energy than just about any other natural occurrence, so it's not surprising that of all the towns in the original Saybrook Colony, Chester and Deep River were the two that developed the most industry.

Not that these towns ever rivaled Pittsburgh, but the cataracts on the Chester, Deep River, and Pattaconk creeks did generate enough power to fuel 50 small factories. Brushes, combs, knitting needles, single-twist ship-building augers, inkwells, cut glass, and lace were all once produced here. And long before anyone thought to worry about the extinction of the world's largest land animal, up to 12,000 pounds of elephant tusks a month were off-loaded in Deep River for use by Pratt Reed & Company, the largest piano key manufacturer in the world. That former factory building is now a condominium complex, complete with piano theme.

The small center of Chester is packed with uniqueness, charm, and beauty—qualities that seem to be on the endangered list these days. Proud residents display bumper stickers proclaiming, "Chester, Connecticut: WE know where it is!" We guarantee that once you visit this one-of-a-kind community and shop, browse, and dine here, you'll never forget where it is, either.

This beauty of a burg also has another claim to fame: the ferry, which runs back and forth across the river, between

Chrisholm Marina's gazebo invites you for a riverside respite. © Maptech

Marine Facilities and Services

All Coast Guard Stations Monitor VHF Channel 16

#	Facility	Phone / Page	Monitors / Working VHF Channel	Transient Berths / Moorings	Seasonal / Year-round	Max LOA	Approach / Dockside Depth at MLW	Hookups: Fresh Water / Phone / Cable TV	110V ★ 220V ▲ 3 Phase ■ Max Amps	Ramp / Dinghy Dock / Launch Service	Rail / Lift / Crane / Trailer: Capacity	Repairs: Propellor / Sail / Rigging / Electronics · Diesel / Wood / Fiberglass	Gas / Diesel Fuel	Fuel Brand	Marine / Groceries / Ice / Bait / LPG / CNG	Restrooms / Showers / Laundry / Pumpout	Public Phone / Restaurant / Snack Bar	Hotel / Pool / Tennis / Golf	Mastercard / VISA / Discover / AmEx
1	Brewer Deep River Marina	860-526-5560 / Inside Back Cover	10/5		Y	50	15/10	FC	★▲50	D	L15	PRGDWFE	GD	Tex	MI	RSP	P	P	All
2	Deep River Town Dock*						*RAMP & SHORT TERM TIE-UP*												
3	Chester marina South Yard	860-526-2227 / p. 219	16	5/	Y	50	6/6	FC	★30	RL	LC25	All	G		MI	RSP	P		MV
4	Chester Auto & Marine	860-526-3823	16/9		Y							PSRWFE							
5	Chester marina	860-526-2227 / p. 219	16/9	20/	S	40	6/5	FC	★▲30	R	L25	PSGDWE			MI	RSP	P	P	MV
6	Hays Haven Marina	860-526-9366		5/	Y	50	6/6	FC	★30	RL	L25	P	GD		MI	RSP	P		MVD
7	Pattaconk Yacht Club*	860-526-5626		1/	Y	37	/3	FC								RS	P		
8	Chrisholm Marina	860-526-5147 / p. 221	9/9	6/	Y	60	8/6	FC	★50		L35	PGDFE	GD		MI	RSP	P		MV

Information in these listings is provided by the facilities themselves. An asterisk (*) indicates that the facility did not respond to our most recent requests for information. (B) represents a BOAT/U.S. cooperating marina.

Painting by Leif Nilsson

Chester

CONNECTICUT

Directions: The left bank of the Connecticut River. Route 9, Exit 6 onto Route 148.

visitchesterct.com

Between New York City and Boston, Chester is a charming unspoiled Connecticut River village known for the quality of its fine shops, arts & antiques, award winning restaurants, and internationally acclaimed theatres.

A unique town that holds the past, present and future in delightful balance.

Chester CONNECTICUT

Painting by Leif Nilsson

Chester is a fine place to spend some time—and a little money, too.
© Maptech

Chester and Hadlyme. It's been in continuous operation since 1768, making it the second-oldest ferry in Connecticut. (The oldest ferry crosses the Connecticut River 25 miles farther north at Glastonbury). Due to icing, the ferry doesn't run in winter, so travelers have to count on the swing bridge in East Haddam—it's the only crossing between Old Saybrook and Middletown.

If you head into downtown Deep River, you'll see a hospitable sign welcoming you to "Deep River: A Nice Town. Come Work, Play, Live with Us." Stroll under the shady trees, past the small shops, the bakery, and the tattoo parlor, then stop in for lunch at one of the homey eateries where nobody's a stranger. See if you're not tempted to accept the sign's invitation.

ACTIVITIES: For a group of tiny towns, Chester, Deep River, and Hadlyme boast a fair amount of stuff to see and do. Mosey through the shops in search of antiques, jewelry, handicrafts, ceramic goods, or a new sweater. If you like the theatre, this is the place to be. A renovated mill in the center of Chester is home to the National Theater of the Deaf (860-526-4971). This wonderful venue features dramas for all audiences, with both sign language and spoken word used. An old knitting needle factory is the Goodspeed at Chester (860-873-8668), a branch of East Haddam's Goodspeed Opera House, where you can see new and experimental plays.

Gillette Castle State Park (860-526-2336) sits atop one of the "Seven Sisters," a row of seven hills on the east side of the river. Built by Shakespearean stage actor William Gillette, the castle is as odd as you might expect from someone who spent his life impersonating Sherlock Holmes. We recommend a visit for the spectacular views of the river as well as the opportunity to spend time in the truly unique building this man called home. Call for openings, as the castle is going through renovations.

The big event in Deep River is the annual Ancient Fife and Drum Muster (860-399-6665), which is held on the third Saturday in July. Thousands of people and dozens of drum corps from as far away as Ohio and Virginia turn out each year to watch the parade and join the fun. You may also want to take a trip on one of the excursion boats operated by Deep River Navigation (860-526-4954), which meets up with the Valley Railroad steam train from Essex and goes upriver to East Haddam.

If you want a change from sea-level life, just wing it! Trade the steam train for a plane and take to the sky aboard a scenic flight out of Chester Airport (860-526-4321).

RESTAURANTS & PROVISIONS: Each of these two riverside villages does the trick for a day's worth of meals. In downtown Chester, try the delightful Fiddlers (860-526-3210), known for seafood and great desserts. Next door is the Wheatmarket (860-526-9347), a small gourmet market and deli, offering primo lunch specials, unique sandwiches, and a few specialty groceries. The daily feature here is a colossal apple pie, weighing in at sixteen-and-a-half pounds—a feast for the eyes as well as the stomach. Around the corner on Main Street, Restaurant du Village (860-526-5301) offers a fine French menu; reservations are suggested. Steps away, the Pattaconk 1850 (860-526-8143) has a more casual atmosphere, including a bar. They serve juicy burgers, sandwiches, and an interesting selection of entrées.

A cab ride will take you to the Sage American Bar & Grill (860-526-9898), serving seafood, filet mignon, pork chops with chutney, and marvelous desserts including vanilla bean crème brulee and dark chocolate mousse. Farther out on Route 148 is the Inn at Chester (860-526-1307), serving continental and new American cuisine in a gorgeous post-and-beam dining room.

For provisions in Chester, head to Basic Goods & Services (860-526-8984). Here you'll find just what the name implies: groceries, newspapers, gift items, a deli counter, and even a fax machine.

The name only scratches the surface at Naturally, Books & Coffee (860-526-3212), across the street. Step around the hand-painted safari animals on the floor and scan the shelves for hand-made cards, soaps, and flannel bloomers. Oh yes—there are books and coffee, too.

Looking north over a bend in the Connecticut River. Chester Marina and other facilities border the river near Chester Creek, to the left of center. Chrisholm Marina is just upriver. © Maptech

In Deep River, drop by the Shortstop (860-526-4146) on Main Street for a bite of breakfast or lunch. For pizza or subs, stop in at Deep River Pizza (860-526-1348). Farther up Main Street, toward Chester, you'll find the Ivory Restaurant (860-526-2528), which serves a varied menu in a casual atmosphere, and the Whistle Stop Café (860-526-4122).

NAVIGATION & ANCHORAGES: Use ChartKit Region 3, page 33A; Maptech™ Waterproof Chart 2; and Maptech™ electronic and NOAA paper charts 12377 (1:20,000). Use tide tables for New London. High tide at Hadlyme is 2 hours 19 minutes later; low tide is 2 hours 23 minutes later. Multiply height of tide at New London by 1.1 for height of tide at Hadlyme. Mean tidal range is 2.7 feet.

The marinas at Chester Creek are 5nm from the docks at the foot of Main Street in Essex, and 3.4nm from the East Haddam Bridge.

From the south, you may approach Deep River from either side of Eustasia Island. On the western side of the island is the old steamboat channel. The concrete base of the old light marking this channel still stands, though the light has been removed. The channel includes Brewer Deep River Marina, which is a clean, full-service yard that has transient slips available. There is plenty of water here for all but

the largest boats, but you will want to favor the western shore to avoid the moored boats and the sandbar which extends 0.5nm north of the island. Paddle or row up Pratt Creek for a pleasant excursion. In spring, brilliant yellow irises beckon. In early summer, giant, pink, swamp mallow roses are out; later in the summer, cardinal flowers pray for attention, while wild rice rises overhead. Don't pick the flowers, but go ahead and grab a handful of rice.

About 0.7nm north of Steamboat Landing are the marinas at the entrance to Chester Creek. Wait until you are due east

Know all the ups and downs of a National Park before you even set foot in it.

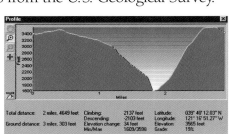

Introducing Maptech® National Park Digital Guides

It's like having a Park Ranger at your elbow, helping you plan your trip.

Simply pop a CD-ROM in your PC or laptop. And up come maps, easy-to-use navigation software, and a fact-filled "electronic guidebook."

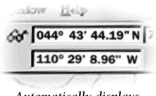

044° 43' 44.19" N
110° 29' 8.96" W

Automatically displays coordinates of your position

By pointing-and-clicking, you can plot a course. Figure out where to stay. Learn about the park's attractions, trails, local geology, wildlife – and a whole lot more.

The maps start with an official National Park Map – but they're combined with detailed, topographic maps from the U.S. Geological Survey. So, you see *exactly* how the land lies.

And there's a special edition of Maptech's Terrain Navigator software that lets you:

- Measure distances and elevations
- Zoom in four levels for "close-ups"
- Print out customized maps to take with you

Call up photos of attractions

Want more out of your park trip? *This* is the place to begin!

Profile

Total distance: 2 miles, 4649 feet
Ground distance: 3 miles, 303 feet
Climbing: 2137 feet
Descending: -2103 feet
Elevation change: 34 feet
Min/Max: 1609/3598
Latitude: 039° 40' 12.03" N
Longitude: 121° 16' 51.27" W
Elevation: 3565 feet
Grade: 19%

Elevation profile lets you check "line-of-sight" to landmarks

If you'd like to know more about Maptech products, and get a free demo, visit our website, at www.maptech.com

Only $29.50 for each park, $69.50 for a region, $179.50 for all 54 National Parks. Available from the Lands' End® catalog, or from Maptech.

For a free demo, go to **www.maptech.com**
Or, for more information, photocopy and mail this coupon or fax it to: **1-603-433-8505.**

To place an order, call: **1-800-627-7236**   FS1298

Name _____

Address _____

City _____ State _____ Zip _____

Phone ( ) _____ Day / Night (*circle one*)

E-mail _____

Maptech, Inc.,
655 Portsmouth Avenue
Greenland, NH 03840
© 1998 Maptech, Inc.

MAPTECH®

of the marinas before heading for the docks. There is a 6-mph speed limit in the channel, and around the marinas at Chester Creek. There are several good facilities that cater to transients in Chester Creek, including Chester Marina. The imposing structure on top of the hill in Deep River is Mount Saint Johns, operated by the Catholic Church since 1907. About three-quarters of a mile from the water is downtown Deep River, where you can purchase anything from fresh pasta to tattoos.

Directly across the river from Chester is Selden Island (Selden Neck on the chart); its 528 acres make it the largest island in Connecticut. Selden was a peninsula until about 1854, when an unusually high freshet overrode the narrow, sandy spit that connected the neck to the mainland, cutting a channel through the sand and forming the island.

Selden Cove is opposite Chester Creek at G C "37." However, it is shallow and best explored by dinghy. If you are looking for a nice gunkhole, your best bet is to approach Selden Neck from the south, enter Seldon Creek about 0.4nm west-northwest of G C "33," and go 0.8nm up the creek. The water is good and deep, and the protection from the wind is complete, but there's not much swing room. It will probably be best to anchor and tie a line to a tree on the shore.

Another beautiful spot to explore by dinghy is Whalebone Creek, just to the south of the ferry slip on the east side of the river. On one side of the entrance to the creek is a high, rock wall of convoluted granite, and on the other is a small, sandy beach, at the point of which is Fl R 45ft and just to the south, Fl R 2.5s 36ft "40," Range A across Potash Bar.

When heading upriver, be sure to leave the ferry plenty of room, and stay away from its backwash, which can easily flip a dinghy. North of the east shore ferry slip in Hadlyme is a ramp at Gillette Castle State Park. You can picnic and hike at the park, and canoes are available for rent at the landing, where there are also portable toilets. Just north of the park, on the west shore, you'll find Chrisholm Marina, a full-service facility with slips available for transients.

Shoreside & Emergency Services
Airport:
—Chester (860-526-4321)
Coast Guard:
—New London (860-442-4471) or VHF 16
Hospital:
—Middlesex Shoreline (860-767-3700)
Police, Fire, Ambulance: 911
Taxi:
—Essex Taxi (860-767-RIDE)
Tow Service:
SEA TOW —24-Hour Dispatch (800-4SEATOW)
—Central Conn. (860-395-0405)
Tow BoatUS —24-Hour Dispatch (800-391-4869)
—Old Saybrook (860-388-4065)

A serene Deep River scene. © Maptech

72°28'

72°29'

Mount Tom

Moodus R.

R

Landing Hill

300

366

SALMON COVE

Scovill Landing

Grass

Grass

Grass

Fl R 4s 29ft 6M "48"

Piling

OVHD PWR CABS
AUTH CL 86 FT

TOWER
OVHD. PWR. CAB.
AUTH. CL. 105 FT.

G
C "47"

TOWER

EAST
HADDAM

200

Grs

Grass

Cones Pt

Outfall Canal

Grass

SCALE 1:20,000

Goodspeeds
Landing

Barricade

R
N "50"

SWING BRIDGE
HOR. CL. 180 FT. (E. DRAW)
HOR. CL. 200 FT. (W. DRAW)
VERT. CL. 22 FT.

Cable

W. TURRET

Ruin

Area

Ramp

Subm piles

Obstr

JOINS ADJACENT CHART TOP

Tylerville

Marsh

Clark Cr.

Ruin

(Abandoned)

Eddy Rock
R "6"
Fl R 4s

SPECIAL ANCH 110.1 & 110.55
(see note A)

Rich I.

Chapman Pond

100

Shoal

SPECIAL ANCH
110.1 & 110.55
(see note A)

Lord I.

350

Marsh

MAGNETIC

VAR 14° 30'W (1996) ANNUAL INCREASE 2'

Fl G 4s 24ft 4M "45"

R
N "44"

200

FLAGPOLE
Middletown Y.C.

Subm
Groin

Ramp

Fl R 4s 30ft 4M
"42"

314

300

Aband

A Tale of Two Williams

In 1913 the famous actor and playwright William Gillette took a rest from the stage and cruised the Connecticut River in his 135-foot houseboat *Aunt Polly*. The Hartford native was so enchanted by the river that he gave up his plan to build on Long Island and bought 122 acres in Hadlyme. Five years and a million dollars later (not pocket change in those days), he set out the welcome mat to his ornate stone castle, every detail of which he designed. While it was being built, the actor lived aboard the *Aunt Polly*.

Before his death in 1937, Gillette directed his executors "to see that the property did not fall into the hands of some blithering saphead who has no conception of where he is." Those trusty executors did their job, and the castle became a state park in 1943. As of this writing, Gillette Castle was closed for renovations (due to reopen in 2002), but the hiking trails remain open.

Gillette's favorite feature was the miniature railway, which he bought to entertain his guests. Two locomotives puffed their way through the woods above the river over three miles of track, ornate bridges, and a tunnel. Although most of the track has been dismantled, as you float past you'll see one of the trestles linking two jutting stone cliffs. There's even talk of someday returning the trains (kept in action for 50 years at Lake Compounce Amusement Park in Bristol, Conn.) to run again at their original home.

East Haddam's other William, William Goodspeed, was a dedicated American entrepreneur: not only did he own a major shipyard and manage a large warehouse in East Haddam, he also ran a steamboat line from New York. It stopped at his shipyard, picked up freight from his warehouse, and let passengers off to see a show at his opera house—after, of course, they did some shopping at his store and had a drink at his bar. The Goodspeed Opera House, or simply 'the Goodspeed,' remains the most popular attraction here.

A rustic autumn display befitting the lovely town of Haddam. © Maptech

ACTIVITIES: The town of East Haddam offers the pleasant opportunity to browse for antiques or gifts, or to grab an ice cream cone and take a stroll. You do not want to miss

	Marine Facilities and Services		Number of Transient Berths / Moorings	Monitors / Working VHF Channel	Approach / Dockside Depth in Feet at MLW	Hookups: Fresh Water / Phone / Cable TV	110V ★ 220V ▲ 3 Phase ■ Maximum Amps	Seasonal / Year-round	Maximum LOA	Rail / Lift / Crane / Trailer / Launch Service	Ramp / Dinghy Dock / Launch Service	Repairs: Propellor / Sail / Rigging / Electronics	Diesel / Wood / Fiberglass / Electronics	Marine / Groceries / Ice / Bait / LPG / CNG	Restrooms / Showers / Laundry / Pumpout	Gas / Diesel Fuel	Fuel Brand	Public Phone / Restaurant / Snack Bar	Hotel / Pool / Tennis / Golf	Mastercard / VISA / Discover / AmEx
1	Chrisholm Marina	860-526-5147 p. 219	9/9	6/	Y	60	8/6	FC	★50			L35	PGDFE	GD		MI	RSP	P	MV	
2	Middlesex Yacht Club	860-526-5634		Y			*PRIVATE—MEMBERS ONLY*													
3	Camelot Cruises	860-345-8591		Y			*SIGHTSEEING CRUISES*													
4	Andrews Marina*	860-345-2286	1/1	S	46	25/5	F	★30	D				G	Hess	MI	RSP	P			
5	DAMAR LTD. MIDWAY MARINA	860-345-4330 p. 227	9/	5/	Y	43	15/10	F	★30	R	LCT15	PSRGDFE			MG	RS	R	MV		

Facilities continued on page 223...

All Coast Guard Stations Monitor VHF Channel 16

marinalife.com
Convenient Online Boat/Slip Reservations

Facilities continued on page 223...

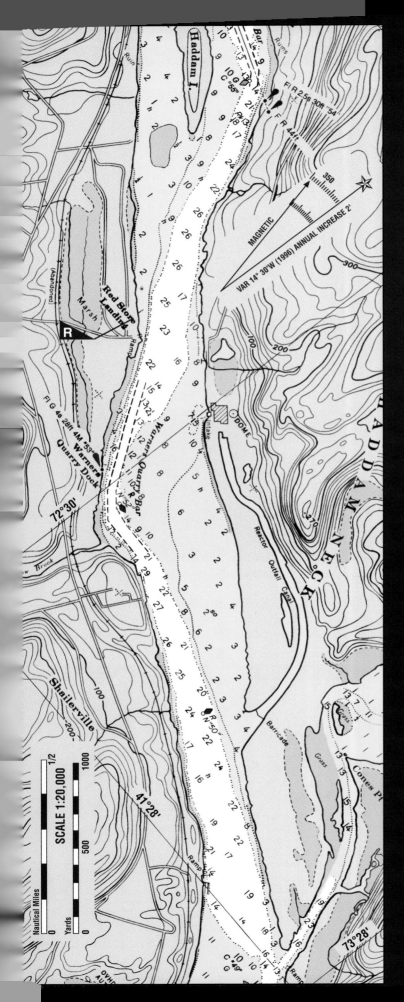

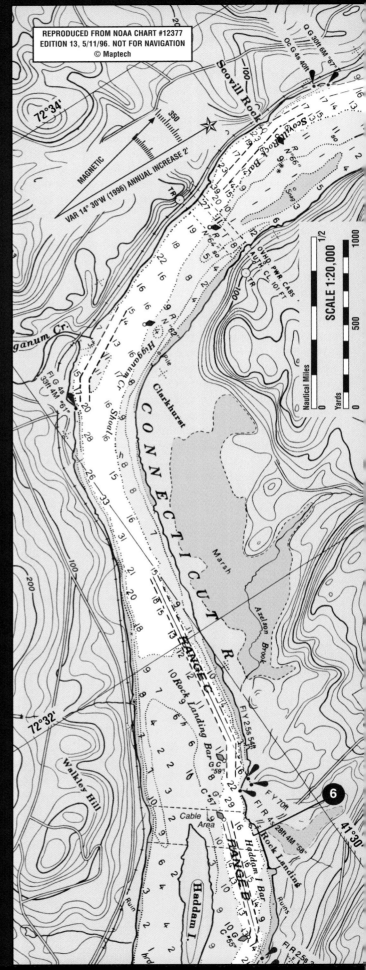

a chance to experience the famous Goodspeed Opera House (860-873-8668), a 400-seat theater dedicated to the American musical. You can also take in a wonderful view of the river in a plane leaving from the Goodspeed Airport (860-873-8568).

Haddam Meadows is also the terminus of the zany Connecticut River Raft Race, usually held on a blistering hot Saturday at the end of July or the beginning of August. Dozens of homemade rafts compete for prizes given to the fastest raft, the funniest-looking raft, and the raft most in the spirit of Tom Sawyer and Huck Finn. There's even a Becky Thatcher award given to the first all-female crew to finish the course.

Another race to watch for is the annual Head of the Connecticut Rowing Regatta held on Columbus Day weekend in Middletown. Call the River Valley & Shoreline Visitors Center (860-347-0020) for information on these events and more. If you're into long-term planning, ask about the calendars they put out every year.

RESTAURANTS & PROVISIONS: The best-known local eatery, The Gelston House (860-873-1411) in East Haddam, offers

Near the Rocky Hill ferry slip, a paddler calls it a morning, but these fishermen are just headed out. © Maptech

very good food in an elegant waterfront setting. Also at the Gelston House, the Beer Garden provides a casual dining patio overlooking the river—it's quite the boater's hangout. Across the bridge in Haddam, about half a mile west, you

	Marine Facilities and Services	All Coast Guard Stations Monitor Channel 16	Monitors / Working VHF Channel	Number of Transient Berths / Moorings	Seasonal / Year-round	Approach / Dockside Depth in Feet at MLW	Maximum LOA	Hookups: Fresh Water / Phone / Cable TV	110V ∗ 220V ▲ 3 Phase ■ Maximum Amps	Ramp / Dinghy Dock / Launch Service	Rail / Lift / Crane / Trailer Capacity (tons)	Repairs: Propellor / Sail / Rigging / Electronics	Diesel / Wood / Fiberglass	Marine / Groceries / Ice / Bait / LPG / CNG	Gas / Diesel Fuel	Fuel Brand	Restrooms / Showers / Laundry / Pumpout	Public Phone / Restaurant / Snack Bar	Hotel / Pool / Tennis / Golf	Mastercard / VISA / Discover / AmEx
6	Rock Landing Marina*	860-267-ROCK	9/	1/	S	40	16/16	F	★30	D							MGI	R		MV
7	Cobalt Marine	860-267-2093	/1		Y	50	6/7	F	★		L25	PWFE					M			
8	Portland Boat Works	860-342-1085		2/	Y	68	12/10	F	★▲50	R	L30	All	G	Tex		M	RS		P	All
9	**YANKEE BOAT YARD AND MARINA, INC.** (B) p. 229	860-342-4735	68/	10/10	Y	50	15/12	All	★▲■	RD	LCT	PGDWFE	GD	Mob		MI	RSP		MVD
10	Riverside Marina	860-342-1911			S	42	20/20	F	★15		L35	All				MI	RS		P	MVD
11	America's Cup	860-347-9999			Y				RESTAURANT—DOCKAGE FOR PATRONS											
12	Harbor Park Landing*	860-343-6620			Y		15/15													
13	**PETZOLD'S** p. 227	860-342-1196	9/72	2/	Y	56	15/15	F	★30		L55	PSWFE	G			M	R		P	MV
14	Middlesex Marine*	860-342-2222			Y					R	BOAT & ENGINE SALES					M	R			
15	Glastonbury Yacht Club*				Y					PRIVATE—MEMBERS ONLY										
16	Hartford Yacht Club*	860-633-9669		3/4	S	34	12/7	F	★30	RD	T									
17	**SEABOARD MARINA** p. 231	860-657-3232	68/	50/	Y	60	15/7	F	★30	RL	L25	All	G	Tex		MI	All		PS	All
18	Wethersfield Cove Yacht Club	860-563-8780		4/	Y		4.5/						G	Gulf			R		P	
19	Charter Oak Landing	860-713-3131			Y	24				R							R			

Information in these listings is provided by the facilities themselves. An asterisk (*) indicates that the facility did not respond to our most recent requests for information. (B) represents a BOAT/U.S. cooperating marina.

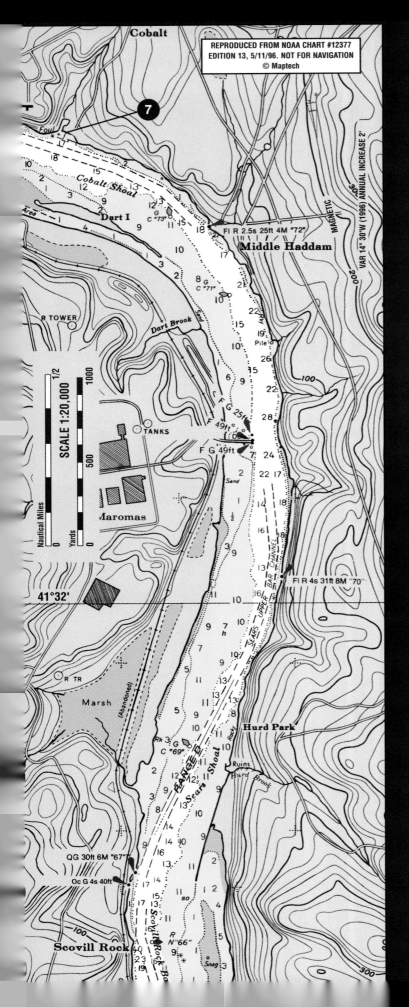
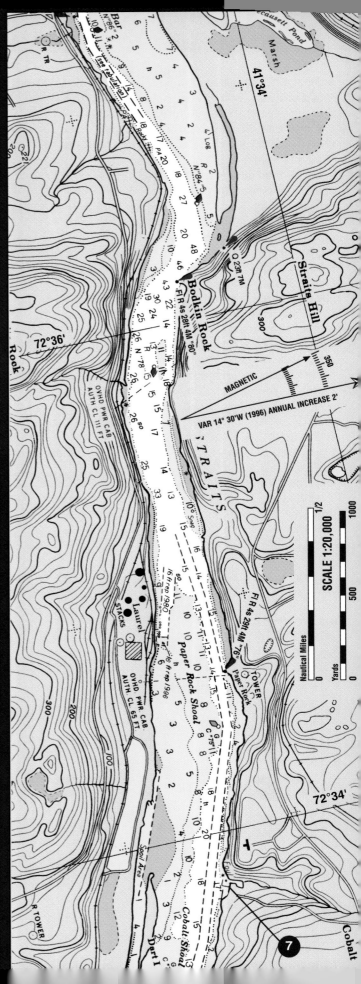

may walk a short distance to Subway (860-345-4600), Country Restaurant (860-345-4229), and Cheeseboard Deli & Pizza (860-345-4418).

For pleasant dining on the water, try Camelot Cruises' (860-345-8591) dinner voyages on its 400-passenger ship. Add a little excitement in the evening by boarding one of their murder mystery voyages. Just upriver, the Blue Oar at Midway Marina (860-345-2994) is open Friday evenings through Sunday for lunch and dinner. Choose from sandwiches, burgers, and chili for lunch and grilled seafood, ribs, chicken, and steak for dinner. The view from the deck is free, and so is the docking.

Upriver in Middletown, you'll find America's Cup (860-347-9999) right on the river, offering a spectacular view from its patio. Specialties include prime rib, seafood, and lobster; dockage is available for patrons. The downtown area serves up a wide variety of eateries. Head to Washington Street for Cornerstones (860-344-0222), serving pasta, seafood, and steaks. Mikado (860-346-6655) is an excellent Japanese grill and sushi bar. Ruby's (860-344-1950) has great sandwiches, and It's Only Natural (860-346-9210) is popular with the health-conscious. On the east side of the river, in Portland, stop in at Farrell's (860-342-4589) for seafood and steaks.

NAVIGATION & ANCHORAGES: Use ChartKit Region 3, pages 33A and 33B; Maptech™ Waterproof Chart 2; and Maptech™ electronic and NOAA paper charts 12377 (1:20,000). Use tide tables for New London. High tide at East Haddam is 2 hours 42 minutes later; low tide is 2 hours 53 minutes later. Multiply height of tide at New London by 1.1 for height of tide at East Haddam. Mean tidal range is 2.9 feet.

The East Haddam Bridge is 3.4nm from Chester Creek, and 8.4nm from the Connecticut River Museum Docks at the foot of Main Street in Essex. The Arrigoni (Route 66) Bridge linking Portland and Middletown is 12.6nm away.

This section of the Connecticut River is easy to navigate. There are quite a few shoals (the tides rise only about 3 feet here, so don't expect too much of a lift if you go aground), but the channel is well marked and easy to follow, with the deepest water on the outside of the turns. Just north of Gillette Castle, on the west shore of the river, you'll see Chrisholm Marina, a full-service facility with transient slips available.

In the 1800s, a hurricane left a huge raft of floating debris that eventually made a permanent land mass, now called Rich Island. Just across from the island is Chapman Pond, uniquely freshwater and tidal; only hurricanes carry the salt water this far north. The first anchorages you'll encounter are to the west of Rich and Lord islands. Between the islands, you'll find a beautiful spot to drop a hook, though it's best left to those in shallow-draft boats. Chapman Pond and the little creek that starts at its southeast tip are too shallow for anything larger than a canoe or dinghy, but the trip around the unnamed island is a pleasant escape from the traffic in the main channel.

Short term tie-up space is available at the Goodspeed Opera House wharf, but you must call first. If you want to

stay longer, you should try Andrew's Marina or Midway Marina on the west side of the river. Maintain "steerage only" speed in the Cable Area near the East Haddam Bridge and the marinas. The bridge has temporary opening restrictions for non-commercial vessels, which include opening only on the hour and half hour, 9 a.m. to 9 p.m., Friday through Sunday, including federal holidays from May 22 to October 31. The bridge will open on demand at all other times. You can contact the bridge tender on VHF 13.

On the east side of the river, below Goodspeed's Landing, is Goodspeed Airport; docking arrangements vary here each year, so call ahead.

The state ramp at the mouth of the Salmon River is 0.9nm north of the East Haddam Bridge. Deep-draft boats can go about half a mile into the cove, but should not pass Cones Point because the channel is nearly impossible to see and the mud is thick enough to grab your keel and hold it for life. However, the bottom does give a good hold, and many local boats successfully weathered Hurricane Gloria here in 1985.

Shallow-draft boats and dinghies are a great way to explore the Salmon River 4nm up to the head of navigation at the Leesville Dam and fish ladder. The Salmon River is Class "A" water, the cleanest in the state, and one of the focal points of the Atlantic Salmon restoration effort.

Be careful of the shallow water near Haddam Island—you can reach the island by foot at low tide. There are two sets of range lights on the east bank above Haddam Island. The pair opposite G C "55" for Range B are F R 44ft over Fl R 2.5s 30ft "54." The pair opposite G C "59" for Range C are F Y 70ft over Fl Y 2.5s 54ft.

Most boaters think that navigation ends at the East Haddam Bridge. But you can continue up to Middletown, a dozen miles farther north, or even to Hartford, nearly 30 miles north of the bridge, to the official head of navigation. Above East Haddam, the Connecticut River is not quite as idyllic as it is to the south. Still, it's remarkably pristine, largely bordered by state parks.

If you're headed upriver to Middletown and Portland, you'll find that the river is well marked with buoys and lights at every bend. The trip upriver will take some time, as it is nearly 12nm from the East Haddam Bridge to Portland. All the service you'll need can be found at Yankee Boat Yard & Marina. Two miles farther upstream takes you to Petzold's, where you can get marine supplies and repairs. Keep an eye on the chart and stay in the channel. The channel is deep, as it runs mostly on the outside corners, but there are shallow spots and rocks outside of the channel all the way. We suggest you don't make this trip at night unless you've already made it once before in daylight. The river gets mighty dark after sunset, and it can be tiring and dangerous to strain your eyes looking for buoys.

If you're on your way up to Rocky Hill, follow the channel—don't be tempted to cut between the west shore of

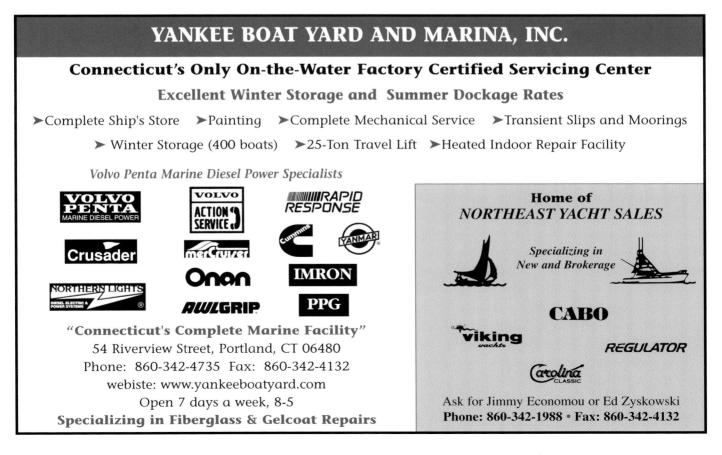

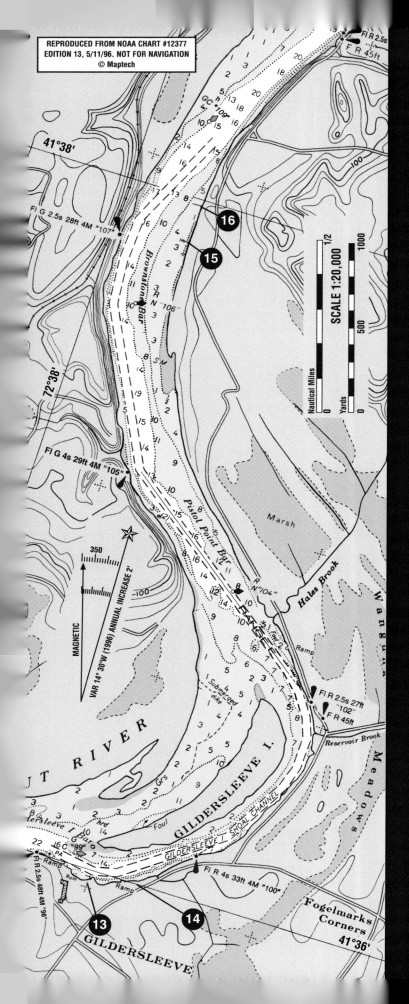
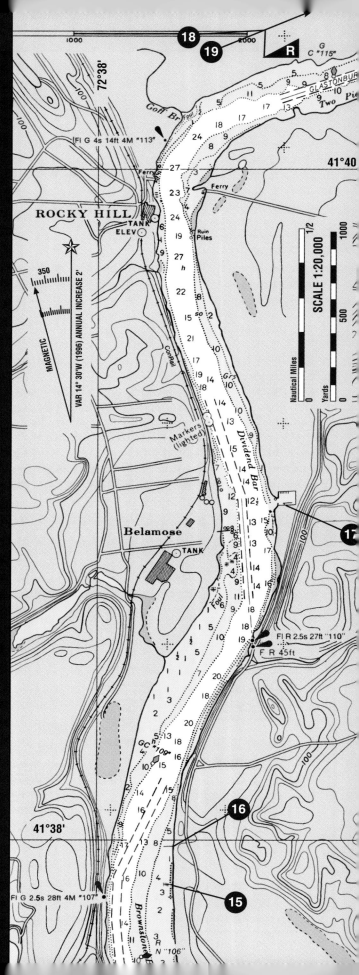

A fog settles over the Connecticut River, north of the East Haddam Bridge. © Maptech/James T. Abts

the river and Gildersleeve Island. The submerged dike that runs almost all the way out to the island catches a few unwary boaters each year. On the east shore, just south of Rocky Hill, you'll see Seaboard Marina which is a full-service marina offering laundry facilities, a restaurant, all repairs, fuel, a playground, and a sand volleyball court. Make dockage reservations early. If you're heading up toward Hartford, keep an eye out for the Rocky Hill Ferry.

Though you won't find much in the way of transient facilities in Hartford, an organization called Riverfront Recapture (860-293-0131) is promoting public use of Hartford waterfront. Parks on both sides of the river offer picnic areas, public docks, and paved launch ramps with plenty of parking.

Shoreside & Emergency Services
Airport:
—Goodspeed (860-873-8568)
—Chester (860-526-4321)
Coast Guard:
—New London (860-442-4471) or VHF 16
—New Haven (203-468-4464) or VHF 16
Ferry: Rocky Hill Ferry (860-566-7635) May-Oct.
Police, Fire, Ambulance: 911
Tow Service:
SEA TOW —24-Hour Dispatch (800-4SEATOW)
—Central Connecticut (203-488-3442)
Tow BoatU.S.—24-Hour Dispatch (800-391-4869)
—Clinton (860-388-4065)

Eastern Connecticut Coast

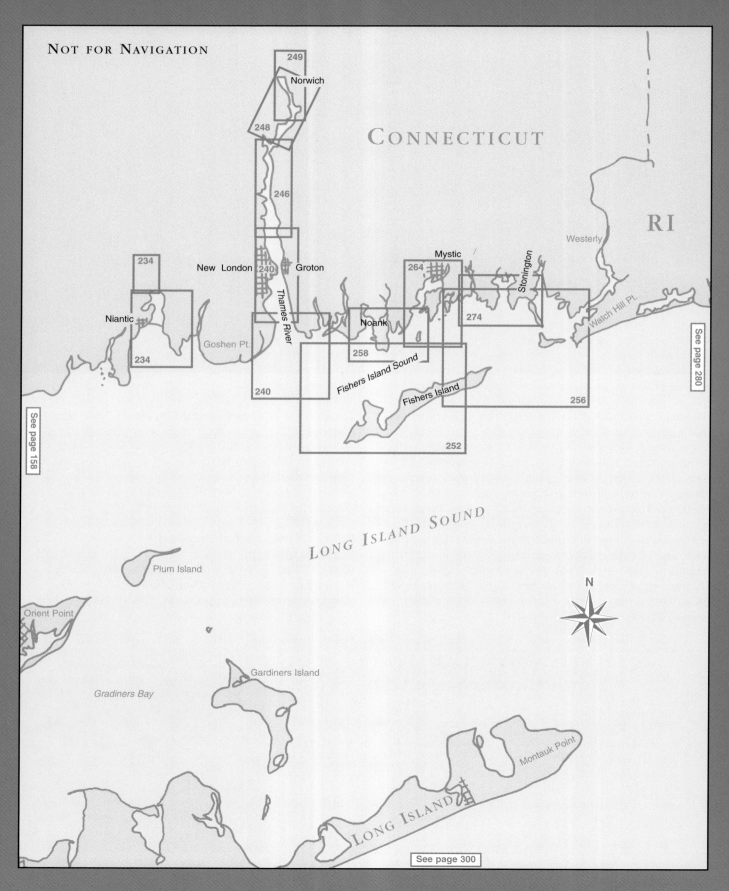

NOT FOR NAVIGATION

249

Norwich

248

CONNECTICUT

246

RI

Westerly

234

New London

240

Groton

Mystic

264

Stonington

Niantic

234

Thames River

Goshen Pt.

Noank

258

274

Watch Hill Pt.

Fishers Island Sound

240

Fishers Island

256

See page 158

See page 280

252

LONG ISLAND SOUND

Plum Island

N

Orient Point

Gardiners Island

Gradiners Bay

Montauk Point

LONG ISLAND

See page 300

Eastern Connecticut begins with **Niantic Bay** and the **Niantic River**, a jewel that many hasty cruisers skip over in a mad rush to get elsewhere. The old whaling port of **New London**, at the mouth of the Thames River, is a bastion of underwater American defense; Electric Boat is a major builder of submarines for the U.S. government. Just upriver, the beautiful buildings of the United States Coast Guard Academy sit on the western shore. The Thames provides a pleasant, uncrowded journey up to **Norwich**, its head of navigation. A top-notch facility and access to Connecticut's famous casinos are reasons enough to make the journey up here.

Although it's only a couple of miles south of the mouth of the Thames, **Fishers Island** is actually part of New York state. Venture over to West Harbor to see what this island life is all about. Directly to the north, the sight of **Noank** means the entrance to the Mystic River. The **Mystic** area has been involved with the ocean since before the nation's conception, and the people's preoccupation with boating remains. You'll find top-notch facilities and repair yards, a pleasant town, and possibly the finest maritime museum in the world. Following the Connecticut shore to the east, **Stonington** is the next neck of land to stick out. Quaint streets and an amiable marina provide reason enough to stop by.

Enjoy the maritime history and top-notch facilities in Eastern Connecticut. © Maptech

Navigating the Eastern Connecticut Coast

From Fl R 4s BELL R "8" southeast of the mouth of the Connecticut River, head 150∞m for 6.1nm to Fl R 4s BELL R "2PG" at Plum Gut. Fl R 4s BELL R "8" is also about 12nm west of New London Harbor. Steer 100∞m toward Fishers Island Sound. About 4nm en route you can begin to head northeast into **Niantic Bay**. Shoot for FL R 4s BELL R "6" on the eastern side of the bay. When approaching Niantic Bay, stay well west of White Rock and Little Rock off the eastern shore, marked by Fl R 4s BELL R "6." *Refer to the Niantic Bay & Niantic River chapter for more information.*

Continuing east, play it safe and stay south of the Bartlett Reef Light (Fl 5s 35ft 9M HORN). Round the light and make way for Fl G 2.5s G "1," which, along with Fl R 2.5s R "2," marks the entrance channel to the **Thames River** and **New London Harbor**. Here, you'll run into commercial shipping traffic and maybe even a submarine. The main channel into the harbor begins at Fl G 2.5s G "1" and Fl R 2.5s R "2." Between Fl R 2.5s R "2" and Race Point on Fishers Island are two ship anchorages, "E" and "F." As you head into the wide-open harbor, you'll see New London Ledge Light (Fl (3) W & R 30s 58ft 14M HORN), a square, brick Victorian building atop a white foundation The light marks a series of ledges that block the harbor. Farther to the west is the beacon of the New London Harbor Light, also known as "Pequot Light" (Iso 6s 89ft 14M), with a red sector marking the near-by shoals. *Refer to the New London Harbor chapter for more information on the entrance, and the Thames River to Norwich chapter for more information about the journey upriver.*

East of the Thames River you enter **Fishers Island Sound**. Fishers Island Sound is well marked (most of the buoys and lights mark dangerous water—usually rocks) and is fairly open for you to pick your own route through. . As always, give all marks a wide berth.

From the entrance to the Thames River, at Fl R 2.5s R "2," head about 110°m toward Fl R 2.5s BELL "2" marking the route to **West Harbor** on **Fishers Island**. Keep Fl R 2.5s BELL "2" to the south and round Fl R 4s R "6" to the east. This marks the beginning to the channel into West Harbor. If you approach Fl R 4s R "6" from the north, your route is clear. The entrance is marked, but keep an eye out for the many lobster pots in this area. *Refer to the Fishers Island chapter for more information.*

Due northeast of West Harbor, on the mainland, **Noank** and the Mystic River are inviting destinations. A series of unlit buoys takes you through a narrow opening on the east side of Ram Island Shoal. The channel up the Mystic River is very well marked and runs along the western side of the river, holding snug to Noank and its fine facilities. Upriver, numerous marine facilities await in **Mystic Harbor**. *Refer to the Noank and Mystic River Entrance chapter and the Mystic Harbor chapter for more information on this area.*

Round Mason Island to the south and follow a series of buoys east and you'll come to the breakwater marking the entrance to **Stonington**. Be sure to round the breakwater's light (Fl G 4s 31ft 5M "5") to the east. *Refer to the Stonington Harbor chapter for more information.*

Connecticut's Secret

Niantic is one secret that we can't keep. Unknown to many Long Island Sound boaters, this protected bay is one of the unknown gems along the Connecticut coast. Never been there? You're not alone. Most boaters are hell-bent on reaching the Saybrook breakwater to the west or the large port of New London to the east, leaving Niantic all but forgotten. Their haste is their loss—and your gain.

The Niantic River raises comparisons to the Connecticut River's Hamburg Cove—a beautiful gunkhole with wooded shores and clear water—though Niantic is less crowded. The river itself is cut off from the bay by a sandbar, keeping it sheltered from overuse.

Niantic gets its name from the Nehantic Indians, a tribe that camped at the river's mouth until 1807, when the opening of the Boston Post Road drove them out. Post Road traffic and ferry stop-overs brought more people through. Many of them liked it enough to stay, and today Niantic is chiefly a residential community.

© Maptech/James T. Abts

Looking southeast over Smith Cove, with the Niantic River entrance in the distance.

To the south, west of Niantic Bay, you'll find the Pattagansett Marshes tucked quietly behind the bluffs of Black Point. The nature preserve here includes the Watts

	Marine Facilities and Services		Number of Transient Berths / Moorings	Approach / Dockside Depth in Feet at MLW	Seasonal / Yearround	Maximum LOA	110V • 220V ▲ 3 Phase ■ Maximum Amps	Ramp / Dinghy Dock / Launch Service	Rail / Lift / Crane / Trailer Capacity (tons)	Repairs: Propeller / Sail / Rigging / Electronics	Diesel / Wood / Fiberglass	Marine / Groceries / Ice / Bait / Gas	Restrooms / Showers / Laundry / Pumpout	Gas / Diesel Fuel	Fuel Brand	Public Phone / Pool / Tennis / Golf	Hotel / Restaurant / Snack Bar	Mastercard / VISA / Discover / AmEx
1	Niantic Bay Yacht Club*	860-739-0558	9/	1/2	S	40	13/		▲■	D	T			I		RS		PS
2	Four Mile River Marina	860-434-8971	9/		S	26	/3	F		R		PF	G		I	RS		P
3	South Lyme Marina*	860-434-9295		2/	Y	23		F	★	R								
4	Bayview Landing	860-739-6604	/9	6/	Y	48	10/4	FC	★▲50	L	C30	All			MI			
5	Boats, Inc.	860-739-6251	71/	5/	Y	32	4/4	F	★30	R	L5	GFE			MI	RS	P	P	All
6	Harbor Hill Marina Inc.	860-739-0331	3/		S	42	6/6	FC	★30	R					I	RS		MVA
7	**PORT NIANTIC MARINA** P. 237	860-739-2155	9/		Y	60	8/7	FC	★▲■50		L35	All	GD	Mob	All	RSP	P	MV
8	Niantic Dockominiums	860-739-8585			Y				PRIVATE FACILITY									
9	**Bayreuther Boat Yard Inc.** p. 238	860-739-6264	9/	2/	Y	60	5/8	F	★	RD	L30	PSRGF	GD		MI	RS	P	PS	MV
9	Smith Cove Yacht Club*				Y				PRIVATE—MEMBERS ONLY									
10	Mago Point Marina	860-442-2710	88/	4/	Y	60	4/4	All	★▲■30		RLC	All	GD	Tex	MGIBL	All		All	MV
11	Niantic Sportfishing Dock	860-444-1434		1/	S	60	9/9	F	★▲50				GD		I			R	MV
12	Capt. John's Sportfishing Center	860-443-7259	13/	2/	Y	100	8/8	F	★15				G	Mob	IB	R		PR	
12	MiJoy Dock	860-443-0663			Y				FISHING CHARTERS									
13	**Niantic Bay Marina Inc.** p. 237	800-782-3774	9/	4/	Y	42	5/5	F	★60	R	LC6.5	PGDFE	GD	Tex	MI	RS		All	MVD
14	Black Hawk Dock	860-739-9296	13/	1/	S				FISHING STATION									

Information in these listings is provided by the facilities themselves. An asterisk (*) indicates that the facility did not respond to our most recent requests for information. (B) represents a BOAT/U.S. cooperating marina.

All Coast Guard Stations Monitor VHF Channel 16

marinalife.com — Convenient Online Boat Slip Reservations

Looking west over the entrance to the Niantic River. To the left, south of the bridge, you'll see Niantic Bay Marina. Port Niantic Marina is just off the page to the right. In the foreground is Mago Point Marina, owned by Niantic Bay Marina. © Maptech/James T. Abts

Island wetlands and the rockier Long Ledge. The marshlands are protected by a primary sand dune stabilized by rocky outcroppings from the west end of Black Point. Bring your binoculars and focus your attention on the nesting platforms that have long attracted osprey, which thrive on the wide variety of life flourishing in the marsh ecosystem.

ACTIVITIES: The clear and calm water of the Niantic River invites all kinds of water activities; in fact, this is one of the few areas on Long Island Sound clear enough for snorkeling. While you're down there, keep an eye out for the blue-eyed scallops in the eelgrass around the shallows. Their "eyes" are actually light sensors.

Today's techno-whiz kids will appreciate the Millstone Information and Science Center (860- 691-4670) on Main Street. It features computer games on energy creation and use, as well as films and exhibits on solar, nuclear, and hydro power. Across the street from the information center is a great old (and inexpensive) movie theater: Niantic Cinema 1, 2, 3, 4 (860-739-6929).

Head east of the bay to Goshen Point to experience the wonder of the 125-acre Harkness Memorial State Park (860-443-5725). The 42-room Harkness mansion, named

Eolia after the Greek god of the winds, is the highlight of the premises, but the real beauty of the park is its vast grounds. You can enjoy the huge lawns, award-winning gardens, and pristine beaches any time. You'll also like the summer music festival held at the park each year. Adjacent land has been turned into Camp Harkness, dedicated to handicapped children.

The Eugene O'Neill Memorial Theatre (860-443-5378) isn't far from Harkness. Thanks to the theatre's graduate program for actors, producers, and playwrights, visitors can witness dramatic readings of works-in-progress.

Near Black Point to the west, Rocky Neck State Park (860-739-5471) presents a serene setting in which to sink your toes into the sand, swim in the clear waters, or hike the trails to a private camp where you can reserve a site for a reasonable fee.

The young mates aboard will find a lot to keep themselves busy at the Children's Museum of Southeastern Connecticut (860-691-1255). Let them dive into the hands-on exhibits, discovery garden, computers, and arts and crafts.

RESTAURANTS & PROVISIONS: As in any good boating port, you'll find that Niantic has a selection of restaurants within walking distance of the water. When on the east bank, you're in Waterford; when on the west, you're in Niantic, which has a much bigger selection. Everything is conveniently located on, or just off, Route 156 in Niantic.

Try Dad's Restaurant (860-739-2113) for an easy, satisfying summer meal, and cap it off with some soft-serve ice cream. Pizza aficionados can choose among Family Pizza (860-739-0466), The Niantic Pizza House (860-739-6062), and Seaview Pizza Restaurant (860-739-4020); if you prefer subs, try one of the nearby delis. For a good American dish, you can't go wrong with Constantine's (860-739-2848).

On the east shore, sit back, relax, and enjoy the traffic passing underneath the bridge on the deck of Sunset Rib Co. (860-443-7427). You can't walk around here without someone recommending Unk's (860-443-2717). Sit out on the deck and feast on a seafood, steak, chicken, or rib dinner. For breakfast, you're sure to feel at home at La Casa Restaurant (860-443-9212).

For provisions, take a short walk to Route 161 (just off Route 156) in Niantic. For cash there are several ATMs; for food, there's Edward's Super Food store (along with several other smaller markets); and for clean clothes, visit Barry's Cleaners and Launderers (860-739-7867).

NAVIGATION & ANCHORAGES: Use ChartKit Region 3, pages 7 and 34; Maptech™ Waterproof Charts 1 and 17; and Maptech™ electronic and NOAA paper charts 13211 (1:20,000), 12372SC (1:40,000), 12354 (1:80,000), and 13205 (1:80,000). Use tide tables for New London. High tide at Millstone Point is 9 minutes later; low tide is 1 minute later. Multiply height of tide at New London by 1.05 for height of tide at Millstone Point. Mean tidal range is 2.7 feet.

It's hard to miss Niantic: the 389-foot, red-and-white stack at the Millstone Nuclear Power Station stands out. Niantic Bay is 8.5nm from the Saybrook breakwater, and 6.5nm from New London Harbor. Plum Gut is 8.1nm from Niantic Bay.

From the west, avoid the shoals at the mouth of the Connecticut River by steering south of Fl R 4s BELL R "8," staying at least 2nm offshore, before turning east-north-east for Niantic. Hatchett Reef is the principal offshore hazard of the summer enclaves of Old Lyme and East Lyme. The reef is well marked by R N "6" to the south and G C "1" to the north. It's best to run south of R N "6" as you head for Black Point.

As you approach Black Point, keep an eye on the chart and locate the Brothers, a cluster of rocky islets inshore. If you're heading into the bight west of Black Point, watch for R N "2" and the rocks north and east of the buoy. East of the Brothers, northwest of R N "2," there's a nice daytime anchorage.

There are three small islands west of Black Point; none of which is open to visitors. Both Griswold Island, to the southwest of Watts Island, and Huntley Island, due west of

Beyond the bridge awaits one of the best kept secrets along the Connecticut coast: the Niantic River. © Maptech

Watts, are privately owned. Watts Island is part of a nature sanctuary and not open to the public.

From the east, there are two approaches to Niantic Bay. Approach via Twotree Island Channel north of Bartlett Reef, staying south of GR C "R" at Rapid Rock and G C "3" at Little Goshen Reef. Pass well north of G C "1" north of Bartlett Reef and G C "3" off Twotree Island, and you'll have a clear shot at Fl R 4s BELL R "6" marking the outer part of Niantic Bay.

Looking east over the entrance to Niantic Bay. © Maptech/James T. Abts

The safest approach is to head south past Bartlett Reef Light (Fl 5s 35ft 12M BELL) and pass south of G C "1A." Boulders sit behind each a mere 3 feet down. Watch your set as you round the light—the current can run as much as 4 knots.

When approaching Niantic Bay, stay well west of White Rock and Little Rock off the eastern shore, marked by Fl R 4s BELL R "6." Niantic Bay is wide enough (1.5nm) for seas to build up, making for an uncomfortable night at anchor if the wind is blowing from any direction but the north. There's a special anchorage east of Crescent Beach, about 0.4nm northwest of Threefoot Rock, marked by G C "7," with good holding ground. The anchorage is marked by Fl 6s 8ft PRIV and is maintained by the Niantic Bay Yacht Club, at the end of the curving breakwater.

Enter the Niantic River via a narrow channel with a controlling depth of 5 feet up to the two bridges that separate the bay from the river. The beginning of the channel is marked by G "1," and it's hard to spot until you're practically on top of it. Your best bet is to travel a course parallel, but well west of, a line between Fl R 4s BELL R "6" and R N "8" at Black Rock until you spot the entrance daymarker. Remember to stay well west of both buoys to avoid White Rock. If you're coming from the west, pass east of Threefoot Rock. With G C "7" dead astern, steer a course of 54°m for 1.1nm to the entrance.

The southernmost bridge at the Niantic River entrance is a railroad bascule with a clearance of 11 feet (mhw), and it's usually open. The northern bridge, a double bascule bridge with a clearance of 32 feet (mhw) when closed, is part of Route 156. In between the two bridges, you can't miss the large, rack-storage facility of Niantic Bay Marina, with transient dockage available.

If you need to open the highway bridge, give one long and one short blast of your horn. Both bridge tenders monitor VHF 13. If you're not used to the tricks the current can play, it's best to enter the river at slack tide, or with the current against you. Plan to spend a few hours above the bridges, taking advantage of the tides for your return. Tidal currents through the bridges normally run 1.6 knots on the flood and about 1 knot on the ebb. However, much greater velocities can occur.

CAUTION: The channel at the railroad bridge is very narrow, and you may have to give way to large boats traveling with the current. A no-wake speed limit is strictly enforced between the bridges.

Beyond the bridges, you'll find a federally maintained channel that zigzags up into the river with a minimum depth of 4.5 feet. Around the point to the east is Mago Point (860-442-2710). Most of the marinas are right next to each other inside the west end of The Bar, including the full-service Port Niantic Marina. The hard part isn't finding the marinas, it's trying to tell which is which in the profusion of docks and yards. The first docks you'll see as the channel turns at R N "10" are those of Boats, Inc. The next docks extending to the channel are those of Port Niantic Marina where you'll find transient berths, a rack storage building, gas and diesel fuel, and marine supplies. The town of Niantic has built a launch ramp near Harbor Mill Marina where visitors may bring their dinghies ashore and leave them on the grass while visiting town.

From the marinas on the lower Niantic, you can go another couple of miles upriver to get away from it all. The entire channel from the entrance up to Smith Cove and beyond is marked with buoys. Though some of the markers are not charted, they should be obeyed, as water is in short supply outside the channel.

The entrance to Smith Cove is marked by privately maintained aids and carries 5 feet of water. Inside, you'll find Bayreuther Boat Yard and the Smith Cove Yacht Club. When entering Smith Cove from the south, be sure not to cut south of G "27." Farther in, it's generally too shallow to anchor.

Good water for anchoring starts about 500 yards north of Smith Cove. You'll find depths of 7 to 19 feet for nearly a mile north of Sandy Point and 8 to 11 feet in Keeny Cove. The peaceful inner bay at Keeny Cove has good holding ground.

Shoreside & Emergency Services
Airport: Groton/New London (860-445-8549)
Coast Guard:
—New London (860-442-4471) or VHF 16
Police, Fire, Ambulance: 911
Taxi: Yellow Cab (860-443-4321)
—Village Cab (860-437-1870)
Tow Service:
SEA TOW —24-Hour Dispatch (800-4SEATOW)
—Eastern Connecticut (860-572-9090)
Tow BoatU.S.—24-Hour Dispatch (800-391-4869)
—Clinton (860-388-4065)

Looking east over the two bridges in Niantic. Niantic Bay Marina sits between the railroad bascule bridge, right, and the highway bridge, left.
© Maptech/James T. Abts

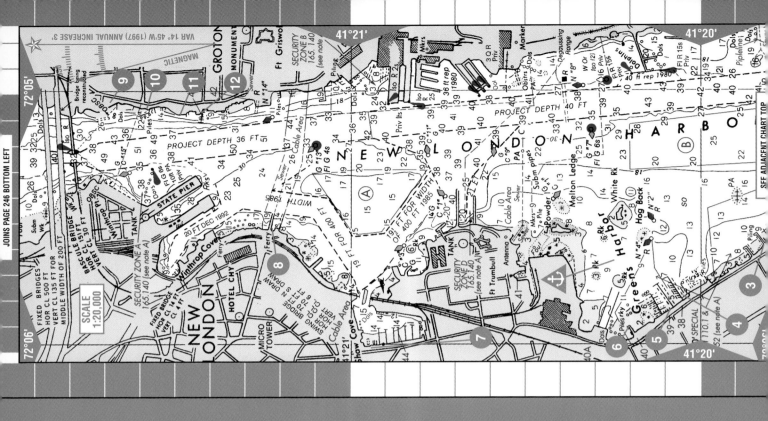

VAR 14° 45'W (1997) ANNUAL INCREASE 3'
MAGNETIC
GROTON

41°21'

41°20'

Ft Griswold

SECURITY ZONE B
165.140

MONUMENT

SEE ADJACENT CHART TOP

Bridge being reconstructed

FIXED BRIDGES
HOR CL 500 FT
VERT CL 135 FT FOR
MIDDLE WIDTH OF 200 FT

SCALE
1:20,000

PROJECT DEPTH 36 FT

PROJECT DEPTH 40 FT

NEW LONDON HARBOR

STATE PIER

SECURITY ZONE A (see note A)
165.140

WINTHROP TANK

NEW LONDON

Winthrop Cove

BASCULE BRIDGE
HOR CL 151 FT
VERT CL 30 FT

HOTEL CHY

FIXED BRIDGE
VER CL 14 FT

SWING BRIDGE
HOR CL 0 FT
VERT CL 6 FT

Shaw Cove

MICRO TOWER

41°21'

Cable Area

Greens Harbor

SECURITY ZONE D
165.140
Ft Trumbull

Melton Ledge
Powder White Rk
Hog Back
Piers

41°20'

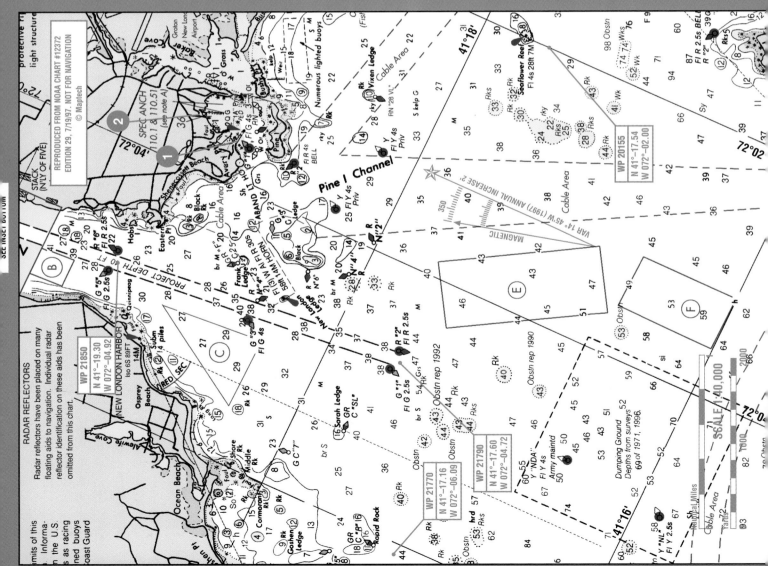

RADAR REFLECTORS
Radar reflectors have been placed on many
floating aids to navigation. Individual radar
reflector identification on these aids has been
omitted from this chart.

protective
light structure

Bolter Cove

Groton
New London
Airport

SPEC ANCH
(110.1 & 110.51)
(see note A)

Pine I Channel

Numerous lighted buoys

Vixen Ledge

Cable Area

41°18'

Seaflower Reef
Fl 4s 28ft 7M

WP 20155
N 41°-17.54
W 072°-02.00

VAR 14° 45'W (1997) ANNUAL INCREASE 2'
MAGNETIC

Cable Area

WP 21850
N 41°-19.30
W 072°-04.92

NEW LONDON HARBOR
Iso 6S 89FT
14M

Osprey Beach

Quinnipeg

PROJECT DEPTH 40 FT

Sarah Ledge

Ocean Beach

Goshen Ledge

Rapid Rock

WP 21770
N 41°-17.16
W 072°-06.09

WP 21790
N 41°-17.60
W 072°-04.72

Obstn rep 1992

Obstn rep 1990

Army maintd

Dumping Ground
Depths from surveys
of 1971, 1996.

Cable Area

SCALE 1:40,000

41°16'

72°04'

72°02'

72°06'

72°05'

Life on the Thames

An unusual and historic light casts its rays on the swells of New London Harbor: the New London Ledge Light. Most offshore lighthouses have cast-iron frames, but the only things cast here are fishing lines and the lantern rising from the top center of the roof. This square brick house—French Second Empire style—was built in 1909, when demand for a navigational aid in New London reached its peak. Residents along the New London shore insisted that a grand lighthouse was needed to match the beauty of their mansions, and they got their wish.

The lightkeepers are also gone; all except for one, that is. The lightkeeper's house is notorious for its ghost. A former keeper of the light named Ernie apparently jumped from the top balcony after his wife eloped with a ferry boat captain. Some claim that Ernie still plays tricks with local ferries.

Once past the New London Ledge Light, the historic Thames River opens wide before you. Of course, it's not the historic Thames of London, but the first colonists here did

Looking northeast over Green's Harbor. In the bottom right, the docks of Thamesport Marina are followed by Burr's Marina. © Maptech/James T. Abts

name this Thames River after the one in London. They may have been short on imagination, or maybe they were just full of pride. Whatever the reason, it took guts to survey this meager settlement with its few miserable log cabins and

Marine Facilities and Services		DOCKAGE						SERVICES				SUPPLIES & AMENITIES								
		Monitors / Working VHF Channel	Number of Transient Berths / Moorings	Seasonal / Year-round	Approach / Dockside Depth in Feet at MLW	Maximum LOA	110V ✴ 220V ▲ 3 Phase ■ Maximum Amps	Hookups: Fresh Water / Phone / Cable TV	Ramp / Dinghy Dock / Launch Service	Rail / Lift / Crane / Trailer Capacity (tons)	Repairs: Propeller / Sail / Rigging / Diesel / Wood / Fiberglass / Electronics	Gas / Diesel Fuel	Marine / Groceries / Ice / Bait / LPG / CNG	Fuel Brand	Restrooms / Showers / Laundry / Pumpout	Public Phone / Restaurant / Snack Bar	Hotel / Pool / Tennis / Golf	Mastercard / VISA / Discover / AmEx
1	Shennecossett Yacht Club	860-445-8211	/2	S	42			PRIVATE—MEMBERS ONLY				GD	Mob			P		
2	PINE ISLAND MARINA (B) p. 244	860-445-9729	68/	/4	S	40	8/5	F	★30	RL	L15	All		MGIB	All		PS	MV
3	Thames Yacht Club	860-443-9933		Y			PRIVATE—MEMBERS ONLY											
4	Thamesport MARINA (B) p. 244	860-437-7022	9/68	30/6	S	130	14/12	FC	■50	D		GD	GD	Gulf	IB	RSP	All	All
5	Burr's MARINA p. 243	860-443-8457	9/78	25/6	S	120	12/9	FC	★▲50	DL	L20	All	GD	Tex	GI	All	P PR	All
6	A.W. Marina	860-443-6076		S	25	10/10	F							B	R			
7	Crocker's Boatyard, Inc. p. 245	860-443-6304	9/10	25/	Y	96	15/12	FP	★▲■100	D	LC75	All	GD	Gulf	GIL	All	P PR	MVD
8	New London City Pier*	860-442-5994	9/	5/	Y	150	20/20	F	★▲						I		P	
9	Groton Oil Co. & Marina	860-445-5336	9/	3/	Y	50	13/7	All	★30				GD	Mob	I	R	P	All
10	Groton Marine Dock*	860-445-4994		S	36	20/15	F	★		PRIVATE DOCK							P	
11	Hel-Cat II Dock	860-535-3200		Y			PRIVATE DOCK											
12	Thames Harbor Inn	860-445-8111	14/	S	40	12/12	F	■	D							RS	H	MVA

All Coast Guard Stations Monitor Channel 16

Information in these listings is provided by the facilities themselves. An asterisk (*) indicates that the facility did not respond to our most recent requests for information.
(B) represents a BOAT/U.S. cooperating marina.

Looking west over the transient-friendly facilities of Crocker's Boatyard. Across the river is Electric Boat.
© Maptech/James T. Abts

was built here in the early 1950s and launched from this site in 1954. In 1981, Electric Boat launched the first of the new Trident-class nuclear attack subs. Each of these 560-foot subs carries 24 missiles that can land within 20 feet of a target located 4,000 miles away.

ACTIVITIES: Two visitor's centers, one next to the city pier and the other on the corner of Golden Street and Eugene O'Neill Drive, will bring you up-to-date with the goings-on in London's namesake. At these visitor centers, you can pick up some information on the local hotspots, as well as an update on the refurbishing New London has undergone in the past several years. Another source of information is the Downtown New London Association (860-444-1879). They can provide a free map of the city and a listing of commercial services. If you're concerned about getting to any of these sights, call a taxi; if you're staying at Burr's Yacht Haven, courtesy rides are available.

Historic sights abound in New London, like the Hempstead House (860-443-7949), oldest in the city (1678), the Huguenot House (1751), and the 1756 Shaw Mansion, now home to the New London County Historical Society (860-443-1209). The handsome New London County Courthouse (1784) is worth a visit, as are the four Greek Revival houses on Whale Oil Row, and the Monte Cristo Cottage on Pequot Avenue (860-443-0051). Just across from the train station is the schoolhouse where Nathan Hale taught in 1775.

At Ocean Beach Park (800-510-SAND), at the foot of Ocean Avenue, a beautiful beach, a water slide, a mile-long boardwalk, miniature golf course, video arcades, and eateries make a day at the beach a priority. Like Napatree Point (in Watch Hill, Rhode Island), Ocean Beach was originally lined with private homes. As at Napatree, all of those homes were washed away by the hurricane of 1938.

West of Avery Point is the equally nice but less developed Bushy Point Beach. Anchor just off the steep, pebbly beach and swim or row a dinghy ashore for a stroll along the water or through the woods at the park. It's a great place for the kids to blow off some steam, but you should check them carefully for ticks afterward—especially the tiny ones that carry Lyme disease.

To check out a history of America's fascination with submarines head to the U.S.S. *Nautilus* Submarine Force Library and Museum (800-343-0079) or sneak a peek through one of its three working periscopes. Built in Groton and christened in 1954, the U.S.S. *Nautilus* was the first nuclear-powered

call it New London—as in London, what was then the greatest city on earth, monetary capital of the world, cultural center extraordinaire, and the home of the King. Optimistic blokes, they were.

Nevertheless, New London has come a long way since those early days. In fact, if those first settlers were to show up now, they might well feel their vision had been fulfilled: the city has become a major shipping, military, and educational center. So far has this river come from its beginnings that one riverside placard reads: "Thames...the streets of dreams and the river of promise."

Yes, the Thames has lived up to its promise by becoming a popular shipping port. Draining across old crystalline rocks in a narrow, crooked valley, the river remains almost sandless. It seems that a glacier left the lower Thames broad and deep, a perfect channel for big ships to come and go. Testament to the harbor's commercial promise, New London's first customs master was appointed in 1659, just 13 years after the town was deeded to Governor John Winthrop Jr. A year later, shipbuilding began along the harbor shores.

New London has never relinquished its position as a major shipping port. At one point during the 1880s, the city laid claim to the second-largest whaling fleet in the nation with 72 ships, one fewer than New Bedford, Massachusetts. More important has been the presence of American armed services in the area. In addition to the Coast Guard Academy located north of the bridges, the river also sports the Electric Boat submarine facility in Groton and the New London Detachment of the Naval Undersea Warfare Center at Fort Trumbull.

Across the river, Groton is known as the "submarine capital of the world." The U.S.S. *Nautilus*, the first nuclear sub,

submarine. Now docked at the museum on permanent display, the submarine is an immensely popular attraction. Unfortunately, there are no tie-up facilities for recreational boaters at the sub base or at the museum, so you'll have to get there by foot or cab.

Upriver a little, the Coast Guard Academy (860-444-8270) majestically looks over New London Harbor from the western shore. The campus is open to the public (after all, your tax money is paying for it) and tours offer an in-depth history of the buildings and the institution. If you're lucky, you'll catch a glimpse of the Coast Guard's sailing vessel, the *Eagle*.

Keep the young mates stimulated at the Children's Museum of Southeastern Connecticut (860-691-1255) or the Science Center of Eastern Connecticut (860-442-0391). Get in touch with the arts scene at the Lyman Allyn Art Museum (860-443-2545) or the Garde Arts Center (860-444-7373), a historic vaudeville/movie house that now hosts performing arts.

The big events in New London and Groton each summer are the annual Sub Festival (the weekend before July 4th), and Sail Festival (the weekend after July 4th). Due to the number of boats, the late hour, and the amount of alcohol consumed, the harbor often gets a bit too exciting during Sail Fest. You may get just as good a view without risking your boat if you watch the fireworks from your slip or on foot in downtown New London. Both sides of the harbor sponsor concerts and other events, and there are sail races in the harbor all weekend.

The newly completed New London Waterfront Park offers a great place to walk along the water, and benches at which to sit and enjoy the view. For the best view of New London and the harbor, climb up to the high ground at Fort Griswold State Park in Groton. New London's Fort Trumbull State Park, open from sunrise to sunset, provides another great view of the harbor and offers a fishing pier and public restrooms. For yet another don't-miss activity, call Harkness Memorial State Park (860-443-5725) for the times of the outdoor classical and pops concerts throughout summer.

Oh yes, that ringing sound you hear in the background? That's just the casinos—Foxwoods and Mohegan Sun—about a half-hour away. Ask the marina you're staying at about where to find transportation there, or head up to Norwich at the head of the Thames, where buses run continuously.

RESTAURANTS & PROVISIONS: A trip up the Thames to New London and Groton is well rewarded with an abundance of places to refuel your boat and your body, in addition to restocking your food locker. Close to Thamesport Marina, Burr's Marina, and all of the marinas along Greens Harbor, you'll find eateries of varying kinds; for a casual meal, try Fred's Shanty (860-447-1301) or Pequot Pizza (860-442-2262). You can't miss Schooners Restaurant (860-437-3801), which features great food and great views of the Thames.

Near Crocker's Boatyard, try the Neon Chicken (860-444-6366) for rotisserie, or Nathaniel's (860-447-8777), a rather elegant eatery. The Bank Street Lobster House (860-447-9398)

The New London Ledge Light serves as an important navigational aid and a nice photo op. © Maptech

serves up everyone's favorite shellfish, among other palate-pleasing fare.

Downtown, you won't be steered wrong with a visit to Captain's Restaurant & Pizza (860-445-9553), where you'll find an assorted menu of Italian and American favorites; leave room for dessert. Across Shaw Cove, Captain Scott's Lobster Dock (860-439-1741) offers lobster, clams, chowder, and fish—all fresh off the boat. The entrées at Timothy's (860-437-0526) have a unique flavor that comes from the chef's way of cooking Italian ingredients with French methods. Try it for yourself. On the other side of the river in Groton, Paul's Pasta (860-445-5276) churns out homemade spaghetti, ravioli, cavatelli—you name it—and other Italian food.

Provisioning is easy if you stay at Burr's Yacht Haven; they'll have groceries delivered right to your boat. In New London you'll find markets throughout town, like Stop & Go Mart (860-442-8926) on Bank Street. There's also an A & P (860-449-1999) in Groton.

NAVIGATION & ANCHORAGES: Use ChartKit Region 3, pages 9, 34, and 34A; Maptech™ Waterproof Charts 1 and 17; and Maptech™ electronic and NOAA paper charts 13213 (1:10,000), 13212 (1:20,000), 12372 (1:40,000), and 13205 (1:80,000). Use tide tables for New London. Mean tidal range is 2.6 feet.

The paired flashers marking the entrance to the New London Harbor channel are 4.5nm from the entrance to Niantic Bay, 3.3nm from Race Rock, and 4.5nm from the approach to Mystic at Morgan Point.

You're going to run into a lot of commercial shipping traffic in New London Harbor. Always give the right-of-way to larger and less maneuverable vessels, especially submarines, which will be on the surface until they reach the open Atlantic.

For all of their awesome capabilities, submarines aren't as maneuverable in tight quarters as you might think. One of our readers, who once served on subs out of New London, tells us they would stop their forward thrust at New London Ledge Light and still have to reverse the turbines to bring the sub to a stop at Electric Boat, 2.5 miles upriver. On rare occasions, you may notice a "pinging" sound running through your hull from sonar transmitters. You may also experience sporadic electrical interference with your instruments.

CAUTION: If you look carefully at the chart for New London Harbor, you'll notice lots of "Security Zone" warnings. Take these seriously. The Navy and Coast Guard do not take kindly to waterborne photographers in the vicinity of the sub base or the shipyards.

The main channel into the harbor begins at Fl G 2.5s G "1" and Fl R 2.5s R "2." Between Fl R 2.5s R "2" and Race Point on Fishers Island are two ship anchorages, "E" and "F." As you head into the wide open harbor, you'll see New London Ledge Light (Fl (3) W & R 30s 58ft 14M HORN), a

square, brick Victorian building atop a white pier. The light marks a series of ledges that block the harbor. Farther up to the west is the beacon of the New London Harbor Light, also known as "Pequot Light"(Iso 6s 89ft 14M), with a red sector marking the nearby shoals.

Also prominent are the microwave tower atop a building in downtown New London and the large sheds of the shipyard on the east side of the river opposite Fort Trumbull. Ferries run in and out of the harbor, moving fast and leaving large wakes. The main entrance has 36 to 40 feet of water, with a mean tidal range of only 2.6 feet, so fixed docks are pretty much the rule.

From the west, you need not enter the channel at the outer channel buoys unless you have a very deep draft. Keep east of GR C "R" at Rapid Rock and G C "7" off Ocean Beach at the west entrance to the harbor, to avoid many rocky patches and boulders. Also stay well east of Quinnipeag Rocks, northeast of New London Harbor Light.

From the east, Pine Island Channel cuts between Avery Point and Black Ledge, marked on the north by G C "3" and Fl R 4s BELL R "2" off Pine Island.

CAUTION: Pine Island Channel has a 10-foot controlling depth and is used by small boats running between New London and Fishers Island, but it's best left to those who are familiar with the area. If you do use it, stay well out from Eastern Point to avoid Black Rock as you come into the main channel.

The currents follow the channel, and are generally not strong. To the east between Avery Point and Pine Island is an enticing small anchorage, home of the Shennecossett Yacht Club. The club has a launch service and serves as the home port for the Groton Police boat.

Pine Island Marina in the Avery Point area offers moorings and slips. Supplies are available at a convenience store about a half mile away, and there is access to a golf course. Just to the east of Shennecossett is the Groton/New London Airport. Depending on the winds and which runway the planes are using for takeoffs, you may not notice the airport at all, or you may find it deafeningly obvious.

The first good anchorage on the west side of the river (in anything but a strong southerly) is Greens Harbor, marked by White Rock just off the main channel. There's a 5-mph speed limit throughout the harbor. Be sure to pass south of R N "2" and R N "4" marking Hog Back Rocks. There are several facilities in Greens Harbor. Burr's Marina is a full-service yard which welcomes transient boaters. Thamesport Marina also offers transient berths.

Upriver beyond Fort Trumbull is Shaw Cove, with 11 to 15 feet of water, entered through a railroad swing bridge. Sound one long and one short blast to open the bridge. Inside the well-protected Shaw Cove, you'll find Crocker's Boatyard, another full-service facility that welcomes transients.

If you want to anchor away from the noise of New London, there are several coves to the east of Avery Point.

When heading toward them and passing in the neighborhood of Seaflower Reef Light (Fl 4s 28ft 7M), be careful of the lobster pots. There's a strong current in the area, so remember that the lines down to the pots may not be directly under the buoys. For a mooring in downtown New London, contact the harbormaster.

Shoreside & Emergency Services
Airport:
—Groton/New London (860-445-8549)
Coast Guard:
—New London (860-442-4471) or VHF 16
Ferry:
—to Martha's Vineyard (860-437-6930)
—to Fisher's Island, NY (860-443-6851)
—to Block Island, RI (860-442-9553) or (860-442-7891)
—to Montauk, NY (860-444-6713)
—to Orient Point, NY (860-443-5281)
Taxi: Blue Cab (860-443-4303)
—Harry's (860-444-2255)
—Yellow Cab (860-443-4321)
Tow Service:
SEA TOW —24-Hour Dispatch (800-4SEATOW)
—Eastern Connecticut (860-572-9090)
TowBoatU.S.—24-Hour Dispatch (800-391-4869)
—New London (860-588-4961)

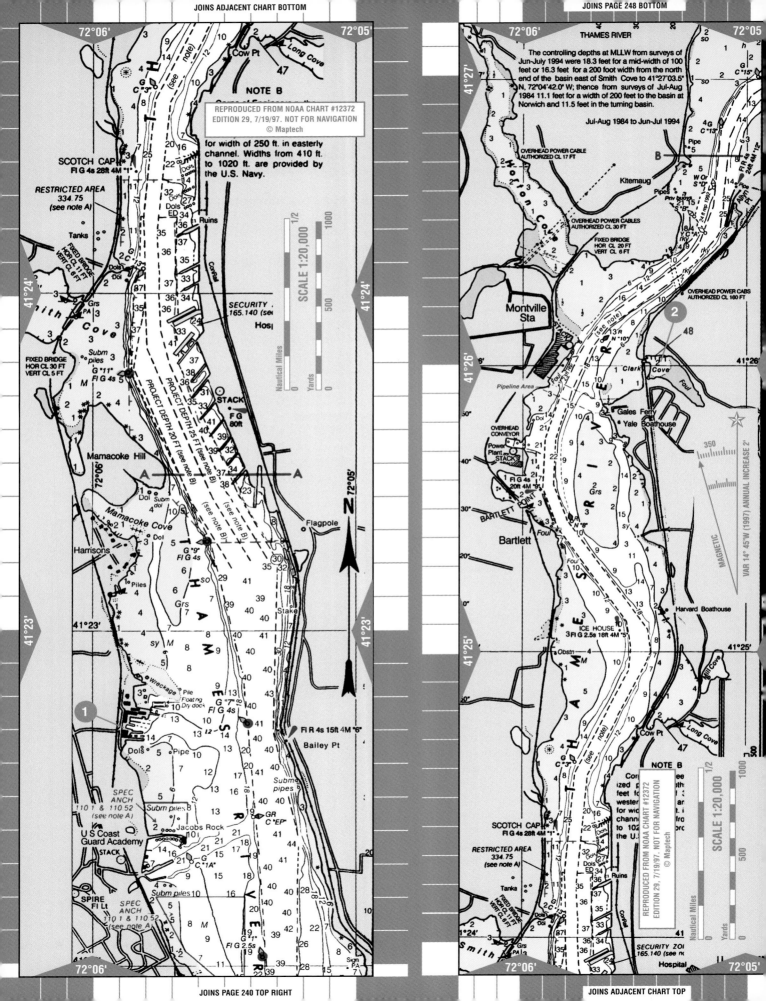

Money at the Head of the River

What's all that money at the head of the Thames River, Captain Kidd's long-lost treasure? No, Captain Kidd never had treasure like that found at Foxwoods Casino & Resort and Mohegan Sun. It's Atlantic City brought to rural Connecticut. It's Las Vegas without all the gaudy flashing lights. Those bells you hear are the constant chimes of slot machines doling out money, and the buzz is the excitement (and disappointment) of the gamblers.

Many are lured up the Thames by the casinos, but not all. The cruise up the river alone is worth it, with sights as rich (in history and beauty) as you hope to become at the casinos. Begin your cruise in New London Harbor at the mouth of the Thames River tidewater estuary. This 12-mile stretch of river mixes fresh and salt water. The watershed of this estuarine river comprises 1,500 square miles, including 43 towns.

The high-tech nuclear subs that ply the waters of the Thames before heading to the Sound have nothing over the Coast Guard's U.S.S. *Eagle*, the 295-foot, three-masted sailing ship just across the river. The Coast Guard Academy was established in 1910 at Fort Trumbull, and didn't move to its present location above the Gold Star Bridge until 1929. The Georgian, red-brick buildings are an impressive landmark on the west bank of the river, though they're hard to see until you have them abeam.

At the head of the river is the city of Norwich. During the Colonial period, Norwich was a transfer point for produce from farms in the backcountry before it developed into a shipping center. Today, the waterfront of Norwich is rebounding after a long period of decline. There's renewed interest in the harbor since the construction of American Wharf, a large marina, restaurant, and office complex on Holly Hock Island. So much has Norwich improved its image that the Connecticut Harbor Management Association named it Harbor of the Year in 1997.

The historic charm of downtown Norwich just might lure you away from the slot machines. Remember, a walk is free! © Maptech

Although the distance upriver does deter some sailors, the area is once again becoming popular with cruising boaters. And if they head to the casinos, some of them may even find treasure up the river.

	Marine Facilities and Services	Phone	Number of Transient Berths / Moorings	Monitors / Working VHF Channel	Approach / Dockside Depth in Feet at MLW	Hookups: Fresh Water / Phone / Cable TV	110V • 220V ■ 3 Phase / Max Amps	Maximum LOA	Seasonal / Year-round	Ramp / Dinghy Dock / Launch Service	Rail / Lift / Crane / Trailer: Capacity (tons)	Repairs	Marine / Groceries / Ice / Bait / LPG / CNG	Gas / Diesel Fuel	Fuel Brand	Restrooms / Showers / Laundry / Pumpout	Public Phone / Restaurant / Snack Bar	Hotel / Pool / Tennis / Golf	Mastercard / VISA / Discover / AmEx
1	Thames Shipyard Inc.	860-442-5340							Y	COMMERCIAL SHIPBUILDING & REPAIRS									
2	Gales Ferry Marina	860-464-2146	2/3	68/9	4/4			45	S	F	★30 / LC35	PGDWFE	MI	G	Tex	RS		P	MV
3	The Marina at American Wharf (p. 251)	860-886-6363	100/	68/68	30/25	All		120	Y	All	★100 / RL / L30	PGDWFE	MI	GD	Tex	All	PG	All	All
4	Thayer's Marina*	860-887-8315	3/	68/68	9/7			26	Y	F	★ / R / L9	PRGDWF	MIB						All
5	Norwich City Landing*								Y										

Information in these listings is provided by the facilities themselves. An asterisk (*) indicates that the facility did not respond to our most recent requests for information. (B) represents a BOAT/U.S. cooperating marina.

All Coast Guard Stations Monitor VHF Channel 16

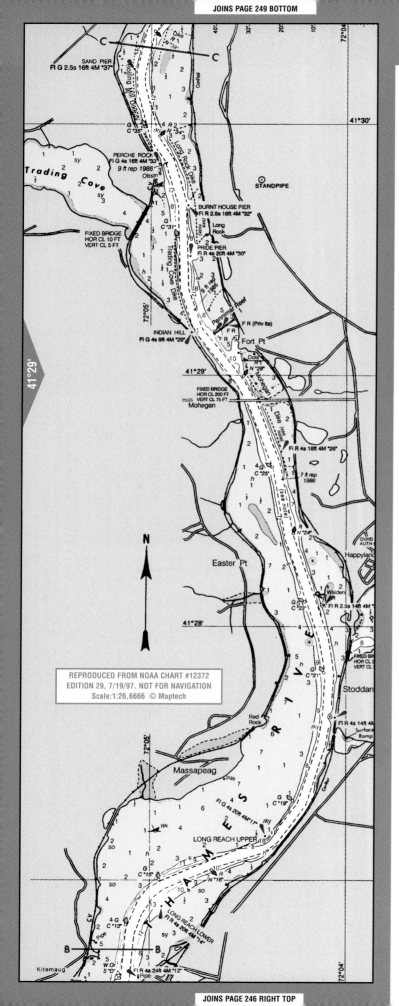

REPRODUCED FROM NOAA CHART #12372
EDITION 29, 7/19/97. NOT FOR NAVIGATION
Scale:1:26,6666 © Maptech

The Marina at American Wharf sits at the head of the Thames River. © Maptech

ACTIVITIES: Scenery on the Thames River is a showcase of contrast. Industry prevails from New London Harbor to a couple of miles north of the bridges, but as you travel farther upriver Mother Nature takes over.

The tall and historic masts of the Coast Guard's U.S.S. *Eagle* at the U.S. Coast Guard Academy in New London can be seen up close on a guided tour. Since you're in the neighborhood, the Coast Guard Academy (860-444-8611) campus is also worth a visit.

Historians and military buffs appreciate the *Nautilus* Memorial & Submarine Force Library & Museum (800-343-0079), next to the sub base. For more information on the *Nautilus* and other sights in the New London area, refer to the previous chapter on New London.

About four miles north of the bridges are the boathouses used by the Yale and Harvard crew teams during their annual (held usually on the first Saturday in June) regatta on the Thames. The Ivy League schools' first regatta was held in 1852 on New Hampshire's Lake Winnipesaukee but has been held on the Thames since 1878. Call Yale University (203-432-5303) for more information about the storied event.

As you make your way toward Norwich, call the Norwich Tourism Office (860-886-4683) for the lowdown on the events that will be taking place while you're there. Partake in the national pastime with some minor league baseball at Dodd Field, home of the Norwich Navigators (800-64-GATOR), a New York Yankees affiliate. For more sports, try Putts Up Dock Mini Golf (860-886-PUTT), at American Wharf. This is no average mini-golf course; it claims to be one of the most challenging in New England.

The city of Norwich sponsors concerts each week at the Howard P. Brown Memorial Park. Located along the riverbank, the park is just a short walk from downtown. There

Embassy Guides

are a number of community events held during the summer at The Marina at American Wharf (860-886-6363), including music, arts & crafts shows, and children's events.

Probably the biggest attractions in these parts are the Foxwoods Casino & Resort (800-PLAY BIG), and the Mohegan Sun Casino (888-226-7711). Both are cities unto themselves, with shopping and eating options galore—and they're constantly getting bigger. Check with Marina at American Wharf for shuttles to each. Who knows: a trip up the Thames may bring you great fortune. Just don't forget who told you about it!

RESTAURANTS & PROVISIONS: There's no need to go far if you're tied up at American Wharf—Americus On-the-Wharf (860-887-8555) at American Wharf serves light, casual fare for lunch and dinner that you can enjoy at the outdoor waterfront café. Also, head for the Chelsea Landing Pub & Galley (860-889-9932), which serves excellent steak and seafood, or to Billy Wilson's Ageing Still (860-887-8733), which has live bands and a bunch of beers on tap.

Start your day with a hearty breakfast at Olde Tymes Restaurant (860-887-6865). Later, if you're in the mood for pizza, the choices are virtually limitless. We recommend Olympic Pizza (860-887-0196) on West Main. The Prince of Wales Dining Room at the Norwich Inn & Spa (860-886-2401) serves fine American cuisine and offers the luxury of eating on an outdoor terrace. You'll need a car or taxi to get there. The casinos offer more than just gambling—there's food, too. Both have eateries that range from buffet to the extremely elegant.

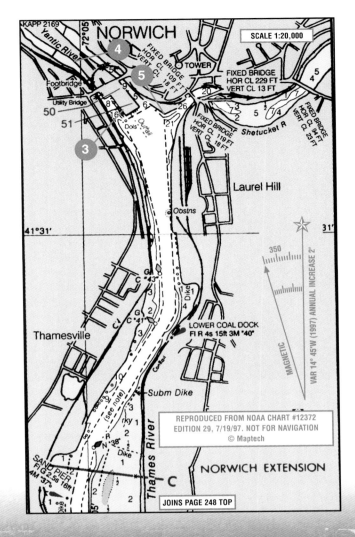

REPRODUCED FROM NOAA CHART #12372 EDITION 29, 7/19/97. NOT FOR NAVIGATION © Maptech

The United States Coast Guard Academy sits on the western shore of the Thames River.
© Maptech/James T. Abts

Race, and 10.0nm from Holly Hock Island in Norwich. About 2 miles above the bridges on the east shore is the U.S. Naval Submarine Base.

A bascule railroad bridge just north of downtown New London separates the upper river from New London Harbor. Give the usual one long and one short blast on your horn, or contact the bridgetender on VHF 13 to open the bridge. Unless your masts are extremely tall, you won't have trouble passing under the next two bridges, with clearances of 135 feet (mhw). The *Eagle* has to house her topmasts (at 147.3 feet) to get under the bridge.

CAUTION: A careful look at the NOAA chart for New London Harbor reveals many "Security Zone" warnings. Take these very seriously. The U.S. Navy and the Coast Guard do not take kindly to photographers near the submarine base or the shipyard. Please encourage your boat's shutterbugs to stow their cameras away for the time being.

It's about a 13.5nm trip from New London Ledge Light to Norwich, so it's best to enter on the flood. You'll find brackish water all the way upriver, but it's fresh enough to kill off the marine growth on the bottom of your boat.

CAUTION: Both Connecticut College and the Coast Guard Academy regularly row on the river. Whenever you see the sleek crew shells, proceed with extreme caution to make sure you don't flip them. Remember that you are legally responsible for any damage caused by your wake.

Stock up on supplies at Shop Rite (860-887-6088), on West Main Street. It also has an ATM at your disposal. Close by is James Laundromat & Dry Cleaners (860-887-9665) if you want to freshen up your garb.

NAVIGATION & ANCHORAGES: Use ChartKit Region 3, pages 34 and 40; Maptech™ Waterproof Chart 17; and Maptech™ electronic and NOAA paper charts 12372 (1:40,000), 13212 (1:20,000), and 13213 (1:10,000). Use tide tables for New London. High tide at Norwich is 13 minutes later; low tide is 25 minutes later. Multiply height of tide at New London by 1.2 for height of tide at Norwich. Mean tidal range is 3.0 feet.

The Interstate-95 bridges across the Thames River are 3.5nm from the New London Ledge Light, 7.8nm from The

Tidal range in the upper Thames River is 3.6 feet, and the 5-mph speed limit is strictly enforced. The channel is well marked and runs at least 11 feet deep all the way to Norwich. The only boating facility between New London and Norwich is Gales Ferry Marina at Clark Cove. There is a fixed railroad trestle at the entrance to Clark Cove with a vertical clearance of 13 feet (mhw), so only smaller vessels will be able to reach this facility.

Farther upriver, the commercial traffic thins out and the river narrows. Nature reasserts itself with trees, somewhat cleaner water, and flocks of birds. You'll see many local boaters trying their luck for bunker, blues, and mackerel.

The warm water produced by the Connecticut Light and Power plant in Montville is especially attractive to fish, and its two tall stacks are a conspicuous landmark.

Poquetanuck Cove would be an inviting spot for exploration if it weren't for the fixed railroad bridge across the entrance (2-foot clearance). There's been talk of replacing this bridge with a taller one or a bascule, but so far no luck.

With prevailing winds out of the southwest in the summer, sailors are often welcomed with an easy, broad reach all the way upriver. The channel is well marked with buoys and range lights, and there are no problems until you pass beneath the 75-foot high Mohegan-Pequot Bridge. Above this bridge, you must be careful of the sea walls and dikes that are invisible at anything over half-tide. These walls were originally built to keep steamships from silting up the channel with erosion from their wash. While the dikes were once above water except at unusually high tides, the river has risen by nearly a foot in the last century, putting the dikes underwater and forming a distinct and unusual hazard to navigation. If you stick to the channel, however, the dikes will pose no problem. Newcomers are advised to head upriver at low tide to get a good look at the location of these obstacles.

Norwich Harbor, at the confluence of the Thames, Shetucket, and Yantic rivers, is well protected by the high hills around it and makes an excellent haven in bad weather. Small boats can anchor above the Norwich bridges, with its clearance of 18 feet (mhw), but larger boats will have to look for space farther south.

A harbor revitalization project on the site of an old coal depot has attracted boaters to what was once a dying waterfront. The Marina at American Wharf has 100 transient slips, some able to accommodate boats as large as 120 feet. It has all of the conveniences and amenities a boater could ask for, including a swimming pool, telephone and cable TV hookups, laundry service, fuel, and a pumpout station. At G C "43," head straight for the gold building until you pick up the privately maintained buoys leading to the marina.

Shoreside & Emergency Services
Airport: Groton/New London (860-445-8549)
Coast Guard: New London (860-442-4471) or VHF 16
Ferry: To Montauk, NY (860-444-6713)
—to Orient Point, NY (860-443-5281)
—to Fishers Island, NY (860-443-6851)
—to Block Island, RI (860-442-9553) or (860-442-7891)
Police, Fire, Ambulance: 911
Taxi: Norwich Taxi & Livery (860-848-2227)
Tow Service:
SEA TOW. —24-Hour Dispatch (800-4SEATOW)
—Eastern Conn. (860-572-9090)
Tow BoatU.S.—24-Hour Dispatch (800-391-4869)
—New London (860-588-4961)

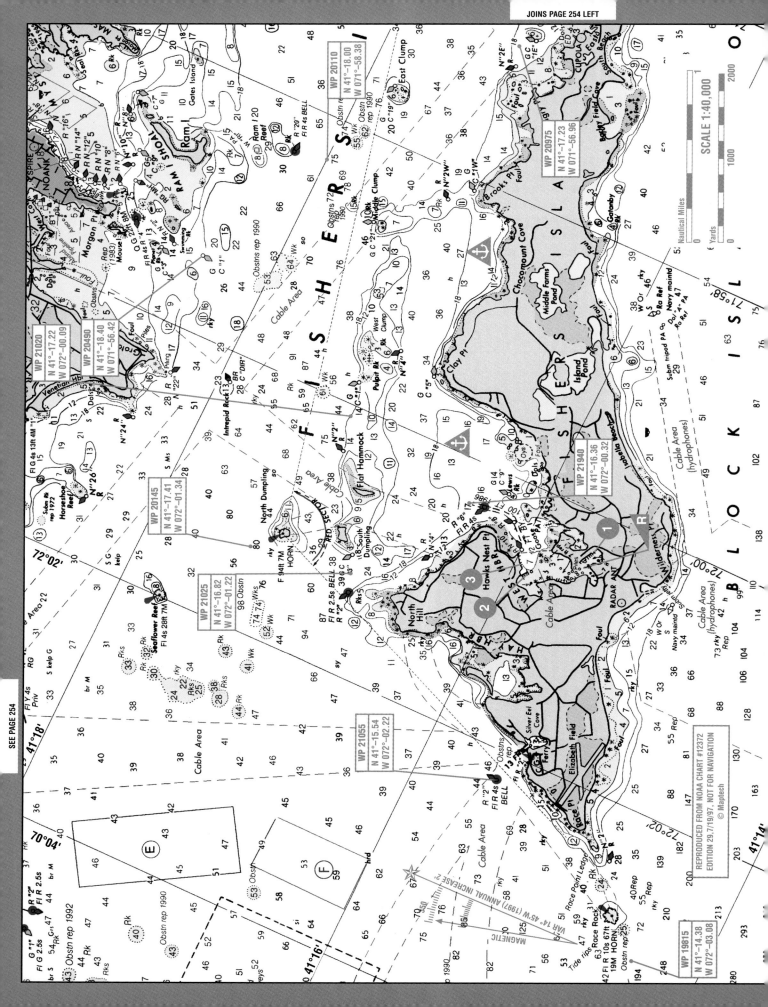

One Tough Race

As you sail past Fishers Island, sneak a glance at the grand houses lining the shores; their size and beauty are spectacular. But don't take your eyes from the water for too long or you may run into trouble, especially as you come through The Race, the treacherous passage marked by Race Rock Light.

The Race is an oceanographic oddity in the northeast, but one that can be explained by simple earth science. The relentless tidal rush through this narrow area has formed a gorge on the Sound's bottom, the cause of all this havoc. The surface may appear calm, but the water beneath is alive. On the flood tides, ocean water rushes into The Race, crashes into the gorge wall, and is catapulted toward the surface. The result is chop, or short waves. If you've never witnessed it before, it's quite a sight—a humbling one.

Tranquil Fishers Island provides a respite from the violent seas around The Race. The origin of the island's name is open to debate: it's so named either because Indians fished on it, or because a Mr. Vischer (a mate of Adriaen Block, who discovered the island) had the island named after him. In any case, it's a peaceful retreat amid the choppy confusion. Most of the island is a retreat for well-to-do summer people, but the harbors and coves surrounding Fishers have more than enough room for your enjoyment.

In 1641, soon after being named the "first governor of the river Connecticut" John Winthrop, Jr. obtained a grant from the Connecticut colony for Fishers Island—then called Munnawtawkin, meaning a place of observation, by the local Indians. After witnessing the massacre of the Pequots at Mystic in 1637, Winthrop was careful not to take advantage of any other tribes in the area and took pains to purchase the island from local natives. By 1646, the governor

Looking northwest over West Harbor. In the foreground you'll see Pirate's Cove Marine, while Fishers Island Yacht Club sits near the entrance, on the left. © Maptech/James T. Abts

had moved his family to the island, and was able to raise a few goats and introduce horses to Connecticut before he returned to New London.

In 1662, Governor Winthrop secured a charter from King Charles II for the Connecticut colony, including Fishers Island. But the Duke of York believed Fishers was part of his domain. The question of which state, New York or Connecticut, had legal possession of Fishers was not settled until 1879. A joint committee from both states decided that the island, like Gardiners and Shelter, belonged to New York. Fishers now has the same area code as Long Island, although the mail goes through Connecticut.

ACTIVITIES: Unless you have resident friends or family, there isn't much for you on the island itself. The eastern two-thirds

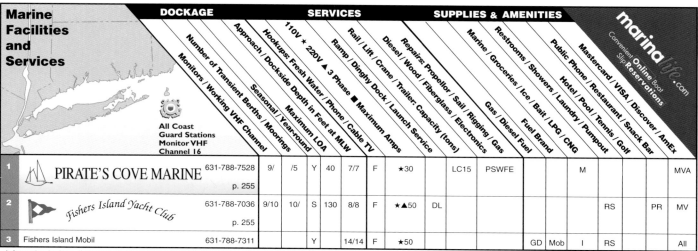

Marine Facilities and Services		DOCKAGE					SERVICES				SUPPLIES & AMENITIES						
	Monitors / Working VHF Channel	Number of Transient Berths / Moorings	Approach / Dockside Depth in Feet at MLW	Seasonal / Year-round	Maximum LOA	110V ★ 220V ▲ 3 Phase ■ Maximum Amps	Hookups: Fresh Water / Phone / Cable TV	Ramp / Dinghy Dock / Launch Service	Rail / Lift / Crane / Trailer: Capacity (tons)	Diesel / Wood / Fiberglass / Electronics	Repairs: Propellor / Sail / Rigging / Electronics	Marine / Groceries / Ice / Bait / LPG / CNG	Gas / Diesel Fuel	Restrooms / Showers / Laundry / Pumpout	Fuel Brand	Public Phone / Restaurant / Snack Bar	Hotel / Pool / Tennis / Golf	Mastercard / VISA / Discover / AmEx
1 PIRATE'S COVE MARINE 631-788-7528 p. 255	9/	/5	Y	40	7/7	F		★30		LC15		PSWFE			M			MVA
2 Fishers Island Yacht Club 631-788-7036 p. 255	9/10	10/	S	130	8/8	F		★▲50	DL					RS		PR		MV
3 Fishers Island Mobil 631-788-7311			Y		14/14	F		★50					GD	Mob	I	RS		All

Information in these listings is provided by the facilities themselves. An asterisk (*) indicates that the facility did not respond to our most recent requests for information. (B) represents a BOAT/U.S. cooperating marina.

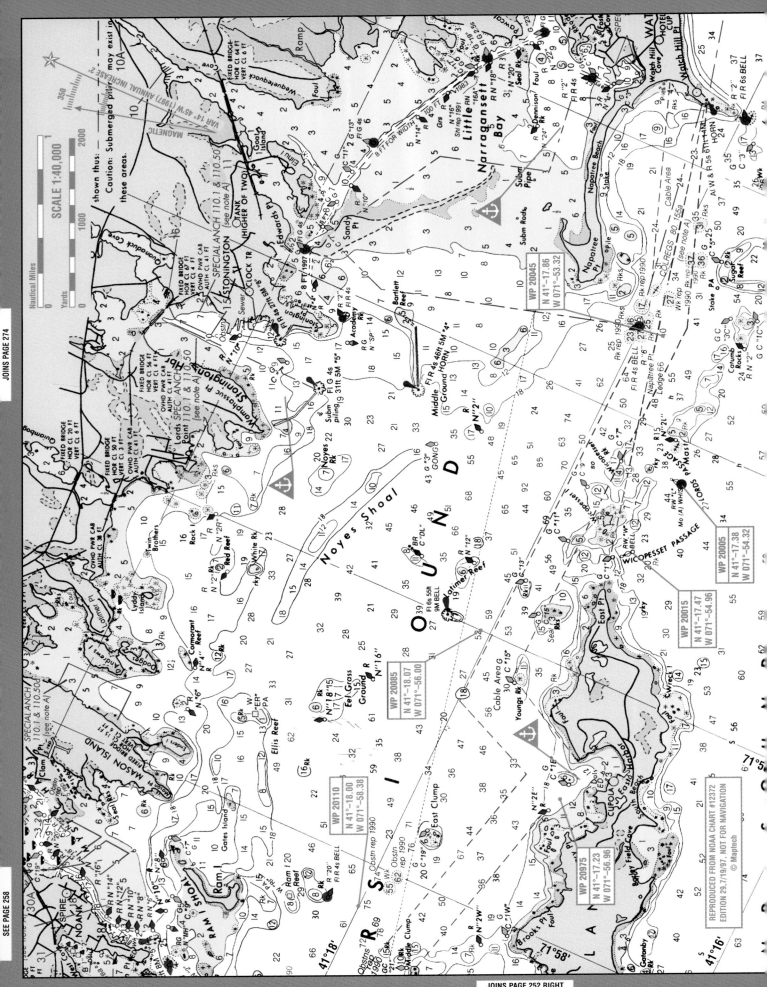

SCALE 1:40,000

Nautical Miles

Yards

Caution: Submerged piles may exist in
these areas.
shown thus:

MAGNETIC
VAR 14° 45'W (1997) ANNUAL INCREASE 2

STONINGTON

Stonington Hbr.

Narragansett
Bay

Little

Noyes Shoal

S O U N D

L O N G   I S L A N D

WP 20045
N 41°-17.86
W 071°-53.32

WP 20005
N 41°-17.38
W 071°-54.32

WP 20015
N 41°-17.47
W 071°-54.96

WP 20085
N 41°-18.07
W 071°-56.00

WP 20110
N 41°-18.00
W 071°-58.38

WP 20975
N 41°-17.23
W 071°-56.96

WICOPESSET PASSAGE

LORDS PASSAGE

Cable Area G

East Harbor

MASON ISLAND

RAM SHOAL

Ram I.

Gates Island

41°18'

41°16'

71°58'

of Fishers Island is private, restricted by a guarded barrier crossing the main road south of Pirate's Cove Marine, but the west end of the island does have a "downtown" for you to stroll around in.

Circumnavigation of the island reveals beautiful beaches along the south shore and snug coves along the north. You can't miss the gorgeous estates that overlook the water, most notably the grand property on the island's east end.

Passing the island to the south, you'll see the remains of Fort Wright, which was built as a naval artillery post during World War I. The old, concrete gun emplacements look like manmade caves dotting the hills.

Drop a hook for fluke and flatfish around Wilderness Point and Isabella Beach. If you're confident enough in your mariner skills, The Race is one of the best bluefishing spots around. The heavy turbulence makes it easy for the vicious blues to catch weaker baitfish.

Hop aboard. © Maptech

RESTAURANTS & PROVISIONS: Your choices are limited on Fishers Island. Many pack a picnic or head to the deli in town. Otherwise, head downtown to the News Café (631-788-7183) for breakfasts filled with pastries and coffee, and weekend buffets. The Pequot Inn (631-788-7246) restaurant gets hoppin' some evenings during the summer.

"Downtown" you also have an ice cream parlor, and a grocery store that can help stock the galley. Pirate's Cove Marine has a ship's store to take care of any nautical needs. For more supplies you're going to have to plot a course for "the mainland," as they call it out here.

NAVIGATION & ANCHORAGES: Use ChartKit Region 3, pages 9, 34A, 34B, and 35; Maptech™ Waterproof Charts 1 and 17; and Maptech™ electronic and NOAA paper charts 13214 (1:20,000), 12372 (1:40,000), and 13205 (1:80,000). Use tide tables for New London. High tide at Silver Eel Pond is 16 minutes earlier; low tide is 4 minutes earlier. Multiply height of tide at New London by 0.9 for height of tide at Silver Eel Pond. Mean tidal range is 2.3 feet.

The channel into West Harbor on Fishers Island, beginning at Fl R 4s R "6" Hawks Nest Point, is 3.9nm from New London Ledge Light (Fl(3) W R 30s 58ft 14M HORN) and 2.8nm from Q G 22ft 8M "5" Morgan Point in Noank. The entrance to Lake Montauk on the tip of Long Island is 11.1nm from Race Rock (Fl R 10s 67ft 16M HORN) at Fishers Island's western shore.

Fishers Island is the plug on the east end of Long Island Sound. Tides entering and exiting Long Island Sound pass by the island's north and south shore, contending with the shallows and rocks and heading through The Race. The area offers both risk and beauty. If you don't take The Race seriously, you'll pay, but a safe trip through these waters reveals the spectacular shores of Fishers Island. Passing the island through Fishers Island Sound is challenging in its own right. On a nice summer day, the sound is packed with boats, especially sailing vessels, and because of its narrow passage, this area suffers its fair share of nasty chop.

CAUTION: Treat The Race with respect. Tidal currents and opposing winds create treacherous conditions in this area, as 25 billion gallons of water swirl through here with every tide. Currents routinely run 4 to 5 knots and sometimes reach 6. The chop will be even worse in a strong easterly or westerly wind. No matter how calm the conditions, the

water shoals so quickly at Valiant Rock that there will always be chop there, so proceed cautiously.

From the west, and heading for West Harbor, stay south of Fl R 5s 45ft 9M Bartlett Reef Light. You have a clear course until you approach South Dumpling. Here, you'll pass between Fl R 2.5s BELL R "2" 0.2nm north of North Hill and G C "3" off South Dumpling. Do not try to pass south of Fl R 2.5s BELL R "2." Continuing on, keep both R N "4" and Fl R 4s R "6" off Hawks Nest Point well west before entering the channel into the harbor.

Boats hailing from Block Island often choose Fishers Island Sound over the rougher waters of The Race. To enter or leave Fishers Island Sound at its eastern end, you must head through one of five passages: Wicopesset, Lords, Catumb, Sugar Reef, or Watch Hill. For detailed descriptions of these areas, see the chapter on Watch Hill.

From the east, be mindful of the current and buoys, especially G C "15," if attempting the Wicopesset Passage. Our tour guide told us of boats hitting pretty hard on Seal Rocks. Moving on, you'll come across East Harbor; it's a small cove with a good deal of foul ground, but a decent gunkhole for exploration by shallow-draft boat.

The entrance is marked, but you'll have to keep an eye out for the many lobster pots in this area. There are no public facilities or access points ashore. When anchoring, be sure to stay at least 200 yards offshore to avoid the rocks. You'll find this a quiet spot, surrounded by an elite—and very private— golf course.

Continuing west, keep an eye out for several obstructions. The Clumps—East, Middle, and West—are each well marked on the chart and are often visible from the water. Pulpit Rock, near West Clump, is difficult to see because it doesn't often break the

© Maptech

Looking east over Fishers Island, with Race Point in the foreground. © Maptech/James T. Abts

water's surface. The rock is marked to the west by G C "1" and should be given a wide berth.

You can pass safely between the Clumps and Fishers Island, but be sure to make your way between R N "2W" and G C "1W" off Brooks Point. From here, Chocomount Cove will be just to your south. You may anchor in this bight between Clay Point and Brooks Point, but it is exposed to the north. Chocomount Hill, southeast of the cove, rises 136 feet and makes for an excellent landmark as the highest point on Fishers Island.

Continuing toward West Harbor, you will want to round Clay Point by passing between R N "4" (off Pulpit Rock) and G C "5." Best to stay as close to the center of this passage as traffic will allow. From here, West Harbor opens just to the southwest. The entire area between Hawks Nest Point and Clay Point offers decent protection from the weather, except when the winds come from the north or the west. The bottom here is a composite of grass, gravel, and mud.

West Harbor is the best anchorage at Fishers Island. The entrance to the harbor is quite wide, surrounded to the east by large estates and to the west by the small village. The eastern channel, marked by private buoys, leads to the inner harbor and Pirate's Cove Marine. The western channel leads to Fishers Island Yacht Club, which has plenty of slips for transients. If you are planning to stay, you may want to call ahead to reserve a slip. Anchoring is allowed outside the mooring area north and east of Goose Island. Be mindful of Lewis Rock, marked by G C "7."

In favorable weather, you may want to lay over on the east side of Flat Hammock, north of West Harbor. This is a popular place to anchor and swim. Keep an ear to the weather channel in case something creeps up. Be sure not to cut between R N "2" and the islet or you'll run aground.

On the west end of Fishers Island, Silver Eel Cove is used by the ferry from New London. You may duck in here during bad weather, but it's particularly difficult to enter during a stiff westerly. The channel entrance is marked by a privately maintained light (Fl R 4s 14ft "2") and a series of pilings. Stay as near mid-channel as possible.

Shoreside & Emergency Services
Airport:
—Elizabeth Field (631-788-7005)
Coast Guard:
—New London (860-442-4471) or VHF 16
Ferry:
—to New London (631-788-7744)
Police, Fire, Ambulance: 911
Tow Service:
SEA TOW. —24-Hour Dispatch (800-4SEATOW)
—Eastern Connecticut (860-572-9090)
Tow BoatU.S.—24-Hour Dispatch (800-391-4869)
—Southeastern Marine Towing (860-536-3128)

Rising a majestic 67 feet above the turbulent water, the Race Rock "Castle" is a remarkable feat of engineering. Built in the 1870s, the light stands right on the reef. After a year of trying to raise a platform of boulders, engineers realized the rocks would never remain in place. Finally, stones from the reef itself were used, and concrete was then poured into this basin to form a secure base. The project took more than six years to complete and cost $278,716— an astronomical sum back in 1879.

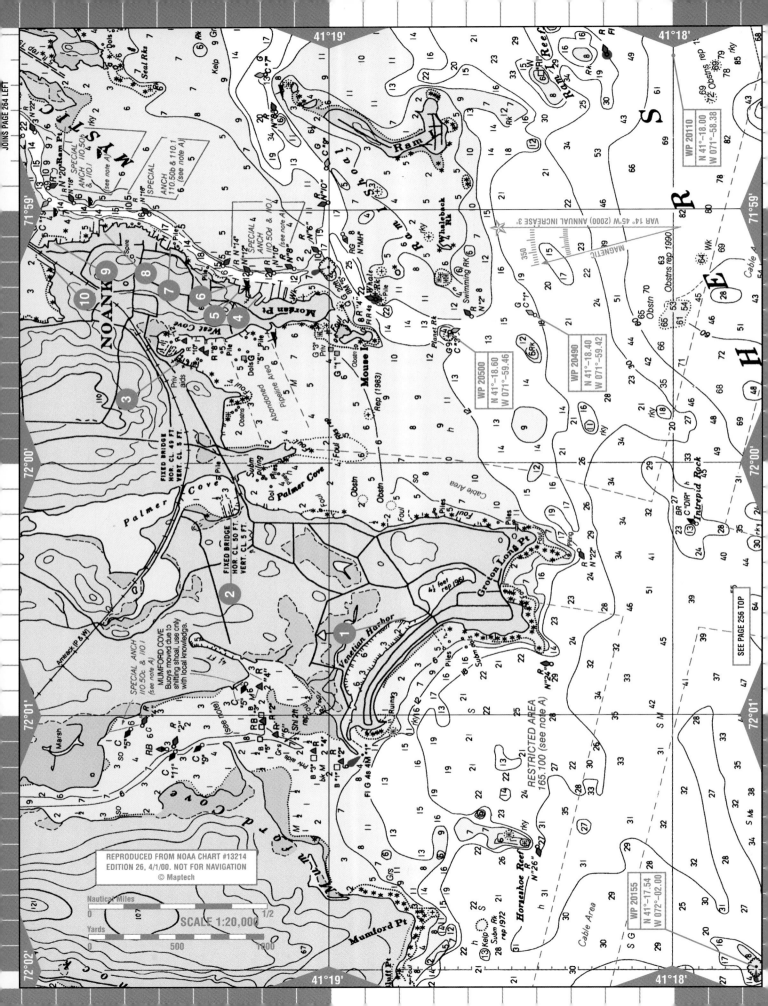

SCALE 1:20,000

Nautical Miles
0   1/2

Yards
0   500   1000

41°19'

41°18'

71°59'

72°00'

72°01'

72°02'

41°19'

41°18'

WP 20110
N 41°-18.00
W 071°-58.38

WP 20490
N 41°-18.40
W 071°-59.42

WP 20500
N 41°-18.60
W 071°-59.46

WP 20155
N 41°-17.54
W 072°-02.00

SEE PAGE 256 TOP

VAR 14° 45'W (2000) ANNUAL INCREASE 3'

RESTRICTED AREA
165.100 (see note A)

SPECIAL ANCH
110.50c & 110.1
(see note)

MUMFORD COVE
Buoys moved due to
shifting shoal, use only
with local knowledge.

FIXED BRIDGE
HOR. CL. 49 FT.
VERT. CL. 5 FT.

FIXED BRIDGE
HOR. CL. 50 FT.
VERT. CL. 5 FT.

NOANK

Venetian Harbor

Groton Long Pt

Palmer Cove

Mumford Pt

Morgan Pt

West Cove

Ram

Cable Area

Get to the Point

To illuminate the way into the Mystic River, the U.S. government established a lighthouse on Morgan Point in 1831. The 25-foot granite tower stood alongside a six-room house, where keeper Ezra Daboll lived with his wife, Eliza. Following Ezra's death in 1838, Eliza took over the keeping duties, and her daughter, the eldest of six children, eagerly lent a hand. The girl expressed her delight by singing in a loud voice as she performed her chores.

But young Miss Daboll's vocal volume could not make up for the fact that Morgan Point Light was too dim to properly serve its purpose. Its 10 lamps and reflectors were replaced with a sixth-order Fresnel lens in 1855. The new lens helped the lighthouse keep up with its brighter neighbors in New London and Stonington, but in 1868 a new lighthouse took over the post until 1919, when it was decommissioned and sold as a private residence.

The Noank Historical Society can show you the town's rich past. © Maptech

ACTIVITIES: Noank's activities revolve around the outdoors: gunkholing, fishing, swimming, and sometimes hiking. The town is centered around an old church on the green and is mostly residential, with streets that criss-cross up and around the hills. The recreation center has a small beach near the town landing at the foot of Main Street. You'll also find tennis and basketball courts as well as a playground. The Noank Historical Society (860-536-3021) is always ready to bring you up-to-date with the town's rich historical past. Call ahead to make an appointment.

There are two state parks in the Noank area. Haley Farm State Park, near the north end of Palmer Cove, offers good hiking trails, while the tidal pools at Bluff Point State Park on Mumford Point, a 750-acre coastal nature preserve, makes a fun diversion. You can pull up to the park in a dinghy from Mumford Cove, and you'll probably be undisturbed, as the road is two miles away.

Marine Facilities and Services

All Coast Guard Stations Monitor VHF Channel 16

marinalife.com — Convenient Online Boat Slip Reservations

#	Facility	Phone	Transient Berths / Working VHF	Seasonal / Moorings	Hookups 110V+	Max LOA	Approach / Dockside Depth	Fresh Water / Phone / Cable TV	Haul / Lift Capacity (★ tons)	Ramp / Dinghy Dock / Launch Service	Rail / Lift / Crane / Trailer Capacity (tons)	Repairs	Gas / Diesel Fuel	Fuel Brand	Marine / Groceries / Ice / Bait / LPG / CNG	Restrooms / Showers / Laundry / Pumpout	Public Phone / Restaurant / Snack Bar	Hotel / Pool / Tennis / Golf	Mastercard / VISA / Discover / AmEx
1	Groton Long Point Yacht Club*				Y		/4	*PRIVATE—MEMBERS ONLY*											
2	Palmer's Cove Marina	860-536-6207	9/72		Y	25	3/3	F		R	L10	DF	G		MI	RS		P	MV
3	Spicer's Noank Marina (B) p. 261	860-536-4978	68/68	24/50	Y	50	7/7	FP	★30	All	L20	All			MGIB	All		All	MVD
4	Atlantic Detroit Diesel-Allison p. 260	860-536-6726			Y						*FULL-SERVICE DETROIT DIESEL, VOLVO PENTA, PERKINS, EMD, MERCRUISER & TWN DSC*		GD						
4	NSY Noank Shipyard p. 262	860-536-9651	9/	1/12	Y	200	14/8	All		DL	LC35	PRGDWFE	GD	Hess	MGIC	All		PR	All
5	Maxwell Boat Yard*	860-536-9076		2/2	S	30	10/10	F	★20	RD	CT10					RS		P	MV
6	Abbott's Restaurant*	860-536-7719			Y			*DOCKAGE FOR PATRONS*									R	R	
7	Ford's Lobsters & Haring's Marine	860-536-2842	18/		Y	150	9/9	F	★30				GD		I				MV
8	Ram Island Yacht Club*	860-536-9014		3/2	S	40	6/6	F	★20	D						RS		P	
9	Noank Village Boatyard p. 263	860-536-1770	72/68	34/30	S	100	5/6	F	★▲50	DL	LCT35	All			I	All		P	MVD
10	Noank Marine Service	860-536-0221		10/15	Y	50	10/7		★	RD	C20					RS			

Information in these listings is provided by the facilities themselves. An asterisk (*) indicates that the facility did not respond to our most recent requests for information. (B) represents a BOAT/U.S. cooperating marina.

Looking north, directly over Morgan Point. © Maptech/James T. Abts

swimming because of the silt. Free jazz, blues, and rock concerts are held here throughout the summer (860-441-6777).

RESTAURANTS & PROVISIONS: Seafood is Noank's specialty, and there are plenty of places to get it. Those staying at Spicer's Noank Marina should try the adjacent Seahorse Restaurant (860-536-1670), offering seafood, beef, chicken, and various daily specials. Also nearby, The Fisherman (860-536-1717) boasts selections of duck, veal, and seafood.

Abbott's Restaurant (860-536-7719), on Morgan Point, is the place for outdoor munching on popular crustaceans. Abbott's will pack fresh lobsters for you as will Ford's Lobsters (860-536-2842), so you can steam dinner on board. At Noank Shipyard, try Costello's Clam Company (860-572-2779), featuring seafood and a raw bar.

If you've had enough fruits of the sea, stop in at Carson's Store (860-536-0059) on Main Street for ice cream to cleanse your palate. Head a few steps up Pearl Street and you'll find the Universal Food and Package Stores (860-536-3767) with groceries and other supplies (including good pizza), plus a post office.

Mumford, Palmer, and Beebe coves are great spots for exploration by dinghy, and each has a reputation for excellent birdwatching. The marshy Sixpenny Island is a popular spot with nesting seabirds. Palmer Cove sports a public park and beach with a snack stand. Esker Point Beach, run by the town of Groton, is good for sunbathing but not for

NAVIGATION & ANCHORAGES: Use ChartKit Region 3, pages 9, 34A, and 34B; Maptech™ Waterproof Charts 1 and 17; and Maptech™ electronic and NOAA paper charts 13214 (1:20,000), 12372SC (1:40,000), and 13205 (1:80,000). Use tide tables for New London. High tide at the Mystic River entrance is 22 minutes earlier; low tide is 8 minutes earlier. Multiply height of tide at New London by 0.9 for height of tide at the Mystic River entrance. Mean tidal range is 2.3 feet.

Morgan Point in Noank is 2.9nm from West Harbor on Fishers Island, and 4.5nm from New London Ledge Light. Stonington Breakwater is 4.6nm away.

Between New London and Mystic, you'll find several gunkholes and anchorages. Mumford Cove and Venetian Harbor, located between Mumford Point and Groton Long Point, are accessible to shallow-draft boats. To approach Mumford Cove, stay halfway between R N "26" marking Horseshoe Reef and R N "24." From here, you have a clear shot north to Fl G 4s 13ft 4M "1" at the entrance to Venetian Harbor. Venetian Harbor is a privately dredged cove hidden behind a bar; there isn't much room, but it is an interesting place to explore.

Continuing into Mumford Cove, keep Fl G "1" well to starboard, and proceed slowly, watching all the while for R "1" and R "2." Even dinghies will have to wait for higher tides to

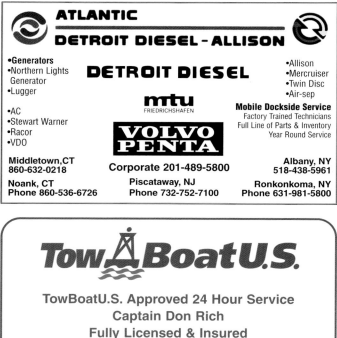

get through here, as there is only about 2 feet of water at low tide, and the tidal range is only about 2.3 feet.

Once you reach R "6," there is a narrow channel with 7 to 9 feet of water, but not much on either side. You can drop a hook wherever there's room. There's also a Special Anchorage area on the east shore inside G "5" and R "4," but this is difficult to reach. The narrow channel is privately maintained, and almost all of the shore, which belongs to Bluff Point State Park, remains undeveloped. The pebbly beaches here are seldom crowded with people, so you will see a fair amount of wildlife.

East of Groton Long Point, Palmer Cove is nice to explore by dinghy, but there are some shallow spots here at low tide. Palmer Cove Marina is a small-boat facility located just inside the bridge (vertical clearance: 5ft mhw) connecting Groton Long Point to Noank.

West Cove, just east of Palmer Cove and west of Morgan Point, is packed with moorings, particularly in the northeast corner, so mind the privately maintained markers in the area. The approach depth in West Cove is about 5 feet. On the west side of the cove, you'll find Spicer's Noank Marina with transient berths, deep-water moorings, and many amenities. Spicer's is well known for its marine store and repairs.

CAUTION: There's a 680-foot breakwater at the entrance to West Cove that does not appear on the NOAA chart.

From the west, the approach to Palmer and West coves is pretty straightforward. Pass south and east of R N "22" off Groton Long Point and turn to the northeast. To enter West Cove, head for privately maintained G "1" just west of Mouse Island. Coming from the east is also straightforward. Pass south of R N "2" at Swimming Rock and south and west of G C "3" marking Planet Rock, giving it a wide berth as you head toward West Cove. West of Morgan Point you may find room to anchor; if you're continuing to Spicer's, leave the breakwater to the west as you enter the channel.

Most facilities in Noank are on the east side of Morgan Point, just outside of the channel to Mystic, so if you're heading into Mystic, watch for boaters coming in and out of the Noank yards. Noank Shipyard, Atlantic Detroit Diesel, Noank Village Boatyard, and Noank Marine Services are among the facilities in the area.

The channel leading along the east side of Morgan Point to Mystic begins at Morgan Point Light (Q G 22ft 8M "5"), which is a privately owned lighthouse at the tip of the point.

From New London and points west, follow a course from Seaflower Reef (Fl 4s 28ft 7M) to G C "1" southwest of Ram Island. Pass south and east of G C "1" before turning north and passing between R N "2" Swimming Rock and G C "3" Planet Rock. Pass west and wide of Fl R 4s R "4" Whale Rock as you turn sharply east for Morgan Point Light (Q G 22ft 8M "5").

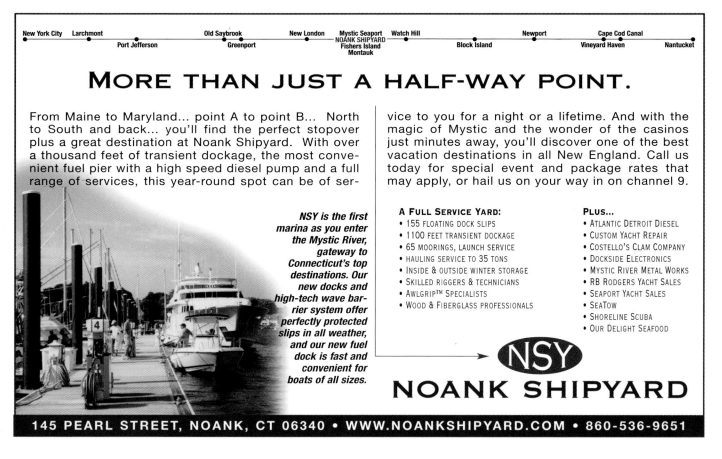

From West Harbor on Fishers Island, you will begin your approach by passing between R N "2" at Flat Hammock and G C "1" at Pulpit Rock. From Flat Hammock, head for G C "1" southwest of Ram Island and follow the main channel as previously indicated.

From East Harbor, a course of about 317°m from R N "2E" for 2.1nm will take you to G C "1" southwest of Ram Island. Make sure to pass well west of East Clump G C "19" and well east of Middle Clump G C "21."

The channel to Mystic can be intimidating, as it is long and twists through shoals and reefs. If you honor the buoys and stay toward the center of the channel, you should have no trouble.

As you head for the channel, be sure to pass south then east of Morgan Point Light. This short turn around the light can sometimes be difficult, as you may not be able to see R N "6" ahead until you're right on top of it—the riprap of the light makes this buoy difficult to pick out. While you may see local boaters cutting west of the light when heading south, you should avoid this side of the light in order to avoid a dangerous rock on the inside.

The first facility you'll see along Morgan Point is Noank Shipyard. As you follow the channel, which holds tight to the Noank shoreline, you'll pass numerous marine facilities. Noank Village Boatyard is the last facility in Noank before you head upriver into Mystic. For more detailed information about Mystic, see the following chapter.

From the east, you'll find that the channel running north of Ram Island is well marked; however, note the 6-foot spot at R N "8." There is a small anchorage on the east side of the island that offers some protection from southwest winds, but you may be tossed about by the wakes of other boats. The bottom is mostly grassy and should provide a decent anchor hold.

The primary anchoring area is between Noank and Mason Island. It is often crowded in the summer, but there should be enough water for you to set anchor with adequate scope. Stay as far east of the channel as possible in order to avoid the heaviest wakes from passing powerboats. Noank has recently joined the ranks of shoreside towns offering floating pump-out service; call VHF 9.

Shoreside & Emergency Services

Airport: Groton (860-445-8549)
Bus: SEAT (860-886-2631)
Coast Guard:
—New London (860-442-4471) or VHF 16
Police, Fire, Ambulance: 911
Taxi: Yellow Cab (860-536-8888)
Tow Service:
SEA TOW —24-Hour Dispatch (800-4SEATOW)
—Eastern Connecticut (860-572-9090)
Tow BoatU.S.—24-Hour Dispatch (800-391-4869)
—Southeastern Marine Towing—(860-536-3128)

The Charles W. Morgan

On July 21, 1841, the full-rigged whaling ship *Charles W. Morgan* was launched in New Bedford, Massachusetts. She was built at the height of the whaling industry, and during her 37 voyages she would catch and process more whales that any other vessel. In all, 54,483 barrels of oil and 152,934 pounds of whalebone, or baleen, were collected.

A typical journey would take the *Morgan* around Cape Horn and into the Pacific and Indian oceans. About 33 men worked tirelessly during the voyages, which would last anywhere from nine months to five years. The crew was an amalgam of races and nationalities, a true representation of the melting pot that was the United States.

The *Charles W. Morgan* sits on the grounds of Mystic Seaport. © Maptech

Marine Facilities and Services

All Coast Guard Stations Monitor VHF Channel 16

#	Facility	Phone	Monitors / Working VHF	Transient Berths / Seasonal / Moorings	Seasonal (S) / Year-round (Y)	Max LOA	Approach / Dockside Depth (ft at MLW)	Hookups: Fresh Water / Phone / Cable TV	110V★ 220V▲ 3Ph■ Max Amps	Ramp / Dinghy / Launch	Rail / Lift / Crane / Trailer (tons)	Repairs: Diesel / Wood / Fiberglass / Electronics	Repairs: Propellor / Sail / Rigging / Gas	Marine / Groceries / Ice / Bait / LPG / CNG	Gas / Diesel Fuel	Restrooms / Showers / Laundry / Pumpout	Fuel Brand	Public Phone / Restaurant / Snack Bar	Hotel / Pool / Tennis / Golf	Mastercard / VISA / Discover / AmEx
1	Ford's Lobsters & Harding's Marine	860-536-2842	18/		Y	150	9/9	F	★30					I	GD					MV
2	Noank Village Boatyard (p. 263)	860-536-1770	72/68	34/30	S	100	5/6	F	★▲50	DL	LCT35	All		I		All		P		MVD
3	Noank Marine Service	860-536-0221		10/15	Y	50	10/7		★	RD	C20					RS				
4	Mystic Shipyard LLC (B) (p. 271)	860-536-6588	9/68	30/	Y	200	15/15	F	★▲50	D	L35	All		I		All		P		MVD
5	Willow Point Marina*	860-536-9873			Y	PRIVATE DOCKAGE														
6	Fort Rachel Marine (p. 269)	860-536-6647	9/13	3/	Y	45	8/8	F	★50	D	L30	All		MI		RSP		P		MVA
7	John I. Carija & Son Boat Works*	860-536-9440			Y															
8	Bayside Diesel Service (p. 268)	860-536-2038		2/	Y		12/10	All	★▲50			All		M		RS				MVA
9	Mystic Downtown Marina (p. 273)	860-572-5942	8/	10/	Y	50	12/8	F	★30	L				I		RSL		P		MV
10	Seaport Marine, Inc. (p. 268)	860-536-9681		6/	Y	125	12/12	All	★▲100		RL100	All				RS		P		
11	Gwenmor Marina	860-536-0281	13/	4/	Y	48	6/6	All	▲50		L30			MI	GDWF	RS		P		MV

Facilities continued on next page...

Follow *My Mystic Belle* up the Mystic River. © Maptech

As the whaling era began to wind down in the early 20th century, the majestic *Charles W. Morgan* still managed to keep busy: it was featured in several Hollywood movies, including *Down to the Sea in Ships*, starring Clara Bow (whom we assume was a big star). But with the development and refinement of petroleum, the whaling industry would soon vanish.

Of the more than 2,200 Yankee whaling ships that plied the oceans, the *Charles W. Morgan* is the sole survivor. She now rests in Mystic, within eyeshot of some of the finest modern marine facilities you'll find along Long Island Sound. It is fitting that she rests here, because here is where you will find the confluence of the old and the new, where history shares every street corner with modern-day convenience.

ACTIVITIES: Downtown Mystic consists of waterside streets lined with shops, boutiques, galleries, and restaurants all packed into a small area just west of the bascule bridge. The town is not so big that you'll get lost, but the Chamber of Commerce (860-572-9578), on Cottrell Street, offers local maps at the railroad depot and Bank Square just in case.

Many people head farther upriver to Mystic Seaport (860-572-0711), clearly the town's greatest attraction. Calling itself "the Museum of America and the Sea," the Seaport captures the very essence of maritime New England. With more than 100 buildings on 17 acres (and growing), the Seaport preserves the history of wooden sailing ships in the atmosphere of a mid-19th century seaside town. Most of the century-old buildings have

	Marine Facilities and Services		DOCKAGE						SERVICES					SUPPLIES & AMENITIES									marinalife.com
			Monitors / Working VHF Channel	Number of Transient Berths	Seasonal / Year-round / Moorings	Approach / Dockside Depth in Feet at MLW	Maximum LOA	Hookups: Fresh Water / Phone / Cable TV	110v + 220v ▲ 3 Phase ■ Maximum Amps	Ramp / Dinghy Dock / Launch Service	Rail / Lift / Crane / Trailer: Capacity (tons)	Diesel / Wood / Fiberglass / Electronics	Repairs: Propellor / Sail / Rigging / Gas	Gas / Diesel Fuel	Marine / Groceries / Ice / Bait / LPG / CNG	Fuel Brand	Restrooms / Showers / Laundry / Pumpout	Public Phone / Restaurant / Snack Bar	Hotel / Pool / Tennis / Golf	Mastercard / VISA / Discover / AmEx	
12	BREWER YACHT YARDS **Brewer Yacht Yard at Mystic**	860-536-2293 Inside Back Cover	9/11		Y	120	15/10	FC	★▲50		LCT35	All	GD		MC	All	P	PS	All
13	Wilcox Marine Supply	860-536-4206 p. 268	18/		Y	MARINE SUPPLIES						R			M				MVD
14	Shaffer's Boat Livery	860-536-8713	68/	10/10	S	25	2/2	F		All			G	Mobil	IB	RS		PS	MV
14	Atlantic Merchants	860-572-7256	16/		Y						RF			M				
15	Brower's Cove Marina	860-536-8864			S	37	4/4	FP	★30	RD	RT20			I	RSP		P	
16	Masons Island Marina	860-536-2608 p. 273	6/2		Y	43	4.5/7	F	★30	D	LC25	PRGDWFE		MI	RS		P	All
17	MYSTIC RIVER MARINA	860-536-3123 p. 270	9/	30/	Y	150	15/6	All	★▲100	D	L35	PGDWF	GD	Tex	MI	All	P	PR	All
18	Mason Island Yacht Club*	860-536-9080			Y													
19	MYSTIC SEAPORT	860-572-5391 p. 267	9/68	40/	S	130	11/11	F	★50	D				I	RSL		All	MVA
20	Mystic Marina	860-536-4930	9/68	15/	Y	55	3/5	All	★▲50		L35	PGDWFE		M	All		PR	MV

All Coast Guard Stations Monitor VHF Channel 16

Information in these listings is provided by the facilities themselves. An asterisk (*) indicates that the facility did not respond to our most recent request for information. (B) represents a BOAT/U.S. cooperating marina.

been collected from New England ports and brought to Mystic for restoration and display. The Seaport also maintains one of the world's largest collections of wooden boats, ranging from skiffs to the aforementioned three-masted whaleship, *Charles W. Morgan*. In mid-July, expect to see even more wooden boats at the Antique & Classic Boat Rendezvous.

Visitors can make an appointment to visit Mystic Seaport's world-class maritime library, or stop in at the planetarium. Most exhibits are manned by guides who will show you how figureheads were carved, riggings maintained, and sails sewn. Completing the Seaport's commitment to education are programs in maritime history, marine biology, sailing, and boatbuilding.

While you're at the Seaport, stop in at the Mystic Seaport Museum Stores (860-572-5386) as they have one of the best nautical bookstores around. If you're looking for nautical art, both the Seaport Store and The Finer Line Gallery (860-536-8339), on the corner of Pearl and West Main streets, have excellent selections.

The Mystic Maritime Aquarium (860-572-5955), a short distance north of the Seaport, is one of the most-visited attractions in Connecticut. More than 3,500 specimens of marine life are displayed in 50 live exhibits, including whale and dolphin demonstrations. Whether you prefer beluga whales, seals, or penguins, you'll find your favorite sea creature here.

RESTAURANTS & PROVISIONS: Mystic takes care of its mariners with a large selection of restaurants. On the west side of the river, you'll find sizzling Mexican dishes at Margaritas (860-536-4589) on Water Street, just south of Route 1. Closer to the marinas, the Capt. Daniel Packer Inne (860-536-3555) serves fine food in a rustic atmosphere, and its tavern downstairs is an especially popular spot. Two blocks away in the opposite direction sits Mystic Pizza (860-536-3700), which inspired the movie of the same name, as well as many delis and pubs.

On the east side of the river you'll find Anthony J's Ristorante (860-536-0448), an Italian bistro serving very good, medium-priced fare. On the corner of Cottrell and East Main streets, look for Bravo Bravo (860-536-3228), offering creative Italian dishes in a casual atmosphere. There's often a line, and it can be a bit pricey, but it's worth it. If you like waterfront dining, S & P Oyster House (860-536-2674) near the bridge has sumptuous seafood choices. At the north end of the Seaport, the Seamen's Inne (860-536-9649) features lunch and dinner in an elegant, colonial atmosphere with an excellent, but costly, menu. Or if you're just looking for a place to grab a hearty breakfast, try Kitchen Little (860-536-2122). They have terrific gourmet specials and homemade breads.

On Route 1, near the Brewer Yacht Yard, the Flood Tide Inn (860-536-8140) has a continental menu, or across the Pequotsepos Brook is Angie's Pizza House (860-536-7300). If you venture out to the Aquarium or Old Mystic Village, you'll have several dining options. The Mooring (860-572-0731) at the Hilton features American nouvelle cuisine, or try The Steak Loft (860-536-2661) for great surf 'n' turf at reasonable prices.

Provisioning in Mystic is fairly easy. West Marine is conveniently located across the street from Mystic Seaport. Or try Wilcox Marine Supply, located on Old Saybrook Road.

NAVIGATION & ANCHORAGES: Use ChartKit Region 3, pages 9, 34A, 34B, and 35; Maptech™ Waterproof Chart 17; and Maptech™ electronic and NOAA paper charts 13214 (1:20,000), 12372 (1:40,000), and 13205 (1:80,000). Use tide tables for New London. High tide at the Mystic River entrance is 22 minutes earlier; low tide is 8 minutes earli-

er. Multiply height of tide at New London by 0.9 for height of tide at the Mystic River entrance. Mean tidal range is 2.3 feet.

The trip up the Mystic River, if you follow it as far as possible, will take at least an hour. There is a no-wake speed limit for most of the trip, and if you get caught waiting for the bridge, your patience will surely be tried. There are many marinas along the river, but you may want to look for space by the mouth and take a taxi from there to save time (although the trip upriver is lovely).

The beginning of the channel up to Mystic, at Morgan Point in Noank, is 2.9nm from the entrance to West Harbor on Fishers Island, and 4.5nm from New London Ledge Light. The breakwater at Stonington Harbor is 4.6nm from Morgan Point, while Murphy Point, at the entrance to the Mystic River, is 2.2nm away.

When speaking of Mystic, you must first define your terms. What's charted as "Mystic Harbor" is known locally as "out there where all the boats are moored" and actually lies between Noank and Masons Island. Most people think of Mystic as the area north of Masons Island, around the bridges, and up to Mystic Seaport.

The channel up to either of these harbors begins at Morgan Point Light (Q G 22ft 8M "5"). Most of the Noank facilities are on the east side of Morgan Point, right off the channel to Mystic, so keep an eye out for boaters coming out of the Noank yards. Entering the channel for the first time can be a daunting experience. The long passage twists and turns through many shoals and reefs, but it proves simple enough if you honor the buoys and stay near the center of the channel.

For detailed information on the approaches to Mystic Harbor from the south or west, see the previous chapter.

CAUTION: Be sure to use up-to-date charts. The latest NOAA edition for this area includes many changes.

From East Harbor on Fishers Island, a course of about 317°m from R N "2E" for 2.1nm will take you to the main channel entrance buoy G C "1" southwest of Ram Island Shoal. Make sure to pass well west of East Clump G C "19" and well east of Middle Clump G C "21."

CAUTION: Do not attempt to cut through the Special Anchorage between Noank and Masons Island. The number of moorings in this area has steadily increased. There are many obstructions, and the eel grass on the bottom may give false readings on a depth sounder.

From the west, follow a course from Seaflower Reef (Fl 4s 28ft 7M) to G C "1" southwest of Ram Island Shoal. Pass south and east of G C "1" before turning north and passing between G C "3" Planet Rock and R N "2" Swimming Rock. Pass west and wide of Fl R 4s R "4" Whale Rock as you turn sharply east of Morgan Point Light (Q G 22ft 8M "5"). Be sure to pass south then east of the light. It's a short turn

around the light, but you won't be able to see R N "6" until it's right in front of you, as it will be blocked by the rip-rap of the light. You may see boaters cutting west of the light on their way south—don't try this, because there is a dangerous rock in the area, and local knowledge is required.

From Stonington and other points east, you'll begin your trip at Fl G 4s 31ft 5M "5" on the breakwater off Wamphassuc Point. Keep south of, but pass near to, R N "2" at Red Reef to avoid the unmarked White Rock, named for the sea gulls that visit here so frequently. Leave R N "4" and R N "6" at Cormorant Reef to the north and head for G C "7" at the north end of Ram Island. Beware of Enders Island and Mason Point to the north and Ellis Reef to the south, which is marked by W "ER" but still catches a number of boats each year. From Ram Island, you can either follow the channel over to Morgan Point and then up to Mystic, or head for the anchorages on the west side of Masons Island. The channel north of Ram Island is well marked. However, take note of the 6-foot spot at R N "8."

From Watch Hill, Wicopesset, or any of the other eastern passages into Fishers Island Sound, stay south of Fl 6s 55ft 9M BELL at Latimer Reef. Once past Latimer Reef, pass south of Fl R 4s BELL R "20" at Ram Island Reef before heading to G C "1" and the approach to the main channel.

Along with its many marinas, Mystic also lays claim to a number of anchorages. There is a nice, quiet spot on the east side of Ram Island, protected from prevailing southwest winds. The island is low in the middle, so this area gets

You'll find the live version of this bronze replica at Mystic Aquarium.
© Maptech

The Mystic River Highway Bridge opens for an incoming sailboat.
© Maptech

eye on the line. Anglers will find many blues and weakfish in this area, as the current is quite strong.

The east side of Masons Island also has some nice anchorages, particularly between Masons Point and the monastery on Enders Island. This area is somewhat exposed to the weather, particularly that from the south, but it offers a nice break from the hectic main anchorage on the west side of the island. Please note that this is a shellfishing/no discharge area.

As for Dodges Island, you may want to have a picnic here, but don't take your boat in close to shore. There's deep water all around, but it's dotted with rocks, so stay at least 200 yards offshore and take a dinghy to the beach.

The primary anchorage is located between Noank and Masons Island. There are usually many boats here, and a number of permanent moorings, so finding a spot may be difficult, especially on a busy weekend. Due to heavy traffic in the channel, you should drop your hook as far east as possible to get away from the wakes. The closer you are to shore, the better view you'll have of the wildlife. We suggest you drop a traditional, old-fashioned anchor to the grassy bottom here, though a plow will serve you well. There is also an anchorage on the north side of Masons Island, north of R N "30," But the water in this area is too shallow for most boats at low tide.

CAUTION: You may see boats anchored south of Sixpenny Island, but you should be cautious about using this area in anything other than a shallow-draft boat. The harbormaster warns us that large boats often go aground here.

enough breeze to cool things off but not enough to rock the boat. The island has a house, a barn, and a lot of sheep—from which the name may have come—and is right in the middle of a high traffic area, so you can get a good rocking from the wakes of passing powerboats. The weedy grass bottom will give a decent hold for your hook, but keep an

The 3.2nm course upriver to the Mystic Downtown Marina and Mystic Seaport runs approximately north by northeast. The deeper water is usually on the Noank side. Don't cut too close to the buoys, as the channel tends to silt up on the edges, particularly around Sixpenny Island where the bottom seems to grab someone every weekend.

CAUTION: Proceed with caution in the area between G C "21" and G C "23." It's very shallow just outside of the channel.

Looking north over the Mystic River.
© Maptech/James T. Abts

The tidal range here is 2.3 feet, so don't expect much help if you stick your keel in the mud. While there are many boats in the area, you'll find surprisingly little dock space for transients. Our best advice is to make reservations well in advance. If you haven't made reservations, call the marinas before you head upriver. Most of the marinas have very good facilities, but it's a long ride back down if you get there and find out there's no space.

Mystic Harbor

At work at Mystic Seaport. © Maptech

About a half-mile north of Masons Island, you'll come to the Amtrak railroad bridge at Fort Rachel. The fort has long since disappeared, and the old rotting barges that once choked this area are going the same way. The railroad swing bridge is usually open to river traffic but closes well in advance of approaching trains. Contact the bridgetender at 860-444-4908 or on VHF 13, or let him know of your presence with one long and one short blast of the horn.

Just north of the railroad bridge you'll find several marine facilities, including Fort Rachel Marine Service and Bayside Diesel Service on the west shore, and Seaport Marine on the east.

On the east side of the Mystic Harbor, the first facility you'll see is Mystic River Marina. Once north of Pine Point, you'll be able to access Masons Island Marina as well as several other facilities. Over on the west shore, at Willow's Point, is Mystic Shipyard. To the east is Brewer Yacht Yard at Mystic.

North of these facilities is the bascule bridge in downtown Mystic. In summer, this bascule bridge opens at 15 minutes past every hour from 7:15 a.m. to 7:15 p.m.; it should open on demand at other times in season. (Note: on weekdays, there is no 12:15 opening in order to facilitate lunchtime street traffic.) From November 1 to April

Looking north up the Mystic River. Mystic River Marina sits on Mason Island in the foreground, with Mystic Shipyard directly across the River. Brewer Yacht Yard at Mystic is in the distance. © Maptech/James T. Abts

30, the bridge is manned between 4 a.m. and 8 p.m., and the tender will require 8 hours' advance notice to open, except for emergencies. There's often a lot of traffic on the bridge, so call in advance (860-536-7070 or on VHF 13) to tell them when you'll need the bridge to be opened. After hours, the police will arrange for an opening (860-599-4411). Remember that the boat moving with the tide has the right-of-way under the bridge.

Since there are two Mystic River bridgetenders within a very short distance of each other, it is important to identify which bridge you want when calling on VHF 13. Ask for either the Mystic River Bascule Bridge or the Mystic River Railroad Bridge. Calls to the Mystic River bridge are largely ignored or may prompt an annoyed reply of: "Which Mystic River bridge?" When the bascule bridge is closed, the channel can become crowded. Some boats raft up, others motor in place, and still others circle around, waiting.

Above the bascule bridge, Mystic Seaport beckons. You can stay right at the Mystic Seaport docks, but this is a popular spot so it's a good idea to make reservations, even several months in advance. Be careful when approaching the docks here—it's especially embarrassing to crash in front of a crowd of camera-carrying tourists. The docking fee includes free entrance to the Museum, and you can even walk around at night, when the paths are empty.

The east side of the river is well-dredged, but the other side is shallow, so don't wander from the channel. Showers and washing machines are available at the New York Yacht Club Station 10 Annex and the Preservation Shipyard.

Although the charts end just above the Interstate-95 bridges, shallow-draft vessels with less than 25 feet clearance can pass under the bridges and continue up the river to a secluded boatyard in the village of Old Mystic. The channel is poorly marked, however, and until you've made it once, the experience can be nerve-wracking. You may wonder along the way if someone hasn't played a nasty joke, but keep going—the quiet is worth the journey.

Shoreside & Emergency Services
Airport:
—Groton (860-445-8549)
Bus:
—SEAT (860-886-2631)
Coast Guard:
—New London (860-442-4471) or VHF 16
Police, Fire, Ambulance: 911
Taxi:
—Yellow Cab (860-536-8888)
Tow Service:
SEA TOW —24-Hour Dispatch (800-4SEATOW)
—Eastern Connecticut (860-572-9090)
Tow BoatU.S. —24-Hour Dispatch (800-391-4869)
—Southeastern Marine Towing (860-536-3128)

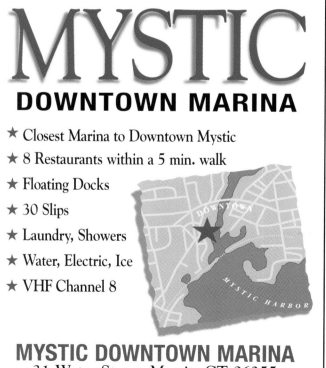

SCALE 1:20,000

Cap'n Nat

Stonington's Nathaniel Palmer, born in 1799, was one of the most daring, respected, and admired sailors of his day. No cargo was too hot for him to handle, no land too distant to explore, and no project too daunting to undertake. As a teenager, "Captain Nat" smuggled goods through the British fleet during the War of 1812. By the time he was 21, he commanded a sealing ship, making seven voyages to the islands at the southern tip of South America. It was during one of these trips that he discovered the Antarctic archipelago that now bears his name—Palmer Land. He ran guns and troops to Simon Bolivar and carried cotton north from New Orleans, and while still in his 30s, he helped design the flat-bottomed transatlantic packet.

Captain Nat's greatest impact on American ship design came when he whittled out the model of the celebrated *Houqua*. Launched in 1844, she was the prototype of the true clipper ship, 143 feet long with only a 32-foot beam. The *Houqua* set a record of 95 days for the run from New York to China. Palmer commanded and supervised a fleet of clippers for the shipping firm of A.A. Low & Brothers. Never a bully, he believed in giving his crew the best of salt beef and pork. His most violent form of anger, in an age of irascible and inhumane captains, was to throw his white beaver hat on the deck and stomp on it. True to form, he remained peaceful in retirement; he hunted on Long Island, raced, bought, and sold yachts, and was a founder of the New York Yacht Club.

ACTIVITIES: Stonington Village is filled with interesting architecture, ranging from colonial Federal-style mansions to Victorian gingerbread homes to contemporary designs. A walk down Water Street from the ornate library in Wadawanuck Park and past Cannon Square to the Old Lighthouse Museum on the point is a must. The community has a long and impressive list of resident artists and writers, many of whom have their work on display in the local galleries. Just about everything from marine supplies and groceries to fine antique shops and restaurants can be found in town, so you'll be rewarded if you take a stroll.

Stonington continues to be intimately connected to the sea and boasts the largest commercial fishing fleet in Connecticut. Many of the fishermen are descendants of Portuguese seafarers who came to Stonington from the

Marine Facilities and Services

#	Facility	Phone	Monitors / Working VHF Channel	Number of Transient Berths / Moorings	Seasonal / Year-round	Maximum LOA	Approach / Dockside Depth in Feet at MLW	Hookups: Fresh Water / Phone / Cable TV	110V★ 220V▲ 3 Phase■ Max Amps	Ramp / Dinghy Dock / Launch Service	Rail / Lift / Crane / Trailer: Capacity (tons)	Repairs: Propellor / Sail / Rigging / Gas / Diesel / Wood / Fiberglass / Electronics	Gas / Diesel Fuel	Fuel Brand	Marine / Groceries / Ice / Bait / LPG / CNG	Restrooms / Showers / Laundry / Pumpout	Public Phone / Restaurant / Snack Bar	Hotel / Pool / Tennis / Golf	Mastercard / VISA / Discover / AmEx
1	Cardinal Cove Marina	860-535-0060	9/16	10/5	S	22	2.5/2.5	F	★30	RD	T		G	Mob	MIB	R		P	
2	Skipper's Dock*	860-535-2000			S	70	10/10			*DOCKAGE FOR PATRONS*									
3	**DODSON BOATYARD** (p. 277)	860-535-1507	9/78	40/118	Y	105	7/7	F	★50	DL	L35	RGDWFE	GD		MGIC	All	All		MVA
4	Wadawanuck Yacht Club*	860-535-0118			S	60	12/6			RD	T	*PRIVATE—RECIPROCAL PRIVELIGES*							
5	Don's Dock	860-535-0077			Y	22	10/5			RD	T		G	Tex	MIB	R			S
6	King Cove Marina	860-599-5864	9/	8/	S	25	5/5	F		R		PDEF			MGIB	RS		P	All
7	Coveside Marina	860-535-2276		5/1	S	25	2/2	F		R	L4	PG	G		MIB	RS		P	MV
8	Whewell's Marina	860-599-4322		2/	Y	24	2/2	F		R	L	All			MI	RS		P	

All Coast Guard Stations Monitor VHF Channel 16

Information in these listings is provided by the facilities themselves. An asterisk (*) indicates that the facility did not respond to our most recent requests for information. (B) represents a BOAT/U.S. cooperating marina.

Looking northwest over Stonington Point and Harbor. © Maptech/James T. Abts

Cape Verde Islands and the Azores aboard whaling and sealing ships. At the fishing pier on the west side of the peninsula, you'll see their big commercial boats.

One of the most colorful events in town is the annual Blessing of the Fleet by the bishop of Norwich. Sponsored by the Southern New England Fishermen's and Lobstermen's Association (860-535-3150), the event includes a parade, concerts, the formal blessing ceremony, and food—lots and lots of it. It's usually held the last weekend in July and attracts more and more people every year.

The Old Lighthouse Museum (860-535-1440) at the foot of Water Street is well worth a visit. It has a fine collection of marine art and rotating exhibits of such wide-ranging subjects as kitchen gadgets and ice-harvesting machinery. You'll also enjoy the view from the top. The grand Stonington home at 40 Palmer Street was built by Nathaniel Palmer with the help of his brother, Alexander. Now owned by the Stonington Historical Society, the house is open to the public.

Just down the hill from the museum on Stonington Point you can beach yourself on DuBois Beach, operated by the Stonington Community Center (860-535-2476) and open to the public. The Community Center has four public tennis courts in town, and sponsors an annual fair, complete with hayrides, auctions, and a magic show, on the first weekend in August at the Village Green.

For those of you who want to sail even when you are in port, join the dinghy races held every Wednesday night by the Stonington Dinghy Club and open to all comers.

If you've brought a bicycle, take a ride to the Denison Pequotsepos Nature Center (860-536-1216), to explore trails, a museum, and a gift shop. For anglers and gunkhole explorers, Don's Dock, just north of the railroad bridge, sells bait and tackle and has small skiffs for rent. Across from Don's, you'll see the magnificent Nathaniel Palmer House (860-535-8445), purchased by the Stonington Historical Society (860-535-1131) in 1994 and now open to the public.

RESTAURANTS & PROVISIONS: Rest assured, you'll never have to travel far to get a bite to eat in Stonington. The Skipper's Dock (860-535-0111) has a large pier for their patrons. It's a real party scene on Saturday afternoons in the summer when the racing yachts tie up. Fresh lobsters are also available right on the pier. There are no electrical or water hookups at Skipper's Dock, so an overnight stay is quite inexpensive.

At Dodson Boat Yard swing over to the Boom (860-535-2588), replete with a full bar and bar menu for those who prefer a light meal, and more sophisticated cuisine for a sit-down meal. Farther down Water Street, Noah's (860-535-3925) serves lunch and dinner in a home-style atmosphere. Head to the Water Street Café & Market (860-535-2122/0797) for light provisions or a dinner menu featuring fresh seafood, steaks, etc. (reservations recommended). The market carries gourmet grocery items including breads and other baked creations. Farther out of town on North Main Street, One South Café (860-535-0418) has sandwiches as well as seafood and pasta dishes.

NAVIGATION & ANCHORAGES: Use ChartKit Region 3, pages 9, 34A, and 35; Maptech™ Waterproof Charts 1 and 17; and Maptech™ electronic and NOAA paper charts 13214 (1:20,000), 12372 (1:40,000), and 13205 (1:80,000). Use tide tables for New London. High tide at Stonington is 32 minutes earlier; low tide is 41 minutes earlier. Multiply height of tide at New London by 1.1 for height of tide at Stonington. Mean tidal range is 2.7 feet.

The tower leads the way to Stonington's Old Lighthouse Museum. © Maptech

Stonington Point is 2.4nm from Watch Hill Point, 3.8nm from Morgan Point in Noank, and 5.6nm from West Harbor on Fishers Island.

Stonington is as picturesque from the water as from land. The shore appears as a cluster of pretty homes packed closely, with masts spiking the foreground As you approach from Fishers Island Sound, the docks are a welcome reprieve from heavy weather. Two of the largest docks offer direct access to restaurants, and services are steps away.

From Mystic, the most direct route to Stonington is by way of the north side of Ram Island, where you'll pass between white daybeacon "ER" on Ellis Reef and R N "4" on Cormorant Reef. Farther east, pass south of, but near to, R N "2" at Red Reef to avoid White Rock.

From R N "2" at Red Reef, head east for the light on the breakwater off Wamphassuc Point (Fl G 4s 31ft 5M "5"). The breakwater creates something of a blind corner, so give it a wide berth and watch for heavy crossing traffic.

From farther west, you will want to stay south of Ram Island Reef, marked by Fl R 4s BELL R "20" and Eel Grass Ground R N "16." Pass north of Fl 6s 55ft 9M BELL at Latimer Reef Light. From Latimer Reef you will have clear passage through the breakwaters. Deep-draft sailboats should keep clear of Noyes Rock and Noyes Shoal to the southwest of the breakwater entrance.

From the east, as from Little Narragansett Bay, follow the channel buoys outbound to Fl R 4s R "2" off Stonington Point. From here, round south of RG N "SP" before turning north-northwest for Stonington Harbor. The channel is very narrow and congested on weekends.

As you can see on the chart, Sandy Point has migrated north and east toward Stonington. There is deep water off the point, but again the channel is narrow and crowded. When connected to Napatree Point, Sandy Point was part of Rhode Island, but since it has moved into Connecticut waters, it's now owned by the Mashantucket Land Trust. The island is a popular swimming, sunbathing, and picnicking spot, but

you'll need a Community Center pass (860-535-2476) to use the beach. Regular patrols enforce the no-camping rule.

Between Fishers Island and Watch Hill Point are the five eastern passages into Fishers Island Sound: Wicopesset, Lords, Catumb, Sugar Reef, and Watch Hill. Watch Hill is generally considered the easiest, and the best marked, and is surely the most used. Wicopesset Passage may be the second-most popular as its rocks are easy to see. (Refer to the Watch Hill chapter for more information).

Many boats cut inside Fl R 4s BELL R "6" at Napatree Point Ledge, but we suggest you avoid this area, there are many rocks near Napatree Point. Stay south of the buoy, then pass south of R N "2," south of Middle Ground, before turning north through the breakwaters. With local knowledge, it is possible to enter the harbor by going to the east of Middle Ground, but it is not recommended. The northeast end of the east breakwater is unmarked and disappears into Bartlett Reef (not to be confused with the reef of the same name near Niantic).

While Middle Ground isn't a great place for sailors to play, it is well known for the huge flatfish and summertime blues, and a favorite spot for diving for lobsters at night.

Stonington's finest anchorage is just inside the west breakwater. Turn to the west after passing Fl G 4s 31ft 5M "5" and snuggle up to the rocks (remember your swing room). Dodson Boat Yard maintains several moorings here and operates launch service throughout the entire harbor. The launch can take you to the waterfront restaurants, for a small round-trip charge (it's free with a mooring rental). If you'd prefer to be dockside, inquire at Dodson or one of the waterfront restaurants about space.

Just north of the mooring area inside the west breakwater is a Special Anchorage area that's likely to be crowded. North of this anchorage, moorings start again and stretch all the way to the northern part of the harbor at the railroad bridge. There are two more Special Anchorage areas just off the docks in Stonington.

If you want to drop your own hook, a traditional, old-fashioned achor or plow anchor will hold best in the grassy bottom. Although the breakwaters add considerably to the protection offered in the harbor, big Atlantic swells still roll in when the wind is out of the south, making parts of the anchorage restless and uncomfortable.

Shoreside & Emergency Services
Airport: Groton (860-445-8549)
Bus: SEAT (860-886-2631)
Coast Guard: New London (860-442-4471) or VHF 16
Police, Fire, Ambulance: 911
Taxi: Yellow Cab Co. (860-536-8888)
Tow Service:
SEA TOW. —24-Hour Dispatch (800-4SEATOW)
—Eastern Conn. (860-572-9090)
Tow BoatU.S.—24-Hour Dispatch (800-391-4869)
—Southeastern Marine Towing (860-536-3128)

Looking southwest over Sandy Point (left) and Stonington. © Maptech/James T. Abts

What's New

Maptech Makes it Simple—Results in Lower Prices

Digital ChartKit 2001

Includes:

- ✦ Official NOAA Digital Charts
- ✦ Selected Navigation & Aerial Photos
- ✦ Coastal Topographic Maps
- ✦ Marine Facilities Locators
- ✦ Tides & Currents
- ✦ USCG Coast Pilot
- ✦ Light List
- ✦ Chart Navigator Software – Making GPS Better

Digital ChartKit 2001 integrates cartography and data from Maptech's extensive resources. It includes all the navigation and aerial photos in Photo Regions CDs, which are now discontinued.

It all comes down to this: combining NOAA charts, photos, coastal topos, data overlays, with great software saves you money. All you need now is in one-box and it's under $200. That's a savings of over $300 if products were purchased individually. There's nothing like it!

Offshore Navigator

- ✦ With the creation of Digital ChartKit 2001, Maptech has simplified its marine chart navigation software. There are two choices: Chart Navigator for at-home planning, which comes with Digital ChartKit, or Offshore Navigator (Cruising Navigator is discounted).
- ✦ Offshore Navigator gives you two major features that are not available in Chart Navigator—real-time GPS tracking and autopilot. Offshore Navigator works seamlessly with Digital ChartKit 2001. Upgrading is simple and straightforward.
- ✦ Save—it's only $199.95 (formerly $299).

Contour Professional 2001

- ✦ See the ocean from the fish's point of view.
- ✦ See what's ahead and what's below for better situational awareness and safer navigation.
- ✦ The new version of Contour Professional 2001 combine's software and 3-D grid charts along with the vector Obstacle Database. You save over $500 from the earlier versions (Contour Planner and Contour Plotter are now discontinued).
- ✦ Also works with Offshore Navigator—see your position on official NOAA charts and 3-D charts side by side. Plot your course in one window and see underwater views in the other. Area coverage is the same as Digital ChartKit regions. Contour Professional is $499.95.

Maptech, Inc., 1 Riverside Drive, Andover, MA 01810-1122
Toll free 1-888-839-5551 • (978) 933-3000 • Fax (978) 933-3030 • www.maptech.com

MAPTECH®

Rhode Island

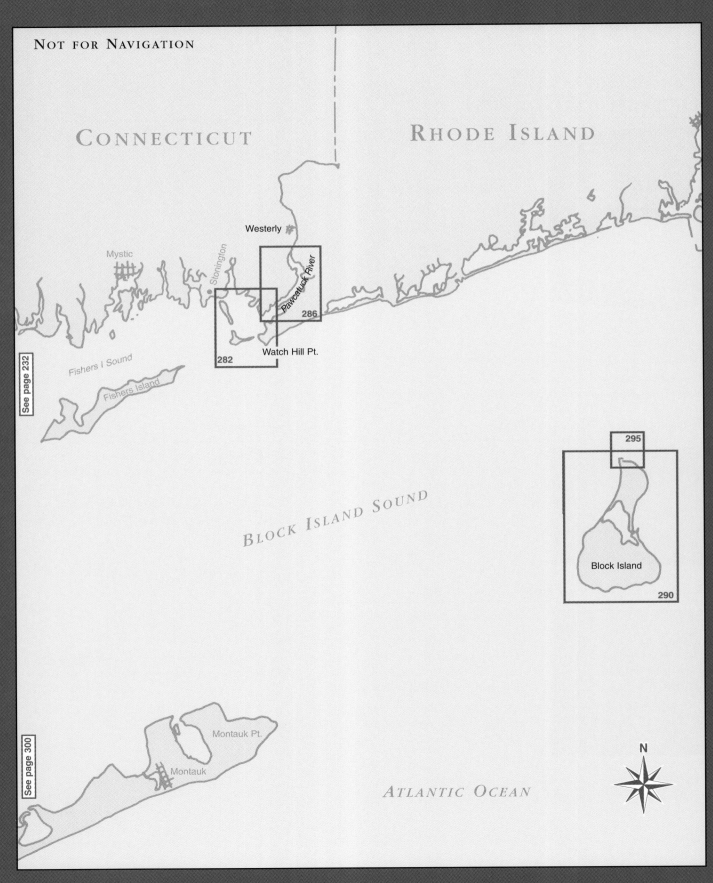

NOT FOR NAVIGATION

CONNECTICUT

RHODE ISLAND

Mystic

Westerly

Stonington

Pawcatuck River

286

Watch Hill Pt.

282

See page 232

Fishers I Sound

Fishers Island

BLOCK ISLAND SOUND

295

Block Island

290

Montauk Pt.

See page 300

Montauk

ATLANTIC OCEAN

N

Welcome to Little Rhody, America's smallest state and also the smallest region in this book. But while it may be small in square mileage, it's big for boating, with scores of natural harbors worth a visit.

Of the three Rhode Island destinations detailed in this book, Watch Hill is the quietest, providing a nice refuge. Like many New England beachfront towns, it rolls up the sidewalks offseason, but when the season's in, you'll find dining options, places to shop, and people to see.

The **Pawcatuck River** is also a quiet area; however, there are plenty of marine facilities to be found, whether you're buying fuel, taking a vacation, or looking for a place to stay while getting repairs made. **Westerly** offers restaurants, food

Heading out into Block Island Sound. © Maptech

stores, and a nice atmosphere for outdoor activities, like swimming in the ocean surf.

Block Island, by nature, stands apart from the rest. It also has a different personality. This island is packed with tourist appeal, and it's a beehive of activity in–season, luring boaters to fill its every slip. A historic atmosphere, complete with Victorian homes, an active night scene, plenty of activities and festivities, and a variety of dining establishments all contribute to the draw of Block Island.

Only Rhode Island's western harbors, including Block Island, are contained within this Long Island Sound book. For details on harbors along Buzzards Bay, refer to *Embassy Guides: Rhode Island, Massachusetts & New Hampshire.*

Navigating Rhode Island

There is one route to reach the marine facilities around Watch Hill and the Pawcatuck River, and that is via the channel that travels around the north end of Sandy Point. The approach to Little Narragansett Bay, including the Pawcatuck River and Watch Hill Cove, begins at Fl R 4s R "2" off Academy Rock at Stonington Point. Academy Rock is 3.2nm from G C "7" between Ram and Mason islands, and 2.1nm from G C "1" off East Point on Fishers Island. From Academy Rock, it's another 2.5nm to the Pawcatuck River and the approach to Watch Hill Cove. When planning a trip to Little Narragansett Bay, take into account the heavy fog that frequently rolls in from Block Island Sound. Late June and early July experience the worst fogs, which generally show up late in the afternoon and clear by 10 the next

morning. *Refer to the Watch Hill Point & Napatree Beach chapter, and the Pawcatuck River to Westerly chapter for more information.*

An exit from Fishers Island Sound requires a trip between Fishers Island and Napatree Point, an area riddled with rocks. Buoys are everywhere and most are unlit, so we don't recommend that you travel through here at night. Whichever passage you choose, be extremely cautious. Stong currents, heavy seas, and hard bottom make a grounding in this area particularly dangerous. There are five channels to choose from: (from west to east) the Wicopesset Passage, Lords Passage, Catumb Passage, Sugar Reef Passage, and Watch Hill Passage. Before attempting to head through, locate exactly where you are and what buoys you are looking at. It can be confusing, and you don't want to make a mistake through here.

Once through this area, it's a straight shot to Block Island. From Fl R 6s BELL R "2," just off Watch Hill Point in Watch Hill Passage, bear 131°m for 13.5nm to reach the entrance to New Harbor (Great Salt Pond), on Block Island. If you prefer to head to Old Harbor, bear 116∞m and round Fl G 4s BELL G "1BI" to the north. From here, bear 161°m to G C "5" WHIS and then 220°m into the harbor. Refer to the Watch Hill Point & Napatree Beach chapter.

Plum Gut, between Long Island's Orient Point and Plum Island is 27.5nm from Great Salt Pond on a bearing of 280°m. This course will take you just north of Gardiners Island, to an area rich with marinas and other facilities for the cruising boater. *Refer to the Region 6 chapters for more information on the Long Island forks.*

LITTLE

NARRAGANSETT

BAY

Sandy Pt

Barn I

Perch I

Pawcatuck Pt

Oyster beds

Seal Rk

Dennison Rk

Rhodes Pt

Foster Cove

Napatree Beach

SPECIAL ANCH AREA (see note A) 110.47 & 110.

Watch Hill Cove

HOTEL

Napatree Pt

WATCH HILL
Al WR 5s 61ft 14M

Watch Hill Pt

Gangway Rk

R "2"
Fl R 6s BELL

R "6"
Fl R 4s BELL

Napatree Pt Ledge

COLREGS DEMARCATION LINE

80.155a (see note A)

WP 20045
N 41°–17.86
W 071°–53.32

Catumb Rocks

Sugar Reef

WATCH HILL PASSA

GONG
Watch Hill Reef

WP 20025
N 41°–17.44
W 071°–51.59

SUGAR REEF PASSAGE

CATUMB PASSAGE

MAGNETIC

VAR 15° 00'W (1994) ANNUAL INCREASE 3'

SCALE 1:20,000

Nautical Miles

Yards

Lookout on Watch Hill

Watch Hill has always been a popular place to watch the sea. Contrary to the leisurely, dream-filled gazes that today's visitors cast, early American colonists took their observations more seriously. The hill atop the entrance to Long Island Sound was of strategic importance during the French & Indian Wars, as well as the American Revolution. The lookout was so important for military and navigational purposes that the federal government bought it early in the 19th century and erected the Watch Hill Lighthouse in 1806.

On the tip of Napatree Point, you'll find Fort Mansfield, built to guard Fishers Island Sound during the Spanish-American War. But the fort only fired its guns in practice, blasting old whale-boats towed behind fishing trawlers. The fishermen often complained that the gunners had notoriously bad aim. The fort closed before the war ended when a visitor noted that a warship could easily anchor off the east side of Watch Hill Point, protected by land, and take out the fort.

However you look at Watch Hill and Napatree Point, it should be with both reverence and caution—these are some of the foggiest waters around.

ACTIVITIES: Take out your kayaks and your canoes, hoist the sails on your sailboard, and fire up those PWCs—the protected shallow waters and long expanses of beach make Little Narragansett Bay a watersports haven. Take care to avoid the runabouts, PWCs, and daysailers here, and don't take your cruising boat through the shallow waters.

The Watch Hill Lighthouse.
© Maptech

If you'd like to do a little fishing, you'll find flounder and other bottom species in the bay or near the Middle Ground breakwater. Surfcasters and fly-fishermen should head to Napatree Point where you'll often find blues, stripers, and maybe a little tunny. Even along the rocks surrounding the lighthouse jumping fish attract land-based anglers.

From Watch Hill Cove or Napatree, you can walk into the town of Watch Hill or to Rhode Island's famous beaches, which stretch 17 miles to the east. The village's sidewalks, across from the beach, are lined with boutiques, and antique and souvenier shops—most open only during the summer. A saunter along Watch Hill's narrow streets reveals a pleasant mixture of summer "cottages" and enormous mansions overlooking the water.

One of the most notable attractions (for kids of all ages) is the 1883 Flying Horse Carousel—it's supposedly the oldest in the country. The Watch Hill Improvement Society controls the granite lighthouse on Watch Hill Point, which is now automated; part is rented as a private residence. It's a nice photo op.

RESTAURANTS & PROVISIONS: Watch Hill boasts a few good restaurants, but if the season is past you'll have to wait 'til May to try them. Facing the cove is the Olympia Tea Room Restaurant (401-348-8211), serving New American cuisine. Overlooking the Atlantic, the huge, yellow Ocean House Hotel (401-348-8161) boasts a spirited American menu. For a quick sandwich try St. Claire's Annex (401-348-8407). All are close to Watch Hill Docks.

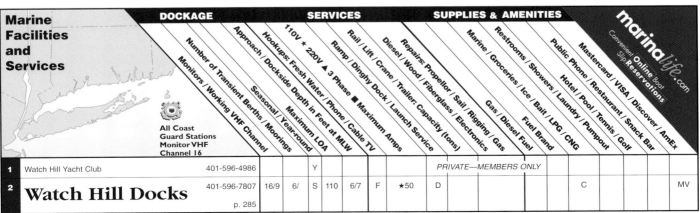

Marine Facilities and Services		Number of Transient Berths / Moorings	Approach / Dockside Depth in Feet at MLW	Seasonal / Year-round	Maximum LOA	110V • 220V ▲ 3 Phase ■	Hookups: Fresh Water / Phone / Cable TV	Maximum Amps	Ramp / Dinghy Dock / Launch Service	Rail / Lift / Crane / Trailer: Capacity (tons)	Diesel / Wood / Fiberglass / Electronics	Repairs: Propellor / Sail / Rigging / Gas	Marine / Groceries / Ice / Bait / LPG / CNG	Restrooms / Showers / Laundry / Pumpout	Gas / Diesel Fuel	Fuel Brand	Public Phone / Restaurant / Snack Bar	Hotel / Pool / Tennis / Golf	Mastercard / VISA / Discover / AmEx
1 Watch Hill Yacht Club	401-596-4986			Y									*PRIVATE—MEMBERS ONLY*						
2 **Watch Hill Docks**	401-596-7807 p. 285	16/9	6/	S	110	6/7		F	★50	D							C		MV

Information in these listings is provided by the facilities themselves. An asterisk (*) indicates that the facility did not respond to our most recent requests for information. (B) represents a BOAT/U.S. cooperating marina.

All Coast Guard Stations Monitor VHF Channel 16

marinalife.com
Convenient Online Boat Slip Reservations

Watch Hill Point & Napatree Beach

A majestic inn atop bubbling shores typifies the coastal scene around Watch Hill. © Maptech

NAVIGATION & ANCHORAGES: Use ChartKit Region 3, pages 9 and 35; Maptech™ Waterproof Charts 1 and 17; and Maptech™ electronic and NOAA paper charts 13214 (1:20,000), 12372 (1:40,000), 13215 (1:40,000), and 13205 (1:80,000). Use tide tables for Newport. High tide at Watch Hill Point is 41 minutes later; low tide is 1 hour, 16 minutes later. Multiply height of tide at Newport by 0.7 for height of tide at Watch Hill Point. Mean tidal range is 2.6 feet.

The approach to Little Narragansett Bay, including the Pawcatuck River and Watch Hill Cove, begins at Fl R 4s R "2" off Academy Rock at Stonington Point. Academy Rock is 3.2nm from G C "7" between Ram and Mason islands, and 2.nm from G C "1" off East Point on Fishers Island. From Academy Rock, it's another 2.5nm to the Pawcatuck River and the approach to Watch Hill Cove.

CAUTION: When planning a trip to Little Narragansett Bay, take into account the heavy fog that frequently rolls in from Block Island Sound. Late June and early July experience the worst fogs, which generally show up late in the afternoon and clear by 10 the next morning.

From the east your passage can be tricky. There are five passages into Fishers Island Sound. From east to west, these are Watch Hill, Sugar Reef, Catumb, Lords, and Wicopesset. All can have a stiff 3- to 4-knot current and will get choppy when the wind and current are opposed.

Coming from the east, we suggest you use Watch Hill Passage. It's nearest the Watch Hill Lighthouse, which is an excellent landmark, especially in the fog. On clear days, also look for the enormous, yellow Ocean House Hotel, northeast of Watch Hill Point. Stay between Fl R 6s BELL R "2" and G C "3," and keep an eye on your set and drift so that the currents don't push you into Watch Hill Reef. GONG G "1" sits on the east side of Watch Hill Reef.

Once through the passage, you should pass south of Fl R 4s BELL R "6" marking Napatree Point Ledge. There are rocks extending nearly 500 yards south of Napatree Point, and the Coast Guard also reports a wreck about 0.3nm east of Fl R 4s BELL R "6."

As for the remaining passages:

1. Sugar Reef Passage is not buoyed and is best left to those familiar with it.

2. Catumb Rocks are marked on the west by R N "2," on the north by G C "3C," and on the east by G C "1C." Because the channel is narrow—only about 200 yards wide—passing on the east side is risky. Better to pass to the west of R N "2" where there's more water; try to stay within 100 yards of the marker, and make course for Fl R 4s BELL R "6" at Napatree Point Ledge. From here, you're home free.

3. Lords Passage is well marked. Look for Mo(A) WHIS R W "L" to the south, R N "2L" to the east, and G C "7" at Wicopesset Rock to the north and west. Stay to the center between the buoys for good water, and do not confuse G C "7" with G C "9" farther north and west, or you'll end up high and dry. Don't attempt to steer the range set up by Mo(A) WHIS R W "L," G C "7" and Fl R 4s 46ft 5M HORN at Middle Ground. This line puts you perilously close to the shoals southeast of Wicopresset Island and Wicopesset Rocks.

4. The western approach through Wicopesset Passage at the eastern end of Fishers Island looks worse than it is, because of the visible rocks near the passage. You may have to punch through some standing waves upon entering, and be careful that the current doesn't set you onto Seal Rocks, marked at the northern end by G C "15." From the south, line up R W BELL "W" and G C "1" and stay east of the buoys as you pass through. Don't turn north until you've passed well west of G C "11." There is one distinct advantage to Wicopesset Passage for sailors: When returning to Fishers Island Sound, the prevailing southwesterlies provide for a nice reach, whereas you might be close-hauled when entering through the Watch Hill Passage.

CAUTION: Whichever passage you choose, be extremely cautious. Strong currents, heavy seas, and hard bottom make a grounding in this area particularly dangerous.

Resist the temptation to cut directly from Napatree Point to Sandy Point. The chart shows good water for most of the distance, but this course will get you in trouble, especially between the Middle Ground breakwater and Sandy Point. The waters around Sandy Point are popular with commercial fishermen, so keep an eye out for large boats and lobster pots.

The safest route from Fl R 4s BELL R "6" off Napatree Point to the channel entrance will take you around the west end of the east breakwater off Stonington Point, marked by Fl R 4s 46ft 5M HORN "4." From Fl R 4s R "2" off Stonington Point, follow the buoys directly. The passage looks worse than it is. You'll find deep water off the point, though the channel here is narrow and often crowded.

From Sandy Point, follow the channel as it heads east and then southeast through Little Narragansett Bay. Don't turn south for Napatree

Looking west over Watch Hill Point and Napatree Beach. © Maptech/James T. Abts

Beach until you've passed Seal Rock and R N "22." The local marinas make a lot of money on repairs for those who cut the last buoy or stray from the channel. Also watch for 4- and 5-foot spots south of Seal Rock, as well as Dennison Rock, marked by R N "24."

Napatree Beach is a sand spit that runs for more than a mile. The holding ground in the anchorage off the north shore is excellent. You'll often find more than 400 boats anchored here. Be aware that a strictly enfored local ordinance requires all boats to anchor at least 50 feet offshore.

Vessels that raft in this area ought to each drop an anchor to avoid smacking hulls when the wind shifts. With summer thunderstorms coming from the north, your boat may swing 180 degrees. Make sure you get a good bite and leave a lot of scope. Little Narragansett Bay is shallow, and with the long fetch from the north, steep waves often build up quickly.

When approaching Watch Hill from the Pawcatuck River, you'll find the channel well marked and easy to follow. From Fl G 4s G "23" off Pawcatuck Point, head southwest toward Fl R 4s R "2" at the entrance to Watch Hill Cove. Don't swing too wide here or you'll run into a couple of shallow spots. From Fl R 4s R "2" you may head south into the cove or west across the lee side of Napatree Beach.

Both Watch Hill Cove and Foster Cove, to the north, are lined with beautiful old summer cottages. Foster Cove is the smaller of the two and is often crowded. There is also a rock in the middle of the anchorage. The large, brown-shingled house on the point at the north entrance of the cove makes a good landmark. The cove entrance is unmarked but simple enough as long as you steer clear of the rocks north and south of the entrance. Don't turn into Foster Cove until you're north of G C "1" at the entrance to Watch Hill Cove.

Watch Hill Docks and the Watch Hill Yacht Club are in Watch Hill Cove, where there depths of 6 to 10 feet mlw. The club warns that the holding ground is poor, making these crowded waters unsafe for anchoring. Contact the Watch Hill Docks for a mooring or slip.

Shoreside & Emergency Services

Airport: Westerly (401-596-2357)
Bus: SEAT (860-886-2631)
Coast Guard: New London (860-442-4471) or VHF 16
Police, Fire, Ambulance: 911
Taxi: Eagle Cab (401-596-7300)
Tow Service:
SEA TOW —24-Hour Dispatch (800-4SEATOW)
—Eastern Conn. (860-572-9090)
TowBoatU.S.—24-Hour Dispatch (800-391-4869)
—Point Judith (401-295-8711)
SAFE/SEA (401-295-8711)

PAWCATUCK

WESTERLY

SPIRE

Amtrack (P&W)

RADIO TOWER (WERI)

JOINS ADJACENT CHART TOP

Nautical Miles

SCALE 1:20,000

1/2

Yards

0   500   1000

350

MAGNETIC

VAR 15° 00'W (2000) ANNUAL INCREASE 3'

RADIO TOWER (WERI)
1230 kHz

Cable Area

1

2

4

TANK

3

R "30" PA Priv

5

Clarks
Village

Major I

Duck Channel

R
"28"
PA Priv

Buoys 19-27A
are private

G "23"
PA
Priv

"26"
4 ltrep
1967

R "24"
PA
Priv

Gavitt Pt

1 Priv

"21" PA
Sewer
W Or

R "22"
1 PA Priv

7

Stanton Weir Pt

R "20"
PA Priv

Thompson Cov

R "18"
PA Priv   6

G "19"
PA Priv

G
"3"
Priv

6

SPEC
ANCHORA

G C "1" I IO.48
Priv

Pawcatuck Rk

G C "17"

R
N "16"

Certain Draw Pt

Mastuxet

R
N "14"

R
N "12"

Rem Pt

Babcock Cove

PAWCATUCK RIVER

(see tabulation)

R
N "10"

14

41°20'

Marsh

SM

Piles

G Piles   9-13
C "7"

10

11

Avondale

8

9

12

Marsh

Barn I

Foul

Foul

Hall I

Foul

R
N "6"

Graves Neck

Marsh

Perch I

2 APR 1962
Z Shl rep 4 1997
2 Rk
C "17"

G "19"
Fl G 2.5s

R
N "16A"

R
N "18"
h

Pawcatuck Pt

Oyster
beds

G
C "3"

Sea Wall (ruin)

R
N "4" 6

Horace I

Colonel Willie Cove

13

ETT

R
N "20"

Seal Rk
Foul

R
N "22"

G "23"
Fl G 4s

Oyster
beds

G
C "1"   10

S

71°50'

71°52'

71°50'

The Westerly Quarriers

Westerly, Rhode Island, has a past carved in stone. Red, grey, and white granite was found near the town long ago and has been quarried for years. The largest quarry in Westerly's history was operated by the Smith Company, which at one time owned a special, narrow-gauge railroad that carried the heavy stone to schooners waiting in the harbor. The finer-grained white granite was often used in constructing monuments and carving sculpture, such as the bear at Brown University. When demand for this high-grade stone dropped off, local quarrymen were forced to cut paving blocks and cobblestones. According to lore, all the streets of Philadelphia and Baltimore were paved with granite from Westerly.

While granite still figures prominently in the local economy, the beautiful stones in the River Bend Cemetery on the east side of the Pawcatuck River stand in mute testimony to the town's stonecutting heritage. Once granite quarrying leveled off in the early part of the century, Westerly turned, like many New England towns, to textiles. At the same time, however, the town had its own, unique source of income: a large greenhouse industry. It was said that if you were searching for food or flowers, you could find them in Westerly, where everything from tomatoes to roses was grown.

Children take advantage of a nice day on the Westerly green. © Maptech

Across the river from Westerly is Pawcatuck, Connecticut, known for many years as Pawcatuck Rock. The town was originally named for the rocky spot where the rope ferry tied up after crossing the river along the course of the Old King's Highway. People still tell stories of the time the first Postmaster General of the United States crossed the river on the local ferry to visit with Mr. Smith, who was the Postmaster of Pawcatuck Rock. You

Marine Facilities and Services	Monitors / Working VHF Channel	Number of Transient Berths	Approach / Dockside Depth in Feet at MLW	Hookups: Fresh Water / Phone / Cable TV	Seasonal / Year-round	Maximum LOA	110V • 220V ▲ 3 Phase ■ Maximum Amps	Ramp / Dinghy Dock / Launch Service	Rail / Lift / Crane / Trailer Capacity (tons)	Repairs: Propellor / Sail / Rigging / Electronics	Diesel / Wood / Fiberglass / Gas	Gas / Diesel Fuel	Fuel Brand	Marine / Groceries / Ice / Bait / LPG / CNG	Restrooms / Showers / Laundry / Pumpout	Public Phone / Restaurant / Snack Bar	Hotel / Pool / Tennis / Golf	Mastercard / VISA / Discover / AmEx
1 Viking Marina, Inc.	401-596-7390		2/	S	40	5/5	F	★30	R	L10	PD			I	RS		R	
2 Westerly Marina	401-596-1727		1/	S	35	10/10	FP	★30		L20	All			MI	RS		P	MVD
3 Pier 65 Marina	401-596-6350	9/68	2/	Y	65	7/6	F	★30	D	LT30	All				RS			MV
4 CONNORS AND O'BRIEN MARINA	860-599-5573 p. 289	9/	/20	Y	30	10/7	F	★	R	T	PRDW			M	R		P	MV
5 NORWEST MARINE	860-599-2442 p. 289	68/68	15/	Y	65	7/7	All	★▲50	D	LCT35	All	GD		MI	RSL		P	All
6 Stonington-on-the-River Dockominiums*	860-599-8728	10/	2/	Y	45	6/6				L25	GD	DOCKOMINIUMS		RSL	P	P		
7 Westerly Yacht Club	401-596-7556			Y		PRIVATE—RECIPROCAL PRIVILEGES													
8 Gray's Boat Yard	401-348-8689	9/	2/2	S	30	3/3.5	F	★30	All	T7	PF			MI	RS		P	
9 Covedge Bait & Tackle	401-348-8888		/3	S	25	2/2	F		R					MIB	RS		P	MV
10 Frank Hall Boatyard	401-348-8005	9/18	2/	Y	47	5/5	All	★▲■30	D	All 25	All	GD		All	All		All	MVA
11 Lotteryville Marina*	401-348-8064	16/	8/6	S	55	6/6	All	★▲100	R	C35	GD			MI	RS		P	All
12 Avondale Boat Yard	401-348-8187	9/8	5/	Y	55	10/7	F	▲50	D	RC35	All	GD	Tex	MB	RS		P	All
13 Watch Hill Boat Yard	401-348-8148	9/	6/5	Y	37	5/5	FP	★30	RD	C35	All			MI	RS		P	
14 Greenhaven Marina	860-599-1049			S	30	6/6	F	★15	RD					I	R		PS	

All Coast Guard Stations Monitor VHF Channel 16

Information in these listings is provided by the facilities themselves. An asterisk (*) indicates that the facility did not respond to our most recent requests for information. (B) represents a BOAT/U.S. cooperating marina.

Looking northeast over Graves Neck and up the Pawcatuck River. © Maptech/James T. Abts

might wonder why one mailman visiting another would cause such a stir. All we can suggest is that while Pawcatuck was just another small town, Benjamin Franklin wasn't just another mailman.

ACTIVITIES: The river from Watch Hill to Westerly is quiet and lined with gracious homes set apart by marshlands. If you follow the water as far as it carries you, you'll find yourself in downtown Westerly, with good eating, shopping, and supplies. The twisting streets of this old, Victorian town are lined with a mixture of frame houses and red brick buildings, perfect for a casual walk or an easy bike ride. For information about events in the city, call the Chamber of Commerce (401-596-7761).

Both Pawcatuck and Westerly have been shaped by their proximity to the river. Crabs, clams, scallops, and fish were once harvested here in abundance and still thrive in local waters. Unfortunately, the river is closed to shellfishing because of the effluent from two sewage-treatment plants upstream. Plans to reopen the area to shellfish beds hinge upon a scheduled upgrade of the treatment facilities.

You'll have no problem finding healthy bass and bluefish, however. Half the boats in the river belong to fishermen, not recreational boaters. The Pawcatuck River is also one of the few sites chosen for reintroduction of shad and Atlantic salmon. After a few small ladders are built, the migrating fish will once again have access to suitable spawning grounds upstream.

RESTAURANTS & PROVISIONS: You need to make it all the way to Westerly before you find a place to eat. Once you

reach downtown Westerly, however, your options multiply.

A stay at Viking Marina makes the choice easy—the Dockside Restaurant serves hardy breakfasts and excellent seafood dinners. They don't have a telephone, so you'll have to take our word for it. On Granite Street, it's not hard to find Happy Holliday Restaurant (401-596-5936), specializing in fresh local seafood, and also offering steak, seafood, sandwiches, and Italian (all available as take-out).

Three Fish (401-348-9700) offers fine dining in a casual atmosphere. A short walk from Norwest Marine and Connors & O'Brien Marina is the Whistle Stop (860-599-5112). Its breakfasts and lunches are quite popular with the boating crowd.

Try the China Village (401-596-2392) for Chinese-American dishes or Dylan's (401-596-4075), on Canal Street, for great steak and seafood. Have one great meal at Three Fish Restaurant (401-348-9700), which serves—you guessed it—a seafood and American menu.

A short walk from the water, Merchant Square offers Rafter's Restaurant & Tavern (401-596-5709), and the Green Marble Coffee House (401-596-2010). In the mood for barbecue? Head to W.B. Cody's (401-322-4070) on Route 1, where you'll also find Mary's Restaurant & Haverstraw Inn (401-322-0444) serving Italian, seafood, and more.

On the Connecticut side of the river, and within walking distance of Connors & O'Brien Marina and Norwest Marine, the Sportsmen's Café (860-599-4246) offers a well-stocked selection of traditional American meals. Take a cab to Prime Time Café (860-599-3840) for seafood. And with a little effort, you'll surely run into one of the many delis and pizzerias.

As for provisioning, you can make one stop at McQuade's Marketplace (401-596-2054) for everything from deli meats to fresh vegetables. McQuade's is on Main Street, which parallels the river.

NAVIGATION & ANCHORAGES: Use ChartKit Region 3, pages 35 and 34A; and Maptech™ electronic and NOAA paper charts 13214 (1:20,000), 13215 (1:40,000), and 13205 (1:80,000). Use tide tables for New London. High tide at Westerly is 21 minutes earlier; low tide is 3 minutes later. Use height of tide at New London for height of tide at Westerly. Mean tidal range is 2.6 feet.

As you head up the Pawcatuck River for the first time, the channel seems narrow and tricky, but after you've done it a couple of times, the ride will be easy and pleasant. Keep some film in your camera and your binoculars at hand to fully enjoy the scenery. Houses line the shores between marshes where you'll see birds seeking their estuarine prey. The no-wake zones on this river are strictly enforced.

The entrance to the Pawcatuck River at Pawcatuck Point is 2.5nm from Stonington Point and 0.6nm from Watch Hill Cove. The head of the river at Westerly is 4.5nm from the river entrance. See the chapters on Stonington Harbor and Watch Hill Point for information about the approaches to the Pawcatuck River.

The first anchorage you'll see is on the west side of the river, between G C "1" and Hall Island. This is a large area with 7 to 8 feet of water. You'll be in a lee when the wind is out of the west, making this a good place to drop a hook—night or day.

Farther upriver, inside Graves Neck, Colonel Willie Cove is a good anchorage; but much of the cove is full to capacity with boats belonging to local property owners or moored at the boatyard.

Graves Neck received its name from a local burial ground. Some graves are of unknown men who washed ashore and had to be buried before they could be identified. To avoid the rocks and Horace Island on the south side, run at least 300 yards northeast of G C "3" (which is south of Hall Island) before turning east into Colonel Willie Cove.

From Graves Neck on, past the marinas and boatyards in Avondale, there is an enforced no-wake zone. The river widens for a short distance off Ram Point, where you'll find a shallow anchorage to the east. It then narrows once again at Pawcatuck Rock, a cedar-covered point jutting out from the Connecticut shore; this is matched by a similar point on the Rhode Island side. Because of the river's narrow width here, the channel remains free of silt—if you hit bottom, you hit rock.

Just upstream from Pawcatuck Rock, you'll see the Westerly Yacht Club at Thomson Cove on the east side. The club welcomes cruisers from other recognized clubs, but dock space is usually scarce. A no-wake zone extends across the area in front of the yacht club, as with all the other clubs and marinas along the river.

Near the River Bend Cemetery opposite Gavitt Point, the channel begins to silt. Also be aware that the passage isn't as wide as it seems on the chart, and buoys 19 to 27A are privately maintained. Don't expect buoys at every bend in the river channel. Heading directly from one marker to the next will surely leave you in the mud. It's best to read the chart carefully and stay to the outside of each curve, where the channel will be deepest. On the west shore, just north of Mayor Island, you'll find slips and amenities for transients at Norwest Marine and Connors & O'Brien Marina.

Above Viking Marina, the river narrows quickly. Time to break out the dinghy or continue in a small powerboat.

Shoreside & Emergency Services

Airport: Westerly (401-596-2357)

Bus: SEAT (860-886-2631)

Coast Guard:
—New London (860-442-4471) or VHF 16

Police, Fire, Ambulance: 911

Taxi: Eagle Cab (401-596-7300)

Tow Service:
SEA TOW —24-Hour Dispatch (800-4SEATOW)
—Eastern Conn. (860-572-9090)
Tow BoatU.S.—24-Hour Dispatch (800-391-4869)
—Point Judith (401-295-8711)
SAFE/SEA (401-295-8711)

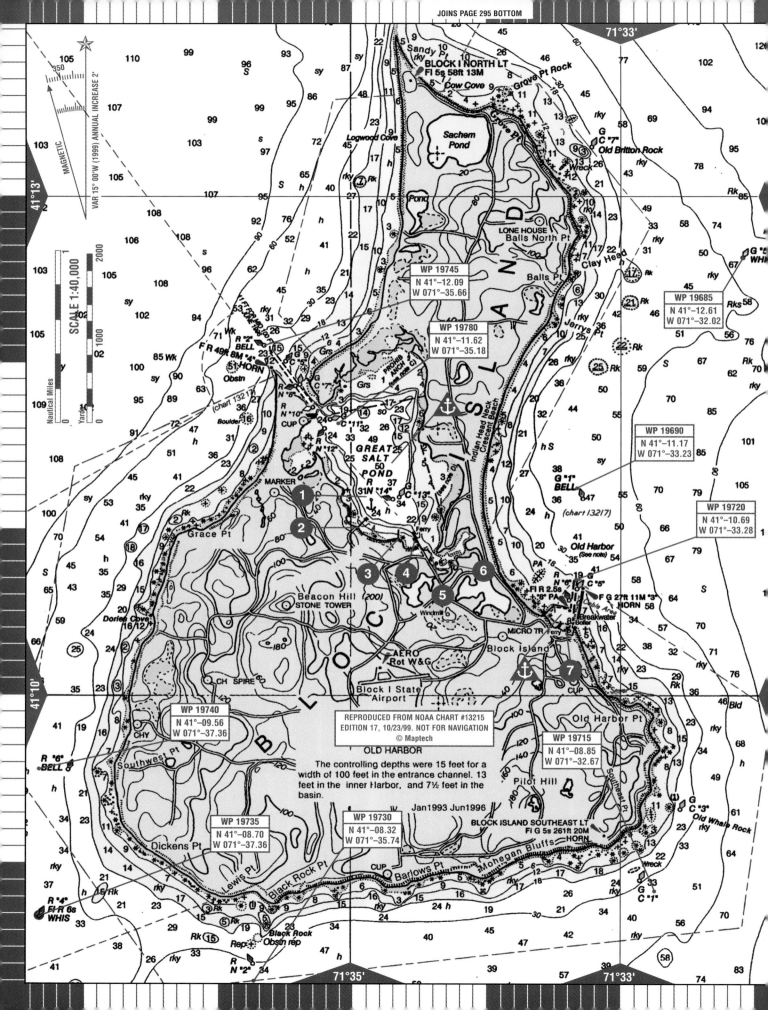

SCALE 1:40,000

VAR 15° 00'W (1999) ANNUAL INCREASE 2'

MAGNETIC

Nautical Miles

Yards

WP 19745
N 41°−12.09
W 071°−35.66

WP 19780
N 41°−11.62
W 071°−35.18

WP 19685
N 41°−12.61
W 071°−32.02

WP 19690
N 41°−11.17
W 071°−33.23

WP 19720
N 41°−10.69
W 071°−33.28

WP 19740
N 41°−09.56
W 071°−37.36

WP 19715
N 41°−08.85
W 071°−32.67

WP 19735
N 41°−08.70
W 071°−37.36

WP 19730
N 41°−08.32
W 071°−35.74

BLOCK ISLAND NORTH LT
Fl 5s 58ft 13M

BLOCK ISLAND SOUTHEAST LT
Fl G 5s 261ft 20M
HORN

REPRODUCED FROM NOAA CHART #13215
EDITION 17, 10/23/99. NOT FOR NAVIGATION
© Maptech

OLD HARBOR

The controlling depths were 15 feet for a
width of 100 feet in the entrance channel. 13
feet in the inner Harbor, and 7½ feet in the
basin.

Jan1993 Jun1996

Stumbling Block No More!

The North Light and Southeast Light not only serve as important navigtion aids, but perfect photo subjects. © Maptech

Nineteenth century mariners may well have laughed at the fact that today's vacationers call Block Island the "Bermuda of the North." To them, the "Stumbling Block" was more like it. Wrought with perilous ledges and thick fog, mariners were literally left in the dark. No lighted buoys. No lighthouses. Between 1819 and 1838, 59 vessels met their demise on or near Block Island.

Enough is enough, the National Lighthouse service finally said. And so Block Island North Light and Block Island Southeast Light came to be two of the four lighthouses erected to mark the entrance to Block Island Sound and Long Island Sound (the other two being Point Judith Light and Montauk Point Light). The northern light is the older of the two, erected in 1829. Shifting sands and mighty storms brought down structure after structure, until the fourth one was erected in 1867. This handsome granite building is the one you see today.

The Southeast Light was a little later in coming. The money appropriated to build this light in 1856 was used to repair the North Light, so it had to wait until 1875 before this end of the island received its beacon. Southeast Light is the highest light in New England, standing 258 feet above sea level. The light was originally designed as a primary seacoast aid to navigation, so it was equipped with very powerful lighting. The light was later equipped with a fog signal device, the present system being installed in 1974.

And so your approaches to Block Island are marked at both ends by lights that are charming, yet utilitarian in

Marine Facilities and Services		Number of Transient Berths / Moorings	Approach / Dockside Depth in Feet at MLW	Maximum LOA	110v ★ 220v ▲ 3 Phase ■ Maximum Amps	Rail / Lift / Crane / Trailer: Capacity (tons)	Repairs: Propellor / Sail / Rigging / Electronics	Marine / Groceries / Ice / Bait / LPG / CNG	Restrooms / Showers / Laundry / Pumpout	Public Phone / Pool / Tennis / Golf	Mastercard / VISA / Discover / AmEx
		Monitors / Working VHF Channel	Seasonal / Year-round	Hookups: Fresh Water / Phone / Cable TV	Ramp / Dinghy Dock / Launch Service	Diesel / Wood / Fiberglass / Electronics	Gas / Diesel Fuel	Fuel Brand	Hotel / Pool / Tennis / Golf		
1	Block Island Town Moorings 401-466-3235	12/	/90	S							
2	CHAMPLIN'S HOTEL, MARINA & RESORT 401-466-7777 p. 293	68/	270/	S	225	24/24	F	★▲ 50	L	All	GD	MGIBC	All	All	All	All
3	Block Island Boat Basin Inc. 401-466-2631 p. 292	9/	85/	S	110	9/9	F	★▲50	DL			MGB	RSP		PR	MV
4	PAYNE'S New Harbor Dock 401-466-5572 p. 294		100/	S	300	18/18	F	★▲50	L		GD	G	RSP		All	MV
5	Smuggler's Cove Marina 401-466-2337	9/	7/	S	45	10/10	P	★30		All		M	RS		R	All
6	Twin Maples 401-466-5547	0/0	0/	Y		/S	FP					C			R	
7	Old Harbor Dock 401-466-3235	12/12	40/	S	120	10/10	FP	★50	D		SRWF	MGIBL	All	H	All	

All Coast Guard Stations Monitor VHF Channel 16

Information in these listings is provided by the facilities themselves. An asterisk (*) indicates that the facility did not respond to our most recent requests for information. (B) represents a BOAT/U.S. cooperating marina.

Just one of many boats that sail into New Harbor. © Maptech

the fourth week of June), it draws hundreds of sailors to the island for this challenging five-day series of races. It's a great event, providing all kinds of water, wind, and current conditions and requiring all types of sails, tacks, and strategies. Between the competition and camaraderie, a good time is had by all. If you'd like to participate or would just like more information, call the Chamber of Commerce (401-466-2982).

While nearly every summer weekend is bound to be packed, you should arrive particularly early if you want even a chance of finding space on Memorial Day weekend, July Fourth weekend, Labor Day weekend, or the politically incorrect Victory Weekend. Celebrated only by Rhode Islanders (another way for the state to milk the tourist cash

purpose. Together they make this former stumbling block into the beautiful, and safe, Block Island you'll love to visit today.

ACTIVITIES: Block Island's moorish landscape brings to mind Scotland or Wales; its rolling hills and rugged ravines make for ideal exploring, be it by bike or foot. The town is full of Victorian hotels, restaurants, shops and galleries, and there are even two movie theaters, including OceanWest Theatre (401-466-2971) at Champlin's Resort on Great Salt Pond.

The island is best seen by bicycle, which can be rented at or near most of the marinas and from various other vendors about town. Mopeds, taxis, and rental cars are also available, as are numerous station wagons masquerading as tour buses.

You'll know the boating season has arrived when Block Island Race Week begins. Held annually (usually during

cow), Victory Weekend is supposed to pay homage to the dropping of the atomic bomb on Japan, an act that brought about the end of World War II. Of course, it ends up being yet another weekend to party. No matter the occasion, all summer long Block Islanders and visitors alike pack the streets and keep the island hoppin' into the wee hours of the morn.

Amble north of Old Harbor to the island's east side and Crescent Beach for a day of sun and surf along a popular, two-mile stretch extending from Old Harbor to Jerry's Point. For a more secluded alternative with stronger surge, head to Southeast Light and descend the wooden stairs from the towering Mohegan Bluffs to the sand and boulders below.

For those who prefer life's calmer, simpler pleasures, like the feeling of sand between your toes and the mesmerizing sound of surf, there are two nice beaches to enjoy near town. While in Great Salt Pond, row to the eastern side,

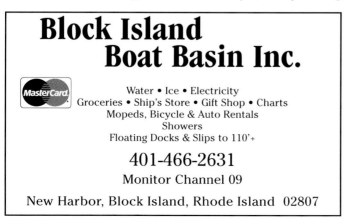
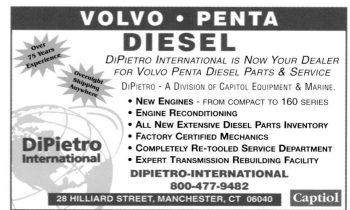

beach your dinghy, and walk across the narrow spit to Crescent Beach. The sand and usually light surf extend from Old Harbor to Jerry's Point, offering excellent swimming and sandcastle opportunities. For a little larger surf, and an opportunity to enjoy a refreshing beverage along with the water (alcohol is not allowed on Crescent Beach), head over to Ballard's Beach on the east side of the Old Harbor breakwater, at Ballard's Inn.

Speaking of buildings close to the ocean, lighthouse buffs will find two don't-miss specimens on Block Island: the Southeast Light on Mohegan Bluffs, and the Block Island North Lighthouse on Sandy Point. Both sites have rich and moving histories, literally. Sitting 201 feet above the ocean, the Southeast Light projected its beam—the most powerful in New England—more than 20 miles out to sea. But the light's strength was no match for Mother Nature, as she eroded the Mohegan Bluffs to within 60 feet of the light. Left perilously close to toppling into the ocean, the Southeast Lighthouse was moved several hundred feet inland in 1993, an awesome feat considering the lighthouse's size. If you make the trip out here, don't forget a snack and your swimsuit—there's an excellent beach at the base of the bluffs that entices surf lovers.

The North Light marks the island's northernmost point and makes you work if you want a close-up view. Whether you travel by bike or car, the road ends at Settler's Rock, the honorary place where the island's first European settlers landed in April 1661. From there, it's about a mile walk over a sand-and-rock beach—terrain that makes it feel longer than it is. It's a rather exhausting hike out there, especially in intense sun, but the view is worth it. When you finish your tour of the renovated lighthouse, recharge on the beach on the point's western shore. Swimming isn't recommended out here, especially off the northern point, where rips can take you out to sea in no time. If you're looking for a peaceful, salt-free dip, you may opt for a freshwater swim in Sachem (pronounced "Sack-em" by Block Islanders) Pond, near Settler's Rock.

Fishing opportunities around Block Island are plentiful for both the young'uns and serious anglers. While in Great Salt Pond, set the young crew members up with a rod, reel, and some fresh bait (clams, squid, etc., available locally). You'll be surprised at the entertaining collection of species dredged up from the depths of the pond (flounder, mackerel, sea robins, spider crabs, and more.).

More serious anglers will be glad to know that striped bass and bluefish swim about Block Island's waters from spring 'til fall. The hotspots vary throughout the season, so the best advice is to get local advice. Twin Maples (401-466-5547) has bait and spin-fishing tackle, while Oceans & Ponds (401-466-5131) on Ocean Avenue carries tackle for spin- and fly-fishermen; both can tell you what's happening where and on what.

Those interested in underwater adventure should consider heading for the Pinnacles. Marked as "Boulders" on the chart, southwest of Block Island, this area is one of the

Finding a place to eat is never a problem on Block Island. © Maptech

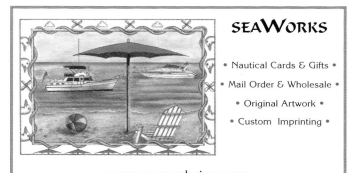
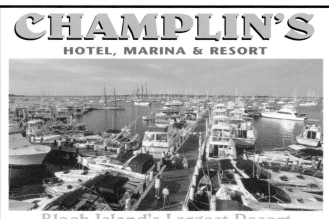

Looking northwest from 2,500 feet above Block Island. Clockwise from left to right are: Great Salt Pond, the long sweep of Crescent Beach, Old Harbor, and Old Harbor Point. © Maptech/James T. Abts

finest dive sites in New England waters south of Cape Cod. The site consists of huge stones piled 50 to 70 feet high. In August, visibility can reach 50 feet and you can swim between the boulders, scouting tropical fish like barracuda and checking out the many wrecks that litter the area. Island Outfitters (401-466-5502) on Ocean Avenue should be able to help you out with any equipment needs that you may have; they also offer charters for those who'd prefer a guide.

These suggestions just touch the tip of the lighthouse when it comes to activities on Block Island. As you can tell, many involve just exploring on your own—so get out there! Contact the Block Island Tourism Council (401-466-5200) or the Chamber of Commerce (401-466-2982) for more information and ideas.

RESTAURANTS & PROVISIONS: On an island that seems to be made for boaters, you won't have far to walk to find something to eat. I In some cases, you don't even have to leave your boat.

"Andiamo! Andiamo!" If you've never stayed the night on Great Salt Pond, this odd sound may alarm you in the morning. But for those of you who are experienced Block Island boaters are probably salivating like Pavlov's dog, for this "let's go" wail emanates from Aldo's floating bakery (401-4666-2198), replete with breakfast fare. Depending on your morning disposition, you'll either love 'em or hate 'em. Either way, there's no question where you are. In Old Harbor, Aldo's Place (401-466-5871) will be happy to serve you too, minus the wake-up call, and you'll also enjoy Ballards (401-466-2231).

If it weren't for the awesome views and island ambience that is crucial to a complete Block Island visit, you could probably spend all your time at Champlin's Marina & Resort

(401-466-7777), where you'll find two eateries of interest. The Dockside Restaurant serves breakfast, lunch, and dinner in a casual atmosphere; or if you're in the mood for a slice, stop in at the Pizzeria. Then again, you may just want to waste away at the Tiki Bar. Walk down the resort's driveway, flanked by feeding horses—there's that ambience—and Samuel Peckham's Tavern (401-466-5458) beckons you inside for a draft and a meal.

The Oar Restaurant (401-466-8820), at Block Island Boat Basin, is appropriately adorned with a colorful selection of pulling devices dangling from the ceiling. The good food, creative decor, and harbor views make for a great combination.

Closer to town, the pairing of Winfield's (401-466-5856) and McGovern's Yellow Kittens (401-466-5855) offers a curious combination of fine dining and one of the island's more famous stomping grounds. On those wild summer weekends, Yellow Kittens can usually be found by following the hum of late-night partiers.

In town, Ernie's Old Harbor Restaurant (401-466-2473) serves a fine breakfast, while Finn's Seafood Bar (401-466-2473), below and in the same building, serves lunch and dinner. Close by and right on the beach is Ballard's Inn (401-466-2231), the Grand Central Station of Block Island. If you've been separated from your friends and are trying to find them before the evening ends, just hang out here for a while and they'll probably turn up.

On Water Street, you'll be sure to find a good meal at the Harborside Inn (401-466-5504) and Mohegan Café (401-466-5911). Don't be turned off by the shack-like appearance of Old Harbor Take-Out—it's a good place for a quick bite. For just a couple of bucks you'll be sitting at your picnic table with a burger, fries, and drink.

Those looking to restock the galley should stop by the Seaside Market (401-466-5876) on the way back from town. It's a bit of a walk to New Harbor, so if you fill the shopping cart, call a cab for a ride. Closer to your boat, both Champlin's Marina and Block Island Boat Basin carry basic supplies and have an ATM.

NAVIGATION & ANCHORAGES: Use ChartKit Region 3, pages 10, 36, and 63; ChartKit Region 2, pages 5 and 30; Maptech™ Waterproof Charts 1 and 19; and Maptech™ electronic and NOAA paper charts 13217 (1:15,000), 13215 (1:40,000), 13218 (1:80,000), and 13205 (1:80,000). Use tide tables for Newport. High tide at Great Salt Pond is 2 minutes later; low tide is 7 minutes later. Multiply by 0.7 for height at high or low water. Mean tidal range is 2.6 feet.

Block Island has become a favorite destination for both yachters and tourists. As such, expect big crowds in town and on the water in summer and especially during Block Island's four big days: Labor Day, Memorial Day, July Fourth, and the oft-forgotten Victory Weekend. On these occasions, don't be surprised to find more than 2,000 boats in New Harbor and more than 200 rafted together in Old Harbor.

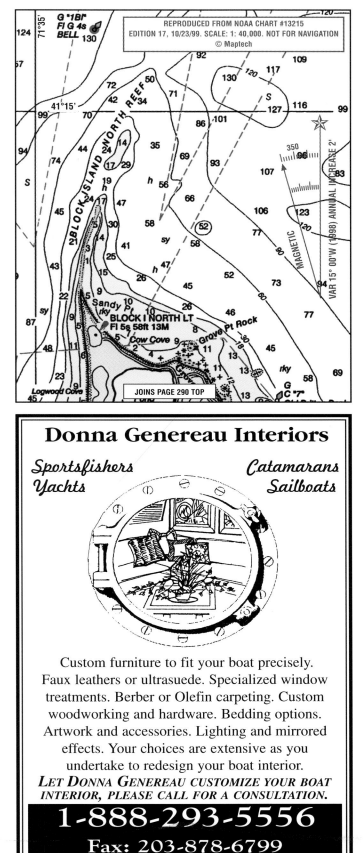

From a distance, Block Island looks like two separate hills, split by the low-lying Great Salt Pond. The north end of the island is marked by the squat tower of the Block Island North Lighthouse (Fl 5s 58ft 13M), about 1.8nm from Fl G 4s BELL G "1BI." The bell is often used as a racing mark and can be hard to round, as you often have to beat back when the wind is out of the southwest.

CAUTION: Do not cut south of Fl G 4s L G "1BI" unless you have up-to-date local knowledge—Block Island North Reef stretches almost all the way from Sandy Point to the buoy. The shoals constantly shift. Standing waves develop around the bell buoy when the wind and tide are opposed, and waves break heavily on the reef.

Block Island Southeast Light (Fl G 5s 261ft 20M HORN) atop Mohegan Bluffs marks the opposite end of the island. In good weather, you can see the light clearly when coming from Montauk or the south. If you're approaching during limited visibility, note that while the fog signal can easily be heard from several miles away, it may be indistinct when nearby.

The perimeter of the island is littered with boulders and should be approached with caution, even by small boats. The Coast Guard recommends keeping 0.5nm offshore except in the marked channels.

Great Salt Pond

From the east, you'll be crossing open water from the mouth of Buzzards Bay. In early summer, the weather can be foggy along this route, and you'll be sailing through long swells from the open ocean. Beginning at the Buzzards Bay Light (Fl 2.5s 67ft 17M HORN), head southwest for 25nm to Fl G 4s BELL G "1BI," north of Block Island. Round this mark to the north and swing south to BELL R "2" at the entrance to Great Salt Pond, about 3.5nm away.

From the north, as from Point Judith, it's a straight shot south-southwest for about 7nm to Fl G 4s BELL G "1BI," marking Block Island North Reef. Again, jog west before marking BELL R "2" at the entrance to Great Salt Pond.

From the west, crossing Block Island Sound to BELL R "2" at the entrance of Great Salt Pond is akin to being in the open Atlantic. There are long swells, heavy fog in early summer, and big-ship traffic.

The entrance to Great Salt Pond is protected by a jetty marked by Fl R 49ft 8M HORN "4." Though the channel shoals, it still carries a respectable 9 feet at mlw. From BELL R "2," it's a straight shot into the harbor—just follow the channel to the paired G C "11" and R N "12."

Great Salt Pond offers good protection, although finding space on big weekends can be a chore. With the varied types of holding ground throughout the pond, your choice of anchor is important. Use a Danforth in the hard bottom found in the middle of the anchorage, and a plow anchor in the soft perimeters. On the far east side of the pond there are some areas where the bottom is covered with oyster shells and other debris. It's best to avoid this area and head out into the deeper water. Anchoring is prohibited in the northern quarter of the pond; you must anchor south of the cylindrical "No Anchoring Buoys." If you have any questions, hail the harbormaster on VHF 12.

Dragging anchor is a real problem here, especially when the wind comes up in the afternoon. When it blows more than 15 knots, boats start to take off. Many people fail to leave enough scope, and a rising tide only exacerbates the problem, especially on the west side of the harbor. Two anchors are recommended.

The Town of New Shoreham is strict about anchoring. It maintains 90 lime-green moorings at $30 a night or $15 for the day. The moorings, located west of R N "14," are allotted on a first-come, first-served basis and fill up quickly. Just pick up a mooring and hail the harbormaster to tell him where you are. If you'd like a chance at a town mooring arrive early—the harbormaster (VHF 12 between 7 a.m. and 7 p.m.) tells us that if you show up Friday afternoon, you won't find space.

You may also look for space in Smugglers Cove—islanders call it the "Hog Pen"—south of the ferry dock. This is the best spot to be in a storm, but it's also cramped. Both Oldport Marine Services and Champlin's Launch can help you ashore once you find a spot.

If you'd prefer to have a slip, try Champlin's Marina, Block Island Boat Basin, Payne's New Harbor Dock or Smuggler's Cove Marina. All have groceries, bike and moped rentals, and restaurants close by. Call ahead for reservations.

The popularity of Great Salt Pond has caused some water pollution problems. As such, the Pond is now a Federal "No Discharge" zone (except for "gray water"—waste water from your sink or shower). If you need a pumpout, contact one of the marinas or the town-operated floating pumpout station. If you don't have a holding tank, you must use the facilities ashore. Recycling is mandatory on Block Island. Separate aluminum cans, glass, and plastic from your trash.

Old Harbor

From the east, it's a straight shot to F G 27ft 11M HORN "3," at the tip of the eastern jetty. This is open ocean, so don't be surprised by big swells and occasional fog during the summer. On the upside, there's little in the way of obstructions.

From the west, you can round Block Island to the north or the south. Your only concern is if you choose the northern route: keep well north and west of Fl G 4s BELL G "1BI" before heading south to Old Harbor.

From the north, as from Point Judith, it's also a fairly simple cruise. Keep east of G C "7" at Old Britton Rock en route to BELL G "1." From this mark, Old Harbor is just 0.5nm to the south.

From the south, let the Block Island Southeast Light (Fl G 5s 261ft 20M HORN) lead the way. Once you approach the island, keep south of G C "1," then east of G C "3" at Old Whale Rock. Continue north about 600 yards offshore as you round F G 27ft 11M HORN "3."

Old Harbor, on the east side of the Block, is a tiny artificial refuge occupied mainly by fishing boats and the ferries. The harbor's breakwater is marked by F G 27ft 11M HORN "3."

Old Harbor may be the more ideal harbor on Block Island because it gives you direct access to "downtown" and is better protected by high bluffs and the breakwater, but most boaters still choose Great Salt Pond. The controlling depth of the channel entering the harbor has been dredged to 15 feet. This is where the ferries dock, so you can be sure of enough water beneath you.

The town maintains a public dock for transients but no reservations are taken. Call the Old Harbor Dockmaster on VHF 12 or come into the inner basin and hail him from your boat. The harbormaster has an office right at the docks if you have any questions. Make sure you have lines and fenders ready. Anchoring is a problem here, as there simply isn't much room. Again, hail the harbormaster and he'll tell you where to go.

One final note: the Town of New Shoreham has been authorized to collect a 50-cent landing fee for each person over the age of 12 visiting Block Island. The fees are to be used along with matching funds from the State to build new facilities for visitors, i.e. showers, toilet facilities, and other services used mainly by boaters in New Harbor. You'll find collection boxes located at all the major marine facilities.

Shoreside & Emergency Services

Airport:
—New England Airlines (401-466-5881)
—Block Island (401-466-5511)

Coast Guard:
—Block Island (401-466-2462) or VHF 16
—Point Judith (401-789-0444) or VHF 16
—Montauk (516-668-2773) or VHF 16

Ferry:
—to Point Judith, RI (401-783-4613)
—to New London, CT (401-783-4613)
—to Providence/Newport, RI (401-783-4613)
—to Montauk, NY (516-668-5709 or 2214)

Harbormaster:
—(401-466-3235) or VHF 12 or 16

Police, Fire, Ambulance: 911

Taxi:
—Wolfie's (401-466-5550)
—Rose (401-466-9967)

Tow Service:
SEA TOW —24-Hour Dispatch (800-4SEATOW)
—Rhode Island (401-294-2360)
Tow BoatU.S.—24-Hour Dispatch (800-391-4869)
—Narragansett Bay (401-295-8711)
SAFE/SEA (401-295-8711)

Looking northeast over Southeast Light and the cliffs of Southeast Point. © Maptech/James T. Abts

Long Island's Forks

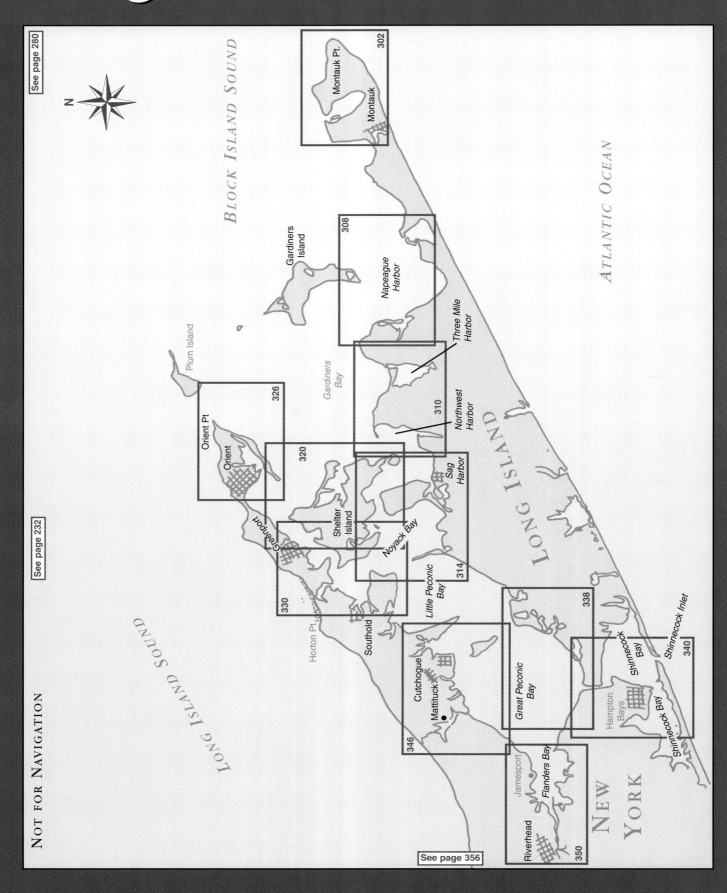

See page 280

See page 232

See page 356

NOT FOR NAVIGATION

BLOCK ISLAND SOUND

ATLANTIC OCEAN

LONG ISLAND SOUND

Montauk Pt.

Montauk

302

Gardiners Island

Napeague Harbor

308

Three Mile Harbor

Plum Island

Gardiners Bay

310

Northwest Harbor

Orient Pt

Orient

326

320

Shelter Island

Sag Harbor

Noyack Bay

Greenport

330

Little Peconic Bay

314

Southold

Horton Pt.

338

Shinnecock Bay

340

Shinnecock Inlet

Cutchogue

Mattituck

346

Great Peconic Bay

Hampton Bays

Shinnecock Bay

LONG ISLAND

Jamesport

Flanders Bay

Riverhead

350

NEW YORK

The charming harbor towns of Long Island's forks attract visitors by the boatload. **Montauk** serves as the unofficial sportfishing capital of the Northeast. It's also a relaxing beach town, with plenty of restaurants and places to dock, buy provisions, and make repairs.

Southwest of Montauk, **Three Mile** and **Northwest harbors** are within easy reach of the exclusive summer community of East Hampton. Equally attractive to boaters is **Sag Harbor**, a historic little town that offers boaters convenient access to amenities.

Between the two forks, **Shelter Island** provides a quiet escape with a reputation for quality boatbuilding. Likewise, **Greenport**, long known as a maritime mecca, has its hand in the marine industry. **Orient** is the end of the north-fork road, so to speak. The Cross Sound Ferry system carries passengers and their cars between here and its home base of New London, Connecticut, saving hours of drive time.

Another time-saver is the **Shinnecock Canal**, a shortcut that allows passage from the Atlantic Ocean and Shinnecock Bay to the Great Peconic Bay. Everything a boater needs is here: places to tie up, gas up, and make repairs. In city-like **Riverhead** you'll find ample activities and provisions. **Mattituck** and **Cutchogue** present a nice place to stretch your legs and cash in on a free wine tasting.

Navigating Long Island's Forks

From Long Island Sound, the approach to **Montauk Harbor** and Mo(A) BELL RW "M" is direct. If you approach from the Atlantic or Block Island you'll need to keep Fl G 2.5s BELL G "7SR" to the south before making your way to Mo(A) BELL RW "M." *Refer to the Montauk & Napeague Harbors chapter for more information.*

From Mo(A) BELL RW "M," steer 256°m toward Mo(A) BELL RW "S," a mark north of Napeague Harbor. **Napeague Harbor** is not marked at all, save for misleading trout stakes and "Tick Infested Area" signs, and there is no anchoring allowed. The approaches are extremely shallow and tight. *Refer to the Montauk & Napeague Harbors chapter for more information.*

Heed the unlit buoys south of the shoals that extend from Gardiners Island. After rounding Hog Creek Point, look for Mo(A) BELL RW "TM," marking the entrance to **Three Mile Harbor.** The well-marked channel enters the harbor between G C "1" and R N "2." The current here runs up to 3 knots. *Refer to the Three Mile Harbor chapter for more information.*

From Mo(A) BELL RW "TM," travel the well-marked route south of Shelter Island. Heed the channel markers once you reach Fl G 4s 4M "7." When you reach Fl G G "11," you can begin your approach to **Sag Harbor**. Do not round the breakwater too closely—keep 10 to 15 feet away—as the water is only about 6 feet deep near its end, although the main channel has 8 to 10 feet of water. *Refer to the Sag Harbor chapter for more information.*

Once the summer crowd departs, you'll have downtown Montauk all to yourself. © Maptech

From Three Mile Harbor and Mo(A) BELL RW "TM," head 007°m to Plum Gut, or 330°m toward Greenport. En route, stop off on Shelter Island's eastern shore at Coecles Harbor. *Refer to the Shelter Island chapter for more information.*

The aforementioned course takes you to Mo(A) WHIS RW "N." From here, head 290∞m to Fl R 4s BELL R "2," south of Long Beach. Follow the channel to reach Greenport to the north, or **Dering Harbor** to the south. There is good water up to the many docks of downtown **Greenport**. Try Stirling Basin if you want an overnight stay here. *Refer to the Greenport chapter for more information.*

Opposite Greenport, you'll find the entrance to Dering Harbor partially blocked by a shoal extending north and east beyond the west shore—enter mid-channel and stay at least 200 yards off Dering Point to avoid the riprap there. Although it's exposed to the north, Dering Harbor is well protected from the east and prevailing southerly winds. *Refer to the Shelter Island chapter for more information.*

Continue west and then south to join **Noyack Bay**. Pass north of Fl G 4s G "17" to enter **Little Peconic Bay**. Round Fl R 4s R "22," south of Nassau Point, to the south and head north into **Cutchogue Harbor**. *Refer to the Mattituck Inlet and Cutchogue Harbor chapter for more information.*

Along the south shore of **Great Peconic Bay**, the entrance to the **Shinnecock Canal** reveals itself at Fl G 4s G "1." When approaching the Shinnecock Canal from anywhere in Great Peconic Bay, look for the jetty that extends 300 yards from the canal entrance. *Refer to the Great Peconic Bay & Shinnecock Canal chapter for more information on traversing the lock.*

Flanders Bay is a paradise for small boats that can skip over its shoals, but it's a somewhat discouraging maze for those with deeper drafts. The destination in this area is the town of **Riverhead,** at the western end of the bay. The Riverhead channel, about 3 miles long, is narrow and built up, but it's well marked. *Refer to the Flanders Bay & Riverhead chapter for more information.*

The Southern Fluke

It is no fluke that Montauk is a travel destination. The groundwork was laid some 18,000 years ago when nomadic glaciers crept south, pushing mineral-rich mounds of rocks and soil with them. Montauk Point, the southern "fluke" of the whale tail of Long Island's east end, is what geologists call a terminal moraine: a heavy load of sedimentary rock bulldozed by the glaciers.

The melting glaciers deposited layers of fertile soil, which the Native Americans farmed. European settlers discovered the point's richness and the vast meadowlands soon spilled over with flocks of sheep and herds of cattle. In 1658, Deep Hollow Ranch became the birthplace of the American cowboy. You can still visit America's oldest cattle ranch and ride the trails of the pre-Revolutionary War pioneers.

Over the years, the town's center of attention has turned from the fields and the herds to focus on the seas and the schools—of fish. In 1926, Carl Fisher paid $2.5 million for 9,700 acres of land with 9 miles of choice waterfront property. Fisher envisioned this as the next Miami Beach, another one of his creations. He planned the golf course, the Montauk Yacht Club, the Manor Hotel, and his high-rise office building in town. His master plan also included cutting a channel from freshwater Lake Montauk to Block Island Sound. This venture would bring boats into Star Island, where

The Atlantic Ocean meets Montauk with a crash. © Maptech

he wanted to put a casino, marina, yacht club, and surf club. Fisher's plan was good for the fishermen, but the 1929 stock market crash decimated his development company as well as his dreams. His legacy remains and so do the Manor Hotel (now a private residence), the Fisher Building, and a harbor bursting with marinas and sportfishing boats.

ACTIVITIES: If you're not interested in deep-sea fishing, don't worry about a thing. Historic museums, nature trails, scuba

	Marine Facilities and Services		Approach / Dockside Depth in Feet at MLW	Number of Transient Berths / Moorings	Monitors / Working VHF Channel	Seasonal / Year-round	Hookups: Fresh Water / Phone / Cable TV	110V ★ 220V ▲ 3 Phase ■ Maximum Amps	Maximum LOA	Ramp / Dinghy Dock / Launch Service	Rail / Lift / Crane / Trailer: Capacity (tons)	Repairs: Propellor / Sail / Rigging / Electronics	Diesel / Wood / Fiberglass	Gas / Diesel Fuel	Marine / Groceries / Ice / Bait / LPG / CNG	Restrooms / Showers / Laundry / Pumpout	Public Phone / Restaurant / Snack Bar	Hotel / Pool / Tennis / Golf	Mastercard / VISA / Discover / AmEx
1	Montauk Yacht Club	631-668-3100	9/	120/	S	180	/6	All	★▲■100	D						I	RSL	HPT	All	All
2	East Hampton Town Pumpout Station*	631-329-3078	16/		S	40	8/8	FREE—SELF SERVE												
3	Star Island Yacht Club and Marina p. 309	631-668-5052	9/10	100/	Y	100	7/7	All	★▲■50	D	L70	PGDFE		GD	Tex	MGIB	RSL	P	All	All
4	Snug Harbor p. 305	631-668-2860	9/		S	50	8/5	FC	★30	D							RSL	HP	P	All
5	Westlake Fishing Lodge	631-668-5600	19/	30/	Y	50	8/6	F	★30							MIB	RS	H	All	MVD
6	DIAMOND COVE MARINA p. 306	631-668-6592	19/19	20/	Y	50	6/5	All	★▲50	L	L40	All		GD	Gulf	MGIB	All		PS	MV
7	Offshore Sports Marina	631-668-2406	19/9	15/	Y	62	9/9	All	★▲■125		L50	PGDWFE		GD	Gulf	MIB	RSL		PS	MV
8	Sportsman's Dock	631-668-5348		3/	S	100	8/6	FP	★▲30								RSL			
9	MONTAUK MARINE BASIN p. 309	631-668-5900	19/69	50/	Y	140	6/6	FC	★▲50		L70			GD	Coas	MGIB	RSL		P	All

Facilities continued on next page...

Looking north over Star Island and the entrance to Lake Montauk. © Maptech/James T. Abts

Hundreds of years of whaling and fishing history is brought to light at the Montauk Point Lighthouse Museum (631-668-2544 or www.montauklighthouse). A keeper's house, old photographs, and varied collection of Fresnel lenses are among the displays. Got your land legs yet? Climb the 130-plus steps (you'll lose count, too!) to the top of the lighthouse. Here you can see for more than 40 miles to Block Island, Rhode Island, Connecticut, and other vistas. A small fee helps defray operating expenses.

The U.S. Coast Guard station (631-668-2773) on Star Island offers tours complete with tales as tall as the cupola, from which you'll enjoy a great view. (Ask the Duty Officer what the "turtle's back" is for, and how it was broken.)

All you cowboys and cowgirls can mosey on over to the oldest cattle ranch in America, Deep Hollow Ranch (631-668-2744). A 4,000-acre spread gives you plenty of room to giddy-up on rustic trails, rolling meadows, and white-sand beaches. The young'uns will enjoy the small petting zoo.

If you happen to have your clubs aboard, try the 18-hole golf course at Montauk Downs State Park (631-668-1234). If you're better at the short game, try miniature golf at Puff & Putt (631-668-4473) in the village. The "Puff" part rents small sailboats on Fort Pond for aspiring skippers. Shallow areas of Lake Montauk and Napeague Harbor are havens for kayaking, waterskiing, and windsurfing. Amagansett Beach & Bicycle (631-267-6325) offers windsurfing lessons and rentals. At night, relax and enjoy first-run films at The Movie (631-668-2393).

diving, and beachcombing are all easily accessible from the harbor by bus, taxi, rental car, or bicycle.

The most popular recreational activity, of course, is fishing. With scores of world-record catches here, Montauk proudly considers itself the sportfishing epicenter of the Northeast. If big game (tuna, marlin, and sharks) grabs your interest, haggle through the marinas where schools of licensed charter captains set their hooks. For about one-tenth the price of a private charter, try the sport and your luck aboard a party-fishing boat. Although it's more crowded, you can swap tales with other fishing enthusiasts on the *Viking Fleet* (631-668-5700) or *Lazy Bones* (631-668-5671), which offer full- and half-day ventures.

Marine Facilities and Services

All Coast Guard Stations Monitor VHF Channel 16

marinalife.com — Convenient Online Boat Slip Reservations

#	Facility	Phone	Monitors / Working VHF Channel	Number of Transient Berths	Seasonal / Year-round / Moorings	Maximum LOA	Approach / Dockside Depth (ft at MLW)	Hookups: Fresh Water / Phone / Cable TV	110V★ 220V▲ 3 Phase■ Max Amps	Ramp / Dinghy Dock / Launch Service	Rail / Lift / Crane / Trailer: Capacity (tons)	Repairs	Gas / Diesel Fuel	Fuel Brand	Marine / Groceries / Ice / Bait / LPG / CNG	Restrooms / Showers / Laundry / Pumpout	Public Phone / Pool / Tennis / Golf	Hotel / Restaurant / Snack Bar	Mastercard / VISA / Discover / AmEx
			DOCKAGE							**SERVICES**			**SUPPLIES & AMENITIES**						
10	Uihlein's Boat Rental & Marina*	631-668-3799	14/	3/	S	48	17/7	All	★▲■100		L25	All	G	Gulf	MGIB	RS	P		All
11	Viking Dock*	631-668-5700			S	140		*CHARTERS & FERRY*											MV
12	Salivar Dock	631-668-2555			Y		6/6											R	
13	Gosman's Dock	631-668-2447			S	60	12/12											All	MVA
14	GONE FISHING MARINA (p. 307)	631-668-3232	19/	30/	Y	50	6/6	FC	★50	R	L25	PGDFE	GD	BP	MGIB	All	P		All
15	Montauk Lake Club & Marina	631-668-5705	19/	9/	S	60	8/8	All	★▲■	D			GD	Tex	I	RSL	P	PR	MVA

Information in these listings is provided by the facilities themselves. An asterisk (*) indicates that the facility did not respond to our most recent requests for information. (B) represents a BOAT/U.S. cooperating marina.

Montauk's beaches are worth combing, especially for those who see picking flotsam and jetsam as a sport. On the north shore, the Block Island Sound beaches are generally rocky, while the Atlantic Ocean beaches on the south side feature smooth, sandy stretches that are fun for walking and swimming. Fishermen often crowd Montauk Point's rocky beachfront with their fishing gear, hoping to pull a big striper from the surf.

RESTAURANTS & PROVISIONS: It would not be surprising to find that Montauk's restaurants serve nothing but fish, but this is not the case. Among the more than two dozen restaurants in the village and harbor, you'll find everything from Italian, French, and American cuisine to seafood, steaks, and vegetarian favorites. Seafood, of course, is a staple here, and while many locals prefer theirs plain, with a little butter or lemon, visitors will also find eateries doctoring it up with tropical salsas, spicy sauces, and other secret ingredients.

If you're in the harbor, visit the elegant and highly-rated Montauk Yacht Club (631-668-3100). Another favorite is the casual restaurant at Star Island Yacht Club & Marina (631-668-5052), offering expansive views of the inlet and of boats returning from the sea.

One of the few places around the harbor that's open early is Montauk Market, across from Viking Dock; it has all your usual provisions plus an ATM. Four Oaks General Store & Bakery (631-668-2534), another early opener, is about a half-mile from Gosman's Dock, at West Lake Drive and Flamingo Road. Pick up fresh bread, pastries, and other baked goodies to take back to the boat.

Late risers don't have to worry about missing breakfast, because it's served all day at John's Pancake House (631-668-2383) on Main Street in the village. Dinner options include Shagwong (631-668-3050), a popular seafood restaurant, and Oyster Pond Restaurant & Bar (631-668-4200). Provisions are plenty in the village, where you'll find banks, pharmacies, supermarkets, clothing boutiques, and specialty stores just a short taxi or bus ride from the harbor.

NAVIGATION & ANCHORAGES: Use ChartKit Region 3, pages 9 and 37; Maptech™ Waterproof Charts 1 and 6; and Maptech™ electronic and NOAA paper charts 13209 (1:40,000) and 13205 (1:80,000). Use tide tables for New London. High tide at the Montauk Harbor entrance is 24 minutes earlier; low tide is 16 minutes earlier. Multiply height of tide at New London by 0.7 for height of tide at the Montauk Harbor entrance. Mean tidal range is 1.9 feet.

High tide at Promised Land, 1.4nm from the entrance to Napeague Harbor, is 13 minutes earlier, and low tide is 8 minutes earlier. Multiply height of tide at New London by 0.9 for height of tide at Promised Land. Mean tidal range is 2.3 feet.

The entrance to Montauk Harbor is 17.3nm from the entrance to Great Salt Pond on Block Island, 13.8nm from Plum Gut and Orient Point, and 14nm from Watch Hill Point, Rhode Island. The entrance to Napeague Harbor lies 6.5nm from Montauk Harbor and 7.4nm from Three Mile Harbor.

From Fl G 2.5s BELL G "7SR," marking Shagwong Reef, a southwesterly course of about 225°m will bring you to Mo(A) BELL RW "M" just off the entrance to Montauk Harbor. If you have a deep-draft vessel, swing wide of Shagwong Reef before heading for the entrance.

Do yourself a favor and reserve a slip or mooring, especially on a weekend. Lake Montauk can be a mob scene on summer weekends. It's an awfully long trip to get there, so be sure you have a place to dock, anchor, or moor.

Montauk Point Light (Fl 5s 168ft 24M HORN), a white and brown stucture on the eastern end of Montauk Point, stands beside a simple, white building and a two-story, shingled keeper's house, plus a World War II machine gun tower. If you're coming in from the east at sunrise, the cliffs that come down from the point take on a bright, reddish hue due to their high iron content.

On the north side of the point is a shoal area that extends about 4nm to the northwest, on which tidal rips develop and waves break. In an ebb current, westbound sailors heading for Montauk Harbor may find the going slow, as they will be fighting the current and waves.

The entrance to Montauk Harbor is between two stone breakwaters marked by Fl R 2.5s 32ft 7M HORN "2" on the west breakwater and Fl G 4s 30ft 4M "1" on the east breakwater. While the current at the harbor entrance is evident—generally 1 to 2 knots—it diminishes dramatically inside. The channel carries a reported depth of 10 feet.

Since Montauk is a busy fishing town, watch out for local fishing boats. The 5-mph harbor speed limit is strictly enforced. With all of the fishing docks jutting in and out, a boat can jump out at you. These boats also tend to kick up a good wake, so it's even more important that you keep a slow and steady pace.

After passing through the breakwaters, you'll see Star Island dead ahead, connected to the mainland by a causeway. The Coast Guard station is on the northern end of the island, next to a town dock where commercial fishing boats tie up.

On the mainland to the west, you'll find a heavy concentration of marinas, restaurants, motels, and charter boats. Follow the privately marked channel, which has a reported depth of 8 feet at mlw. From south to north, transients can choose from among Snug Harbor Motel and Marina, Diamond Cove Marina, and Montauk Marine Basin, all of which have excellent facilities for transients. Across the channel, on the west side of Star Island is Star Island Yacht Club and Marina, offering repairs and other services.

Just east of the Coast Guard station on Star Island is the East Hampton Town Pumpout Station. The free pumpout, available April to November, is self-service. Boats nearing 40 feet long and drawing 4 feet or more should steer in bow first at the end of the floating dock, where the depth is 10 feet. Where the floating dock meets a fixed dock, the depth shoals up to a range of 3 to 4 feet.

The most conspicuous landmark on the eastern side of Star Island is the lighthouse tower of the Montauk Yacht Club. Gone Fishing Marina, across the channel, is an excellent full-service marina with a high-capacity lift.

If you're heading for one of the marinas on the eastern side of Lake Montauk or the designated anchorage area, keep Star Island to starboard. Stay close to the island to avoid the sandbar (marked by G C "3," G C "5," and G C "7") that reaches out from the eastern shore of the mainland.

Be aware, too, that the speed limit south of Star Island,

Embassy Guides

in the lake, is 25 mph and 45 mph for waterskiing, so keep your eye out for fast-moving vessels and fallen skiers. The channel to the anchorage area is clearly marked. Stay in the middle of it, as there are some shallow spots—as low as 3 feet—just off the buoys. The East Hampton Bay Constable reports that the channel has more than the reported 4 feet of water on the chart, but if you have any doubts, hail him on VHF 16.

After passing G C "7," swing to the southeast, where you'll find about 8 feet of water and a charming anchorage. However, the grass and mud bottom of the harbor is considered poor holding ground.

CAUTION: The southern half of Lake Montauk, south of G C "7," has shoaled up to less than the 8-foot depth reported on the NOAA chart. The harbormaster warns against anchoring in this shallow area unless your draft is minimal or your keel is strong, or you do your scouting by dinghy.

If you are looking for a quiet and deep anchorage, head for Fort Pond Bay, 3nm west of Montauk Harbor. From Fl G 2.5s BELL G "7SR", take a southwesterly course of 240°m. Swing wide of Shagwong Reef and Culloden Point before turning south into the bay. The original Montauk Village was located here before being destroyed in the 1938 hurricane. Much of the area is private property; however, there is a ramp for a seaplane and an abandoned

Navy pier for access to land. The beach is small, and there are no lifeguards or any services here. Montauk Village is approximately 1.5 miles south by foot or taxi.

Napeague Harbor

In contrast to Montauk, **Napeague Harbor** is not marked at all, save for misleading trout stakes and "Tick Infested Area" signs, and there is no anchoring allowed. The approaches are extremely shallow and tight.

When visiting Napeague Harbor, come only in a small boat or dinghy, and only on a rising tide.

If you're coming **from the west**, follow the Promised Land Channel, the buoyed passage south of Gardiners and

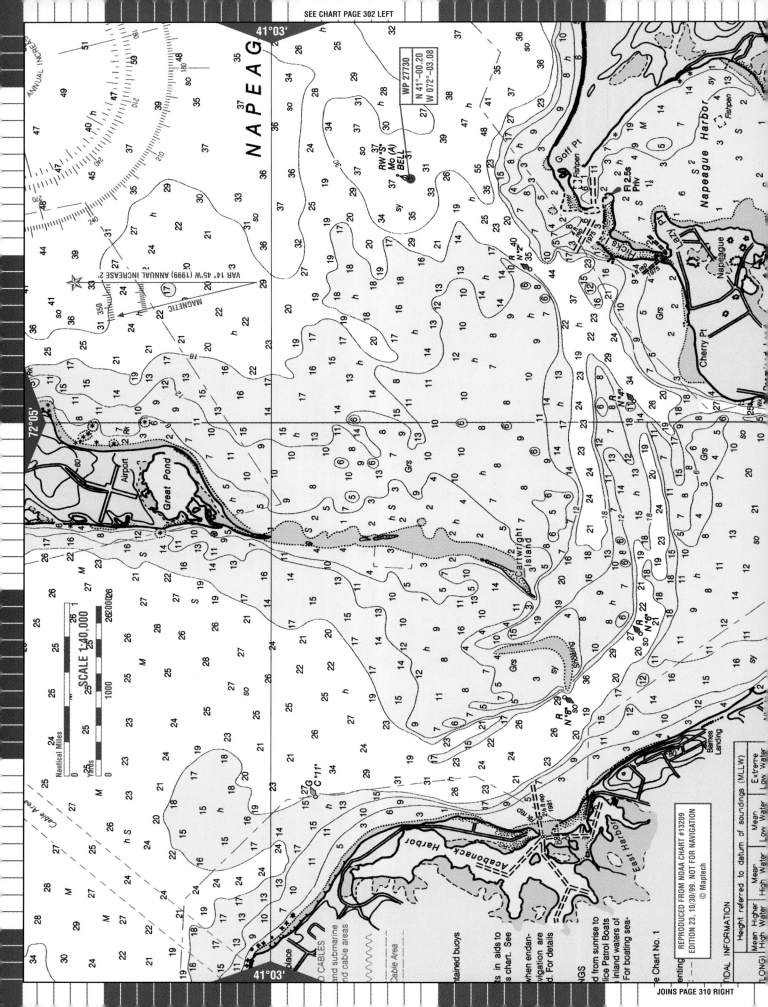

NAPEAG

WP 27730
N 41°—00.20
W 072°—03.08

RW "S"
Mo (A)
BELL

VAR 14° 45'W (1999) ANNUAL INCREASE 2'

MAGNETIC

Golf Pt

Napeague Harbor

Cherry Pt

Napeague

Hick's Pt

SCALE 1:40,000

Nautical Miles

Yards

Airport

Great Pond

Cable Area

Cartwright Island

Shoaling

Barnes Landing

East Harbor

Accabonack Harbor

TIDAL INFORMATION

Height referred to datum of soundings (MLLW)

Mean Higher High Water	Mean High Water	Mean Low Water	Extreme Low Water

41°03'

41°03'

72°05'

Cartwright islands. Tidal velocity in the channel averages 1.5 knots.

Approaching **from the east or west**, wait until you're at least 400 yards southwest of R N "2" before heading toward the entrance. It is very shallow off Goff Point, so don't enter from the north. The harbor's mouth is marked by a large sign that reads "No Anchoring" in no uncertain terms.

CAUTION: The currents in and out of this harbor are quite strong and should not be underestimated; in an opposing wind they can be downright hellacious. Be ready to compensate quickly when making the turn.

If your boat draws less than 4 feet, you can enter on a rising tide, but keep at least 125 feet from shore and follow the shore's curve. Even under the best conditions, the channel is less than 12 feet wide, so don't be a cowboy. You'll know you've successfully reached this secluded site when you see the markers for shellfish hatcheries.

Keep your speed way down when entering the harbor, and cautiously feel your way through the 4-foot deep channel, turning hard to port when going around the bar.

There's another entrance on the west side of Hicks Island, which has shoaled to a depth of less than 4 feet. The channel is very narrow and, as the tides change, the current is swift. The entrance is mainly for local boaters who use the town ramp on Lazy Point. It is best to enter here at half or full tide.

The bottom contours on the chart for Napeague Harbor are not entirely in accordance with the actual depth, so if you have a depth sounder on board or a spare hand to watch the bottom at the bow, use 'em. This would be a great place to swing the lead line.

Once inside, you'll find shoals and marsh to the west. Stay at least 200 yards off the eastern shore for plenty of deep water.

Acabonack Harbor, just west of Cartwright Island, has a narrow channel with privately maintained markers. You'll be making your turn from the Promised Land Channel about 800 yards northwest of R N "8," taking care to watch for the rock on the south side of the entrance. The channel is 2.5 feet deep, but there is more water inside.

Shoreside & Emergency Services
Airport: Montauk (631-668-3738)
—Montauk Seaplane Base (631-878-1125)
Coast Guard: Montauk (631-668-2773) or VHF 16
Ferry: Block Island, RI, Viking Line (631-668-5700)
Police, Fire, Ambulance: 911
Taxi: Great White Taxi (631-668-3545)
Tow Service:
SEA TOW. —24-Hour Dispatch (800-4SEATOW)
—Eastern Long Island (631-765-5300)
Tow BoatU.S.—24-Hour Dispatch (800-391-4869)
Train: Long Island Railroad (631-822-5477)

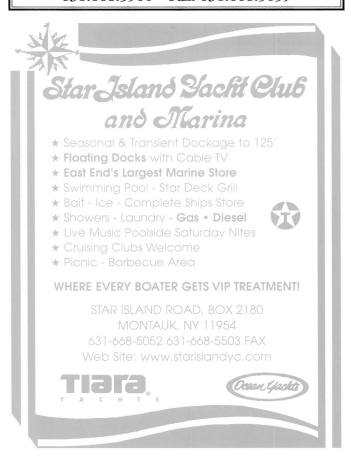

41°02'
41°00'

72°10'

THREEMILE HARBOR

SUBMARINE PIPELINES AND CABLES

Charted submarine pipelines and submarine cables and submarine pipeline and cable areas are shown as.

Pipeline Area

CAUTION

Channels marked by privately maintained buoys from May to November.

Temporary changes or defects in aids to navigation are not indicated on this chart. See Notice to Mariners.

During some winter months or when endangered by ice, certain aids to navigation are replaced by other types or removed. For details see U.S. Coast Guard Light List.

SMALL CRAFT WARNINGS

Small craft warnings will be displayed from sunrise to sunset from Suffolk County Marine Police Patrol Boats underway in the coastal and navigable inland waters of Suffolk County Long Island New York. For boating season only.

For Symbols and Abbreviations see Chart No. 1

COLREGS: International Regulations for Preventing Collisions Demarcation lines are shown thus:

WP 27775
N 41°-02.66'
W 072°-11.31'

Hog Creek Pt

Threemile Harbor

POLLUTION REPORTS

Report all spills of oil and hazardous substances to the National Response Center via 1-800-424-8802 (toll free), or to the nearest U.S. Coast Guard facility if telephone communication is impossible (33 CFR 153).

VAR 14° 45'W (1999) ANNUAL INCREASE 2'

MAGNETIC

SCALE 1:40,000

WP 28235
N 41°-03.25'
W 072°-14.02'

WP 28255
N 41°-01.05'
W 072°-16.16'

REPRODUCED FROM NOAA CHART #13209
EDITION 23, 10/30/99. NOT FOR NAVIGATION
© Maptech

Northwest Harbor

WP 28245
N 41°-02.37'
W 072°-15.95'

Cedar Pt

Barcelona Neck

Northwest Creek

AIDS TO NAVIGATION

72°15'

41°00'

Money, Money

There are people with money to burn, and then there are people who summer in the Hamptons. Wealth can be seen in every direction. East Hampton's main drag looks like a cleaner, smaller version (much smaller, of course) of New York City's Fifth Avenue. Three Mile Harbor's marine facilities follow suit and offer luxurious amenities to boaters.

Originally called "Maidstone," for the English town whence most of the first residents came, the village of East Hampton began as a farming community and later developed a reputation as a home-away-from-home for many. In the early 20th century workers erected lavish summer homes ("cottages") along East Hampton's shores for the fashionable and wealthy. Gentility lives on in this place—a place so nice, you may want to make this your home sweet home.

ACTIVITIES: In Three Mile Harbor, the water is clean and good for swimming, thanks to a strict no discharge policy. The best swimming area, other than off the side of your boat, is the north side of Sammy's Beach, west of the entrance jetties.

Looking north over Three Mile Harbor. © Maptech/James T. Abts

Across the channel and on the bay side, Maidstone Beach has restrooms, a cabana, barbecues, and a ball field.

Cedar Point County Park (631-852-7620), a long spit, sandy on one side and stony on the other, is three miles west of Three Mile Harbor and forms the northern breakwater for Northwest Harbor. Small boats can be rented at

Marine Facilities and Services

All Coast Guard Stations Monitor VHF Channel 16

#	Facility	Phone	Monitors/Working VHF	Transient Berths/Moorings	Seasonal/Year-round	Max LOA	Approach/Dockside Depth (MLW)	Hookups (Fresh Water/Phone/Cable TV)	110V✴/220V▲/3-Phase■ Max Amps	Ramp/Dinghy Dock/Launch Service	Rail/Lift/Crane/Trailer Capacity (tons)	Repairs (Prop/Sail/Rigging/Gas/Diesel/Wood/Fiberglass/Electronics)	Gas/Diesel Fuel	Fuel Brand	Marine/Groceries/Ice/Bait/LPG/CNG	Restrooms/Showers/Laundry/Pumpout	Public Phone/Pool/Tennis/Golf	Hotel/Restaurant/Snack Bar	Mastercard/VISA/Discover/AmEx
1	Sunset Cove Marina	631-329-1431	16/9	5/	S	24	3/3	F	★30									HT	
2	Harbor Marina (p. 313)	631-324-5666	9/10	5/	Y	67	12/6	F	★▲50	All	LT15	All	GD	BP	MGIB	RSP		All	MVA
3	East Hampton Commercial Dock*		16/12	/8	Y	100	10/6.5	F				R					P		
4	Maidstone Harbor Marina	631-324-2651	9/	10/	Y	80	10/8	All	★▲■100			All			MGI	All	P	PR	
5	East Hampton Point Marina (p. 312)	631-324-8400	9/	12/	Y	100	7/7	FC	★▲50	D	LT25	All	GD	Tex	MGI	All	PT	All	All
6	Shagwong Marina	631-324-4830	9/	1/	Y	48	6/6	All	30	D	T					RSP	P		
7	Halsey's Marina Inc.	631-324-9847	9/	1/	S	80	6/6	FC	★▲■50							RSL	P		
8	Gardiner's Marina (p. 313)	631-324-9894	9/10	5/	Y	85	8/6	FP	★▲50	D		All			I	RS			MVA
9	Three Mile Harbor Boat Yard, Inc. (p. 312)	631-324-1320	9/	20/	Y	60	10/10	All	★▲50	D	L40	All			MIB		P		All
10	Three Mile Marina*				Y	55	9/5	FP	★30	RD	CT6								
11	East Hampton Marina	631-324-4042	9/10		Y	30	5/7			D	L6	PGDWFE	G	Gulf	MI	R			MVA

Information in these listings is provided by the facilities themselves. An asterisk (*) indicates that the facility did not respond to our most recent requests for information.
(B) represents a BOAT/U.S. cooperating marina.

the park's store for exploring Alewife Pond and Creek. The beach is great for quiet bathing, sunning, and strolling.

If you like to see the sky light up with color, this is a good place for it. July Fourth fireworks are fired from the Devon Yacht Club and at the Main Beach at East Hampton. Then in mid-July fireworks are launched over Three Mile Harbor in a spectacular display reflected in the water. The event is a fund-raiser for Boys Harbor, a local camp, so don't be surprised if someone pulls up to your boat for a donation.

History aficionados often start at John Howard Payne's own Home Sweet Home museum (631-324-0713), an 18th-century house filled with Americana. The East Hampton Historical Society (631-324-6850) runs a marine museum and boat shop worth checking out. The Marine Museum

(631-267-6544) on Bluff Road in Amagansett, recalls the history of Long Island fishing and whaling, complete with artifacts and dioramas.

The Hook Windmill at the north end of Main Street is open to the public for a small fee during July and August. The Guild Hall Museum & John Drew Theater (631-324-0806), beside the flagpole at the other end of town, has changing art and stage presentations. And a stone's throw from the museum you'll find the perfect place to spend a rainy day: East Hampton Cinema (631-324-0448).

RESTAURANTS & PROVISIONS: Although the nearest large commercial area is the Village of East Hampton, there are plenty of restaurants around Three Mile Harbor. Michael's at Maidstone Park (631-324-0725) is closest to the beach and offers an American menu and a lively bar. One block west, the Maidstone Market (631-329-2830) on the corner of Flaggy Hole and Three Mile Harbor roads, is open long hours, especially in the summer. This little general store and gourmet shop sells homemade soups and fresh breads

For medium-priced dining with a water view, seat yourself on the covered deck or inside Bostwick's Seafood Grill & Oyster Bar (631-324-1111) at The Harbor Marina. If you're staying at Maidstone Harbor Marina, you can't go wrong with Monterey Seafood Grille (631-324-0000). Without question, the most elegant eatery is the East Hampton Point Restaurant (631-329-2800). The building and bar are beautiful, the wine list extraordinary, and the food fabulous. Uncork your wallet and enjoy yourself.

At the south end of the harbor, Janine's (631-324-9024) dishes out generous portions in an easygoing atmosphere.

NAVIGATION & ANCHORAGES: Use ChartKit Region 3, pages 8 and 38; Maptech™ Waterproof Charts 1 and 6; and Maptech™ electronic and NOAA paper charts 13209 (1:40,000), 12358 (1:40,000), 12354 (1:80,000), and 13205 (1:80,000). Use tide tables for New London. High tide at the Three Mile Harbor entrance is 22 minutes later; low tide is 2 minutes later. Multiply height of tide at New London by 0.9 for height of tide at the Three Mile Harbor entrance. Mean tidal range is 2.4 feet.

The entrance to Three Mile Harbor is 6.6nm from Sag Harbor, 7.5nm from Plum Gut, and 11.5nm from Lake Montauk.

From Fl G 4s GONG G "1GI" north of Gardiners Island, a course of 210°m will take you by R N "14" west of Crow Shoal to Three Mile Harbor which is marked by Mo (A) A BELL R W "TM" about 0.6nm offshore. Beware of fish traps close to shore on the east side of the entrance. The entrance channel begins between G C "1" and R N "2." There are usually a number of fishermen on the jetties at the entrance, the jetties being privately marked at the outer ends with Q R 10ft on the west and Q G 27ft on the east. When you approach at night, the channel is so well marked you feel you're heading down a runway, and it has good depth, having been dredged to 12 feet in 1997. There is a current in the entrance channel of up to 3 knots—enough to make you cautious.

CAUTION: A sandbar extends at least 0.5nm farther south from Sammy's Beach than is marked on the chart, and it is unforgiving to those who try to cut it. Do not turn to the west until you've passed R N "22," about 100 yards south of East Hampton Point Yacht Club.

South of East Hampton Point Marina depths are good in the channel and in the anchorage area to the west. The channel is well marked but narrow and crowded on weekends. A 5-mph speed limit is enforced throughout the harbor and especially in the channel.

Harbor Marina is the first big marine facility on the east side as you enter Three Mile Harbor. They offer transient slips and repair services. Immediately to the south are the town's commercial dock and boat ramp, the harbormaster's office, and a free, self-serve pumpout station. The dock is primarily for commercial fishermen, but you can tie up in an emergency.

You'll find the largest yachts in the harbor tied up at the East Hampton Point Marina & Boatyard. The entrance channel to Maidstone Harbor Marina runs along the Point's northern bulkhead. Contact the marinas on VHF 9 for instructions before you come in for food, fuel, or a slip. South of the Point, there is an unmarked shoal extending about 30 yards west of the dolphin. As long as you stay well north of the dolphin there should be no problem.

Once south of R N "22," you can make a slow turn into the anchorage and find deep water as far as the western shore.

The mud bottom is good holding ground throughout, and there is a large area for anchoring, well protected by the hills to the south. Eight transient moorings (white balls with black "T") line the western side of the channel. You can pick one up on a first-come, first-served basis; the Marine Patrol (VHF 16) will swing by in the morning to pick up the $25 fee.

Continuing south, the channel leads to more marinas and a gorgeous, totally protected cove at the head of the harbor. There you'll find Three Mile Harbor Boat Yard and Gardiner's Marina, both of which welcome transients.

Shoreside & Emergency Services
Airport: East Hampton (631-537-1130)
Bus: Suffolk County Transit (631-852-5200)
Coast Guard:
—Montauk (631-668-2773) or VHF 16
Harbormaster:
—Marine Patrol (631-329-3078) or VHF 16
Police, Fire, Ambulance: 911
Taxi: Bill's Taxi (631-329-5019)
Tow Service:
SEA TOW —24-Hour Dispatch (800-4SEATOW)
—Eastern Long Island (631-765-5300)
Tow BoatU.S.—24-Hour Dispatch (800-391-4869)
—Peconic Bay (631-728-2743)
Train:
—Long Island Railroad, Amagansett (631-822-5477)

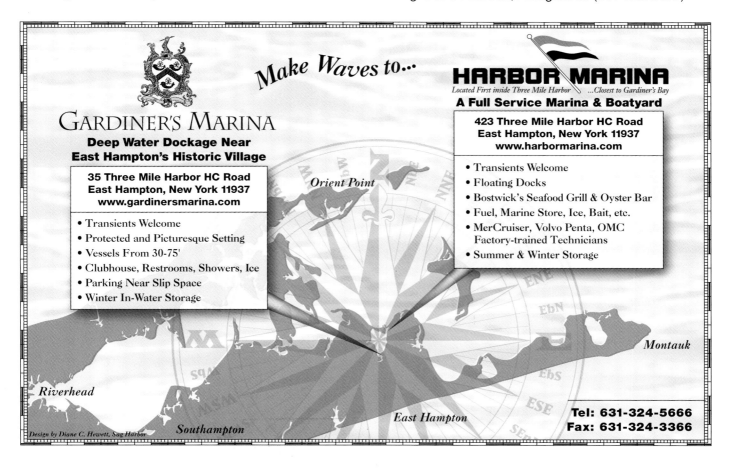

A Whale of a Town

When George Washington helped establish Sag Harbor as a port of entry, he ensured that it would be one of Long Island's more significant villages. People looked at Sag Harbor and saw another New York City on the rise. For a time at the end of the 18th century, the harbor was not only clearing more tonnage than New York but also had more ships.

Whaling aided the harbor's spectacular climb; a fleet of 63 whaling ships jammed the already tight harbor by 1840. The village population of about 4,000 rose and fell like a sea swell because seamen made up nearly half the population. Herman Melville used whaling Capt. David Hand as the source for Ahab in *Moby Dick*. James Fenimore Cooper found characters like Leather Stocking among these men and wrote his first novel, *Precaution*, while living in town as an agent for a whaling company.

Like every harbor tied to the whales, Sag Harbor's fortunes sank with the decline of whaling. It wasn't until after World War II that Sag Harbor was rejuvenated by the tourist trade (although in the 1920s and '30s rum-running helped a bit), which remains strong today.

Main Street in Sag Harbor reveals the town's past through Colonial brick buildings that disappear into twisting trees hovering over benches, and tiny, timeworn whalers' homes adorn the side streets. At night, the street brightens with

You won't find much for 5 and 10 cents these days, even at this Sag Harbor store. © Maptech

Marine Facilities and Services		DOCKAGE					SERVICES				SUPPLIES & AMENITIES							
		Monitors / Working VHF Channel	Number of Transient Berths	Seasonal / Moorings	Approach / Dockside Depth in Feet at MLW	Maximum LOA	110V • 220V ▲ 3 Phase ■ Maximum Amps	Hookups: Fresh Water / Phone / Cable TV	Ramp / Dinghy Dock / Launch Service	Rail / Lift / Crane / Trailer Capacity (tons)	Repairs: Propellor / Sail / Rigging / Electronics	Diesel / Wood / Fiberglass	Marine / Groceries / Ice / Bait / LPG / CNG	Restrooms / Showers / Laundry / Pumpout	Gas / Diesel Fuel	Fuel Brand	Public Phone / Pool / Tennis / Golf	Hotel / Restaurant / Snack Bar	Mastercard / VISA / Discover / AmEx
1	SAG HARBOR YACHT YARD p. 317	631-725-3838	10/10		Y	70	13/13	F	★▲30	D	L35	All		MIC	RS		P	All
2	SAG HARBOR YACHT CLUB p. 319	631-725-0567	9/	15/	Y	200	10/10	All	★▲■200				GD	MB	RSP		P	MVA
3	Breakwater Yacht Club Community Sailing Ctr.*	631-725-4604			Y													
4	Sag Harbor Municipal Dock	631-725-2368	9/	30/10	S	110	10/10	F	★▲50	RD					RSP			MV
5	Malloy Waterfront Marina	631-725-3886	9/11	20/	S	175	10/10	FC	★▲■100					I	RS		P	MVA
6	Bayview Seafood Market	631-725-0740			S					R				GIB				MV
7	Long Wharf Village Pier	631-725-2368	9/		Y	190	10/10										P	MV
8	Malloy Sag Harbor Cove East Marina	631-725-1605	9/	20/	S	75	9/7	All	★▲50					I	RSL		PR	All
9	Ship Ashore Marina	631-725-3755	9/9		Y	35	3/3	F	★20		L30	All	G	MIB	RSP			MV
10	Malloy Sag Harbor Cove West Marina	631-725-3939	9/11	10/	S	60	10/7	FC	★▲50				G	Gulf	I	RSL	P	MVA
11	Hidden Cove Marina	631-725-3333		2/	S	20	6/4	F		R	T7			MIB	R		S	MV
12	Mill Creek Marina	631-725-1351		1/	S	42	4/4	F	★15	L	L25	All	G	Gulf	IB	RS	PR	MVA
13	Shalium Yacht Basin	631-749-1030			Y	40	6/6	F	★30	RD				MI	RSL			
14	The Island Boatyard (B)	631-749-3333	9/	45/	Y	60	6/6	F	■30	RD	L25	All	GD	Tex	MI	All	P	PR	MV

All Coast Guard Stations Monitor VHF Channel 16

Information in these listings is provided by the facilities themselves. An asterisk (*) indicates that the facility did not respond to our most recent requests for information. (B) represents a BOAT/U.S. cooperating marina.

Looking north over Sag Harbor, with Shelter Island in the background. © Maptech/James T. Abts

cast-iron gas lamps. There is a persistent sense of elegance and worldliness in the nooks and crannies of Sag Harbor.

ACTIVITIES: Few ports-of-call on Long Island are as polished as Sag Harbor. The village is small and manageable, the perfect stop if you enjoy a good walk through calm and pleasant streets. Start at the information booth in the mock windmill just off Long Wharf and get a walker's map of the town, courtesy of the Chamber of Commerce (631-725-0011). The tourist center can also provide you with a list of the historic houses in town that are open to the public.

Whaling's influence on the town has left a few memorable impressions, among them the seasonal Whaling Museum at the Benjamin Hunting House (631-725-0770). After making your entrance through the massive jawbones of a whale that arch over the main door, you will find a collection of flensing knives, blubber spades, harpoons, and "try-works," the huge vats used to boil whale blubber. With a curatorial style like grandma's attic, the contents of the museum are fascinating.

An architectural memento from bygone days is the Whalers Church, originally topped with a spyglass steeple that was blown off in the hurricane of 1938 and never replaced. The trim is reputed to have been carved by the town's whalers.

The Bay Street Theatre's (631-725-9500) summer season runs Memorial Day through Labor Day; weekend performances are held in the off-season. For "reel" fun, head to the Sag Harbor Cinema (631-725-0010), which is noted for its classic movies and second-runs.

If you want to venture away from the harbor area, Bike Hampton (631-725-7329) rents bikes. Allow extra time if traveling by taxi to Noyack Bay or other areas surrounding Sag Harbor. In summer, the cabs are long in demand and short in supply.

Embassy Guides

Take the kids to Havens Beach, just east of the breakwater. The beachfront park has restrooms, a lifeguard, swing set, and slide. Bay Point Beach Park on Noyack Bay has lots of running room for youngsters and joggers, and is open until 9 p.m.

The Morton Wildlife Refuge (631-725-2270) on Jessup Neck is manned full-time by a naturalist from the U.S. Fish & Wildlife Service who will be glad to answer any questions you may have about the place. The Neck has a varied wooded terrain with many kinds of flora and, of course, good beach walking. It's a prime spot for watching warbler migration in the spring when the woods are also beautiful with daffodils.

RESTAURANTS & PROVISIONS: Sag Harbor may be small, but there is no shortage of fine places to dine. You'll find the best ones on Main Street.

At the village pier, be sure to try the eclectic Southern-influenced wonders of B. Smith's (631-725-5858), named for the culinary queen who owns it. Barbara Smith also hosts a television cooking show, using her Sag Harbor home as the set.

At the American Hotel (631-725-3535), you can dress up a bit and dine in a perfectly classic setting. On some nights, especially in the off-season, the restaurant offers dinner with a movie at the local cinema. Il Capuccino Ristorante (631-725-2747) is your best bet for Northern Italian cuisine and a robust Chianti; it's only open for dinner. If you prefer Japanese cuisine, Sen (631-725-1774) will satisfy your yen; start out with a sushi roll, move on to an exquisite entrée, and wrap up the experience with a scoop of green tea ice cream.

The Dockside Bar & Grill (631-725-7100), across from the docks at the American Legion Post, is relaxing, friendly and affordable. At the head of Main Street, the Corner Bar and Restaurant (631-725-9760) is a local watering hole offering moderately-priced lunch and dinner in a good ol' saloon atmosphere.

The Main Street area is also a shopper's haven. Right off the waterfront, you'll find antique shops, boutiques, and art galleries. Conveniences such as a liquor and grocery store, laundromat, pharmacy, bookstore, hardware store, banks, and ATMs are readily available downtown.

If you're staying around Mill Creek in Noyack, try the Inn at Mill Creek (631-725-1116) for continental-style cuisine in a casual atmosphere. Provisioning in Mill Creek is limited. The Mill Creek Marina (631-725-1351) has seafood for sale, but you'll have to walk a half-mile south to the corner of Harry's Lane and Noyack Road to find a delicatessen. For nautical provisions, try Sag Harbor Yacht Yard's ship's store. Also, Henry Person & Sons (631-725-1900) can satisfy your hardware needs.

NAVIGATION & ANCHORAGES: Use ChartKit Region 3, pages 8 and 38; Maptech™ Waterproof Charts 1 and 6; and Maptech™ electronic and NOAA paper charts 12358 (1:40,000) and 12354 (1:80,000). Use tide tables for New London. High tide at Sag Harbor is 1 hour later; low tide is 48 minutes later. Use height of tide at New London for height of tide at Sag Harbor. Mean tidal range is 2.5 feet.

The Whaling Museum pays tribute to the town's early industry. © Maptech

High tide at Noyack Bay is 2 hours 6 minutes later; low tide is 1 hour 44 minutes later. Multiply height of tide at New London by 0.9 for height of tide at Noyack Bay. Mean tidal range is 2.3 feet.

Sag Harbor is 4.2nm south-southeast of West Neck Harbor on Shelter Island, and 2.5nm southwest of the light at Cedar Point, where a picturesque abandoned lighthouse guards the approach.

When a northeast wind blows across Gardiners Bay, very rough seas can build up around Cedar Point as the waves converge on the shallower and more constricted passage.

If you're headed past Sag Harbor toward Smith Cove or West Neck Harbor on Shelter Island, you can stay to the north of the sand spit. Keep at least 350 yards off Mashomack Point. Leave R N "8" and W Or C "S" well to the south and head directly for Fl G 4s G "15" off Tyndal Point on North Haven. Three ferries run back and forth across the channel between the North Haven Peninsula and South Ferry Hills on Shelter Island, and they don't give way for recreational boaters.

CAUTION: Pay careful attention to your charts and course when entering Sag Harbor. The harbormaster tells us that inattentive boaters will end up on the rocks.

From the east, round south of R N "8," and the Sand Spit Light (Fl R 4s 10ft 4M "10A"), both south of Mashomack Point on Shelter Island, in order to avoid the sand spit, rocks, and shoals that they mark. There is very shallow water south of G C "9," so honor the markers and stay in the channel.

From the north and west, keep Fl G 4s G "15" off the northeast tip of North Haven Peninsula to the south and west when rounding Tyndal Point, and then keep west of R N "14" and R N "12" as you head southeast.

None of these passages should be attempted in the dark, and even in daytime you must steer carefully between the markers. Whichever way you are approaching Sag Harbor, look for Fl G 4s G "11" 0.4nm northeast of the Sag Harbor breakwater, and G R "SH" mid-channel marker 200 yards to the west. Between these buoys lies the only safe approach to the harbor. Trying to save time by cutting buoys, especially if you're coming from the east, is not useful because you'll lose even more time waiting for your hull repairs at a local boatyard.

Keep west of the rocks, marked with W Or C, as you make your way to the breakwater. Fl G 2.5s 12ft 4M "1SH," on the northwest end of the long Sag Harbor breakwater, marks the harbor entrance.

It's tight and busy inside Sag Harbor, so it's a good idea to know ahead of time where you are going. Call the marinas first (or the harbormaster) for assistance. In addition, an ordinance requires sailboats with engines to be under power within harbor limits.

When coming into the harbor, do not round the breakwater too closely—keep 10 to 15 feet away—as the water is only about 6 feet deep near its end, though the main channel has 8 to 10 feet of water. Dead ahead you'll see Long Wharf, between you and the windmill.

Part of the town marina stretches east from Long Wharf. Transient slips are available on a first-come, first-

Looking northwest over Northwest Harbor and Cedar Point. © Maptech/James T. Abts

served basis. The harbormaster can be reached on VHF 9 to find out if space is available. (Since there are no finger piers, and the ladders from the water up to the main pier are built into the bulkhead, be sure to back into the berth.) The Sag Harbor Yacht Club offers transient slips, not to mention fuel.

No anchoring is allowed inside the harbor. Anchoring outside of the breakwater, to the south and east of the harbor entrance, is recommended in the high season. For a small fee, you can use the marina facilities (showers/laundry) even if you anchor out. Be aware of the rock (now marked by an obstruction buoy) less than 1500 feet southeast of the entrance, just off the breakwater. The gap in the breakwater is wide and deep enough for dinghies to sneak through.

The town of Southampton, of which Sag Harbor is a part, offers free pump-out. Just call them on VHF 73, and they'll come to you. As you might expect in the Hamptons, it's a spotless operation. (You might show your appreciation with a tip to the attendant.) Sag Harbor Yacht Yard has no berths, but they specialize in yacht restoration and conversion.

Sag Harbor Cove, to the west of Long Wharf, is fine for power boats that can go under the 20-foot-high fixed bridge. Follow a privately maintained, seasonal set of buoys to the marinas inside. There's another section of the town marina here, 300 yards inside of the bridge.

Just past the bridge, the Town of Southampton allows free anchoring for the first 72 hours, after which you'll be charged $25 for each additional 72 hours. The speed limit inside the cove is 5 mph. Most of the property surrounding the cove is private, and the only place you can land is on the eastern shore of Long Beach.

Ship Ashore Marina offers haul-out in the cove, but sailboats will have to be met outside the fixed bridge, where they will be dismasted. A barge used for this procedure also provides towing into the cove.

Noyack Bay, on the western side of North Haven Peninsula, provides unobstructed deep water as long as you stay a half mile from shore. The northwest corner of Noyack Bay is marked with Fl G 4s G "17" off Jessup Neck.

Noyack Bay provides no protection in a northerly wind, but there is plenty of room to escape from a southerly. With only a few rocks and a slightly muddy bottom, the anchorage is highly recommended by readers. If you've been dying to take a dip, here's your chance; the water quality is very good.

Mill Creek, at the southern end of Noyack Bay, is a cozy anchorage with several marine facilities. The approach is a straight shot south from Shelter Island Sound. Don't cut too close to Gleason Point if you're coming from the east, or too close to Jessup Neck from the west.

Mill Creek is entered by a 6-foot deep channel marked by private, seasonal lights and buoys. Inside is a town dock and ramp, on the east side directly opposite Fl G "5." Transients may tie up for 2 hours, but a permit is needed

to use the ramp. Call the Southampton Town Hall (516-283-6000) for permit information.

The shellfishing is good in Noyack Creek at the base of the point, but no facilities will be found. Shellfishing permits are available at the Southampton Town Hall. Anchoring in Noyack Creek is for residents only, with a town permit.

Shoreside & Emergency Services
Airport:
—East Hampton (631-537-1130)
Bus:
—Suffolk County Transit (631-852-5200)
Coast Guard:
—Montauk (631-668-2773) or VHF 16
Ferry:
—to North Haven Peninsula (631-749-1200)
—to Haddam, CT (passenger only) (860-345-4507)
Police, Fire, Ambulance: 911
Taxi:
—Ocean Limousine & Taxi (631-324-0077)
—Dependable Taxi (631-537-1800)
Tow Service:
SEA TOW —24-Hour Dispatch (800-4SEATOW)
—Eastern Long Island (631-765-5300)
Tow BoatU.S.—24-Hour Dispatch (800-391-4869)
—Peconic Bay (631-728-2743)
Train: Long Island Railroad (631-822-5477)

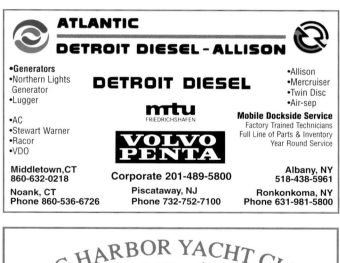

A Speedy Pursuit

There's a great old story they tell on Shelter Island. In 1804, England and France were embroiled in one of their interminable wars. The French held England in check with a blockade. Word spread in Norfolk, Virginia, that a cargo of 1,000 barrels of flour had to be carried to Liverpool, and the owners let it be known that any captain willing to run the French blockade would receive a guinea per barrel, a tempting price. But the risk was great: death or imprisonment.

Enter Captain Sam Lord, the wealthy, crusty head of the Lord family from Shelter Island. Captain Sam was in Norfolk with his swift schooner, *Paragon*. He didn't really need the money, but the prospect of a guinea a barrel was too much for his proud Yankee heart to refuse.

Looking north over Dering Harbor, with Shelter Island below and Greenport in the distance.

© Maptech/James T. Abts

The night the flour was loaded, *Paragon* sailed for Britain. The fifteenth night out was black, a blockade runner's best friend. All lights aboard were extinguished, and not a word passed between the men. Captain Sam steered the *Paragon* hard to starboard and swiftly past a French frigate. By dawn the Shelter Island men were in the Irish Sea headed for Liverpool. They had run the blockade! Soon all England was abuzz, and Captain Sam was invited to a banquet with the Lord Mayor and the brightest lights of Liverpool.

The next day the *Paragon* left for home, 1,000 guineas safely stored in Captain Sam's cabin. Running the blockade again was easy, but on the third day out a man-o-war was sighted in pursuit. The winds died and the frigate gained on *Paragon*. When the chase was over, the mysterious ship

Marine Facilities and Services

All Coast Guard Stations Monitor VHF Channel 16

#	Facility	Phone	Monitors VHF / Transient Berths	Approach/Dockside Depth	Seasonal (S)/Year-round (Y) · Moorings	Maximum LOA	Hookups: Fresh Water/Phone/Cable TV	110V★ 220V▲ 3Phase■ Max Amps	Ramp/Dinghy Dock	Rail/Lift/Crane/Launch Service	Repairs	Gas/Diesel Fuel	Fuel Brand	Marine/Groceries/Ice/Bait/LPG/CNG	Restrooms/Showers/Laundry/Pumpout	Public Phone/Pool/Tennis/Golf	Hotel/Restaurant/Snack Bar	Mastercard/VISA/Discover/AmEx
1	Shelter Island Yacht Club*				Y				*PRIVATE—RECIPROCAL PRIVILEGES*									
2	Jack's Marine	631-749-0114	9/	3/15	S	60	10/10	F		D					MGIB	R		
3	Town Dock/Dering Harbor*				Y				*2 HOUR TIE UP—LOADING & UNLOADING*									
4	**PICCOZZI'S** dering harbor marina (p. 323)	631-749-0045	9/7	50/13	Y	150	12/12	F	★▲100	D			GD	Mob	MGIBL	All		All	All
5	**COECLES HARBOR** MARINA & BOATYARD INC. (p. 325)	631-749-0700	9/68	25/20	Y	65	6/8	F	★▲50		L30	All	GD	Mob	MGILC	All	P	PS	MV
6	Town Dock/Coecles Harbor*		16/		Y	24	3/3		★20	R								
7	Ram's Head Inn	631-749-0811	/10		S		8/5			D						R	HT	PR	MVA
8	Island Boatyard	631-749-3333	9/	30/	Y	60	6/6	F	30	RD	LT25	All	GD	Tex	MI	All		PR	MVA

Information in these listings is provided by the facilities themselves. An asterisk (*) indicates that the facility did not respond to our most recent requests for information.
(B) represents a BOAT/U.S. cooperating marina.

proved to be British. Her commander demanded to know whom she had caught. "The *Paragon* from New York, three days out of Liverpool!" cried Captain Sam.

"You lie, sir!" came the sharp reply.

The British captain was astonished when handed a Liverpool newspaper from the day *Paragon* sailed. Never had he known a ship to come so far so fast.

The *Paragon,* it turns out, would not be the last of Shelter Island's speedy vessels. In 1996, Coecles Harbor Marina & Boatyard built and launched a revival of sorts— the Shelter Island 38 Runabout, a boat that combines the classic elements of a lobster boat, a 1940's commuter express, and a Prohibition-era rum-runner. This boat, inspired and funded by singer Billy Joel and designed by Doug Zurn of Marblehead, Massachusetts, has attracted many wealthy new clients to Coecles Harbor Marina & Boatyard, each wanting his or her own speedy creation. No doubt, these boats won't be running blockades, but it's safe to say that even today's captains will be astonished at the speeds they can travel with dual, 415-hp inboards pushing them.

ACTIVITIES: Shelter Island's name is appropriate—the harbors and coves here are protected, peaceful, and surrounded by wooded hills and stunning houses that look out over the water. The roads that wind their way through these hills are great for bicycling, so when you come ashore, rent a bike at Piccozzi's in Dering Harbor or Coecles Harbor Marina and take to the hills.

A brisk game of tennis can be had at the tennis courts run by the Shelter Island Heights Association (631-749-8897), just up the road from Piccozzi's; call to reserve a court. If golf is your game, there's a 9-hole course at the Shelter Island Country Club (631-749-0416).

The more nature-oriented pursuits on Shelter Island can be found on the 2,000-acre Mashomack Preserve (631-749-1001) on the southwestern point of the island, off Route 114, about four miles from Dering Harbor. Operated by the Nature Conservancy, the preserve offers more than 15 miles of trails taking you through woodland, beaches, and salt marshes. Note that only hiking is allowed; no bicycling or jogging is permitted.

Swimmers will be in their glory on Shelter Island: Crescent Beach runs from Jennings Point to Shelter Island Heights, on the northwest side of the island. Alas, one of our readers from the island writes us: "An old pair of sneakers might come in handy...a lot of the beaches are not exactly sandy." Leave the beach behind with a little help from Shelter Island Kayak Tours (631-749-1990), offering guided nature tours.

If you are looking to delve into the history of Shelter Island, you can visit the Manhanset Chapel Museum (631-749-1116) or the Havens House (631-749-0025) with its period rooms and aromatic herb garden. Or you may decide on a peaceful stroll through the Quaker burial grounds on Route 114 (North Ferry Road) near Dering Harbor. Meetings are held outdoors on Sundays—as they were originally—in the summer.

Looking east over West Neck Harbor. © Maptech/James T. Abts

Special events, including fireworks, road races, concerts, and flower and craft shows, are held throughout the summer. Ask around town, or call the Chamber of Commerce (631-749-0399) for more information.

RESTAURANTS & PROVISIONS: You'll find more than shelter in Shelter Island's inns. The Dering Harbor marinas are only a short walk away from the Chequit Inn (631-749-0018), serving seafood, New York sirloin, and well-dressed pasta followed by desserts to die for.

Out on Ram Island is the Ram's Head Inn (631-749-0811), which maintains a few moorings for its patrons. Here, you can enjoy elegant appetizers, fowl, seafood, and chops with innovative accompaniments. Both inns also offer a selection of Long Island spirits: microbrews from Southampton Publick House and plenty of local wines.

Back in town, you'll find The Dory (631-749-8871), a watering hole with a hearty American menu. Nearby, are Cogan's Country Restaurant (631-749-2129) and Michael Anthony's (631-749-3460), which has a great fillet mignon dinner.

At the Island Boatyard, Alfred's Place (631-749-3355) serves light pub fare, while Dockside Deli (631-749-3366) offers breakfast and lunch. Near Crescent Beach, The Island Grill (631-749-1808) serves French cuisine at The Shelter Island Resort. Most marinas on the island will arrange transportation to island restaurants.

For groceries, head to George's Market on North Ferry Road, up the street from Shelter Island Marina. Other needs can be filled at Shelter Island Heights Pharmacy (631-749-0445), Jack's Marine, Bait, & Tackle Shop (631-749-0114), Shelter Island Hardware (631-749-0097), and Bliss' Department Store (631-749-0041). Also, Coecles Harbor Marina has some nautical supplies.

NAVIGATION & ANCHORAGES: Use ChartKit Region 3, pages 8 and 38; Maptech™ Waterproof Charts 1 and 6; and Maptech™ electronic and NOAA paper charts 12358 (1:40,000) and 12354 (1:80,000). Use tide tables for New London. High tide at Greenport is 1 hour and 5 minutes later; low tide is 49 minutes later. Multiply height of tide at New London by 0.9 for height of tide at Greenport. Mean tidal range is 2.4 feet.

Shelter Island is an island of many harbors. At the northwest side of the island, Dering Harbor is 7.7nm from Plum Gut, 3.5nm from Coecles Harbor, and 13.5nm from the Shinnecock Canal.

Coecles Harbor is 6.5nm from Plum Gut and 4.3nm from Three Mile Harbor. The entrance to West Neck Harbor on the south side of the island is 2.7nm from Dering Harbor, and 3.2nm from Coecles Harbor.

Directly opposite Greenport, Dering Harbor usually has a handsome complement of yachts. The harbor is picturesque enough so that imagining it in a postcard setting is no trouble at all. Nor is there a problem making its entrance.

From the east, keep well south and west of Long Beach Point, as the reported shoaling extends a bit farther than the charts let on. Follow the channel around Long Beach Point to the harbor, not cutting any of the markers, and you've got it made.

The entrance to Dering Harbor, however, is partially blocked by a shoal extending north and east beyond the west shore—so most boats enter in mid-channel. (Although some boats anchor outside the entrance to Dering Harbor, the harbormaster warns that it is an unprotected and hazardous area.) When entering the harbor it's best to stay at least 200 yards off Dering Point to avoid the riprap there. Although it's exposed to the north, Dering Harbor is well protected from the east and prevailing southerly winds.

Anchoring is prohibited in the harbor, but moorings and berths are available at Piccozzi's Dering Harbor Marina or one of the other facilities. Make reservations well in advance; the harbor can get quite crowded in the summer. The yacht club has moorings and a launch service (VHF 9) available only on a reciprocal basis with other clubs.

Next to Piccozzi's is the town dock where you can tie up for 2 hours. Jack's Marine, a complete chandlery, has a floating dinghy dock where you can also tie up a small boat.

A short walk from the yacht club is the ferry to Greenport, which runs every 20 minutes, putting you in touch with, among other things, a supermarket and more restaurants.

Shelter Island

Coecles Harbor

Southeast from Dering Harbor is **Coecles Harbor**, one of the most pleasant places on the island. If you are coming in from the west, as from Greenport or Dering Harbor, stay well to the north of Fl G 4s G "7" north of Cornelius Point. The shoals to the south of it have a tendency to grab sunstruck early risers. Again, leave a good margin between you and Long Beach Point. Follow the curve of the channel east to Mo (A) WHIS RW "N" before turning south for Fl G 4s G "1" at the entrance to Coecles Harbor.

At Fl G 4s G "1" you'll turn west into the harbor. This passage is narrow and has a tendency to shoal. The privately-maintained navigational aids can be difficult to see when Gardiners Bay sets up a chop; they are also small and sometimes out of order. Upon entering, be sure to stay in the channel, which carries a reported depth of 7 feet at mlw.

Once inside the harbor, you'll see G C "7" to the west, and the remains of a lighthouse on a point called Taylor Island by the local residents, but marked "CUP" (for cupola) on the chart; give the point and the surrounding rocks a wide berth. G C "7" is well placed, marking the end of a rocky shoal off the point. The sandbar connecting it to the mainland is submerged at high tide, so stay clear.

Dockside in Shelter Island. © Maptech

Inside Coecles Harbor, there are several choices for anchoring. Note that aside from two Special Anchorages at Shelter Island, all anchoring is restricted to three hours May 15 to September 15. One of the Special Anchorages is the bight south of the channel as you enter Coecles Harbor, between Sungic Point and the cupola. Here, you can anchor up to 48 hours in any 72-hour period between May 15 and September 15. (The other Special Anchorage is at West Neck Harbor.)

CAUTION: A common mistake made by boaters who enter this harbor for the first time is that they travel past G C "7" and then turn south toward this anchorage area, cutting between the cupola and G C "7." This is a good way to lose the bottom of your boat.

If you draw less than 5 feet, you can go behind Little Ram Island, up into the northern bight. Keep R N "10" to the north and give it a wide berth—at least 200 feet—since there's only 4 feet of water immediately surrounding it. From R N "10" there are privately maintained markers to Coecles Harbor Marina and Boatyard. The anchorage area is north of R N "12."

There is a small town marina inside Congdons Creek in the southwest corner of the harbor, used mainly by residents with small boats. While the marked channel has a reported depth of about 5 feet, the water can be as low as 3 feet dockside.

Coecles Harbor generally has good holding ground of grass and mud and is a popular anchoring area. Weekends, you will certainly have company, but you shouldn't have any trouble finding room to swing at anchor. The northwest-southeast axis of the harbor means that it can get choppy when the wind blows along the same direction, especially in an opposing current. In such a case, head into one of the bights for a smoother night. (On warm summer nights, keep the bug spray handy.)

Keeping the water clean is important to Shelter Islanders, and the town's Chief of Police is quite strict with polluters. Help keep the water clean by not littering or discharging.

Coecles Harbor is also popular with windsurfers and beachcombers. You may see a few people clamming inside the point, but the privilege is extended to New York residents only. Swimming in the harbor can be good, but watch out for jellyfish that sometimes drift in.

West Neck Harbor

West Neck Harbor is another protected, peaceful spot to drop anchor. Coming from Dering Harbor, the traffic and currents can be quite heavy. Stay alert. Refer to the Greenport and Southold chapter chart for a detail of the following passage. The jaunt between Shelter Island Heights and Jennings Point is pleasant, as Greenport is to the north, and the woods, beaches and inns rise to the south. After you've passed west of Fl G 4s G "11" off Jennings Point, make for Fl R 4s R "12" between Paradise Point and West Neck. Make sure to pass east of the buoy or you'll be looking for a tow off of Paradise Point.

You can now head directly for Fl R 4s R "16." Pass south of the buoy before turning north-northeast for Fl R 4s R "2" at the entrance. Be sure to keep at least 250 yards off Shell Beach as you make your approach.

West Neck Harbor has plenty of good water inside, but there is a bar at the entrance, narrowing considerably an otherwise wide opening. The entrance is very close to the seaward end of the gravel point, locally called Shell

Looking east over the entrance to Coecles Harbor. © Maptech/James T. Abts

Beach. The Special Anchorage is just inside the harbor to the south.

The harbor may look as though you will never get into it if you draw more than 2 feet, but vessels with 5-foot drafts regularly pass over the bar. To do this, come in on a rising tide and come in very carefully. Upon entering, hug close to shore as there isn't as much water near Fl R 4s R "2." About 300 yards inside the point, to the north, is a privately-maintained and very well-marked channel to the marinas. Call The Island Boatyard and Marina for available slips or supplies.

Shoreside & Emergency Services
Coast Guard:
—Montauk (631-668-2773) or VHF 16
Ferry:
—To Sag Harbor from South Ferry (631-749-1200)
—To Greenport from Dering Harbor (631-749-0139)
Police, Fire, Ambulance: 911
Taxi:
—Fleetwood (631-477-0078)
Tow Service:
SEA TOW —24-Hour Dispatch (800-4SEATOW)
—Eastern Long Island (631-765-5300)
Tow BoatU.S. —24-Hour Dispatch (800-391-4869)
—Orient Point (631-323-2645)
Train: Long Island Railroad (631-822-5477)

The Far End of Long Island

Looking northeast over Long Beach, with Plum Gut and Plum Island in the distance. © Maptech/James T. Abts

Rising off Orient Point is the cast-iron Orient Point Light, also called the "Coffee Pot" by sea-weary navigators. This testament to the town's preservation efforts was beginning to rust through in the 1970s and the Coast Guard decided to demolish it, but citizens rallied to save the historic structure. In 1999 the Coffee Pot celebrated its 100th birthday—now that's a lot of cups of java. The light has operated automatically (running non-stop on caffeine, perhaps?) since its rehabilitation.

Set back several miles from the tip of Orient Point, Orient was a favorite hideaway for honeymooners early in the 20th century. Suffolk County acquired a large tract of land here in 1988 in order to preserve environmentally fragile areas. The land is open to the public, and there is a footpath to the point.

One place that is most definitely not open to the public is Plum Island. Purchased from the Indians for a coat, a container of biscuits, and 100 fish hooks, the island is used by the Department of Agriculture for its Animal Disease Laboratory. Research is conducted on harmful insects and contagious animal diseases, such as swine fever and hoof-and-mouth disease; the public is not allowed on the island.

Nelson DeMille's 1997 best-selling novel *Plum Island* revolved around the fictional murder of two biologists believed to have stolen invincible viruses from the island. While DeMille's murder-mystery was a work of fiction, the sense of mystery surrounding the island's off-limits status has caused some active imaginations to dream up notions of what actually goes on there, and rumors abound.

Marine Facilities and Services			DOCKAGE						SERVICES					SUPPLIES & AMENITIES							
		Number of Transient Berths / Moorings	Monitors / Working VHF Channel	Seasonal / Yearround	Approach / Dockside Depth in Feet at MLW	Maximum LOA	Hookups: Fresh Water / Phone / Cable TV	110V ★ 220V ▲ 3 Phase ■ Maximum Amps	Ramp / Dinghy Dock / Launch Service	Rail / Lift / Crane / Trailer: Capacity (tons)	Diesel / Wood / Fiberglass / Electronics	Repairs: Propellor / Sail / Rigging / Gas	Marine / Groceries / Ice / Bait / LPG / CNG	Gas / Diesel Fuel	Fuel Brand	Restrooms / Showers / Laundry / Pumpout	Public Phone / Restaurant / Snack Bar	Hotel / Pool / Tennis / Golf	Mastercard / VISA / Discover / AmEx	
1	**Orient By The Sea** RESTAURANT & MARINA 631-323-2424 p. 329	9/	10/	S	50	6/8	F	★30	R			WFE		GD			I		RS		PR	MVD
2	Narrow River Marina 631-323-2660		6/	Y	28	4/4	F		R			GDWFE					R				
3	Orient Yacht Club*			Y			*PRIVATE-MEMBERS ONLY*														

All Coast Guard Stations Monitor VHF Channel 16

Information in these listings is provided by the facilities themselves. An asterisk (*) indicates that the facility did not respond to our most recent requests for information. (B) represents a BOAT/U.S. cooperating marina.

Long Beach Bar Light. © Maptech

serves a variety of seafood specials, and they're all good—it just depends what you're in the mood for. In Orient Village, you'll find the Orient Country Store (631-323-2580).

For a wider range of provisioning options, hail a cab down to Greenport, which has all the amenities for the touring boater.

NAVIGATION & ANCHORAGES: Use ChartKit Region 3, pages 8 and 38; Maptech™ Waterproof Charts 1 and 6; and Maptech™ electronic and NOAA paper charts 12358 (1:40,000), 13209 (1:40,000), and 12354 (1:80,000). Use tide tables for New London. High tide at Plum Gut is 28 minutes later; low tide is 16 minutes later. Use height of tide at New London for height of tide at Plum Gut. Mean tidal range is 2.6 feet. High tide at Orient Harbor is 37 minutes later than New London; low tide is 36 minutes later. Use height of tide at New London for height of tide at Orient Harbor. Mean tidal range is 2.5 feet.

The neighboring Great Gull Island is a healthy sanctuary for a large population of roseate terns, an endangered species. The island is co-owned by the American Museum of Natural History and the Linnaean Society. The birds need peace and space to propagate, so landing is prohibited there, too.

ACTIVITIES: Orient is an unassuming pearl of a town, full of charming old houses, farmland, and marsh. It's a great place to explore on foot or bike, but don't expect to find an abundance of activities.

The town is somewhat off the beaten path, so there is a minimum of boutiques, restaurants, and the like. The Oysterponds Historical Society's (631-323-2480) seven-house complex includes exhibits of marine paintings and scrimshaw, among other things. The museum is a block north of the Orient Yacht Club. At the entrance of the tidal creek just north of the yacht club is a small town landing, for access to the museum and a quaint country store with ice and ice cream. The only public phone is on the main road, about a half block to the east.

You're in luck if you've brought your bike along. Once away from town, the roads meander through farmland, along marshes, and past a vineyard or two. Another restful panorama is seen from Orient Beach State Park (631-323-2440). The 342-acre park is a long sand spit with 10 miles of waterfront on Gardiners Bay. While there is deep water off the beach, boats must stay 1,000 feet off the swimming area and 500 feet off the rest of the beach. If you visit the park by land, you'll find a food stand, bathhouse, and picnic areas with hibachis.

RESTAURANTS & PROVISIONS: The Orient by the Sea Marina & Restaurant (631-323-2424) at the Cross Sound Ferry dock

Having crossed the Sound, chances are you'll choose to pass through Plum Gut to get to Orient Point. Plum Gut is 9.9nm from New London Harbor entrance and 9.5nm from Dering Harbor on Shelter Island. Three Mile Harbor is 7.5nm to the south.

From the Saybrook bar marked by Fl R 4s BELL R "8," a course of about 150°m will take you between Plum Island and Orient Point.

CAUTION: Use extreme care when entering Plum Gut. The tide rips can be worse than The Race, though more short-lived. Pick a clear, calm day if you're going through here for the first time.

From Long Island Sound it is absolutely necessary to check the tide tables in order to time your passage through the Gut for slack water or ebb tide. If you don't, you very well might end up sailing backward. Pay close attention to the wind and current; pick a time when they're not fighting each other, because in the Gut it can turn into a brawl.

From Gardiners Bay, take the passage at slack or flood tide. Pass well east of Fl 5s 64ft 17M HORN off Oyster Pond Reef.

The channel through Plum Gut is 0.6nm wide and plenty deep; there is one spot where the bottom plunges from about 35 feet to nearly 200. It can look spectacular, as well as scary, on the depth sounder.

The velocities of flood and ebb tide in the Gut range from slack to 4.5 knots, but can go much higher under the right conditions. The flood sets northwestward and the ebb southeastward. During flood, a countercurrent develops along the north shore of Plum Island, and it gets quite nasty within half a mile of shore.

Also watch the wind, because it can do hair-raising things; be careful you don't lose your steerage as you lose headway in the chop. Keep an eye out for what the water does, too. It is not uncommon to encounter an 8-foot standing wave poised in front of you like a fist.

Orient Point is marked by Fl 5s 64ft 17M HORN. The foghorn can be difficult to hear in a rumbling easterly wind. Stay well east of the light because Oyster Pond Reef is strewn with boulders and is only about 2 feet deep at mlw. Watch out for fishermen in this area, as well as around Middle Ground (off Plum Island) and Midway Shoal, just south of Plum Gut. Also be on the lookout for commercial trawlers, which will usually identify themselves with a metal basket hanging from the mast. Keep in mind that they may be trailing nets as far as 50 yards astern, and that they have right-of-way over you, even if you're sailing.

Ferryboats travel the channel so regularly that they have little patience with small craft. Their sheer size makes for a lack of maneuverability, so it's up to you to steer clear of them. Be aware that they often make unexpected moves when playing the currents. (If you happen to be passing through the Gut in a high sea, and are in a power boat, follow the ferry through at a safe distance, as its wake flattens the water considerably.)

Be careful sailing parallel to the shores anywhere in this area. You should stand out a good distance and know which way the tides are running so that you aren't set onto the rocks and shoals off Orient Point.

As you round Orient Point and come into Gardiners Bay, you'll see the ferry slips just southwest of the point. The marinas in the area are good, but often crowded because of their proximity to the traffic at Plum Gut and the lack of other facilities nearby. You can anchor anywhere along the sandy spit of Orient and Long Beach for a swim, but the harbormaster has informed us that this area is part of Orient State Park, and that there is a no-landing rule in effect here. Remember to stay 1,000 feet off the swimming area and 500 feet off the rest of the beach.

Heading southwest directly toward Shelter Island, stay at least 500 yards offshore to keep from running over the many fish weirs close to the beaches. Also, keep clear of Long Beach Point, as a shoal extends south from it and has built up enough to be a danger even to small boats. Note that Fl 4s Long Beach Point Light (a.k.a. Bug Light) has been rebuilt. The best course is to steer between Fl R 4s BELL R "2" and G C "3" south of Long Beach Point.

From Fl R 4s BELL R "2," head directly for, and pass north of, Fl G 4s G "7" off Cornelius Point on Shelter Island. This is also the gateway to Greenport, Southold, and Dering Harbor. If you're heading for anchorage north of Long Beach Point, follow the same course and make sure you round the point keeping off at least 800 yards. The currents are also strong here, so be sure you aren't set up to the shoal. Once you're around the point and heading northeast, there's a pleasant anchorage dead ahead. Keep clear of the fish stakes, some of which may be broken off below water. This is a fair-weather anchorage and is entirely exposed to the southwest. Across the bay is Orient Harbor proper, well-protected to the north but wide-open to the south.

To the east, between Long Beach and Peters Neck Point, is the entrance to Hallock Bay. The bay is shallow and the entrance is tight, blocked with pilings and shoals, so it should be attempted only in a dinghy or a boat with very shallow draft. It is, however, quite peaceful and has good holding ground. A channel marked by pilings hugs the western shore along Browns Point.

Orient by the Sea Marina & Restaurant offers some repair services and also sells fuel. You'll get a great deal on overnight dockage—just $25. Transient slips are also available at Narrow River Marina, inside the bay. It's a moderate walk to town from there.

Shoreside & Emergency Services

Coast Guard: Montauk (631-668-2773) or VHF 16
—New London (860-442-4471) or VHF 16
Ferry: Cross Sound to New London, CT (631-323-2525)
Police, Fire, Ambulance: 911
Taxi: Fleetwood (631-477-0078)
Tow Service:
SEA TOW —24-Hour Dispatch (800-4SEATOW)
—Eastern Long Island (631-765-5300)
Tow BoatU.S.—24-Hour Dispatch (800-391-4869)
—Orient (631-323-2645)

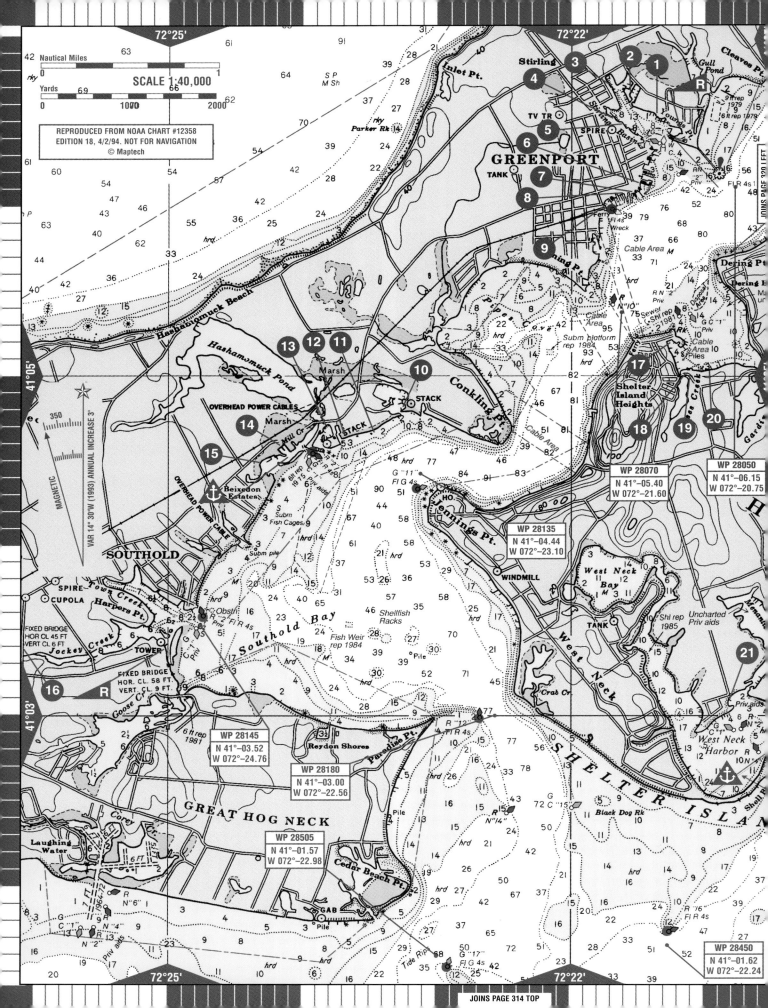

A Quick Fix

Settled as "Hashamomuck" by "seekers of spirit resin" (turpentine) in 1636, Southold is the oldest English-speaking settlement in "Nieuw Amsterdam." More spread out and suburban than Greenport, and with an all-private waterfront, downtown Southold doesn't have quite the nautical flavor of the Greenport, but is a pleasant place nonetheless.

Greenport's boatyards have always reaped the rewards of a town closely connected with the sea. Following the days of the great sailing ship era, Greenport's fishing fleet increased, and so did the need for those vessels to be fixed. Then came Prohibition in the 1920s when Greenport turned its attention to rum-running. The illegal activity was so popular that a Coast Guard Station was opened in the village to police the activity. And of course, the rum-running boats and Coast Guard chasers needed to be fixed once in a while.

A multi-colored sailing vessel graces a Greenport dock. © Maptech

Marine Facilities and Services		DOCKAGE						SERVICES				SUPPLIES & AMENITIES									marinalife.com
		Monitors / Working VHF Channel	Number of Transient Berths / Moorings	Approach / Dockside Depth in Feet at MLW	Seasonal / Yearround	Hookups: Fresh Water / Phone / Cable TV	110V • 220V ▲ 3 Phase ■ Maximum Amps	Maximum LOA	Ramp / Dinghy Dock / Launch Service	Rail / Lift / Crane / Trailer: Capacity (tons)	Repairs: Propellor / Sail / Rigging / Electronics	Diesel / Wood / Fiberglass	Marine / Groceries / Ice / Bait	Gas / Diesel Fuel	Restrooms / Showers / Laundry / Pumpout	Fuel Brand	Public Phone / Restaurant / Snack Bar	Hotel / Pool / Tennis / Golf	Mastercard / VISA / Discover / AmEx	
1	Brewer Yacht Yard at Greenport *Inside Back Cover*	631-477-9594	9/	15/	Y	60	8/7	F	★▲50	D	L70	RWFE			MIC	All	P	PS	All	
2	STIRLING HARBOR MARINA *p. 333*	631-477-0828	9/10	30/	Y	125	13/10	FP	★▲50		L50	All	GD		I	RSL	PT	All	MVD	
3	Triangle Yacht Club*	631-477-2341			Y				*PRIVATE—MEMBERS ONLY*											
4	TOWNSEND MANOR MARINA *p. 337*	631-477-2000	9/	51/	S	50	10/8	FC	★▲50	D			G		I	RSL	HP	All	All	
5	Hanff's Boat Yard	631-477-1550			Y	45	10/6			RC20		All								
6	Greenport Yacht & Shipbuilding Co.	631-477-2277			Y	110	16/12			RL350		All						P		
7	EST. PRESTON'S 1880 *p. 335*	631-477-1990			Y	150	20/10			D					M				All	
8	Claudio's Marina	631-477-0627	9/	35/	S	290	40/15	F	★▲100				GD		MGIB	All		All	MV	
9	Greenport Visitors' Dock*			10/	Y				D									P		
10	Brick Cove Marina	631-477-0830		5/	Y	50	6/6	F	★▲50	R	L30	All			MI	All	PT	P	MVA	
11	The Old Barge Bar & Restaurant*	631-765-4700		4/	S	50	4/4								R		PR	MVA		
12	Mill Creek Basin	631-765-3653		4/	Y	35	3/4	F	★▲50			PRE			RS		PR			
13	Goldsmith's Boat Shop	631-765-1600	16/		Y	40	8/15	F	★15	R	LT11	WFE	G		M	RP		P	All	
14	Port of Egypt	631-765-2445		20/	Y	44	6/4	F	★	R	L7	All	GD		MIB	All	HP	All	MVA	
15	ALBERTSON Marine, inc. *p. 337*	631-765-3232	16/18		Y	42	4/4	F	★		L26	PSRFE			M	RP		P	All	

All Coast Guard Stations Monitor VHF Channel 16

Facilities continued on next page...

Anyone who visits Greenport ends up at S.T. Preson's. © Maptech

Greenport took a patriotic role in patrolling the seas during World War II when the town equipped itself with its own navy. "The Hooligan Navy" was a hodgepodge of dandy boats, schooners, ketches, motorsailers, and others lent by residents to the U.S. Coast Guard. The flotilla was outfitted with submarine detection devices and commissioned to patrol for German U-boats. Wind-powered and made of wood, "the Corsair Fleet," as it was officially called, was virtually undetectable by the enemy.

The war effort was also vigorous ashore. At one point the Greenport Shipyard employed as many as 2,000 men—an incredible total considering the size of the town—to build minesweepers, sea sleds, and landing barges. Following the war, things settled down to the old routine of fishing and farming. Stirling Basin was dredged in the 1960s and has become the focus of Greenport's recreational marine industry. To be sure, there are a few repair yards here to mend your vessel even today.

ACTIVITIES: There is an unmistakable look about Greenport: sand in the streets, big captains' houses half-hidden by trees, small fishermen's cottages with lobster pots in the yard, funky antique shops, fried food, and salty bars.

Downtown, every street lets out at the water. Main Street is no exception; it ends in the heart of town, with a pair of east end institutions: S.T. Preston's chandlery (631-477-1990) on one side, and Claudio's restaurant on the other. Even if you're not in need of marine supplies, charts, books, gifts, or nautical clothing or accessories, be sure to stop in to soak up the atmosphere.

In Greenport, you'll find most conveniences within a five-minute walk from the dock, and you can also watch the commercial fishermen unload their catch (some of which will go to the local restaurants). Follow the golden horseshoes painted on the street one block east to the Grumman Carousel. One buck gets you on the gentle broncos for a spin and chance at the brass ring. Next in line and next door is the Railroad Museum (631-477-0439) for a look at the town's history of rail shipment to New York City dating back to 1850.

For some maritime heritage, visit the East End Seaport Maritime Museum (631-477-0004), located at the end of

Marine Facilities and Services

All Coast Guard Stations Monitor VHF Channel 16

#	Facility	Phone	Monitors/Working VHF Channel	No. of Transient Berths / Moorings	Seasonal/Yearround	Max LOA	Approach/Dockside Depth (ft MLW)	Hookups: Fresh Water/Phone/Cable TV	110V+220V ▲3 Phase ■ Max Amps	Ramp/Dinghy Dock/Launch	Rail/Lift/Crane/Trailer Capacity (tons)	Repairs: Propeller/Sail/Rigging/Electronics	Diesel/Wood/Fiberglass	Gas/Diesel Fuel	Fuel Brand	Marine/Groceries/Ice/Bait/LPG/CNG	Restrooms/Showers/Laundry/Pumpout	Public Phone/Restaurant/Snack Bar	Hotel/Pool/Tennis/Golf	MC/VISA/Discover/AmEx
16	Southold Marine Center	631-765-3131		5/	Y	25	3/3	F			L6	PRGF				M	R			MV
17	Shelter Island Yacht Club*				Y					*PRIVATE—RECIPROCAL PRIVILEGES*										
18	Jack's Marine	631-749-0114	9/	3/15	S	60	10/10	F		D						MGIB	R			
19	Town Dock/Dering Harbor*				Y					*2 HOUR TIE UP—LOADING & UNLOADING*										
20	**PICCOZZI'S** dering harbor marina p. 323	631-749-0045	9/7	50/13	Y	150	12/12	F	★▲100	D				GD	Mob	MGIBL	All		All	All
21	The Island Boatyard (B)	631-749-3333	9/	45/	Y	60	6/6	F	■30	RD	L25	All		GD	Tex	MI	All	P	PR	MV

Information in these listings is provided by the facilities themselves. An asterisk (*) indicates that the facility did not respond to our most recent requests for information. (B) represents a BOAT/U.S. cooperating marina.

You could end up spending your entire cruise here.

(It happens all the time!)

Some people just decided to stop in at the last minute. Still others had read the Offshore Magazine review which gave Stirling Harbor its highest rating. It called us "…one of those special places that is kept nestled in your memory. It is worth a visit." Either way, they ended up staying a lot longer than planned.

The reasons were many. A park-like setting with scores of trees and fieldstone fireplaces. A four-star restaurant, pool and mini spa in a country club setting. Full security and privacy. Plus every important feature any cruising boater could ever need including complimentary electricity, water, and shuttle service into town, plus full-service shipyard facilities and more.

All situated in a spot-often called the "crossroads of boating." A place where fishing villages meet farm fields and vineyards. Just one visit will convince you that Stirling Harbor is not just a place to stop, but a destination.

Chosen as one of the Top 10 Marinas on the East Coast by Waterway Guide 2000.

• FULL SERVICE SHIPYARD & MARINA
(Mechanical, Electrical, Fiberglass & Wood Repair, Metal Electro plating-Chrome, Gold, Silver)

- Full-length fixed & floating fingers
- Free 30 & 50 Amp electric service
- Free water
- Free membership in our Pool & Cabana club
- Free Coffee & Danish daily
- Use of Resort Spa & Fitness Center: *(Full Gym, Massage Therapy & Water Aerobics)*
- *Shuttle service into town*

- Concierge service
- Full security
- Storm Safe Harbor: free installation of owner's extra bumpers & lines
- Fuel dock & Shipyard *open 7 days a week*
- Mechanic On-Premises
- Fully tiled private bathrooms & showers
- Laundry Delivery Service or use our Laundromat
- Barbecue and Picnic areas
- Tennis Court

- New York Times available
- Interior/Exterior boat cleaning service-*reservations required*
- Wine Tasting & Lectures - see Calendar of Events
- Four Star Restaurant
- Group tours & wine tasting arranged
- Open Year Round
- Winter & Summer Storage Available

YOUR HOME AWAY FROM HOME

STIRLING HARBOR MARINA

1410 MANHANSET AVENUE GREENPORT, NEW YORK 11944 (631) 477-0828 FAX (631) 477-0847
e-mail-dockmaster @ stirlingharbor.com

Third Street by the ferry dock. If you're in town on the last weekend in September, be prepared for the annual two-day maritime harbor festival (631-477-0004) with boat and crab races, survival suit swims, helicopter rescue demonstrations, and visiting tall ships. There are dozens of other events put on by the museum and the local marinas, so call in advance of your trip to get the latest schedule.

Take a swing and stroll at the Islands End Golf Course (631-477-0777), a cab ride east on the main road towards Orient. Attire is strict: "No shorts with inseams less than 5 inches." Shorts are fine at the town playground and beach at Fanning Point, where you will find restrooms, swings, basketball courts, picnic tables, and a small dock.

There are 16 wineries and vineyards within a short cab ride west of town. For more information on winery tours and events, call the Long Island Wine Council (631-366-5889).

For sightseeing in Southold, the New York State Archaeological Association runs the Indian Museum (631-765-5577), offering "A Flashback to Indian Days," as their brochure announces. Aside from an impressive collection of

artifacts, some of which date back 10,000 years, the exhibits also show how the Algonquins "hunted, fished, farmed...[and] gambled."

The Southold Historical Society (631-765-5500) maintains a cluster of historic buildings on Main Road that includes the Victorian Ann Currie-Bell House, a corncrib, icehouse, buttery, blacksmith shop, and carriage house. The Society also maintains the Horton Point Lighthouse and museum on the Sound side, two miles from the docks at Mill Creek. The light is picturesque and accented by ever-present beach anglers. To heighten the experience— especially at sunset—walk among the giant boulders strewn along the beach. Or, stare at the stars through the Custer Institute's celestial telescope on Saturday evenings after dark (631-765-2626).

A less rocky beach to stroll is Cedar Beach Point on the southeast tip of Great Hog Neck, a county preserve. The beach is crowded in the summer, but fun to visit because of the thousands of shells that wash ashore. They come in practically every color of the spectrum. There are also a lot

Long Island Windmills Keep Four Sheets to the Wind

He was three sheets to the wind, mate. You should've seen 'im," might be a sailor describing the antics of the previous evening. Three sheets to the wind? Stumbling drunk, of course.

There was a time, however, when the sheets were the sails mounted on the arms of a windmill. Four "sheets" to the wind were okay; the windmill was balanced. Try three sheets and the windmill shuddered out-of-balance in the wind, much like an inebriated person. But it's no surprise that most people don't think of this meaning today when windmills are mostly historic relics, standing firm yet rarely powering the grinding of grain, pumping of water, or sawing of wood.

There are 11 of these wooden windmills still standing on Long Island, making up the largest single group of surviving windmills in the United States. All of them are smock windmills, with the cylindrical shape of the body resembling the shape of a smock. They feature a stationary body and machinery topped with a rotating cap that turns the arms toward the wind.

Most remaining Long Island windmills sit on the south shore, but there are windmills still standing today on Gardiners Island and

Shelter Island. Both were built by millwright Nathaniel Dominy V from East Hampton. The Shelter Island Windmill was built in 1810 in Southold on the North Fork. It has since been moved twice. In 1839, it was transported to Shelter Island's village center. In 1926, it was moved to the grounds of Sylvester Manor, where it stands as a landmark today. It is the only surviving windmill actually built on the North Fork.

The Gardiners Island Windmill was built even earlier, in 1795, and was probably the first windmill Dominy built. It is relatively small and believed to be a part of John Lyon Gardiner's rejuvenation of Gardiners Island after the Revolutionary War; the windmill was frequently used for grinding livestock feed. After a hurricane blew the structure over in 1815, Dominy was hired to rebuild it.

As it turns out, the Gardiners Island windmill is an excellent landmark for mariners. It can be seen from afar, reminiscent of an era of wind-powered technology when mounted sails tackled moving masses of air. Except for once in a while, that is, when a sail would tear or not be replaced properly, and the windmill would find itself with little control—three sheets to the wind.

of gulls here, no doubt interested in the pretty mollusks. Wear a hat. For your own sake.

RESTAURANTS & PROVISIONS: Greenport's four-block downtown (Main to 3rd, Front to Center streets) has at least one of everything you will need including restaurants (a dozen), banks, ATMs, a pharmacy, hardware stores, a laundromat, chandleries, liquor stores, a movie theater, and a supermarket.

Owned and operated by the same family since 1870, Claudio's (631-477-0627) is a cornerstone of Greenport. This sizable, family-style restaurant is actually three eateries and displays nautical memorabilia from such ships as the *Enterprise*, the 1930s America's Cup defender, on the walls. Seafood is the main brace here, with lobsters the specialty. Claudio's is right on the water and offers free dockage to patrons.

Once known for its French cuisine, Aldo's took on a Japanese flair and is now called Sushi & Aldo's (631-477-1699). It now has a fully Japanese menu. To get that famous biscotti, just head across the street to Aldo's, Too (631-477-2859). If your sweet tooth is still aching, there are three ice cream stands and a pastry shop within a block. To cap off the night, the Rhumb Line (631-477-9883) is the sailors' saloon in town, and also serves good food at reasonable prices.

At Stirling Harbor Marina you'll find Bistro Blue (631-477-3940) very classy and reasonably priced. A view of the Brewer Yacht Yard parking lot (boats and water in the distance) serves as a backdrop for the Antares Café (631-477-8839), a somewhat upscale eatery, serving contemporary American dishes—try the Peconic Bay Bouillabase. In the west end of town, try Porto Bello (631-477-1717) for fine Italian fare.

Missed the ferry to Shelter Island? Then jump into the Chowder Pot Pub (631-477-1345) for guess what? Sip a pint or watch a game on the tube at the bar while you wait for another, and another (ferry).

In Southold, around the marinas at Hashamomuck Pond, you'll find other Southold eateries including the Seafood Barge (631-765-3010), with a great view of Mill Creek and Southold Bay. On the east end of Mill Creek Bridge, Hollisters (631-765-5113) serves reasonably-priced daily specials in a comfortable country setting.

Downtown Southold is about four blocks long and located at the head of Town Creek. Unfortunately, there are no convenient public landings. Come by car for access to Main Street essentials (they are all there).

NAVIGATION & ANCHORAGES: Use ChartKit Region 3, pages 8 and 38; Maptech™ Waterproof Charts 1 and 6; and Maptech™ electronic and NOAA paper charts 12358 (1:40,000) and 12354 (1:80,000). Use tide tables for New London. High tide at Greenport is 1 hour 5 minutes later; low tide is 49 minutes later. Multiply height of tide at New London by 0.9 for height of tide at Greenport. Mean tidal range is 2.4 feet.

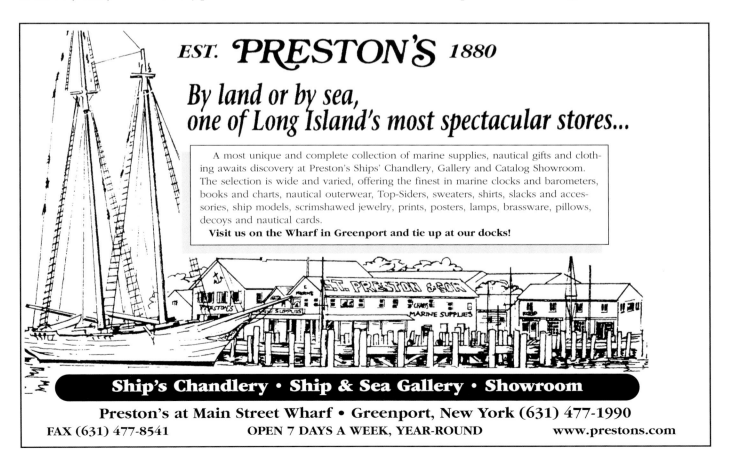

Greenport Harbor is opposite Dering Harbor on Shelter Island, about 8.8nm southwest of Plum Gut, and 3.2nm northeast of Mill Creek in Southold.

From Gardiners Bay, proceeding southwest directly towards Shelter Island, head for Fl R 4s R "2" located southeast of Long Beach Point. Passing south of the buoy, turn northwest to pass between Fl R 4s R "2" and G C "3." You may see boats "cutting the corner" around Long Beach Point, but we recommend you stay in the marked channel as a shoal extending south of the Point has built up enough to be a danger to even small boats. An important landmark will be the completely rebuilt Long Beach Bar "Bug" Light (Fl 4s) off the southwestern end of Long Beach Point. Aim northwest and pass north of Fl G 4s G "7," toward the rusty, white shipyard buildings on Cleaves Point to round Shelter Island's Hay Beach Point.

Looking a bit like the backyard canals of Fort Lauderdale, Gull Pond is just to the west with 6 to 7 feet of water, but no place to go unless you've got a friend there with an empty dock. If the pond doesn't do, steer southwest toward Fl R 4s 19ft 4M "8A" on the breakwater off Youngs Point which protects the entrance to Stirling Basin and Greenport Harbor.

There is good water up to the many docks of downtown Greenport. The port is not really an anchorage since it is too busy and too open, but it's a good place to tie up to see the old fishing town. S.T. Preston's chandlery has free dockage during the day, but you should know there is heavy channel wash. Some people, however, find docking more comfortable next door at Claudio's—at the cost of a meal. There is also a small visitors' dock just east of the ferry dock.

The best place for an overnight stay in Greenport itself, if you can find room, is inside Stirling Basin, where there's a reported channel depth of 8 feet. After you pass the breakwater at Young's Point and Fl R 4s 19ft "8A" turn west and pass south of R N "2" (priv). Align yourself toward a pair of privately maintained buoys at the Stirling Basin entrance; G C "1" and W Or C. G C "1" marks foul ground; once beyond it, turn to the northwest and stay close to the west shore. Don't cut too close to "the thumb" of sand extending out from Monument Point on the east shore. On the other hand, as long as you don't pester the nesters (piping plovers and osprey) the beach is a perfect place for your fledglings to fly kites, swim, or stretch their legs.

You'll find numerous berths on the west shore at the all-transient Townsend Manor Inn & Marina. On the east side, Brewer Yacht Yard at Greenport and Stirling Harbor Marina are both full-service yards with excellent transient facilities and good restaurants. The only down-side is that they are on the wrong side of the harbor if you want to go into town. But don't fret, both Stirling Harbor Marina and Brewer's will arrange land transportation for you. The harbormaster (631-477-0392) controls mooring and anchoring in the basin; reservations are a must for weekends. The transient moorings

Looking west over the marinas located west of Conkling Point. Hashamomuck Pond sits in the background with Port of Egypt Marina and Albertson's Marine at its entrance.
© Maptech/James T. Abts

have two lobster pot-style floats tied to them: one orange, another green.

Some cruising yachtsmen occasionally moor in Dering Harbor on Shelter Island (anchoring is no longer permitted) and take the ferry across ($1/trip) to Greenport to shop, sightsee, or eat. The three ferries operate continuously, so if you are staying at one of the nearby marinas, try to get a slip away from the channel wash and noise.

Pipes Cove, between Greenport and Conkling Point, is OK for lunch but is ringed with shallows and wide open to wakes from the nearby channel. Don't stay here overnight.

The entrance to Southold Bay is two miles southwest of Greenport, between Conkling and Jennings points. At night, the low, marshy, and unmarked Conkling Point can be hard to see, thus causing difficulties for mariners who fail to give it a wide enough berth. Mill Creek, opposite Jennings Point, is a pleasant little anchorage with a marina and a small restaurant.

Keep well off Jennings Point, which is surrounded by rocks extended out 150 yards. The channel narrows at this point to as little as 700 yards, and the traffic can be very heavy, as can the currents. Keep your eye on the chart and your wits about you. The town of Southold, which includes Greenport and Orient Point, enforces a 5-mph speed limit within 500 yards of the shore.

The channel into Mill Creek is a reported 4 feet deep and then 3.5 feet farther inside. Inside, Port of Egypt Marina and Albertson's Marine keep a number of slips open for transients. Follow the privately maintained markers and lights. East of Mill Creek is a small, unnamed inlet with a reported depth of 4 feet up to the marina inside. The channel is marked by privately maintained aids.

Jockey Creek and Town Creek, which make up Southold Harbor, share the same entrance with bulkheads and sandy beaches on each side. A white tower on the south side of Jockey Creek is a good range to head for after rounding Jennings Point, but as you get closer, look for Fl R 4s priv. R "2" paired with G C "1," which mark the entrance. (Both buoys are seasonal and privately maintained.)

Stay close to G C "1" to avoid the shoal on the north side of the entrance. The channel may be less than the 6 to 8 feet shown on your chart. Several marinas and marine service centers are around the harbor.

Goose Creek, a little farther south, is suitable only for small boats. It has a fixed bridge with a height of 9 feet and shallow water. You can drop a lunch hook anywhere in Southold Bay, but the open anchorage suffers from the same problems as Pipes Cove. You'll want to head for a more secure anchorage at night. Take care when rounding Paradise Point off Great Hog Neck. Stay east of Fl R 4s R "12" which is actually closer to Shelter Island, and hence, many boaters miss the mark and get toasted on the sand spit.

Shoreside & Emergency Services
Airport: Mattituck Airbase (631-298-8330)
Bus: Suffolk County Transit (631-852-5200)
Coast Guard:
—Montauk, NY (631-668-2716) or VHF 16
—New London, CT (860-442-4471) or VHF 16
Ferry: Greenport to Shelter Island (631-749-0139)
Police, Fire, Ambulance: 911
Taxi: Fleetwood/Greenport (631-477-0078)
—Maria's/Greenport (631-477-0700)
—Southold (631-765-2221)
Tow Service:
SEA TOW —24-Hour Dispatch (800-4SEATOW)
—Eastern Long Island (631-765-5300)
Tow BoatU.S.—24-Hour Dispatch (800-391-4869)
—Orient (631-323-2645)
Train: Long Island Railroad (631-822-5477)

72°25'

North Sea

Tuckahoe
Tv Tr

1 WP 28750
N 40°-57.07
W 072°-27.00

2 WP 28820
N 40°-55.20
W 072°-27.57

3

Scallop Pond

Cow Neck Pt.

Cow Neck

West Neck

West Neck

Bullhead Bay

Ram I.

Little Sebonac Cr.

DUTCH WINDMILL

Sebonac Neck

Cold Spring Pond

4 Shinnecock Hills

Shinnecock-Hills

"DANGER ROCKS"

Rodgers Rock

R "30"
Fl R 4s

5 WP 28850
N 40°-54.15
W 072°-28.81

OVERHEAD POWER CABLE
AUTHORIZED CL

FIXED BRIDGE
HOR CL 148 FT
VERT CL 23 FT
OVHD PWR CAB
AUTH CL 38 FT

FIXED BRIDGE
HOR CL 106 FT
VERT CL 22 FT

LOCK
WIDTH 41 FT.
LENGTH 250 FT.

FIXED BRIDGE
HOR CL 112 FT

P E C O N I C   B A Y

MAGNETIC

ANNUAL INCREASE 3'

VAR 14°15' W (1993)

6 WP 28860
N 40°-54.16
W 072°-30.26

Shinnecock

7 Canoe Place
OVHD PWR CAB
Rep cl 48 ft

SHINNECOCK CANAL

Squiretown

Squire Pond

SEE PAGE 338 TOP

Y "BB"
Fl Y 2.5s
Priv

Fl R 4s
Priv

The controlling depth at mean lower
low water in the canal was 6 feet in Aug 1978.
Caution - Swift current exists when gates
are open.

SCALE 1:40,000

Nautical Miles

Yards

Between the Flukes

Great Peconic Bay is not hard to find. Picture this: Long Island is a giant whale (an oddly-shaped one at best) beached on the shores of the Atlantic. Between the two great flukes of its tail—the 50-mile-long north and south forks of Long Island—lie the Peconic bays. Little Peconic Bay, about five miles long, is ringed with fascinating creeks and gunkholes. Great Peconic Bay is more circular, about five miles in diameter, with extensive shoals along its southern and northern shores.

To the southeast of Great Peconic Bay, the village of Southampton, settled in 1640, is one of the oldest towns on Long Island. In the mid-19th century, summer visitors flocked here, and the arrival of the railroad in 1870 attracted thousands more. Southampton remains a very busy summer community, and the village has retained some of the past with road names like Ox Pasture and Meeting House Lane.

The three-quarter-mile-long Shinnecock Canal connects Great Peconic Bay with Shinnecock Bay. As early as 1650, the residents of Southampton and Canoe Place (the little hamlet on the west side of the present-day canal) recognized the commercial potential of turning landlocked Shinnecock Bay into a saltwater bay suitable for commercial fishing. Canoe Place is so named because the local Indians portaged their canoes from bay to bay across the narrow strip of land. Some even suggest the Indians dug a primitive canal of their own at one time.

Over the centuries, several futile attempts were made to cut a canal to Shinnecock Bay from Great Peconic Bay

Dried fish nailed to this piling make a curious portrait. © Maptech

Marine Facilities and Services — *All Coast Guard Stations Monitor VHF Channel 16*

#	Facility	Phone	Monitors / Working VHF Channel	No. of Transient Berths	Seasonal / Year-round / Moorings	Maximum LOA	Approach / Dockside Depth (ft at MLW)	Hookups: Fresh Water / Phone / Cable TV	110V★ 220V▲ 3Phase■ / Max Amps	Ramp / Dinghy / Launch	Rail / Lift / Crane / Trailer (tons)	Repairs	Gas / Diesel Fuel	Fuel Brand	Marine / Groceries / Ice / Bait / LPG / CNG	Restrooms / Showers / Laundry / Pumpout	Public Phone / Restaurant / Snack Bar	Hotel / Pool / Tennis / Golf	Mastercard / VISA / Discover / AmEx
1	Peconic Marina Inc.	631-283-3799		4/	Y	36	5/5	F	★20		L10	GF	GD	Tex	MIB	RSP		All	All
2	Conscience Point Marina*	516-283-8295	16/	26/	S	46	6/4	F	★▲30				GD	Gulf	I	RS			All
3	Dave Bofill Marine Inc.	631-283-6736			Y		4/3				L12	All							MVA
4	The Lobster Inn*	516-283-1525		4/	s	30	6/4	F	★30	*DOCKAGE FOR PATRONS*							R		All
5	Shinnecock Canal Boat Basin	631-854-4949		27/	Y	45	5/5	F	★30							RSP		PS	
6	**Modern Yachts** (p. 343)	631-728-2266		8/	Y	60	10/5	All	★▲50		L40	All	GD	Gulf	MI	RS	P	PS	All
7	**SPELLMAN'S MARINE** (p. 342)	631-728-9200		8/	Y	30	7/3	F	★15		L25	PDFE			MB	RS		PR	All
8	**Jackson's Marina** (p. 345)	631-728-4220	68/	20/	Y	76	8/6	All	★50		L75	All	GD	BP	MGIB	RS		P	All
9	**MARINER'S COVE MARINA** (p. 344)	631-728-0286	68/	12/	Y	65	8/6	All	★▲■50	R	T6	All			MGIB	RSP		All	MV

Facilities continued on page 341...

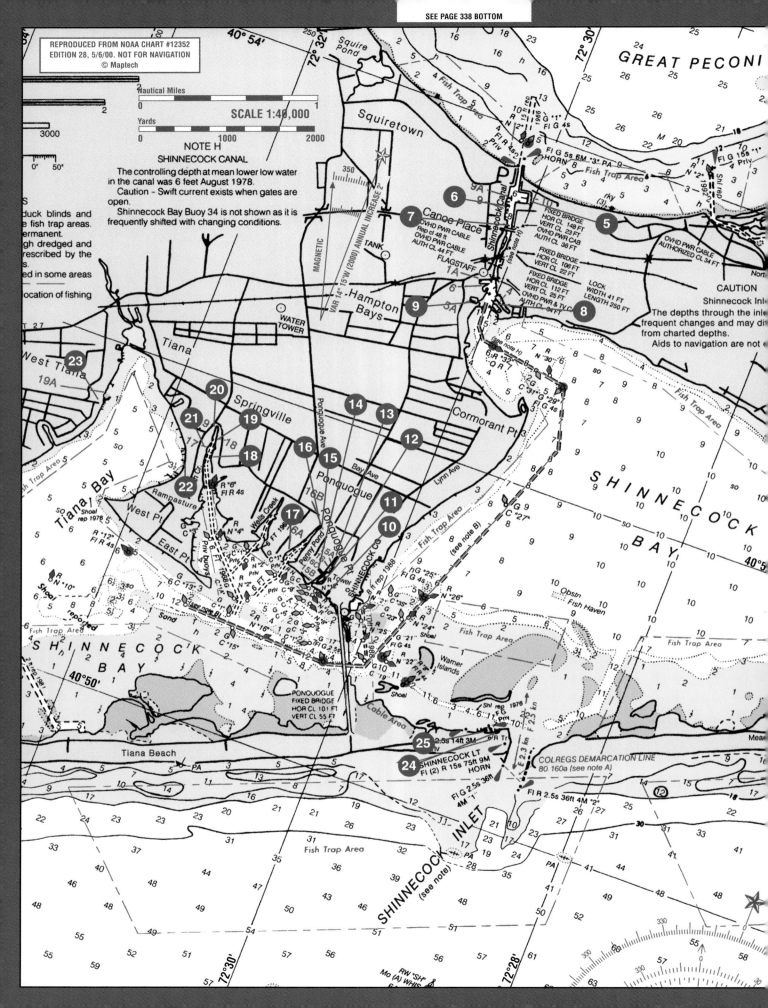

and to cut an inlet across the sandy beaches separating Shinnecock from the Atlantic. In 1826, a state engineer proposed a canal with a lock that would serve a dual purpose: saltwater could flow south from Great Peconic Bay into Shinnecock Bay, and the lock could be used to keep the water level high in Shinnecock Bay. Should an inlet from the ocean ever be dug, the tides could be manipulated to keep the inlet from filling with sand.

Sixty-six years later, after a decade of half-hearted attempts, the state succeeded in opening the Shinnecock Canal, but the lock wasn't added until 1919. Local fishermen were delighted to see a dramatic rise in the shellfish population in Shinnecock Bay.

The final act—an unplanned one at that—in the Shinnecock Canal drama came in September 1938 when the Great Hurricane created the Shinnecock Inlet and

Looking west over the entrance to the Shinnecock Inlet. © Maptech/James T. Abts

opened the southern bay to the ocean. This was the sole positive result of a storm that killed 700 people and left 63,000 homeless.

Over the years, the canal has been rebuilt and improved, and today is traveled by thousands of boaters. Sailors, however, are galled from time to time because

	Marine Facilities and Services		Monitors / Working VHF Channel	Number of Transient Berths / Moorings	Seasonal / Year-round	Approach / Dockside Depth in Feet at MLW	Maximum LOA	Hookups: Fresh Water / Phone / Cable TV	110V ★ 220V ▲ 3 Phase ■ Maximum Amps	Rail / Lift / Crane / Ramp / Dinghy Dock / Launch Service	Diesel / Wood / Fiberglass / Electronics Repairs: Propellor / Sail / Rigging / Gas	Gas / Diesel Fuel	Marine / Groceries / Ice / Bait / LPG / CNG	Fuel Brand	Restrooms / Showers / Laundry / Pumpout	Public Phone / Restaurant / Snack Bar	Hotel / Pool / Tennis / Golf	Mastercard / VISA / Discover / AmEx
10	Ponquogue Marina	516-728-2264		3/	Y	42	4/12	F	★30		L30	All			RS		MV
11	Mill River Boat Works	631-728-6768		1/	Y		3/3	F	★▲50	R		All					MV
12	Tully's Harbor Restaurant	631-728-9043		2/	S	25	4/6		★120		*DOCKAGE FOR PATRONS*			R		R	MVD
13	Baywatch Motel & Marina	631-728-4550	19/	12/	Y	32	4/3	F		R				I	RS	HP	P	MV
14	Molnar's Landing*	516-728-1860			Y												
15	Bel-Air Cove	631-728-0416		3/	Y	23	5/2	F	★							HP	All
16	Shinnecock Bay Fishing Station	631-728-6116		5/	Y	40	3/3	F	★30			G	IB		RS		PR	All
17	Harrison Boatyard	631-728-2467			Y												
18	Hampton Watercraft & Marina* (B)	516-728-0922			Y	25	6/6					PRWFE			I	R		All
19	Hampton Boat Works (B)	631-728-1114		8/	Y	50	/5	F	★30		L	All			RS		MV
20	Frank's Landing of Hampton Bays Inc.	631-728-0619			Y	25						G	M	R		MV
21	SPELLMAN'S MARINE p. 342	631-728-1341			Y	30	5/4	F	★15		L25	GWF		M	RS	P	All
22	Tiana Bay Estates-Beach & Yacht Club	631-728-1488			Y												MV
23	Colonial Shores Resort & Marina Inc	631-728-0011		5/	S	23	4/4	F		R					HP	MVA
24	Oakland's Restaurant & Marina	631-728-6900	68/	8/	S	50	10/6	FP	★▲50			GD	Tex	MIB	RS	PR	All
25	Pell's Dock*	516-728-5100	68/	5/	Y	70	12/10	F	★▲■50		L	GD	BP	MGIB	RS	All	MVD

Information in these listings is provided by the facilities themselves. An asterisk (*) indicates that the facility did not respond to our most recent requests for information.
(B) represents a BOAT/U.S. cooperating marina.

they must unstep their masts to pass under the 22-foot high bridge over the canal.

ACTIVITIES: If you like to plan out things, give the Long Island Convention & Visitors Bureau (800-441-4601, ext. 200) a call for a guide on what to see and do while on the island. Otherwise, begin your stay in the region with a trip to some of the historic sites. The Old Halsey Homestead in Southampton Village, about five miles southeast of the Shinnecock Canal, is considered the oldest frame house in the state. The Southampton Historical Museum (631-283-2494), in the former home of a whaling captain, offers exhibits highlighting local history.

The Parrish Art Museum and Arboretum (631-283-2118) specializes in American art of the 19th and 20th centuries and holds more than 2,500 paintings in its permanent collection. The centerpieces of the museum are collections of two renowned residents of Southampton, William Merritt Chase and Fairfield Porter.

Don't be surprised to see the banks of the Shinnecock Canal lined with fishermen sitting in groups, spinning tales of the one that got away. The local fishermen tell us the flounder (in April) and the weakfish (especially in early May) are plentiful here. Go ahead; drop a hook while you're ashore, but if you're inclined to fish by moonlight, you'll need a permit (631-854-4949). Another good fishing spot is out on Shinnecock Inlet. Alongside the huge fishing

trawlers docked there, you'll find a number of surf fishermen and those casting from the jetty.

If sunbathing is more your speed, there's a small beach about a mile west of the north end of the canal. Be careful when approaching it, and dink to shore. There are rocks just offshore (marked on the charts) that give the marinas lots of lower-unit repair work. In the other direction, next to the Shinnecock Canal Boat Basin, you'll find the Meschutt Beach County Park. Don't worry if the surf and sand give you an appetite: there's a snack bar.

RESTAURANTS & PROVISIONS: Nearly anywhere you come ashore here, you'll have a few dining options. There are several seafood restaurants near the Shinnecock Canal, within walking distance of Modern Yachts, Jackson's Marina, Spellmans Marine, and Mariner's Cove Marina. Or while in the canal, pull up to Rip Tide Restaurant (631-728-7373) and enjoy the canal-side view and your meal. Nearby is Giorgio's Ristorante (631-728-2500), offering an Italian menu.

For seafood in a casual setting, it's a short cab ride to Villa Paul (631-728-3261). If you're staying at the Peconic Marina, you'll find the Coast Grille (631-283-2277), where you can sample lobster and clam specialties.

In the Shinnecock Bay and Inlet area, there are several places right on the water. Buy some fresh fish at Shinnecock Fish Dock, Inc. (631-728-0004), or stop by Oakland's Restaurant & Marina (631-728-6900) for a prepared meal. Close by is Pell's Dock Marina with the Sunset Deck Restaurant (631-728-1040). They serve moderately-priced seafood and American dishes. To the west of Ponquogue Point, you'll find Tully's Harbor Restaurant (631-728-9043), which also has dock-and-dine facilities.

Many of the marinas in the area have boating supplies, but for extensive supplies, head to All Points Marine Supplies (631-728-0012). For provisions you'll need to grab a cab.

NAVIGATION & ANCHORAGES: Use ChartKit Region 3, pages 39 and 52B; Maptech™ Waterproof Charts 1 and 16; and Maptech™ electronic and NOAA paper charts 12358 (1:40,000), 12352SC (1:40,000), and 12354 (1:80,000). Use tide tables for New London. High tide at the Shinnecock Canal is 2 hours 34 minutes later; low tide is 2 hours 31 minutes later. Multiply height of tide at New London by 0.9 for height of tide at the Shinnecock Canal. Mean tidal range is 2.4 feet. At the Shinnecock Inlet, use tide tables for Sandy Hook. High tide is 51 minutes earlier; low tide is 1 hour 6 minutes earlier. Multiply height of tide at Sandy Hook by 0.6 for height of tide at the Shinnecock Inlet. Mean tidal range is 2.9 feet.

The Shinnecock Canal, on the south side of Great Peconic Bay, is 7.7nm from Riverhead, 7nm from Cutchogue Harbor, and 5nm from the Shinnecock Inlet, which connects Shinnecock Bay to the Atlantic Ocean.

Bear in mind that all harbors in both Little and Great Peconic bays are artificial, so the depth at the entrances varies according to the accumulation of sand and the frequency of dredging. The creeks are fun to explore, but be prepared for a little bump and grind, even in a dinghy. Because of the size of Great Peconic Bay and its shallow water, a steep chop can build up quickly when the winds kick in.

When heading through Little Peconic Bay **from the east**, you'll pass south of Fl R 4s R "22" south-southeast of the high bluffs of Nassau Point. You can find protection from an easterly on the west side of Little Hog Neck.

The southwest side of Little Peconic Bay has several anchorages. Wooley Pond, 1.7nm southeast of Nassau Point, is difficult because of its concealed entrance, swift currents, and visible shoals, but the harbor is cozy and well protected. The channel is marked by private, seasonal buoys and a private light on the north side of the entrance, and marine services are available for boats drawing less than 5 feet. There is no anchoring overnight unless you have a holding tank.

To the west, North Sea Harbor also appeals mainly to small craft seeking refuge. Holmes Hill, a prominent sandy bluff just west of the entrance, is a good landmark. The reported 4-foot channel is marked by G C "1" and Fl R 5s "2," about 300 yards outside the entrance. Though the harbor is shallow inside, its soft bottom is good holding ground.

You'll find two marinas on Conscience Point, the small, bird's-head shaped point at the southwest corner of North Sea Harbor. The town of Southampton (not to be confused with the Village of Southampton) maintains a ramp on Conscience

Point and a town dock on Towd Point, to port as you enter the harbor. The center of Southampton is 3 miles away.

When you enter Great Peconic Bay, you'll pass Robins Island. Two marked channels surround the island, the preferred one being the southerly. Stay south of Fl R 2.5s R "26," off the southern tip of the island, to avoid the tide rips and shallow spots.

On the south shore of Great Peconic Bay is Sebonac Creek, which is the entrance to Bullhead Bay. This is the closest you'll get to the Village of Southampton, the most famous of all Long Island summer resort areas. There's at least 5 feet of water inside the privately dredged channel, which has an entrance marked by Fl 5s R "2" PRIV and G C "1." Because of a serious shoal on either side of the channel, stay at least 250 yards west of the entrance buoys until you've lined up the channel for a run straight down the center.

Inside Sebonac Creek, there's a town dock at West Neck, northeast of Ram Island and just opposite G C "7." You can tie up for 2 hours for loading or unloading. The best anchorage is also in this area.

Cold Spring Pond is dinghy and canoe territory—no more than 2 feet at low tide. It's about 1.6 miles southwest of Sebonac Creek and 1.1nm east of the Shinnecock Canal. Stay out of Cold Spring Pond, even in a small powerboat. Your chart shows cable clearance as 34 feet but The Lobster Inn, which has transient space for patrons, says it has been

Looking north over the Shinnecock Canal. © Maptech/James T. Abts

Many boaters are intimidated by the currents and the lock, but getting through the Shinnecock Canal can be quite simple if done at the right time. The lock is 250 feet long and 41 feet wide, with a depth of 12 feet over the sills. It consists of a set of lock gates and a set of tide gates parallel to and westward of the lock gates.

The gates are constructed so tidal action opens them to allow the current to set south through the canal and closes them to prevent water from Shinnecock Bay flowing back into Great Peconic Bay. The lock is tended 24 hours and the gates can be opened mechanically when the current is flowing northward to allow the passage of boats. The two sets of gates are articulated separately so a south-bound vessel can be lifted from the level of Great Peconic Bay to the level of Shinnecock Bay, or a north-bound vessel can be dropped down to the level of the Great Peconic Bay.

raised to 44 feet. That doesn't matter much though, since a large boat can't fit in here.

Southwest 1.1nm from the Cold Spring Pond entrance is the entrance to the 3/4-mile-long Shinnecock Canal and the eastern end of the 29-mile inland water route along the south shore of Long Island.

When approaching the Shinnecock Canal from anywhere in Great Peconic Bay, look for the jetty that extends 300 yards from the canal entrance—one of our readers tells us he can see the jetty with binoculars from Robins Island. Closer in, you'll see Fl G 4s G "1" off the end of the jetty, paired with R N "2." Stay at least 0.3nm north of the entrance buoys until you have the channel lined up. There's good water throughout the canal (approximately 6 feet), but make sure you understand the currents in the canal before entering.

When the tide gates are open, currents can make your trip south very fast and tricky. Currents of more than 4 knots are possible right after the lock opens. If you'd rather not quicken your pulse, just wait an hour or two until the currents are manageable. South of the lock, at the railroad bridge, you may encounter some tricky eddies. The currents are especially important if you're headed north. When the tide gates are open and the southbound current is at its peak, you'll need a fair amount of power to motor your way through.

Call the lock house (516-852-8299) for more information or some friendly advice. The lock tender will probably tell you when the lock was last opened and that you should add 6 hours to find the time it will close. Another way to figure out the status of the lock is to employ a trick the local fishermen use: the tide gates will close 3-1/2 hours before high water at Sandy Hook, and open 2-1/2 hours after high water at Sandy Hook.

The safest way to make the passage is to "lock through" during the period when the gates are closed. You needn't worry about the current inside the lock—it's like a pond. Inside, you can tie up or simply hold on to one of the many steel rungs attached to the bulkhead, while waiting to motor out of the lock.

CAUTION: If you're in a sailboat, you'll have to unstep your mast to pass under the 22-foot clearance of the lowest bridge; there are two self-service "mast-unsteppers,"

one located in the boat basin and one located south of the lock on the west side of the canal.

North of the lock, there's a basin on the east side where you can tie up and wait. There are also several marinas and restaurants in the area. Modern Yachts is located on the west side of the canal and is a full-service facility with transient slips available. Meschutt Beach County Park is on the northeast side of the canal next to the basin. On the southern end of the canal, you'll find Mariner's Cove, a full-service facility that welcomes transients.

Not many sailors use the canal because they must unstep their masts, but the trip around Long Island is lengthy. However, one of the nice things about the trip is that when the weather is good, you can shoot out of one of the inlets and cruise on the open Atlantic. If the weather isn't so good, you can duck into the protected waters of the inland waterway. Two things you'll want to consider before taking such a cruise: the state channel is dredged to a depth of 6 feet, and most of it has a speed limit of 5 to 10 mph to avoid wakes.

If you're headed out to the open ocean, the most direct access is through the Shinnecock Inlet. The inlet should be approached with caution, as the channel depths are uncharted because they frequently shift, and the entrance can get very rough. A strong southerly breeze will set up large breakers that make the inlet dangerous, especially during ebb tide. Your best bet is to use the inlet on a calm day at slack tide.

Shinnecock Light (Fl (2) R 15s 75ft 9M HORN) marks the west side of the entrance; privately maintained lights are on both of the jetties, and uncharted buoys mark the channel itself. Be especially careful of the shoaling in the outer bar area. If you are not familiar with the inlet, check with one of the local marina operators about the latest channel conditions, or follow one of the local sportfishermen—the more local, the better.

There's no need to go searching for a pump-out around here. The township of Southampton provides free pump-out service, and they'll come right to your boat.

Shoreside & Emergency Services
Airport:
—Suffolk County (631-852-8095)
Bus:
—Suffolk County Transit (631-852-5200)
Coast Guard:
—Shinnecock (631-728-1171) or VHF 16
Harbormaster:
—Southold Police (631-728-2600)
Police, Fire, Ambulance: 911
Tow Service:
SEA TOW —24-Hour Dispatch (800-4SEATOW)
—Moriches/Shinnecock (631-653-6361)
Tow BoatU.S.—24-Hour Dispatch (800-391-4869)
—Peconic Bay (631-728-2743)
Train: Long Island Railroad (631-822-5477)

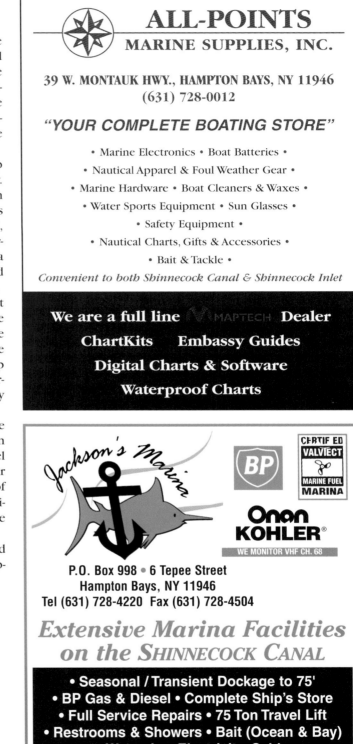

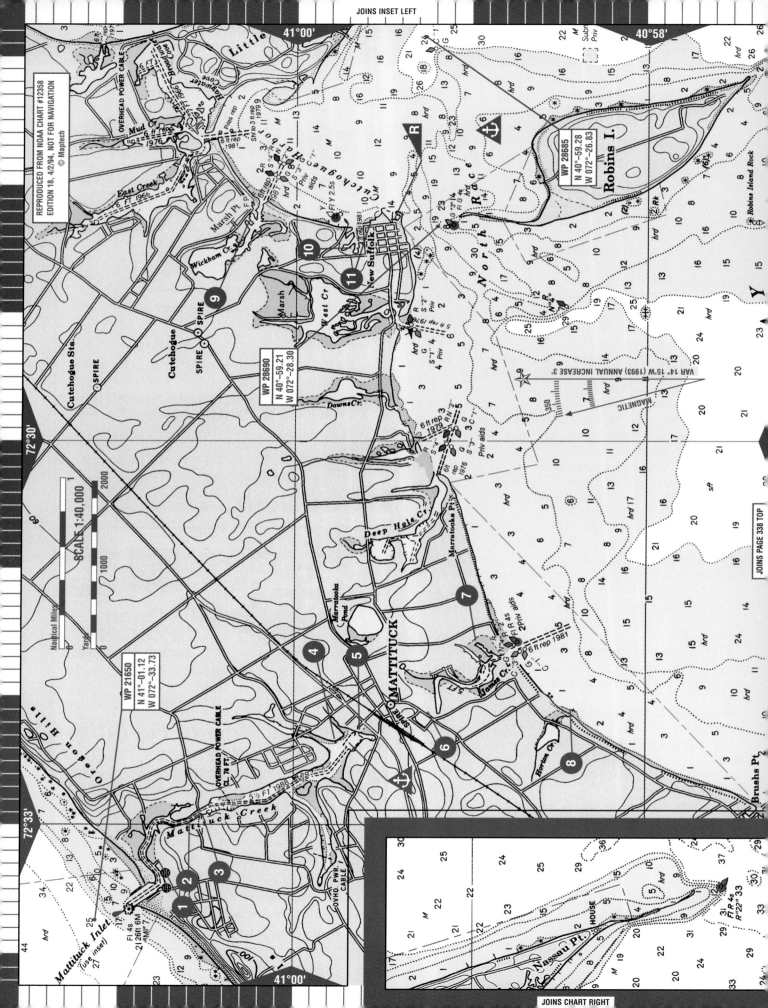

Long Island's Napa Valley

You can't see them from the water, but they're there: grapevines, more than 1,000 acres in all. They're not wild, but expertly cultivated by local wineries. In recent decades, the forks of Long Island have become a haven for quality wine—the Napa Valley of the Northeast, if you will.

Mattituck, the only Sound-side harbor east of Mount Sinai, is the only town on the north shore that boaters can reach from both sides of the northern fluke of the whale's tail. It's cut deep on both sides: by Mattituck Inlet to the north of town and James Creek to the south. On the south side of the north fork lies Cutchogue Harbor. Cutchogue's earliest farmers were known for producing crops of potatoes, but like other eastern Long Island farmers, they have, in recent years, staked their claims in grapes. On the west side of Cutchogue Harbor is New Suffolk, a town that resembles a Maine fishing village.

You may ask, "Why hasn't a canal been cut across the 500-yard stretch of land from Mattituck Inlet to James Creek, thereby joining Long Island Sound and Great Peconic Bay?" Good question; here's the answer: Such a marriage would make traveling more convenient, but it would cause all sorts of ecological trouble. The idea is even more

Looking north up James Creek. In the distance are the marinas in Mattituck Creek and Mattituck Inlet. © Maptech/James T. Abts

preposterous considering that a canal would cut through Route 25 and the center of town.

ACTIVITIES: In Mattituck, a modest, residential town where you'll see people on porches and tire swings in the yards,

	Marine Facilities and Services		Monitors / Working VHF Channel	Number of Transient Berths / Moorings	Approach / Dockside Depth in Feet at MLW	Seasonal / Year-round	Hookups: Fresh Water / Phone / Cable TV	Maximum LOA	110V ★ 220V ▲ 3 Phase ■ Maximum Amps	Ramp / Dinghy Dock / Launch Service	Rail / Lift / Crane / Trailer: Capacity (tons)	Repairs: Propeller / Sail / Rigging / Electronics	Diesel / Wood / Fiberglass / Electronics	Marine / Groceries / Ice / Bait / LPG / CNG	Gas / Diesel Fuel	Restrooms / Showers / Laundry / Pumpout	Fuel Brand	Public Phone / Restaurant / Snack Bar	Hotel / Pool / Tennis / Golf	Mastercard / VISA / Discover / AmEx
1	Mattituck Fishing Station	631-298-8399				S	21		F							G				
2	Old Mill Inn	631-298-8080				Y	40		RESTAURANT—DOCKAGE FOR PATRONS ONLY											
3	Mattituck Inlet Marina	631-298-4480	68/68	5/		Y	100	10/6	FC	★▲50			L70		GD			RS	P	All
4	Matt-A-Mar Marina (B) p. 349	631-298-4739		40/		Y	75	7/5	F	★▲			L50	All	GD	BP	MI	RSP	P	All	All
5	Mattituck Park District Marina	631-298-9103				Y												RS		
6	Village Marine	631-298-5800		4/		Y	28	6/6	F	★15	R			GDFE			M		P	All
7	Strong's Marine	631-298-4770	68/68	5/		Y	40	4/4	F	★30	R	L2	PRGDWFE	G		MI	RSP	P	MVA
8	Mattituck Yacht Club*	631-298-8974				Y			PRIVATE—RECIPROCAL PRIVILEGES											
9	Cutchogue Harbor Marina (B)	631-734-6993	9/	15/		S	50	6/6	All	★▲■50			All		GD		MIB	All	P	All
10	New Suffolk Shipyard p. 349	631-734-6311				Y	40	5/6	F	★30	D	L15	All	G		MI	RSP	P	MVA
11	Capt. Marty's Fishing Station*	631-734-6852				S			BOAT RENTALS					P						

Information in these listings is provided by the facilities themselves. An asterisk (*) indicates that the facility did not respond to our most recent requests for information. (B) represents a BOAT/U.S. cooperating marina.

All Coast Guard Stations Monitor VHF Channel 16

© Maptech

the transient boater can get basic provisions and marine supplies. It's also a fishing town with a small fleet of trawlers. For all its charming provinciality, there's something almost refined and urbane about Mattituck, the way towns that grow good wine carry themselves.

Potatoes were long the primary crop in these parts, but over the last decade wine grapes have become more popular. The well-drained, sandy soil and the moderate temperatures are perfectly suited for growing grapes. Sixteen wineries are spread throughout the area, and many have tastings and tours of their facilities. Pindar Vineyards (631-734-6200), located in the village of Peconic, is the largest with a 650-acre spread. Stop by their Harvest Festival in Fall.

In Cutchogue alone, you'll find Bedell Cellars (631-734-7537), Bidwell Vineyards (631-734-5200), Gristina Vineyards (631-734-7089), Hargrave Vineyards (631-734-5158), Peconic Bay Vineyards (631-734-7361), Pellegrini Vineyards (631-734-4111), and Pugliese Vineyards (631-734-5983). Plan your wine-tasting visit ahead of time by visiting www.liwines.com.

If you've brought the dinghy, fishing or exploring the numerous smaller creeks at Cutchogue Harbor is an ideal way to get into nature for a while.

RESTAURANTS & PROVISIONS: If you're looking to dock and dine, you can do so on the Sound side, up Mattituck Inlet, at the Old Mill Restaurant (631-298-8080). They specialize in seafood that the fishing armada brings in daily. Toward the end of the inlet, get tasty Italian cuisine and seafood at the Touch of Venice (631-298-5851), right next to Matt-A-Mar Marina. For a quick and casual lunch, try one of the delis in town along Love Lane.

Coming ashore at James Creek doesn't land you at a restaurant, but you can call a cab and make your way to Route 25, where you'll find The Apple Tree (631-298-4180) for Italian and seafood dishes.

In Cutchogue, ask for the Fisherman's Rest (631-734-5155) on Main Street. Like most of the other restaurants in this area, it also serves a lot of seafood and Italian.

Provisions are easily found in Mattituck. On Love Lane there's Barker's Pharmacy (631-298-8666) and a hardware

store for repair supplies. You'll also find a couple of small markets selling limited groceries. For an even bigger selection there's an A&P in the Mattituck Plaza. Also, Love Lane Laundromat (631-298-4651) can freshen up your clothes while you're in town.

NAVIGATION & ANCHORAGES: Use ChartKit Region 3, pages 8 and 52B; Maptech™ Waterproof Charts 1 and 6; and Maptech™ electronic and NOAA paper charts 12358 (1:40,000) and 12354 (1:80,000). Use tide tables for Bridgeport. High tide at Mattituck Inlet is 4 minutes later; low tide is 4 minutes earlier. Multiply height of tide at Bridgeport by 0.8 for height of tide at Mattituck Inlet. Mean tidal range is 5.2 feet. For Cutchogue Harbor, use tide tables for New London. High tide at New Suffolk is 2 hours 27 minutes later; low tide is 2 hours 11 minutes later. Use height of tide at New London for height of tide at New Suffolk. Mean tidal range is 2.6 feet.

Mattituck Inlet is 14.5nm from Clinton, Connecticut, or 6.8nm from Horton Point Light. The entrance at James Creek is about 16nm from Greenport, and 8.5nm from Riverhead. Cutchogue Harbor is 7.2nm from the Shinnecock Canal, and about 4nm from the James Creek entrance.

At the risk of gross understatement, Mattituck Inlet is hard to spot from the Sound. From Fl (2+1) R 6s RG "TE" south of Sixmile Reef, steer a course of about 210°m for about 8nm to reach the entrance to Mattituck Inlet.

CAUTION: As you approach the Mattituck Inlet entrance you'll notice the huge, battleship-like structure directly east of Roanoke Point Shoal. It's an oil platform with pipelines running to the shore at Jacobs Point. There is a 500-yard restricted area around the pipeline head.

While GONG G "3A" is located a mile offshore to help you locate the inlet, it will be difficult to spot Fl 4s 25ft 6M "MI" atop the western breakwater, especially in the morning with the sun in your eyes. A better landmark is the long break in the bluffs and two large oil tanks on the west side of the entrance.

In a fresh northerly or westerly, you may find the entrance a rough experience, especially with an outgoing tide. Though shoaling is apt to occur at the entrance, the sandy channel has a reported depth of 4 to 6 feet. The channel is unmarked and, thus, not so easy to find either, so proceed slower than the 5-mph limit.

The beach to the east, at the entrance of the channel is submerged at high tide, but we've seen at least one boat sitting high and dry, anchor still firmly holding ground, when the tide went out. Don't be put off by the initial "industrialness" of the inlet; it quickly fades into modest houses, neat marinas, including transient-friendly Matt-A-Mar Marina, and lots of trees.

The channel is well marked only after you pass the Old Mill Restaurant to the west. The current at this point will hit you fast and strong, like a diminutive Hell Gate. This is because the channel bottom plunges to 40 feet, rises suddenly to 15, and drops again to 40; it's this damming effect that can damn your boat if you're not careful, especially in bad weather, with the tide and wind opposed. We've heard stories about 4-foot standing waves at this junction in angry weather.

The channel continues to a free federal anchorage basin offering perfect protection and 7 feet of clean water. At the head is a transient dock and bathing beach operated by the Mattituck Park Commission. While there's fresh water available at the bathhouse nearby, there is no dockmaster. You can stay up to three hours.

Off the main channel are tiny inlets with up to 6 feet of water. Once you're anchored, docked, or moored, the town is a short dinghy ride or walk away.

On the Great Peconic Bay side, Nassau Point is 5.6nm east of James Creek. Fl R 4s R "22" off Nassau Point marks the eastern approach to Cutchogue Harbor. Don't cut between the flasher and Nassau Point due to the shoals that stretch 0.5nm south of the point.

Cutchogue Harbor is well enclosed, although a southeasterly can make it uncomfortable. In Cutchogue Harbor, head to New Suffolk Shipyard to satisfy your repair needs.

Robins Island divides the 5-mile wide Great Peconic Bay to the west from Little Peconic Bay to the east. Given the prevailing southwest winds, the bight on the north side of the island makes a very nice anchorage. Do not land on the 2-mile long, seemingly deserted island, as there are "No Trespassing" signs posted.

When rounding the north side of Robins Island, keep north of Fl G 4s G "3," because a long sand spit extends well into the North Race.

If you're headed from Nassau Point to the Shinnecock Canal or Riverhead (6nm and 12.5nm, respectively) you'll want to continue southwest past Robins Island and through the deeper water of the South Race.

CAUTION: Tide rips can develop near the southern tip of Robins Island, especially when tide and wind are opposed, so you'll also want to favor the Cow Neck side while keeping an eye out for the charted rocks and shoals.

The village of New Suffolk is mostly residential, although you'll find a few marinas and a grocery there. For anchoring, Haywater and Broadwater coves are ideal, as are Mud Creek and East Creek; all share the same entrance on the north side of Cutchogue Harbor.

Although the narrow channels at these four little creeks are generally 4 to 6 feet deep, their common entrance tends to shoal, so explore here only in a dinghy or shallow-draft boat. The positions and depths of these channels vary considerably, depending on recent storm activity.

There are a number of other creeks and inlets between Mattituck and Riverhead. Most are successfully tackled only by residents.

Shoreside & Emergency Services
Airport: Mattituck Airbase (631-298-8330)
Bus: Suffolk County Transit (631-852-5200)
Coast Guard: New London (860-442-4471) or VHF 16
—New Haven (203-468-4464) or VHF 16
—Shinnecock (631-728-1171) or VHF 16
Harbormaster: Bay Constable (631-765-2600)
Police, Fire, Ambulance: 911
Taxi: Keri (631-727-0707) or (800-727-5374)
Tow Service:
SEA TOW. —24-Hour Dispatch (800-4SEATOW)
—Moriches/Shinnecock (631-653-6361)
Tow BoatU.S.—24-Hour Dispatch (800-391-4869)
—Peconic Bay (631-728-2743)

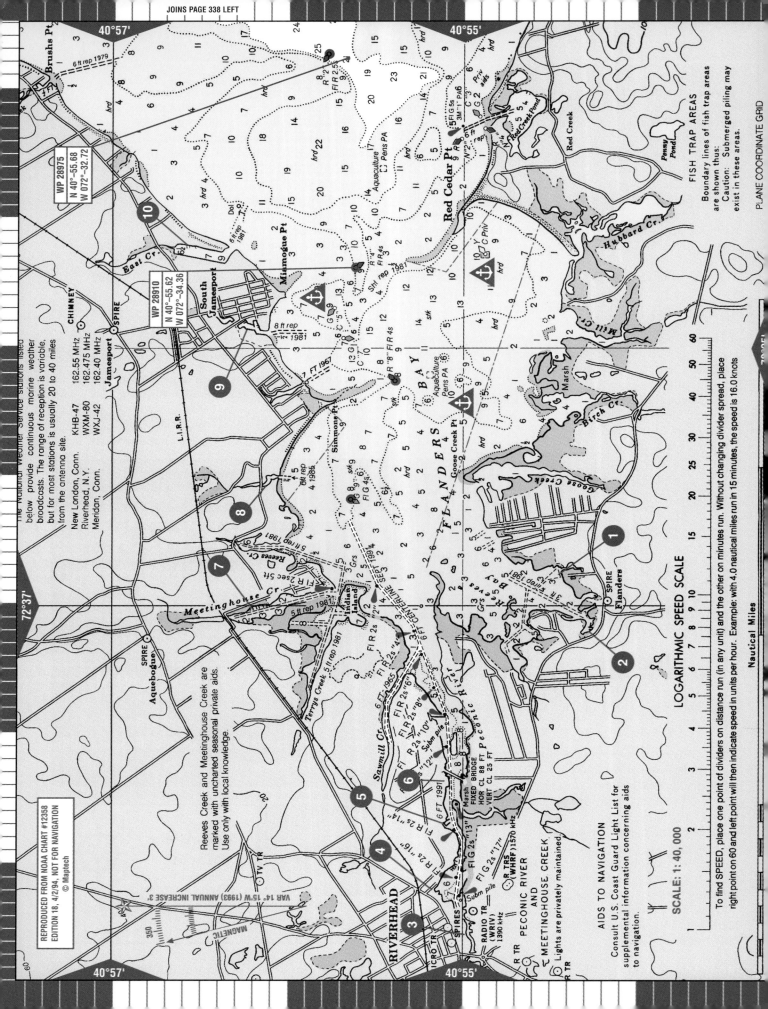

The Seat of Suffolk

Despite its city atmosphere, Riverhead had a bucolic beginning. It used to be a center for potato and cauliflower farming and for raising the famous Long Island ducks once popular on the menus of choice New York restaurants. The snow-white fowl found their way to America when Ed McGrath, a New York merchant, returned from Peking, China, with some eggs. Once the hatchlings grew up and got plump, the Long Islanders found out just how tasty they were, so a few were kept alive for breeding. Riverhead's Sound-side location was great for farming ducks since the young ones fattened up on fish (most older ducks were fed only grain, as fish-eating ducks yielded fishy-tasting meat) as their primary feed.

Alas, in recent years the duck business has lost most of its feathers, and Riverhead's focus now is its role as the seat of Suffolk County. As such, you'll find plenty of government buildings and civic-minded people, all of which contribute to Riverhead's status as the most densely populated area on Long Island's "whale's tail." With its busy streets, shopping center, restaurants, and overall city feel, Riverhead seems like a small, urban outpost amid the pastoral New England-style villages scattered around the east end of Long Island.

ACTIVITIES: Once called "Occabog," Riverhead sits right where its name suggests: at the head of the Peconic River.

In her imagination, this child is swimming with the sea lions at Atlantis Marine. © Maptech

	Marine Facilities and Services		Monitors / Working VHF Channel	Number of Transient Berths / Moorings	Approach / Dockside Depth in Feet at MLW	Seasonal / Yearround Maximum LOA	110V • 220V ▲ 3 Phase ■ Maximum Amps	Hookups: Fresh Water / Phone / Cable TV	Ramp / Dinghy Dock / Launch Service	Rail / Lift / Crane / Trailer: Capacity (tons)	Diesel / Wood / Fiberglass / Electronics	Repairs: Propeller / Sail / Rigging / Gas	Marine / Groceries / Ice / Bait / LPG / CNG	Gas / Diesel Fuel	Fuel Brand	Restrooms / Showers / Laundry / Pumpout	Public Phone / Pool / Tennis / Golf	Hotel / Restaurant / Snack Bar	Mastercard / VISA / Discover / AmEx
1	B & E Marine	631-727-8619			S	25	3/3						All						
2	Gateway Marine	631-727-1028		5/	Y	35	4/3	F	★30	RD	L15	All		G	Gulf	MI	R		All
3	Peconic Riverfront Marina*	631-727-3200 ext. 276		40/	Y	1	10/5	All	★▲50							MGIB	P	HPG	All
4	TREASURE COVE RESORT MARINA p. 353	631-727-8386	9/	25/	S	50		All	★▲50			All		G	Tex	MIB	All	P	RS	All
5	Riverside Marina	631-673-1049			S	55	6/6	FC	★▲50								RS		
6	Riverhead Yacht Club*	631-369-0944			Y				*PRIVATE—MEMBERS ONLY*										
7	LARRY'S LIGHTHOUSE MARINA p. 355	631-722-3400		20/	Y	65	6/8	All	▲50	D	L35	All		GD	BP	MI	All	P	PR	All
8	Dreamer's Cove Motel	631-722-3212		16/	Y	35	6/6	F	★▲■								H	P	MVA
9	Great Peconic Bay Marina p. 355	631-722-3565		10/	Y	55	6/6	FP	★50	D	L50	All		GD		MGI	RSP		P	MV
10	East Creek Marina of Jamesport	631-722-4842		10/	S	60	8/12	F	★30	RD	C	G				MGIB	RS	TG	PS	MVA

Information in these listings is provided by the facilities themselves. An asterisk (*) indicates that the facility did not respond to our most recent requests for information. (B) represents a BOAT/U.S. cooperating marina.

Flanders Bay & Riverhead

It's a good destination if you're cruising Flanders Bay, because of all it has to offer: shopping, historic sites, restaurants, and provisions.

If you plan on staying for an extended period of time, or if you want some help deciding what to do while in town, grab a copy of the Downtown Reporter, which contains listings of all local events. You can find it at the information booth near the Riverhead riverfront dock.

Atlantis Marine World (631-208-9200), Long Island's first large-scale aquarium, opened in June 2000 under the watchful eye of King Poseidon, who welcomes visitors into his Lost City kingdom to learn about the creatures of the sea. Check out Ray Bay, where you can pet the smooth, rubbery skin of the stingrays, and the other touch tanks, where you can pick up a starfish, clam, or snail. When we visited, the staff members were abuzz with contagious excitement over the hatching of a tiny baby shark the previous day. Your crew will be excited as well, whether they're watching the sea lion show, participating in the stingray feedings, or riding the simulated submarine ride.

It's always a good time to pull into port when a town is having a fair or festival, and Riverhead has a few. The Polish Fair is a cultural event usually held the second weekend in August in Polishtown, a district in Riverhead. Try some ethnic food and witness an authentic Polish wedding. You'll need to grab a transient space well ahead of time if you're going to catch the Country Fair, held on the Sunday of Columbus Day weekend. Blocks of streets and waterfront area are blocked off for carnival rides, street vendors, and live entertainment. Nearly 50,000 people pack the streets, to watch tractor pulls and needlepoint and baking contests, as well as a contest for the biggest vegetable. Call the Riverhead Town Hall (631-727-3200) or the Long Island Farm Bureau (631-727-3777) for information.

A short walk away is the Suffolk County Historical Museum (631-727-2881), which offers a look at Eastern Long Island traditions and local genealogy. The story of Suffolk County from its pre-Columbian days to the Revolution is told through dioramas, a gun room, collections of ship models, whaling artifacts, dolls, and toys. If you like artwork, try the East End Arts Council Gallery (631-727-0900) with its changing exhibits, paintings, photography, and crafts.

Explore the tranquil Peconic River and rent kayaks, paddle boats, or canoes at Treasure Cove Resort Marina (631-727-8386). If you'd prefer to spend some time on terra firma, Treasure Cove also rents bikes for exploring Riverhead. The Peconic Paddler (631-727-9895) has kayaks and canoes for you to rent, too. Or simply hand the controls over to someone else and enjoy a relaxing riverboat trip on Peconic River Cruises (631-369-3700), departing from the Riverhead village pier. They have a few different options, including lunch and dinner cruises with good grub, rollicking entertainment, singing, and dancing.

Your other fun-time options are a bit farther out of town. Shoppers will find it worth the cab fare to get to

Looking west over Flanders Bay, with the city of Riverhead at its terminus. © Maptech/James T. Abts

TREASURE COVE
RESORT MARINA

A Beautiful Getaway!

At Treasure Cove Marina, transient boaters will enjoy the beautiful waters of the Peconic River and Peconic Bay. Situated at the center of Long Island's twin forks, offering easy access to popular boating and entertainment spots on Long Island.

150 Boat Slips tucked away from crowded waterways. Enjoy quiet mornings or evenings surrounded by nature's beauty. Well sheltered, floating docks accommodate powerboats up to 65ft. Docks are equipped with up to 50 amp electric and cable TV. Laundry and shower facilities are also available.

Treasure Cove Marina is a "full service" marina. Enjoy the 30' x 50' private pool, restaurant & clam bar, ships store, gas dock, mechanic on duty, kayak rentals and private barbecue/picnic areas.

Call ahead, reservations are suggested.

Next door to Treasure Cove Marina is Atlantis Marine World Aquarium, Long Island's number one educational entertainment facility. We're also conveniently located near Tanger Outlet Mall, Splish Splash Water Park, Riverhead Raceway, Golf Courses and all the Long Island Vineyards.

call for more information and a brochure

631-727-8386

VHF CHANNEL 9

469 East Main Street • Riverhead, NY 11901

www.treasurecoveresortmarina.com

353

Looking northwest over Meetinghouse Creek and Larry's Lighthouse Marina.

© Maptech/James T. Abts

choice. Also among these restaurants are a number of smaller eateries and pizza places for you to grab a quick bite to eat.

The Meetinghouse Creek Inn (631-722-4220), just across from Larry's Lighthouse Marina in Aquebogue, serves seafood in a casual, tablecloth setting. It's quite convenient and is the only restaurant within walking distance in that area.

Once in South Jamesport, you'll find what some local residents refer to as the "world famous" Cliff's Elbow Room (631-722-3292), with a selection of steaks and seafood.

Near the water in Riverhead, West Marine (631-369-2628) can take care of your nautical needs. A hardware store is also close by for those repairs that can't wait, and the galley can be stocked at Stop & Go Mini Mart. Laundromats and ATMs are found among the busy streets.

Tanger Factory Outlet Center (631-369-2732), three miles east of town. Farther out of town, Splish Splash Water Park (631-727-3600) will cool off the crew with a good soaking with water slides, lazy river rides, and other watery wildness.

For water fun in the natural setting, the shallow Flanders Bay is excellent for watersports, but be careful where you take your sailboard or PWC. The border between Riverhead (to the north) and Southampton (to the south) runs right down the middle of Flanders Bay and the Peconic River. In Southampton waters, no water-skiing or PWCs are allowed within 500 feet of the shore, and PWCs may only be launched from Southampton town ramps.

The aquatic life is plentiful in these parts, so drop a hook and try landing a weakfish, blue, or flounder. Oystering and clamming used to be excellent, but conditions vary widely, so you'll have to talk to local fisherfolk to find out the state of things at any given time. Check with one of the local town halls for a shellfish permit.

RESTAURANTS & PROVISIONS: Riverhead may be the only port that offers a bulkheaded McDonald's just waiting for dock-and-diners. Try it for the fun of it, but if you prefer a more substantial meal, head downtown to a wide selection of eateries. Digger O'Dell's (631-369-3200) and Hyting Restaurant (631-727-1557) are right next to each other downtown. Digger's is an Irish pub known for its prime rib, while Hyting has a fine Chinese menu.

A stop at Treasure Cove Resort Marina will land you at Jerry's Restaurant & Clam Bar (631-727-8489). Sit down and enjoy seafood, chicken, steak, or pasta; but you can't leave the place without trying Jerry's famous buffalo wings.

If you're a beef eater, a stop at Rendezvous Restaurant (631-727-6880) is a must—it's the best known steak house around. The Riverhead Grill (631-727-8495) is also a fine

NAVIGATION & ANCHORAGES: Use ChartKit Region 3, pages 6 and 52B; Maptech™ Waterproof Charts 1 and 6; and Maptech™ electronic and NOAA paper charts 12358 (1:40,000) and 12354 (1:80,000). Use tide tables for New London. High tide at South Jamesport is 2 hours 33 minutes later; low tide is 2 hours 40 minutes later. Use height of tide at New London for height of tide at South Jamesport. Mean tidal range is 2.7 feet.

The entrance to Flanders Bay, between Red Cedar and Miamogue points, is 4.1nm from Shinnecock Canal, and 18.2nm from Greenport Harbor. The entrance to the Peconic River is 2.3nm away.

Before you come into Flanders Bay proper, you'll pass Red Creek Pond just east of Red Cedar Point. Red Creek Pond is a lovely little gunkhole with a 6-foot dredged channel and 4 to 5 feet in the harbor. The channel entrance is marked by Fl G 5s 3M "1" and R N "2." R N "2" and R N "4" are well off the channel to the west, so favor the east side of the channel. Inside are a number of private moorings.

On the other side of the entrance to Flanders Bay, just north of Miamogue Point, is East Creek, dredged to 8 feet (6 feet on the approach). There's a state launching ramp and beach there, as well as a marina with a playground and nature area. When on the beach, try not to disrupt the nesting roseate terns, an endangered species.

Flanders Bay is a paradise for small boats that can skip over its shoals, and a somewhat discouraging maze for those with deeper drafts. If you draw more than 4 feet, stay out of Flanders Bay except at half or full tide. Most of the bottom is soft mud or sand, with only a few rocks and no strong currents. Wherever you go, unless you're in a small outboard or dinghy, follow the twisting channels and keep an eye on your depth finder. Most of the creeks are best navigated by dinghy.

South Jamesport and Riverhead can both be reached easily if you follow the buoys and take frequent soundings. Approaching South Jamesport, leave Fl R 4s R "4" to the north and G C "5" to the west. There is an anchorage west of Miamogue Point, and the channel carries a reported depth of 8 feet, though there is only 5 feet on the approach. In South Jamesport, Great Peconic Bay Marina offers transient dockage and a marine store.

If you're looking for anchorages, there's good protection and plenty of water in the area west of Red Cedar Point, a little less than a mile south and west of Fl R 4s R "4." You can also drop your Danforth as much as 1,000 yards south of Fl R 4s R "8." Stay well north and west of the shoal extending 0.5nm northwest of Red Cedar Point. Farther south you'll find Birch, Mill, and Hubbard creeks, which the Southampton Bay Constable aptly described as "dinghy water."

Proceeding past South Jamesport, pass north of G C "7" and head south-southwest toward Fl R 4s R "8" off of Simmons Point. Stay south of the buoy unless you're interested in mud—lots of it, all over your keel.

At Fl R 4s R "8" turn hard to the northwest and look for Fl G 4s G "9," which marks the entrance to the Flanders Bay channels. As you pass north of the buoy you'll see Reeves Creek, Meetinghouse Creek, and Terry's Creek off to the west. Meetinghouse Creek, which leads to the village of Aquebogue, has piles and Fl R 2s 5ft to guide you. Three cans lead up the creek to Larry's Lighthouse Marina with plenty of transient docking in about 5 to 6 feet of water.

Terry's Creek is good gunkholing for small boats only, as depths are generally below 6 feet, and there are no facilities. Reeves Bay, on the southwest side, leads into the town of Flanders via a privately dredged channel with a reported controlling depth of 3 feet. At the head of the creek there's a huge, old oak tree that is said to have been a landmark and meeting place for Indians. To this day, farmers in the vicinity routinely plow up arrowheads.

Your destination in this area is the town of Riverhead, at the western end of the bay. The Riverhead channel, about 3 miles long, is narrow and built up, but it's well marked by a series of red and green 2s flashers. The river is impassable for sailboats after the first mile because of a 25-foot-high fixed bridge. After that you'll find a town in the process of revitalizing itself. A recently rebuilt town boardwalk and the hospitable Treasure Cove Resort Marina await.

Shoreside & Emergency Services
Airport: Mattituck Airbase (631-298-8330)
Bus: Suffolk County Transit (631-852-5200)
Coast Guard: Shinnecock (631-728-1171) or VHF 16
Harbormaster: Bay Constable (631-287-5717)
Police, Fire, Ambulance: 911
Taxi: Riverhead Cab (631-727-6088)
Tow Service:
SEA TOW —24-Hour Dispatch (800-4SEATOW)
—Moriches/Shinnecock (631-653-6361)
Tow BoatU.S.—24-Hour Dispatch (800-391-4869)
Train: Long Island Railroad (631-822-5477)

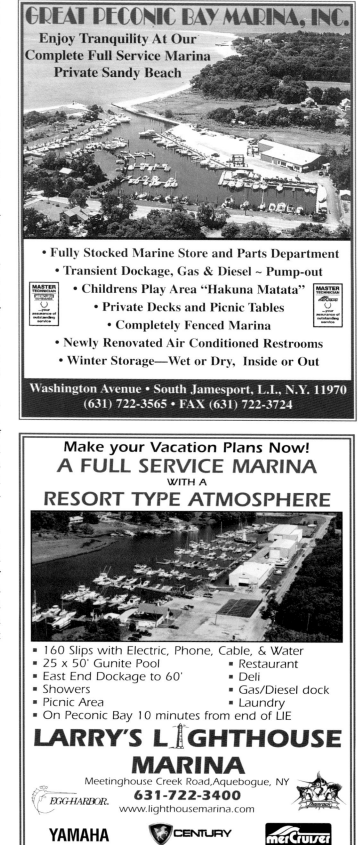

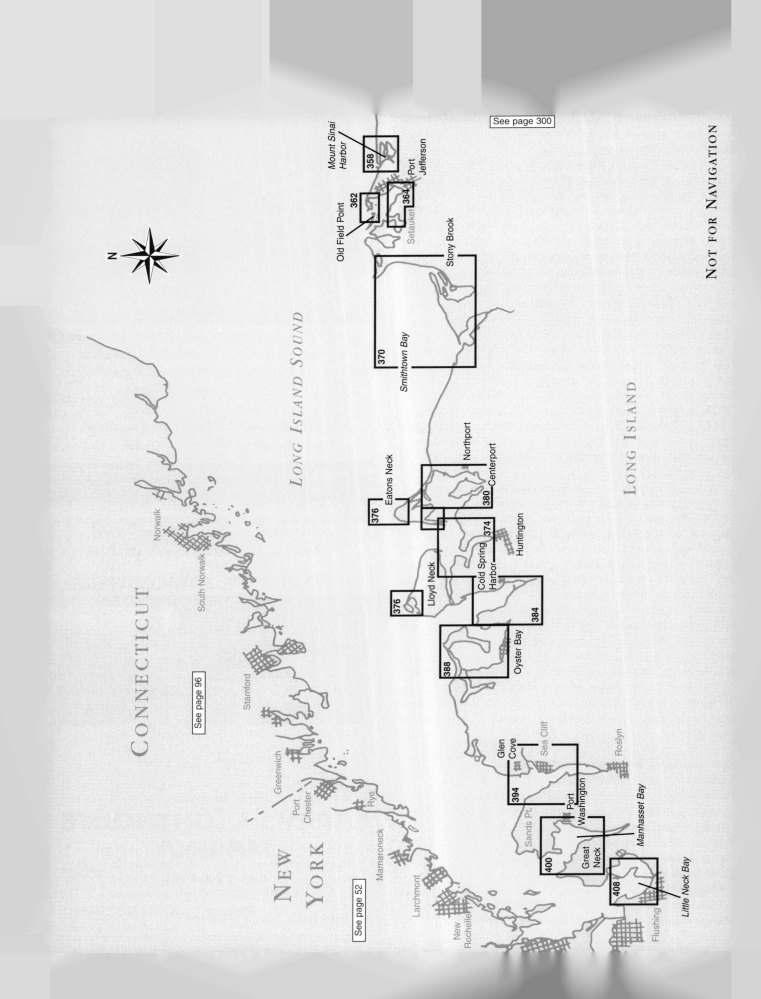

CONNECTICUT

NEW YORK

LONG ISLAND SOUND

LONG ISLAND

See page 96

See page 52

See page 300

Norwalk

South Norwalk

Stamford

Greenwich

Port Chester

Rye

Mamaroneck

Larchmont

New Rochelle

Mount Sinai Harbor

358

362

Old Field Point

364

Setauket

Port Jefferson

370

Smithtown Bay

Stony Brook

376

Eatons Neck

Northport

380

Centerport

374

Cold Spring Harbor

Huntington

376

Lloyd Neck

384

Oyster Bay

388

394

Glen Cove

Sea Cliff

Roslyn

Sands Pt.

Port Washington

Manhasset Bay

400

Great Neck

408

Little Neck Bay

Flushing

Cruise along the north shore of Long Island with its quiet coves abutted by high hills; you'll see why wealthy 19th-century families made this area the Gold Coast. The haves (and a few have-nots) of that era considered it the ideal getaway on steamy days that were even steamier in the city. Some came to the beaches by steamboat for just the day, but others built large manors atop the hills, granting them a grand view as well as water access.

Not much has changed, as affluent families still favor the hilly shores of places like **Mount Sinai Harbor, Lloyd Neck,** and **Oyster Bay.** The business districts of larger harbors, including **Huntington** and **Port Jefferson,** balance out the sleepier Gold Coast communities and provide commercial support with amenities and shopping. Put together, it makes for ideal cruising territory, as you can travel in and out of natural harbors, each with its own place in history, and enjoy first-class dining, shopping, and sightseeing.

Navigating Region 7

Long Island's north shore is relatively sparse between Mattituck Inlet and Port Jefferson. Fom GONG G "3A" head 277°m toward G C "11," north of Mount Misery Shoal. Southeast of that mark, you can sneak into pleasant Mount Sinai Harbor. Head for RW SP "M" and then Fl G 5s 20ft Priv.

The entrance depth varies from 9 to 23 feet between the breakwaters; play it safe and stick to the middle of the channel. Also take note of the 6-foot tidal rise and fall in the harbor. With strong currents between the breakwaters at the change of tides, expect a bit of a push. *Refer to the Mount Sinai Harbor chapter for more information.*

Round Mount Misery Shoal and G C "11" to the north before heading to Port Jefferson. The current runs quickly past Mount Misery Shoal. Steer for Fl R 2.5s BELL R "2," which marks Port Jefferson's entrance channel. On the east side of the harbor entrance is a popular anchorage, Mount Misery Cove, offering good all-around protection. Once inside Port Jefferson Harbor, you'll be in a well-protected, deep-water harbor; you may drop your anchor anywhere outside the channel. There's a 12-mph speed limit to the first charted mooring, then a 5-mph limit to Port Jeff. *Refer to the Port Jefferson chapter for more information.*

Continuing west, keep GONG G "11A" well to the south. Round Crane Neck Point, and you'll see Fl G 4s G "1" marking the entrance to Stony Brook Harbor. Strong currents produce tide rips around both Eatons Neck and Crane Neck points, so give each plenty of room. Shoaling in this area can be terrible, exacerbated by a vigorous current heightened at full or new moon. *Refer to the Smithtown Bay and Stony Brook Harbor chapter for more information.*

Your next destination is Huntington Bay. From GONG G "11A" head 280°m. Keep G C "13" to the south and steer for Fl R 4s BELL R "8." To enter Huntington Harbor, first pass between Huntington Light (Iso 6s 42ft 9M HORN) and Fl G

The eye-pleasing view from Centerport Yacht Club. © Maptech

4s G "1." Follow the channel as it passes between West Neck and Wincoma Point; it's a narrow passage with a strong current. Enter Lloyd Harbor north of the Huntington Light and stay between G C "3" and R N "4" to avoid the nasty reefs south of East Beach. *Refer to the Eatons Neck, Lloyd Harbor & Huntington Harbor chapter for more information.*

The markers that run along the north shore of Lloyd Neck will keep you away from the rocks. The channel into Oyster Bay Harbor carries more than 30 feet of water to Moses Point; west of the point the channel narrows, but it's well marked with a row of nuns and cans. *Refer to the Oyster Bay chapter for more information.*

From Fl G 4s GONG G "15," north of Lloyd Point, head 258°m toward Fl G 4s GONG G "21." Keep that mark to the south and you can head into Hempstead Harbor, home to Glen Cove on the eastern shore. Stay north of R N "2," marking Old Hen Rock. Glen Cove Creek, about a half mile south of the breakwater, has a channel running from Mosquito Cove about 0.6nm to the head. The creek contains three marinas and attracts many boaters. A good landmark for Prospect Point is a large, white house with columns, designed by the famous architect Stanford White. *Refer to the Hempstead Harbor & Glen Cove chapter for more information.*

To reach Manhasset Bay, pass northwest of Fl G 2.5s G "25" and GONG G "27" before turning south toward the bay. East of Plum Point, marked by Fl G 4s G "1," is Manorhaven. The deepest-water approach to the marinas is between the buoys G C "3" and R N "4". *Refer to Manhasset Bay & Port Washington chapter for more information.*

Round Hewlett Point offshore of Fl G 4s G "29" before running along the shore toward R N "2" and R N "4," northwest of Great Neck. Pass southeast of, but close aboard, each of these buoys before rounding Kings Point and entering Little Neck Bay. West of Little Neck Bay and R N "2" at Willets Point, lies the East River. *Refer to the Little Neck Bay chapter for more information.*

MT SINAI HARBOR

CEDAR BEACH

SCALE 1:10,000

Nautical Miles
0   1/4

Yards
0   250   500

VAR 13° 45'W (1990) ANNUAL INCREASE 4'

MAGNETIC

Old Man & the Mount

The Native Americans named this area Nonawantuck, but how it came to be called Old Man's is a mystery. When community officials asked for installation of a post office in 1840, they were told that Old Man's was not an acceptable name for a town. For a brief spell they called it Mount Vernon, until they realized that the name was already taken by a New York City suburb.

So the townsfolk gathered at the church and grumbled, "Why, anybody could pick a better name than that by opening the Bible and sticking his finger anywheres upon a page!" That's exactly what the postmaster did, using a knitting needle rather than his finger. The needle landed smack upon Moses' descension from Mount Sinai.

Capping 40 miles of unbroken bluffs, Mount Sinai is the only harbor on the north shore between Port Jefferson and Mattituck. Most of the north section of the harbor is manmade, and in the 1950s it became a sparring ground for sand and gravel companies, environmentalists, fishermen, boaters, and the town officials. Each group had a different plan in mind for the surrounding salt marsh. To appease everyone as best as possible, two-thirds of the marshland was kept as a nature preserve and the remainder was dredged, making a harbor. Beaches, fishing piers, ramps, and a marina were also created.

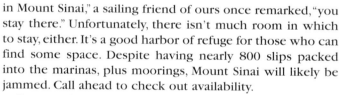

People try their luck at fishing as a sailboat motors past. © Maptech

ACTIVITIES: Although Mount Sinai offers a great deal of outdoor recreational opportunities, it's isolated. "When you stay in Mount Sinai," a sailing friend of ours once remarked, "you stay there." Unfortunately, there isn't much room in which to stay, either. It's a good harbor of refuge for those who can find some space. Despite having nearly 800 slips packed into the marinas, plus moorings, Mount Sinai will likely be jammed. Call ahead to check out availability.

Once you've secured the boat, grab a towel and pull up some sand. Cedar Beach gets its name from the dense growth of cedar trees to the east. At the western end of the beach is a fishing pier (a local mariner reports that good size fluke, flounder, and stripers can be caught right off the docks), and between them is a nature preserve with a small

Marine Facilities and Services

All Coast Guard Stations Monitor VHF Channel 16

#	Facility	Phone	Monitors / Working VHF Channel	No. of Transient Berths	Seasonal / Year-round Moorings	Max. LOA	Approach / Dockside Depth (ft at MLW)	Hookups: Fresh Water / Phone / Cable TV	110V ★ 220V ▲ 3 Phase ■ Max Amps	Rail / Lift / Crane / Trailer	Ramp / Dinghy Dock / Launch Service	Repairs: Propellor / Sail / Rigging / Gas / Diesel / Wood / Fiberglass / Electronics	Gas / Diesel Fuel	Fuel Brand	Marine / Groceries / Ice / Bait / LPG / CNG	Restrooms / Showers / Laundry / Pumpout	Public Phone / Restaurant / Snack Bar	Hotel / Pool / Tennis / Golf	Mastercard / VISA / Discover / AmEx
1	RALPH'S MARINA & FISHING STATION (p. 361)	631-473-6655	67/67	4/6	Y	50	13/13	FP	★30		All	PGDWFE	GD	BP	MIB	RS	PS		All
2	Mount Sinai Yacht Club	631-473-2993	9/	10/6	Y	50	10/15	F	★▲50		D		GD		I	RSP		All	MVA
3	OLD MAN'S BOATYARD (p. 361)	631-473-7330		3/1	Y	55	12/12	F	★30	LC25	D	All			M	RP			
4	Mount Sinai Marina	631-928-0199		20/	S	45		F	★30		R					R	PS		

Information in these listings is provided by the facilities themselves. An asterisk (*) indicates that the facility did not respond to our most recent requests for information. (B) represents a BOAT/U.S. cooperating marina.

Looking northwest over Mount Sinai Harbor. As you enter the harbor, you'll first pass by Ralph's Marina & Fishing Station, then Old Man's Boatyard.
© Maptech/James T. Abts

walking trail, and indoor and outdoor exhibits on Old Man's and the salt marsh.

At the preserve, pick up a map for a bicycle tour of Mount Sinai (be prepared for some hills), following part of the route taken by Major Benjamin Tallmadge and his troops in 1780, as they marched from Mount Sinai Harbor to attack the British in Mastic and Coram. En route, you'll see a glacially-formed kettle-hole lake, an Indian encampment area, and a pine barrens where trees grow barely above eye level because of the poor soil.

If lounging about isn't your cup of chowder, call a cab and head down to Port Jefferson, just over three miles away. See the Port Jefferson chapter for more information on activities there.

RESTAURANTS & PROVISIONS: You can get quick, easy, hand-held meals at The Roost, a take-out counter with outdoor deck at Ralph's Fishing Station; Cedar Beach also has a snack bar in summer. Mount Sinai Yacht Club's grill, open to members and guests (including transients), serves burgers and sandwiches. For sit-down service, take a quick cab ride to Savino's Hideaway (631-928-6510), serving Italian favorites and steaks in a relaxed atmosphere, or Dublin Delights (631-331-4848) for Irish dishes,

including shepherd's pie so good it'll make you shout, "Oh, begorrah!"

The marinas have marine supplies if you need them, but your best bet is to call that cab again for the three mile ride to Port Jefferson. Again, refer to the Port Jefferson Harbor chapter for more eating options.

NAVIGATION & ANCHORAGES: Use ChartKit Region 3, page 24; Maptech™ Waterproof Charts 1; and Maptech™ electronic and NOAA paper charts 12362 (1:10,000), 12364 (1:40,000), and 12354 (1:80,000). Use tide tables for Bridgeport. High tide at Mount Sinai Harbor is 4 minutes later; low tide is 18 minutes later. Multiply the height of tide at Bridgeport by 0.9 for the height of tide at Mount Sinai. Mean tidal range is 6 feet.

The entrance to Mount Sinai Harbor is 3.2nm from the Port Jefferson Harbor entrance, 22.2nm from Mattituck Inlet, and 17nm from the breakwaters at New Haven, Connecticut. From Fl R 4s BELL R "2" at the southern tip of Middle Ground, a course of about 165°m for 5.7nm will take you to the entrance of Mount Sinai Harbor. Mount Sinai is easily approached from both the east and west, but it can be hard to spot from a distance.

From the east, stay 1.5nm offshore to avoid the occasional rocks and shoals until you're north of Fl G 5s 20ft

PRIV marking the eastern breakwater. When approaching from this direction, take note of Millers Rock, about 0.5nm offshore and 2nm east of the nasty breakwater, which provides much of the business for the harbor's repair shops.

From the west, stay to the north of GC "11" at Mount Misery Shoal, 1.9nm to the northwest, and then head for RW S P "M," about 0.3nm north of the breakwater. Note, the privately-maintained light on the east breakwater has been known to go out.

The entrance depth varies from 9 to 23 feet between the breakwaters, and is marked by a low break in the beach. Along the east side of the entrance is a fishing pier, usable by non-residents for a fee. The two breakwater jetties are awash at high water, so use caution when rounding them. Play it safe and stick to the middle of the channel.

CAUTION: There's at least a 6-foot tidal rise and fall in the harbor, with strong currents between the breakwaters at the change of tides, so expect a bit of a push.

As you turn east to head behind Cedar Beach and enter the harbor proper, you'll want to stay as far north as traffic will allow to keep off the shallows to the south. The channel is buoyed by a row of nuns and a few cans maintained by the town, and the fishing pier is lighted during the summer.

You'll be well protected in the harbor, and your best bet for finding an anchorage is in the harbor's extreme eastern end as the rest is filled with moorings.

There's good dinghy exploring in the marshes south of the town marina, but the mud can be very treacherous, so even in your dink you should wait until high tide to go into the marshes. No landing is allowed anywhere in the harbor, except at the marinas. There's a 6-mph speed limit, so water-skiing is prohibited.

If you want a mooring or a slip at the town marina, contact the harbormaster (631-928-0199), but don't get your hopes up. You may have better luck at Old Man's Boatyard or Ralph's Fishing Station, full-service facilities with a handful of transient berths. You can buy gas and diesel at Ralph's, the westernmost facility on Cedar Beach, or the Mount Sinai Yacht Club.

Shoreside & Emergency Services
Airport: MacArthur (631-467-3210)
Bus: Suffolk County Transit (631-852-5200)
Coast Guard:
—New Haven (203-468-4464) or VHF 16
—Eatons Neck (631-261-6868) or VHF 16
Harbormaster: (631-928-0199) or VHF 16
Police, Fire, Ambulance: 911
Taxi: Port Taxi (631-475-5959)
Tow Service:
SEA TOW —24-Hour Dispatch (800-4SEATOW)
—Port Jefferson (631-473-2869)
Tow BoatU.S.—24-Hour Dispatch (800-391-4869)
Train: Long Island Railroad (631-822-5477)

"Nauti" word

Scuttlebutt: *Informal* n. gossip or rumor; idle talk

Many moons ago, the drinking water on ships was kept in a receptacle, or **butt**, from which the crew could draw their rations. So that the men wouldn't exceed their measly share, a **scuttle**, or hole, was made in the butt so that it could only be filled halfway each day. Thus the water would last through a voyage.

Naturally, as the thirsty men waited in line they traded the gossip of the day (we can't imagine how many fresh rumors came up in such a situation, but we're not digging deep). After all, it was about the only time that they had to socialize a little.

Of course, this water-cooler gossip still occurs, undoubtedly in your own workplace. And today's meaning of *scuttlebutt*—idle talk, especially that exchanged around a drinking fountain—reflects that.

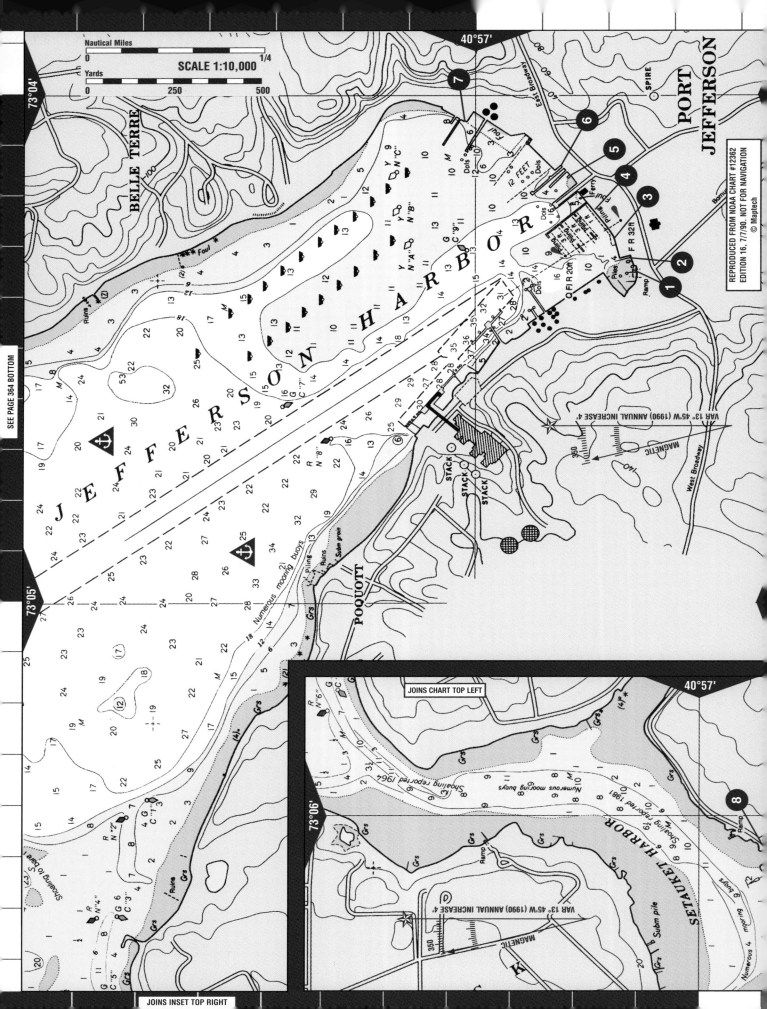

Nautical Miles
0 _____ 1/4
SCALE 1:10,000
Yards
0 _____ 250 _____ 500

40°57'

73°04'

BELLE TERRE

JEFFERSON HARBOR

JEFFERSON

POQUOTT

PORT
JEFFERSON

VAR 13° 45'W (1990) ANNUAL INCREASE 4'

MAGNETIC

Numerous mooring buoys

JOINS CHART TOP LEFT

40°57'

73°06'

SETAUKET HARBOR

Shoaling reported 1964

Numerous mooring buoys

Shoaling reported 1981

VAR 13° 45'W (1990) ANNUAL INCREASE 4'

MAGNETIC

Steep Stuff

Hike around Port Jefferson for an afternoon and you'll come away from your jaunt with sore legs and a newfound respect for the area's topography—the hills on both sides of the harbor are killers.

Back around the turn of the 20th century, East Broadway (vertical drop: 230 feet) was the site of a series of popular automobile hill climbs. Designers and drivers (including Henry Ford, who didn't do any better than 16th place) came from far and wide to test their vehicles against Port Jeff's steeps. Local drivers even managed to pull off a few surprise victories over the years. In 1910 a locally-built car, the 12-horsepower O.N.L.Y., finished second to a beastly 200-horsepower Fiat. In 1925 local Allison Vandall fared even better in a modified F.R.P. touring car, beating that year's winner of the more prestigious Pikes Peak Hill climb. If you can get your hands on a car and wish to test your driving skills against East Broadway today, keep in mind that the enforced speed limit in town is a relatively tame 30 m.p.h.

Long before cars existed, Port Jeff was building a strong maritime heritage. The sails for *America*, the yacht that changed the name of the Louis Vuitton Cup to the "America's Cup," were made here by R.H. Wilson and Sons in 1856. In the early 1800s, P.T. Barnum helped found a burgeoning ferry service between Port Jeff and his circus' base of operations 14 miles across the Sound in Bridgeport, Connecticut. Many of the ferries, including the original *MV Park City* (1898), were built in Port Jeff.

A view of Port Jeff Harbor, with its signature stacks. © Maptech

In the 1950s and '60s, Port Jeff became more and more industrial and less and less appealing. Today, the massive power plant on the southwest side of the harbor is one of the few reminders of this period. A successful revitalization effort in the 1980s revived the charm of this old fishing village. Interesting shops, excellent restaurants, a first-class hotel and conference center, and easy access to the harbor make Port Jeff a great stopover.

Nearby Setauket, settled in 1655 by a small group of emigrés from Connecticut, distinguished itself in the field of espionage. After the execution of Nathan Hale during the American Revolution, the need for better intelligence and surveillance of the British became apparent. Setauket

	Marine Facilities and Services		Monitors / Working VHF Channel	Number of Transient Berths	Approach / Dockside Depth in Feet at MLW	Seasonal / Year-round Moorings	Maximum LOA	110V ★ 220V ▲ 3 Phase ■ Maximum Amps	Hookups: Fresh Water / Phone / Cable TV	Ramp / Dinghy Dock / Launch Service	Rail / Lift / Crane / Trailer Capacity (tons)	Repairs: Propellor / Sail / Rigging / Electronics	Diesel / Wood / Fiberglass	Marine / Groceries / Ice / Bait / LPG / CNG	Gas / Diesel Fuel	Fuel Brand	Restrooms / Showers / Laundry / Pumpout	Public Phone / Restaurant / Snack Bar	Hotel / Pool / Tennis / Golf	Mastercard / VISA / Discover / AmEx
1	The Boat Place	631-473-0612		Y	45	9/5	F	★30	R	L25	All				MIB		PS	All
2	Caraftis Fishing Station	631-473-2288		S		4/4										R		All
3	Port Jefferson Yacht Club	631-473-9864	68/	S	40	5/5	F	★30		*PRIVATE—RECIPROCAL PRIVILEGES*					RS		All	All
4	Port Jefferson Town Marina	631-331-3567	16/9	15/20	S	42	12/8	F	★30	R				GD	bp		RP	P
5	Port Jefferson Launch Service	631-751-5035 or 516-702-9122	68/68	/30	S					L	*HARBOR LAUNCH SERVICE*							
6	Danford's Inn & Marina	631-928-5200	9/	35/	S	125	18/9	All	★▲■30	D		All	GD	Gulf	MI	RS	H	All	All
7	Setauket Yacht Club	631-473-9890	68/	/24	S		15/13			DL					I	RS		P	MV
8	Setauket Harbor Boat Basin*	631-941-4640		S			★▲■30	All	T	All				RS			MV

All Coast Guard Stations Monitor VHF Channel 16

marinalife.com — Convenient Online Boat Slip Reservations

Information in these listings is provided by the facilities themselves. An asterisk (*) indicates that the facility did not respond to our most recent requests for information. (B) represents a BOAT/U.S. cooperating marina.

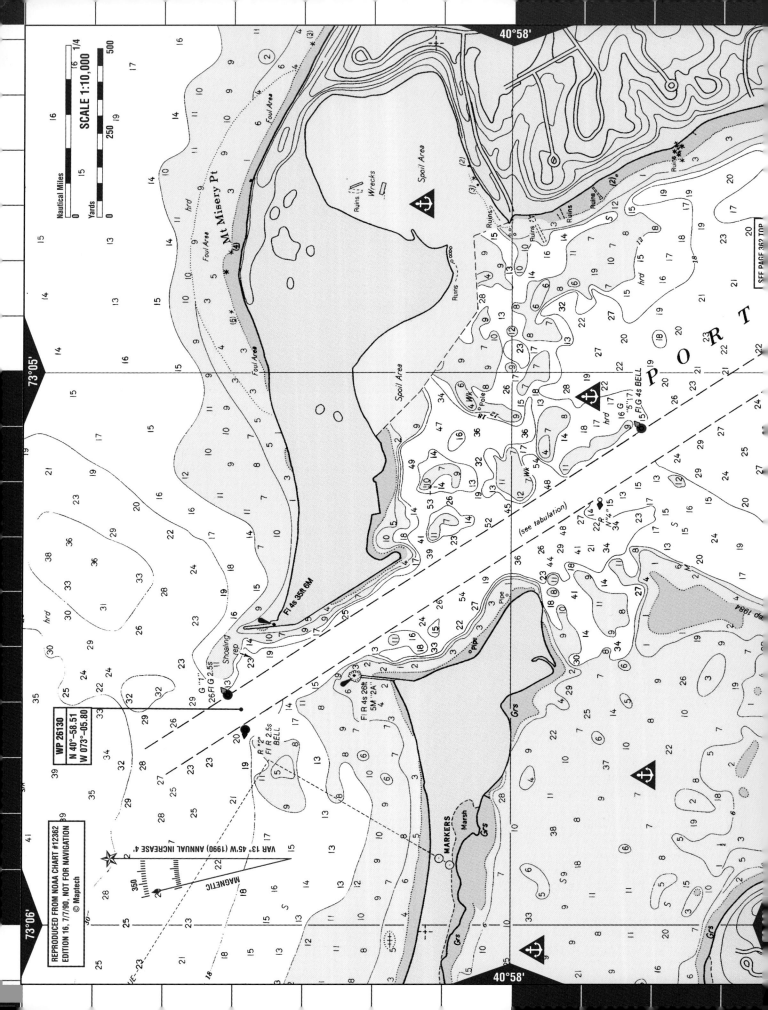

Patriots set up a spy ring right under the noses of a group of local Tories, and long-boats made midnight excursions up and down the Sound to check on British troop movements. Messages were signaled to other Patriots by a local woman who strung a certain number and combination of red or black petticoats and white hand-kerchiefs on a clothesline.

Befitting its location in a secluded cranny of Port Jefferson Harbor, Setauket is a snug, charming little town. Laundry still hangs drying in backyards on warm, sunny days, signalling not a blessed thing.

ACTIVITIES: With the concentration of businesses around the waterfront and the comings and goings of huge ferries at the dock, Port Jeff presents an extremely busy façade. But walk a few blocks inland, and you'll see

A couple and their dogs enjoy a waterside stroll near Mount Misery Cove. © Maptech

it's also a quiet and beautiful residential town. Still, Port Jefferson's layout indicates that this town was made with the transient boater in mind. Restaurants, markets, inviting shops and boutiques, art galleries, and antique stores are all within easy walking distance.

Call the Port Jefferson Chamber of Commerce (631-473-1414) for a rundown of the latest happenings in this active, waterside town. Every Memorial Day weekend, Port Jefferson brings out the colors and celebrates the coming of summer with a street fair. Also during summer, there are July Fourth festivities as well as free concerts put on by the recreation department (631-473-4778) every Thursday evening.The chamber, located on West Broadway next to the ferry slips, gives out a free map and brochures for a town walking tour.

Drama fans, don't miss a performance at Theater Three (631-928-9100), one of Long Island's better-known repertory theaters. This year-round playhouse, founded in 1969, is right on Main Street, and it features a variety of musicals and plays, including educational dramas for children.

For a walking tour of old ship captains' houses and the Barnum house, pick up a map at the Historical Society of Greater Port Jefferson (631-473-2665) located at the Mather House, or at the Chamber of Commerce. At the Society's museum on Prospect Street, a few blocks from the harbor, there's a charming collection of paintings by William M. Davis, a 19th-century genre painter from Port Jefferson. If you'd rather stroll by historical places than visit them, a walk down East Main Street is certainly in order.

P.T. Barnum doesn't have his circus in Bridgeport any longer, but his ferry from Port Jeff to Bridgeport still runs. The Bridgeport & Port Jefferson Steamboat Company (631-473-0286) crosses the Sound on a regular basis throughout the year. Best of all, they offer day trips via a ferry/motor coach combo package: you take the ferry from Port Jeff to Bridgeport, then a motor coach takes

you to any of a number of New England attractions, including Connecticut casinos, Boston, and the Newport Mansions. Contact the ferry office's New England Tour Department for details, or visit their website (http://www.pagelinx.com/bpjferry/daytour.htm).

RESTAURANTS & PROVISIONS: In Port Jeff, grub is never far from the water—that's the way a seafaring port should be. When you step off your boat, you'll see several restaurants staring at you.

It's only natural that a historical place like Port Jefferson has an establishment as quaint as 25 East Bistro at Danford's (631-928-5200, ext. 170). Located next to the ferry landing, Danford's fine restaurant serves specialties such as lamb and veal chops, Long Island duck, and original pasta creations; on Sundays there's a terrific brunch. Docking is available for patrons at the marina, and on show nights they offer a dinner and theater combination in conjunction with Theater Three.

Across from the ferry terminal is the Steamroom (631-928-6690) for chowder and bisque, fried seafood, steamers, and boiled lobsters. Be sure to try the onion loaf, a golden nest of

onion rings fried in batter to a crisp, heavenly perfection. Also facing the waterfront is Dockside Restaurant (631473-5656), known for its outstanding bouillabaisse. The menu changes daily, so walk up to their front door and check out what seafood specialties are on the docket. Cut through the municipal lot behind the Steamroom to get to the Tiger Lily Café (631-476-7080). At this "alternative eatery," as it bills itself, you can choose from a variety of soups and sandwiches made from whole grains, vegetables, lean meats, and tofu, then top it all off with a fruit smoothie.

The Village Way (631-928-3395), on Main Street, features a selection of American favorites, as does the Broadway Grill (631-473-1220), which also offers a vegetarian menu. Folks also flock to the Elk Street Grille (631-331-0960), where the more unusual menu items are kielbasa and sauerkraut, bison chili, and smoked salmon salad. For quick and easy eats, pull up a stool, sip on a longneck, and munch a burrito at Salsa Salsa (631-473-9700).

Those of you with a sweet tooth can grab a treat at La Bonne Boulangerie (631-473-7900), a bakery on Broadway, or go for an egg cream or ice cream at Port Jefferson Frigate (631-474-8888), in the small plaza opposite the ferry dock. There's also a Starbuck's (631-476-3791) a few steps up the hill on Main Street.

All the amenities you'll need can be found on Main and East Main streets, both of which run perpendicular to the waterfront. For provisions, try Moore's Gourmet Market & Deli (631-928-1443) on Main Street or Village Grocery on the corner of Maple Place and Main.

NAVIGATION & ANCHORAGES: Use ChartKit Region 3, pages 23 and 25; Maptech™ Waterproof Charts 1 and 16; and Maptech™ electronic and NOAA paper charts 12362 (1:10,000), 12364 (1:40,000) and 12354 (1:80,000). Use tide tables for Bridgeport. High tide at Port Jefferson is 6 minutes later; low tide is 5 minutes later. Use height of tide at Bridgeport for height of tide at Port Jefferson. Mean tidal range is 6.6 feet.

The entrance to Port Jefferson Harbor is 8.1nm from Stony Brook Harbor and 4nm from Mount Sinai Harbor. From Fl R 4s BELL R "2" south of Middle Ground (Stratford Shoal), a course of about 190°m for 4.7nm takes you to the entrance channel for Port Jefferson Harbor.

Approaching Port Jefferson, stay well offshore to clear the rocks and shoals off Old Field and Mount Misery points. The current runs quickly past both points and has scooped away the sand, leaving large and dangerous piles of boulders no longer marked by buoys. Mount Misery Shoal shows a charted depth of 7 feet, but the depth can be less. Depending on your course, your landmark may be Old Field Point Light (Al R G 24s 74ft 12M) or RW "PJ" Mo(A) WHIS RW "PJ".

From the east or northeast, other landmarks are the 60-foot-high sand bluffs of Mount Misery to the east of the entrance jetties. Also clearly visible are the two smokestacks of the Long Island Lighting Company power plant at the south end of Port Jefferson Harbor.

CAUTION: Be careful not to confuse these 2 stacks with the 4 stacks of the power plant at Northport, 12 miles to the west.

Looking northwest over Port Jefferson Harbor. Old Field Point is located in the upper right.© Maptech/J.T. Abts

If the tide is ebbing and the winds are out of the north (prevailing summer winds are from the southwest), rough seas can build up outside the jetties, with currents up to 2.6 knots. Sailboats are best off motoring in.

Once inside Port Jefferson Harbor, you'll be in a well-protected, deep-water harbor; you may drop your anchor anywhere outside the channel. There's a 12-mph speed limit to the first charted mooring, then a 5-mph limit down to Port Jeff.

Inside the entrance to the west is a very popular anchorage behind Old Field Point and Old Field Beach, but don't look at the chart and think there's plenty of water right off Old Field Beach at the entrance; many boats get hung up here. Make your turn to the west on either side of R N "4," but be sure to make it sharp to avoid the

Looking north over Setauket Harbor. © Maptech/J.T. Abts

shoal about 400 yards south of the grassy point. You can go westward all the way up to the entrance of the grass-filled Conscience Bay at the Narrows. There is no marked channel, so pick your way carefully. It's wisest to try it for the first time on a rising tide. You'll be well-protected except in a southeasterly, due to the fetch across the harbor.

On the east side of the harbor entrance is another popular anchorage, Mount Misery Cove, offering good all-around protection and adequate hold (use a Danforth anchor for best results). Although the chart doesn't give any soundings, this manmade cove has an average depth of 11 to 15 feet (mlw). If you draw more than 4 feet, your best route in is to round Fl G 4s BELL G "5" and approach from the south to avoid the shoals between the jetty and the buoy. You'll see boats anchored just 100 yards east of the channel, but there's probably shoaling between them and the channel, so make sure you pass south of Fl G 4s BELL G "5" before making your turn.

If you are not interested in beaches or birds and just want to get out of a blow, anchor anywhere out of the channel. There's plenty of room and deep water in the "Upper Landing" section of Port Jefferson Harbor. If you'd rather tie up to a cleat than drop anchor, several marinas await in Port Jefferson Harbor. There are also some moorings in the harbor, provided by Port Jefferson Launch Service.

CAUTION: Don't go near the Bridgeport-Port Jefferson ferry slip. While it may look tempting for a quick run into town when the ferry is away, you'll have a horde of angry crewmen yelling at you and risk having your boat crushed when the ferry comes back.

On the subject of ferries, give them and the tugs and barges a wide berth. They aren't double-ended, so they must turn around inside the harbor before heading out.

Setauket Harbor is a snug, but shallow, anchorage between Tinkers Point and Strongs Neck. The harbor is apt to be crowded with moored boats, including quite a few flat-decked clammers. Boats drawing more than 5 feet should enter only at high tide, and keep faithfully to the channel. Also note, the long pier at the south end of Setauket Harbor no longer sells gas.

CAUTION: The channel into Setauket Harbor is only marked by three green cans. When entering and exiting the harbor, keep them close abeam as it gets shallow quickly to the north.

If you decide to sample Setauket Harbor, you'll be pleased with the water's calmness and cleanliness. Keep an eye open for commercial traffic and the Bridgeport-Port Jefferson ferry, especially when you're leaving the harbor.

Shoreside & Emergency Services
Airport:
—MacArthur (631-467-3210)
Bus:
—Suffolk County Transit (631-852-5200)
Coast Guard:
—Eatons Neck (631-261-6868) or VHF 16
Ferry:
—Bridgeport & Port Jefferson Steamboat Co.,
   (631-473-0286)
Police, Fire, Ambulance: 911
Taxi: Call-a-Cab (631-473-0707)
Tow Service:
SEA TOW —24-Hour Dispatch (800-4SEATOW)
—Northport (516-624-3483)
Tow BoatUS.—24-Hour Dispatch (800-391-4869)
Train: Long Island Railroad (631-822-5477)

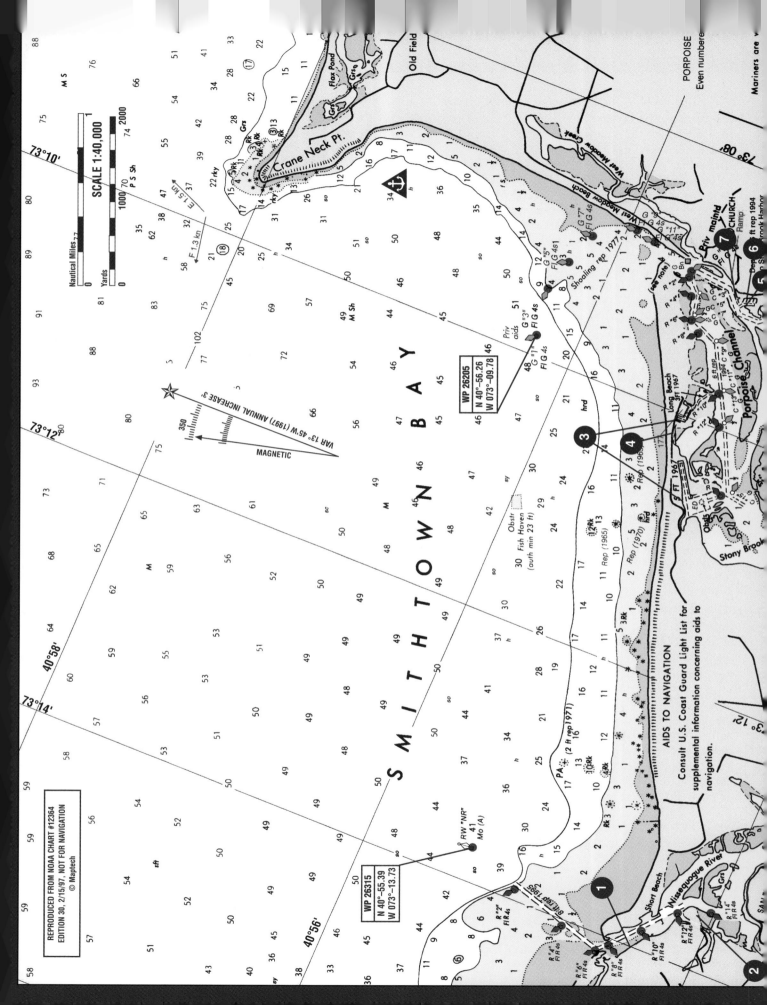

A Man with a Plan

Stony Brook displays such a prim tidiness that it almost makes visitors wonder if little elves come out in the night to keep things straightened up. The town owes its current pristine condition to the vision and ample bank account of one man: Ward Melville.

Young Melville began summering with his parents in the Three Village (Stony Brook, Setauket, and Old Field) area in 1900, when he was 13. In those days Stony Brook was a bit unrefined, and it remained so until the late 1930s when the middle-aged Melville, by that time a tycoon, decided he wanted the town to resemble a classic New England village. And so, true to his word, he set forth the plan that put the "tony" into Stony Brook.

Melville called a town meeting at the Three Village Inn and more or less bought the town from its residents. By 1941, he had cleaned it up, moved some buildings around, and built the Village Center, the nation's first shopping plaza. In the process, he left enough open space for a new town green and opened up access to the harbor.

Melville also contributed much of his own cash to build what was supposed to be a classic, ivy-covered college for the State University of New York at Stony Brook. Unfortunately, he died before the plans for the college were complete, and the state's bureaucrats instead built a modern campus, spanning 1,100 acres. Even without the climbing vines, SUNY-Stony Brook has made a name for itself with highly-ranked engineering and marine science programs and an on-campus teaching hospital. The medical school is so big you can see it all the way across the Sound, making it a good landmark for mariners headed for Smithtown Bay.

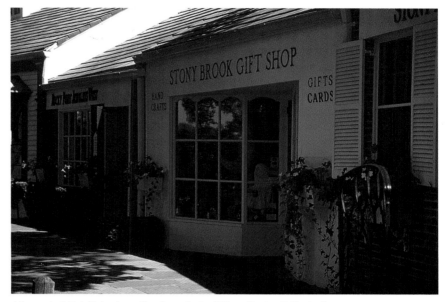

All a part of Melville's plan—the shops in the Village Center. © Maptech

ACTIVITIES: Stony Brook is picture-perfect, with its charm preserved by an appreciation and respect for what Melville accomplished. For instance, electric signs are not permitted in the Village Center, preserving it as a unique and inviting place where residents running errands mingle with browsing out-of-towners.

In the center of it all is the original Stony Brook Village Center, fronted by a sloped green dotted with shade trees. Completed by Melville in 1941, the center houses 30 specialty shops, outlet stores, and a few eateries. While there, be sure to keep your eyes peeled for the mechanical eagle atop the post office—its wings flap on the hour.

The Hercules Pavilion, on the creek shore right across Main Street, houses a 3,000-pound figurehead of the Greek hero. It was taken from the U.S.S. *Ohio*, the first ship

Marine Facilities and Services		DOCKAGE					SERVICES					SUPPLIES & AMENITIES					
All Coast Guard Stations Monitor VHF Channel 16		Monitors / Working VHF Channel	Number of Transient Berths / Moorings	Approach / Dockside Depth in Feet at MLW	Seasonal / Year-round	Hookups: Fresh Water / Phone / Cable TV	110V + 220V ▲ 3 Phase ■ Maximum Amps	Maximum LOA	Ramp / Dinghy Dock / Launch Service	Rail / Lift / Crane / Trailer Capacity (tons)	Diesel / Wood / Fiberglass / Electronics	Repairs: Propellor / Sail / Rigging / Electronics	Marine / Groceries / Ice / Bait / LPG / CNG	Restrooms / Showers / Laundry / Pumpout	Gas / Diesel Fuel	Fuel Brand	Public Phone / Restaurant / Snack Bar	Hotel / Pool / Tennis / Golf	Mastercard / VISA / Discover / AmEx
1	King's Park Bluff	631-360-7643			Y				DOCK & RAMP FOR RESIDENTS ONLY								R	
2	Kings Park Yacht Club	631-544-9679			Y			PRIVATE—MEMBERS ONLY										
3	Smithtown Long Beach Marina*	631-584-9679	16/	25/	Y	50	4/8		★50	R		All	G	Gul	MGIB	RSP		PS
4	Smithtown Bay Yacht Club	631-584-9680			Y			PRIVATE—MEMBERS ONLY										
5	Stony Brook Boat Works Corp.	631-751-1230	2/		Y	30	2/4	F	★30	T15		All				R		
6	Stony Brook Yacht Club	631-751-9873			Y			PRIVATE—MEMBERS ONLY										
7	Brookhaven Town Dock	631-360-7643			Y			20 MINUTE TIE-UP										

Information in these listings is provided by the facilities themselves. An asterisk (*) indicates that the facility did not respond to our most recent requests for information. (B) represents a BOAT/U.S. cooperating marina.

Looking west over Stony Brook Harbor. © Maptech/James T. Abts

Waitresses dressed in colonial garb add to the charming setting, and there's entertainment on weekends.

You'll find the bulk of eateries in the Stony Brook Village Center. Try Pentimento (631-689-7755) for contemporary Northern Italian cuisine; you can only get dinner on Sundays, but lunch and dinner are served every other day of the week. The center also contains Robinson's Tea Room (631-751-1232), offering light meals and a British high tea, and a casual restaurant, The Brook House (631-751-4617), where families like to go for comfort foods and ice cream. You can eat in or take out pastries, coffee, sandwiches, soups, and more at the Golden Pear Café (631-751-7695) or the Village Delicatessen (631-751-0019). Another dining option in town is the Country House Restaurant (631-751-3332), across from the museums on Main Street.

The Village Center has few choices for stocking the galley, except for limited groceries at the Village Delicatessen. Call a cab and head into Setauket.

launched from the Brooklyn Navy Yard in 1820. After the ship was dismantled in Greenport, the figurehead—carved from a single piece of cedar—was purchased by the owner of the Canoe Place Inn at the Shinnecock Canal, and was then taken to Stony Brook.

A short stroll down Main Street from the Village Center takes you to the Mill Pond and park where families gather to feed the ducks. Across the street is the most fully-equipped grist mill on Long Island—the Stony Brook Grist Mill (631-751-2244), built in 1751. For a small fee, you can watch millers at work, and afterward, browse the Mill Store. Pick up some pancake mix and syrup to take home, or get some cracked corn to feed to the ducks.

On Wednesday afternoons at 2:50 p.m. (June through September) the Stony Brook Community Fund (631-751-2244) offers a free walking tour of downtown Stony Brook. The Fund also sponsors a series of free summer concerts on the Village Green, Sunday evenings at 8 p.m. in July and August.

Farther down Main Street at the intersection of Route 25A, discover the Museums at Stony Brook (631-751-0066). The nine-acre site includes the History and Carriage Museums as well as four historic buildings. Exhibits feature antique decoys, miniature rooms, horse-drawn carriages, costumes, toys, and the paintings of William Sydney Mount, the famous 19th-century genre artist.

RESTAURANTS & PROVISIONS: Hungry seafarers boating in this area don't have far to walk to sate their appetites. Across the street from the marinas is the Three Village Inn (631-751-0555), offering three meals daily (and brunch on Sunday) from an epicurean menu of Long Island and New England dishes, including duckling, lobster, and prime rib.

NAVIGATION & ANCHORAGES: Use ChartKit Region 3, page 24; Maptech™ Waterproof Charts 1 and 16; and Maptech™ electronic and NOAA paper charts 12364SC (1:40,000), 12363 (1:80,000), and 12353 (1:80,000). Use tide tables for Bridgeport. High tide at Smithtown Bay is 7 minutes later; low tide is 10 minutes later. Multiply the height of tide at Bridgeport by 0.9 for height of tide at Smithtown Bay. Mean tidal range is 6.1 feet.

Smithtown Bay stretches for 10.5nm between Crane Neck Point and Eatons Neck. The entrance to Stony Brook Harbor is 1.8nm from Crane Neck Point and 8.1nm from the four stacks of the LILCO power plant at Northport. The stacks line up almost exactly on a bearing of due south magnetic, making them the best landmark for boaters heading here.

From the north and Fl R 4s BELL R "2" at the southern tip of Stratford Shoal (Middle Ground), a course of about 225°m will take you past Crane Neck Point. To the south will be Fl G 4s G "1," your main marker into the harbor.

Strong currents produce tide rips around both Eatons Neck and Crane Neck points, so give each plenty of room. The large boulders in this area host a variety of marine life. Divers consider Crane Neck one of the best scuba sites in the western Sound. The waters off the point are also a favorite haunt of fishermen in search of flounder and bass. A good summer anchorage, sheltered from easterly winds, can be found in the bay a mile south of Crane Neck Point. Be sure to stay at least 0.4nm off the point when rounding.

Crane Neck Point is unmarked and can obscure the light on Old Field Point (Al R G 24s 74ft 12M). About a mile west of Fl G 4s G "1," marking the entrance to Stony Brook Harbor, is a manmade "fish haven" where you may see a few anglers. The artificial reef was built in 1978 for use by SUNY marine biologists studying reef-building. It's not used for research much anymore, but blackfish, porgies, flounder, bluefish, weakfish, and lobsters love it.

Stony Brook Harbor can be a nasty navigational problem. If you haven't been here before, don't expect a serene trip into peaceful marshland. Shoaling in this area can be terrible, exacerbated by a vigorous current heightened at full or new moon.

Before battling the current or negotiating the shallows, you'll have to find the harbor entrance. This is no picnic as it's poorly marked. NOAA charts indicate a green daymark at the harbor entrance; there really isn't anything aside from a broken plaque atop a stake. The harbor must be entered over a bar extending almost a mile from land.

CAUTION: At mean low water, the depth at the entrance to Stony Brook Harbor is about 3 feet, and a fresh nor'wester can wipe out most of that. The tidal range is 6.1 feet, so getting in or out is easy enough as long as you do it within 3 hours on either side of high water.

From Fl G 4s G "1," steer east to the first of five privately maintained, lighted green buoys; follow the channel to the last buoy off West Meadow Beach; then, just west of the daymark (G Bn) continue south into the harbor. Though you may see some local boaters passing inside of the green buoys, follow them at your own risk. Shoaling may extend farther out into the bay than indicated on the chart.

CAUTION: This row of markers can cause confusion. The most common mistake is to keep too far off these buoys and run aground. The channel is narrow and the buoys are right on its edge, so hug them closely. You can almost touch the beach on your port side when entering.

Your problems aren't over once you have made the entrance. If the tide is going out, you've come at the wrong time, since a 3- to 4-knot current starts building as soon as you pass the half-baked daymark. Navigating these shallows can be tricky even if they're marked, because the current can easily push you to the shore. As in Napeague Harbor near Montauk, it might help to have someone at the bow keeping a lookout for the bottom, because a depth sounder is sometimes rendered ineffective by the shallowness.

The channel divides at Fl G 4s G "1," one half going south toward the town, and the other, the Porpoise Channel, heading west behind Long Beach. Here at the fork, the first 300 yards of both channels were dredged to a 6-foot controlling depth in the winter of 1996. Heading south, you'll come to the town ramp next to the Stony Brook Yacht Club, which has a float for visitors.

You can anchor anywhere out of the channel, but beware of shoaling, especially at low tide. You'll find more room to anchor farther west in Porpoise Channel, which is well marked and privately maintained. The buoys are removed over the winter.

You can anchor in the southern end of Stony Brook Harbor, but keep an eye on the depth sounder and come in at high water because of the shallow entrance. There is 6 feet of water in parts of the anchorage. (You'll also see some pretty sizeable sailboats here, but rest assured that few spots are deep enough for 6-foot drafts or greater.)

Throughout the harbor there's a 5-mph speed limit, enforced with radar. Personal watercraft, like Jet-Skis, in the harbor can make the channel even more dangerous. The town has alleviated the problem by building a PWC ramp on the Sound side of Long Beach.

Unless you're at a marina on the southern channel, you're not within walking distance of town. If you've gone westward to the Smithtown Long Beach Marina, you'll either have to take your boat or call a taxi. The closest grocery store is in Setauket, a 4-mile drive to the east.

The Nissequogue River is 4.5nm west of Stony Brook and separated from it by a high sand bluff. The Northport Basin is about 5.2nm to the west of the Nissequogue River. As at Stony Brook, shoals extend almost three-quarters of a mile offshore, so stick to the dredged channel. The channel runs for about 1.4nm, with about 5 feet of water and strong tidal currents. There's a town dock with a 10-minute tie-up limit. There are no guest moorings or services, but there is a small restaurant and cocktail lounge across the parking lot and the river has good anchorages. The launching ramp is for residents only. The red brick, green-roofed SUNY hospital complex is a prominent landmark.

The Nissequogue is a beautiful river, and popular with canoers and fishermen. Farther south, next to the huge SUNY hospital complex, are two small, private yacht clubs. The extensive salt marshes surrounding the river offer refuge to a great deal of wildlife, particularly wading birds and their favorite hors d'oeuvres, mosquitoes.

The harbor is well protected, but big enough that some onshore winds develop, making for nice small boat sailing. Keep an eye on changing tides or you may find yourself sailing nowhere fast in the mud. Clamming is not allowed in the river.

Shoreside & Emergency Services
Airport: MacArthur (631-467-3210)
Bus: Suffolk County Transit (631-852-5200)
Coast Guard: Eatons Neck (631-261-6868) or VHF 16
Police, Fire, Ambulance: 911
Taxi: Lindy's Taxi (631-265-2727)
Tow Service:
SEA TOW. —24-Hour Dispatch (800-4SEATOW)
—Port Jefferson (631-473-2869)
Tow BoatU.S.—24-Hour Dispatch (800-391-4869)
Train: Long Island Railroad (631-822-5477)

40°54'

VAR 13° 30'W (1993) ANNUAL INCREASE 4'

MAGNETIC

HUNTINGTON BAY

HUNTINGTON
NECK

EAST

WP 26680
N 40°-55.00
W 073°-24.48

WP 26530
N 40°-54.93
W 073°-25.85

Huntington Yacht Club

Huntington Town Dock

HUNTINGTON HBR

SPECIAL ANCHORAGE
I/IO 60 & I/O I (see note A)

Channel marked by
private aids from
buoy 9 thru buoy 18.

SPECIAL ANCHORAGE
I/IO 60 & I/IO

REPRODUCED FROM NOAA CHART #12365
EDITION 25, 1/31/98, NOT FOR NAVIGATION
© Maptech

1:10,000
1:20,000

Wincome Pt

SEAWALL

SEAWALL

Fl R 4s 5ft 4M "6"
HUNTINGTON HBR

CUPOLA

73°26'

Cable Area

HUNTINGTON HBR
Iso 6s 42ft 9M
HORN

Cable Area

SCALE 1:20,000

Nautical Miles

Yards

HARBOR

Cable Area

Cable Area

JOINS PAGE 378 LEFT

Winkle Pt

WP 26690
N 40°-54.83
W 073°-24.00

Price Bend

Priv aids

Crab Island

Hobart Beach

West Beach

MILE COURSE

Obstr
MARKER

40°55'

73°28'

40°55'

"Oh Huntington! My Huntington!"

Looking northwest over Huntington Harbor. © Maptech/James T. Abts

Famed American poet Walt Whitman called this beautiful pocket of Long Island his home in the 19th century. Whitman's ancestors owned 1,400 acres just south of Huntington Village, having settled in the area in the mid-17th century.

A few years after Walt's birth, the family moved to Brooklyn, where his father labored as a house builder. Young

Walt attended school in Brooklyn, then took a job as a printer's devil for the Long Island Patriot. By 1835 he was working as a printer in Manhattan, but economic depression forced him back to Long Island, where he farmed and taught school for a couple of years before returning full time to writing.

Lloyd Harbor was named for the extended Lloyd family, who owned a sizeable estate on Lloyd Neck. Thanks to a

	Marine Facilities and Services		Number of Transient Berths / Moorings / Monitors / Working VHF Channel	Approach / Dockside Depth in Feet at MLW / Seasonal / Year-round	Hookups: Fresh Water / Phone / Cable TV / 110V ★ 220V ▲ 3 Phase ■ Maximum Amps	Maximum LOA	Ramp / Dinghy Dock / Launch Service	Rail / Lift / Crane / Trailer: Capacity (tons)	Repairs: Propellor / Sail / Rigging / Diesel / Wood / Fiberglass / Electronics	Marine / Groceries / Ice / Bait / LPG / CNG	Gas / Diesel Fuel	Fuel Brand	Restrooms / Showers / Laundry / Pumpout	Public Phone / Restaurant / Snack Bar	Hotel / Pool / Tennis / Golf	Mastercard / VISA / Discover / AmEx
1	Gold Star Battalion/Coneys Marine	631-421-3366	9/	15/	Y	50	17/8			L			I	RSP	P	MV
2	Harbor Boating Club	631-351-9312			Y		PRIVATE—MEMBERS ONLY									
3	Wyncote Club	631-351-9521	10/	15/6	S	50	10/10	F	★30	DL		G	BP	All	RS	P	MVD
4	Knutson West Marine	631-549-7842	9/		Y		20/	FP	★▲	L	RLCT	All		M	RSL		MVA
5	Long Island Yacht Services, Inc. p. 377	631-549-4687	72/72	25/	S					L30	GDE						All
5	West Shore Marina p. 375	631-427-3444	9/		Y	150	18/18	FP	★▲■100	L35	All		MGI	All	P	PS	MV
6	Mill Dam Marina & Ramps*	631-351-3095	16/9		Y		6/6			R					P		
7	Willis Marine Center	631-421-3400	9/	10/25	Y	65	15/14	F	★▲■50	RL	L35	All	GD	Tex	MGI	RS	P	MVA
8	Huntington Yacht Club p. 377	631-427-4949	68/68	10/20	S	85	11/7	FC	★▲■50	DL	T		GD		I	RSP	All	All
9	Knutson's Yacht Haven	631-673-0700	8/	2/10	Y	120	10/10	FC	★▲50	All	LC35	All			MGIB	All		All

West Shore Marina — Resort Pool

All Coast Guard Stations Monitor VHF Channel 16

Facilities continued on next page...

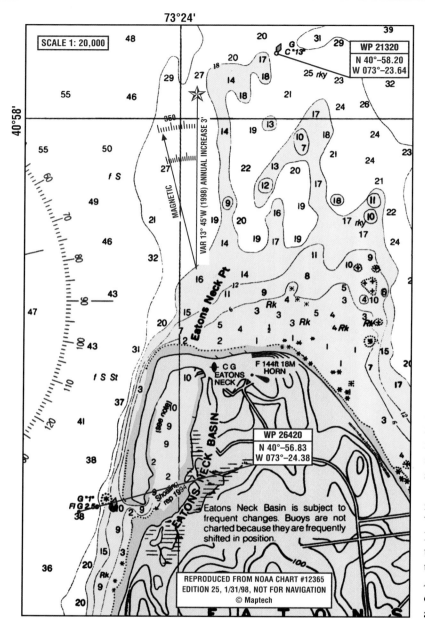

SCALE 1: 20,000

WP 21320
N 40°-58.20
W 073°-23.64

VAR 13° 45'W (1998) ANNUAL INCREASE 3'

MAGNETIC

CG EATONS NECK

F 144ft 18M HORN

WP 26420
N 40°-56.83
W 073°-24.38

Eatons Neck Basin is subject to frequent changes. Buoys are not charted because they are frequently shifted in position.

REPRODUCED FROM NOAA CHART #12365
EDITION 25, 1/31/98, NOT FOR NAVIGATION
© Maptech

steamboat dock built in 1852 by Henry Lloyd IV, the last Lloyd to hold the property, New Yorkers could come on summer days to sun themselves and swim. The original Lloyd property has since changed hands several times, accommodating in the 20th century such luminary lessees as Charles Lindbergh and Billy Joel.

Lloyd Neck's neighbor, Eatons Neck, was also highbrow from the start. Settled by Connecticut people and named for Theophilus Eaton, a New Haven politician, the resort community consisted of large estates inhabited by prominent residents, among them Eugene O'Neill and Henry Sturgis Morgan, grandson of J.P. Morgan and founder of Morgan Stanley.

Mariners acquainted with these waters know about the strong tides and the reefs extending offshore. Huntington Bay's most infamous disaster was the wreck of the steamer *Lexington* in 1840, when 120 people were lost in an inferno. Eatons Neck Light, built in 1799 to forestall such shipwrecks, is the second oldest lighthouse in New York. It's no surprise that Eatons Neck was the site of one of the first life-saving stations in America.

ACTIVITIES: The Huntington area is packed with manmade activities in the form of museums, restaurants, and shops. If you'd rather go water-skiing, swimming, fishing, or exploring in your dinghy, you also have lots of choices.

Walt Whitman's birthplace (631-427-5240) includes a museum and a library devoted to Whitman's career. The internationally known Heckscher Museum (631-351-3250) has a collection of American and European paintings, photographs, and sculptures. Founded in 1920 by August Heckscher, the museum also offers a noncirculating art library and gift shops for adults and children.

	Marine Facilities and Services		Number of Transient Berths / Moorings	Approach / Dockside Depth in Feet at MLW	Seasonal / Year-round	Maximum LOA	Hookups: Fresh Water / Phone / Cable TV	110V ★ 220V ▲ 3 Phase ■ Maximum Amps	Rail / Lift / Crane / Trailer: Capacity (tons)	Ramp / Dinghy Dock / Launch Service	Repairs: Propellor / Sail / Rigging / Electronics	Diesel / Wood / Fiberglass / Electronics	Gas / Diesel Fuel	Fuel Brand	Marine / Groceries / Ice / Bait / LPG / CNG	Restrooms / Showers / Laundry / Pumpout	Public Phone / Restaurant / Snack Bar	Hotel / Pool / Tennis / Golf	Mastercard / VISA / Discover / AmEx
10	Huntington Town Dock	631-351-3255	9/		S	5/5									*1 HOUR TIE-UP*				
11	Halesite Marina	631-351-3255	16/		Y	6/6												P	
12	Ketewomoke Yacht Club	631-351-9762	9/	/2	S	40	10/8	★▲■100	D		*PRIVATE—RECIPROCAL PRIVILEGES*								
13	Co Co's Water Café*	631-271-5700			Y	60	8/8				*RESTAURANT—DOCKAGE FOR PATRONS*								
14	Coneys Marine	631-421-3366	9/	/10	Y	42	15/8	F	★30	L	L20	All				MGI	All		MV

Information in these listings is provided by the facilities themselves. An asterisk (*) indicates that the facility did not respond to our most recent requests for information. (B) represents a BOAT/U.S. cooperating marina.

West Shore Marina

Resort Pool

All Coast Guard Stations Monitor VHF Channel 16

Down the road, on New York Avenue, the IMAC (Inter-Media Arts Center) (631-549-2787) sponsors jazz and folk music concerts. For another form of entertainment, try the New Community Cinema (631-423-3456) on the village green. This movie house screens little-known masterworks, foreign films, and works by contemporary filmmakers; they've even been known to screen a boating series.

The former Lloyd Harbor estate of Marshall Field III, the highly successful newspaper publisher and grandson of the department store magnate, is now Caumsett State Park (631-423-1770). The 1,500-acre park has trails for hiking and biking. Picnicking is allowed as long as you take your trash with you, but camping, swimming, and pets are prohibited. The Target Rock National Wildlife Refuge (631-271-2409) on the eastern end of Lloyd Neck includes a 10-acre formal garden open to the public.

Most of Huntington Bay beaches are restricted to residents, but there are public beaches on the eastern end of Lloyd Harbor, and at West Beach, to the south of Eatons Neck. There's great bass and blue fishing on the east side of Eatons Neck. Proceed with caution: swift currents and submerged boulders make the area dangerous, especially for sailboats. Target Rock, on the west side of Huntington Bay, offers excellent year-round flounder fishing.

RESTAURANTS & PROVISIONS: From Huntington Harbor you can walk to an array of eateries. Mediterraneo Ristorante (631-549-3422), a family-owned operation, specializes in Northern Italian cuisine at moderate prices. CoCo's (631-271-5700), on the waterfront, is a loud, popular spot for the singles set; tasty pasta dishes and nightly dancing keep the place packed. If you tie up at CoCo's dock and go in for a few drinks, be sure to appoint a designated skipper first. One of our readers recommends Piccollo's (631-424-5592) for traditional Italian fare.

Near Knutson's Marina, try the Shamrock (631-427-4221) or grab a sandwich at one of the delis: Bay Deli (631-421-4250), Halesite Harbour Deli (631-351-9340), or Surfside Deli. The fine folks at West Shore Marina keep an up-to-date list of restaurants in the area, and they're happy to share it with anyone who asks. For groceries, head to King Kullen, which is within walking distance of Huntington Harbor.

A couple of miles away, downtown Huntington makes the trip worthwhile with several blocks of shops, restaurants, cafés, and banks. There's even a 24-hour pharmacy and a full-sized natural grocery store. Any nautical needs can be taken care of at Compass Rose Marine Supplies, located right at the base of Huntington Harbor.

NAVIGATION & ANCHORAGES: Use ChartKit Region 3, pages 23 and 25; Maptech™ Waterproof Charts 1 and 16; and Maptech™ electronic and NOAA paper charts 12365 (1:20,000), 12364 (1:40,000), and 12363 (1:80,000). Use

tide tables for Bridgeport. High tide at the Lloyd Harbor entrance in Huntington Bay is 2 minutes later; low tide is 3 minutes later. Multiply the height of tide at Bridgeport by 1.1 for the height of tide at the Lloyd Harbor entrance. Mean tidal range is 7.4 feet.

High tide at Eatons Neck Point is 2 minutes after Bridgeport; low tide is 8 minutes later. Use the height of tide at Bridgeport for the height of tide at Eatons Neck Point. Mean tidal range is 7.1 feet.

The wide entrance to Huntington Bay is 13.5nm from Stony Brook Harbor, 5nm from Oyster Bay, and 7nm from Stamford, Connecticut.

NOTE: The greater Huntington Bay area, including Northport and Centerport, is a no-discharge area. Take advantage of one of the many inexpensive or free pumpout stations. For details, see the facility table or call the harbormaster.

From Fl R 4s BELL R "28C" south of Cable and Anchor Reef, a course of about 195°m will take you to Fl R 4s BELL R "8" marking Target Rock.

Huntington Bay, the largest bay on the north shore of Long Island, is the gateway to Northport Bay and to Lloyd, Huntington, Centerport, and Northport harbors. Even with the high tidal range in this area, current velocity in the bay is generally less than 0.7 knots. However, around Eatons Neck, it can reach 2 knots.

From the east, keep to the north of G C "13" north of Eatons Neck Point to avoid the shoals north of the point. Hundreds of smart seamen have foundered here, so stay north of the can.

From the west, approaching Huntington Bay is easy as long as you stay off the rocky, shallow waters of the north coast of Lloyd Neck. The shoals are well marked by 3 nuns—R N "2," R N "4," and R N "6," and by Fl R 4s BELL R "8" off Target Rock at East Fort Point.

As you head south into Huntington Bay, you'll pass Eatons Neck Basin (also called Eatons Neck Cove) on the northwestern tip of Eatons Neck. Once a popular swimming spot, the beach is now closed to the public, as it is a bird sanctuary for the endangered least tern.

Make sure you enter Eatons Neck Basin from the west to avoid the sandbar that extends west and north from the shore. Pass near to, but south of, Fl G 2.5s G "1" as you enter the extremely narrow channel between the jetties, which are usually submerged at half tide.

The channel carries 7 feet, but the cans in the basin are uncharted because the fierce tides change the channel regularly. Although the buoys aren't charted, don't ignore them. Those who cut corners without local knowledge will likely run into trouble. The west shore offers the best anchorage.

At the end of the basin is Eatons Neck Light (F 144ft 18M HORN), signaling sailors for nearly 200 years. In thick weather the loud foghorn makes overnight stays unbearable.

Enter busy Huntington Harbor through the southern end of the bay. The entire southwest corner, near West Shore Marina, has been dredged to a mean depth of 20 feet. You'll find at least 9 feet of water in the channel most of the way down. Although this harbor is rather crowded, the channel is wide and well marked.

To enter Huntington Harbor, first pass between Huntington Light (Iso 6s 42ft 9M HORN) and Fl G 4s G "1." The light is a square, concrete tower attached to what looks like a dwelling.

Follow the channel as it passes between West Neck and Wincoma Point; it's a narrow passage with a strong current. Watch out for a bar extending west from Wincoma Point and favor the west side when entering. However, stay clear of the shoal north-northeast of Fl R 4s 5ft 4M "6" LIGHT on West Neck.

The channel is about 100 feet wide at the entrance, and well marked. Make sure to stay west of Fl G 4s G "7" south of the harbor entrance, or chances are you'll be aground.

There is little room for anchoring, but many marinas, including Huntington Yacht Club and West Shore Marina, offer full amenities and ample transient facilities. Across the street from West Shore Marina you'll find Long Island Yacht Services, offering parts and some repairs.

You can tie up at three yacht clubs and two town docks, about 2 miles from the harbor entrance. The town of Huntington also runs the Halesite and Mill Dam marinas, for residents only.

South of Eatons Neck, Price Bend offers anchorage in a sheltered bight behind West Beach. The sandy spit is popular for swimming, camping, and weekend boating.

To reach Price Bend, pick up Fl G 4s G "1" south of the spit, and follow the channel east. Swing north after passing south and east of G C "3." Don't stray to the northwest in your eagerness to get to the beach, because you may hit bottom first—there are several shallow spots and unmarked shoals in the area.

CAUTION: Sand City Island used to be a dredging center, hence its name. An old mining structure there is irresistible to kids, but it's extremely dangerous.

There is good holding ground around Sand City, but boats drawing more than 3 feet should be especially careful of the

Embassy Guides

extreme tidal range and rocks. Also, keep an eye out for water-skiers enjoying the calm waters of Price Bend. You can anchor east of Sand City Island or as far north as the spit that creates the small cove. Just north of that spit is a small public boat ramp, reached by a clearly marked channel. Give a wide berth to the charted wreck off the spit.

Lloyd Harbor is shaped like a champagne glass turned on its side. It's a fine anchorage, except in an easterly wind as there is quite a fetch across the bays. The harbor runs westward from Huntington Bay up to Oyster Bay; trees conceal the large estates on three sides.

Enter Lloyd Harbor north of the Huntington Light and stay between G C "3" and R N "4" to avoid the nasty reefs south of East Beach. There's a good anchorage, reserved for transients only, to the south along the West Neck shore, well protected from the prevailing southwest winds. Bordered on the north by G C "3" and on the east by Huntington Light, the anchorage extends roughly 400 yards west of the lighthouse. If you anchor outside this area without a resident permit you'll probably be ticketed.

To reach the transient anchorage, turn to the southwest after you pass G C "3." In there you'll find depths of 7 to 11 feet and a good mud bottom. A 5-mph speed limit is enforced everywhere except in the water-skiing area (in the northwest part of the harbor), and no rafting is allowed after sundown.

The northeastern "rim" of Lloyd Harbor, near East Beach, is packed with moorings for residents with permits only. Keep an eye out here for water-skiers.

The western arm of Lloyd Harbor begins at the privately maintained G C "5" and R N "6." You can paddle a dinghy up the harbor through a quiet, narrow passage to the thin strip of land that separates Lloyd Harbor from Oyster Bay, clamber over the causeway, and take a dip in Cold Spring Harbor. Quiet Lloyd Harbor prohibits powerboats; you'll be quickly nabbed if you enter under power. If you want to land and stretch your legs, try East Beach, which marks the east end of Lloyd Harbor.

Shoreside & Emergency Services
Airport:
—Long Island MacArthur (631-467-3210)
Bus:
—Suffolk County Transit (631-852-5200)
Coast Guard:
—Eatons Neck (631-261-6868) or VHF 16
Police, Fire, Ambulance: 911
Taxi:
—Crown (631-427-1166)
Tow Service:
SEA TOW —24-Hour Dispatch (800-4SEATOW)
—Huntington (631-423-0882)
Tow BoatU.S.—24-Hour Dispatch (800-391-4869)
—Train: Long Island Railroad (631-822-5477)

Heart of Gold

During the War of 1812 Northport began its rise as a valuable shipbuilding center. Within a few decades the industry dominated the town, with several yards churning out commercial sailing ships. The advent of steel hulls struck a heavy blow to Northport's business, but the tide had already begun to turn, anyway, as the Long Island Railroad came to town and affluent visitors discovered the Gold Coast of Long Island.

Some of America's wealthiest people summered in Northport, once known as Cow Harbor, and Centerport, which was once called Little Cow Harbor. The most prominent among them was William Kissam Vanderbilt II who built a mansion, *Eagle's Nest*, on Little Neck. An avid sailor, Vanderbilt named his fabulous yacht *Alva* for his mother, and some furniture from the yacht is on display in the Vanderbilt Museum (see the Activities section).

If Long Island's north shore is its "Gold Coast," then Northport Harbor could very well be its heart of gold. The village, especially the downtown waterfront, is reminiscent of Sag Harbor (albeit on a smaller scale) with its shops, restaurants, and historic atmosphere. Trolley tracks still line the center of the street, adding to the flavor of the past.

ACTIVITIES: Next to the Northport Village Docks is the lovely town park. The modest swatch of green, which was designated as a park in 1932, is bordered by oaks, the harbor, and Seymour's Boatyard and crowned with a perfect bandshell: a whitewashed, octagonal structure with a red roof. Main Street, perpendicular to the harbor, is a solid row of shops and restaurants, enough for a pleasant afternoon of browsing.

Welcome to Northport Harbor. © Maptech

Don't miss the Vanderbilt Museum (631-854-5555, closed Mondays) on Little Neck. The 43-acre mansion complex has been turned into a public exhibit and planetarium. During his extensive world travels, William K. Vanderbilt II collected rare birds, fish, and plants, some of which are on display in the

#	Marine Facilities and Services		Monitors / Working VHF Channel	Number of Transient Berths	Seasonal / Year-round / Moorings	Approach / Dockside Depth in Feet at MLW	Maximum LOA	110V • 220V ▲ 3 Phase ■ Maximum Amps	Hookups: Fresh Water / Phone / Cable TV	Ramp / Dinghy Dock / Launch Service	Rail / Lift / Crane / Trailer: Capacity (tons)	Repairs: Propellor / Sail / Rigging / Gas	Diesel / Wood / Fiberglass / Electronics	Marine / Groceries / Ice / Bait / LPG / CNG	Gas / Diesel Fuel	Fuel Brand	Restrooms / Showers / Laundry / Pumpout	Public Phone / Restaurant / Snack Bar	Hotel / Pool / Tennis / Golf	Mastercard / VISA / Discover / AmEx
1	Centerport Boatworks*	631-757-8576	68/68	10/10	Y	45	6/3.5	F		▲20	All		CT20	PSGDWFE			IB	R		P
2	Northport Yacht Club*	631-261-7633			Y				*PRIVATE—RECIPROCAL PRIVILEGES*											
3	Centerport Yacht Club	631-261-5440			Y				*PRIVATE—RECIPROCAL PRIVILEGES*											
4	Seymour's (B)	631-261-6574	68/68	4/20	S	50	7/7	F		★30	L		R30	PSRGDWF	GD	BP	I	R		P	MVD
5	Northport Town Dock*	631-261-7502			Y	150					R									
6	Woodbine Marina*	631-351-3255			S	40	7/4	F		▲								SP		P
7	BRITANNIA YACHTING CENTER p. 381	631-261-5600	9/	25/	Y	70	6/6	All		★▲■50			LC55	All	GD	Tex	MB	RSP	PT	All	All
7	Tidewater Marine Supply p. 381	631-754-0160			Y				*MARINE SUPPLIES*								M			

Information in these listings is provided by the facilities themselves. An asterisk (*) indicates that the facility did not respond to our most recent requests for information. (B) represents a BOAT/U.S. cooperating marina.

All Coast Guard Stations Monitor VHF Channel 16

Looking north over Northport Harbor. © Maptech/James T. Abts

museum's Memorial Wing. He often brought an artist on these expeditions to record the coloration of specimens brought up from the depths before the sunlight faded their hues.

For more information on local history, particularly shipbuilding, visit the Northport Historical Society and Museum (631-757-9859). Just a five-minute walk from the town dock, it's open every day except holidays. The best swimming in the area is at Asharoken Beach, due north of Northport Harbor, and at West Beach, at the entrance to Northport Bay.

RESTAURANTS & PROVISIONS: Northport's Main Street is packed with enough restaurants and bars to suit every appetite and budget.

If price is not your concern and you've got proper attire aboard, you'll relish a meal at the Bay View Bistro (631-262-9744). A mere glance at the menu will start you salivating, from the appetizers and epicurean entrées to the heavenly desserts, including flourless chocolate cake.

There's truly a nautical atmosphere at the Northport Ship's Inn (631-261-3000), but rest assured, the food is much better than your typical tugboat galley's. Try Golden China (631-754-2811) for Asian favorites, or for a burger and brew, try Skipper's Pub (631-261-3589). Other palate-pleasers are Tim's Shipwreck Diner (631-754-1797) and Season's Café (631-474-5533). Also worth a visit is Sea Shanty (631-261-8538) on Woodbine, serving fresh seafood in a casual setting. A block or so down Woodbine, opposite the town dock, you'll find the Ritz Café (631-754-6348).

Craving a cool treat on a hot afternoon? Head to Lics (631-757-9099), Incredible Ices (631-261-8939), or Victorian Pizza & Ice Cream (631-261-7565). Coffee and pastry fans should try Orbit (631-757-6169) or the Copenhagen Bakery (631-754-3256). If Spot is aboard, make tracks for Bark Ave., Ltd., on Main Street, and get your paws on some "non-essential niceties" (a.k.a. freshly-baked dog treats).

There are plenty of places to pick up galley supplies on Main Street, with a market, Organically Yours (631-754-2150) health food store, a pharmacy, and hardware store.

The Clothes Line Laundromat is what you need to clean those khakis.

In Centerport, you can walk to a small plaza from Centerport Boatworks (you'll need a cab if you're coming from Centerport Yacht Club). Within the plaza you can get sandwiches and provisions at Centerport Deli (631-261-7944), while your choice for a sit-down meal, Nicky's of Centerport (631-757-7277), serves lunch and dinner, specializing in lobster. To pick up some nautical products. as well as fishing gear and tackle, try Bowman's Sporting Goods (631-261-6611).

NAVIGATION & ANCHORAGES: Use ChartKit Region 3, pages 23 and 25; Maptech™ Waterproof Charts 1 and 16; and Maptech™ electronic and NOAA paper charts 12365 (1:20,000), 12364 (1:40,000), and 12363 (1:80,000). Use tide tables for Bridgeport. High tide at Northport Bay is 2 minutes later; low tide is 8 minutes later. Multiply the height of tide at Bridgeport by 1.1 for the height of the tide at Northport. Mean tidal range is 7.3 feet.

The village dock in Northport is 2.8nm from West Beach at the entrance to Northport Bay. Huntington Harbor is 4.4nm from Northport Harbor. See the chapter on Eatons Neck, Lloyd Harbor, and Huntington Harbor for the approaches to Huntington Bay and thence to Northport Bay.

Fl G 4s G "1" off the West Beach spit marks the entrance to Northport Bay, due east of Lloyd Harbor. Northport Bay leads to Price Bend (see the preceding chapter), Centerport, Northport, and Duck Island Harbor. While the tidal range in the area is a hefty 7.3 feet, the current velocity is only about 0.5 knots because the area is so open.

From the west, be sure to stay well north of RN "4" to avoid the shallow spot just west of the buoy. The first anchorage area is in Duck Island Harbor. To reach it, pass south of Fl G 4s G "1" and G C "3," and then head for the quartet of red-and-white, 600-foot-tall stacks of the LILCO power plant east of the bay. If you can't see them, you're either hopelessly lost or in a very thick fog.

A shallow cove between Duck Island and Eatons Neck, Duck Island Harbor can be a dream of an anchorage, even though it's open to the southwest. From the east side of Fl R 4s R "8," head due north magnetic towards the southern tip of Duck Island, and then turn west when you're about 250 yards off the point. This way you'll avoid the nasty rocks and shoals surrounding Duck Island, as well as the rocky shoal extending 0.4nm east of Winkle Point. Follow the chart carefully, stay in the deep water, and don't anchor close to shore. The harbormaster may check to see if you have a holding tank (to comply with the no-discharge rule), and no landing is allowed. The perimeter of the harbor is set aside for water-skiers, whose wakes can send you rocking and spoil your solitude.

Asharoken Beach, on the northeast side of Northport Bay, provides a good open anchorage. There's a public ramp on the east end of the beach. Use of holding tanks is required.

Centerport Harbor, south of Duck Island Harbor and across the Little Neck peninsula from Northport, is about 6 feet deep down to where the charted channel ends. This is roughly even with Camp Alvernia, a summer camp on Little Neck. From there the channel carries approximately 3 feet to Centerport Marine at the head of the harbor.

The entrance to Northport Harbor is wide and easy. If you have a deep-draft boat you'll need to hug the east side, but otherwise it's open water to the dock.

The village dock is marked by the charted flagpole and an amber light that may be impossible to see if there are too many boats anchored in the harbor. The dock, right smack in the middle of the village, is open for 2-hour tie-ups until 8:00 p.m. Use fenders to guard against too much grind while you're gone. The Centerport Yacht Club on Little Neck allows only a 15-minute tie-up at the docks, but both the Centerport and Northport yacht clubs usually have moorings available to members of reciprocating clubs.

You can also anchor in the southwest corner of Northport Harbor. The bottom is soft but adequate except when the wind is out of the north or northwest. If you're headed down the channel from the village dock to the facilities and wharves at the south end of the harbor, you should have no trouble. Here, you'll find the Britannia Yachting Center, a large, full-service marina with transient slips, and Tidewater Marine Supply, a great place to satisfy your boating needs.

The pipeline area marked on the chart is also a hazard. The "sewer" spot marks an outflow pipe that sits just below the surface, and the charted wrecks are very real. The island is a bird sanctuary (appropriately named "Bird Island" by area residents), so it should be admired but not trod upon.

If you want a closer look the LILCO power plant, the largest oil-fired power plant in the U.S., there is a small-boat basin and town launching ramp at the plant. Approach from Long Island Sound, and look for the Northport oil pumping station. The station is about 1.7nm north of the plant and 2.4nm east of Eatons Neck Point and is surrounded by large mooring buoys.

The channel into the basin is marked by private aids. The basin does not serve as an anchorage except in emergencies. By the way, those big towers will give you an almost perfect magnetic north-south bearing when they're aligned.

Shoreside & Emergency Services
Airport: Long Island MacArthur (631-467-3210)
Bus: Suffolk County Transit (631-852-5200)
Coast Guard:
—Eatons Neck (631-261-6868) or VHF 16
Harbormaster: (631-351-3255) or VHF 16
Police, Fire, Ambulance: 911
Taxi: Harbor (631-261-6385)
—Northport (631-757-3564)
—Quinlan's (631-261-0235)
Tow Service:
SEA TOW —24-Hour Dispatch (800-4SEATOW)
—Huntington (631-423-0882)
Tow BoatU.S.—24-Hour Dispatch (800-391-4869)
—Northport (631-624-3483)
Train: Long Island Railroad (631-822-5477)

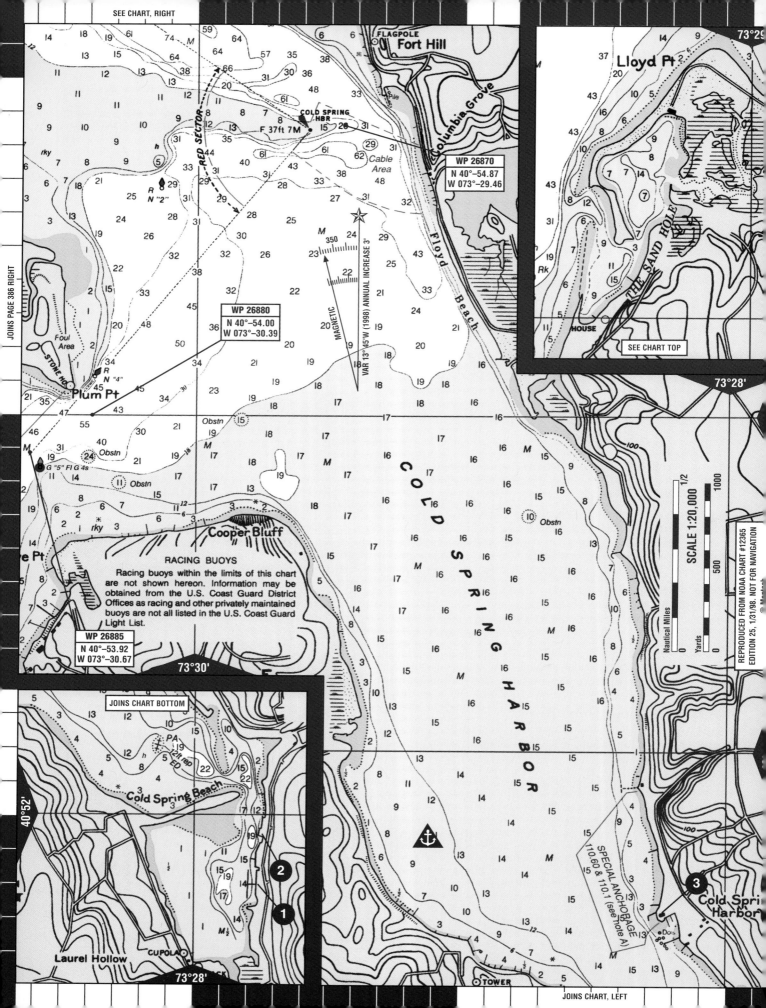

FLAGPOLE
Fort Hill

Lloyd Pt

COLD SPRING
HBR
F 37ft 7M

Columbia Grove

WP 26870
N 40°–54.87
W 073°–29.46

THE SAND HOLE

HOUSE

Cable
Area

Floyd Beach

R
N "2"

WP 26880
N 40°–54.00
W 073°–30.39

MAGNETIC

VAR 13°–45'W (1998) ANNUAL INCREASE 3'

Foul
Area

STONE HO

R
N "4"

Plum Pt

JOINS PAGE 386 RIGHT

Obstn

Obstn

Obstn

G "5" Fl G 4s

Obstn

Cooper Bluff

RACING BUOYS

Racing buoys within the limits of this chart
are not shown hereon. Information may be
obtained from the U.S. Coast Guard District
Offices as racing and other privately maintained
buoys are not all listed in the U.S. Coast Guard
Light List.

WP 26885
N 40°–53.92
W 073°–30.67

C O L D   S P R I N G   H A R B O R

SCALE 1:20,000

Nautical Miles

Yards

JOINS CHART BOTTOM

PA

Cold Spring Beach

Laurel Hollow   CUPOLA

SPECIAL ANCHORAGE
110.60 & 110.1 (see Note A)

Cold Spring
Harbor

TOWER

From Rowdy to Refined

It'd be a challenge to find a more tasteful business district than Cold Spring Harbor's Main Street, and it's even more difficult to believe that this rather refined road was once nicknamed "Bedlam Street." It was named so in honor of the rowdy behavior of sailors who frequented it in the 19th century, when the community had several brothels in operation.

Things have certainly changed for the better in Cold Spring Harbor: the brothels are out and sophisticated shops are in. Visiting sailors are courteous, not coarse, and the community is a highly desirable bedroom and summer community. The tourist boom in that late 1800s brought an influx of affluent people, sending real estate prices steeply skyward over the decades, yet there was still a time when a mere dollar made a difference.

In 1790, George Washington was passing through town on his way to Oyster Bay in a horse-drawn coach when he happened upon townspeople hard at work on Cold Spring Harbor's first schoolhouse. Our first president reached into his pocket and contributed to the project with a silver dollar. Considering the era, that buck probably helped a lot. A dollar went a long way in a certain 20th-century transaction, as well. A squat, wooden lighthouse (circa 1889) perched on a cast-iron and concrete foundation once marked a shoal just south of the stream on the east side of Centre Island. It was decommissioned in 1965 by the Coast Guard, who intended to burn it. They got as far as pitching it into the water when a local person spied the structure and promptly offered to buy it. The Coast Guard was happy to get rid of the problem and sold it for a dollar. The floating hulk was towed to its present site and after substantial renovations, converted to a boathouse.

ACTIVITIES: The main attractions are the excellent (if limited) shopping and the Cold Spring Harbor Whaling Museum (631-367-3418) on Main Street. The Museum includes a 19th-century whaleboat fully equipped with original gear, an extensive scrimshaw collection, ship models, and a hands-on, marine mammal bone display.

South of Cold Spring Harbor, on Route 25A, is the Cold Spring Harbor Fish Hatchery (631-692-6768), where different species of trout are raised to stock private ponds and turtles are raised for release into the wild. Founded in 1883, the hatchery includes an aquarium section exhibiting nearly every freshwater species found in the area: small fish and all kinds of turtles, frogs, toads, and snakes. The privately-owned complex has a friendly, park-like setting and offers educational programs for all ages, even an annual birthday party for the trout.

At the southwest corner of Cold Spring Harbor is the campus of Cold Spring Harbor Labs (631-367-8397). This major biological and cancer research institution is headed by Nobel Prize winner James Dewey Watson, one of the discoverers of DNA. The DNA Learning Center (631-367-5170) offers educational programs and exhibits for all ages.

Main Street's well-kept shops make for great browsing. © Maptech

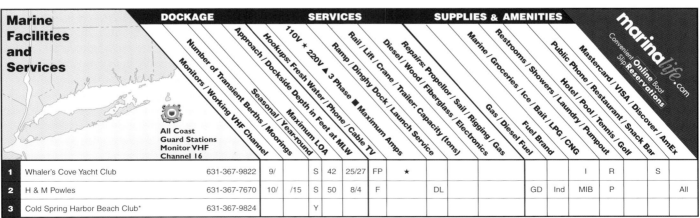

#	Marine Facilities and Services		Monitors/Working VHF Channel	Number of Transient Berths/Moorings	Seasonal/Year-round	Maximum LOA	Approach/Dockside Depth in Feet at MLW	Hookups: Fresh Water/Phone/Cable TV	Repairs	Gas/Diesel Fuel	Fuel Brand	Marine/Groceries/Ice/Bait/LPG/CNG	Restrooms/Showers/Laundry/Pumpout	Public Phone/Restaurant/Snack Bar	Mastercard/VISA/Discover/AmEx
1	Whaler's Cove Yacht Club	631-367-9822		9/	S	42	25/27	FP	★				I	R	S
2	H & M Powles	631-367-7670		10/ /15	S	50	8/4	F	DL	GD	Ind	MIB	P		All
3	Cold Spring Harbor Beach Club*	631-367-9824			Y										

Information in these listings is provided by the facilities themselves. An asterisk (*) indicates that the facility did not respond to our most recent requests for information. (B) represents a BOAT/U.S. cooperating marina.

Cold Spring Harbor & the Sand Hole

If you walk along the beaches of Cold Spring today at high tide, you won't find any springs. Come back a few hours later, though, and you'll notice cold, fresh water bubbling up through the ground. The springs and deep water make the harbor unusually cold, like swimming in Maine in March. If you do take to the water, you'll find it an invigorating experience. Many beaches in the area are free and open to the public. If you come to a private section, the law allows you to walk along the wet sand portion of the beach, below the high-tide line.

RESTAURANTS & PROVISIONS: Amid the shops in Cold Spring Harbor you'll find Wyland's Country Kitchen (631-692-5655), serving soup, sandwiches, and American favorites, and the Trattoria Grasso Due (631-367-6060), serving northern Italian cuisine at lunch and dinner. The upscale Inn on the Harbor (631-367-3166), on Harbor Road, serves an impressive menu of rather exotic items (rabbit, duck, frogs' legs) prepared with a Continental flair; brunch is served on Sunday. For a quick lunch or picnic supplies, try Cold Spring Plaza Deli (631-367-3533). If you need supplies on a larger scale, catch a cab to Huntington Village.

NAVIGATION & ANCHORAGES: Use ChartKit Region 3, page 23; Maptech™ Waterproof Charts 1 and 16; and Maptech™ electronic and NOAA paper charts 12365 (1:20,000), 12364 (1:40,000), and 12363 (1:80,000). Use tide tables for Bridgeport. High tide at Cold Spring Harbor is 7 minutes later; low tide is 8 minutes later. Multiply the height of tide at Bridgeport by 1.1 for the height of tide at Cold Spring Harbor. Mean tidal range is 7.4 feet.

Oyster Bay, about 4.5nm from Eatons Neck Point, serves as the entrance to both Cold Spring Harbor and Oyster Bay Harbor. Fl G 4s GONG G "15" off Lloyd Point is 4nm from Eatons Neck Point. GONG G "1" off Whitewood is another 2.3nm away; the lighthouse off Fort Hill is about 0.8nm away.

From Fl R 2.5s BELL R "32A," marking the 26-foot shoal, a course of about 155°m should take you to Cold Spring Harbor Light (F 37ft 7M).

From the east, it's wise to stay more than 0.5nm off the high, yellow bluff of Lloyd Neck. A rocky shoal extends north from Lloyd Point.

CAUTION: Morris Rock, about 0.5nm east of Lloyd Point, is covered by only 2 feet of water and is poorly marked by W Or. A 6-foot spot slightly to the north and west is not marked at all. The latter is usually forgotten about—and hence more often hit—as mariners concentrate on missing Morris Rock.

If you are not familiar with the area, we recommend that you follow the buoy line for Huntington out to Fl G 4s GONG G "15," then turn southeast for Oyster Bay. Local boaters will often cut inside Morris Rock to save a few minutes and get away from the current. Leave this route to those with local knowledge.

From the west, pass well north of BELL G "17," 0.9nm north-northeast of Rocky Point. Beware of the foul area that runs from Rocky Point out to the bell. Traveling another 1.9nm to the southeast will take you to Cold Spring Harbor Light (F 37ft 7M), and the approaches to Oyster Bay Harbor and Cold Spring Harbor. Be sure to stay north of the shoal that extends westward from the light.

CAUTION: Beware of the large (6-foot diameter), unlighted, steel mooring buoys for the sand barges between the Sand Hole and GONG G "1."

On the northwest side of Lloyd Neck is the Sand Hole, a great gunkhole also known as "Sand Diggers." From a distance the Sand Hole would be difficult to spot if it were empty, but it rarely is, therefore all you have to do is look for a group of masts sticking out of the sand like a stand of dead pines.

CAUTION: The bar to the north of the Sand Hole channel entrance extends much farther west than the chart indicates. If you're coming from the north, be sure to swing well west, or stay at least 400 yards off the coast, before heading due east into the channel.

The entry to the Sand Hole is not marked. Again, watch out for the reef on the north side, off the north point, and swing wide around it before you turn east. Then stay close to shore as you round the south point and make your turn to the north. It's best to enter the Sand Hole at high water, although at that time the breakwater that forms the southwest side of the harbor probably won't be visible. There is also a sandbar that extends north of the breakwater, so stay close to that northern point.

If you're here for the first time, don't be surprised if the entrance confuses you. It's hard to spot, very tricky, and unmarked. You may want to wait until you can follow a deeper draft boat in and let its keel take the risk. The entry to the channel is not very deep, so if you draw more than 2 feet you may have trouble getting through the inlet at low tide. Deeper-draft boats should only try entering at full tide. Inside, there's plenty of water for anchoring.

The Sand Hole has two places to anchor, one on the south side and another around the point to the north. The depths drop off sharply just off the beach, so if you keep an eye on your depth sounder and go slowly, you may be able to scoot in very close to the shore.

On weekends you'll find the Sand Hole jammed with motorboats, in spite of the fact that it is now a bird sanctuary where you can no longer go ashore. The holding ground is good, with depths running from 4 to 15 feet. You will have more company in the northern end, but if you like exploring by dink, you will also be close to the tidal creeks and the incredible variety of little critters and birds you can find in the marshes.

Heading south down Oyster Bay, you'll find a shoal marked at its eastern end by Cold Spring Harbor Light (F 37ft 7M), a large iron caisson, off Fort Hill. The 37-foot light, which marks a wrecked barge of bricks as well as the shoal, has fixed red and white sectors that are helpful for night approaches. (You'll see the red sector marked on the chart.) Pass east of the Light before turning southwest for Oyster Bay Harbor.

If you're in a shallow-draft vessel (less than 6 feet) and decide to pass west of the harbor light, beware of the 5-foot spot 175 yards north of RN "2."

Oyster Bay is a lovely area, with unspoiled beaches and wooded hills. It's also one of the cleanest harbors on the Sound. The mean tidal range is 7.3 feet, and because the harbor is so deep and wide with an unrestricted entrance, the current velocity at Cold Spring Harbor Light is only 0.7 knots or less.

The Cold Spring Harbor Beach Club on the east side of Cold Spring Harbor is 2.5nm south of the harbor light. From the beach club it's about a mile to town. Cold Spring Harbor lies about 3 miles south of Lloyd Point and is separated from Oyster Bay Harbor by Cove Neck. It offers plenty of room and good protection except in a northerly wind. You'll notice the lack of buoys—they're not needed much because of the harbor's depth, size, and few facilities.

CAUTION: Commercial vessels do transit through Cold Spring Harbor enroute to a busy oil and gas terminal just south of the charted Special Anchorage area.

You can anchor almost anywhere and find good holding ground. You may see boats anchored off Cooper Bluff to the north, but this is a pretty wide-open spot and subject to some channel wash. A favorite spot is off the north side of Cold Spring Beach, a 600-yard long sand pit extending across the southern tip of the harbor.

The dredged inner harbor below Cold Spring Beach is even more protected. It can get a little tight for cruising boats but is well used by runabouts. There's a town launching ramp directly opposite the eastern tip of Cold Spring Beach, as well as a small yacht club and an even smaller marina, H & M Powles. If you're headed for Main Street in Cold Spring Harbor, this is the most convenient place to leave your boat.

Shoreside & Emergency Services

Airport: Long Island MacArthur (631-467-3210)
Bus: MTA Long Island Bus Information (631-766-6722)
Coast Guard: Eatons Neck (631-261-6959) or VHF 16
Harbormaster: Oyster Bay (516-624-6201) or VHF 9
Police, Fire, Ambulance: 911
Taxi: Orange & White (631-271-3600)
Tow Service:
SEA TOW —24-Hour Dispatch (800-4SEATOW)
—Western L.I. Sound (914-698-6523)
Tow BoatU.S.—24-Hour Dispatch (800-391-4869)
—Northport (516-624-3483)
Train: Long Island Railroad (631-822-5477)

Looking north over Cold Spring Harbor. Cold Spring Beach cuts across the middle. On the eastern shore you'll find Whaler's Cove Yacht Club and H & M Powles in the foreground, and Cold Spring Harbor Beach Club in the distance. © Maptech/James T. Abts

A Shell-tered Place

It's a good thing that Oyster Bay's residents, officials, and environmentalists had their wits about them in the 1970s. Developer Robert Moses, the man behind the Triborough Bridge, the Cross-Bronx and Brooklyn-Queens expressways, Jones Beach, Shea Stadium and Flushing Meadows Corona Park, among other projects, wanted to build a bridge linking Oyster Bay to Westchester County. The opposition prevailed, protecting the community's quiet pace.

Centre Island, a 600-acre piece of land bordered by Cold Spring Harbor, Oyster Bay Harbor, and Long Island Sound, was originally the site of a brickworks (hence the name of the island's southwest point). Exploiting the island's ample clay deposits, the Smith Brothers plant manufactured three million bricks on the island in 1860. Soon after, in the Long Island Gold Coast rush, affluent city dwellers moved in and built elaborate summer homes on what was previously fertile farmland.

In 1871, a number of these folks formed the Seawanhaka Corinthian Yacht Club, dedicated to returning the sport of yachting to amateurs (wealthy amateurs, to be sure). Along with the North Shore Yacht Club in Port Washington, Seawanhaka shares the distinction of being the oldest club on the Sound. On the club's 125th anniversary it won back the Seawanhaka International Challenge Cup from the Royal Yacht Club of Tasmania, Australia. It was Seawanhaka's 17th victory, the most of any country since the race series began in 1895.

But Oyster Bay's main claim to fame is its famous, former resident, Teddy Roosevelt. Roosevelt, the 26th president of the United States, lived at Sagamore Hill on Cove Neck, only

Without a shadow of a doubt, you've reached Oyster Bay. © Maptech

a few miles from the village. Used as a summer White House during his presidency, Sagamore Hill has been preserved and is open to the public.

ACTIVITIES: Folks come from all over for the festivals that take place year-round in Oyster Bay. Call the Chamber of Commerce (516-922-6464) to get the scoop on such events as the Mozart Festival on Memorial Day or the Long Island Jazz Festival in August. Every October the town celebrates Teddy Roosevelt's birthday with an Oyster Festival, a two-day street fête featuring lots of activities and gobs of food. Roughly 25,000 oysters are consumed at the event. If nothing's on the calendar during your visit, fear not: the village is packed with shops and restaurants, for your browsing and dining pleasure.

Not surprisingly, Roosevelt's name adorns quite a few parks and sites. Walk the self-guided trails of Theodore

Marine Facilities and Services		Number of Transient Berths	Seasonal / Year-round	Approach / Dockside Depth in Feet at MLW	Maximum LOA	Monitors / Working VHF Channel	110v ★ 220v ▲ 3 Phase ■ Maximum Amps	Hookups: Fresh Water / Phone / Cable TV	Ramp / Dinghy Dock / Launch Service	Rail / Lift / Crane / Trailer: Capacity (tons)	Repairs: Propellor / Sail / Rigging / Gas	Diesel / Wood / Fiberglass / Electronics	Gas / Diesel Fuel	Marine / Groceries / Ice / Bait / LPG / CNG	Fuel Brand	Restrooms / Showers / Laundry / Pumpout	Public Phone / Restaurant / Snack Bar	Hotel / Pool / Tennis / Golf	Mastercard / VISA / Discover / AmEx
1	Seawanhaka Corinthian Yacht Club 516-922-6305					Y				*PRIVATE—MEMBERS ONLY*									
2	**OBMC** Oyster Bay Marine Center 516-922-6331 p. 389	71/	2/10	S	180	17/22		F	★▲50	L		C	All	GD	BP	MI	RSP	PS	MV
3	Sagamore Yacht Club 516-922-0555	78/	/15	Y		10/7		F	★30	DL		C2			MI	RS	P	All	
4	Roosevelt Memorial Park Marina* 516-624-6203	9/		S		5/5		F	★				GD			RP	P		
5	**BRIDGE MARINA** 516-628-8688 p. 391	1/2		Y	38	8/8		F	★▲40	All		L14	PGDFE		MIB	R		All	All

Information in these listings is provided by the facilities themselves. An asterisk (*) indicates that the facility did not respond to our most recent requests for information.
(B) represents a BOAT/U.S. cooperating marina.

All Coast Guard Stations Monitor VHF Channel 16

Looking northwest over Oyster Bay Harbor. The full-service Oyster Bay Marine Center sits along the harbor's southern shore, in the left-center of the photo. © Maptech/James T. Abts

Roosevelt's Memorial Bird Sanctuary (516-922-3200) with your eyes peeled for winged friends, then visit the small museum. The final resting place of the president and his wife is close by at Young's Memorial Cemetery. His estate,

Sagamore Hill (516-922-4447), is now a museum that serves to enlighten the American people about Mr. Roosevelt's personality and achievements. The 23-room Victorian frame-and-brick home is filled with the furnishings and memorabilia of a national family at play. Also on the estate is the former home of General Theodore Roosevelt, Jr. The estate is a good distance from the waterfront, so a cab or bike is a must.

Another landmark is Raynham Hall (516-922-6808), which was built in 1738 by a Quaker merchant and later served as the headquarters for the British army of occupation during the Revolution. The Victorian wing was built on in 1851.

Within a short cab ride of Oyster Bay, enjoy the natural splendors of the great outdoors. The Planting Fields Arboretum (516-922-9201) sits on 409 landscaped acres of greenhouses, gardens, and natural habitat. The rhododendron and azalea collections contain more than 600 species. A 65-room Tudor Revival mansion called Coe Hall (516-922-0479) also on the grounds is quite a sight with its stonework, patterned chimney, and carvings. Folks from all over flock to the Planting Fields during the summer to take in the sights and sounds of Friends of the Arts (516-922-0061), specializing in world-class music and performing arts.

From any of the marinas around Mill Neck Bay, it's an easy bike ride to the town of Bayville. Bayville is mostly residential, but you'll find a few restaurants and small markets (see the following section).

RESTAURANTS & PROVISIONS: For a meal outside of your galley, you'll have to stretch your legs a few paces from the waterfront into Oyster Bay Village. Take your empty stomach to Canterbury Ales Oyster Bar & Grill (516-922-3614) and enjoy the chowder house atmosphere as you pore over the

Oyster Bay Harbor

Looking west over Bridge Marina. © Maptech/James T. Abts

Mean tidal range is 7.3 feet. High tide at Bayville Bridge is 12 minutes after Bridgeport; low tide is 20 minutes later. Multiply height of tide at Bridgeport by 1.1 for height of tide at Bayville Bridge. Mean tidal range is 7.4 feet.

Plum Point, at the entrance to Oyster Bay Harbor, is 10.2nm from Hempstead Harbor at Weeks Point, 7.8nm from Fl R 4s BELL R "8" at Huntington Bay to the east, and 7.2nm from the entrance to Stamford Harbor.

From Fl R 2.5s BELL R "32A," a course of about 155°m will take you within sight of the Cold Spring Harbor Light (F 37ft 7M). After passing east and south of the light, rounding Plum Point is easy; just spot Fl G 4s G "5," marking the shoal's edge north of Cove Point.

For many yachtsmen, Oyster Bay Harbor ranks as the queen of harbors on Long Island. This long, crooked arm on the west side of Oyster Bay is big enough to accommodate a navy.

From Fl G 4s GONG G "15" off Lloyd Point it's 2.3nm south-southwest to GONG G "1" off Whitewood Point ("N.W. Bluff"), and from there it's another 0.8nm southeast to Cold Spring Harbor Light (F 37ft 7M) off Fort Hill.

From the east, it's wise to stay more than 0.5nm off the high yellow bluff of Lloyd Neck. A rocky shoal extends north from Lloyd Point.

CAUTION: Morris Rock, about 0.5nm east of Lloyd Point, is covered by only 2 feet of water and is poorly marked by W OR C. A 6-foot spot slightly to the north and west is not marked at all. It is usually forgotten (and hence more often hit) as mariners concentrate on missing Morris Rock.

Newcomers should be sure to honor Fl G 4s GONG G "15" before making the turn south into Oyster Bay, even though local boaters will often cut inside Morris Rock to save a few minutes and get away from the current. Leave this route to those with local knowledge.

From the west, pass well north of BELL G "17," 0.9nm north-northeast of Rocky Point. Beware of the foul area between this buoy and Rocky Point. Traveling another 1.9nm to the southeast will take you to Cold Spring Harbor Light (F 37ft 7M), and the approaches to Oyster Bay and Cold Spring harbors. Be sure to stay north of the shoal that extends westward from the light.

On the northwest side of Lloyd Neck is the Sand Hole, a great gunkhole also known as "Sand Diggers." (For information on navigating the Sand Hole, please see the chapter on Cold Spring Harbor.)

CAUTION: Beware of the large (6-foot diameter), unlighted, steel mooring buoys for the sand barges between the Sand Hole and GONG G "1."

extensive menu offering loads of seafood in traditional and Hawaiian style, plus ribs, chops, steaks, and pasta. Wash it all down with a huge variety of domestic and imported beers or uncommon spirits, but be sure to leave room for dessert.

Nearby, Fiddleheads (516-922-2999) will wow you with their presentation of contemporary entrees, dominated by seafood, and impressively original desserts. If you happened to pack your nice clothes, try the Mill River Inn (516-922-7768) on Mill River Road. Reservations are suggested at this award-winning, continental restaurant. Sprinkled among these are a few pizzerias and seafood joints.

West of Oyster Bay, a short distance by cab, is the village of Locust Valley, where Barney's (516-671-6300) serves rather expensive New American cuisine in a refurbished firehouse. Bayville, north of Mill Neck Creek, is home to the highly recommended Crescent Restaurant (516-628-3000), with a great view of the Sound and a menu of healthful, innovative dishes. Close to Bridge Marina you'll find the Bayville Luncheonette (516-628-8636) and the Taste of China II (516-628-2288).

Also in Bayville, you may dine waterside at the clam bar at Bridge Marina. Within walking distance of here you'll find CoCo Jumbo's Produce (516-628-9285), Bayville Deli (516-628-2063), and Bayville Meat Center (516-628-2139), along with a couple of convenience markets.

Besides the ship's store at Oyster Bay Marine Center, you can pick up your nautical supplies at Oyster Bay Marine Supply (516-922-8010) on South Main. Hop in a cab, and a few miles up Route 106 you'll find a supermarket and pharmacy, plus a McDonald's.

NAVIGATION & ANCHORAGES: Use ChartKit Region 3, page 23; Maptech™ Waterproof Charts 1 and 16; and Maptech™ electronic and NOAA paper charts 12365 (1:20,000), 12364 (1:40,000), and 12363 (1:80,000). Use tide tables for Bridgeport. High tide at Oyster Bay Harbor is 7 minutes later; low tide is 13 minutes later. Multiply height of tide at Bridgeport by 1.1 for height of tide at Oyster Bay Harbor.

Eastward from Rocky Point, reaching nearly all the way across Oyster Bay, is a shoal marked at its eastern end by Cold Spring Harbor Light (F 37ft 7M), a large, iron caisson, off Fort Hill.

The 37-foot light, marking the shoal and a wrecked barge of bricks, has fixed red and white sectors that are helpful for night approaches. (You'll see the red sector marked on the chart.) Pass east of the light before turning southwest for Oyster Bay Harbor.

If you are in a shallow-draft vessel (less than 6 feet) and you decide to pass west of the harbor light, beware of the 5-foot spot 175 yards north of R N "2."

The entrance to Oyster Bay Harbor really begins with RN "4" off Plum Point to the north and Fl G 4s G "5" to the south, off Cove Point. Centre Island separates Oyster Bay from West Harbor. From Fl G 4s G "5," aim for the big, brightly-colored oil tanks at Oyster Bay Village, and you'll end up at the main channel entrance.

The channel into Oyster Bay Harbor carries more than 30 feet of water to Moses Point; west of the point the channel narrows, but it's well marked with a row of nuns and cans. At the east end of this channel, look for Q G GR "B," marking the beginning of the channel down to the village wharf. This channel, like the main east-west channel, is also well marked. This channel is flanked on both sides by numerous moorings. Keep a sharp lookout for tug and barge traffic entering or exiting this channel, as there is very little room to maneuver.

CAUTION: There's a no-wake speed limit in this area, and it's strictly enforced. Remember that you're liable for any damage caused by your wake.

Several good anchorages can be found in this uncrowded and unspoiled harbor; one is the bight west of Plum Point, on the east side of Centre Island, marked by a small stone tower. You might find some room to anchor near the yachts of the Seawanhaka Corinthian Yacht Club on Centre Island, but reservations are suggested.

Picking up just any empty mooring is not a good idea. If the harbormaster nabs you, he'll tell you to move on unless you have a written letter of authorization from the owner of the mooring. Except for the yacht club, there are no boating facilities on the island, so if you want to dine out or reprovision, you'll have to go ashore at the village.

The bight between Cove Neck and the Oyster Bay wharf offers another good, tree-lined anchorage just off the channel to Oyster Bay Village. There's a jetty on Cove Neck, on the east side of this anchorage, where you can land your dinghy and walk up to Sagamore Hill, less than a mile away.

On the east side of the wharf, near the oil tanks, is a row of sunken barges. Another channel runs west to the Oyster Bay Marine Center. Gas, diesel, and transient slips are available, and a free pump-out station is nearby. One of the reasons Oyster Bay is so clean is that the harbormaster strongly encourages boaters to use the pump-out station. You can't

beat the price, so take advantage of it. Contact the Roosevelt Memorial Park Marina on VHF 9 for more information.

The Long Island Railroad station is just a stone's throw away from the wharf, as is downtown Oyster Bay. Oyster Bay Marine Service and the Sagamore Yacht Club both offer launch service (at Sagamore, for members only).

There's a Special Anchorage southwest of Moses Point, at the south end of Centre Island, but most of it is taken up with permanent moorings. Pass south of R N "12," and keep at least 0.2nm off Brickyard Point to avoid unmarked rocks. Some oystering continues in Oyster Bay, but not at the level of former years. Old oyster stakes broken off just below the waterline remain a hazard for unwary boaters.

In West Harbor, west of Centre Island, you'll be heading north again and can drop your anchor just about anywhere off Mill Neck to the west or off Centre Island to the east. As one of our readers put it, this is a "hurricane hole extraordinaire," usually jam-packed with boats. You can sail well up into the harbor and then dink over to the beach at the head of the bay. Don't try landing on Centre Island, as visitors are not welcome.

Mill Neck Creek, in the northwest corner of the harbor, is spanned by a bascule bridge with a clearance of 9 feet (mhw). The area west of the bridge has depths of 6 to 13 feet. Here you'll find Bridge Marina, a full service facility with a few transient moorings. Just outside the entrance to the creek is a special mooring area for Bayville residents only.

Shoreside and Emergency Services
Airport: MacArthur (631-467-3210)
Bus: Suffolk County Transit (516-360-5700)
—MTA Long Island Bus Information (516-766-6722)
Coast Guard: Eatons Neck (631-261-6959) or VHF 16
Harbormaster: (516-624-6201)
Police, Fire, Ambulance: 911
Taxi: Oyster Bay Taxi & Limo (516-921-2141)
Tow Service:
SEA TOW.—24-Hour Dispatch (800-4SEATOW)
—Western Long Island Sound (914-698-6523)
Tow BoatU.S.—24-Hour Dispatch (800-391-4869)
—Oyster Bay (516-624-3483)
Train: Long Island Railroad (516-822-5477)

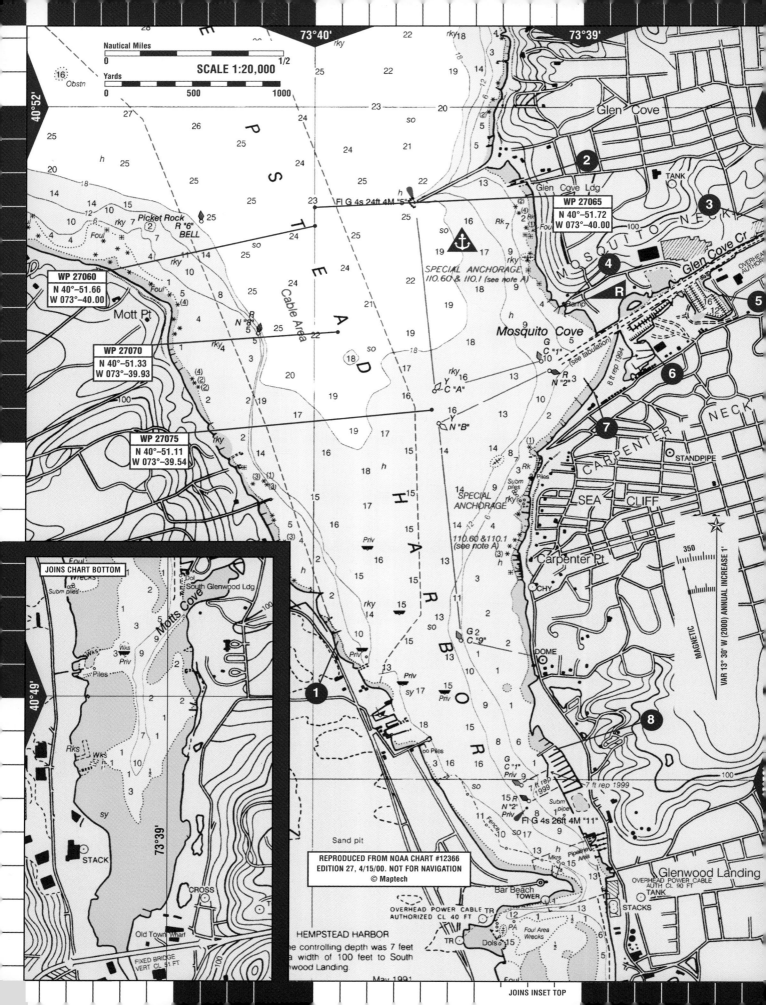

The Making of a Boating Destination

Ah, boating destinations. Massachusetts has Nantucket. Rhode Island has Newport. Connecticut has Mystic. And New York has…. Glen Cove? No, Glen Cove is not the first name that pops into your mind when you think of New York boating meccas, but that's where the city wants to go. Though it's filled with history, sights, and activities, the city has never been particularly accessible for the transient boater. That's all beginning to change.

Take a snapshot of Glen Cove Creek right now and come back in a few years and compare. Chances are you won't be able to. State and local funding is expanding the Glen Cove waterfront near the business district and improving waterfront access while beautifying the landscape. The city aspires to be mentioned in the same breath as Nantucket, Newport, and Mystic. Although that may be a ways off, Glen Cove is making a concerted effort to make its shoreline as appealing as the residential hills that tower above it.

Glen Cove's hills offer a wonderful view of Hempstead Harbor. © Maptech

ACTIVITIES: There are three transient-friendly marinas amidst the revitalization effort, and despite a somewhat rough exterior, Glen Cove offers quite a few activities to make your stay worthwhile. You will need a cab or rental car to get to many destinations, but downtown Glen Cove, with all its shopping opportunities, is a short walk from the marinas.

Docked at Jude Thaddeus Glen Cove Marina is the *Thomas Jefferson* (516-744-2353), an 80-foot replica of a 19th-century paddleboat. Hop on board and listen to the period-dressed crew narrate a tour of the Gold Coast. We're told the 150-passenger steamer is a popular wedding setting.

Just north of Glen Cove Creek you'll find the Garvies Point Museum & Preserve (516-671-0300), devoted to the culture of Long Island Indians and the area's fascinating geology. A self-guided nature trail helps you work off your sea legs and learn a bit about nature and geology in the process. Particularly fascinating are the rocky beach, characteristic of glacial terrain, and the cliffs above—one of the few places on Long Island where you can see sedimentary soil beneath the glacial moraine that created the island.

To peruse the city on four wheels, rent a car at Enterprise (516-674-4300), Budget (516-759-3333), or Rent-A-Wreck

	Marine Facilities and Services		Monitors / Working VHF Channel	Number of Transient Berths / Moorings	Approach / Dockside Depth in Feet at MLW	Seasonal / Yearround	Maximum LOA	Hookups: Fresh Water / Phone / Cable TV	110V ★ 220V ▲ 3 Phase ■ Maximum Amps	Rail / Lift / Crane / Launch Service	Ramp / Dinghy Dock	Diesel / Wood / Fiberglass / Electronics	Repairs: Propellor / Sail / Rigging / Gas	Marine / Groceries / Ice / Bait / LPG / CNG	Restrooms / Showers / Laundry / Pumpout	Gas / Diesel Fuel	Fuel Brand	Public Phone / Restaurant / Snack Bar	Hotel / Pool / Tennis / Golf	Mastercard / VISA / Discover / AmEx
1	Beacon Hill Marina*	516-883-5050		4/5	S	35	6/5				R			All				MI		MV
2	Glen Cove Yacht Club*	516-767-9450		/2	S	40	12/6			DL		T						RS	P	
3	Glen Cove Angler's Club*	516-767-9794			Y															
4	Hempstead Harbour Club	516-671-0600		/4	S		15/6			DL		*RECIPROCAL PRIVILEGES*						RS	P	
5	**The Jude Thaddeus Glen Cove Marina** (B) p. 395	516-759-3129	9/71	10/	Y	65	6/6	FP	★▲■50		L35	PGDWFE	GD	Gulf	MI	RS	P	All		
6	**Brewer Yacht Yard at Glen Cove** Inside Back Cover	516-671-5563	9/	22/	Y	55	7/8	F	★▲50		L60	All	GD	Tex	MIC	RSP	P	P	All	
7	Sea Cliff Yacht Club	516-671-7374			Y						*PRIVATE—MEMBERS ONLY*									
8	Harry Tappen Boat Basin	516-674-7101		2/	Y	44	7/7	F	★30		R					RP		P		

All Coast Guard Stations Monitor VHF Channel 16

Information in these listings is provided by the facilities themselves. An asterisk (*) indicates that the facility did not respond to our most recent request for information. (B) represents a BOAT/U.S. cooperating marina.

A September morn at the Tappen Beach Marina. © Maptech

(516-759-1001); or call a cab. Then, roll over to the 200-acre Welwyn Preserve, where you can hike the beautiful nature trails. Just because you're having fun doesn't mean you can't learn something. At the preserve, stop by the Holocaust Museum (516-571-8040) for an educational tour. It's open Monday through Friday 10 a.m. to 4 p.m., and Sundays from 11 a.m. to 4 p.m.

If you're out at sea all summer, you have to make the best of your time on land. Why not go golfing? Try Glen Cove Golf Course (516-676-0550) for 18 holes beautifully sprawled along the water. If golf is too strenuous (ahem), take a seat at Cineplex Odeon Theaters (516-671-6668) to catch the latest flicks.

If you feel like staying on the water, fishing is fantastic in this area. It's so good in these parts that fishing charters from City Island make their way here regularly. In Hempstead Harbor you'll find just about every species of fish that lives in the Sound. Drop your hook just north of the jetty, north of Glen Cove Creek.

In 1904, the 238-foot, side-wheel steamer *Glen Island* caught fire off Matinecock Point, burned, and sank. With scuba gear you can dive to the wreck, but be careful of the tidal currents off the point, as they can be quite strong.

With the ongoing revitalization, it's not a bad idea to give the mayor's office (516-676-2004) or the Chamber of Commerce (516-676-6666) a call to find out what's new. Or hop on-line at www.glencove-li.com.

RESTAURANTS & PROVISIONS: If there's one thing Glen Cove does pretty well, it's restaurants. Whether it's McDonald's, take-out Chinese, or multiple courses at a four-star restaurant, Glen Cove can accommodate all kinds of appetites. In Glen Cove proper, you'll find an array of international restaurants within walking distance of each other, but a cab ride away from the marinas.

At Jude Thaddeus Glen Cove Marina, you'll find the Steamboat Landing (516-759-3129). If pasta and pizza are what you like, you've come to the right place. Stangos Italian Restaurant (516-671-2389), Ciros Pizza (516-759-0793), and Delicious Pizzeria & Restaurant (516-676-3488) are all recommended.

China King (516-676-8181) has some of the best Chinese around, but it's take-out only. For an all-American dish, make tracks for Henry's Luncheonette (516-671-3222). The food is good, and the homemade cheesecake and ice cream are out of this world.

You don't have to leave the comfort of your boat at mealtime. Call Black Tie (516-676-0909) and, for a percentage of the total sale, they'll pick up your order and deliver it to your boat.

Farther afield, head to Roslyn, in the southern end of Hempstead Harbor. This is where you'll find Friend of a Farmer Restaurant & Café (516-625-3808), Laguna Café (516-625-7771), and Poco Loco (516-621-5626).

The ship's stores at the marinas can tidy up your nautical cabinet, but to stock the galley you'll have to hop in a cab. Head to Farmer's Bazaar (516-759-1440) or Rising Tide (516-676-7895), a health food store, for a varied selection to keep the crew fed and happy.

NAVIGATION & ANCHORAGES: Use ChartKit Region 3, page 20; Maptech™ Waterproof Chart 1 and 16; and Maptech™ electronic and NOAA paper charts 12366 (1:20,000), 12364 (1:40,000), and 12363 (1:80,000). Use tide tables for Willets Point. High tide at Glen Cove is 5 minutes earlier; low tide is 8 minutes earlier. Use the height of tide at Willets Point for the height of tide at Glen Cove. Mean tidal range is 7.3 feet.

Fl G 4s 24ft 4M "5" on the breakwater at Glen Cove Landing is 10.7nm from Cold Spring Harbor Light, 6.2nm from Plum Point in Manhasset Bay, and 4.6nm from Mamaroneck Harbor.

From Fl G 4s GONG G "21" off Matinecock Point, a course of about 225°m will take you west of Weeks Point and into Hempstead Harbor's broad entrance.

Hempstead Harbor offers good holding ground in everything but a strong northerly wind. This may not be a problem during the summer, but if you're coming into the harbor in fall or winter, you could be in for a beating. Like Manhasset Bay next door, the harbor gets narrower and shallower as you head south. The mean tidal range is 7.3 feet, with weak currents except at the channel at Bar Beach, where the velocity can reach 1 knot.

From the east, it's wisest to stay south of Fl G 4s GONG G "21" off Matinecock Point.

From the west and Execution Rocks, it's best to stay outside all the buoys off Manhasset Neck from Fl G 4s GONG G "23" at Sands Point all the way to R N "8" off Mott Point in order to clear the many rocks and shoals along the shore.

The Jude Thaddeus Glen Cove Marina.

The most protected Full Service Marina on Long Island. Within walking distance to **Shops, Theatres, Museums, & The High Speed Ferry**. Also featuring Glen Cove's **First and Only Waterfront Restaurant, Steamboat Landing operated by John Ferarra**.

The Jude Thaddeus Glen Cove Marina has over **350 slips** ranging from **20 ft. to 90 ft.** and over **1000 ft. of transient dockage**. All slips have 30 or 50 amp. electric service and fresh running water.

Steamboat Landing
Restaurant features **Live Entertainment nightly**, **over 1000 ft. of docking space** for those coming by boat, also offering catering for private parties of any size and all occasions.

Opening in 2001
Bait and Tackle shop, Breakfast & Deli Nook, and Waterfront Boutiques.

76 Shore Road, Glen Cove, NY 11542 • Phone: 516-759-3129 • Fax: 516-759-3306

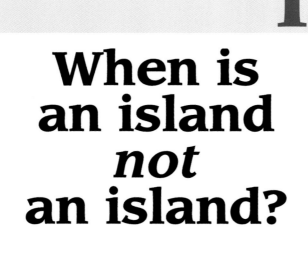

When is an island *not* an island?

Take a deep breath and say this quickly 20 times: If the river is a river, the island isn't an island and the sound isn't a sound. If the river isn't a river, the island is an island and the sound is a sound. If the river isn't a river, the island isn't an island, and the sound isn't a sound, why are they called a river, an island and a sound?

Anyone who has tried to walk to Queens or Brooklyn from Manhattan would agree that Long Island is an island. Everyone that lives on Long Island knows it's an island, but the U.S. Supreme Court says it isn't.

A historic accident dating back over 350 years was part of the basis for the Court's decision. It seems that the illustrious Dutch explorer Adriaen Block, who discovered Long Island Sound, wasn't so good at identifying the places he found. Block discovered the Sound by sailing through New York Harbor, which he erroneously assumed was fed by two great rivers, the Hudson River and what he called the "East River." That was his first mistake. Block's second mistake was to call Long Island Sound a river because he thought it was an extension of the East River. Others later realized that the Sound was a different beast entirely.

As the centuries passed, the current names—Long Island Sound, Long Island, and East River—became permanent, though the last is technically inaccurate. In the early colonists' defense it must be said that when you're fighting for survival in a virgin wilderness, matters of proper nomenclature aren't of great importance.

According to the experts, the Sound is a sound because it is a "long passage of water connecting two larger bodies [as a sea with the ocean] or passing between the mainland and an island." The East River, however, is really a tidal strait because it carries salt water back and forth between New York Harbor and the Sound, has no head, and drains no watershed; therefore, Long Island is an island.

But the law is not made by oceanographers. In 1985 the U.S. Supreme Court considered Long Island's commercial and political links to the mainland and made a curious ruling: "We agree . . . that Long Island, which indeed is unusual, presents an exceptional case of an island which should be treated as an extension of the mainland."

The obvious question is why the Supreme Court is getting involved when the old names worked perfectly well after three and a half centuries. The answer is, of course, money. In the 1960s and 1970s when surveyors started exploring a seabed in search of minerals and oil, a squabble broke out between New York and Rhode Island over the rights to the area between Orient and Montauk points in New York and Point Judith, Rhode Island. Whether Long Island was considered an island or a peninsula would determine which state would get the lion's share of the disputed area. One specially appointed judge tried to resolve the issue by dividing it up between the two states and the Federal Government: All three parties appealed. New York eventually won by arguing that Long Island isn't an island, and gained the seabed and the authority to regulate shipping in the disputed area.

If Long Island is redefined as a peninsula, Long Island Sound becomes a bay, and we have the perplexing situation in which Long Island isn't an island, the East River isn't a river, and Long Island Sound isn't a sound.

Given the above, we're left with the question of whether or not to rename Long Island, Long Island Sound, and the East River. There doesn't appear to be much interest in such a move—there would be far too many maps to change, and somehow the name "Long Peninsula Bay" just doesn't have the same sound.

Coming from Manhasset Bay or Throgs Neck, a good landmark for Prospect Point is a large, white house with columns, designed by the famous architect Stanford White. Stay north of R N "2," marking Old Hen Rock.

The long breakwater north of Glen Cove Landing, marked by Fl G 4s 24ft 4M "5" on its west end, provides a nice anchorage for small boats. This is a free, federal mooring field, one of the last around. In the south end of the harbor, be sure not to anchor in the pipeline area between Glenwood Landing and Bar Beach.

On the western side of the harbor, above Bar Beach, you will see the large sand and gravel pits that supply commercial barges. Dredged channels off to the west of the harbor allow the barges to come in close to the sand pits for loading. The barges are kept on two large, steel mooring buoys located on the western side of the harbor, across from Carpenter Point. There can be as little as two or as many as 20 barges on each of these moorings at any given time. Pay close attention if you are transiting at the change of the tide; the vessels take up a lot of real estate when they swinging on the moorings.

NOTE: Glen Cove Creek was dredged to a depth of 10 feet up to Jude Thaddeus Glen Cove Marina by the Army Corps of Engineers in the fall of 1996.

Glen Cove Creek, about a half mile south of the breakwater, has a channel running from Mosquito Cove about 0.6nm to the head. The creek contains three marinas and attracts many boaters. Brewer Yacht Yard at Glen Cove offers slips for transients. Next door, Jude Thaddeus Glen Cove Marina also offers transient slips and amenities. There's a ramp just north of the creek entrance for residents only.

There are anchorages inside both Y C "A" and Y N "B," marking the approach to Glen Cove Creek. If you want to anchor southeast of Y N "B," watch the chart carefully. Go too far south and you'll be one of the many boaters who have to be pulled off the mud around Carpenter Point.

From Sea Cliff south to Glenwood Landing, a shoal extends 400 yards off the east shore to G C "9." The eight stacks of the large power plants at Glenwood Landing are easy to spot. It's not uncommon to see vessels anchored just outside of the swimmers' rope floats to the north of Bar Beach, especially during summer. However, if you decide to join them, be prepared to move as this is part of the approach to a busy oil/gasoline terminal at Glenwood Landing.

From Glenwood, a dredged channel continues south. However, shallow water (less than 4 feet), industrial sites, and commercial traffic make it unappealing to most

Looking northwest over Hempstead Harbor. Both Brewer Yacht Yard at Glen Cove (left) and Jude Thaddeus Glen Cove Marina (right) are easily accessible. © Maptech/James T. Abts

boaters. The Glen Cove Harbor Patrol operates as a mini-Coast Guard and is attentive to the needs of yachters.

Shoreside & Emergency Services
Airport: MacArthur (631-467-3210)
—Port Authority of NY/NJ (800-AIR-RIDE)
Bus: MTA Long Island (516-766-6722)
Coast Guard: Eatons Neck (631-261-6959) or VHF 16
Harbormaster: Harbor Patrol (516-671-4263)
Police, Fire, Ambulance: 911
Taxi: Arena Car Service (516-671-1848)
—The Taxi (516-671-0707)
Tow Service:
SEA TOW —24-Hour Dispatch (800-4SEATOW)
—Western Long Island Sound (914-698-6523)
TowBoatUS—24-Hour Dispatch (800-391-4869)
—City Island (718-885-3420)
Train: Long Island Railroad (516-822-5477)

The Sands of Time

As you cruise Long Island's north shore, you may wonder why Manhasset Bay, once known as Cow Bay, lacks those stunning shoreline hills that you see along much of the Gold Coast. Well, the glaciers did leave behind hills, lovely, towering sandmounts that provided great views from atop as well as below, but they've since moved on to the big city.

You see, Port Washington's sand was exceptional—too good, certain people thought, to just leave there. After its "discovery" in 1865, the uncommonly fine-grained sand was coveted by New York City concrete companies, who paid a mint to get certified Cow Bay sand for building skyscrapers and paving the sidewalks in front them. Many Long Islanders vehemently protested the mining—to no avail, of course, because money talks (and Manhattan money talks even louder). The sand-mining continued for nearly a century, with millions of tons dug out and carted off. Today part of the flat land supports a golf course, and some abandoned pits remain, a sad testament to many who wax bitter when they think what the shore might look like had it been left in peace.

The sand hills remain untouched at Sands Point, named not for those regal grains but for one of the original settlers of Block Island. Here the very, very rich once showed the nation how to live well in Irish castles and Norman mansions built high atop imposing bluffs. One of the mansions, owned by Harry Guggenheim, sheltered young Charles Lindbergh from the press hounds after his famous 1927 flight across the Atlantic.

Heading down the dock for an afternoon outing. © Maptech

	Marine Facilities and Services		Number of Transient Berths	Seasonal / Year-round	Approach / Dockside Depth in Feet at MLW	Maximum LOA	110V • 220V ▲ 3 Phase ■ Maximum Amps	Hookups: Fresh Water / Phone / Cable TV	Ramp / Dinghy Dock / Launch Service	Rail / Lift / Crane / Trailer: Capacity (tons)	Repairs: Propeller / Sail / Rigging / Gas	Diesel / Wood / Fiberglass / Electronics	Marine / Groceries / Ice / Bait / LPG / CNG	Restrooms / Showers / Laundry / Pumpout	Gas / Diesel Fuel	Fuel Brand	Public Phone / Tennis / Golf	Hotel / Pool / Tennis / Snack Bar	Mastercard / VISA / Discover / AmEx
1	**Brewer Capri Marina East and West** *Inside Back Cover*	516-883-7800	9/71	40/10	Y	150	8/8	All	★▲100	DL	L75	All	GD	BP	MB	All	P	All	MVA
2	North Shore Yacht Club	516-883-9823			Y			*PRIVATE—MEMBERS ONLY*											
3	W & W Marine	516-944-9200		10/4	Y	70	6/6	F	★▲50	D	L20	All			I	R		P	All
4	Toms Point Marina (B)	516-883-6630	71/	10/	Y	45	6/5	All	★▲60	All	T15	PSRGDWF			B	All		P	MV
5	Manhasset Bay Sportsmen's Club Inc.	516-883-9689	68/		Y	24		*PRIVATE—MEMBERS ONLY*											
6	Sigsbee Sailing Center	516-767-0944			Y	60	7/7	*BOAT RENTALS & SAILING SCHOOL*											All
7	Randazzo Yacht Mechanics	516-767-1666			Y			*DISTRIBUTOR OF MARINE BATTERIES*											MVD
8	Haven Marina Inc.	516-883-0937		4/	Y	42	5/5	FP	★30	RD	C45	All			MI			P	MVA
9	*Manhasset Bay Marina* (B) p. 401	516-883-8411	9/71	20/2	Y	110	8/6	All	★▲■50		LC70	All	GD	Tex	MB	All		PR	All
10	Gulfway Marine Service	516-767-0113			Y	35	7/7	F	★30		C18	All			M	RS		P	

All Coast Guard Stations Monitor VHF Channel 16

Facilities continued on next page...

who by 1857 were ready to call their hometown something else. The 21st-century Port Washington is a sought-after commuter community, a great place for New York City professionals to escape to for their evenings and weekends—especially if they're boaters.

ACTIVITIES: Manhasset Bay's busy waterfront and commercial districts are surrounded by quiet residential areas ranging from middle-class to affluent. It's a nice suburban area indelibly stamped with New York City. In this popular harbor you'll find more marinas, yacht clubs, restaurants, and fine shopping than almost anywhere else on the Sound.

For a glimpse at the lifestyles of the rich (and sometimes famous), take in the Sands Point Preserve (516-571-7902), which contains the restored Guggenheim family homes and a 209-acre forest. Castlegould, built in 1902, is a huge stone castle (the Irish one) that once served as a stable; it now houses a dinosaur exhibit. Falaise, built by Captain Harry F. Guggenheim in 1923, is an elegant manor house

Manhasset Bay attracts a good mix of power and sail. © Maptech

As Manhasset Bay was once Cow Bay, Port Washington was called Cow Neck. There's no record of George Washington's having visited, by boat or buggy, this sound-side community that now bears his name. He did stop in Roslyn, though, on a return trip from Oyster Bay in 1790, and that was close enough for the residents of Cow Neck,

Marine Facilities and Services

#	Name	Phone	Monitors / Working VHF Channel	Number of Transient Berths / Seasonal / Moorings	Hookups	Maximum LOA	Dockside Depth in Feet at MLW	Ramp / Dinghy Dock / Launch Service	Rail / Lift / Crane / Trailer Capacity (tons)	Repairs	Marine / Groceries / Ice / Bait / LPG / CNG	Gas / Diesel Fuel	Restrooms / Showers / Laundry / Pumpout	Fuel Brand	Public Phone / Restaurant / Snack Bar	Hotel / Pool / Tennis / Golf	Mastercard / VISA / Discover / AmEx
11	North Hempstead Town Dock	516-767-4622	16/	/200	Y	25	9/4								P		
12	Louie's Shore Restaurant	516-883-4242		10/	Y	50	5.5/5							I	R	PR	All
13	Brewer Capri Marina at Inspiration Wharf — Inside Back Cover	516-883-7800	9/71	30/	Y	60	7/3	All	★▲■30	D	LC35	All	GD	BP	RS	All	MVA
14	Knickerbocker Yacht Club	516-883-7655			Y				PRIVATE—MEMBERS ONLY								
15	MANHASSET BAY SHIPYARD — p. 403	516-767-7447	68/		Y	50	6/6	F	★50	D	LT35	GDW				P	MV
16	Manhasset Bay Yacht Club	516-883-8411			Y				PRIVATE—MEMBERS ONLY								
17	Port Washington Yacht Club	516-767-1614			Y				PRIVATE—MEMBERS ONLY								
18	Kennilwood Yacht Club	516-482-2393			Y				PRIVATE—MEMBERS ONLY								
19	Broadlawn Harbour Yacht Club	516-482-9793			Y				PRIVATE—MEMBERS ONLY								
20	Shelter Harbour Marina	516-482-9085	69/	3/	S	100	15/7.5		★▲■50	D				I	RS	PT	P

All Coast Guard Stations Monitor VHF Channel 16

Information in these listings is provided by the facilities themselves. An asterisk (*) indicates that the facility did not respond to our most recent requests for information. (B) represents a BOAT/U.S. cooperating marina.

Embassy Guides

(the Norman one) with original furnishings and the owner's aeronautical memorabilia. Tours are by escort only, so be sure to call ahead. Hempstead House (it's Tudor) is the former main residence.

Execution Rocks excels as a favorite fishing spot, but the strong current can set you onto those rocks if you're not careful, and there's a good deal of commercial traffic. To anchor and fish, come in close on the south side. Don't try the west side, especially at low tide when you're likely to bang your keel on the rocks.

Manhasset Bay's hardy sailors race year-round. Three yacht clubs of the Cow Bay Racing Association sponsor an open regatta in the spring called "Thirsty Thursday." Fall fanatics favor the Frostbite Regatta, a dinghy event that the Manhasset Bay Yacht Club hosts over the New Year's holiday.

A cab ride will take you to Route 25A at the foot of the harbor and to the "Miracle Mile," a strip of expensive shops where many a sailor and his money have taken different tacks. If your means are more modest, however, fear not; there are plenty of very nice (and somewhat less expensive) shops and restaurants just a short walk from the harbor.

RESTAURANTS & PROVISIONS: You'll find no shortage of edibles in Port Washington, as it is jam-packed with restaurants and delis. Nobody arriving by water passes by Louie's Shore Restaurant (516-883-4242), the local institution for the boating crowd. It has a dock for transients and nearly everyone recommends it for its tasty food and nice view.

The Brewer Capri Marina East and West yards each have an eatery: a snack bar at the West yard and P.W.'s Chowder House (516-767-7924) at the East yard. On the other side of the harbor you'll find a Chinese restaurant at Brewer Capri Marina at Inspiration Wharf. Just to the east you can try the steaks and seafood at Bill's Harbor Inn (516-883-3554). If the usual burgers and fish have bored you to tears, try Diwan (516-767-7878) for Indian cuisine or Finn MacCool's (516-944-3439) for Irish dishes.

For hearty Italian and American fare, try the very popular LaMotta's (516-944-7900) at the Manhasset Bay Marina. The marina snack bar also serves breakfast and lunch, and dockage is available for patrons. On Main Street, not far from the town dock, well-regarded Pomodoro (516-767-7164) serves up tasty, innovative pasta dishes in a somewhat loud atmosphere. Have lunch at the Seaport (516-883-3030) or stay for dinner to catch the sunset over Manhasset Bay. Of course, if you're in a hurry, Mayview Deli (516-883-7788) can whip you up a quick sandwich and deliver it right to your boat.

Take care of your provisioning needs at the Grand Union or King Kullen, each within walking distance of the harbor.

Looking north over Manhasset Bay. © Maptech/James T. Abts

NAVIGATION & ANCHORAGES: Use ChartKit Region 3, pages 20 and 21; Maptech™ Waterproof Charts 1 and 16; and Maptech™ electronic and NOAA paper charts 12366 (1:20,000), 12364 (1:40,000), and 12363 (1:80,000). Use tide tables for Willets Point. High tide at Port Washington is 5 minutes later; low tide is 9 minutes later. Use the height of tide at Willets Point for the height of tide at Port Washington. Mean tidal range is 7.3 feet.

Barker Point, marking the east entrance to Manhasset Bay, is 5.5nm from the Glen Cove breakwater in Hempstead Harbor, and 4.2nm from the Throgs Neck Bridge. City Island is 2.1nm away, and Mamaroneck Harbor is 4.1nm away.

From GONG G "27" at Gangway Rock, a course of 195°m will take you into the broad entrance of Manhasset Bay.

NOTE: There are two active oil terminals in Manhasset Bay. One is located in Port Washington, the other at the southern end of the bay. Use caution when in close proximity to the tug/barge units.

From the east, to reach Barker Point stay north of Fl G 4s GONG G "23" at Prospect Point, as the shoal extends about 0.4nm north of the point and then falls off quickly to a depth of 60 feet. Stay west of Fl G 2.5s G "25," west of Sands Point. A reef marked by GW Bn extends about 0.3nm off Sands Point, and at low water the boulders show for some 300 yards. You can't miss the brownstone tower of the old Sands Point Lighthouse, which was built in 1809.

In the bight between Sands Point and Barker Point is Half Moon Beach, one of the best on the Sound. Although the area is too exposed for a night anchorage, you can sail in, drop a hook, and swim or take your dinghy to shore. Since the current runs across the two points, the bight is also a good area to tack into to avoid the tides.

Barker Point, 1nm south-southwest of Sands Point, is a high bluff on the northeast side of Manhasset Bay. If you are bound for the bay, avoid going inside Gangway Rock, marked by Fl G 6s 40ft 6M "27A" on the northwest end of the rocky shoal extending 0.6nm northwest of Barker Point. There appears to be room to cut through on the chart, but local navigators have enormous respect for Barker Point, and you should too, so pass west of GONG G "27."

From the west, the approach to Manhasset Bay from Stepping Stones Light (Oc G 4s 46ft 8M) is straightforward. Always stay well to the north and west of the light. Pass north of Fl G 4s G "29" off Hewlett Point. (There is an inside route on the east side of Stepping Stones, south of RN "4" and RN "2" off Kings Point, but this is not recommended for boaters new to the area.)

In the summer, when the prevailing winds are southwesterly, Manhasset Bay is well protected and easy to enter by day or night. However, if you're hardy enough or crazy enough (as we were one year) to go in during November, you'll find that the prevailing northerlies and shallow water may conspire to make you question your sanity. In a good blow, the vicious chop can make the bay even more uncomfortable than the Sound itself.

The depths in the northern part of Manhasset Bay range from 12 to 17 feet, and 7 to 12 feet in the southern part, with little current. The extreme south end is shallow and riddled with extensive mudflats, although 2 to 6 feet of water can be carried in the natural channel almost to the head of the bay.

About a mile in you will pass Plum Point, marked by Fl G 4s G "1," about 150 yards southwest of the point. If you're coming in after dark, keep an eye out for the large, unlighted, speed-limit sign off the point. Running into it will surely slow you down.

Plum Point was the site of the old Sands Point Beach & Tennis Club. It burned down years ago, and the future of the site is still in question. To the east of the point is Manorhaven and the well-equipped and transient-friendly Brewer Capri Marina's East and West yards.

Less than a mile east of Plum Point, Toms Point guards the entrance to Port Washington. There is an 8-foot channel to the town docks, and another channel running to a bight northeast of the point.

Port Washington offers an array of facilities for boaters. Manhasset Bay Marina welcomes transients and has one of the largest lifts around. They also boast a restaurant and a snack bar. You may tie up on the west and south sides of the town dock for a half-hour with permission from the harbor patrol.

The least crowded anchorages are on the south end of the bay and on the west side off Great Neck, which has several yacht clubs lying at the feet of impressive estates. Here, just north of the Manhasset Bay Yacht Club, you'll find the Manhasset Bay Shipyard, which can handle a number of repairs.

Slightly farther north, Brewer Capri Marina at Inspiration Wharf has a restaurant on the grounds and plenty of slips for transients. They also offer repairs, and they sell gas and diesel.

The anchorage between Plum Point and Toms Point is a good one, although the majority of the space is taken up with moorings. The bay's soft bottom affords good holding ground.

CAUTION: Watch out for the commuting seaplanes that frequently take off or land in special No-Anchoring areas clearly marked on the charts. Don't be surprised if you see a seaplane coming in just to fuel up.

Shoreside & Emergency Services
Airport:
—Long Island MacArthur (516-467-3210)
—Port Authority of NY/NJ (800-AIR-RIDE)
Bus: MTA Long Island Bus Information (516-766-6722)
Coast Guard: Eatons Neck (631-261-6868) or VHF 16
Police, Fire, Ambulance: 911
Taxi: Deluxe Taxi (516-883-1900)
Tow Service:
SEA TOW —24-Hour Dispatch (800-4SEATOW)
—Western Long Island Sound (914-698-6523)
Tow BoatUS —24-Hour Dispatch (800-391-4869)
— City Island (718-885-3420)

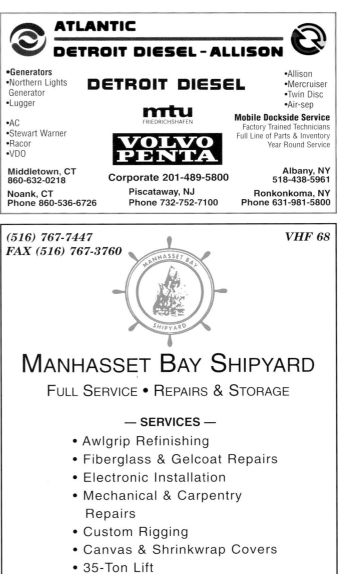

your passions are

NavPhotos

Digital
Aeronautical
Charts

Digital Topographic Maps

National
Park
Guides

Paper Cruising
Guides

our business

Easy-to-use Navigation software

Digital Nautical Charts

Waterproof charts

3-D Charts & Maps

ChartKit Paper Charts

MAPTECH

FLAGPOLE
Yacht Club
Hospital
Crocheron Park
Y N "D"

73°46'

WP 21505
N 40°-49.52
W 073°-46.75

④

Stepping Stones
Oc G 4s 46ft 8M
Cable Area

Obstn

SPECIAL ANCH
110.60 & 110.1
(see note A)

R N "2"

R N "4"

Elm Pt

WP 27160
N 40°-49.02
W 073°-46.05

①

Kings Point
Park

STACK

U.S. Merchant
Marine Academy
FLAGPOLE 172 FT

○ Kings Point

Iso 2s 102ft
Priv

350

VAR 13° 30'W (2000) ANNUAL INCREASE

MAGNETIC

100

CUP ○

Piles

⑤

Obstn
Obstn
Obstn

REPRODUCED FROM NOAA CHART #12366
EDITION 27, 4/15/00. NOT FOR NAVIGATION
© Maptech

Udalls Millpond

SPIRE

R N "2"

Willets Pt

CG

L I T T L E

N E C K

B A Y

Dam

Village Park

SCALE 1:20,000

Nautical Miles
Yards
1/2
1000
500

WP 27175
N 40°-47.26
W 073°-45.77

Cross Island Parkway

RW
SP "LN"

⚓

Y N "A"

Sewer

40°48'

40°47'

73°46'

73°45'

SPECIAL ANCHORAGE
110.60 & 110.1
(see note A)

Tides To Power A Mill

While the seven- to nine-foot tides in Little Neck Bay are annoying to mariners, one colonial-period entrepreneur used them to power his grist mill on the east side of the bay. A dam across the inlet to his millpond forced the tides through a narrow channel and under a waterwheel. As long as the tide was flowing, the mill had power. With the coming of steam, oil, and electrical power, the mill was neglected and it deteriorated badly. Recently, however, the mill has been completely restored, and it's now run by Nassau County and open to the public.

Of course, the bay was also used for boating. The Douglaston Yacht Club was organized in 1891 and it actively encouraged racing on the Sound. But due to the silting of the bay and the danger of mines around Fort Totten during the Spanish-American War, the club changed its name to the Manhasset Bay Yacht Club and moved one bay to the east in 1899.

The Throgs Neck Bridge stands 157 feet tall to the west, marking the terminus of Long Island Sound. Beyond that, the boroughs of the Bronx and Manhattan line the horizon, as do the towering skyscrapers of New York City. To the east of the span lies the quiet anchorage of Little Neck Bay—as quiet as you can get around the Big Apple. The bay has silted up over the years, and though it is dredged regularly, it has an average depth of only 6 to 8 feet. You'll find that most of the boats using the special anchorage near Douglaston are of the shallow-draft variety.

ACTIVITIES: The United States Merchant Marine Academy (516-773-5000) on Kings Point in Great Neck trains officers for the merchant marine and welcomes groups for guided tours of its facilities from August through June. While on campus, visit the mansion of the late Walter P. Chrysler, now the Academy's administration building, and the American

This inviting walkway invites residents into Stepping Stones Park. © Maptech

Merchant Marine Museum (516-466-9696), which was once the home of William Barstow, inventor of the electric meter and the illuminator of the Brooklyn Bridge. The museum features ship models, rare navigational instruments, marine art, and a gallery on the wartime merchant marine. Only alumni are allowed to dock at the Academy.

If you're thinking of leaving your boat and venturing into the Big Apple, your best bet would be to get a slip in Throgs Neck or Manhasset Bay. Then call the New York City Travel Authority (718-330-1234) for information on public transportation in the five boroughs.

RESTAURANTS & PROVISIONS: If you're starving and the larder is bare, head to Manhasset Bay for a couple of cleat-and-eat options. Also, City Island is just a short 2.5nm journey across Long Island Sound, and it's filled with restaurants as well. See the chapters on those harbors for detailed eatery information.

NAVIGATION & ANCHORAGES: Use ChartKit Region 3, page 20; Maptech™ Waterproof Charts 1 and 16; and Maptech™

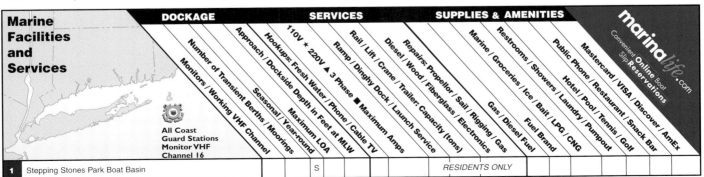

	DOCKAGE				SERVICES				SUPPLIES & AMENITIES			
1 Stepping Stones Park Boat Basin			S			*RESIDENTS ONLY*						

Information in these listings is provided by the facilities themselves. An asterisk (*) indicates that the facility did not respond to our most recent requests for information. (B) represents a BOAT/U.S. cooperating marina.

electronic and NOAA paper charts 12366 (1:20,000), 12364 (1:40,000), and 12363 (1:80,000). Use tide tables for Willets Point. Mean tidal range is 7.1 feet.

Willets Point, marking the western entrance to Little Neck Bay, is 0.8nm east of the Throgs Neck Bridge, 2.4nm south of City Island, and 4.4nm from Plum Point in Manhasset Bay.

If you're heading into or out of New York Harbor, see the Throgs Neck and East River chapters.

From Hewlett Point and Manhasset Bay, it is safest to pass well north and west of Stepping Stones Light (Oc G 4s 46ft 8M), a brick, Victorian structure about halfway between Elm Point and City Island.

CAUTION: According to the Coast Guard and the New York City Harbor Police, the stretch of foul ground between the light and R N "4" and R N "2" is the place where visitors have the most trouble. If you take the southern passage along the shore just off Elm Point, stay south of the nuns. This passage may save you some time if you're traveling along the north shore of Long Island, but don't try it until you are familiar with the area, and then watch out for the tide rips.

South of Elm Point is Kings Point, the home of the U.S. Merchant Marine Academy. A good landmark is the Academy's steel flagpole, which is said to be the country's tallest—the top is 216 feet above the water.

All of Little Neck Bay is a restricted anchorage, so use caution, especially at night when moored and anchored boats may not be lighted. Depths in the bay are 7 to 12 feet, decreasing gradually to the head of the harbor, about 2nm to the south where the bay divides into muddy flats.

The harbor offers a convenient jumping-off place for a trip up the Sound, but it is open to weather from the north. Though thickly settled with many private boat landings, Little Neck Bay is not used much as an anchorage. Watch out for boulders close to shore, especially in the southern part of the bay.

Shoreside & Emergency Services
Airport: Port Authority of NY/NJ (800-AIR-RIDE)
Bus:
—MTA Long Island Bus Information (631-766-6722)
Police, Fire, Ambulance: 911
Taxi: Little Neck (718-229-5454)
—Great Neck (631-482-0077)
Tow Service:
SEA TOW —24-Hour Dispatch (800-4SEATOW)
—Huntington (631-423-0882)
Tow BoatU.S.—24-Hour Dispatch (800-391-4869)
—Sound Tow (718-885-3420)

Rainbow/red sky at morning: sailors take warning.
Rainbow/red sky at night: sailors delight.

These two verses pertain to the amount of moisture in the air. Morning or evening, a lot of moisture in the air will sometimes produce a low rainbow at the antisolar point, i.e., in the west in the morning or in the east in the evening. If the morning sun reveals moisture in the west, then the prevailing westerly wind will bring rain in the course of the day. If the rainbow is in the east, opposite the setting sun, the wind is taking the rain away from the ship.

Evening red, morning grey: speeds the sailor on his way.
Evening grey, morning red: rain falls on the sailor's head.

The "red sky" refers to a brilliant, red-orange band on the horizon that betrays moisture in the air. As the day warms up after sunrise, more moisture ascends, provoking stiff winds as it rises, and once the air is saturated, the moisture may fall out of its own weight as a torrential rain. By contrast, in the evening, the air gains no more heat and, therefore, no more moisture. Hence, clear weather the next day.

If the sun goes pale to bed, rain tomorrow—so 'tis said.

Here, the sun is obscured by high atmospheric moisture, enough of which will fall to the decks and stir up a breeze as it cools the air.

sailor's delight

Looking northwest over Little Neck Bay. The Throgs Neck Bridge and Manhattan are in the background. © Maptech/James T. Abts

Index

My great-grandfather R.G. Brewer of Mamaroneck opened his chandlery and hardware store in 1879, beginning a long tradition of personal service to professional and recreational boatowners, sailors and fishermen.

In 1967 our family aquired the boatyard out back. It became known as Post Road Boat Yard — and the first of 18 Brewer Yards now located from New York to Maine.

Over the next 34 years we learned the importance of having a professional staff and immaculately maintained facilities, top flight riggers, carpenters and mechanics, constant formal training and the best equipment. We learned to anticipate our customers' needs, and pay close attention to detail. We learned how to get things right the first time.

See for yourself what 120 years of service experience can mean for you and your boat. Stop in and spend the night, and be sure to ask for a tour of the facilities. You'll be glad you did.

John (Jack) Brewer Jr.

SERVICE YOU CAN COUNT ON.

Mechanical
   Expert trouble shooting
   Engine rebuilding
   Air conditioning
   Plumbing & Sanitation
   Refrigeration
   Heating systems
   Propping & Shafting
   Repowering
Carpentry
   Interior modifications
   Planking & framing
   Wooden spars
   Teak decks & trim
Painting
   Gelcoat
   Color matching
   Awlgrip, Imron coatings
   Osmotic blister repair
   Traditional wood finishes
   Brightwork without equal
Rigging
   Deck modifications
   Furling systems
   Hydraulic systems
   Winches & windlasses
   Running rigging
   Standing rigging
Major Hull Work
   Structural modifications
   Vacuum forming
   Wooden boat restoration
   Keel upgrades
   Salvage
Major Metal Work
   Radar arches
   Fuel and water tanks
   Rigging fittings
   Spar modifications & repairs
Storage
   Indoor, outdoor
   Decommissioning
Electronics
   Repair and Installation

SURVEY
Brewer Yacht Yards were voted #1 for Best Marina, Boatyard & Services and Maintenance in the 2000 Offshore Magazine Reader's Survey.

BENEFITS YOU CAN USE.

THE CLUB
The Brewer Customer Club offers great benefits from free dockage to chandlery discounts. Call us for more information.

Clean bathrooms

Hot showers

Washers and dryers

Sparkling swimming pools

Spas and whirlpools

Floating docks

Cable television

Electrical hookups

Well maintained channels

Recreational areas

Playgrounds

Exercise facilities

Well-stocked marine chandleries

Shoreside activities

Easy access to restaurants and shops